ALSO BY ED CRAY

≡

General of the Army: George C. Marshall, Soldier and Statesman

American Datelines
(ed. with Jonathan Kotler and Miles Beller)

The Erotic Muse: American Bawdy Songs

Chrome Colossus: General Motors and Its Times

Levi's

Burden of Proof: The Trial of Juan Corona

The Enemy in the Streets

In Failing Health

The Big Blue Line

CHIEF JUSTICE

A BIOGRAPHY OF EARL WARREN

Ed Cray

SIMON & SCHUSTER

SIMON & SCHUSTER
Rockefeller Center
1230 Avenue of the Americas
New York, NY 10020

Copyright © 1997 by Ed Cray
All rights reserved,
including the right of reproduction
in whole or in part in any form.

SIMON & SCHUSTER and colophon are registered trademarks
of Simon & Schuster Inc.

Designed by Liney Li

Manufactured in the United States of America

1   3   5   7   9   10   8   6   4   2

Library of Congress Cataloging-in-Publication Data
Cray, Ed.
Chief justice: a biography of Earl Warren/by Ed Cray.
p.   cm.
Includes bibliographical references and index.
1. Warren, Earl, 1891–1974.   2. Judges—United States—Biography.
3. Governors—California—Biography   I. Title.
KF8745.W3C73   1997   97–2984   CIP
347.73'2634—dc21
[B]
ISBN 0-684-80852-8

CONTENTS

PART III. THIS HONORABLE COURT

PART IV. THE WARREN COURT

IN MEMORIAM

ALBERT EASON MONROE
1909–1975

ABRAHAM LINCOLN WIRIN
1900–1978

FRIENDS, MENTORS

AND
ELAINE CRAY POTTER
1936–1991
MY SISTER

CIVIL LIBERTARIANS ALL

He will judge your people with righteousness

And your poor with justice.

—PSALM 72:2

INTRODUCTION

He was like an Old Testament prophet, a conscience to remind us that this nation could be a more perfect union, that we individually could be better, even more noble.

To millions at home and abroad, he stood for the great self-evident truth, that all men are created equal. For many in the so-called Third World, Earl Warren stood as the very embodiment of the American promise.

To millions more, fearful, distrusting those liberties they so often claimed for themselves, Earl Warren was a man despised.

How he came to be this larger-than-life figure is an American story, his evolution a reflection of the American nation in the first seven decades of the century.

Earl Warren was more than symbol, more than icon.

For all his forthright nature, Warren was a man of contradictions. "Only Abe Lincoln had such a strange departure as Warren," said a onetime critic. "You expect one direction and another emerges."

A bluff, outgoing politician, he appealed to millions—at the same time hiding a private, inner man revealed to only a very few. Not a legal scholar, he nonetheless led a legal revolution; his court added enduring catch-phrases to the American vocabulary: "Separate is not equal"; "One man, one vote"; "Read him his rights."

This former prosecutor fashioned majorities in case after case to protect the rights of the accused. A former governor who believed in states rights, he personally wrote a Supreme Court decision that would permanently alter the shape of state government. One of the first local officials secretly to amass files on suspected subversives, he later led the high court to a series of decisions that curtailed the Red Scare of the 1950s.

In case after case, Earl Warren helped to reshape the very meaning of the Bill of Rights, and to insist that states too honor the rights assured every citizen. Poet and lawyer Archibald MacLeish concluded that the fourteenth chief justice had "restored the future."

Outside his family, even those who knew him best, did not truly understand the man or his career. Robert Kenny, good friend, reluctant political rival, lawyer, and fellow Californian, early on recognized the changes in the man, but decided, "There was no sudden conversion like Saul of Tarsus." Newspaper columnist Drew Pearson, who would become an equally close friend and summer traveling companion, deliberately compared the Chief to Saul on the road to Damascus.

Their disagreement is understandable, for Warren's career was a tangle of seeming contradictions. He was deliberate in making decisions, so much so that some despaired at his seeming ignorance. Yet one old pol, who knew him for four decades, claimed, "Warren is and always was about two jumps ahead of where you thought he was. He'd anticipate what you were thinking about."

He was in many ways old-fashioned in his values, even prudish. Yet this man voted to permit the publication of books and showing of motion pictures that provoked him to say he would kill the man who showed such material to his daughters.

He was a model of those "family values" his opponents in the Republican Party would later seize as a political slogan. He remained happily married to the same woman for forty-nine years, fretting he might leave his widow unprovided for. No wisp of scandal, sexual or financial, attached itself to him throughout a lifetime of public service.

With his appointment to the Supreme Court in 1953, liberals groaned in dismay, fearful of reactionary decisions to come. Sixteen years later, conservatives cheered his resignation while liberals bemoaned the nation's loss.

For sixteen years he led the brethren through those very legal thickets scholars insisted were best avoided. And for those sixteen years he confounded those same critics. The man whom one of the more astute political observers of his time said would "never set the world on fire" had, by the end of his career, proved himself one of the most influential Americans of the twentieth century.

The president who appointed him later muttered that choice was "the biggest damn fool thing I ever did"; the president against whom he ran in 1948 never ceased praising his onetime political rival.

And the president who appointed Warren's replacement never understood how the fourteenth chief justice of the United States had achieved enduring greatness.

The justices with whom Warren served on the high court were agreed;

the man they called Chief had left his mark on history. Waspish, conservative Felix Frankfurter, with whom Warren often disagreed, reportedly said the Californian "will be remembered as a great Chief Justice." The equally prickly liberal, William O. Douglas, decided "he will rank with Marshall and Hughes in the broad sweep of United States history." William Brennan nicknamed him "Super Chief," after a crack streamliner.

Not everyone shared that opinion. Richard Nixon, less than three years before his fall, was both "surprised and bewildered" when a magazine poll of sixty-five academics ranked his longtime nemesis among the twelve great- est of the ninety-eight justices who had sat on the Supreme Court to that time.

Alabama Governor George Wallace sputtered, "Earl Warren does not have enough brains to try a chicken thief in my home county!" One now-forgotten retired marine lieutenant colonel in an address before an equally forgotten anticommunist organization proclaimed impeachment too good for the CJ; the colonel, like a splenetic syndicated columnist before him, recommended hanging.

Some of the criticism stung, but it did not deter Warren. On the wall of the library in Apartment I-140 at the Sheraton Park hung the original drawing of Phil Interlandi's *New Yorker* cartoon depicting Whistler's mother embroidering on a doily, "Impeach Earl Warren."

For sixteen years he presided, first among equals, over the Supreme Court of the United States. There he wrought a revolution, guided not by closely reasoned legal argument, but by a simple moral compass: Is it fair?

Not all of their decisions would stand, he knew. Some would be over- turned by later courts, some trimmed back. But the core would remain.

And at that center was a decency, a sense of ethics, of righteousness, Earl Warren the voice of that rectitude, the Old Testament prophet gently guid- ing us to decency, chiding us for our past failures, but resolutely showing his nation, his people a better way.

Warren was modest in that achievement. Late in his life, his second son, himself a lawyer and judge, asked his father just what he had accomplished. The white-haired man who had spent his adult life in public service replied, "History is going to have to tell us that."

The history is here, in these pages.

Part I

THE LAST
PROGRESSIVE

CHAPTER 1

THE CHILDREN WERE VERY
WELL MANNERED

THROUGH THE HOT SUMMER NIGHTS, THEY COULD HEAR THE FAINT music tumbling from the dance halls and the occasional gunshots ending an argument on K Street. Though the good people of Bakersfield, California, like Chrystal Hernlund Warren, did not speak openly of the fancy houses and saloons near 19th Street and Chester, their children nevertheless understood there was something unsavory about those places and the people who frequented them.

If Chrystal's husband, Matt, was more tolerant of the worn men nursing their beer at the Arlington Saloon or the Palace, it was only because he worked with some of them in the Southern Pacific repair shops across Baker Street. Matt Warren did not throw away hard-earned money on five-cent beers, no matter how hot the summer sun in Bakersfield.

Kern County—as big as all of Massachusetts, locals boasted in these last years of the century—was growing. The census of 1900 would record sixteen thousand citizens, not counting the transient railroad workers and farmhands, or the oil roustabouts who dropped from the Los Angeles express each night to seek work in the new-sprung fields northeast of the county seat.

Bakersfield was raucous boom town and bustling community. The city boasted good water, a public library, schools, clubhouses, and newspapers. The streets were newly paved, with sewers laid down; Power Transit and Light's open streetcars would soon link Bakersfield and the SP division point of East Bakersfield two miles away. The city directory of 1899, Bakersfield's first, listed ten churches, nine liquor stores, a racetrack, and an Odd Fellows Hall.

Young Earl Warren, astride his docile burro Jack, found it all a great place for exploration, especially the stone courthouse with its lofty cupola and crowning statue of Columbia. The tow-headed youngster enjoyed the trials, perhaps because they reeked of evil revenged and villainies redressed, perhaps because the paneled courtrooms in summer were usually cooler than the 100-degree temperatures outside.

East Bakersfield, where the Warren family lived, suited young Earl's father. Listed in that first directory as a "car inspector," Matt Warren had worked himself up to foreman on the night crew in the Southern Pacific shops.

As a master car builder, he had steadily squirreled away money from his rather handsome $70-per-month salary. He spent little, and squandered nothing. "Son," he warned young Earl, "never let yourself be caught broke. Saving is a habit, like any other, and once established will last you a lifetime."

Matt Warren's thrift laid a stern discipline upon the small frame house on Niles Street. "He never spent an unnecessary dollar on himself. He lived a Spartan life, which meant a more or less Spartan life for my mother also," Earl Warren later said.

On one cause only was Matt Warren generous: his children's education. Earl and his older sister, Ethel, had all the books they wanted.

So the Warren family gradually prospered in East Bakersfield. With his savings, Matt bought first one, then a second weathered house, hammered them into shape, then rented them to itinerant workers. As the family's fortunes improved, they moved, from M Street to Beale Avenue, and finally to what young Earl thought of as the family home at 707 Niles Street, across the dusty road from the Southern Pacific shops.

The Warrens doggedly pursued the American dream. Hard work and thrift, laced with education and moral rectitude, led to financial security, Matt and Chrystal taught. When the children faltered, punishment was swift, their son recalled. "My father wasn't exactly a failure at handling the birch rod."

Old-fashioned values they were, but the Warrens were old-fashioned folks.

Born in Stavanger, Norway, in 1864, Matt was brought to the United States two years later. The family of Halvor Varran settled first on a farm in Leland, Illinois, amid relatives from Stavanger. Halvor Varran, sometime farmer, sometime carpenter, became Harry Warren, and his son Methias, Matt.

Four years after arriving in the United States, young Matt's mother died. With three young sons to raise, his father quickly remarried and moved the family to a farm in Eagle Grove, Iowa. In time there were eight more children and too few dollars in the crowded home. Sent to live with neighbors, Matt and his older brother Ole did farm chores in exchange for bed, board, and schooling. According to the custom of the country, on July 4, the boys received a fifty-cent piece from their employer.

Matt managed to stay in school through the seventh grade, longer than did most children in this last quarter of the nineteenth century and preserved his interest in education. A generation after, his son and daughter easily summoned the memory of wiry Matt Warren at the dining room table hunched over bookkeeping and accounting books from the International Correspondence School.

Together Ole, seventeen, and Matt, fifteen, left the farm in Eagle Grove, the younger boy vowing to his stepmother, "I am going to have a home of my own some day, and my wife has to have more money than you've got." They crisscrossed the Midwest working as farmhands in the country and as skilled handymen in the towns.

Eventually, the two brothers made their way to Chicago. There Ole contracted a virulent form of tuberculosis; hacking bloody sputum, he died in his brother's arms on a bleak Christmas Eve, 1884.

Matt Warren would never escape the guilt he felt, blaming Ole's death on their inability to hire a doctor. "Having lost the one most near and dear to him and being broke in a strange city, my father later told me, he then swore that as long as he lived he would never be broke again," Earl recalled.

Left alone, Matt Warren made his way in 1885 to Minneapolis and the large Scandinavian community in that city. There he found work in the rail yards repairing freight cars, and met brown-haired Christine Hernlund, an attractive seventeen-year-old schoolgirl born in Hälsingland, Sweden. Like Matt, "Chrystal"—as she preferred to be called—had come to America as an infant. The Hernlund family had settled first in Chicago, but was burned out in the great fire of 1871 and moved on to Minneapolis.

Common background and common values drew Matt and Chrystal together. Raised in a Christian family, Chrystal disapproved of alcohol and tobacco. A quiet woman, she too believed in hard work. A year after they met, Matt Warren, twenty, and Christine Hernlund, eighteen, were married. Their first child, Ethel, was born the following year in Minneapolis.

Anxious about his health—tireless Matt was slight and, according to his daughter, feared an early death like Ole's—the new father succumbed to railroad advertisements touting the healthful climate in Southern California. In 1889, Warren packed his wife and daughter onto a crowded Atchison, Topeka and Santa Fe train bound for San Diego.

Matt Warren found work as a "mechanic" at the Coronado Hotel, a grand resort perched in whited splendor on an island in San Diego Bay. The following year Warren again packed up his family, moving 125 miles north, to Los Angeles, for a job in the Southern Pacific Railroad's car repair shops. He rented a shabby five-room house at 457 Turner Street, not far from the city's original plaza.

There, on March 19, 1891, a midwife delivered their second child, a son, christened Earl. When later the boy asked why he bore no middle name, his father snorted, "My boy, when you were born I was too poor to give you a middle name."

Founded literally on thin air, Southern California's land boom could not last. By 1891 jobs had grown scarce.

The stock market crash of 1893 made matters worse, much worse. Across the country, almost 500 banks failed, and 15,000 businesses closed their doors. A third of the nation's overvalued railroads lay mired in bankruptcy. Three million workers were unemployed. Uncomprehending men like Matt Warren grew fearful of implacable economic laws they could neither under-stand nor control.

The depression wore on, month after grim month. In the company town of Pullman, Illinois, the Pullman Palace Car Company summarily slashed wages by one-quarter; workers were left with as little as a dollar to feed their families for two weeks after the paymaster had deducted rent for the houses in which they lived.

The angry Pullman workers flocked to join the new American Railway Union, headed by a balding ex–railroad fireman from Vincennes, Indiana, Eugene Victor Debs. On May 10, 1894, the company fired three members of an ARU grievance committee; the next morning the desperate workers voted to strike. When a quarter of a million railroad workers walked out in sympathy, the twenty-six rail lines snaking from Chicago lay empty of traffic. The ARU had brought the nation to "the ragged edge of anarchy," the attorney general of the United States fumed.

The strike spread. By June 27, an alarmed *Los Angeles Times* headlined, "Through Travel Suspended for the Time Being." Matt Warren was among the 3,000 Southern Pacific and Santa Fe workers who downed tools at the Arcade and Le Grande yards that day. Southern California was isolated by what newspapers had taken to calling "The Debs Rebellion."

In response, the railroads started a blacklist of strikers, while taking "large numbers of applications for the positions vacated by the strikers," the *Times* reported.

The walkout in Los Angeles remained peaceful, though striker Matt Warren's three-year-old son Earl vividly recalled seeing "a large group of men" hang a straw effigy from the flagpole at nearby Ann Street school one night. The jeering of the unidentified men and the stuffed figure swaying in the light of a bonfire sent the boy scurrying into his mother's arms. Fear of the mob would remain with him all his life.

On July 3, the federal government called out troops to put down the strike. Five companies of the First Regiment, U.S. Infantry, were dispatched to Los Angeles from the Presidio of San Francisco with orders to reopen the railroads.

City by city, the great railway strike of 1894 was broken. Rail service resumed. The railroads summarily fired the men who had walked out.

Cautious Matt Warren found himself out of work and blacklisted by the Southern Pacific. Leaving his family in Los Angeles, Warren traveled to San Bernardino, sixty miles to the east, where the Santa Fe maintained repair shops. He worked there briefly, before learning of a better job with the Southern Pacific in labor-short Kern City in the San Joaquin Valley.*

Kern City had begun life in 1874 as Sumner, an SP division point 230 miles south of San Francisco at the foot of the fertile valley. Beyond lay the Tehachapi Mountains, the east-west tail of the southern Sierra Nevada, rising four thousand feet above the valley floor; it would take almost two years to push the railroad through eighteen tunnels, around a famed loop of track that ever after attracted photographers, then over the steep grade and into the barren desert that led to Los Angeles.

For almost a quarter-century, the Southern Pacific—the "Octopus" of Frank Norris's angry novel—had enjoyed a monopoly in the valley. Unchecked, it fixed extortionate freight rates, bought votes in the state legislature, and effectively controlled life in the Golden State.

The SP went unchallenged in central California until the rival Santa Fe opened a parallel route from Oakland into Bakersfield in 1896. Overnight SP's freight charges in the San Joaquin Valley dropped 20 percent.

That year Matt Warren moved his family to Kern City. Earl was not yet six.

Kern City, no more than a sun-baked, clapboard town, offered few amenities. It was "the other side of the tracks," a place for rough-edged railroad workers and the standoffish Basque and French sheepherders who came down from the hills during the winter.

A few blacks lived scattered here and there in town, their American Methodist Episcopal church around the corner from the Warren home. The Chinese who had escaped employment on the railroad remained rigidly segregated on L Street in Bakersfield, just a block from the whorehouses on K, where their money was not welcome, for even moral outcasts needed pariahs to scorn.

The Warrens arrived in this rough-and-tumble community just as oil drillers brought in the discovery wells of the Kern River fields. The rowdy railroad town remade itself into an even more raucous, thoroughly corrupted oil town. Decades later, Warren easily recalled a shotgun duel on a Sunday morning in April, 1903, in which Sheriff's Deputy Will Tibbett, the father of future operatic baritone Lawrence, was killed.

With growth, Bakersfield and nearby Kern City—renamed East Bakersfield in 1900 and nine years later annexed by the county seat—demanded respectability. Matt and Chrystal Warren guided their children in the paths of righteousness. Ethel and Earl "were very well mannered, clean looking,

---

* Devoted son Earl believed his father was in sympathy with the strikers, but there is some hint in later documents that Matt Warren may have been a spy for the company. His reward would have been a job out of town at twice the salary of oil field workers and farmhands. At least one man who knew Matt Warren in Bakersfield described him much later as "a labor-hating so-and-so." See Steve Murdock, "The Making of a Demagogue—Warren," *People's World*, September 27, 1948.

blonds, and never did anything shocking or earth shaking," a schoolmate recalled.

They were taught right from wrong, older sister Ethel explained later. If her younger brother was a little more daring than Ethel, he seemed to know just how far he could go. A lie was not acceptable in the Warren home. It was "a major crime," Ethel said.

The boy favored his mother's looks, blue-eyed, fair of hair and complexion. He also seemed to favor her friendly nature, sister Ethel reminisced. "He always liked people. He made friends with everyone. Mama used to say that if she missed him, she'd just look for a group of people and he'd be in the middle of it."

His father prevailed upon school authorities to let Earl enter the first grade at Baker Street Elementary School in September, 1896, because his son could already read and print his letters. Those skills also prompted Principal Leo G. Pauly to move Earl into the third grade at the end of the first year. It was the last time the boy would reveal any particular academic gift.

"Earl was an average student," Pauly said later, "a very docile fellow who attended strictly to business." Naturally left-handed, the lad learned to write with his right hand as proper Palmer penmanship demanded. For the rest of his life, he wrote right-handed, but otherwise favored his left.

Young Warren would go through the public schools of Kern County at least one year, sometimes two or three years, younger than his classmates. A succession of schoolyard fights over his "sissy" ringlets led his mother eventually to agree to a haircut. Otherwise, Pauly said, "there was no special promise of a brilliant career."

The boy was industrious. For three stifling summers he worked seven days a week on Ethen Zumwalt's ice wagon, delivering ten-pound blocks to homes on the iceman's regular route. The job paid twenty-five cents a day, with a welcome block of ice for the Warren home thrown in. The money he carefully put away for a college education, at his father's insistence.

Money in the Warren household went for serious things, like a copy of Professor L. DuPont Syle's anthology of English poetry, *From Milton to Tennyson,* which Earl Warren carefully inscribed a month after his thirteenth birthday.* Though most of the poems were probably beyond a boy's interest, on the fly leaf he wrote the imperfectly remembered Edward Lear limerick:

> *There was Hindo who does the best he kindo*
> *He sticks to his cast from the first to the last*
> *And for pants, he makes his skin do.*

---

* Warren kept the book in his personal library for the next forty-eight years. It is now in the Bancroft Library, University of California.

Chautauqua speakers provided the Warrens with edification and entertainment alike. For the rest of his life, Earl would often recall the Reverend Russell H. Conwell's popular homily celebrating local boosterism and the gospel of success, "Acres of Diamonds." He would not, however, heed the tent-lecture moral that riches were to be found at home.

Earl was thirteen in September, 1904, when he entered Kern County High School, one of seventy members of the Class of 1908. Because most of those who completed the eighth grade immediately went to work, the high school enrollment was not large. Earl enrolled in the college preparatory sequence.

Shorter than his classmates and still in the hated knee pants his mother demanded he wear, young Warren was shy around girls. None in any event seemed interested in spooning with the youngest and smallest kid in the school.

Despite his parents' disapproval—"Father thought you went to school to learn"—Earl went out for sports. In his senior year, he played right end on the second or "B" football team. A less than gifted athlete, he became instead an avid spectator. He considered himself "shortchanged" because he was so small he could never fully participate in high school sports. *His* children would not skip grades.

Kern County High School's pedagogy rested more on firm discipline and a rigid curriculum than any love of learning. The forbidding principal, C. C. Childress, "Old C-Cubed," saw to that. The handful of students like Earl in the academic program took four subjects a semester: two years of Latin or French, four of English, and a year each of ancient, medieval, English, and American history.

Warren was little more than an average student, as he wrote in his memoirs. He did well in the classes he enjoyed, especially in history where he earned a grade of 94 in his senior year. Unlike his father, he could not grasp mathematics. His lowest grade during his four years at Kern was a 70 in advanced algebra. He did little better in the required physics class, one of his classmates recalled.

Though his grades did not reflect it, her brother "had quite an analytic mind," Ethel Warren recalled. "At home Dad and Earl used to take opposite views of things. I think Dad was drawing Earl out to see what he was thinking."

Both Earl and his sister took music lessons after school, Ethel on the piano and Earl on the clarinet. Playing in the Bakersfield town band with his one close friend, Albert Cuneo, and the jobs Earl held were his most memorable experiences during these high school years.

He worked on a baker's delivery wagon early in the mornings. Instead of ice he took home cookies. He delivered *The Bakersfield Californian*. He drove a mule team pulling a grocery wagon for two summers. The next he kept books for the Ardizzi-Olcese Company, general merchandiser. He tutored a onetime SP brakeman who had lost a foot in a railroad accident, helping the man pass his college entrance examinations.

While old acquaintances from Baker Street School were already familiar with the adult world, young Warren hung back. He avoided the teenager's ritual initiation with the black prostitutes on K Street, though classmate Frank Vaughan hinted that the gangly Warren got his first taste of "Old Wide-Eye" while in high school.

In the summer of 1907, Earl and Albert Cuneo took the train to Los Angeles on railroad passes to see the sixteen warships of Theodore Roosevelt's Great White Fleet moored in San Pedro harbor. The two boys followed the flotilla north to Santa Barbara before returning to Bakersfield. It was the first time he had been away from home.

Still, the most fun came from playing in the town band with his buddy Albert. They marched in ceremonial parades, furnished the music for political rallies and torchlight parades, and performed Saturday night concerts during the summer.

Warren was just fifteen when he and Albert were invited to become charter members of Local 263 of the American Federation of Musicians. "It wasn't that my playing was so good," he joked later. "It was just that the union needed members." He served as secretary at the organizational meeting and carried a union card for the rest of his life.

Beginning in his junior year of high school, the year he shot up to almost six feet in height, Earl went to work for the Southern Pacific as a call boy. It was his job to round up the crews scheduled to man trains leaving town. Since many of the men were single, Warren came to know the Owl and Standard dance halls, the Southern Hotel and the Mint Saloon, the bawdy houses where classmate Omar Cavins assured him he would "get an eyeful," the saloons with their illegal gambling games upstairs, all places his protective mother had shielded him from.

It was a jarring lesson in that era of virtually unrestrained laissez-faire. "I was dealing with people as they worked for a gigantic corporation that dominated the economic and political life of the community. I saw that power exercised and the hardship that followed in its wake": men laid off without warning to increase stock dividends; others mutilated in industrial accidents and left jobless without compensation; the Chinese immigrants held in virtual slavery to perform manual labor for the railroad. "I witnessed crime and vice of all kinds countenanced by corrupt government." The memory of stacks of $20 gold pieces on the gambling tables was keen, and indelible.

He worked hard as a call boy. Warren was proud that he never delayed a train for failing to round up a crew. Moreover, he covered for the men who were drunk or otherwise unavailable, invariably listing them as "sick" and thereby saving their jobs for them.

As busy as his after-school hours were, Earl Warren in dark suit with long pants, his hair parted carefully in the center, was among the six men and eleven women who graduated Kern County High School in the June, 1908, ceremonies at Scribner's Opera House. In the class yearbook, his mock last testament stated, "I, Earl Warren, will to Lorraine K. Stoner my ability to slide through, doing as little work as possible." The teasing class prophecy foretold his future selling "Warren's New Hair Dope" on street corners.

Two months later, seventeen-year-old Earl Warren boarded a train for Berkeley and the campus of the University of California. He was escaping, never again to live in stifling Bakersfield.

CHAPTER 2

PINKY'S WAY

THE JOURNEY FROM BAKERSFIELD TO OAKLAND WAS LONG, HOT, and dusty. For thirteen hours gawky Earl Warren sat sweating in the grimy SP coach, watching the San Joaquin Valley pass his open window.

His father had bid him a gruff goodbye: "Well, my boy, you are going away from home. You are a man now, and I am sure you are going to act like one." That farewell left Matt Warren's son apprehensive, uncertain of what the University of California held in store.

There would be few familiar faces on the Berkeley campus. Warren was the first from East Bakersfield to attend the university. While four of his fellow Kern County High School graduates were going to the university, two, Reginald Stoner and Wilfred Forker, were privileged, and popular athletes, not the sort of men to chum around with unprepossessing Earl Warren.

His father had once urged Earl to study mining at the university. There was a good school of mining there, and plenty of jobs to be had in a state rich with mineral deposits and oil fields. Stoner, Forker, and Omar Cavins, who would work a year before joining them, were all going to study at Mining, destined for careers with Standard Oil.

Earl cherished a different dream. He knew he wanted to be a lawyer, a trial lawyer, like the men he had seen arguing cases in the courthouse on the way home from school. He could never recall exactly when or how he made that decision. At one time he had considered medicine, his sister remembered, "for a doctor could help people. . . . But once he made up his mind to be a lawyer, he never changed it."

It was a strange career choice for a youngster who found it difficult even to recite in class. Perhaps it was the very fluency of the attorneys, the practiced ease of their arguments, that attracted him. Perhaps he too could achieve that casual mastery in law school.

The eager youth who hefted his suitcase from the overhead rack as the train slowed to a halt in Oakland was exceptionally fortunate. Few people in the United States attended colleges or universities in this first decade of the century. The children of immigrants rarely went to college; the census of 1900 reported that just 86,000 of the 687,000 people still in school after the age of eighteen had one or more foreign-born parents. Matt and Chrystal Warren's thrift had overcome long odds.

For the first time in his life, Earl Warren felt free. He had saved $800 from his part-time jobs, a goodly sum when an oil field roustabout made $12 per week. The money was Earl's to do with as he wished; Matt Warren had undertaken to pay for his son's education.

The SP train stood, sighing steam, on the great pier thrust a thousand yards into a San Francisco Bay washed red with the sunset. At the head of the pier waited a ferryboat that would take Earl Warren across the calm waters to San Francisco. He intended to stay his first night away from home in the biggest city in the state.

On this Saturday evening in August, 1908, Warren made his way forward. "As I stood on the bow of the ferryboat, surveying the beautiful bay and looking over to the Golden Gate, I filled my lungs with refreshing air and said to myself, 'I never want to live anywhere else the rest of my life.' "

The city itself was sobering. The wreckage of the great earthquake and fire of April, 1906, was still everywhere to be seen. Here and there new buildings sprouted along Market Street amid cleared lots and heaps of broken bricks. There was a sense of spirit, of new life. Seventeen-year-old Earl Warren, the boy from the frontier railroad town, was captivated by the romance, the sheer grandeur of a shattered city rebuilding itself.

The following morning Warren retraced his way to Oakland on the ferry and boarded an interurban train to Berkeley, home of the University of California. He was to enroll as one of 842 members of the freshman class, on a campus with 3,100 students and a faculty approaching 300.

He ate breakfast in a restaurant on Oxford Street across from the campus, marveling at the size of the buildings, the dense groves of live oak, and the stands of eucalyptus on the hills east of the university. After breakfast he walked across campus, with its odd blend of traditional ivy and tropical palm trees, through the wild grasses beyond the newly opened Hearst Memorial Mining Building, past the bare steel frame of the rising campanile that would tower over the campus and its new library. Young Earl Warren was swept up in the excitement of a state university, founded just thirty-nine years before, poised at the beginning of a great expansion; for the rest of his life he would be the most loyal of alumni.

That same day he made a second lifelong attachment. He moved into the

La Junta Club, a block from the campus, recommended to the fraternal living group by a family friend. La Junta men were serious about their studies, and often self-supporting.

In the manner of these affairs, freshman and upperclassmen appraised each other. At the first Sunday meeting of the semester, Warren recounted in his memoirs, he was asked about his high school days. He proudly recounted the "cat and mouse relationship" the students had with C. C. Childress, the ever-snooping principal of Kern County High School. Since old "C-Cubed" even penalized classes on suspicion of cheating, the boys, in turn, tried to outwit him with ever more clever methods of cheating.

Senior Herbert Whiting that evening gravely invited the freshman to dinner in Oakland later in the week. In a "fatherly way," Whiting reproved Warren for his childish behavior. "This was not the way things were done at the university. He said the university operated on the honor system; that there was no spying; that students were entrusted with self-government, and that they were expected to be honorable in taking examinations as in all other things."

Moreover, Whiting added, cheating unfairly penalized fellow students since most professors graded on a class average. If someone unfairly raised that average by cheating, the honorable would receive poorer grades.

Warren was acutely embarrassed. He promised Whiting never to violate the honor code.

A few weeks later Warren was invited to join the La Junta Club. He would live with that group for the next six years, reveling in the companionship then, and cherishing in later years the friendships made there. The La Junta Club was a secure den in an institution almost overwhelming, so bustling with ideas and people, and a place of heady freedom for Earl Warren. He was a member still four years later when La Junta became a chapter of the older Sigma Phi fraternity.

The new political science major—his course chosen with an eye on matriculating to law school—was not a particularly serious student. He had no craving for knowledge, he conceded later. "No book or professor had a profound influence on me . . ."

Warren fit in easily. To fulfill a military training requirement, he joined the fifty-two-piece university band, one of three men playing second clarinet, dutifully working his way to first clarinet in the next three years. He also earned pocket money playing for campus proms, prim affairs at which the Junior Prom Committee prohibited the increasingly fashionable turkey trot, grizzly bear, and back-walking.

The youngster known around La Junta as "The Freshman" matured. His features hardened and he put on weight, his hair now parted on the left side. Warren spent much of his time playing cards at La Junta, or drinking ten-cent beers at such popular campus gathering places as Gus Brause's. The companionship meant more to him than his studies.

Less skilled than game, he also took up sparring with the athletic Walter

Arthur Gordon, the grandson of a slave. The two men would remain lifelong friends.

He read a fair amount outside of class; Rudyard Kipling, Robert Louis Stevenson, and Charles Dickens were favorites, as were three Americans, Upton Sinclair, Jack London, and Frank Norris. Significantly, two of the three were Californians, and all were progressive social reformers.

Earl acquired a nickname, bestowed on him by a nurse at the university infirmary where he had gone to be treated for pinkeye. Friends heard her call, "Come on, Pinky, it's time for your medicine." The name stuck, in part because of his fair complexion and the tendency of his skin to burn in the sun.

He was invited to become a member of the secretive Gun Club that gathered on Thursday nights at Pop Kessler's Rathskeller in Oakland to drink beer and read the poetry of Robert Service, Rudyard Kipling, Gelett Burgess, and Bret Harte. Warren would be remembered there for declaiming "The Sinking of the Mary Gloucester" and "Leave the Lady, Willie," but his own favorite was W. E. Henley's "Invictus":

> It matters not how strait the gate,
>   How charged with punishments the scroll,
> I am the master of my fate;
>   I am the captain of my soul.

Membership in the society, based on companionship rather than social standing, nurtured Warren's idealism. As a member, he strove to earn "a love between men who would put virtue and honor and loyalty above all else," as a later member put it.

Here too he learned to honor the homily of the university's football coach, Andy Smith: "It is better to lose than to win at the sacrifice of an ideal." Here too he found affirmation in the boyhood lesson that "the only thing that matters in a man is character. Character is determined by his refusal to lie." Popular on campus, in his last year he was invited to join the select honor society Skull and Keys.

With friends Warren trooped down to the Oakland–Alameda estuary to talk with wintering salmon fishermen or hang out in the First and Last Chance saloon where writer London told outrageous adventure stories to anyone who would buy him a drink. Other times Warren and classmate John Quinn would take a ferry across the bay to savor the spiked punch and free lunches served at the Waldorf Bar.

"Pinky" Warren considered these undergraduate years at Berkeley uneventful. His studies were none too demanding. Summers he returned to Bakersfield to labor as a mechanic's helper in the Southern Pacific roundhouse.

While no professor had a lasting impact on him, Berkeley in this second decade of the century burned with the fires of Progressive reform. Thomas

Harrison Reed, a young and dynamic political science professor, was lecturing in class on weekdays and from the pulpit of the Congregational Church on Sundays regarding social questions.

Reed's fervor seeped across the campus. Reform would henceforth be infused with a religious strain for Warren; "throwing the rascals out" was not only good government, it was the moral thing to do.

Politics interested Warren. He took part in elections for student government, promoting one or another friend's candidacy, but ran for no office himself. In his sophomore year, he attended rallies at San Francisco's Dreamland Rink for Progressive gubernatorial candidate Hiram W. Johnson, then spent election night as a poll-watcher in San Francisco's Mission District. As a junior, Warren cheered a student demonstration for Socialist John Stitt Wilson, later elected mayor of Berkeley.

Warren's nascent Progressivism evolved from the native Californian's antipathy to the dominant Southern Pacific Railroad and from his father's identification with the reform-minded small businessmen who sought a share of the prosperity the great corporations had hoarded.

He himself became a confirmed Progressive in 1912—the year in which he cast his first presidential vote—after traveling to Sacramento to hear Wisconsin Senator Robert La Follette, Sr., "pour out his heart" futilely campaigning for the Republican nomination.

As governor of Wisconsin, "Fighting Bob" had pushed through a succession of political, economic, and social reforms that made him a champion of the up-and-comer, the go-getter, ambitious young men like Earl Warren.

Decades later, Warren could still quote the reform-minded senator: "The supreme issue, involving all others, is the encroachment of the powerful few upon the rights of the many."

La Follette left a lasting impression:

> He was called a radical, a disrupter, a socialist, a subverter, and perhaps the only reason he was not called a Communist was because that term had not then been popularized as a term of opprobrium. But he was a lifelong Republican, steeped in the tradition of that party. . . . He believed in the party system . . . and his party in particular as a party of the people—farmers, workmen, small-business men; not as an oligarchy of dominant interests.

At the end of his third year at Berkeley, Warren entered the Department of Jurisprudence in newly opened Boalt Hall. He may well have been the least promising of the seventy-nine enrolled students.

The school's rigid curriculum provoked quiet rebellion in the first-year student. Under the leadership of Dean William Carey Jones, Boalt had adopted the casebook method of study recently pioneered at Harvard. The five members of the faculty presided over the required courses, slavishly following the Harvard model of contracts, torts, property, criminal law, and common law pleading. All were read from casebooks that began with Old English law and plodded toward the twentieth century.

There was no introductory course to the practice of law and no practical training whatsoever, Warren grumbled. Students who might have sought a broader education were prohibited from working in a law office; nothing was to interfere with their indoctrination by the Boalt faculty.

"The law school made a fetish of discouraging the acquisition of practical knowledge; and they were so committed to the case system that they denied you opportunity of seeing things in perspective." The discontented Warren held his tongue until the end of the first year when he received his bachelor of law degree.

Dean Jones frankly attempted to discourage Warren from continuing his law studies. "You will never graduate," he warned.

Why? asked the young man. Hadn't he passed all of his examinations?

He had, yes, but he had not once raised his hand to speak out in class, Jones replied.

Was it obligatory? No.

Was the class ever informed? It was assumed.

"Well, then, Dean, as I was never told, and it is not obligatory and I am passing my examinations, I am going to graduate," Warren firmly concluded.

He did. Contrary to the school's rules, Warren took an afternoon job in a Berkeley law office, serving court papers, handling nontechnical matters, and studying the interminable casebooks when he was not busy. The job offered an insight into the everyday practice of law that was missing from the Boalt Hall curriculum.

His grades during his last two years at Boalt were acceptable, but not good enough to qualify him for the new law review's staff. Neither did he make the legal honorary societies. He turned in his thirty-four-page thesis, "The Personal Liability of Corporation Directors in the State of California," on time in May, 1914.

He was undistinguished in all ways, one of fifteen men and one woman to receive their doctor of jurisprudence degree that year. Even in graduating, he was erroneously identified by *The Blue and Gold* annual as "Carl" Warren.

A week later, the class was routinely admitted to practice in California, without examination, on motion of a member of the law school faculty before the District Court of Appeal.

Graduation raised a major problem. His father expected Earl to return to Bakersfield to practice law. The prospect, after six years in Berkeley, seemed to him a loss of freedom.

He weighed a move to Sacramento. There were jobs for a lawyer in a state capital. But it would be difficult to explain to his father a move from the heat of Bakersfield to the heat of Sacramento.

Instead, he chose to remain in the San Francisco Bay area. Intent on gaining the practical training he had missed in law school, he joined the two-lawyer legal department of the Associated Oil Company in San Francisco. The pay was a scant $50 per month.

He was twenty-three, a light blond with lighter whiskers, big at 6 feet 1 inch, but rawboned. "I guess I must have looked awfully young to people," Warren conceded.

Warren quickly grew disillusioned with his job. The oil company's chief counsel, Edmund Tauske, was irascible or demeaning by turns. He issued peremptory orders, gruffly dispatching Warren to fetch a half-dozen Coronas from the cigar store downstairs. Tauske verbally dismissed his assistant's legal research, then adopted it without change when advising management on a point of law. Frustrated, the younger man would have soon quit but did not want to embarrass the friends he had used as references.

His spirits fell even more when he contemplated the sorry state of the practice of law in San Francisco. Almost daily he visited the temporary county courthouse and observed the day-to-day workings of the law. He soon realized the majority of the judges and prosecutors were hacks, creatures of the Southern Pacific Railroad and the city's political bosses. "The atmosphere surrounding them was anything but inspiring," Warren wrote later.

Reform had come slowly to freewheeling San Francisco. Until 1907, the city was firmly in the hands of a canny, cultured politician, Abraham Ruef. Republican Abe Ruef controlled all eighteen seats on the Board of Supervisors that governed the city and county.

Ruef was both boss and bagman. He spread among the supervisors his lucrative legal fees from the city's street railway, and the water, telephone, gas, and electric utilities. The graft system worked smoothly until the earthquake and fire of 1906.

The corruption that slowed the city's recovery sapped the public's tolerance. Prodded by a crusading newspaper publisher, the district attorney appointed a special prosecutor to root out corruption. But prosecutor Francis J. Heney's reformist zeal spurred him beyond caution. He indicted the executives of the companies that had bribed Ruef, and the business community abruptly turned on their pet thieftaker.

Heney himself ran for district attorney in 1909—the city election that Warren had crossed the bay to monitor—only to learn the great lesson of reform politics: The "very best people," who provide the money for bribes, also provide the money for election campaigns. Heney was defeated.

The new district attorney, Charles M. Fickert, immediately dropped the graft prosecutions. In a city of scoundrels and bribe-takers, only the go-between, Abe Ruef, would eventually serve time in San Quentin.

San Francisco's brief spasm of good government produced one significant result. A group of idealistic reformers in Los Angeles prevailed upon Ruef's prosecutor, Hiram W. Johnson, to run for governor in 1910. Johnson and his supporters in the newly organized Lincoln-Roosevelt League swept into office on an anti-railroad, reform platform, and captured the Republican Party machinery from the Old Guard of corporate interests.

Then nineteen, Earl Warren had cheered Johnson's campaign—no one who grew up in the shadow of the Southern Pacific in East Bakersfield could do otherwise. Johnson toured the state in an automobile, promising in speech after speech to expel the corruptors. As part of that extirpation, Johnson also pledged "to kick the Southern Pacific Railroad out of politics."

Sworn into office in 1911, Johnson and his Progressives instituted a wide-ranging series of social and political reforms. Most notably, they introduced the referendum and citizen initiative. They also stripped political parties of the power to endorse candidates. Without the authority to select candidates and enforce discipline, the political parties and their bosses withered.

Johnson brought flowers to the funeral by pushing through the legislature a primary election system that permitted a candidate from one party to run in the primary of another. "Cross-filing" was to have a profound impact on the careers of California officeholders for the next half-century.

Johnson deliberately broadened his appeal to attract Democratic Party voters by pressing for social reforms. He supported workman's compensation laws, the regulation of child labor, an eight-hour day for women, a minimum wage, and factory inspections. With unanimous votes in both houses, he rammed through laws that empowered the state railroad commission to set railroad rates. Similarly, Johnson secured comprehensive regulation of public utilities. While such radical notions may have alienated conservative Republican backers, he gained more votes than he lost.

Johnson and his fellow Progressives brought a spiritual certainty to their cleansing of the temple. They were crusaders, temperance-minded, opposed to racetrack gambling and slot machines, quick to condemn the vices of the lower classes. A later historian would label their efforts "Onward, Christian capitalists."

First La Follette, now Johnson captured Warren's imagination. This son of a workman, and to that extent a likely Democratic voter, became instead a lifelong Republican.

Party label mattered not at all in San Francisco, where the courthouse cronyism and wink-of-the-eye favoritism was endemic, and so disillusioning to Warren. Further, his job in Associated Oil's Legal Department offered no more than unrewarding scut work. Only one incident stood out in that dreary year.

He was dispatched to obtain a routine order from Frank M. Angellotti, the chief justice of the state Supreme Court. As Warren entered the justice's private office, Angellotti graciously rose from his chair behind the desk and crossed halfway to the young man, extending his hand.

"Mr. Warren, I am happy to see you," the justice announced.

The simple gesture of courtesy by the highest judicial officer of the state made a lasting impression on the disheartened young attorney.

Warren hung on unhappily for a year with Associated Oil, then announced he was leaving—after finding his replacement. He had no other job lined up; he simply had to get out.

Within days Warren had secured another position, clerking for the Oakland law firm of Robinson and Robinson. Warren began his law career over again, at a salary of $75 per month. He kept the firm's calendar of court appearances, handled minor matters at the wood-frame county courthouse, and did legal research for the senior partner. Unlike his experience in San Francisco, Warren enjoyed his trips to the Oakland courthouse. Judges, clerks, and other lawyers, particularly such younger men as Oliver D. Hamlin in the district attorney's office, were friendly.

He was happy here. Oakland was a thriving city of 150,000, rife with opportunity, personal and professional. Warren took the lead in organizing the younger attorneys into a social club that met at the Peerless Cafe on 13th Street. When this Young Lawyers' Club of Oakland with its hundred members petitioned the inactive bar association to call a reorganization meeting, Warren unexpectedly found himself elected vice president of the third largest bar association in the state.

He was just twenty-six, less than three years out of law school, hardly more than a law clerk with one carefully pressed blue serge suit to his name. His salary was still a fledgling's $75 per month which he supplemented by tutoring a group of men for the state bar exam.

He rented a room from his sister Ethel, who had moved to Oakland with her husband, Vernon Plank, an SP storekeeper. They lived a short ride on the electric interurban from the courthouse.

Eighteen months after going to work at Robinson and Robinson, Warren and two classmates from Boalt Hall, Chris Fox and Thomas Ledwich, decided to open their own practice. The three approached an older trial lawyer, Peter J. Crosby, about forming a partnership, with Crosby to get the majority of the profits while the young men did a majority of the work. Crosby agreed.

The would-be partners were looking for office space when on April 2, 1917, President Woodrow Wilson asked Congress for a declaration of war against Germany. The world, the President told Congress, "must be made safe for democracy."

Earl Warren's job prospects changed dramatically.

The young lawyer was one of thousands of patriotic men who volunteered to attend a hastily set up officers' training camp. Passed over for the first group admitted, Warren was accepted for the second levy. Doctors discovered, however, that he had hemorrhoids and disqualified him.

Intent on serving, Warren promptly checked into an Oakland hospital to have the hemorrhoids removed. He underwent the discomfiting operation, but fell victim to ether pneumonia.

By the time he was discharged from the hospital three weeks later, officer enlistments had closed. Instead, a nationwide draft had been inaugurated. Warren asked to be drafted as an enlisted man.

He found himself in charge of the first group of draftees to leave Oakland on September 5, 1917, bound for Camp Lewis, Washington, near Tacoma. At newly opened Camp Lewis, Warren was assigned to I Company of the 363rd Regiment, 91st Infantry Division.

Mobilization had taken by surprise an army unprepared either for war or for large groups of recruits. The men of I Company were issued no uniforms for weeks; bedding was in short supply. They lived "almost in squalor for weeks until some new issues arrived," Warren recalled.

The company commander appointed Private Warren acting first sergeant of I Company. The assignment was his as much for sheer size as for any military training in the school band. A member of the regiment, fellow Californian Leo Carrillo, remembered his former first sergeant as "a big man mentally and physically, a great hulking, strong, sturdy soldier without any pettiness."

Exempted from the wearying four-mile marches to American Lake and the mindless close-order drill with wooden guns, Warren was responsible for the administration of the 250-man training company. He would later describe that as his most valuable training in the army. He would also make two lifelong friends at Camp Lewis, Carrillo and Tatsu Ogawa, a volunteer from the Hawaiian Islands.

In January, 1918, Warren volunteered to go through the three-month officers' training program. He remembered the training as a grueling ordeal since his desk-bound duty as first sergeant had hardly put him in the best physical shape. Though 40 percent of the trainees washed out, Warren survived the course and on May 1, 1918, he returned to I Company at Camp Lewis.

Secret orders sent the regiment by fast train across the continent to Camp Lee, Virginia, the men certain they would be shipped to France as infantry replacements. Instead, the 363rd was assigned to training draftees. Newly commissioned Second Lieutenant Earl Warren was to spend the rest of his army career in the United States.

Mustered out less than a month after the November armistice, newly promoted First Lieutenant Warren returned to Bakersfield to spend Christmas with his family.*

He had greatly changed since leaving for the university ten years earlier. His army experience had toughened him and had bolstered his confidence after a lackluster start in the law. He had grown to his full height of six feet, one inch, and added twenty-five pounds. No longer the gawky kid, he now weighed a solid two hundred pounds.

---

* Warren remained in the Officers Reserve Corps until December 5, 1934. He rose to the rank of captain before his commission was terminated by a budget-conscious Congress.

At such moments, men take stock. He was twenty-seven and had little to show for it. The $60 mustering-out pay in his pocket represented his entire worldly wealth. His law career had been anything but outstanding, and his plans were shapeless. Only one thing was certain to First Lieutenant Earl Warren. He could not live in confining Bakersfield.

CHAPTER 3

THE DEPUTY

S TILL IN UNIFORM, EARL WARREN RETURNED TO OAKLAND AT THE
end of 1918. He moved in with his sister and brother-in-law on
Brighton Street, undecided about his future, but eager to find work.
Oakland had grown. The thriving city, third largest in the state, would
record a population of more than two hundred thousand in the 1920 census.
New industries like Chevrolet were flourishing, and Moore Shipbuilding
had grown to be the largest employer in all of northern California. Meanwhile, adjacent Berkeley, with 56,000 residents and ten thousand students
at the burgeoning university, contributed to the feeling that Alameda
County was a lively metropolitan area, a good place to open a practice as a
trial lawyer.

Warren was weighing just that course when he encountered Leon E.
Gray, a former associate at Robinson and Robinson. Gray asked about
Warren's plans.

They were in "a state of flux," Warren allowed. He had nothing definite.

Gray was suddenly enthusiastic, brimming with ideas. He had been
elected to the state Assembly the previous month, he explained. Each legislator was entitled to a deputy, and Gray had not yet picked his. The pay was
$5 per day for the duration of the session. The job would give Warren a
few months to readjust to civilian life, and figure out what he wanted to do.
Was Warren interested?

When was Gray leaving for Sacramento?

Tomorrow, the assemblyman replied.

As suddenly as that, Earl Warren entered public service.

He would not work as Gray's administrative assistant for very long. Shortly after arriving in Sacramento, Warren bumped into Charles Kasch, newly elected to the Assembly from Ukiah in northern Humboldt County. A member of the La Junta Club at Berkeley while Warren had roomed there, Kasch proposed that he and Gray find a better job for their friend.

Two days later, Warren was named clerk of the powerful Assembly Judiciary Committee. The salary was $7 per day.

This would not be an "inspirational" legislative session, as Warren himself put it with droll understatement. California appeared to be worn out by its spasm of Progressive reform. Without Johnson to whip them along—he had been elected to the United States Senate in 1917—many legislators fell back upon slothful habits. The legislature, indeed the entire state, teetered on the brink of reaction cloaked in impassioned patriotism.

The legislature convened for its biennial session on the first Monday in January, 1919, amid a blast of antiradical speeches and draconian bills to curb "Reds," "communists," "anarchists" and "subversives." Warren's sponsor, Charlie Kasch, was particularly outraged by the militant Industrial Workers of the World, which was organizing lumberjacks in the redwood and cedar forests of his district.

Two well-publicized acts of terrorism had stripped California's labor unions of respectability and vital middle-class sympathy. In 1910 a bomb laid by union organizers exploded in "Ink Alley" behind the *Los Angeles Times* building, killing twenty-one printers. Six years later a suitcase bomb killed ten spectators watching a business-sponsored Preparedness Day Parade on San Francisco's Market Street; suspicion promptly, even conveniently, alighted on two union men outspoken in their opposition to United States participation in the war in Europe. The eventual conviction of socialists Tom Mooney and Warren K. Billings seemed to prove that unions were filled with un-American, cowardly terrorists.

Meanwhile, from Arizona, from Idaho, from Washington, from a dozen different localities in California, there arose a more fearsome menace, the Industrial Workers of the World. The "Wobblies," as members of the IWW were known, drew their strength from unskilled migratory harvest workers, miners, and lumberjacks. They were "womanless, voteless and jobless." They were poor. They were militant.

Once the United States declared war, the Wobblies—who refused "to fight for any purpose other than industrial freedom"—became sport for patriotic vigilantes. Business organizations and a partisan press saw an evil link between the threat at home, the IWW, and the enemy abroad. Now there were editorial assertions that the IWW was financed by the kaiser, or by the newly come to power Soviet Reds. "The IWW are worse than the Germans," the *San Francisco Chronicle* shrieked, "a brand of people associated for the sole purpose of destruction."

The hysteria ran on. The legislature and newly elected governor, William

D. Stephens, joined in the obliteration of the IWW, those "Huns of industry," in California.

A bill intended to curb "criminal syndicalism," defined as using violence or terror to change industrial ownership, moved quickly through the legislature early in 1919. The measure made it a crime to advocate criminal syndicalism, or even to be a member of an organization that advocated, taught, or abetted such beliefs.

Friends of labor held it up briefly in the Assembly, but only long enough to be assured that the legislation applied only to radicals, and not good American laboring men. The Assembly voted 59–9 for the measure. Patriotism prevailed, even when one critical assemblyman charged, "I don't think any of you know what syndicalism means."

The first returned veteran to work for the state legislature, still wearing his army uniform until he could afford a new suit, Warren was troubled by the hysteria surrounding the session. Panic, he concluded, did not lend itself to reasoned debate or sound legislation.

Warren rather quickly adapted to the convoluted political turnings in the state capital. He came to believe he could distinguish between the independent legislators and those who had sold out to special interests. He also became adept at spotting the opaque "cinch bills" introduced by corrupt legislators to squeeze money from special interests.

However disillusioned he might be, the gregarious Warren readily made friends among Sacramento's politicians. He lived with Gray and the rest of the Alameda County delegation in the Hotel Sequoia on K Street. There he became especially close to the slight, dark-haired Frank W. Anderson, who at thirty was beginning his third two-year term in the Assembly.

Anderson encouraged Warren to look into the opportunities with the Alameda County district attorney's office. The DA, Ezra Decoto, had asked the Assembly to authorize an additional deputy for his office. It was just the right job for Warren, a patriotic veteran, Anderson noted pointedly. The Alameda legislators promptly agreed to push for the staff position, providing it went to their friend Warren.

Decoto protested. He had a man, Wade Snook, the son of a former district attorney, trained for the job already. The Alameda County legislators insisted the post go to Warren. No Warren, no funding.

Warren himself broke the deadlock. He explained to Decoto that he had nothing to do with the effort to force the DA to hire him. He wanted the job, but not under these circumstances. He was withdrawing his name.

A relieved Decoto promised to keep Warren in mind for the first available position in his office. Warren accepted the pledge, though the members of the Alameda County legislative delegation later chided him. He would not hear from Decoto anytime soon, they told him.

As the end of the biennial session approached, Earl Warren once more faced unemployment. Again Leon Gray came to Warren's aid.

Gray had accepted a job as a deputy city attorney in Oakland, a position that permitted him to practice law on the side. He proposed they share a law office in the Bank of Italy building in downtown Oakland. As an inducement, Gray promised to steer some business to Warren, just to help him get on his feet. With no real alternative, Warren acceded.

When the legislative session adjourned in April, 1919, the two men moved back to Oakland. They hardly had time to put their names on the door when Gray learned there was an unexpected opening in the Oakland city attorney's office. Assemblyman–Deputy City Attorney Gray recommended his good friend Earl Warren, former chief clerk of the Assembly Judiciary Committee.

City Attorney Hugh L. Hagan immediately recognized the value of having another contact with the budget-dealing state legislature. He offered the $200-per-month job to Warren, advising him to supplement that with a private practice. Warren promptly accepted.

The next months were satisfying, though the raw deputy city attorney recalled that his first appearances in civil court were trying. "I was then so tense that on the streetcar down to the courthouse, I hoped the car would be wrecked so that I wouldn't have to appear in court."

As a deputy city attorney, he advised various city boards and officials on points of law. He wrote advisory opinions, and he dealt enough with the civil courts finally to consider himself a lawyer. Additionally, the private practice cases he was carrying for Gray supplemented his salary by $150 each month.

In the spring of 1920, District Attorney Ezra Decoto telephoned Warren. Warren's acquaintance, Oliver Hamlin, had announced he was going into private practice. There would be an opening in the office on May 1, and when Decoto had finished shuffling people around, the least senior position on the staff would be open. Did Warren want it?

Though it paid only $150 per month, less than he was making in the city attorney's office, Warren accepted. Here finally was the sort of job he had been seeking. Here was criminal trial experience, all he could hope for, covering the justice courts from San Leandro to the Santa Clara County line.

Warren was elated. "I had a sense of liberation such as that which possessed me when I entered the University of California."

The office of the district attorney of Alameda County was a busy one, the deputies divided between prosecuting serious crimes, serving as staff attorney for various county agencies, and representing the county in civil cases. It was all intriguing to Warren, all challenging.

Disdaining the private practices that other deputies maintained, Warren became a tireless volunteer on both the criminal and the civil sides. He intended to work perhaps eighteen months as a deputy district attorney, acquiring the experience that would make him a great trial lawyer, then set off on his own.

His days—"happy days," he said later—stretched longer and longer. Rarely did he get away before midnight. He had a magpie memory, tucking away curious facts about a case or noting the odd legal citation that solved problems. Warren also began to study the office itself, its organization and its relationship to other county agencies.

Appointed district attorney by the county Board of Supervisors in 1916, Decoto had since been twice reelected. He was a man of limited horizon, honest to be sure, but hardly a vigorous prosecutor, and certainly no reformer. Alameda County was shot through with prostitution, illegal gambling, bootlegging, and police corruption.

Emeryville, conveniently adjacent to the university town of Berkeley and thriving Oakland, ran wide open. "Everything went in Emeryville," county Supervisor John Mullins acknowledged.

Decoto ignored the sins of tiny Emeryville since the voters did not seem particularly concerned. If local police failed to enforce the law, Decoto did nothing to spur them on.

Nor did he press his own deputies, who let their cases slide in preference to their private practices. After all, public service paid little, and in booming Alameda County private practitioners were doing quite well. The office had more and more vacancies as skilled deputies left for better-paying positions in private firms.

Their departures raised problems. Who knew about the cases left hanging? Decoto asked. The unfailing answer was "Warren." The longer Warren stayed, the more valuable he became to the office, and the more responsibility fell to him.

"I would frequently ask him on Saturday morning if he could find me some law on a case in the office in the course of the next few days," Decoto remembered. "Monday morning there would invariably be a memorandum on my desk setting forth all the law on the subject involved."

Constantly involved in work he found engrossing, Warren's eighteen-month deadline began to slip. He worked both civil and criminal courts, gaining trial experience. In his very first criminal case, Warren assisted Snook, now a senior deputy district attorney, in the prosecution of a Wobbly.

Warren had private reservations. He felt uneasy about the use of "some repulsive informers" in the case—a convicted burglar and draft dodger; a military deserter; and an admitted embezzler. The three informers, already well practiced, would testify repeatedly up and down the state, becoming no more than professional witnesses for the prosecution.

Meanwhile "the defendant was an ideological radical, but I never could believe he was a terrorist." Injustice was the likely product of convictions based on the testimony of paid informants, Warren decided.

There were few distractions from the work of the office for Warren. He lived with his sister and brother-in-law, occasionally eating dinner with Assemblyman Frank Anderson or one of the younger men on Decoto's staff.

From time to time, he met his college sparring partner, Walter Gordon, now a Berkeley policeman attending law school at night.

He played handball at the Athens Athletic Club a few blocks from the courthouse. In warmer weather he might take a quick noonday swim at one of the bathing clubs that lined the bay, then cap that with a sandwich and milkshake before rushing back to work. On pleasant Sunday afternoons he took his set of left-handed golf clubs out to the Sequoia Golf Club in a futile effort to break ninety. At other times he gathered with college chums at one or another city park to play baseball; Warren played the game with more enthusiasm than skill.

He went to dances and parties, met various women, but dated infrequently and not seriously. Then, about a year after joining the district attorney's office, friends invited him to a Sunday-morning birthday party at the Piedmont Baths in Oakland. There he spied a young woman splashing about in the plunge. Struck by her appearance, Warren asked their hostess to introduce him.

The red-cheeked woman was Nina Elisabeth Meyers, twenty-eight, a widow responsible for her three-year-old son, Jim, and for a widowed stepmother. She managed a women's specialty shop in Oakland.

Earl Warren, who had not thought at all about marriage, was suddenly smitten, head over heels in love.

They were well met. Nina—who preferred "Ny-na" to "Nee-na"—was one of three daughters of a Swedish Baptist minister and sometime osteopath, Nils Peter Palmquist. Born in Sweden, she had been brought to the United States as an infant. The Reverend Palmquist moved his family to San Diego for the mild climate; his first-born, Enoch, was sickly. In 1898, Nina's mother died of uremic poisoning, leaving her father to care for their three young daughters, Eva, Nina, and Hannah, and two sons. Nina was just five years old.

The Palmquists moved on to Oakland, the city Nina would call home. There the Reverend Palmquist remarried.

Illness was to ravage the Palmquist family. The reverend died of tuberculosis in 1907, his two sons in 1919 and 1920. Only reluctantly would Nina Warren speak of those times. "We were so poor, and everybody was dying. We didn't have pleasant memories."

Without financial support, the three daughters of Nils Peter Palmquist were forced to make their way. Each studied at Heald's Business College at night. Each in turn took a secretarial job at a local plumbing supply house. Each moved on to better positions and worked until they married.

The Baptist Church of their stepmother figured large in their lives. Earl's high school acquaintance and Berkeley classmate Frank Vaughan, himself the son of a Methodist minister, recalled meeting Nina in 1912 on a church cruise about the bay. Older sister Eva married a missionary and moved to China, where they would serve near the Tibetan border for the next twenty-five years.

Nina married Grover Cleveland Meyers, a classically trained pianist who had taken up the new popular music called jazz. "Cleve" Meyers would also die of tuberculosis, three weeks after the birth of their son, James, in 1919. Her husband's illness had drained their meager savings, forcing the widow Meyers to return to work.

Two years later, Nina Meyers bobbed in shoulder-high water at the Piedmont Baths on a Sunday morning in April, covertly watching the sandy-haired man with keen blue eyes standing on the edge of the pool. She was as much taken with him as he was with her. His smile seemed so warm, and he was so big, so healthy-looking, she thought.

"I spotted him just as quickly as he spotted me," she said later. "Actually, he took a big chance that day," she told a friend. "All he could see of me was my head above the water."

Petite Nina Meyers, just five feet two and one-half inches tall, was attractive. She was also—and this certainly appealed to the man who shyly came calling—an old-fashioned girl. She was as dedicated to her job, managing the women's store, as Warren was to his in the county courthouse. And unlike him, she had responsibility not only for herself but for her son and stepmother as well.

Theirs was a cautious courtship; in matters of the heart Earl Warren moved slowly. She loved him immediately, she told an interviewer later, but as a widow with a child she "was in no position to take things for granted."

They set aside Saturday evenings, usually for the theater or for dinner and dancing afterward. Occasionally he was a guest for Sunday dinner. In time the relationship ripened, and the two tentatively discussed marriage. They decided they wanted a big family, three boys for him, three girls for her.

The pair came to consider themselves engaged. Marriage would have to wait, he insisted, until his salary in the district attorney's office rose enough to support them. Each of them made $250 a month, but Warren would have felt humiliated had Nina continued to work. He desired both a family —indeed, he wanted to adopt Nina's son when they were married—and a wife at home. He could be patient.

They might have married earlier, but Warren had become attached to public service and no longer considered opening his own practice. He also declined to build a private practice since it would detract from the time he spent learning the intricacies of the district attorney's office.

Three and one-half years after Warren joined Decoto's staff, the district attorney placed him in charge of the civil side of the office. Decoto also assigned the thirty-three-year-old Warren to be legal adviser to the county Board of Supervisors.

Warren now held the most important position in the office after the DA's own, a job that thrust him into county politics. Until then he had shown no special interest, though he had volunteered to be campaign manager for his friend Frank Anderson when the assemblyman ran for a sixth term in 1924. But that had been a special circumstance.

Quiet Frank Anderson, the man they teased for never having given a speech in the state legislature, was gravely ill with tuberculosis. Though Anderson did not know it, doctors had determined he would not live to see the 1925 session open. Anderson's parents, fearing to shatter their son's morale, turned for advice to Anderson's good friend, big, stolid Earl Warren.

Warren proposed they continue as if they expected Anderson to recover. Warren would manage Anderson's campaign until the assemblyman could get back on his feet.

Warren ran a low-key campaign against Anderson's seven opponents. Warren periodically released statements on Anderson's behalf, and called occasional "strategy" meetings at Anderson's bedside. Friendly reporters played along with the charade.

The election was close, Anderson eking out a scant sixty-vote victory when the last two precincts were counted. Warren himself went to Anderson's home, woke him early in the morning and reported the outcome.

Through the day friends came by to congratulate a contented Anderson. He died the following day.

Earl Warren had proved himself a good party man. He was a Republican regular in a county once Progressive, now leaning Republican. Like the nation as a whole, in the wake of war, Deputy District Attorney Earl Warren had grown more conservative in his politics. In the 1924 presidential election he publicly supported Republican Calvin Coolidge against Democrat John W. Davis and Senator Hiram Johnson's choice, Robert La Follette, nominee of the fading Progressive Party. In the privacy of the voting booth, however, Warren cast a last, sentimental ballot for the man who had so inspired him, "Fighting Bob."

Warren had also attracted narrow-eyed attention in what reporters of the day habitually called "powerful circles." Because of his earlier experience in the legislature, the state's district attorneys asked him to lobby during the 1923 legislatve session for reform legislation.

Warren "had a lot of friends in Sacramento," recalled Fletcher Bowron, then Governor Friend W. Richardson's executive secretary. "He didn't get all he wanted, but he did get some changes in old laws, and some new laws" that aided prosecutors.

His success as a lobbyist marked him as a comer in law enforcement circles, a man to be watched.

More important, Warren and Bowron became friends. It was Bowron who introduced the deputy district attorney to the governor.

Former newspaper publisher Friend Richardson was from Alameda County, and naturally took special interest in his political base. He was a conservative or regular Republican, anxious to hold the rival Hiram Johnson Progressives in check. And he knew that District Attorney Ezra Decoto, secure in a $10,000-per-year private practice, had his eye on a less demanding public office.

Young Warren just might be the man to replace Decoto—if they could maneuver it. Alameda County political boss Mike Kelly, holding court after Sunday mass in the lobby of the Hotel Oakland, had another candidate in mind.

CHAPTER 4

THE BOY SCOUT

P OLITICS IN ALAMEDA COUNTY WAS COMPLICATED, OSCAR JAHN-
sen would explain with a laugh, "unless you were brought up with
it, and then it's very simple."

None of the three political factions in the county—conservative or "regular" Republicans, Progressive Republicans, and Democrats—had votes
enough to govern alone; any two could frustrate the third. Consequently,
the disagreements remained gentlemanly and the alliances constantly shifting.

The former county treasurer, now superintendent of the United States
Mint in San Francisco, Michael Joseph Kelly, was the nominal political boss
of Alameda County. "In every county there's a guy like that who says, 'Well,
you have to come to me if you want to be a judge,' " said James Walsh, who
often accompanied his ambitious father to Kelly's Sunday audiences in the
lobby of the Hotel Oakland.

Unlike eastern bosses, Mike Kelly controlled no patronage or lucrative
contracts. He could not reward supporters with sinecures; a new charter
had placed most county jobs under civil service. His power flowed from
persuasion and the token contributions he could direct to favored candidates.

A Progressive, Kelly had only one rival, former Congressman Joseph R.
Knowland, a conservative or "regular" Republican. "Silk Hat Joe" Knowland had begun his political career as a state legislator in 1898; then, with
the blessing of the Southern Pacific Railroad, had moved to the United
States Congress in 1912. Two years later he split the Republican vote with

Progressive Francis J. Heney and allowed Democrat James Phelan to capture a vacant United States Senate seat.

Knowland returned to Oakland, purchased an interest in *The Oakland Tribune,* and, with George Cameron of the *San Francisco Chronicle,* regrouped the remnants of the Southern Pacific coalition into a conservative force in the Bay Area.

Ezra Decoto's pending departure had triggered jockeying among the five members of the Board of Supervisors who would vote for a new district attorney. In years past, Mike Kelly might have been expected to deliver the three-vote majority to his man, Frank W. Shay, the chief deputy district attorney on the criminal side. This time "Irish" Johnny Mullins and Silk Hat Joe Knowland had other ideas.

Mullins, supervisor from the fifth district, had taken a liking to Earl Warren over the past year of Monday-morning meetings with their counsel. Warren had drafted resolutions for the supervisors, written ordinances and the bond proposals for Highland Hospital, the Veteran's Memorial, harbor improvement, and the tunnel to run under the estuary dividing the cities of Alameda and Oakland.

Johnny Mullins was impressed with the bluff, hardworking Warren. Too many of the men in public life, he complained, "looked like they'd come out of a pool parlor. He looked as if he'd come out of a church."

Warren advocated energetic law enforcement, and he had the guts to clean up wide-open Emeryville as well, Mullins decided.

Joe Knowland agreed. With Warren, at thirty-three, attractive and vigorous, a veteran to boot, they might regain control of the GOP in Alameda County.

In mid-1924, Mullins confidently assured Warren, "Kid, you're the next district attorney of Alameda County."

"Well, Johnny, that's only one vote," Warren cautioned.

Until then, Warren had not seriously considered the district attorney's post. He had joined the DA's office, expecting to remain there no more than eighteen months, before going into private practice. Those eighteen months had stretched to more than four years.

Almost a year earlier he had heard rumors that Decoto was looking for a new job. Warren's name had been mentioned as a possible successor but he had done nothing to encourage the talk. For one thing, he was a Mason; Kelly and Shay were Catholics. For another, he lacked the political leverage.

Now Mullins was offering his support, ignoring religious ties, ignoring the fact that "those weren't easy days for the Irish and we stuck together." To make sure Alameda County got cleaned up, he would support someone who could stand up to the political pressure.

Still, getting the two additional votes necessary would be difficult; Kelly held the other four on the Board of Supervisors for Shay. It was nothing personal, Kelly assured Warren. "My only objection to your being appointed to fill out the term is that you have not earned it politically." Kelly owed Frank Shay a debt of loyalty.

Mullins got his back up. He went public, asking his supporters to back Warren for the unexpired term. He buttonholed his colleagues, coaxing, cajoling, arguing the merits of tough Earl Warren over go-along Frank Shay.

Mullins worked hard on the Warren appointment. He recruited Republican regulars, in particular Oliver Hamlin, whose position Warren had filled more than four years before. Hamlin's father, Oscar, a former president of the influential California Medical Association, also rallied to Warren's cause; the elder Hamlin would divide the once solid support that Kelly had counted on from the doctors, dentists, and pharmacists.

Two others played a role in the appointment. California Governor Friend Richardson made telephone calls on Warren's behalf. And *Oakland Tribune* owner Joe Knowland assigned his most sophisticated political operator, state Senator Edward J. Tyrrell, to work on the Kelly men in the state legislature. Gregarious Ed Tyrrell, an Irish Catholic and a veteran campaigner, would also instruct Warren in the political niceties.

Warren was quick to learn. He dropped by the pressroom in the courthouse, reporter Mary Shaw recalled, "because he was ambitious. Everyone who's ambitious does that. . . . Earl wanted to be up with everything. He wanted to be considered by every group to be on top."

Mullins realized the risk in alienating Kelly, a force to be reckoned with in Mullins's own district. "I knew that it meant political suicide for me. But I loved Alameda County and thought that Warren could do better than anyone else in fighting all the crooks in it."

Undaunted, Johnny Mullins and Ed Tyrrell pasted together a coalition with the two supervisors from the predominantly agricultural districts in the southern part of the county. When Mullins offered to support local improvements, Charles Heyer of the second district around rural Hayward agreed to back Warren. They needed a third vote.

A cooperative Governor Richardson stalled. He declined to appoint Ezra Decoto to the state Railroad Commission and thereby create a vacancy in the district attorney's office until Mullins had the three votes for Warren. Decoto waited impatiently.

The third vote came with the November, 1924, election of Police Judge Ralph V. Richmond from Pleasanton to the board. Mullins offered a sweet deal to the new supervisor: He would vote for anyone Richmond nominated for any office in Richmond's district. Mullins was effectively offering the new supervisor virtual patronage powers in his district.

Richmond leaped to accept. In exchange he proposed, "Your program will be mine."

"Well, I don't think I'll ever ask you for anything important other than the appointment of Earl Warren as district attorney."

"That'll be my man, Johnny; I'll stand with you," Richmond promised.

Johnny Mullins had his majority.*

On Monday morning, January 12, 1925, Governor Richardson named Ezra Decoto to the Railroad Commission. Before the morning was out, the Alameda County Board of Supervisors voted behind closed doors 3–2 for Warren. In a spirit of reconciliation, the public vote that afternoon was announced as unanimous.

Earl Warren had been elected to his first public office. He would fill out the remaining two years of Decoto's term; his annual salary jumped from $5,000 to $7,000.

Warren accepted the appointment with a stern credo: "I believe the quality of any county government can be measured by the prevailing standard of law enforcement in that county, and it will therefore be my constant aim to see that all the laws of the land are enforced strictly and uniformly."

He had made no promises regarding the conduct of the office to the members in exchange for their votes, Warren continued. "This leaves me free to be guided only by my conscience." The whorehouses, speakeasies, and illegal distilleries of Emeryville were on notice.

Warren moved into "the bird's nest," his high-ceilinged office carved out of a disused second-story courtroom on the north side of the courthouse at Fifth and Broadway. There he began reorganizing the staff. He set up a master calendar for the criminal courts and insisted that his deputies be prepared to go to trial within thirty days of arraignment; continuances would no longer be routine. Neither would they plea-bargain cases merely to clear a congested docket.

Warren expended a bit of his political capital, persuading the Board of Supervisors to give him his own investigative staff—since Sheriff Frank Barnet had little interest in rooting out vice. With the $180-per-month salary the supervisors appropriated, Warren hired a young Internal Revenue Service agent, Oscar Jahnsen.

Jahnsen was an energetic, determined ferret. He had crammed a wealth of dubious experiences into his twenty-five years; as a youth he had been an elevator operator in the San Pablo Hotel, where he got an education "about the worldly ways that a boy of my age should never have been acquainted with." A former undercover informant for the Oakland Police, a naval intelligence agent, then an IRS agent, Jahnsen knew most of what there was to know about gambling, prostitution, and bootlegging in the Bay Area. Oscar Jahnsen's special knowledge would be immediately put to use.

Warren quickly reorganized his staff and the work. He abolished time cards and check-in times but in return demanded that his deputies put in

---

* In later years, on the wall of the entry hall of Mullins's modest home in Oakland hung a picture of Earl Warren in his robes as chief justice of the United States. Mullins's oral history quotes the inscription: "To John F. Mullins, the first sponsor and for thirty years the most loyal supporter in public life of his friend, Earl Warren."

whatever hours were necessary to get their jobs done. The deputies might still maintain their private law practices, but their public responsibilities were to come first.

The job, one longtime deputy recalled, was "altogether too demanding and too strenuous" for many of his coworkers. "We had a very rapid turnover of people in the office because of this," Warren Olney III noted.

Those who stayed worked hard, often into the night, then sat down to a steak-and-potatoes dinner around midnight. Warren relished the pace. "It's a great feeling," he reminisced four decades later, "to go to bed after a hard day's work and never hear a sound until morning."

The new DA pressed his staff to tighten the administration of criminal justice. He inaugurated Saturday morning instruction about new appellate court decisions. He insisted on strict accountability.

At a time when police work was anything but professional, Warren's men "took pride in making intelligent, painstaking investigations and preparing coherent, unambiguous reports. They scorned trickiness or any unfairness to a defendant." Warren's deputy district attorneys promptly earned a reputation around the courthouse as "Boy Scouts."

Ten days after his election, Warren announced an investigation of reported fraud in the Berkeley school board accounts; $10,000 was reported missing. Three weeks later, he obtained a grand jury indictment on forgery and embezzlement charges against the board's business manager, and secured a guilty plea. The disgraced business manager quickly received a sentence of one to ten years in state prison. Warren had sent a message.

Stern with malefactors, the "Chief," as his staff came to call him, was also compassionate. When stenographer Lorraine Redicher fell ill, Warren instructed one of the investigators to take Redicher's elderly mother to and from the hospital each day. Similarly, when a staff member's wife lay dying at Merritt Hospital, Warren ordered him to stay by her side for the woman's last three months.

While he set high standards for his deputies, he conformed to them himself. He gave up drinking and curtailed his social life on the grounds that he could not "honorably prosecute liquor violators in the daytime and then go to parties where hard drinks were served in the evening." When the disdainful reporters in the pressroom downstairs poured a shot of bootleg whiskey for him, "he would toy with his glass, try to be one of the boys—and throw the drink in a wastebasket or phone booth when we weren't looking."

It was an easy decision, though it would restrict Warren's social calendar until the repeal of Prohibition in 1933. Nina Meyers was unruffled; she was a teetotaler. Further, there was little time for parties between her job at the specialty shop, her son James, and the weekend hours spent quietly with Earl.

For all their efforts to improve the administration of criminal justice, they found themselves snarled by the entrenched bail bond system in Alameda County. Bondsmen and attorneys kicked back to each other, paid off cops for steering arrestees to favored lawyers, and cut jailers in for a piece when they held up a prisoner's release until the "right" bondsman put up bail.

The tidy arrangements extended to the district attorney's office. If an arrestee jumped bail, Decoto and Shay would agree to repeated delays of hearings at which judges would have ordered bondsmen to forfeit posted bail. In some cases, deputy DAs arranged to drop charges on bail jumpers, thereby sparing the bondsmen forfeitures. At election time, the bondsmen, especially Charlie Meyers and his partner, Jack Rohan, were generous with campaign contributions.

Warren wanted no part of it. He demanded the bondsmen pay for the long-lapsed bonds. The brokers dismissed his request.

The standoff continued for months until the biggest of the bondsmen slipped up. Charlie Meyers had long before posted bond for a convicted burglar who then jumped bail. The court had never asked Meyers to make good on his bond.

Eventually the fugitive was caught and sent off to San Quentin. His wife then asked Meyers to return the deed on her house that the onetime fugitive had put up to guarantee his appearance. Told that the bail had been forfeited and the home sold to repay Meyers, the wife complained to Warren.

Here was the lever Warren needed. Meyers had not actually forfeited the bail; therefore, he was not entitled to reimburse himself by selling the home. Clearly, he had committed fraud.

The district attorney himself presented the case to the grand jury. "Meyers was promptly indicted," Warren recalled proudly, "and when he was arrested an hour or so later, it was as if the foundations of City Hall had shattered."

By the next morning, Meyers and his partner, sometime coal dealer "Fullsack" Jack Rohan, and the other delinquent bail bondsmen had paid their accounts in full.

Warren then asked the grand jury to investigate the corrupt arrangements between bondsmen, jailers, and attorneys in Alameda County. A number of police officers and sheriff's deputies chose to find other employment—some of them with the thriving bootleggers, then running 10,000 cases of hooch into the county each month. Headlines accompanied the DA's every move.

Even as he turned county administration on its head, Warren's personal life changed drastically. He and Nina had been keeping company for four years and had considered themselves engaged for the last two. In all that time, Warren had steadily visited Nina and her son, James, now six years old, in their upstairs flat across the street from the Yellow Cab garage.

Assured of an annual income sufficient to support a family, the district attorney and his fiancée planned an early marriage. Matt especially approved of his son's choice; he judged Nina "the most efficient person I ever met."

The patient couple were instead forced to postpone their wedding. Warren's mother had moved to Oakland to live with her daughter, Ethel, while undergoing a series of eye operations, then she had to enter the hospital for what Warren delicately called "an abdominal operation." She was not well enough to attend a marriage ceremony until October 14, 1925.

The wedding that day was small, intended only for the immediate family, the mothers of both the bride and groom, Warren's sister Ethel and brother-in-law Vernon Plank, and their daughter.

Two outsiders crashed the noon ceremony at the First Baptist Church of Oakland: friend and former deputy district attorney Oliver Hamlin and the manager of the county garage, George C. Feldman. Tipped off by a clerk in the marriage license bureau, Hamlin and Feldman were sitting in an automobile across from the church when Warren arrived for the ceremony. The district attorney shrugged and invited them in; for years after they teased Warren about their "engraved invitations."

Unknown to Warren, however, Hamlin and Feldman as a prank had arranged to have the entire county highway patrol on motorcycles waiting along nearby streets to escort the Warrens to the county line. With sirens blaring, the motorcycle brigade ushered the newlyweds in their black Buick off to a honeymoon in British Columbia.

They returned to Oakland two weeks later, to move into a rented upstairs apartment on Greenwood Avenue. The day after moving in, Warren came home to find his wife admiring a piece of jade jewelry. It had been sent as a wedding gift by a friend of Earl's, she assumed, since she did not recognize the name on the card.

Warren did. Lim Ben was the county's most prominent Chinese lottery operator. Two of Warren's investigators returned the gift to Lim the next day.

The Warrens "started housekeeping from scratch," Nina Warren recalled. The payments on the portable washing machine, the china, crystal, vacuum cleaner, and *Encyclopaedia Britannica* came to $35 per month. "It took a long time to pay off this indebtedness," she wrote much later.

Domestic life suited Earl Warren. For young James, "Earl" immediately became "Dad," the attachment between the two so strong that "James never wanted you to say he was a stepson." Bonding them as a family, Warren adopted the boy.

To the Greenwood Avenue apartment, the Warrens took home their firstborn child, Virginia, in 1928. The new husband and father gave up golf in favor of spending Sundays with the children.

Their Sunday jaunts, with cookies, toys, diapers, and bottles stuffed into the family automobile, gave Nina an afternoon to herself. Even as more children came—four more in the next six years—the Sunday trips continued. Nina would "marvel how he could take care of so many little ones, but he looked forward to these outings."

However arduous the Sunday outings to Aunt Ethel's or grandmother's or the zoo, they were pleasant diversion from the office and the approaching election. Warren faced a difficult reelection campaign in 1926.

Mike Kelly had been open about it. He had nothing against Warren personally, but Kelly's organization would be backing Oakland attorney and former deputy district attorney Preston Higgins in the 1926 primary. Warren believed Kelly had amassed a $25,000 war chest to use against him. In the face of that, he "had to work up a lot of foam, a lot of steam in order to get some recognition," Oscar Jahnsen said.

Barely sworn in as district attorney, Warren had begun giving talks to local civic organizations. To "his comrades" in the American Legion, he pledged to go after illegal gambling and bootlegging. "I believe that a man should take his pay home with him and not leave it at some bootlegger's or gambling place," he proclaimed with a mixture of paternalism and moral outrage.

Similarly, he intended to go after the confidence men who preyed on the naive. He hated bunco men worse than murderers, a member of his staff insisted. "When a victim of a crook, especially an elderly victim, is stripped of his life's savings, the prolonged frustration from which he cannot recover is often worse than death."

There was too much crime, he lectured members of the Exchange Club, in part because "a man with a great deal of money can commit any kind of crime and keep out of prison almost indefinitely. . . . He can carry his case through the lower courts up to the highest and then start all over the same route again on some legal technicality."

The United States was the most lawless of any civilized nation, Warren scolded the Lions Club. He blamed some portion of the crime on easy probation. "It has come to the point here where three out of four criminals who plead guilty are given probation."

He wanted sure, firm justice, the new district attorney assured the Oakland Electric Club. The escape of two murderers from San Quentin proved the need for capital punishment, he contended.

Guided by state Senator Ed Tyrrell, Warren broadened his political base. He secured endorsements from the superintendent of the Anti-Saloon League, a Women's Christian Temperance Union spokesman, and half a dozen local churchmen. He added memberships in fraternal societies and the anti-Oriental Native Sons of the Golden West, and took active roles with the Masons and the American Legion.

With all his efforts, the 1926 election was to be "a pretty strenuous" campaign, as one deputy described it. It was a race made more difficult by the murder of beautiful, seemingly modest Elizabeth Ferguson who lived with her mother in a wood-frame house on a quiet street in Oakland. She disappeared in 1925 after telling her anxious mother she was going out that evening with Alameda County Sheriff Frank Barnet.

"Bessie, you leave him alone; he is too powerful for you to handle," her mother advised.

"Don't worry, Mother, he will pay like all the rest of them."

Mother Ferguson had good reason to worry. The beauteous Bessie was an accomplished blackmailer who passed off a sister's baby as her own. At

least three married men, each with a position in the community to maintain, were paying Bessie monthly sums to support "their" child.

Bessie failed to come home from her date with Sheriff Barnet that night.
Five days later, a teenager in neighboring Contra Costa County found
hanging from a tule reed in a marsh a blond curl with a piece of scalp
attached to it. A search of the area turned up pieces of clothing identified
as belonging to the missing woman.

Two days later a bridge tender spotted a canvas sack floating in the oily
estuary that divided Oakland and Alameda. Retrieving the sack, he discovered in it a dismembered skeleton. The flesh had been stripped from the
bones with acid, probably by someone with a knowledge of anatomy, perhaps a veterinarian, the coroner theorized. Dental records identified these
as the sorry remains of Elizabeth "Bessie" Ferguson.

Newspaper editors gave the "Tule Murder Case" big play while law
enforcement officers futilely scrambled for leads. They had little to go on
beyond the hearsay evidence of the distraught mother; the woman's testimony, pointing to Sheriff Barnet's complicity, leaked to the press.

A new organization now weighed in. In the years after the Great War, the
long-dormant Ku Klux Klan had enjoyed a revival, posturing as defenders
of Christian morality. Klansmen charged law enforcement—including the
district attorney—with a cover-up to protect the sheriff.

Mike Kelly decided to cut his losses; the cigar-smoking, diamond-
studded Frank Barnet was tainted and getting dirtier. Kelly abruptly turned
his back on Sheriff Barnet to line up behind the Klan's candidate, Piedmont
Chief of Police Burton F. Becker.

Warren formally announced his candidacy on July 8, 1926, "with the full
knowledge that it will provoke determined opposition from the underworld."

Unnamed "criminal and vice elements" had contributed $25,000 to see
him defeated, Warren alleged. Careful to avoid the assertion that either
Kelly or Higgins had solicited the money, Warren charged that Higgins had
resigned from the district attorney's office in December, 1923, "for the
avowed purpose of representing the bail bond brokers in the Police Court
litigation which they controlled."

Since then, Higgins had gone on to defend more than 250 bootleggers,
gamblers, and prostitutes, of whom more than 90 percent were convicted,
Warren charged. Meanwhile, Warren and his Boy Scout deputies were
prosecuting 499 felony cases in court, and achieving a conviction rate of 83
percent—compared to the statewide rate of 66 percent.

Warren stressed his independence. In keeping with that stance, Warren
insisted upon running alone; he avoided appearances with Barnet, and
declined even to endorse John Mullins.

The embattled supervisor generously considered Warren's strategy the
correct one. "It was more important for him to win than for me. It wouldn't
have done any good for him to endorse me."

Warren was his own man even to the point of personally financing his reelection campaign. He accepted only three campaign contributions, each of $150, from his three top deputies. With Nina's agreement, Warren invested in his career $7,000, a year's salary, from the money they had been saving to buy a home. He was, in effect, betting one dollar of their savings to make four in future salary—not good odds unless he was already weighing a long career in public service.

Few decisions Warren would make in his public career appear as critical as this. Incumbency alone gives a candidate a formidable advantage over his rivals; moreover, the longer the incumbent is in office, the harder it is to unseat him. This first reelection campaign was crucial.

The political independence his savings bought allowed Warren to carry water on both shoulders. Deemed a member of the Knowland or conservative wing of the Republican Party, Warren could nonetheless endorse a new county charter. The endorsement cast him as reform-minded, for the proposed charter created a public defender's office to represent indigents in criminal cases brought by the district attorney.

At the same time, he backed a state constitutional amendment that ostensibly imposed "the federal plan" to reapportion state legislative districts. In fact, it was a clever scheme to retain political power for conservative northern businessmen and Central Valley agricultural interests—the core of the Republican Old Guard—in the face of obstreperous Los Angeles's rapid growth.

Warren, meanwhile, ran his comparatively underfinanced, homemade campaign against Higgins. He posted no billboards or placards; instead, friends wrote letters on his behalf. With Nina at his side he made repeated public appearances. When she was asked to address one such gathering, Warren told the laughing audience, "We have a strict rule in our family. I do all the speaking in public and Mrs. Warren does it all at home."

Warren brought a Progressive's moral fervor to a conservative law-and-order campaign, posing as a political David taking on the Goliath-like bosses. The myth was potent.

"I managed to win that election by meeting and talking to more voters than any candidate had ever talked to before," he boasted. By sheer force of personality, Earl Warren swept to a landslide victory on August 31, 1926, with 70,435 votes to Higgins's 26,615.

Irish Johnny Mullins was not so fortunate. After a quarter-century as city councilman and county supervisor, he was turned out of office.* So too Sheriff Frank Barnet, besmirched by the unsolved Bessie Ferguson murder. In Barnet's place stood the Ku Klux Klan's exemplar of Christian morality, Burton F. Becker.

---

* Friends arranged for Mullins to become manager of the Oakland municipal auditorium; he supplemented that stipend by opening an insurance agency. Earl Warren placed all his personal insurance with him until Mullins's death in 1968.

CHAPTER 5

A CERTAIN AMOUNT

OF RESPECT

SHERIFF BURTON BECKER WAS UNYIELDING. THREE TIMES IN THE FIRST months of 1927 he coolly dismissed District Attorney Earl Warren's warnings about corruption.

"You take care of your business and I will take care of mine," Becker snapped at their last meeting in March.

Warren intended to do just that. Candidate Becker had posed as an advocate of tough law enforcement. Sheriff Becker was reorganizing the corruption for his own benefit.

Two of Warren's Emeryville informers, "Diamond Lil" and "Gloomy Gus," reported Becker had agreed to protect slot machines brought in by what they called Kansas City and Cleveland interests. The payoffs from bootleggers—twenty-five cents a gallon—the whorehouses, and the lottery operators were to go to Becker's bagman, a sometime Willys-Overland auto dealer and Ku Klux Klansman, Fred Smith.

An infuriated Warren intended to take on Becker, even if it meant angering the potent Ku Klux Klan. But first the DA had to protect his flank.

Warren privately warned both Mike Kelly and Richard Carrington, publisher of the *Oakland Post-Enquirer* and William Randolph Hearst's man in the county. Their boy, Burton Becker, was dirty. Warren did not want them to think any prosecution of Becker was politically motivated.

Warren began a well-publicized anti-vice campaign. He dispatched Oscar Jahnsen to pick up slot machines in unincorporated areas—despite the protection money paid to Becker. The machines were destroyed while newspapers ran pictures of the stern Earl Warren looking on.

Other district attorneys preferred to leave enforcement of unpopular Prohibition laws to federal agents. Not Warren. His investigators crashed in on stills and warehouses, dumping thousands of gallons of illegal spirits into the sewers. His men raided a country club where wealthy drinkers had enjoyed an alcoholic immunity. The district attorney himself went to court to lift a license from a resort where "boys and girls were carousing." He was back soon enough seeking revocation of a permit awarded an inn that hosted "rum orgies."

He mounted a coordinated raid on twenty lottery parlors in Emeryville, then requested and got an appropriation of $30,000 from the county Board of Supervisors to hire temporarily ten more investigators. He disliked taking on the job of policing the county, Warren told the supervisors, but they risked the rot spreading to local police departments unless he acted swiftly.

In the face of Warren's campaign, the ambitious Becker expanded his grasp. He installed Undersheriff William Parker as an Oakland road commissioner; Parker was to skim one-half cent per square foot of paving laid at inflated prices by favored contractors in the city of Oakland.

Warren worked for three years to build a case against the boodlers. Then *San Francisco Examiner* reporter Bill Mason, independently investigating the paving scandal, offered to help. Mason would merely ask Parker about rumors that Warren was pursuing an investigation of corruption in the award of paving contracts. Warren agreed it was worth a try.

In an interview in the next day's *Examiner,* Parker demanded an opportunity to answer the vicious rumors circulating about him. Parker asked for a grand jury inquiry, directly challenging Warren either to indict or exonerate him.

Free now of even the appearance of political bias, Warren called Parker's bluff. He subpoenaed Parker to appear before the grand jury.

Once there, Parker refused to answer questions on the constitutional ground of self-incrimination. Warren pressed ahead, laying out the entire paving fraud for the grand jury. Not only had three of the five commissioners connived to cut themselves in on the payoff, but the favored contractors had used substandard materials billed at inflated prices. The grand jury indicted Parker and two other city road commissioners.

Warren turned next to the prominent executives of the companies that had distributed their bribes in weekly checks to the commissioners. His strategy here was unorthodox—and politically dangerous. Reformers might prosecute corrupt public officials; they were not, however, expected to go after the influential businessmen who furnished the bribes.

Confronting a solid wall of secrecy and constitutional refusals to testify, Warren announced he would release a daily transcript of the embarrassing grand jury testimony. If he could not convict them, Warren meant to publicly shame these pillars of the community. According to one of his deputies, "Reputations were ruined right and left."

Each day the newspapers ran damning extracts from the transcript. Each day another of the distinguished businessmen who declined even to state his address on constitutional grounds appeared in print to be arrogant or defiant. Each day another of the men Warren might have looked to for political support found himself held up to public scorn.

"I would not recommend for today the vigorous cross-examination we gave to those prominent paving company people when they exercised their right against self-incrimination," he wryly wrote in his memoirs almost fifty years later.

Warren's prosecution of the paving contractors in Superior Court was equally tough. His examinations of witnesses were piercing, the conclusions he drew inexorable in their logic. He appeared effective, implacable, and self-serving.

"Earl Warren would convict his own grandmother if he thought it might help him politically," one newspaperman sitting in the press row snapped.

In Sacramento, Warren met Franklin Hichborn, doyen of the reform-minded Progressives who had raised Hiram Johnson to public office in 1912. The old-time reformer warned the district attorney that procedural delays and a relaxed court calendar had sapped earlier graft prosecutions. "The prosecution had been worn out; the community had been worn out. The defense had shown greater staying qualities than either peace officers or community."

Warren made certain that similar defense stratagems would not deflect *his* cleanup. He pressed for expedited hearings on procedural motions and prepared briefs for instant filing. He personally prosecuted Parker, the director of the contractors' association, the three contractors, and a clutch of minor players.

Only the three contractors escaped. Apparently impressed by the reputations of the defendants and their equally prominent lawyers, the trial judge instructed the jury to bring in a directed acquittal. (Despite the judge's order, the dubious jury members debated for four hours before complying.)

Hardly pausing, Warren turned from the bribe-taker Parker to his sponsor and protector, Sheriff Becker. A succession of bootleggers, pimps, and petty racketeers testified before the grand jury that they had regularly paid off Sheriff Becker. The collector or bagman was Oakland attorney J. Cromwell Ormsby, who had earlier served as finance chairman for Warren's 1926 opponent for district attorney, Preston Higgins. Day after day the evidence of pervasive corruption in Alameda County piled up.

For three years he had futilely pursued the case against the corrupt Burton Becker. Despite telling friends earlier he intended to return to private life, Warren instead announced he would run for reelection this year. "If I quit, with an election coming up, it would have looked as though I hadn't meant what I'd been saying," he told Deputy District Attorney J. Frank Coakley.

The August, 1930, election lay but months off, with Becker seemingly protected by well-placed Klansmen on the grand jury. Still Warren refused to settle for anything less than an indictment of the sheriff.

When the grand jury reconvened to report to the presiding judge only its indictment of Ormsby, the bagman, Warren moved to dismiss the charges. "I can't see how I can prosecute a man who collected the graft and paid it to the sheriff and not prosecute the sheriff, and the grand jury has declined to indict the sheriff."

The presiding judge dismissed the indictment, and ordered the grand jury back into immediate session.

Warren promptly subpoenaed Sheriff Becker to testify. Rather than chance a perjury indictment, the once blustering Becker cautiously invoked his Fifth Amendment privilege against self-incrimination.

Becker's fellow Klansmen on the grand jury were furious with the sheriff. Before Warren could call another witness, their leader conceded. "Well, go ahead and prepare your indictment. If the so-and-so won't take care of himself, well, he can't expect anyone else to." The grand jury voted unanimously to indict.

Warren personally prosecuted Becker and Ormsby in a trial, Warren wrote later, "spectacular only in the diversity of the graft it disclosed." Still the prosecution was symbolic; the day before his closing argument, Warren announced he would seek a second full term as district attorney. He was tying his fate to what local papers had taken to calling "the most sweeping exposé of graft in the history of the county."

Until Becker and Ormsby were convicted, the anti-graft cases filled his days. Evenings he spent campaigning as the August, 1930, election drew near; he reserved Sunday for Nina and a growing family.

The district attorney's office "became my preoccupation." He did not so much decide upon a career in public service as slip gradually into it, he maintained later.

He discovered he enjoyed the day-to-day stuff of politics, the handshaking, the endless civic meetings. His invariable greeting was a booming, "How are ya? Glad to see ya." If it was someone he knew or thought he had met before, he invariably added, "How's the family?"

Blessed with a memory for names, Warren was "a hell of a politician!" exclaimed one of his investigators. "The best single-handed politician that Alameda County has ever seen!"

He missed few opportunities for the publicity that fueled a successful public career. A member of the clerical staff kept scrapbooks of news stories about the DA sent in by a clipping service; year by year the scrapbooks bulked larger and larger, a measure of Warren's concern for his public image.

Running as an anticorruption candidate, Warren had only token opposition in the 1930 election. He spent no money, yet won by the largest majority any district attorney had garnered, 94,745 to 18,482.

Reelected, Warren barely slackened. Unlike many elected officials, Warren kept his office rigidly nonpolitical. "You do your job and I'll do the politics," he ordered his staff.

That concept of justice exempted no one. He was the son of stern

Methias Warren, criticizing juvenile delinquents and "the attitude of fathers who, to maintain their own personal peace, buy every luxury demanded by their children rather than inconvenience themselves to the extent of exerting discipline."

When he learned that one of his own undercover agents, B. F. "Bill" Jones, had perjured himself in order to secure convictions in bootleg cases, Warren personally prosecuted Jones. As the convicted agent boarded the ferry bound for San Quentin, Warren righteously told reporters, "I hope that Jones' fate will be a warning . . . not to use illegal methods in attempting to convict supposed law violators."

A two-month investigation of the Oakland Police Department in the fall of 1931 turned up "systematic graft on such a well-organized scale that it could qualify as 'big business.' " As many as 150 officers were dividing $50,000 each month to protect 250 speakeasies. The "system," as Warren called it, was so well-constructed that police were selling to bootleggers at twice the going rate liquor seized in earlier raids. Some bootleggers were simply ransoming their own stock.

The widespread corruption among the police led Warren to consider the quality of men who joined the force. That in turn led him to weigh the improvement of their training. He would return to these questions again and again, first in speeches to local civic organizations, later with legislation in Sacramento.

Under Warren, the district attorney's office went after a succession of bunco artists and confidence men who had flourished amid the easy-money atmosphere in these last years of the Roaring Twenties.

Two deputies, J. Frank Coakley and Miss Cecil Mosbacher, were to gain national reputations for their dogged prosecutions of these con artists and business frauds. Mosbacher, the daughter of a well-to-do Bay Area family, was especially effective in dealing with oil stock frauds.

Coakley and Mosbacher were but two of the deputies Warren hired in a continuing effort to build a professional staff. He preferred to take on young attorneys, often fresh from local universities. Warren might have on his staff as many as six of these newly minted law school graduates, working without salary, waiting for an opening and, if nothing else, gaining valuable trial experience.

Having those young lawyers trained and at the ready when a position opened up served another purpose. It allowed him to deflect nominations from other politicians—and to keep his office relatively free of political favors.

Warren took pains in selecting his staff. Candidates were subjected to a comprehensive background check, including, in the 1930s, inquiries into their politics. Any hint of radicalism in that radical era might bring discredit on his office.

He favored those he knew and had tested. Some, like fellow Master Mason Clarence Severin, he had befriended years before, "but when you went to work for him, he demanded and commanded respect. And he got it," Severin said firmly. In the office "no one ever called him by his first name. He was either 'Mr. Warren' or, as we always called him, 'Chief.'"

The Chief inspired a camaraderie among his deputies they would long remember. "We shared friendship, confidence, devotion, work," one insisted. "It was the closest thing to blood brothership many of us had ever known," said Helen R. MacGregor, a 1922 Boalt Hall graduate who served as Warren's executive secretary.

The DA set strict standards of conduct. Christmas gifts, no matter how small, were to be returned. Clerks were warned not to accept even the long-customary bag of groceries from bondsmen or attorneys. Neither would deputies fix traffic tickets, even for themselves. Those who broke the rules were promptly fired; few did.

During the Depression years, the men and women who joined Warren's office tended to be from comfortable backgrounds. Only men like Warren Olney III, son of a state Supreme Court justice, could afford to tithe the long months of the unpaid tryout without vacations. Arthur Sherry worked sixteen months as the "bottom deputy" in the depths of the Depression, living with his parents, before going on the payroll for the beginning $50-per-week salary.

As the Depression eased, Warren hired less affluent men: J. Frank Coakley, the son of Irish immigrants, had worked the night shift at Moore Shipyards to put himself through Boalt Hall. Nathan Miller worked his way through the university as a streetcar conductor; at Warren's behest, Miller held on to his membership in the carman's union.

Warren wanted that union contact, just as he appreciated Miller's membership in Sinai Temple and B'nai Brith. Warren expected his deputies to maintain ties in the community; Miller's special responsibility was contacts in the black neighborhoods of West Oakland. Similarly, Agnes Polsdorfer joined Warren's staff, "representing interests of women in the County"; Coakley was to maintain contact with the Catholic diocese.

If a prominent Catholic became entangled in the law, Warren, a Mason, made certain that Frank Coakley, a Catholic, tried the case. If it was a Jew, Miller or Mosbacher handled the matter. "So they couldn't say that they were being persecuted . . ."

Beyond that, he paid no attention to race or religion. In 1931 he was an organizer of the Alameda County chapter of what would become the National Conference of Christians and Jews. "With Warren you just never felt that he had any sense of prejudice," Nathan Miller's widow stressed.

The Chief took an active part in his office's law enforcement. His son Earl remembered taking mysterious telephone calls at home from cryptic men who ordered, "'Tell your father I'll meet him at such and such at 9:00 P.M.'"

"He'd walk out and meet some real hard people, murderers and people like that," Earl Junior said.

Sometimes the callers were not friendly. At least one gruffly warned Nina the children might suffer if her husband did not drop a case. Nina coolly told the man, "Thank you. I'll give Mr. Warren your message when he comes home." The two parents decided to ignore the threat on the grounds they could not live in fear.

Warren himself remained aloof during working hours, even avoiding lunches with his staff. The staff did not fraternize a great deal after hours, partly because they often worked until late at night. Near Christmas, Warren hosted a party at the Sequoia Country Club; until 1933 and the repeal of Prohibition, the parties were dry. In later years, Warren would have a social drink or two. Nina, who tended to avoid all but the obligatory affairs, favored Coca-Cola.

"He ran a good office, a good strong district attorney's office," one of his chief trial deputies said later. His conviction rate ran well above the state average, yet Warren avoided a conviction-at-any-cost policy. He approved dropping cases when a prosecutor or investigator said he lacked evidence to convict. "Let's not fool with it. If the man's violating the law, he'll do it again."

The newly appointed county public defender—who owed his very office to the charter revision Warren had endorsed in 1926—promptly worked out a modus vivendi based on mutual trust. Brother Mason Earl Warren was generous, Willard W. Shea acknowledged.

Shea and Warren reached a case-by-case arrangement for plea bargaining. "If you have a man you really believe is innocent," Warren told Shea, "come in and see me and I'll show you all the facts we have on him. If then you still believe him to be innocent, we'll go together to the judge and we'll dismiss the charges."

When Shea could present an alibi for a client, Warren dismissed the case. Twice Shea, who had no investigators on his staff, took unexplored leads that might exonerate a client to the DA; the prosecutor's reports helped the public defender, Shea said.

As rough as the district attorney might be in court, convictions were never so important that he cut corners, Shea insisted. Other defense attorneys had a different view. According to one, Warren was "a very tough DA, a convicting DA, a real prosecutor who was considered as a man who would leave no stones unturned, do right or wrong to get a conviction."

Warren's efforts in strengthening his office, in demanding the highest professional standards, gained first statewide, then national attention. His decision to assign a deputy district attorney to monitor bills introduced in the state legislature affecting law enforcement led other prosecutors in California to look to Warren for leadership. Alameda County's DA would become the district attorneys' lobbyist in Sacramento.

In 1931, Columbia University's Raymond Moley—later a prominent journalist—surveyed law enforcement departments across the nation and concluded that Alameda County had in Earl Warren "the most intelligent and politically independent district attorney in the United States." Alameda County had few gangsters "because criminals know that there is little 'bargain counter' justice there."

Warren himself was, in Moley's judgment, "quiet, almost stolid in temperament, matter of fact, efficient, cautious, slow, secretive."

The stern prosecutor was an entirely different man at home, with a family that grew steadily in the next years. Virginia was born in 1928, Earl Junior in 1930, Dorothy the following year, Nina Elisabeth—who would be known from infancy as "Honey Bear"—in 1933, and finally Robert in 1935. In all, there were five children in little more than six years. At the birth of each, his wife teased, Warren wheedled his way into the delivery room and then turned as white as the hospital gown he wore.

In 1935 Warren bought a grandly furnished, otherwise unaffordable home at 88 Vernon Street from a banker who had fallen on hard times. Family memory has Warren generously insisting the strapped banker accept a profit of $1,000 more than the bare foreclosure price.

"Eighty-eight," just over the hill from Lake Merritt and downtown Oakland, would be the family home of fond memory, long after the children had scattered. Three stories tall, the slate gray, Classic Revival home sat in stolid comfort below deep cornices on a sloping lawn large enough for the boys' touch football games. Across Vernon Street lay a big vacant field with leafy fruit trees and "plenty of places to build forts in."

Christmas at Eighty-eight was a special time for the Warren children. Each of them, from "Jimbo" down to little "Bobby," had his own Christmas tree in the large basement, the trees graduated in size, each with that child's gifts arranged around it. And each year before the trees came down, the Shriners' band would gather on the morning of the Shrine charity football game to serenade the master Mason and his wife who served such fine pregame breakfasts.

Nina had her hands full caring for the house and family. On her husband's salary, raised now to $7,200, she maintained the family budget. She also cleaned seven bedrooms, a richly paneled study on the third floor, a parlor and solarium, breakfast and dining rooms, and a kitchen. Eventually the Warrens would hire a maid to help Nina about the house.

Her children remembered her as always in motion with kids or Brownie, the aging springer spaniel, underfoot, cleaning, baking, cooking, or dressing the little ones. Oldest daughter Virginia recalled with pride that her mother's angel's food cakes and her fudgelike penuche were special favorites at charity bake sales and raffles for church and schools.

The Warrens lived simply. They entertained infrequently, preferring evenings at home with the children. Dinner for the children was at 5:30; their father and mother ate later, usually the plain food he preferred—stews, chops, leg of lamb, or steak.

After dinner, Earl fell into the habit of visiting Holmes Book Store in downtown Oakland, to browse among the piles of used books. One by one the children joined their father on his visits, one by one graduating from comic books to children's books to their own special interests—Jim in graphic arts; Earl Junior in animal husbandry and chemistry; Virginia in poetry; Dotty in children; Nina and Bobby in horses.

Until her death in May, 1940, on other nights father and children would visit grandmother Chrystal in her nearby apartment. Despite failing sight and hearing, she often went shopping with Virginia, who decades later remembered the buttery bags of popcorn she and her regal grandmother shared on the ferry to San Francisco. On Saturdays, Earl Junior would visit, delivering a bunch of violets bought with the nickel his mother had slipped into his pocket earlier that morning.*

Each week, after Sunday school at the Baptist church, the best district attorney in the nation piled the children into the family automobile for an outing to the zoo, or to Lake Merritt or to visit Aunt Ethel and cousins Dorothy and Warren, trips that gave Nina an afternoon to herself.

Occasionally, Virginia recalled, their father showed off his growing family to friends George Feldman or Oliver Hamlin. If they drove over the newly opened Bay Bridge to San Francisco's Chinatown—a favorite of the children—they ate always at the Four Seas Restaurant, sitting upstairs in the curtained booths.

Over time, "we got to know every amusement place around Oakland," he told newspaper columnist Drew Pearson years after. "I've ridden thousands of miles on merry-go-rounds. It was a lot of fun, but before the day was over it could be wearing, and made me appreciate my wife more than ever."

Adjudicating the inevitable squabbles and correcting their behavior seemed no problem, the child known as Honey Bear said. They were not spanked. Discipline meant being sent to their room until their father came to talk to them.

Such stern measures were enough. The children were trusted, even at a young age, and, being trusted, were careful not to abuse their independence.

Just what Earl and Nina Warren expected of the children was largely determined by a liberal religious sensibility. The Warrens sent their children to Sunday school at the local Baptist Church, not for doctrinaire purposes, but to master the precept that "if one believes in the principles learned through the Gospel and tries to abide by them, it is bound to affect one's actions and reactions."

Warren himself was not a faithful churchgoer. He read Scripture, and thought himself religious, but not in a sectarian sense. Earl Junior finally decided his father "felt that everybody's Supreme Being is personal to that person and maybe no two people have the same exact concept."

---

* Of his mother's death at age seventy-two, a closely guarded Warren said only, "I felt we should have been able to have her for many years." Quoted from EW to Tom Dewey, December 11, 1954, in Dewey papers, Series 10, Box 46, File 5, University of Rochester Library.

Warren the district attorney was Warren the father at Eighty-eight. He did not bring work home. "Home is for living," he insisted. "It belongs to the family."

Furthermore, children were impressionable, he told an old friend. "I've always hated crime and the sordid accompanying business of arrests, convictions and imprisonments. I never believed it was a proper picture to expose to growing children."

As his political activities increased, so too did the demands on him. He instructed his executive secretary, Helen MacGregor, to set aside times for the most important events in the lives of his children. Turning down a speaking invitation in May, 1935, he told a supporter that son James would be promoted to Eagle Scout at a Court of Honor. "I feel I must not miss it."

Weeknights, when he was home, he helped the children with their homework. "Inevitably we'd get into something that would be debatable or controversial," James reminisced, "and he'd take the other side, on purpose, to make you prove your point." Sometimes it was just easier doing the homework without Dad's help.

As Methias was to Earl, so Earl was to his six children. Each was expected to be independent, to think for himself. They were expected to defend their ideas. "Unless you had thought it out," Earl Junior said, "he would chop that plan to ribbons. But if you had thought it out, you could come to him with something that he thought was doomed to failure and . . . he'd say, 'You've got my blessing.' "

Proving yourself was important to Warren. When you started something, you finished it, he lectured. "I didn't dare quit until I became an Eagle Scout," James conceded. "Once you start something, you never quit, no matter what."

Earl and Nina Warren expected their six children to work hard. No "lick and a promise" for them, James told an interviewer years later. "I remember 'slacker' was a big word when I was a kid. . . . Give, give, give—all you've got—to whatever it is that you want to be."

When his children did earn merit badges in scouting or win blue ribbons in swimming competitions, their proud father beamed, clucking, "Well, well, well, isn't that fine." He attended their high school sporting events and plays, their recitals, and watched proudly as Honey Bear and Bobby became competition riders.

Implicitly, the pressure on the children to succeed was considerable. James entered the University of California at Berkeley much later, "one scared kid. To get into college and stay in college was to me . . . one of the toughest things that anybody was ever expected to do." Failure would have meant failing his father, who was by then a prominent and active member of the Alumni Association.

His father did not overemphasize grades as such. Anybody could get a grade of C, an average mark. A B average was acceptable. "In fact, it was a lot better to have a B average and to participate in a lot of other activities than it was to get all A's and not participate in anything else. He was really for the well-rounded individual."

Nonetheless, when Jimbo received a C in a high school class, his father made him attend summer school to take a typing class. Jim had not done his best.

For all their achievements, there was one final lesson in humility for all the children, his oldest son recalled: "He used to talk a lot about the fact that a boy who can't be comfortable with books but who can do great things with his hands should never be put in a class that should make him feel inferior. 'We need both,' he'd say, and then he'd look at his own hands and say, 'I can't even drive a nail or draw a picture of a straight line.' "

Whatever their father's shortcomings as a carpenter or artist, he had proved himself an exceptional public servant and local politician. With that, ambitious Earl Warren began to look beyond Alameda County, to the state and the nation—alert to the looming threat of radicalism in Depression America.

CHAPTER 6

THE RADICALS

T HE DEPRESSION STRUCK HARD IN BLUE-COLLAR OAKLAND. AL-most three of every ten workers shuffled about the city, jobless men gray with despair. Month by month, the layoffs increased. Workers came to dread payday, when pink slips were clipped to a final paycheck.

Between 1929 and 1932, Alameda County's welfare caseload doubled, doubled again, then yet again. Homeless men and women huddled in the great cement pipes stored in American Concrete's yard at the foot of 19th Avenue. An Oakland workforce once described by the boastful Chamber of Commerce as "the least susceptible to radical agitation" raged between anger and desperation.

Labor organizers, increasingly bold and increasingly successful, moved among the ramshackle "Hoovervilles" that lined the mudflats of the bay. Revolution was in the air; county law enforcement officials fretted, then boosted orders for tear gas with which to control the expected mobs. On May Day, 1930, truncheon-swinging Oakland police swooped down on a communist demonstration at the intersection of 10th and Broadway, ripped placards from the peaceful marchers, and arrested a dozen, including a plucky fifteen-year-old girl attempting to give a speech in the midst of the brawl.

The Depression wore on, seemingly endless. In stricken San Francisco on July 5, 1934, police confronted 6,000 dock workers picketing along the Embarcadero. The line of longshoremen held until police fired first tear gas canisters then their pistols. Two workers were killed, sixty injured.

When the leader of the striking longshoremen, Harry Bridges, called for a general strike throughout the Bay Area, city and state officials panicked. Conservative Governor Frank F. Merriam tacitly conceded in a nationwide broadcast that longshoremen might have legitimate grievances, but insisted those were being exploited by communists and professional agitators. Merriam called out the National Guard to keep the peace on San Francisco's waterfront.

The alarm spread across the bay. The frightened mayor of Oakland, a city untouched by labor violence, railed, "Our government, our institutions, and our very lives have been menaced." Vigilantes, themselves a particular Bay Area tradition, roamed the county, demanding that "radical" workers be replaced by real Americans.

Berkeley, Alameda, and Oakland police stocked up on tear gas; so did Earl Warren's DA office, which purchased $1,300 worth of the canisters as a precaution. Alameda County deputized more than 400 men, mostly veterans recruited through the American Legion, to reinforce private factory guards.

The crisis subsided, averted by an unprecedented agreement between shipping companies and longshoremen. Warren sent a personal letter on office stationery to the special deputies and security guards thanking them for "protecting life and property from the activities of Communists during the recent general strike."

Still Warren remained on the alert. "We made it our business to know what was going on in the Communist movement around the bay," Warren acknowledged later, "and used undercover people for that."

The chief assigned investigator Chester Flint to compile files on communists, the German-American Bund, and the militant Japanese Black Dragon Society. Those files District Attorney Warren shared with other law enforcement agencies and, occasionally, with political allies.*

Amid the labor turmoil, Warren strove to be evenhanded. He negotiated ground rules with union officials for peaceful picketing, and sought to check the most aggressive of the anti-Reds in county law enforcement agencies.

When Oakland police arrested fifteen students from the University of California who had marched in support of a Woolworth clerks' strike, Warren was livid. "This is no way of doing this kind of thing!" he raged. "You tell the chief of police we issue no more complaints on any of these things until further notice!"

---

* On November 30, 1937, Roy E. Dunn, Republican national committeeman from Minnesota, asked Warren for a report of the speech Minnesota's "extremely radical" governor, Elmer A. Benson, was to give in San Francisco on behalf of long-imprisoned Tom Mooney. Warren instructed his executive secretary, Helen R. MacGregor, to comply. She forwarded two reports from Flint's files citing a number of Benson's activities: speeches, articles he had written, contributions, and associations. All had been publicly reported and all were well within First Amendment protection. (See file 201 in the Warren papers in the California State Archives.)

As much as Warren personally disliked the New Deal's National Recovery Act, he began cooperating in May, 1934, with federal compliance officers seeking to moderate farm labor disputes. He wanted no repetition of the bloody melees and mass arrests that had scarred the lettuce harvest in the Salinas and Imperial Valleys earlier that year.

Warren dispatched Deputy District Attorney Richard Chamberlain and investigator Oscar Jahnsen to mediate disputes between growers and pea pickers. The two also kept close watch on the farm labor contractors, notorious for underpaying their field hands. When pea growers reported they had enough pickers, Warren publicly announced there was no employment that year for latecomers. He wanted no pool of jobless migrants shifting about his county, desperate for work, prey to radical organizers or wage-cutting growers.

He was proud that these impartial efforts averted violence—while assuring that farmworkers were paid promptly and the perishable crops moved to market. "The workers have been working very cheerfully," he smugly wrote later, "and each year attempts are made to continue the improvement of the working conditions of the migratory workers."

Warren by 1930 had reshaped the district attorney's office. It would be firmly nonpartisan; the twenty-five deputies would be imbued with a sense of professionalism. With some pride, Warren's political mentor, the former congressman turned newspaper publisher Joseph R. Knowland, noted:

"No one ever told Warren what to do in the line of duty, at least not more than once. I lost several friends who asked me to intervene in some important matter with Warren, and wouldn't believe me when I told them I couldn't influence Warren, and that if I tried to interfere it would only hurt them or their friends."

Warren sought evenhanded justice. Whether dealing with communists or common criminals, he demanded his investigators hew to the letter of the law. "You don't break the law to enforce the law."

It might be bent however. His men made use of wiretaps for investigative leads, according to one of his inspectors. In accordance with federal law that prohibited disclosure of tapped conversations, Warren never produced evidence of the taps in court.

Instead he professed a horror of such evidence. "I would have burned every scrap of the record and shot everybody who knew of its existence!" he snapped at a *San Francisco Examiner* reporter who asked him about use of wiretapping equipment in a case.

Warren gave orders that suspects were to be treated with care; there were to be no coerced confessions. A police officer would be present during interrogations, but only to protect the deputy district attorney and stenographer taking any statement.

Some spirit of Progressive reform remained to inspire Warren. He took an active role in founding the Bay Area Legal Aid Society to provide lawyers in civil actions for those who could not afford them.

In 1932 he became an unpaid research associate in the University of California's Bureau of Public Administration; the bureau was to undertake a comprehensive study of the work of a district attorney. Warren's office, already dubbed "the best in the country" by Columbia's Raymond Moley, was to be the model. Later, with Works Progress Administration money, Warren revamped the county's antiquated criminal records system.

He turned his attention to penology. Warren proposed that new sheriff Mike Driver open a prison farm for nonviolent prisoners and alleviate crowding in the county jail. In coming years Warren would return often to the question of prison reform.

Warren increasingly advocated professionalism of law enforcement. Police needed instruction, including university classes, he maintained. At his urging, San Jose State College agreed to create the nation's first police science curriculum.

Warren traveled widely to meet with police, "a run-down-at-the-heel bunch of social misfits," according to one reform-minded law enforcement officer. Warren attended their often drunken conventions, "cultivating them, and just being with them. . . . I attributed it as purely political," Bakersfield Chief of Police Robert Powers said.

Warren did not lecture, Powers noted. "Deep down in his guts he understood the problems and realized that they couldn't be any better than they were under the circumstances."

In short order, Warren became a spokesman for law enforcement in California. Appointed to the board of managers of the state's Bureau of Criminal Identification in 1926, Warren became chairman five years later. Meanwhile, he prompted the revitalization of the statewide District Attorneys' Association and served as its Sacramento lobbyist from 1931 to 1939.

He opposed a succession of bills that would weaken the regulation of bail bondsmen, loan sharks, and bookmakers. Describing himself as "the biggest lobbyist they had," Warren appeared before legislative committees as law enforcement's spokesman, "just arguing one bill after another, one bill after another." No measure became law over the combined opposition of this new law enforcement lobby, he proudly claimed.

He formed an advisory Anti-Racket Council of businessmen, newspaper publishers, and representatives from police departments across the county. Amid a fanfare of publicity, Warren's council also organized a "Kidnap Squad." The newspaper coverage was excellent, one former investigator recalled, "but it wasn't slowing down any kidnappings. He'd get the publicity. He'd milk it out. . . ." News stories helped, but put an end to neither rackets nor bunco schemes in Alameda County.

His reputation as an innovator spread far. United States Attorney General Homer Cummings in 1933 invited Warren to join a weeklong meeting to recommend legislation to curb interstate crime. There Warren learned that the head of the Federal Bureau of Investigation, the natty bulldog J. Edgar Hoover, was also anxious to professionalize law enforcement.

Sharing similar ideas, the two were soon "Earl" and "Edgar." Hoover placed Warren on a special correspondents' list and provided an FBI car and driver whenever the DA visited Washington. Meanwhile, a clutch of Warren's proposals, including the suggestion that the FBI be given the power to carry weapons and to make arrests, were enacted into federal law.

Warren's activities, perhaps inevitably, prompted speculation about his political future. As early as March, 1934, *The Oakland Tribune* reported "increasing discussion of District Attorney Earl Warren as a candidate for governor or lieutenant governor." Warren was uninterested.

Warren was slow to come to partisan politics. His office, indeed, all of local government in California was nonpartisan; he ran without party label. As a result, though he considered himself a Progressive, he "was a Republican simply because California was then an overwhelmingly Republican state."

Joe Knowland, publisher of the important *Oakland Tribune,* intended to change that. "Earl represents the younger group," Knowland wrote to influential Ventura County rancher C. C. Teague in 1934, "and is a man of splendid character, and the kind of leader we could well put to the front this year."

Knowland knew his man. He had earlier tapped Warren to be an alternate delegate to the Republican convention in Kansas City in 1928. Although the position was little more than honorific, it served to introduce the handsome district attorney with the hearty handshake to political figures from other parts of the state. Appointment to the delegation effectively marked him as a comer.

During the presidential campaign that year, Warren served as county campaign chairman and as the nominal president of the short-lived Hoover College Club of California. (Meanwhile, Deputy District Attorney Frank Coakley was Alameda County chairman for Hoover's Democratic opponent, Al Smith. When irritated Republican partisans asked why Warren did not enforce discipline in the ranks, he mildly explained that the district attorney's office was nonpartisan; Coakley was as free to support Smith as Warren was to back Hoover.)

For all his indifference, Warren's political prospects grew with his reputation as a hard-hitting crimebuster. He followed the graft trials with the conviction of a member of the Berkeley Board of Education for embezzlement. He brought charges against the administrator of a county hospital for the mentally ill who was physically abusing some patients while selling narcotics to others. Warren personally prosecuted police and sheriff's deputies who were peddling both drugs and illegal furloughs to ease the rigors of the county jail. All the while he sought to curb vice; Bay Area newspapers periodically proclaimed, "Warren Declares 'Fight to Finish' with Racketeer Elements."

While he tried fewer cases himself, Warren the politician remained busy —with the office, with addresses to a succession of civic organizations at lunch, with the Elks, the Masons, the Moose, the Native Sons of the Golden West in the evenings. He learned to take catnaps, falling asleep at his desk or in a conference room chair for five minutes, then awakening fully refreshed, and ready to work again.

His oldest son, James, recalled Warren in the crowded days after repeal of Prohibition. The two would talk about the youngster's baseball practice while Warren changed clothes in the bathroom after work. From a bottle of bourbon in the medicine cabinet, Warren would pour a drink "while we stood there, while he was changing his clothes, and this was his cocktail hour.

"If Dad had gotten home and we didn't see him we'd say, 'Where's Dad, Mother?'

"And she'd say, 'Oh, he's up having his medicine.' "

In 1932, as a regular delegate to the Republican National Convention in Chicago, Warren cast a dutiful vote for Herbert Hoover. The Great Humanitarian, utterly weary, stood discredited in this, the third year of the Great Depression.

On the last day of the 1932 campaign, Warren watched bystanders hurl rotting vegetables as a presidential motorcade drove through the streets of Oakland. "Hoover was a beaten man. I felt so sorry for him. . . . Politics is the art of doing the possible and Hoover tried for perfection."

The following day, Earl Warren cast his vote in a forlorn cause. Franklin D. Roosevelt, capturing all but six states, retired the bewildered Hoover to his home in Palo Alto, California.

Roosevelt's landslide victory in California, 58 to 42 percent, dramatically rewrote the political equation in the state. California Democrats that year picked up ten congressional seats and substantially trimmed Republican holdings in the state legislature.

Warren's own Alameda County, once a secure Republican stronghold, went Democrat by a margin of 54 to 46 percent. Only the election to the state Assembly of his friend William Knowland, the son of J.R., eased the sting of the sweeping Roosevelt victory.

A committed partisan by now, Warren was disturbed by the rush of remedial legislation that the Democratic Congress adopted in what became known as the Hundred Days. The budding Republican politician scored the National Industrial Recovery Act as "the first major effort to change by stealth the greatest free government of all time into a totalitarian state wherein men are but the pawns of a dictator." He was delighted when the Supreme Court of the United States unanimously struck down the act in the "Sick Chicken" case on May 27, 1935.

At the same time, Warren was furious when the high court voted 5–4 in February, 1935, to uphold President Roosevelt's order to back gold certificates not with bullion but with cheaper dollars—thereby effectively lowering the gold content of the dollar.

"Extreme radicalism," he raged, stomping about his office. He kept closing the stack of open law books on a deputy's desk and fuming, "They're no good anymore. Forget them. Contracts don't mean anything anymore."

Under the influence of the conservative Joe Knowland, Warren had become a hard money man.*

Warren's horizons, and ambition, had shifted in these thirteen years in the district attorney's office. Once, briefly, he had weighed a lucrative offer from a private law firm, but decided against it. The Warrens continued to scrape by.

As the Depression worsened, opportunities narrowed drastically; the only job offer Warren received was as a bank trust officer. With Nina's concurrence, he turned it down.

Finally it was too late. "I knew I was spoiled for private practice because of the satisfaction I had had from public service."

He became interested in the state attorney general's stagnant office. Early in 1933, Warren called on the Republican incumbent, Ulysses Sigel Webb, a somnolent time-server routinely reelected every four years since 1902. As attorney general, Webb had little responsibility beyond offering legal advice to the governor, and representing the state in civil suits. His law enforcement functions were limited to those criminal appeals that local district attorneys chose not to handle.

With his salary long pegged at $5,000—less than Warren's $7,200 at the time—Webb devoted himself to his flourishing private practice. Meanwhile, fifty autonomous deputies, earning but $200 per month, did no more than their boss.

Warren saw potential in the attorney general's office, particularly if its law enforcement responsibilities could be increased. Nonetheless, he assured Webb he would not run against him. "But if you should ever decide to retire, I would appreciate it if you would advise me of your intention to do so, because I want to succeed you," he frankly told the old man.

Webb, then seventy-one, promptly announced that he intended to file once more for his prestigious sinecure. The younger man would have to wait his turn.

Warren had no desire to challenge a Republican Party stalwart, and risk a bruising intramural fight. Warren instead chose to bide his time.

He ran a third time for district attorney, endorsed by law enforcement and a variety of civic organizations, including no less than thirty-four labor unions. Warren swept to victory in the August, 1934, election, once more burying his perennial opponent, T. L. Christianson.

While waiting for Webb to serve out his term, Warren broadened his own political base. He even went so far as broadcasting on local radio station

---

* Warren was virtually repeating the tirade delivered by Associate Justice James C. McReynolds from the bench when the decision was announced: "It is impossible to overestimate the result of what has been done this day. The constitution as many of us have understood it, the constitution that has meant so much is gone." See Walter F. Murphy, *Congress and the Court,* p. 54 fn.

KYA a nightly analysis of the testimony in the trial of Bruno Hauptmann, accused of the kidnapping-murder of the Lindbergh baby.

Meanwhile, Warren and two politically astute deputies, R. H. Chamberlain and Warren Olney III, drafted for the ballot a group of constitutional amendments that would radically alter the office of the state attorney general. As Warren himself put it, "I did aspire to and plan for the office of attorney general. I could see a great opportunity for developing it into an extremely important arm of the state government."

Warren personally wrote the key proposed amendment, one he considered "revolutionary at the time." Intended in part as an anti-corruption measure, it substantially broadened the responsibilities of the attorney general's office. Under its terms, the attorney general would become California's chief law enforcement officer, empowered to displace any sheriff or district attorney who failed to enforce the law. The amendment elevated the attorney general, in practical effect, to be the second most powerful officeholder in the state.

The constitutional amendment would also transform the position of attorney general into a full-time job. In exchange for a salary equivalent to that of a state Supreme Court justice, then $11,000 per year, the attorney general would be barred from maintaining a private practice while in office.

Chamberlain and Olney meanwhile wrote three more constitutional amendments as part of this sweeping law enforcement reform package. One permitted defendants to enter guilty pleas at their arraignment in lower courts, and thus avoid serving what they called "dead time" while awaiting trial; the second provided that prosecutors and judges could comment in court on the defendant's failure to testify or deny his guilt.*

The last of the proposed amendments created a civil service and personnel board to remove most state offices from political patronage. (The Republican-dominated State Employees Association, fearing a Democratic election victory and wholesale firings of longtime state workers, circulated the petitions to place the initiative on the ballot. The employees promoted the proposition as an anti-boss measure.)

With Warren their strongest advocate—he wrote the ballot arguments for the measures—the proposals received backing from organizations as varied as the American Legion, the State Bar, and the League of Women Voters. The initiatives, urged on the public with the admonition to "curb crime," passed by greater than 2 to 1 margins on November 6, 1934.

This 1934 election campaign was to be pivotal for forty-three-year-old Earl Warren. Cast as the embodiment of vigorous law enforcement and an

---

* The amendment permitting prosecution comments was Warren's attempt to bring to California a New Jersey practice approved by the United States Supreme Court in *Twining v. New Jersey,* 211 U.S. 78 (1908). Warren was on the high court when *Twining* was struck down as unconstitutional in 1953, but he took no part in the decision.

opponent of corrupt political patronage, this well-regarded district attorney emerged the most prominent "Good Government" figure in the state.

A fine political future loomed.

Warren's opportunity came at the Republican state convention in late September, 1934, where Joe Knowland, *San Francisco Chronicle* publisher George Cameron, and *Los Angeles Times* political operative Kyle Palmer staged a putsch. These dominant powers in the GOP decided that John McNab, slated to take over the chairmanship of the Republican State Central Committee, was too closely identified with the discredited Herbert Hoover.

Abandoned by the kingmakers, McNab abruptly withdrew. Earl Warren, untainted by past intramural feuding and already marked as a political comer, was elected chairman of the Republican Party.

Warren was assuming a nasty chore. Franklin Roosevelt's landslide in 1932 had set evil times upon the GOP.

In California, a state that had not elected a Democrat as governor since 1896, Democratic voter registration was fast rising. Younger Republicans, particularly in the south, stormed that the older, Hoover conservatives who controlled their party could not respond to the Democratic challenge.

Then on June 2, 1934, less than three months before the primary election, popular Republican Governor "Sunny" Jim Rolph died. The GOP had lost its certain nominee and unifying force.

Lacking even token leadership, the party fell upon itself, liberal versus conservative, north against south, youth opposed to age. After a sharp primary fight with the newly elevated liberal wing of the party, Lieutenant Governor Frank F. Merriam, a former Iowa state auditor and sometime Ku Klux Klan kleagle, snared the 1934 Republican nomination for governor.

Conservative Frank Merriam was "an affable, rather ponderous old gentleman with few strong convictions." He was also "drinking himself into paresis, and petting his movie mistress in automobiles in the public streets," his Democratic opponent, Upton Sinclair, mocked. Further, Merriam was tenuously linked with the bitter Herbert Hoover, who was sulking in his Palo Alto home, dreaming of a political comeback.

Complicating matters for the Republicans, the general election that year was to be a three-way contest. Raymond Haight, running on the fading Progressive Party ticket, threatened to drain liberal Republican votes from the more conservative Merriam.

Summoning the righteous fervor that had fired the Progressives of old, Haight waded into the campaign with an embarrassing accusation: Merriam's campaign had accepted a $250,000 donation in exchange for calling out the National Guard to suppress the San Francisco general strike in July. Merriam himself had pocketed $30,000, Haight charged, naming both the oil company donor and the bank where Merriam's account was kept.

Meanwhile, Democratic voters had nominated Upton Sinclair, a spirited muckraker, prolific novelist, and general irritant to the financially powerful. A lifelong socialist, Sinclair had first registered as a Democrat less than a year before the August 28, 1934, primary. He announced his candidacy in a stunning sixty-four-page tract, "I, Governor of California, and How I Ended Poverty."

Sinclair was an energetic, sternly moral candidate for a party that was itself split between Catholics and "Kluxers," that is, southern Baptists; between urban workers and rural farmers. If there was anything that bound these fractious Democrats together, it was their shared poverty. Sinclair's "End Poverty in California" program appealed widely in a state gloomed by Depression.

Some 800 local EPIC clubs sprang up, dedicated to Sinclair's proposal of creating a state-sponsored agricultural-industrial-mercantile system that would put the unemployed back to work. While Sinclair's concept of "production for use" ranged between impractical and utopian, EPIC terrified those with a vested interest in the capitalist system.

As Republican Party chairman, onetime Progressive Earl Warren sang in the GOP choir during the anti-Sinclair campaign of that fall. He had been elected on September 28, 1934, only after assuring the party's conservatives that "he could provide the punch and leadership of the strenuous campaign being planned for Merriam."

Promises aside, Joe Knowland's protégé had little impact on the campaign. He had been elected just six weeks before the general election, too late to have a hand in the campaign planning. Further, under reforms wrought by the Progressives two decades before, political parties had little actual influence. They could not contribute directly to candidates and could not even endorse in primary campaigns; candidates consequently built their own, personal organizations.

The candidates themselves, not their political parties, ran the campaigns. So, left to their own devices, Merriam's managers, a crafty husband-and-wife team of San Francisco press agents, Clem Whitaker and Leone Baxter, were to create the first political campaign in which a candidate was promoted like a commercial product.

State law and custom delegated little responsibility to the new party chairman, Earl Warren. He found himself, instead, busy as a peacemaker soothing wounded egos within party ranks.

Warren confronted multiple problems as he set out to revitalize the party. Hoover's "Old Guard" distrusted him for his role in dumping John NcNab. Merriam, the accidental governor, found Warren a bar to Merriam's grip on the party apparatus. At the same time, the Progressive or liberal wing remained wary of Warren's ties with conservative Joe Knowland.

Warren the politician fell in with the expedient alliance between the Merriam campaign and conservative Democrats frightened by Sinclair's "Red" menace. In his first statement as party chairman, Warren pointedly wooed those defecting Democrats with the assurance that "the issues confronting us transcend party and personality of the candidates."

Warren's comments grew more partisan as the campaign wore on. Sinclair's "election would mean a threat to private industry, small or large—a menace to every investor, be his investment only a few cents on an insurance policy. It means chaos to California."

This was no mere political campaign, but "a crusade of Americans and Californians against Radicalism and Socialism," Warren thundered. Merriam billboards shrieked, "Take California out of the red; the Red out of California."

In a statewide radio address, party chairman Warren raked Sinclair's program as un-American. "The battle is between two conflicting philosophies of government—one that is proud of our flag, our governmental institutions and our honored history, the other that glorifies the Red Flag of Russia and hopes to establish on American soil a despotism based upon class hatred and tyranny."

Sinclair inadvertently helped Merriam with a joking aside overheard by a reporter for the *Los Angeles Times*. If he were elected and his EPIC program adopted, Sinclair laughingly told federal relief administrator Harry Hopkins, "Half the unemployed of the United States will come to California."

The next day, the *Los Angeles Times* bannered, "Heavy Rush of Idle Seen by Sinclair." Whitaker and Baxter through constant repetition were to transform a flippant joke into a dark menace.

Republican-dominated newspapers of the state erupted in a rash of editorial cartoons warning of the "Bum's Express." Newspapers reported fanciful censuses of indigents, and having reported them as true, quoted each other with solemn authority. Two thousand billboards across the state screamed: " 'If I am elected governor, I expect one-half the unemployed in the U.S. to hop the first freight to California.' More competition for your job."

The campaign was bitter and long rankled Sinclair's supporters, "for the billboards, thousands and thousands of them, lied," one wrote two decades later.

Warren ran with the baying hounds. As chairman of the Republican Party, he funneled money into a dummy Democrats for Merriam committee—whose chairman promptly asserted Sinclair "would Russianize California and inflict on our people the curse of Communism."

As party chairman, Warren piously telegraphed an appeal to federal relief authorities to stop the imagined migration of the unemployed to California. Then he demanded that federal relief laws be amended "to protect us from being overwhelmed by these hordes.

"We are unable to care for the poor of the nation," Warren's telegram continued. "Heralding of freakish political theories from California can only have pitiful results."

Sinclair's radical crusade peaked, and fell short. Merriam eked out a narrow victory; he polled 1,138,620 votes, 49 percent of the ballots cast, to Sinclair's 879,537. Progressive Raymond Haight received 302,519, mostly from anxious Democrats who could not bring themselves to vote for a lifelong Socialist.

A conservative Republican was once more governor. At the same time, Democrats increased their representation in the state legislature, from twenty-five to thirty-seven in the Assembly, from five to eight in the Senate. A number of the new officeholders had enjoyed EPIC endorsements.

Earl Warren the party chairman pronounced himself satisfied with the election returns. "The people of California," he said in a congratulatory statement released to the press, "have repelled the attacks of extreme radicalism and have declared that California is still a progressive and not a radical state."

Warren the potential candidate privately deemed the vote tabulation sobering. Merriam's total was less than that of his two more liberal opponents. Moreover, registered Democrats outnumbered Republicans for the first time in history. In a state tending more and more Democratic in registration, a Republican candidate for statewide office would survive only if he appealed to a significant number of Democrats.

The lesson was not lost. Earl Warren was to remake himself politically once more.

CHAPTER 7

OLD JOE'S BOY

E ARL WARREN'S ELECTION AS STATE CHAIRMAN OF THE REPUBLICAN
Party was a mixed blessing. It marked him a leader in the Republican Party, true, but of a party in shambles. Moreover, he took up
the daunting task in the face of an upcoming presidential election with a
Democratic tide running.

The Roosevelt landslide of 1932 had broken the long Republican-
Progressive hegemony in California. More than half of the state's twenty
congressmen now were Democrats. With the election of 1934, the Democrats had jumped from three to thirty-seven seats in the eighty-seat Assembly. In the state Senate, they had picked up the single seat from huge Los
Angeles County.

Moreover, Warren had a big stake, but a small bankroll, in what a be-
mused political reporter called "the deuces-wild game of California politics."

Two decades before, Hiram Johnson's Progressives had effectively destroyed political parties in California. Under the guise of good government,
they had passed laws that stripped political parties of the right to select,
endorse, or financially support candidates for state office. The party column
on the ballot was also eliminated, thereby ending the one-lever, party-line
vote.

Then, city, county, and judicial offices, one after the other, were declared
nonpartisan; finally civil service was extended to ever more jobs once held
by political appointees. One by one, the ties that bound together the dominant political machines of the East and Midwest were cut in California.

But the most powerful of the Progressive reforms came to be cross-filing, enacted by constitutional amendment in 1913. Cross-filing enabled a candidate, without designating his own political affiliation, to appear on the primary ballots of more than one party.

The beauty of cross-filing, in the eyes of incumbents, instantly became clear in the first primary after the amendment went into effect. One state legislator was reelected by running in, and winning the Republican, Democrat, Progressive, Prohibition, and Socialist primaries.

Twenty years later, Progressive and Republican officeholders, familiar to voters by name if not party designation, had settled firmly in their seats, and personal, local organizations had replaced party machinery. No fewer than sixty-eight of the eighty members of the state Assembly were returned to office in the 1930 primary. All were Republicans.

Franklin Roosevelt had broken the Republican hammerlock. Even with politics on a personal rather than a party basis, Warren wrote an old acquaintance early in 1936, the GOP could prosper only as long as it was the majority party.

With Democratic registration outstripping Republican, he continued, "it behooves us to vote as a body if we are to be successful. Animosities must be forgotten and we must all strive for one end, namely, to defeat the New Deal."

In another era, the party would have fallen in behind its ranking officeholder, Governor Frank Merriam. But Merriam was not "an outstanding candidate whom a majority of our Republicans were interested in having as our standard-bearer," Warren confidentially conceded.

Merriam was not interested in the Republican Party "on other than a purely personal basis," Earl Warren wrote former President Herbert Hoover. Merriam harbored ambitions for higher office, perhaps the vice presidency on a ticket with the GOP's putative nominee, Kansas Governor Alf Landon, or, if Landon faltered, the presidency itself.

Four factions coveted the soul of the Republican Party: Merriam's reactionaries; Hoover's conservative Old Guard; the year-old, unofficial California Republican Assembly stuffed with restless young turks; and a loose coalition of conservative pragmatists who put winning elections ahead of ideology or immediate personal aggrandizement.

A north-south rivalry—of old California versus new, of water-rich north versus water-poor south, of rural north versus urban south—further snarled allegiances.

Party chairman Warren sympathized with the young rebels; he was secretly underwriting with party funds the $500 monthly costs of organizing the CRA.* Still, as party chairman, he necessarily stood with the pragma-

---

* Because it was an unofficial organization, the CRA could legally circumvent state law, and support selected Republican candidates. The CRA's early endorsement was intended to dissuade the unendorsed from entering the primary, and thus enhance party unity.

tists: George Cameron of the *San Francisco Chronicle,* Joe Knowland of *The Oakland Tribune,* and the *Los Angeles Times*'s Harry Chandler. In an age when the endorsements of their newspapers generally determined state elections, these publishers brooked no challenge.

Least of all were they prepared for a challenge from one of their own, the publisher of four of the five largest newspapers in the state, William Randolph Hearst. The lord of San Simeon would turn the 1936 presidential campaign in California into a struggle between the dominant newspapers in the state for control of the Republican Party.

Hearst the Imperious had supported Roosevelt in 1932. He fell out primarily over the president's "soak-the-rich" tax policy; now from his rococo castle shrouded in the coastal mists above San Simeon, Hearst, a lifelong Democrat, was meddling in Republican Party affairs.

If Hearst hated Roosevelt, he despised Herbert Hoover more. To help block Hoover's renomination in 1936, Hearst put his twenty-six daily newspapers and nine national magazines in support of the affable, moderate Governor Alfred M. Landon.

Hearst also moved to assure the Kansan would get California's forty-four convention votes. He proposed that Merriam abandon his favorite-son candidacy and announce for Landon. In turn, Landon would not run in the California primary, leaving Merriam the unquestioned leader of the party in California and a vice presidential contender.

The Merriam switch stunned Hoover. Whatever hope of redemption the former president cherished lay in preventing Merriam from capturing California's delegation to the national convention.

Shortly after the beginning of 1936, Hoover settled upon an adroit counterploy. He quietly proposed that friends organize an "uninstructed" slate to run against the Merriam delegation.

On February 15, twenty-three people, opaquely calling themselves the Committee of Republicans, met at the Biltmore Hotel in Los Angeles. They were assembling to form "a united front" against the New Deal, state chairman Earl Warren announced.

Though Warren sought to represent various factions in the party while selecting the committee, Governor Merriam refused to participate in a unity slate. A primary battle was assured.

With that, first Ulysses S. Webb, pleading his advanced years, and the others successively named as possible chairmen of an unpledged delegation bowed out. In their stead, the committee turned to the most attractive front man it could find: Earl Warren.

He *was* state chairman; that lent an "official" cachet to his slate. Unlike Merriam, he had alienated no one in the party.

He was young. He was energetic. As grand master of the Masons in California the previous year and as lobbyist for the District Attorneys' Association, he had statewide contacts. His future was bright.

Disavowing any personal political ambition, Warren accepted the chair-

manship "for the sole purpose of securing unity of action. . . . The delegation or delegates will be free to act as their own conscience should
determine at the convention."

It was an odd campaign. The relatively unknown district attorney of
Alameda County was stumping the state against a well-known, if unloved
governor. Further, that governor was openly supporting the leading candidate for the Republican nomination for president, Alf Landon. Warren, for
his part, could promise only that his delegates would vote their conscience.

The primary campaign settled into an "unpopularity contest" between
William Randolph Hearst and Herbert Hoover for control of the party. The
Hearst press discharged daily stories condemning the "mysterious" Warren
delegation as no more than a stalking horse for the still ambitious Hoover.
An editorial cartoon in the *San Francisco Examiner* portrayed Warren as a
ventriloquist's dummy sitting on Hoover's knee. Another drew his delegation as a wooden duck decoy.

This was to be an uphill battle. Even as the Warren people sought to
organize their campaign, former lieutenant governor and campaign adviser
H. L. Carnahan warned, "Hearst is running away from us."

The Merriam slate benefited from its link to front-runner Alf Landon.
The unpledged Warren slate, meanwhile, appeared indecisive or to be backing the unpopular Herbert Hoover.

Confronting a loss of the primary and with it control of the party, Joe
Knowland, Cameron, Hoover, and Warren met for lunch at the *Chronicle*
office in early April. Their campaign seemed to be worsening, Warren
reported.

"What do you think can be done to save it?" Hoover asked.

Though Warren suspected that Hoover had not truly forsworn political
ambition, the party chairman frankly answered: "Well, Mr. President, there's
only one thing that I can see that would save us, and that would be if you
were to say that you are not a candidate and you would not *be* a candidate
for the Republican nomination."

Hoover exploded. He would not be disfranchised, regardless of the consequences. "I have never seen anyone so sore," Warren remarked later.

Relations between the former president and the party chairman were
never again cordial.

The Warren delegation continued to slip in the polls. Prodded by Warren,
the press counterattack against Hearst, particularly in the *Times, Chronicle,*
and *Tribune,* finally lumbered into gear in April.

Daily the editorial writers and cartoonists raged against "the affrontery
[sic] of Hearst as a Democrat in trying to steal the Republican delegation."
George Cameron ordered the list of unpledged delegates be printed every
day in his *Chronicle* until election day. "One morning, to our dismay,"
Warren recalled, "we found it in the obituary column."

In the last weekend of the campaign, against the advice of friends who
warned that Hearst would never forgive him, Warren delivered a radio

address notable for its frank depiction of Hearst. "He had never been a Republican and, secondly, that it was arrogant of him to try to control politics in California because he had publicly repudiated his California citizenship and transferred it to New York to avoid paying our taxes on his enormous income."

Charges that his unpledged delegation was secretly in Hoover's pocket "is a downright lie," Warren stormed. "Mr. Hoover had absolutely nothing to do with the selection of this delegation and is not considered to be a candidate for the Republican nomination at Cleveland for it."

Warren's attack on Hearst, and by implication on the Merriam faction that had compacted with the Devil, was "not the usual thing to be done" in a campaign, Warren's friend Bill Knowland conceded later. But just such forceful language turned the tide.

On May 5, 1936, the little-known district attorney of Alameda County, California, defeated Landon, 350,410 to 260,170. He won, Warren acknowledged, because Republicans voted against Merriam rather than for Warren. Local issues had taken precedence over national.

The stunning upset transformed Earl Warren into a national figure within the Republican Party, the man who had beaten the presidential nominee. Still, the party's convention in Cleveland during the second week of June was anticlimactic, a Landon coronation. As he had promised, Warren immediately freed the delegates. Warren placed trusted members of the CRA at the end of each row to prevent Hoover supporters from mounting an embarrassing demonstration on behalf of their fallen hero.

Earl Warren enjoyed the role of national party leader. On the last day of the convention, the California delegation nominated its state chairman to serve simultaneously as national committeeman; Warren would replace an archconservative who had backed Herbert Hoover to the end. With that, leadership in California passed to a younger generation of men.

Warren returned home to campaign doggedly on behalf of Landon, striving to unite a shattered party with brave speeches. Warren had never been so partisan.

FDR's "spending orgy" and the burgeoning bureaucracy of the federal government would bankrupt the nation, he charged. Republicans had to stay alert.

He had never been so strident. The National Recovery Act, though struck down by the Supreme Court, was but the New Deal's "first major effort to change by stealth . . . the greatest free government of all time into a totalitarian state . . . which clothes dictators and their bureaucracy with an air of benevolence and respectability."

This, Warren's first statewide campaign, was a tutorial in politics. As state chairman, he signed checks for everything from office furniture to billboards to a press clipping service—learning the mechanics of organizing a partisan political campaign as he did so.

But for all of Warren's efforts, the Republican ticket had little chance in a state where one out of ten was on relief. President Roosevelt chose not to campaign personally in California, allowing an estimated half-billion dollars in federal relief since 1932 to speak for him. It was more than enough.

Franklin D. Roosevelt rolled up a November 3 national landslide. Across the country he polled 27.7 million to Landon's 16.6 in the popular vote. The Democratic tide swept in 75 percent majorities in both houses of the Congress, and twenty-six of thirty-three state houses up for election.

In California, Roosevelt crushed Landon, 1,766,863 to 835,713. Democrats also earned a majority in the state Assembly and picked up ten more seats in the state Senate. At the same time, twenty of twenty-four congressional seats went to Democrats.

A rueful Earl Warren could only conclude in a letter to the party's national chairman, John D. M. Hamilton, "Our defeat was overwhelming." While he spoke of rebuilding the GOP "into a living, vibrant organization," he acknowledged in a confidential party questionnaire how far they had to go.

"I believe that the Republican Party is 'dying on the vine' for want of an adequate set of principles and policies that are capable of solving the great economic and social problems that are confronting the American people today. If we are unwilling to do this or unable to because of too much self-interest then we do not deserve to win and we won't."

Reviving of the party would have to wait. In the last week of the presidential campaign Warren returned to the courtroom to try the most controversial case of his thirteen-year career as district attorney.

The body of Chief Engineer George W. Alberts was found Sunday morning, March 22, 1936, stuffed in the bunk of his cabin aboard the freighter S.S. *Point Lobos* at Encinal Terminal in Alameda. Alberts had been hit around the head and shoulders, then stabbed repeatedly. Knocked senseless, he bled to death from a severed artery in the left leg.

Alberts's death was one of a series of murders linked to union activities around the waterfront. The engineer had a reputation as a strong company man, loyal to Swayne and Hoyt, "Sweat and Hungry," an antiunion company that owned the *Point Lobos.*

His death came as militant unions girded once more for negotiations with the shipping companies, including Swayne and Hoyt, which insisted "ships made money at sea, not at port." The word on the Embarcadero said union enforcers were responsible for Alberts's murder.

Warren took a special interest in the case. Even before Alberts's bloodless body was removed from the vessel, Warren had dispatched Oscar Jahnsen and the office's murder prosecution team to take over the case. By the second day of the investigation they had decided that "Alberts had been firing Communists and that this was a Communist murder."

They would work on the case for the next five months, assisted by the American Legion–based American League Against Communism, the shipping company, and the Pinkerton Detective Agency. "Pinkops" at Warren's direction provided investigative help, including surveillance of labor union leaders. The agency also paid expenses of the DA's investigators when they left the county.

In early August, Lloyd Jester, one of Warren's investigators, turned up an informant in San Francisco's Tenderloin district who fingered Alberts's killers. Waterfront rumors named two members of a Marine, Firemen, Oilers, Watertenders and Wipers Union "beef squad" based in San Pedro. For $7 per day, Ben Sakovitz and George Wallace imposed discipline upon stool pigeons, strikebreakers, and scabs. The word on the waterfront had it that Ben Sakovitz and George Wallace had dropped out of sight since the death of Alberts.

Jester's informant led him to Matthew G. Guidera, a delegate on the *Point Lobos* for the American Federation of Labor's Marine Cooks and Stewards Union. According to Guidera, his roommate, the assistant secretary-treasurer of the MFOW, had admitted helping one of the reputed killers, George Wallace, skip town. The roommate, Albert Murphy, had also received a letter from Wallace implicating Earl King, MFOW vice president, in the murder.

Jahnsen and Chief Deputy District Attorney Ralph Hoyt secreted a microphone in the room that Guidera and Murphy shared in the grimy Terminal Hotel. (Eavesdropping was still legal, as long as agents did not tap telephones.) For three days Guidera sought to draw Murphy out while the DA's men and a stenographer listened down the hall.

Guidera invited unsuspecting Earl King, secretary of the MFOW local, up to his room, while Warren's men listened in. King, twenty-five years a union man and one of the most effective labor leaders on the waterfront, gave away nothing.

Eventually Guidera, a militant anticommunist, convinced the equally anticommunist Murphy to talk, explaining that the district attorney's people had been listening all the while. A nervous Murphy implicated King; a second MFOW member, Ernest G. Ramsay; and the two members of the traveling beef squad, Wallace and Sakovitz. King and Ramsay were in San Francisco, while Wallace hid in Brownsville, Texas, hoping to slip over the border. Sakovitz had vanished.

Warren dispatched investigators with arrest warrants for Wallace in Brownsville. They picked up the frightened man, then secretly returned with him to California by train.

Fearing union attorneys would try to keep Wallace from talking, the two investigators and their prisoner dropped off the train in the sun-parched town of Barstow; there they met two Alameda County sheriff's cars. Sirens fired up, the two cars dashed northward on the two-lane highway through the Central Valley on to Oakland.

They arrived late in the afternoon of Sunday, August 30, 1936, delivering Wallace to the Hotel Whitecotton in Berkeley. Jahnsen immediately settled Wallace in a rented room, then began quietly to interrogate him. By now

Wallace was more afraid of possible union retribution for talking to law enforcement officers than he feared any possible legal consequences.

Told that Murphy had confessed and had fingered him as the killer, Wallace agreed to give a statement. It was slow going. Raised in Germany, Wallace spoke English with a heavy accent; he was as inarticulate as he was beefy.

With Jahnsen and Hoyt's help, Wallace eventually produced a statement that corroborated Murphy's story. According to Wallace, he and Ben Sakovitz had been sent to Encinal Terminal to "tamp up" the chief engineer by Earl King, vice president of the MFOW, and Ernest G. Ramsay, who was responsible for handling grievances. At King's direction, Frank J. Conner, a member of both the union and the *Point Lobos* crew, had pointed out Alberts's cabin to Sakovitz and Wallace. Sakovitz had killed Alberts, Wallace claimed. Wallace had merely served as lookout.

The statement taken, at 8:20 P.M. Jahnsen and Hoyt finally booked Wallace in the county jail. Law enforcement officers quickly arrested King and Ramsay, and tucked them away in the little city of Piedmont jail to keep their attorneys from finding them. Conner and Sakovitz remained at large.

Though five union men were implicated in the murder, the major defendants were "Red"—for his hair—Ramsay, former organizer of the Fish Reduction Union on the Pacific Coast; and Earl King, black sheep son of a prominent Canadian family. According to one supporter, after Harry Bridges of the longshoremen's union, King was "the second most important man on the waterfront as secretary of MFOW, a very able labor leader, idealistic, honest."

Within hours of the arrests, District Attorney Earl Warren released a press statement asserting radical union activity lay behind Alberts's murder. "Alberts was an outspoken man, and had voiced his bitter opinion on seamen's union troubles and against Communistic activities, and thus apparently incurred the animosity which brought about his death."

Through the night, King refused to talk, even to a decoy placed in his bugged cell. He asked to see his lawyer but was refused. Kept from the others, Ramsay gave a statement without implicating anyone.

The following morning, Warren went before the county grand jury to seek murder indictments against all five: King, Ramsay, Conner, Wallace, and Sakovitz. Announcing the indictments, a Warren statement baldly charged, "It was a paid assassin's job, and the basis of the plot was communistic."

The story dominated Bay Area newspapers for the next week. "S.F. Union Chief and 3 Others Jailed in Murder on Oakland Waterfront," Hearst's *San Francisco Examiner* shrilled. "The murder is definitely hooked up with a campaign of terrorism and sabotage by Communists to gain complete control of West Coast marine unions."

Federal agents arrested the thirty-nine-year-old Frank Conner in Seattle on the night of August 31 and charged him with traveling in interstate commerce with the intent to avoid prosecution. (That federal law, coincidentally, had been enacted by Congress after District Attorney Warren proposed it to a national conference on kidnapping two years before.)

Delivered to the Hotel Whitecotton, Conner spent the next day handcuffed to a chair, repeatedly questioned and denied sleep. Though not physically struck—Warren insisted confessions be free and voluntary—Conner was under great pressure. Suffering from stomach ulcers, a cold, and a painful lacerated leg from an auto accident, Conner was held incommunicado.

Conner was impressionable. He was inexperienced in union affairs, no more than a shop steward for the *Point Lobos* black gang. Further, he had a bad drinking problem that undermined his emotional stability. In custody twenty-one hours, questioned all but four and one-half of those, Conner caved in.

Feeling abandoned and vengeful, Conner gave Warren a confession. According to Conner, Wallace and Sakovitz, sent by Ramsay, had come across the bay intending only to thrash Alberts. "I would never have pointed out his door to them if I knew they was going to kill him," Conner protested.

Earl Warren now had his case.

What became known as the King-Ramsay-Conner case became another cause for embattled left-wing and labor activists. Fifty unions funded a defense team, charging the defendants were victimized by a shameless frame-up.

Warren's participation in the Shipboard Murder Case was unusual. "I certainly was an eager beaver," he acknowledged, particularly since years of experience had cooled any "burning desire to be frequently in the courtroom."

Moreover, he acknowledged, he "never heard the jury foreman say, 'Guilty of murder in the first degree' without having a feeling of nausea. The taking of human life, even by the law in retribution for an unlawful killing, is so awesome and gruesome that it becomes a traumatic experience. . . ."

Finally, he was running a considerable political risk by personally involving himself in the case. The murder trial of King, Conner, and Ramsay offered a politician with his eye on higher office the opportunity for statewide publicity. At the same time, prosecuting three union officers for the murder of an antiunion man in a state ever more Democratic could be destructive to a political career.

When courthouse gossip hinted that Warren would not risk trying the Shipboard Murder Case, the district attorney took the whispers as a direct challenge. "Well, I guess I've got to go down there," he acknowledged to one of his deputies.

If the King-Ramsay-Conner case was a frame-up, as the waterfront unions claimed, they themselves were not blameless. "Slugging" squads roamed the West Coast, hiring out to other unions with discipline problems.

Now a member of the beef squad was on trial and, worse still, preparing to testify for the prosecution. Union representatives offered Wallace $5,000 with which to retain an attorney, but he refused. He had instead selected Alameda County's public defender, Willard Shea, the man prisoners called "Old Cop-a-Plea."

Even more ominously, it was the district attorney himself who made the announcement of his friend Shea's appointment. When other defense lawyers sought to interview Wallace, Warren, not Shea gave permission.

To the defense, the final proof of a well-prepared frame-up came with the assignment of the case to Frank MacDonald Ogden's courtroom. Ogden had been Earl Warren's first appointment to deputy district attorney. In 1930, with less than five years' experience at the bar, he was appointed to the Superior Court on Warren's recommendation. In vain the defense sought Ogden's removal.

If the waterfront unions considered Warren's case a frame-up, the prosecution was equally convinced the defendants were communists to be extirpated from society. King, Wallace, and the missing Sakovitz were all said to be members of the party; even the creation of the King-Ramsay-Conner Defense Committee was a common ploy of the Reds.

Chester Flint periodically issued sweeping reports on the "communist" organizations supporting the committee. Other investigators tailed defense attorneys, noting pointedly that one had entered a communist book store. Repeatedly, futilely, investigators attempted to link the union, the Communist Party, and the string of unsolved murders on the waterfront.

The more union supporters charged frame-up, the more Warren came to see the case as a personal struggle against an encroaching evil. The more union supporters claimed Warren a tool of big business and the shipping interests, the more Warren saw the Red hand behind the criticism.

He repeatedly protested this trial was not an attack on the working man; after all, he had been a union member himself. "There is no one in this courtroom that [sic] believes any more firmly in the principles and the general aims of Union Labor than I do," he argued.

The trial, the most controversial of Warren's career, opened on October 26, 1936, in the second-story courtroom of Department 5. Outside the decaying Second Empire courthouse, hundreds of demonstrators marched around the building, under the eye of the redwood statue of Justice, her sword and scales blown away in some long-forgotten storm.

The marchers would be there for the next three months while Earl Warren tried his last case.

CHAPTER 8

A FIRST-CLASS MAN

THE TRIAL STRETCHED ON AND ON, THE WEEKS MARKED BY SPO-radic picketing in front of the courthouse and the Warren home at 88 Vernon. Jury selection took a full month and exhausted four jury panels before six retired men and six housewives were seated in the box.

With his courtroom tense and placard-carrying pickets circling the courthouse, Judge Ogden ordered the jury sequestered. For the next three months, over Thanksgiving, Christmas, and the New Year, the nervous jurors lived in a local hotel, courtesy of Alameda County, guarded by sheriff's deputies. To speed the trial, the judge ordered court sessions three nights a week.

The tension screwed tighter with a muttered threat on the Warren home telephone. The district attorney detailed Chester Flint to drive the five youngest children to school; Oakland police staked out the house from a car parked up the street. (Nina came eventually to favor letting the address painted on the curb weather away.)

Looking for car bombs, detectives took to checking the automobiles of the three prosecutors trying the case. Police escorted them in and out of the courthouse through the jeering pickets.

Warren sought first-degree murder convictions for all four defendants on the settled principle that participants in a conspiracy to commit murder were guilty even if they were not present when the deed was done.

Tough Charles Wehr carried the burden of the trial for the prosecution, but there was no doubt that the DA himself was running the case. Warren sat at the prosecution's table, but only rarely involved himself in the day-today scuffles with the four members of the King-Ramsay-Conner defense team. When he did, said one of the opposing counsel, he appeared to be "somewhat of an orator."

The attorneys fought bitterly throughout the nine weeks of the trial. Long after the conclusion of the case, defense attorney Aubrey Grossman could recall the prosecution's sheer determination. "I know that Earl Warren and the police and the sheriffs in Alameda County went way beyond what one would do if one was simply a vigorous prosecutor or a vigorous police-man or a vigorous sheriff."

Defense attorney Myron Harris was even more emphatic about Warren's role. "I don't think that there was anything he wouldn't do to convict somebody." Gestures or courtroom courtesies routinely extended in the past to the friendly, tractable Willard Shea, Warren withheld from the King-Ramsay-Conner team.

Warren's assurance, his very competence, angered those who sided with the unionists. To defend the confession he had taken from Conner, Warren twice put himself on the witness stand and twice endured cross-examination by the defense. "It was one of the most beautiful performances I saw," said one supporter of the defendants. "He sat there with a righteous look. *Oh, he was good at it.*"

Because he relentlessly pressed his conspiracy-to-commit-murder theory —the only way to implicate the union leaders—Warren appeared no more than a tool of management. To those on the political left, the trial marked Warren as "the arch-enemy, a profoundly anti-union man" who saw all unions as gangs of criminals and thugs.

Labor organizers judged him "a reactionary Republican red-baiter" and "just another cog in the Knowland machine." Warren "was hated by the labor movement," a union activist concluded much later.

Over the course of the trial, defense attorneys would raise questions about the use of the planted microphone; about the confession they alleged had been coerced from Conner; about the denial of counsel to King, Ramsay, and Conner when they were first arrested; about Judge Ogden's seeming bias; and about the DA's refusal to reveal the existence of exculpa-tory witnesses.

Judge Ogden shifted the trial for its last week to the newly dedicated Streamlined Moderne courthouse built by the federal Works Progress Ad-ministration on the shores of Lake Merritt. It was in the new courthouse that Earl Warren gave the prosecution's closing argument, a three-hour statement that sought to separate the defendants from the union movement in general, to review the evidence against them, and enlist the jurors in his cause.

The trial had been long, unnecessarily long, he began. The defense, he charged, "dragged in the red herrings on the issue of Communism and union labor. This is not a case against union labor, it is a case against four men. Labor unions don't stand for murder."

Taking advantage of a 1934 amendment to the California Constitution, an amendment he had written, Warren pointed out that the defendants had not taken the stand to deny the accusations of Albert Murphy, "a law-abiding American citizen," or of their fellow defendants, Frank Conner and George Wallace.

"All I want is the law enforced," Warren thundered in wrath. "All I want to see is life and property safe in this community. . . . Ladies and gentlemen, I just want to say this to you: That you never have and never will sit in a more important case than this case right here and what you do in this case will mean much to the future of this county."

Judge Ogden stepped forward now as the prosecution's "ace in the hole," according to a pamphlet published by the defense committee. Another of the 1934 amendments to the state constitution permitted the trial judge, ostensibly the only impartial observer at the trial, to comment on the evidence and the credibility of the witnesses.

In the words of the *San Francisco Examiner,* Ogden the former prosecutor "bluntly stated, in effect, that the prosecution had established that the responsibility for the murder of Alberts last March 22 rested on Earl King, Ernest G. Ramsay, Frank J. Conner and George Wallace."

Wallace's barely coherent confession, Ogden advised the jury, "is to my mind strong evidence of the criminal responsibility of all defendants for the death of George W. Alberts." The exculpatory testimony of defense witnesses he brushed aside, repeating that the defendants had declined to testify.

Conner's confession to Warren, recanted the following day, was voluntarily made, Judge Ogden continued, and corroborated Wallace's in details. Judge Ogden all but compelled the jury to vote convictions.

The jury took just over four hours to return with convictions for second-degree murder on January 5, 1937. The verdict suggested that the jurors believed the defendants had meant only to "tamp up" Alberts, not to kill him. The four defendants would receive five-year-to-life sentences, the actual length to be set by a state Board of Prison Terms and Paroles.*

The news coverage during the trial and the resultant verdict transformed

---

* Ben Sakovitz was never tried. He disappeared, according to Oscar Jahnsen, into the Abraham Lincoln Battalion to fight for the Republicans in the Spanish Civil War. When the International Brigades were disbanded, Sakovitz apparently joined the French Foreign Legion in North Africa. After the Allied invasion of North Africa in November, 1942, the Legion went over to the Allies, and Sakovitz sought to enlist in the United States Army. Sakovitz was discovered by American authorities and put aboard a ship returning to the United States. While under guard, and in mid-ocean, he disappeared—presumably, Warren suggested, "through the assistance of members of the same union which had brought about the killing" of Alberts. Jahnsen hinted that those union members just might have done in the embarrassing Sakovitz, and disposed of his body at sea. Deputy DA Coakley said rumor had Sakovitz fleeing to Russia, where he was killed fighting for the Soviets. Fifty years later, Sakovitz was still considered by the FBI a fugitive from justice. (See Warren, *Memoirs,* pp. 115–16; Coakley, *For the People,* p. 87; and the Jahnsen oral history, p. 112.)

Earl Warren into the most prominent law enforcement officer in California. He was a man poised for higher office.

Just when he set his eyes on that greater vision Earl Warren never quite made clear. Throughout his career he masked his personal ambition, claiming he ran for office only in response to a "draft." Whatever the occasion, Warren had come to believe "there was a lot more in the real world that needed changing," his son, Earl Junior, said.

Shortly after the end of the Shipboard Murder Case, the doddering state attorney general, Ulysses S. Webb, summoned Warren to his office in San Francisco. Webb intended to retire, he told Warren, but would delay a public announcement to give the district attorney a head start in organizing his campaign before others jumped in.

Warren was poised to run when Webb announced in January, 1938, that he would not stand for reelection in November. Instantly the district attorney was "prominently mentioned" in the press as a potential candidate. Two days later he was described as the one man who could garner support both north and south. Then came a series of endorsements for the Alameda County district attorney. Finally, on February 10, a leaked story announced he would run.

Warren publicly announced his candidacy on February 17 with a bit of spread-eagled oratory. "I am convinced that the future of our democracy depends upon the quality of our local and state governments and upon whether or not we have an honest, fearless and uniform enforcement of the law."

Warren elaborated in a letter advising the national chairman of the Republican Party that he would soon resign as national committeeman. In a veiled allusion to the corrupt district attorney of Los Angeles County who also coveted Webb's seat, Warren wrote,

> *As you know my great interest is in law enforcement work and the office of Attorney General with its recently enlarged powers offers one of the greatest opportunities in the country along this line. . . .*
>
> *[I]f I do not run for the office, no one who is active in this phase of the public service and who is sincerely interested in law enforcement will make the race. There are powerful underworld influences in the State which would take the office over, bag and baggage, and practically by default . . .*

In purely political terms, Warren was a strong candidate, surely the Republican front runner. He was forty-seven, a family man, and physically imposing. As district attorney he had directed a highly praised office. He had broad support, in both the party and among law enforcement officers.

By nature a Progressive reformer, he had moved rightward in a political sense. He dealt easily with such conservatives as Joe Knowland, and shared enough of their views to be acceptable.

Equally important, Warren had made a number of friends across the state. He was active in the University of California Alumni Association, and his seminars on public administration at Berkeley introduced him to the faculty as something more than another lawyer.

Warren's fellow members of the American Legion viewed him as a staunch anticommunist because of the *Point Lobos* case. Active in the Masons, he had been grand master for California in 1935; 150,000 members knew him by name, many had shaken his hand. Less actively, he was also involved with the xenophobic Native Sons of the Golden West and a clutch of athletic and social clubs in the Bay Area. Finally, he was both state chairman of the Republican Party and national committeeman, positions that helped spread his reputation amongst political activists.

Warren was more than prepared. By the end of February, 1938, he had put together a personal campaign organization. Its independence and stubbornly held amateur status—Warren's committees would disband after each election—combined to give the candidate a reputation as a political loner.

Warren and his closest advisers were painstaking in enlisting people to work in the campaign. Independence was everything. "They'd bleed over this so . . . finding someone who . . . wasn't *just* completely honest—but wasn't *beholden* to anybody," said one close observer.

His steering committee consisted of San Francisco attorney Jesse Steinhart, recognized for supporting bright young men for public office; two deputies from his own office, Cecil Mosbacher and Tom Coakley; San Francisco law partners Eustace Cullinan, an old-time Progressive, and William T. Sweigert, active Democrat and past state deputy of the Knights of Columbus; and a professional publicist, George Linn. Helen R. Mac-Gregor, Warren's executive secretary, filled the same role in the campaign.

His earliest supporters were significant for their diversity: Democrat Tom Storke, the aging publisher of the *Santa Barbara News-Press* who shared Warren's affection for the state; Walter Haas, like Warren a devoted son of Berkeley, now president of Levi Strauss and Co. and an influential member of San Francisco's wealthy Jewish community; the old-money Mailliard family of that city; and state senator T. H. "Ted" deLap, who maintained close ties with agricultural associations.

Altogether, Warren's campaign raised $32,912.97—$7,000 of which Warren borrowed from his father—for the vital primary campaign. A few contributions were large, but the greatest number came in the form of $20 to $50 checks. He spent $26,524.

Warren's campaign strategy was based on the fact that Governor Frank Merriam, at the top of the ticket, was "a terrible candidate," as party functionary McIntrye Faries put it.

Asa Call, fast rising as a Republican leader in Los Angeles, agreed. "I didn't think Merriam could be elected for a second term." In the face of that, Call realized that "if Earl Warren didn't get both nominations that year, he might get lost in the shuffle because [Democrat Culbert L.] Olson was going to be governor, and he'd take with him the attorney generalship."

The key was for Warren to cross-file. If he could appear as a nonpartisan, he might secure both Republican and Democratic nominations in the primary. The general election would become pro forma.

On April 5, 1938, Warren resigned as Republican national committeeman with the explanation that he believed the attorney general's office should be nonpartisan. He was something less than frank. Warren, after all, had held both the state chairmanship and the national committee post while serving in the equally nonpartisan district attorney's office.

His true motive was likely founded on self-serving camouflage: The sitting Republican national committeeman could hardly appeal to Democratic voters in the August primary.

He would stress four issues during the next months: the rising crime rate in California, rehabilitation of prisoners in state prisons, coordination of law enforcement activities, and reshaping the office into a true Department of Justice.

With a small war chest, much of his campaign was based on snaring newspaper publicity from cooperative editors. (His newspaper support was virtually unanimous, including editorial endorsements from the major Democratic papers.)

He also toured the state, making personal appearances. Edith Balaban remembered her husband, Deputy District Attorney Nathan Miller, and his boss on campaign trips to solicit support from Jewish and labor groups that summer. "Whenever you saw him, you felt like you were just renewing a friendship again," Mrs. Balaban concluded.

Meanwhile, the endorsements rained down from organizations as wide ranging as the District Attorneys' Association and the Musician's Union. Half a dozen of the more conservative American Federation of Labor locals backed him. The president of the California Medical Association urged his election; so too Public Defender Willard Shea.

Warren's support thus stretched from the Republican right through the center of the political spectrum to the conservative wing of the Democratic Party. It also included California's ethnic minorities.

When eleven "Japanese" residents of Alameda County endorsed Warren, the campaign placed ads reprinting their letter in various Japanese-language newspapers. Warren, they wrote, "is too big a man to stir up racial prejudice against Japanese . . . [and] not the kind of man to go out of his way to try to create trouble for the Japanese people of this state."

Even the chief justice of the California Supreme Court, William Waste, took the unusual, if timely, step a month before the August primary of praising Warren's "outstanding qualifications and unquestioned character, which eminently fit him for the higher office he now seeks." Waste did not quite urge voters to cast their ballots for Warren, but neither did he praise Warren's rivals.

Finally, one day before the primary election, the venerable Ulysses S. Webb endorsed Warren as the "logical choice" to succeed him.

As the primary neared, Warren could be reasonably confident of the Republican and Progressive nominations. But even with a crowded field of six, he could not be so sure of the Democratic nomination. To broaden his appeal, he made a deliberate bid for liberal Democratic union votes.

At the suggestion of Los Angeles attorney Grant Cooper, Warren met with Los Angeles Superior Court judge Robert W. Kenny. Kenny, or so Cooper assured Warren, "is anxious to support you provided he can satisfy himself and in turn satisfy his liberal friends and followers as to your stand on civil liberties."

A lifelong Progressive, the liberal Kenny had switched party registration to Democrat just weeks before and become Southern California treasurer for the likely Democratic nominee for governor, Culbert Olson. At the same time, he was himself running for the sole Los Angeles seat in the state Senate.

Were he to endorse Warren, Kenny would not only cross party lines, but he would risk alienating his natural base among liberal Democrats. The sticking point was the prosecution of King, Ramsay, and Conner, which had damaged Warren's standing amongst liberals.

At Kenny's invitation, Warren met him on June 16 for lunch at the exclusive California Club in Los Angeles. In view of the *Point Lobos* case, Kenny asked for a statement "that would make my endorsement understandable to my civil liberties friends."

Warren not only mailed Kenny the requested letter stating his position on civil liberties; he delivered the same statement publicly at a fund-raising luncheon at the Biltmore Hotel. The candidate told the gathering:

> *I believe the preservation of our civil liberties to be the most fundamental and important of all our governmental problems . . .*
>
> *I believe that there is a grave danger in this country of losing our civil liberties as they have been lost in other countries. There are things transpiring in this country today that are definitely menacing our future; among which are the activities of Mayor Hague and other little Hagues throughout the country.* These activities are so basically wrong and so menacing to our institutions that every citizen and particularly every public official should oppose them to the limit of his strength.*

---

* Autocratic Jersey City Mayor Frank Hague, boasting "I am the law," arbitrarily denied parade and meeting permits to prevent union organizing in his city: "We hear about constitutional rights, free speech and free press. Everytime I hear these words, I say to myself, 'That man is a Red, that man is a Communist.' " (See Walker, p. 110.)

As Attorney General I would do my best to prevent Hagueism from gaining a foothold in California. . . . I believe that if majorities are entitled to have their civil rights protected they should be willing to fight for the same rights to minorities no matter how violently they disagree with their views. Further, I am convinced that this is the only way they can be preserved.

Kenny was delighted with the sweep of the statement. "Civil rights, in the context of that period, meant the rights of labor to most people. It meant the right to picket and march. It meant freedom to protest. Warren, I think, went beyond this. He was saying that the Bill of Rights was an essential—if not the essential—part of the Constitution and, as Attorney General, he would see that it wasn't violated."

Kenny was not the only Democrat to support the Republican Warren. Civil rights attorney Loren Miller, who published Los Angeles's fiercely liberal, black newspaper, *The California Eagle,* endorsed Warren on July 21. Three weeks later, retired Superior Court judge Isaac Pacht, doyen of Los Angeles's Jewish community, added his support.

In Kenny's opinion, the endorsements of these staunchly liberal Democrats were crucial to Warren's victory in the August 30 primary. As expected, the district attorney handily captured both the Republican and Progressive nominations.

At the same time, Warren's margin of victory in the Democratic primary was very close. He polled 308,500 votes to second place Carl Kegley's 280,408. (Another 423,000 ballots were distributed among five other candidates.) Kegley too agreed that liberal support for Warren had made the difference.

In the general election of November 8, 1938, Culbert Olson handily defeated Frank Merriam, to become the first Democrat elected governor since 1894. Had Kegley earlier won the Democratic primary, he might well have ridden into office on Olson's coattails.

But for Warren, his election as attorney general came as a bittersweet triumph, a "hollow climax," as he wrote later.

On May 15, in the midst of the primary campaign, a handyman had discovered the gaunt body of Matt Warren lying in a pool of blood, his skull crushed by an unknown assailant. Police had no good leads and a wealth of suspects.

In Matt Warren's last years, determined thrift had warped into miserliness. Troubled by cataracts and partially deaf, his wife had moved to Oakland to be near their son and daughter, near the grandchildren and good medical care. Since 1932, when Chrystal left him, he had lived alone in the weathering house at the corner of Niles and Baker.

As police reconstructed the murder, Matt had been sitting in a large leather chair pulled close to the gas stove on a cool Saturday night, reviewing his ledgers under a dangling bulb. The murderer had threaded his way through the discarded plumbing and appliances in the backyard, crept in through an open door, then struck the old man on the left temple with a short length of lead pipe picked up in the littered yard. Shattered glasses and a half-read ledger page had spilled to the floor near the chair.

The intruder had dragged the stunned Matt to the bed, rifled his pockets, and taken his wallet. Police found the murder weapon in a pile of fresh feces, the noisome hallmark of the professional burglar.

The murderer might be anyone who knew that this shabby old man kept fair sums of cash about his house, perhaps a tenant or even a disgruntled employee. Or the killer might have been a passing transient who stumbled on a hapless old man in a darkened house.

District Attorney Warren received a telegram informing him of his father's murder on Sunday morning, May 14, 1938, during a campaign appearance at a Masonic breakfast in Berkeley. Stunned, Warren visited his mother, gently telling her only that Matt was dead.

While Warren consoled his mother and widowed sister, a quickly assembled team of four deputies and investigators under Oscar Jahnsen's direction flew to Bakersfield in a chartered airplane.

The following day, the district attorney arrived in Bakersfield to discover that half a dozen law enforcement agencies had voluntarily dispatched detectives to aid in the investigation. Expecting to find a small town force over its head and beleaguered by ravening reporters, the new arrivals discovered instead a rare professional chief of police, Robert Powers, insisting that *he* would be in charge.

Warren met with the reporters in his Bakersfield hotel room on Monday, sitting on the edge of the bed, trying to answer questions, choked with remorse.

"Since he was seven years old my father worked hard, much of his life with his hands," the district attorney told reporters. "He took no pleasure for himself. He tried to give that to his children and their children."

He was crying as he continued. "At seventy-three, after hanging on through the depression years, he was getting on his feet, beginning to see light again, able to rest a little."

The reporters, like the volunteer investigators, were protective. When a photographer took a picture of Warren wiping away tears, the newsmen in the room immediately ordered him to pull the plate from his Speed Graphic and expose the sheet film.

The investigators had little to go on. "Casual, simple crimes are often more difficult to solve than those that are carefully planned," Warren noted. Matt's killer had blundered into murder, "obviously without planning."

Powers's investigators eventually developed a lead, the son of onetime Warren tenants recently convicted of a string of assault and robberies. Powers suggested they plant a stool pigeon and an eavesdropping device in the convict's San Quentin cell.

Warren refused. "I don't believe in Dictaphones," he told Powers firmly.

The chief of police was surprised. "It was the first time I'd ever heard anybody object to underhanded methods that we generally and proudly used to catch criminals."

The murder of Matt Warren would never be solved. His son stayed one last, sad week in Bakersfield, arranging the funeral and following the fruitless investigation. He returned to Oakland and the interrupted campaign on May 25.*

Deputy District Attorney Nathan Miller, recuperating from a heart attack, volunteered to prepare Matt's tangled estate for probate. Earl Warren's decisions in handling the estate and the inheritance taxes impressed the Millers. "That's why we know that Earl Warren was an honorable individual," Miller's wife insisted. "He was so darned honest, it's just marvelous." †

Warren returned to Oakland, the primary campaign, and a *Point Lobos* case that would not rest quietly. Defense attorneys had turned up evidence that Warren's trial deputy, Charles Wehr, had a personal relationship with a juror on the case. If true, King, Conner, and Ramsay were entitled to a new trial.

Mrs. Julia Vickerson had testified during her voir dire that she scarcely knew Wehr. Unchallenged by the defense, Mrs. Vickerson took her seat in the jury box.

Neither Warren nor Chief Deputy Ralph Hoyt had wanted Mrs. Vickerson on the jury—Warren because she was "quarrelsome," Hoyt because she was "undependable and a peculiar character." Wehr, who was carrying the main burden of the prosecution, insisted she be seated.

Only after their clients were convicted did the defense learn Mrs. Vickerson and "Bucket of Blood" Wehr were more than passing acquaintances. Wehr may have handled some legal affairs for the woman, who was heavily involved in real estate transactions. She had certainly lent him money, at least $600, and perhaps as much as $8,500, without asking for security. Some even whispered that the deputy district attorney was the father of her small child.

---

* In December, 1966, Warren told newspaper columnist Drew Pearson he had recently been approached by a man purportedly writing a book about the death of Matt Warren. The book would pin the murder on Warren. Fearing blackmail, Warren asked the FBI to investigate. The bureau's third-ranking official, Cartha DeLoach, told Warren "they had talked to the man in question and that they had reason to believe that the book was not going to be published." (See the Drew Pearson Diary, December 2, 1966, in the LBJ Library.)

† Though press speculation set Matt Warren's estate as high as $700,000, it was officially valued at $177,653. He had acquired a number of mineral rights in the Bakersfield area for fees as low as $2 per year, "none of which panned out. He hit nothing," grandson Earl Junior stated in an interview on February 21, 1991. The small houses Matt had purchased over the years went to his wife, providing an annual income of $5,000, and to Ethel. After his mother's death in 1941, Earl received $6,500 from her estate. He and Ethel sold the properties to San Bernardino County; a new courthouse was built on land Matt had once owned, his grandson said. Whatever profits Ethel and Earl realized were small. "I don't know of any money made from development of the properties," Earl Junior said.

Julia Vickerson hardly seemed the "slight acquaintance," as she had testified. Charlie Wehr had a "plant" on the jury.

Warren's successor, newly elected District Attorney Ralph Hoyt, would have to deal with it if the defense raised the issue on appeal. On December 29, 1938, forty-seven-year-old Earl Warren took the oath of office as attorney general. He was now the chief law enforcement officer of the state of California.

CHAPTER 9

COMMON NUISANCES

EARL WARREN STRODE PURPOSEFULLY FROM THE ELEVATOR IN THE crowded quarters the attorney general maintained in the state capital. On this second day of the new year, 1939, his first in office, the newly sworn-in attorney general had "decided to behave like a new broom and get to the office at nine o'clock sharp."

He arrived flanked by the cadre of trusted deputies he had asked to accompany him to Sacramento: Oscar Jahnsen, the resourceful investigator; Charles Wehr, the hard-nosed prosecutor; and Helen R. MacGregor, the petite lawyer who served as Warren's personal chief of staff.

Each had a particular assignment in reshaping the somnolent office that Ulysses S. Webb had left them. Jahnsen as chief investigator was to infuse the police arm of the office, Criminal Investigation and Identification, with Warren's strict standards. Wehr, the new chief of criminal prosecutions, was to do the same with the thirty-six deputy attorneys general scattered about Los Angeles, Sacramento, and the major office in San Francisco. MacGregor meanwhile would have responsibility for the administration of the office; her first task was to clear the calendar of cases left to languish during the casual Webb years.

Warren himself would have the biggest job. He intended to implement the reforms envisioned in the ballot propositions adopted in 1934.

At the same time, Warren also offered California as a laboratory to FBI director J. Edgar Hoover—"to use the State of California with his help for any program you wanted to try out in connection with ideas for the advancement of law enforcement work . . ."

He was particularly concerned about tracking subversive activities, he wrote Hoover. Law enforcement files in that field were "unverified and of questionable reliability." (Despite that, early in his term, the new AG was to offer Naval Intelligence the cooperation of his office in combating Japanese efforts to spy on the maneuvers of the Pacific Fleet.)

Two telephone messages awaited the attorney general when he sat down at his desk moments after nine o'clock. One message was from the editor of *The Sacramento Bee,* Walter P. Jones, the other from Joseph Stephens, a member of the state Board of Prison Terms and Paroles.

"Here are two friendly calls," he said to himself, "so I'll show them I am already in business."

He first telephoned Jones, who urgently asked if Warren had yet talked to Stephens. Stephens had something of great importance to pass on.

Within minutes Stephens was dealing Warren his first problem. Outgoing Governor Merriam's private secretary, given a midnight appointment to the Superior Court in Alameda, had peddled last-chance pardons to prisoners. The chairman of the parole board could confirm Stephens's story.

In a sworn statement made later that day in Warren's office, newly installed Judge Mark Lee Megladderry, Jr., glibly insisted he was innocent. The money he took was either a campaign contribution to the retiring governor or a legal fee for preparing pardon applications.

Warren seethed. He personally telephoned the presiding judge of the Superior Court in Oakland to see to it that Megladderry heard no cases until the matter was cleared up.

When the Sacramento district attorney declined to take the case to the grand jury for political reasons, Warren turned the whole matter over to his former chief assistant, Ralph Hoyt. As newly elected district attorney of Alameda County, Hoyt eventually tried Megladderry and secured a conviction.

Megladderry was just the beginning. By the end of Warren's first month in office, he was investigating eight other charges of "pardon sales," implicating legislators as well as the governor's office.

Over the past twenty years gubernatorial pardons had gone to those with influence or money, Warren charged. "You will find very few who have been pardoned solely because of the merit of their claims." It was hardly a politic statement; five Republican governors had served successively in those twenty years.

Moral outrage would also power Warren's next move. He intended to root out organized gambling, "the most corruptive influence in local government."

Gambling flourished because police and sheriffs tolerated it. As "the chief law officer of the State," Warren had authority to step in whenever local police, sheriffs, or district attorneys failed to enforce the law. He intended to use that power.

In the weeks before taking office, Warren had received a number of letters complaining of illegal dog tracks operating in South San Francisco, in Tracy and Susanville; of bookies and gambling parlors in Santa Ana and Yreka; and of slot machines scattered across San Diego County. Their very existence offended Warren's acknowledged "ingrained bias"—learned in Bakersfield where bars and brothels plucked the workingman's dollar at the expense of wives and children.

The dog tracks that ringed the San Francisco Bay Area were particularly blatant. Though illegal, they openly operated with a wink and a nod from tolerant law enforcement officers. The owners hewed to a share-the-wealth schedule so that only one track was open at a time.

Three months after taking office, Warren moved against the only dog track open, in Contra Costa County, adjacent to Warren's Alameda. The track was run by John J. Jerome, nicknamed "Black Jack" for his unsavory activities as a professional strikebreaker.

Warren advised Jerome that his El Cerrito dog track was illegal and must be closed. Jerome could do it himself or face an expensive law suit—after which a judge would order him shut down.

Jerome held a whispered conference with his attorney, a man who had often opposed Warren in court.

"Do you intend to treat all dog tracks the same?" the attorney asked Warren. "Or are you closing Jerome's track because he is Jerome?"

It was not personal, Warren assured them. All dog tracks were illegal and all dog tracks would be closed.

The attorney turned to his client. "I have known this man for many years, and if he says everyone is to be treated the same, he will do just that."

Jerome nodded. Could he operate until Saturday night?

Warren could not, of course, approve of an illegal dog track operating but, since this was Wednesday, he judged he could not institute legal proceedings before Saturday.

That night, patrons heard the announcement on the public address system that Saturday would mark the last night of the season. Jerome's was the last dog track to operate in California.

Next Warren turned to slot machines. In a letter to every district attorney and sheriff in the state, he quietly offered to indict "any slot-machine operator . . . too solidly entrenched in any community to be prosecuted successfully by local authorities." The warning was implicit and clear.

Finally, in July, 1939, his anti-gambling crusade in full cry, the attorney general turned to "the biggest nuisance operated in the nation," offshore gambling.

Festooned with strings of light bulbs, gambling ships had operated in the waters off Southern California for over a decade. Protected by a succession of court rulings that held the vessels were anchored in international waters, the gambling ships thrived in the sheltered calm of Long Beach Harbor and Santa Monica Bay.*

The vessels were as a mote in Warren's eye. "With things like this going on, nobody can take us seriously when we're talking about dog tracks and gambling houses on the shore," he complained.

Some 30,000 citizens each week rode water taxis to the gambling ships. As many as 3,000 eager guests aboard the *Rex,* the busiest of the four vessels, wagered $400,000 each day.

The owner of the ship, onetime bootlegger Tony Cornero, brought a keen sense of exuberant public relations to a once furtive business. His newspaper advertisements promised, "All the thrills of Biarritz, Riviera, Monte Carlo, Cannes—surpassed." In the ever blue skies over the city, skywriting biplanes urged the sporting crowd to "Play on the S.S. *Rex.*" Freeloading Hollywood columnists invariably described the *Rex*—its salon, dining room, and casino refurbished at a cost of $250,000—as a sumptuous pleasure dome.

Neither the county of Los Angeles nor the cities of Santa Monica and Long Beach showed any great interest in curbing Cornero. Warren instead solicited a request to intervene from Los Angeles reform mayor Fletcher Bowron, whose jurisdiction did not extend to Long Beach, Santa Monica, or their offshore waters.

Warren dispatched Oscar Jahnsen to warn Cornero, an acquaintance from the days of the Great Experiment. Jahnsen advised Cornero he could surrender now and have safe passage for his gambling equipment from California to Nevada or suffer the loss of his investment.

Trusting an appellate court ruling that placed his ship beyond Warren's reach, Cornero declined the offer. His smug confidence so goaded Warren, the attorney general turned to a measure he had earlier rejected in the investigation of the murder of his own father.

Warren approved placing a tap on the telephone in Cornero's Beverly Hills home. The tap was illegal, Warren Olney III reminded the agent in charge of the FBI's San Francisco office. Were it discovered, "because of political ramifications it would be most embarrassing for the Attorney General's office, and for Mr. Warren personally." †

On July 28, 1939, Warren's office served notices of abatement on the owners of the four gambling ships.

The complaint thundered with biblical rectitude. Warren charged that

---

* As a Superior Court judge, Robert Kenny once refused an injunction against the water taxis that ferried customers to the gambling ship *Johanna Smith*. If it was lawful for the Southern Pacific to haul passengers by land to Nevada where gambling is legal, he held it equally permissible to ferry passengers beyond the three-mile limit where gambling was also legal.

† The tap apparently yielded no vital information. They did learn that the vice consul of Luxembourg was running gambling games in the consulate. Warren apparently arranged for the story to leak with the expectation that embarrassed consular officials would shut down the gaming. (See the *San Francisco Examiner,* September 7, 1939.)

the vessels induced people of limited means "to spend upon wagers the money necessary for the support and maintenance of their minor children and aged parents." They had contributed to the delinquency of minors "by openly glorifying, in their eyes, gambling and the evasion of the laws of the State, and by inducing them to lead idle and dissolute lives." Finally, they had caused the loss of jobs "by reason of the idle and dissolute habits encouraged and developed by gambling."

Such nuisances could be abated by law.

Operating in secrecy for fear corrupt law enforcement officers would tip off the gambling ship operators, Olney and Jahnsen assembled a motley squadron of state Fish and Game vessels and rented water taxis. At 3:00 P.M. on August 1, 1939, "Oscar's Navy" fell upon the unsuspecting gambling ships.

The unprepared *Tango* and *Showboat* off Long Beach surrendered immediately. The *Texas* in Santa Monica Bay briefly resisted before Jahnsen's boarding party clambered aboard; the raiders gleefully pitched $25,000 worth of slot machines, roulette wheels, and gambling tables overboard while news photographers took pictures from circling motorboats.

Aboard the *Rex,* Cornero bellowed defiance to Warren's "pirates." He ordered his crew to turn high-pressure fire hoses on the circling powerboats when they drew near the gambling ship. Oscar's Navy settled down to wait.

Edition by edition, chortling newspapermen turned the battle of Santa Monica Bay into a tongue-in-cheek saga of the high seas. "Three of the four gambling barges off Santa Monica and Long Beach have surrendered and all are 'sunk' as far as carrying on further gambling activities are concerned," reporters quoted Warren.

Eight hours after the raid, Cornero and Olney negotiated a deal that permitted the 600 weary patrons trapped aboard the *Rex* to go ashore. Cornero himself held out for eight more days before surrendering, still defiant and vowing to settle the matter in court.

The legal issue was simple: Did the large Santa Monica Bay lie entirely within state waters? Cornero contended the three-mile limit followed the shoreline, allowing him to anchor three miles offshore yet still lie within the sheltering headlands. Olney argued that the bay lay within state waters and was, in fact, what sailors and mapmakers called a bight.

If Olney was correct, then international waters began three miles from a line drawn from headland to headland, or ten miles farther from the landing. A water taxi trip of that distance would be long, and "the anchored ship in the open Pacific swells would cause so much seasickness that most people would lose all desire to gamble," Warren wrote later.

In December, 1939, Olney prevailed over Cornero, history, and maritime custom alike. The state Supreme Court unanimously determined that Santa Monica Bay was a bight entirely within state waters.

Cornero folded his hand. He would forfeit the money found aboard the *Rex,* pay the state's $13,000 expenses, another $4,200 in taxes, and $7,500 in fines for operating a water taxi service without a license. Las Vegas, where gambling was legal, beckoned.*

For a month Earl Warren had been prominently featured in the newspapers of populous Los Angeles County. If closing a popular public entertainment cast him as a spoiler to some, Warren's sense of righteous purpose appealed to the thousands of churchgoing folk who lamented the decline in public morality.

As much as he thrived on the publicity, Warren could not devote all his time to pursuit of the antic criminal. More mundane tasks demanded his attention.

The legal agenda in the attorney general's office was far broader than he had dealt with in Oakland, the issues ranging from admiralty law to Indian rights, from the education code to fish and game laws. He was of necessity no longer a trial or even an appellate lawyer, but the administrative head of a large law firm, with its main office in San Francisco and thriving branches in Sacramento and Los Angeles.

He brought to the job the work habits developed as district attorney. He expected his deputies to put in a full week; they would be in the office on Saturday mornings. Deputies were no longer to represent private clients before state agencies. Further, they were to keep their private cases out of the office.

"As the chances of private practice while using state facilities diminished, more vacancies occurred, and I was able to reorganize the office into a manageable unit," Warren noted later.

The days filled. On trips from his sixth-floor office facing San Francisco's Civic Center, he took to dictating correspondence to Helen MacGregor or revising her drafts of speeches while a state policeman drove the spacious black Buick that Warren favored.

The woman he invariable addressed as "Miss MacGregor" lifted the routine burdens from the "General." His time ever more in demand, she repeatedly cautioned staff members, "He doesn't want you to reflect what *he* thinks. He wants you to give him your best advice, and he will make up his mind whether or not he will follow it."

Quite as capable and confident as the General himself, the forty-two-year-old MacGregor had attended the University of California Law School. She passed the bar in 1922, but was unable to get a job in a law office. "I think they weren't making any efforts to accommodate a woman," she decided.

---

* Cornero went on to build the Stardust Hotel in Las Vegas, while his nautical adventures inspired a Cary Grant motion picture, *Mr. Lucky,* and a subsequent television series. He made a second attempt in August, 1946, to open a gambling ship off Long Beach but ran afoul of federal navigation laws. In July, 1955, he suffered a fatal heart attack after an all-night crap game. Warren and his former attorney general, Robert Kenny, drank a toast to "Admiral" Tony's memory. Lamented Warren, "The crooks don't seem the same anymore. They don't have any fun."

MacGregor, who "looked like everybody's idea of a librarian," according to Earl Junior, eventually found work as secretary and law clerk to an appellate court judge. When he died thirteen years later, she joined Warren's office in Oakland as his personal secretary.

She was to make herself invaluable. "She was an immensely important person in the family," Earl Junior recalled. "Dad could not have done many of the things he did in the political arena without her."

In addition to MacGregor, two others came to figure in the administration of the office, one on the criminal side, the other the civil—and both almost by accident.

With Charles Wehr stricken by the leukemia that would shortly kill him, Warren asked another of his former Oakland deputies to take charge of the criminal docket. Warren Olney III agreed, bringing to the AG's office a commitment to public service as resolute as the General's own.

Son of a former state Supreme Court justice, the soft-spoken, dapper Olney had struck first a professional relationship, then a friendship with Warren. With shared values they complemented each other, Warren the public figure, Olney content to work in the background, "the consummate gentleman, a courteous man, just a fine human being."

In 1937, Olney's father had resigned from the state court and asked his son to join him in private practice. Then–District Attorney Warren urged the younger man to accept. "It is a great tribute to you. You can never tell how long your father has to live, and if anything happened to him, you'd never forgive yourself." There would be a job waiting for Olney when he returned, Warren promised.

Upon the death of his partner-father, the younger Olney closed the firm in favor of public service. He rejoined Warren in May, 1939, for the $5,000 annual salary of the assistant attorney general.

Nine months later, Warren made the last of the key appointments when he persuaded his former campaign adviser, William T. Sweigert, to take charge of civil litigation in the attorney general's office.

Depressed by the death of his wife, Sweigert had resisted Warren's earlier offers. Finally the thirty-nine-year-old Sweigert relented and in his new post found renewed energy and commitment. Within a fortnight, two longtime deputies resigned to devote themselves to their time-consuming private practices; others would follow until Sweigert had reshaped the staff in Warren's image.

As willing to delegate authority as he was, Earl Warren remained the boss. James Walsh, doubling as a clerk while he attended law school, recalled the Warren of those years as "rather intimidating. He had presence with a capital 'P.' "

To the men and women in the office, Warren "was polite, and somewhat courtly," friendly, but reserved, Walsh added. "He always held something back. I don't think he calculated everything; I just think it was half natural," the mask of the professional politician.

As politicians will, Warren tended to divide his life into professional and personal ambits. He made professional acquaintances easily, but few became personal friends.

On a succession of visits to Sacramento, he did strike up a passing friendship with a state policeman, a young black man who always seemed to be reading at his desk. Edgar "Pat" Patterson explained that he alternated reading the state penal code and the Bible. He was trying to resolve the conflicts.

On subsequent visits, the attorney general would stop to chat with the young man, sometimes to discuss the conflicts between scripture and law. Over the next three years, "we got to be very, very close," Patterson later said.

Patterson was the exception. The men with whom Warren occasionally hunted or faithfully attended University of California football games were social companions only.

Meanwhile, he discussed political problems with a handful of tight-lipped men: Joe Knowland and, increasingly, Knowland's son, Bill; *Sacramento Bee* editor Walter P. Jones; attorney Jesse Steinhart, a fixture in San Francisco's influential Jewish community; and with his old college friend, Robert Gordon Sproul, who had risen to president of the University of California. Significantly, these advisers spanned the political spectrum from conservative Republican to New Deal Democrat.

As attorney general, Warren handled two cases in the United States Supreme Court that posed significant issues of states' rights.* In the first, California secured a judgment of $17 million on behalf of Indians in the state who had sued the federal government for failure to ratify solemn treaties with various tribes.

The second case was anything but a victory.

When the crops were ripe, California agriculture welcomed migrant workers like Fred E. Edwards, a sometime preacher at the federal Farm Security Administration camp south of Marysville. The more migrants ready to work, the lower the wages. In the slack winter months, however, when they might apply for welfare, the migrants found that welcome withdrawn.

A special investigator for the state controller arrested Edwards on a misdemeanor charge of transporting indigents into the state: his sister, her husband, and two children. Edwards was convicted, then dealt a six-month suspended sentence. Worried that the conviction might bar him from lucrative work in the mushrooming defense industry, Edwards accepted the American Civil Liberties Union's offer to appeal his case.

Representing the state of California, Earl Warren had precedents dating

---

* Warren first appeared before the high court on January 6, 1932. He won a unanimous decision for Alameda County in a suit brought by the Southern Pacific Railroad dealing with the infringement of a county road on the SP's right-of-way.

to the Elizabethan Poor Laws. He had a century of United States Supreme Court decisions in his favor. He had a friend-of-the-court brief from the attorneys general of the twenty-seven states with similar laws barring the transport of indigents.

Both precedent and necessity, this son of Scandinavian immigrants asserted in his brief before the Supreme Court, gave California authority to keep "an influx of paupers" from overburdened relief rolls.

The Supreme Court disagreed with Warren's states' rights argument. The Court, in effect, held the constitutional right of travel from state to state inalienable. A penalty—the denial of welfare—could not be imposed for exercising that right.

Warren took the loss with equanimity. California's pioneers, he reminded reporters, "came here to seek opportunity, and that is the reason the present migrants come." He had not forgotten his own roots.

Matt Warren's son continued to attract national attention. In 1940, he was elected president of the National Association of Attorneys General. Shortly after, disaffected New Dealer Raymond Moley, in an article promoting the presidential candidacy of New York Republican Thomas E. Dewey, enthused, "Only Earl Warren of Oakland, Calif., now Attorney General of that state, has ever approached Dewey's achievement as D.A."

That year Warren made just two token political appearances in the Republican presidential campaign—in keeping with his pledge to remain a nonpartisan law enforcement officer. But even a token gesture was sufficient to provoke Democratic governor Culbert Olson.

The friction with Olson had begun almost with the inauguration two years earlier. Both sons of immigrants, both stubborn, both Progressive-minded reformers in their youth, they had since gone their separate ways. Warren favored individual entrepreneurship and the Republican Party, Olson the New Deal's program of collective responsibility.

Olson at sixty-two was lean, tall, fair-complected, with clear blue eyes and snow-white hair, "type cast for the role of governor," said one supporter, author Carey McWilliams. Running against the discredited Frank Merriam, Olson was an easy winner.

Olson's first act as governor was simultaneously moral and politically ill-advised. He freed Tom Mooney from the state prison.

Mooney and a fellow union organizer, Warren K. Billings, had been convicted of murder in San Francisco's Preparedness Day bombings in 1916; ten people had died in the blast of the suitcase bomb set off near the parade's starting point on Market Street.

Mooney, his wife Rena, Billings, and two others presented credible witnesses who placed them a mile from the explosion. Amid charges of a frame-up by a politically ambitious district attorney, Billings was sentenced to life imprisonment. Mooney's death sentence was commuted to life.

Twenty-two years later, Number 31921 was easily the most celebrated prisoner at San Quentin. Labor unions, particularly the more radical, had transformed the crusade of "Free Mooney!" into a proof of working class loyalty.

Despite evidence of perjury and suppressed evidence, a succession of Republican governors declined to issue pardons to the two "labor martyrs." Eventually, the decision fell to Democrat Culbert Olson.

Attorney General Warren conceded he had no knowledge of Mooney's guilt or innocence, and held no bias against the man. However, as the highest law enforcement officer in the state, Warren asked that Olson not criticize the prosecution of the case.

The governor disregarded Warren's request. Climaxing a tearful ceremony in the crowded state Assembly chamber, Olson proclaimed Mooney an innocent man convicted "on perjured testimony presented by representatives of the State of California." Mooney walked from the Capitol a free man, twenty-two years, five months, and twelve days after his conviction.

Warren took out his anger on the hapless Billings.

Because of a prior felony conviction for possession of dynamite, Billings could not be pardoned without a recommendation from a majority of the state Supreme Court. The Court, in turn, would be guided by a nonbinding statement from the state Pardon Advisory Board. By virtue of his office, Warren sat as one of five members of the board.

In February, 1939, the board voted 3 to 2 not to recommend a pardon. Warren; Folsom warden Clyde I. Plummer, the former head of the San Diego Police Department's "Red Squad"; and Clarence Morrill, director of the Bureau of Criminal Investigation and Identification, and Warren's subordinate, voted against Billings.*

Warren's votes when the Advisory Board took up the *Point Lobos* case appeared even more partisan and self-serving.

CIO unions had supported Olson with the understanding that he would reexamine the convictions of King, Conner, and Ramsay. The three labor leaders were in San Quentin, with more than five years to serve on their sentences.

The King-Ramsay-Conner Defense Committee prepared a brief for the governor detailing the exculpatory evidence, in particular new details of an intimate relationship between the dead Charles Wehr and juror Julia Vickerson. Olson bucked the file to his Pardon Advisory Board.

The board met on April 11, 1940, in Lieutenant Governor Ellis Patterson's cramped San Francisco office. As Patterson recounted the meeting, Warren promptly announced he was "convinced that any lessening of the sentences meted out to these criminals would subvert the ends of justice."

Patterson told Warren he should not vote when the prisoners' petitions

* The state Supreme Court eventually recommended that the governor grant Billings a commutation of sentence. On October 16, 1939, Olson complied, apologizing that he could not issue a full pardon. That pardon was eventually granted in 1961, after Governor Edmund G. Brown, Sr., secured the Supreme Court's assent. By then, only Billings, age sixty-nine, cared.

came up. As district attorney, Warren had prosecuted them; as attorney general, he was not likely to approve their release.

Warren prevailed. The board voted 4 to 1 against recommending that pardons be granted.

Under increasing pressure from labor unions, Olson traveled to San Quentin to interview King, Conner, Ramsay, and Wallace. Four days later he announced to reporters that he had found only "a very slim thread connecting the three men with the murder." (Wallace was another matter entirely.)

The trial evidence, Olson asserted, was "largely conflicting and impeached. I can't figure them out as the type of men who would deliberately participate in the murder of anyone." Olson acknowledged that he was weighing a pardon for King, Conner, and Ramsay.

Warren was livid. He denounced Olson's suggestion as "shocking. . . . Every good citizen of California should resent it." Olson intended to "appease the revolutionary radicals by pardoning for this crime Earl King, leader of the most murderous element of the Communist radicals in San Francisco and his hirelings."

As for the "slim thread," Warren continued, "I challenge the Governor to say on his honor that he has read the evidence in the case, which consists of 4,275 pages." Though he had spent half a day talking to the prisoners, Olson certainly had not discussed the case with any of the prosecutors, Warren sneered.

"Heretofore, I have never said one word against the Governor or any of his official acts, but silence on my part in this matter would be cowardice. These men are assassins—proven to be so."

There would be no pardon. Instead, Olson's Prison Board of Terms and Paroles on November 28, 1941, voted 4–1 to grant King, Conner, and Ramsay paroles. They had served four years and nine months. (Wallace, the admitted murderer, would stay on in San Quentin until paroled in 1949.)

Normally so controlled, Attorney General Warren exploded with the release of the three unionists. "The murderers are free today," he raged in a prepared statement, "not because they are rehabilitated criminals, but because they are politically powerful Communistic radicals.

"Their parole is the culmination of a sinister program of subversive politics, attempted bribery, terrorism and intimidation which has evidenced itself in so many ways during the past three years."

Warren's role in the King-Conner-Ramsay case alienated California's small and politically impotent radical left. A second of Warren's personal feuds—this over the nomination of Max Radin to the state Supreme Court —soured his reputation with what remained of the Democratic New Deal.

Max Radin was accounted a brilliant legal scholar, a superlative teacher, and an engaging popular lecturer. He took delight in challenging conventional wisdom, or twitting such organizations as the American Legion for their readiness to label any social criticism as "communistic." Frequently tarred as a communist himself in the frightened years of the 1930s, Radin publicly challenged his accusers to prove it. He was neither communist nor socialist, he claimed, but stood "left of center . . . the ideal position from which one may toss a few rocks at those too far right of it."

Warren had once thought well of Radin, a professor of law at the University of California since 1919. In 1935, then–District Attorney Warren had declined to recommend Radin, "our old friend," for a seat on the federal bench only on the ground that Warren was the *Republican* national committeeman. "I am sure," Warren wrote a mutual friend, "that Max Radin would reflect honor on the bench, if he should receive the appointment . . ."

Olson's election three years later prompted rumors that Radin would be appointed to the state Supreme Court, "slated to be 'the Felix Frankfurter of California.' "

When Olson did finally nominate Radin to the high court in June, 1940, the outcry was strident. He was an "extreme leftist" and, worse, the author of an "atheistic" college textbook, according to one Christian fundamentalist organization.

By the terms of a constitutional amendment Warren had supported in 1934, all nominations to the bench were to be ratified by a Commission on Judicial Qualifications. The commission's three members included the chief justice of the state Supreme Court, the senior presiding judge of the courts of appeal, and the attorney general.

Chief Justice Phil Gibson had served as Olson's director of finance and had worked closely with Radin in the first year of the administration. He was a safe Radin vote. The senior presiding justice on the appellate court, conservative Republican John T. Nourse, was just as adamant in his opposition to the nominee. Warren's would be the deciding vote.

Warren had challenged Olson's first appointment to the Supreme Court, Jesse Carter, on narrow legal grounds, and lost—with Radin defending the appointment. The second of Olson's nominations, Phil Gibson, Warren silently affirmed. The third nominee, Max Radin, was another matter entirely.

Warren never publicly explained why he opposed the nomination of his "old friend." Privately, Warren told some close associates that Radin lacked a judicial temperament. As attorney general, Warren "couldn't go along with the appointment," he told a deputy. "The man was impractical, a visionary."

While even Radin's acquaintances shared that opinion, Warren had another, unspoken reason. Democrat Radin had crossed Republican Warren one time too many in the past five years.

Radin had publicly opposed Warren's assertion that a state legislative committee was entitled to subpoena lists of union members. The professor had also contributed $20 to the King-Ramsay-Conner Defense Committee, and had stated publicly that he considered Conner innocent of the murder. Moreover, Radin had defended the governor's pardon in the Mooney case, had supported Olson in opposing sweeping subpoena powers for state legislators, and had defended Olson's first nomination to the Supreme Court.

Radin himself was to provide Warren whatever rationale the attorney general needed to vote against the appointment.

On June 3, 1940, eighteen employees of the Stockton office of the State Relief Administration refused to answer questions put to them by a state Assembly committee investigating communist infiltration of the agency. The eighteen were arrested for contempt of the committee and tried. Radin then wrote letters on law school letterhead to two former students requesting that they "speak a word for a light sentence to the judge" if the eighteen were convicted.

When the letters came to light, the chairman of the investigating committee protested. Radin's letters, Assemblyman Samuel W. Yorty claimed, "tend to corroborate testimony previously adduced before your committee in which he was named as a 'campus contact' of subversive groups."

Radin denied he had done anything improper in attempting to "soften the blow." Writing the letters was "a perfectly legal practice," he insisted.*

The Commission on Judicial Qualifications met behind closed doors on July 22, 1940, to consider Radin's nomination. The three members reviewed statements that Warren, as its secretary, had taken regarding Radin's fitness, a statement from Radin himself, and a sharply critical report from a three-member panel from the Governors of the California State Bar.

After two hours, Warren emerged to announce Radin had been rejected, declining even to report the vote was 2 to 1 against the nomination. Warren gave no reasons for the rejection.

His coveted appointment lost, Radin blamed Warren, damning him as "a compound of Ku Klux, antisemitism, witch hunting, Republican partisanship, and . . . general cussedness." The attorney general, whatever his pretensions as a nonpartisan, was revealed as "a thoroughly unreliable and slippery politician," Radin charged.

Warren's rejection of Max Radin was personal and visceral. Five months after the vote rejecting the professor for the court, Warren still fumed about Radin's nomination.

In a private meeting with University of California president Robert Gordon Sproul, Warren "launched forth in a vigorous denunciation of Professor Radin, which very evidently contained a good deal of personal animus." According to Sproul's notes, the attorney general asserted that both Radin's brother and daughter were communists; that Radin "constantly gives aid and comfort to Communists and other radicals, particularly

---

* Such letters are routinely solicited by defense attorneys. Warren himself seems to have intervened after a guilty verdict in a Los Angeles criminal trial. D. M. Reynolds wrote Warren on January 15, 1942: "The boy was before the Court this morning and was given five years' straight probation, without having to serve any time. This would not have happened if it had not been for the support which you were kind enough to give in this matter." (See EWP/S 17943.) Warren acknowledged he did write such letters. (See Pearson, p. 279.)

in free speech and civil liberties cases"; that Radin had sought lenient sentences for the state relief workers in Stockton.

Warren was especially upset, Sproul noted, that such a man should have been appointed to the prestigious John Boalt chair of law. When Sproul asked his old friend what he proposed, Warren could only request lamely that the "University cease to favor Radin and glorify him at every opportunity."

There the matter rested, "a black mark" on Warren's record, Warren's friend Robert Kenny concluded. Radin continued as a member of the law school faculty. Warren meanwhile would be swept up in the more pressing crisis of a world gone mad.

CHAPTER 10

THE MENACE

F OR MOST AMERICANS, EARL WARREN AMONG THEM, WAR HAD ONCE
seemed far off. Manchuria, Ethiopia, even Spain were hardly more
than newspaper headlines or static-ridden radio "talks." Few gave
them more than passing attention amid the anxieties of Depression America.

Yet hardly more than a year after taking office in January, 1939, California's attorney general was caught up by the gathering furies. In Europe,
Hitler had shattered the brittle peace of Versailles. Poland, Norway, Holland,
Belgium, Denmark, and France fell one after the other. As Great Britain
steeled itself for invasion, President Roosevelt declared a national emergency.

Slowly, slowly a nation wary of foreign entanglements roused itself to
rearm. Military appropriations reached $4.3 billion annually, and Congress
grudgingly passed the nation's first peacetime conscription program; 1.2
million draftees and 800,000 reservists were to receive military training.

California's economy throbbed with federal dollars. Carpenters swarmed
over a dozen military bases from San Diego to Sacramento, throwing up
barracks, mess halls, and churches. Deserts bloomed with airfields and
bombing ranges. Aircraft plants and shipyards hung up help wanted signs;
they would not come down for five years.

A veteran of the Great War and retired reserve captain, Warren favored
the rearmament program. "We must realize the importance of putting ourselves in a condition to make total defense against any kind of assault that
may be made upon us," he cautioned in a speech to the influential Associated Farmers at the end of 1940.

But as the most prominent Republican officeholder and the nominal party leader in California, Warren trod a careful path. He rejected the sclerotic isolationism of the Old Guard and its distrust of President Roosevelt's motives in fostering rearmament. At the same time, the attorney general echoed the conservatives with bold proposals to curb subversion—particularly from the left.*

"While the most cherished part of our democracy is that Bill of Rights, still we must adjust ourselves to present conditions, abandon outmoded criteria, and not permit foreign conspirators to wrap the flag and the Constitution around themselves as a cloak to protect them while destroying our nation." War was coming, and Earl Warren was preparing.

Threats foreign and domestic prompted the state of California to erect its own civil defense structure in 1939. Governor Culbert Olson formed a council of defense with himself as chairman, then asked an official from the League of Cities to serve as its director.

Richard Graves was reluctant to accept, fearing he would be saddled with a clutch of Democratic timeservers. Only after Olson assured him the defense council would be free of politics did Graves accept the post.

Olson then reneged. Once Graves had ushered through the state legislature a $5 million appropriation bill for civil defense, the governor asked him for a list of jobs and salaries. Olson was apologetic, explaining "he was under such terrible pressure . . . that he just had to find a way to take care of some of his people."

At Warren's suggestion, Graves resigned. Like the attorney general, he believed national defense was too important to be left to hacks.

As California's chief law enforcement officer, Warren convened a statewide conference to coordinate police, fire, military, and FBI activities. He then lobbied through the legislature a sabotage prevention bill and a Mutual Assistance Act, which authorized local fire departments to assist each other.

A sense of increasing urgency drove Warren to devote ever more time to civil defense. And the more effort he put into civil defense, the more Governor Olson resented him.

Olson suspected "that the Attorney General's movements throughout the state were aimed at building a political machine which would enable Warren to supplant him in 1942." For his part, "Warren didn't think Olson was a very good governor," concluded a deputy attorney general who was close to the AG.

Warren and Olson, attorney general and governor, broke off meeting personally. Instead, they clashed often and openly in the legislature and the press.

Olson asked the legislature in December, 1940, to establish a California

---

* Warren was privately critical of Democratic Congressman Martin Dies's Special Committee on Un-American Activities as "more interested in publicity than it is in ascertaining the true facts." (See EW to J.R. Knowland, April 5, 1941, in EWP/S 17835.)

State Guard. Warren argued that a state guard would be illegal. Anticipating that the National Guard's 40th Armored Division would be mobilized in the event of war, the legislature granted Olson authority to establish the state guard he sought.

Olson responded by asking the legislature for an additional $17 million for the guard, and $4 million for a discretionary emergency fund. When the Republican-dominated Economy Bloc trimmed the appropriation, Olson retaliated by refusing to fund $214,000 to cover the civil defense responsibilities of the attorney general's office.

In a clumsy ploy to usurp Warren as the state's chief law enforcement officer, Olson also moved to appoint officers from the State Guard to command public safety in each of the regions Warren had earlier set up.

Warren fought off the coup by arguing that Olson would need a declaration of martial law to supplant local authorities. "Any effort on the Governor's part to declare martial law will be illegal, and as attorney general, I will consider it my duty to fight it."

The struggle over civil defense, according to Graves, turned Warren into "an active candidate early" for governor. Until then, Warren had resisted the notion of higher office, explaining that the only way for him to be governor was to be the best possible attorney general.

By Sunday, December 7, even civility had fled.

Warren was at Eighty-eight with his family when they learned of the Japanese attack on Pearl Harbor that morning. Almost as if to defuse his anger, he slashed across the page of his appointment book for December 7: "War broke out."

The following day at a hastily summoned state conference on defense in Los Angeles he wrote in his appointment book: "War declared on Japan." Law enforcement now extended to such unfamiliar subjects as insurrection and invasion.

The Japanese attackers meanwhile disappeared into the vastness of the ocean, leaving the hulks of the Pacific Fleet smoldering in the oily waters of Pearl Harbor. In California, nervous citizens waited the next blow, sure it would fall on their undefended coastline.

San Francisco endured three air raid alerts on Monday, December 8, hardly assured by the flustered military commander of the Western Defense Command, Lieutenant General John DeWitt, that "death and destruction are likely to come to this city at any moment."

Governor Olson promptly declared a state of emergency. "Enemy forces for invasion from air or sea may be hovering about us."

He was wrong, but in the anxious days after Pearl Harbor, when the Navy secretly conceded it had but two destroyers to guard the Pacific Coast, any rumor passed from general to governor became the basis for action.

The nation's defenses were even worse than the attorney general had imagined, he learned in a meeting with the naval commander on the Pacific

Coast. "We don't have anything, General, to defend the West Coast!" Admiral John Greenslade told him.

"Well, my God!" Warren replied. "We have thousands and thousands of Japanese here. We could have an invasion here."

The Japanese military did not realize how thinly defended was the coastline, Admiral Greenslade continued. They agreed they would say nothing publicly to suggest how defenseless they were. From then on, Warren would speak only of the danger of sabotage, never of invasion.

Meanwhile, using preprepared lists, federal agents on the West Coast began a roundup of enemy aliens deemed security risks. The well-publicized arrests of the 595 Japanese and 186 Germans and Italians seemed to confirm the possibility of subversion.

Panic took hold. Japanese fishermen and farmers were said to be waving lights mysteriously along the shoreline, Los Angeles mayor Fletcher Bowron claimed. Bowron and half a hundred other politicians were ready to believe even the wildest rumor of Oriental treachery.

For more than forty years, anti-Asian sentiment had wormed its way through California politics. Well before the turn of the century, unions had inveighed against Chinese and Japanese as cheap labor undercutting American workers. The state Grange had picked up the cry, demanding laws to keep Japanese from acquiring agricultural land; then-Governor Hiram Johnson had signed just such a bill in 1913.

Eight years later, V. S. McClatchy, publisher of *The Sacramento Bee,* organized a California Joint Immigration Committee composed of representatives from the state Federation of Labor, the Grange, the Native Sons of the Golden West, the American Legion, and Attorney General Ulysses S. Webb, who had drafted the Alien Land Law.

That committee would reach its peak of influence when it successfully lobbied Congress to attach a ban on Oriental immigration to the Immigration Act of 1924. From then until the attack on Pearl Harbor, the committee dwindled to a handful of soured old men prattling that "all people of Japanese extraction are sly, sinister, ruthless, unprincipled, aggressive, biologically more fertile than the white man, and totally incapable of genuine loyalty to the United States."

Though Warren the politician was a member of both the American Legion and the Native Sons, he said nothing to indicate he agreed with them that "the 'Yellow Peril' was here and going to take over," as some have concluded.

In his December, 1940, speech to the Associated Farmers convention, Warren cautioned against bigotry:

It should be remembered that practically all aliens have come to this country because they like our land and our institutions better than those from whence they came. They have attached themselves to the life of this country in a manner that they would hate to change and the vast majority of them will, if given a chance, remain the same good neighbors that they have been in the past regardless of what difficulties our nation may have with the country of their birth. History proves this to be true. . . . We must see to it that no race prejudices develop and that there are no petty persecutions of law-abiding people.

With his election as attorney general, Warren assumed Webb's ex officio seat on the Joint Committee in December, 1938; he resigned eight months later, never having attended any meetings, saying only, "it would be better for all concerned if I am not a member . . ."

If the attorney general harbored any particular concern about aliens, it was for those who took advantage of constitutional rights to advocate what Warren deemed subversive doctrines. Aliens might "point with loving pride to the joys of communism and fascism . . . [and] advocate overthrow of the government by violence" yet avoid deportation.

Now helpless California numbly awaited its fate as lurking submarines impudently attacked shipping within sight of the California coast. The *Agriworld* limped into Monterey harbor, the *Emidio* went down off San Diego. The Union Oil tanker *Montebello* was torpedoed within sight of Hearst Castle; the *Larry Doheny* was shelled by a submarine riding on the surface. The very coast appeared to be blockaded.

Meanwhile, Japanese forces landed in Malaya and Thailand. Imperial Marines waded ashore in the Gilbert Islands. Bombers struck at Singapore and Hong Kong, at the Philippines, at Guam, Midway, and Wake islands. Daily the headlines shrieked of disaster and defeat.

On December 15, Secretary of the Navy Frank Knox returned from a hasty inspection of shattered Pearl Harbor to tell a Washington press conference that "the most effective fifth-column work of the entire war was done in Hawaii. . . ." While there was no evidence that Japanese residents of the islands had aided the attack, Knox's confusion of *espionage* by Japanese consulate officers with *sabotage* by Japanese Americans seemingly underscored the threat to the mainland.

By Christmas, California was awash in bizarre rumors of sabotage at Pearl Harbor. Japanese-owned trucks were said to have blocked vital roads or rammed aircraft sitting on the runway at Hickam Field. Japanese landowners allegedly cut arrows in their sugarcane fields to point the way to Pearl Harbor. A milk truck or trucks drove onto military bases, then let down its sides to reveal a machine gun that slaughtered hundreds of unarmed troops.

Those reports gained credibility in Warren's office. "We were told that we were getting word from the military in the Hawaiian Islands about widespread sabotage," then–Deputy Attorney General Adrian Kragen recalled.

The rumors swirled around General DeWitt, who vowed not to be caught short like the military commander in Hawaii.

Day by day, the tension increased. On January 4, 1942, Hearst newspaper columnist Damon Runyon reported, erroneously, that a radio transmitter had been discovered secreted in a rooming house that catered to Japanese. Who could "doubt the continued existence of enemy agents among the large alien Japanese population"?

Ten days later, Republican Congressman Leland M. Ford of Santa Monica wrote both the War and Justice departments insisting that "all Japanese, whether citizens or not, be placed in inland concentration camps." The truly loyal among them, Ford reasoned, would be pleased to go and thus prove "he is patriotic and is working for us."

Ford's demand was match to tinder. Before the end of the month, the entire California congressional delegation was pressing for action.

The Los Angeles Board of Supervisors passed a resolution asking that the 13,000 Japanese aliens living in the county be evacuated. The American Legion demanded all 93,000 people of Japanese extraction in California be interned.

The city and county of Los Angeles dismissed ninety-five Japanese-American civil servants on the grounds it was "impossible to distinguish between loyal and disloyal . . ." * The chief of police of Los Angeles insisted the second generation Nisei, American citizens after all, posed a more difficult problem than did their alien parents. How to judge their true loyalty, when "you have racial characteristics, that of being a Mongolian, which cannot be obliterated from these persons, regardless of how many generations are born in the United States"?

Growing panic drove out reason. Governor Olson in a radio address on February 4 stated that it was "much easier" to determine the loyalty of Italian and German aliens than of Japanese and Japanese Americans. "All Japanese people, I believe, will recognize this fact."

On Sunday, January 25, the White House released the text of a report on the Pearl Harbor attack prepared by a committee chaired by Supreme Court Associate Justice Owen Roberts. The report of the five-member committee erroneously found there had been widespread espionage before the attack both by Japanese consular officers and "persons having no open relations with the Japanese foreign service." Though the charge was not documented, suspicion fell instantly upon Japanese residents of Oahu.

In the next week, General DeWitt and Governor Olson met twice to weigh the impact of the Roberts report, deciding,

There's a tremendous volume of public opinion now developing against the Japanese of all classes, that is aliens and non-aliens, to get them off the

---

* Some of those advocating the evacuation were motivated by less than patriotic reasons. The manager of the influential Grower-Shipper Vegetable Association acknowledged, "We're charged with wanting to get rid of the Japs for selfish reasons. We might as well be honest. We do. It's a question of whether the white man lives on the Pacific Coast or the brown man." (Quoted in Grodzins, p. 27.)

*land. . . . As a matter of fact, it's not being instigated or developed by
people who are not thinking but by the best people of California. Since
the publication of the Roberts Report they feel that they are living in the
midst of a lot of enemies. They don't trust the Japanese, none of them.*

Attorney General Warren too was alarmed by the Roberts report. Anyone who read it, he decided, "must realize that we have a tremendous
problem in California to protect the State against fifth column activities."

The presence of the Japanese in California provided the opportunity for
"a repetition of Pearl Harbor," he told reporters.

Once stated, the fear became the reality. Hearst newspapers' columnist
Henry McLemore on January 29 questioned the loyalty of the Japanese and
urged their "immediate removal. They are a serious menace and you can't
tell me that an individual's rights have any business being placed above a
nation's safety." McLemore in successive columns would grow more and
more shrill.

Four days later the Oregon and Washington congressional delegations
joined the Californians in demanding that an evacuation plan be created.

In San Francisco that same day Attorney General Earl Warren convened
a conference of one hundred law enforcement officers from around the
state. Military and naval authorities had advised him that a Pearl Harbor–
like attack on California was possible, Warren told the group.

The very fact that there had been no attacks suggested "it was a studied
effort not to have any until the zero hour arrives . . . It would be inconsistent with everything the Axis has ever done, if it was not planned for us in
California." Though warning against vigilante action, Warren cautioned,
"Every alien Japanese should be considered in the light of a potential fifth
column . . ." *

Warren asked the assembled law enforcement officers to prepare maps of
their counties detailing land holdings of both the Issei and their children,
the Nisei. When completed by Deputy Attorney General Herbert E.
Wenig, the assembled maps suggested an ominous pattern of Japanese-
owned lands dotted about strategic installations and facilities.

It was suspicious, Kern County District Attorney Tom Scott noted, that
Japanese-American truck farms surrounded Muroc Dry Lake, a bombing
practice base set in "what we call jack rabbit land, just sagebrush and alkali."
The land holdings in Santa Barbara County formed an even more dire
pattern, District Attorney Percy C. Heckendorf told Warren.

Eventually, the assembled maps indicated "that from Point Reyes south,
virtually every feasible landing beach, air field, power house, oil field, water

---

*Warren apparently picked up this theme of sinister inactivity from General DeWitt. Nine days
before, on January 24, 1942, DeWitt told the Army's provost marshal, "The fact that nothing
has happened so far is more or less . . . ominous." DeWitt had concluded that the lack of
sabotage indicated "there is control being exercised and when we have it it will be on a mass
basis." (See Conn, p. 132.)

reservoir or pumping plant, radio station and other points of strategic military importance had several and usually a considerable number of Japanese-occupied properties in their immediate vicinity," Assistant Attorney General Olney concluded.

Warren called upon the district attorneys to enforce the state's Alien Land Law, which prohibited those ineligible for citizenship—in effect, first-generation Japanese immigrants—from owning land.

The assembled law enforcement officials adopted a resolution calling for the evacuation of all *alien* Japanese. Warren personally favored the evacuation of at least the alien Japanese, he told the unofficial California Joint Immigration Committee in Sacramento on February 7. General DeWitt could remove "any or all Japanese out of the combat zone . . . and I am rather of the opinion that that should be done."

The military had the authority in time of war, Warren continued, "to tell me to get back 200 miles if it wants to do it, and as a good American citizen I have no right to complain. Now, if a good American citizen cannot complain, I don't see why the Japanese should complain." *

For Earl Warren, retired Army Reserve captain, there was no doubt. The United States was in danger and the military would have to take appropriate measures—even if it meant old friends like Tatsu Ogawa, his comrade wounded in the first war, had to be interned.

The decision for evacuation was the War Department's to make, Warren advised the joint committee. But General DeWitt and Admiral Greenslade were susceptible, even open to pressure, Warren noted.

Whatever their course, Warren insisted, it had to carried out legally. When the State Personnel Board ordered that all descendants of alien enemies be discharged from civil service, Warren raised constitutional objections.

The rule, he wrote, "discriminates against naturalized citizens and citizens by birth of the first generation, in favor of those citizens whose forebears have lived in this country for a greater number of generations."

The cost was too high, he told *The New York Times*. "We'd be in a bad way if we won the war and lost our civil liberties."

Ten days later, he ruled against the Department of Agriculture's arbitrary revocation of state licenses issued to Issei and Nisei produce dealers. (First- and second-generation Japanese Americans owned three-quarters of the distributors of agricultural foodstuffs.)

On February 12, nationally syndicated columnist Walter Lippmann— who had discussed the situation five days before with Warren—warned of "an imminent danger" of attack. Furthermore, Lippmann continued, "from

---

* Warren appears to be discriminating between alien and citizen. Just when he decided the entire Japanese population must be evacuated is unclear. General DeWitt reported to Washington by telephone on January 29 that Warren favored a mass evacuation. (See Conn, p. 133.) But the law enforcement meeting he convened on February 2 called only for the evacuation of alien Japanese.

what we know about Hawaii and about the Fifth Column in Europe, this is not, as some have liked to think, a sign that there is nothing to be feared. It is a sign that the blow is well organized and that it is held back until it can be struck with maximum effect."

This was not an ex–sports reporter like Henry McLemore. Walter Lippmann spoke to and for what a later generation would call "The Establishment."

Lippmann's column triggered a flurry of national comment. Hearst columnist Westbrook Pegler, never one to preach with moderation, raged that if Lippmann's fear was real, "the Japanese in California should be under armed guard to the last man and woman right now and to hell with habeas corpus until the danger is over."

Sentiment in favor of evacuation spread throughout the western states. The attorney general of Idaho, Bert Miller, insisted in a meeting with Army G-3 Colonel Dwight Eisenhower that "all Japanese be put in concentration camps, for the remainder of the war." Lest there be any doubt, he added, "We want to keep this a white man's country."

Troy Smith, attorney general of the state of Washington, wired *United States News* that he favored a declaration of martial law and the evacuation of "citizens of Japanese extraction." The governor of Oregon, Charles A. Sprague, concurred.

Under pressure, Washington inched toward a decision. On February 11, President Roosevelt—assuming extra-constitutional power—verbally approved an evacuation if the military deemed it necessary.

Alert to public opinion, General DeWitt made his decision. In a letter to the War Department dated February 14, 1942, he recommended that all persons of Japanese descent be removed from "sensitive areas."

Five days later, on February 19, the president signed Executive Order 9066 formally authorizing the military to clear sensitive areas of "any and all persons" and to restrict the right to enter, remain in, or leave such areas. DeWitt had his carte blanche.

Santa Barbara District Attorney Heckendorf immediately congratulated Warren: "I have no doubt that the presidential order stems back to the article written by Lippmann following talk with you."

The issue of evacuation had been decided by February 21, the day Representative John Tolan convened a hearing of his Select Committee Investigating National Defense Migration in San Francisco. Warren sat at the witness table before the three members of the committee, official-looking maps prepared by local law enforcement officers at his elbow. At his side in the crowded hearing room in the San Francisco Post Office sat his assistant, Warren Olney III, and Herbert E. Wenig, who had prepared the maps.

"For some time," Warren began, I have been of the opinion that the solution of our alien enemy problem with all its ramifications, which include the descendants of aliens, is not only a Federal problem but is a military problem."

Fifth column activities and organized sabotage would be "the greatest danger to continental United States" for a long time, he told the committee. "I am convinced that the fifth-column activities of our enemy call for the participation of people who are in fact American citizens . . ."

That there had been no sabotage, Warren again took as "the most ominous sign of our whole situation. It convinces me more than perhaps any other factor that the sabotage that we are to get, the fifth-column activities that we are to get, are timed just like Pearl Harbor was timed."

What Warren termed the "day of reckoning" loomed. When it would come, they did not know "but we are approaching an invisible deadline."

Warren, by far the most authoritative government official to speak that day, insisted that "opinion among law-enforcement officers of this State is that there is more potential danger among the group of Japanese who are born in this country than from the alien Japanese who were born in Japan."

There were twice as many Nisei as Issei, 66,000 to 33,000 thousand, in California. They were younger and many had received part of their education in Japan.

Congressman Laurence Arnold of Illinois interrupted: Did they have any way of knowing who among them was loyal?

"Congressman, there is no way that we can establish that fact," Warren replied crisply. With "the Caucasian race," they could "arrive at some fairly sound conclusions. . . . But when we deal with the Japanese we are in an entirely different field and we cannot form any opinion that we believe to be sound."

The Japanese were insular and tight-lipped. At his earlier meeting with sheriffs and district attorneys, Warren told the committee, he had asked if any Japanese or Japanese-Americans had volunteered any information on subversive activities or disloyalty. "The answer was unanimously that no such information had ever been given to them." *

Warren kept private his doubts about the Japanese evacuation. In a letter to J. Edgar Hoover on March 30, 1942, the attorney general wondered if "we are not straining out the grat [sic] and swallowing the camel" in ignoring German and Italian aliens.

While Warren applauded President Roosevelt's exclusion order, the coastal ban did nothing to curb the "many, many Japanese who are now roaming around the State," he cautioned the Tolan committee. Feeling against the Japanese ran high; their very presence in the community "will unquestionably bring about race riots and prejudice and hysteria and excesses of all kinds."

To put enemy aliens "on the road indiscriminately . . . would be an un-

---

* In fact, the minutes of the meeting of law enforcement officers on February 2 report Warren telling one inquirer, "We got a number of instances, five or six, throughout the group, who said some individuals had dropped in to give them some information." (See Grodzins, pp. 98, 144–45.)

speakable situation for our country." For their own safety, the evacuees would have to be confined.

Warren turned to the maps resting on the witness table. "These maps show to the law enforcement officers that it is more than just accident[al] that many of those ownerships are located where they are. . . . You can hardly grow a jack rabbit in some of the places where they presume to be carrying on farming operations close to an Army bombing base."

As if to underscore the threat, on Monday evening, February 23, a Japanese submarine surfaced off unguarded Ellwood Beach twelve miles north of Santa Barbara and fired as many as sixteen shells from a deck gun at the Bankline Oil Company's small field. In this first wartime attack on United States soil since 1812, a single derrick toppled, causing $500 in damages.

The attack was doubly suspicious. Ellwood was one of the sites that District Attorney Heckendorf had marked on his map as home to Japanese truck farms. The undefended oil field had been spared only because of poor gunnery.

Newspaperman Verne Scoggins, later to become a Warren press relations officer, suddenly recognized "there was fear, especially in Los Angeles and along the Santa Barbara coast, of an invasion."

The fear verged on hysteria by the early morning of February 25, when antiaircraft batteries scattered about Los Angeles began firing wildly into an overcast sky at unidentified aircraft. Five people died in traffic accidents or of heart attacks in "the battle of Los Angeles."

Nervous Naval Intelligence advised that an attack could be expected within the next ten hours; defense installations went on a yellow alert. California was seemingly imperiled.

The clamor for evacuation of all persons of Japanese descent was irresistible. On March 2, General DeWitt—who had earlier told reporters that three intruders had, in fact, flown over Beverly Hills a week earlier—designated the entire western half of California, Oregon, and Washington as a military area from which those of Japanese ancestry were to be removed "in the interest of military necessity."

More than 110,000 people, two-thirds of them citizens of the United States, would be summarily evicted from their homes and confined in ten internment camps for the next three and one-half years.*

---

* A generation later, the injustice of the evacuation is clear. There was no evidence of either sabotage or even cooperation with the Japanese military by either Issei or Nisei at Pearl Harbor. Underscoring the irrationality of the evacuation was the anomaly that the Japanese residents in Hawaii were not evacuated, and the fact that German and Italian aliens, who might move more freely about, were never considered for mass evacuation. (As Grodzins, p. 297 fn. 63, points out, Germany and Italy had no less interest than did Japan in sabotaging aircraft production in West Coast plants.) Congress eventually passed an indemnification act, apologizing, and granting survivors $20,000 for the injustice done to them by the forced evacuation.

Few protested. People of Japanese descent, citizen and non-citizen alike, neighbors, were put aboard trains and shipped away.

"Nobody seemed to stand up and say, 'You can't do that.' They just said, 'What a shame, I guess.' And they went on looking for marauding Japanese planes," reporter Richard Bergholz pointed out.

Though he was only one of many calling for an evacuation, and hardly the most strident, Warren had played a pivotal role in the ultimate decision. As attorney general, he took the lead in compiling the opinions of California's law enforcement officers—and he spoke for them. He had met with Walter Lippmann, whose later column cast the evacuation not as racism unleashed but as prudent military necessity.

The maps Warren ordered Herbert Wenig to prepare became justification a year later in DeWitt's final report for an evacuation; Warren's own arguments paraphrased in that report provided the rationale.

Through real panic and imaginary crisis, Warren had appeared to be firm and self-assured. His was the voice of reason in a time of fear. Where Olson had vacillated, Warren was decisive; the attorney general had become California's most prominent public figure.

CHAPTER 11

THE VICTOR

ARL WARREN AND CULBERT OLSON, HAD THEY BEEN DIFFERENT MEN, might have smoothed over their political disagreements. But the attorney general was stiff-necked and the governor fiercely partisan. Conflict was inevitable.

They skirmished first over a "hot cargo" bill, which would have banned the picketing of goods shipped to market during a labor dispute. Olson vetoed the measure on the grounds it was unconstitutional, and the legislature asked the attorney general's legal opinion.

In response, Warren's office wrote an opinion holding that the "hot cargo" bill was constitutional; secondary picketing might be banned, as strike-plagued agricultural interests wanted. Olson immediately interpreted Warren's legal opinion as personal opposition.*

They crossed swords a second time over a bill requiring mandatory flag salutes in public schools. Warren signed another solicited opinion stating the law was constitutional and children who refused to salute the flag might be expelled.

Despite that ruling, Olson pocket-vetoed the bill with the explanation,

---

* As governor in 1947, Warren permitted a "hot cargo" bill adopted by the legislature to become law without his gubernatorial signature. He was taking a "neutral stance," he explained to reporters, content to leave the issue to the courts. Twelve years later, Chief Justice of the United States Earl Warren changed his mind. He dissented from a majority opinion holding that such "hot cargo" acts were constitutional. The majority opinion, Warren wrote in dissent, would destroy one of labor's historic rights.

"I thought it more important to have children learn to love the flag than to force them to salute it." (In fact, Warren was legally correct, but little more than a year later the U.S. Supreme Court would rule that children could not be compelled to salute the flag.)

Because each was his party's highest ranking elected official, the disagreements on legal questions necessarily transformed them into political rivals.

As early as May, 1939, Warren's friend and close adviser Jesse Steinhart had conceived a plan to elect Warren governor. Steinhart's ploy simply was to portray Warren as a reluctant candidate.

"You played hard to get," as one man who saw the confidential document paraphrased the advice. Then the hesitant candidate yielded to a "draft" by citizens eager for him to run.

Because such drafts had to be carefully arranged, Joe Knowland convened a meeting with Warren's Southern California political operative McIntyre Faries and two fund-raisers, San Francisco securities broker Charles Blyth and Anglo-Crocker Bank's Jerd Sullivan.

As Warren sat listening, Knowland coolly laid out his reasons for tapping the attorney general as their best candidate. First of all, Warren was reliable. "Nobody thought of him as in any way radical," as Faries put it later.

Warren was also a proven vote-getter, and publicity surrounding his crackdown on the gambling ships had enhanced his reputation. No other Republican had Warren's broad political appeal.

Knowland proposed they raise seed money to promote a Warren candidacy. The northerners were prepared to put up $15,000 to launch a Warren candidacy. Faries was to sniff out a similar amount in Southern California.

Warren had reservations about the campaign. "What do you want out of it, Charlie?" he pointedly asked Blyth.

"All I want out of it is honest government," the broker reportedly replied.

Warren could not have asked for more. By the end of the meeting, Warren had assented to a quiet exploratory campaign.

Joe Knowland's son Bill would be the point man. He traveled about the state, discreetly promoting Warren, meanwhile goading the attorney general that unless he ran they would have to endure another four years of Olson.

The north fell into line. The south waited until May, 1941, when the *Los Angeles Times*'s influential political editor, Kyle Palmer, signaled agreement: "Should Attorney General Earl Warren set aside his personal preferences, [he] would be one of the strongest challengers the Republicans could put up against any Democrat."

Though Warren remained uncommitted, Knowland the missionary pressed on. "A large number of our friends in the south are champing at the bit," Knowland reported on September 21, 1941.

Late that year, a private poll identified Warren as the party's most attractive candidate. Warren also ran ahead among the pivotal independent and Democratic voters by a 4 to 1 margin.

When his advisers pressed him to announce his candidacy, Warren declined with a surprise announcement. He intended to accept a commission as a colonel in the army.

Jesse Steinhart urged he run first. "What have you got to lose? If you run and lose, you can go in the army then; the war's going to last a long time. If you run and win, you could be a tremendous asset to the country as governor of this state."

Warren still hung back. "Why, I couldn't afford to run for governor," he explained later. "I had six children and they were all of school age."

As attorney general, his salary was $11,000 per year; as governor, he would earn a constitutionally fixed $10,000. The family budget was tight; unlike other California officeholders, Warren had no "slush fund" contributed by supporters for his personal use.

Warren suggested they enlist a substitute. Fearful of a rising Democratic tide, both Los Angeles mayor Fletcher Bowron and University of California president Robert Gordon Sproul declined.

Late in March, 1942, a frustrated Earl Warren gave in.

Having denied two weeks earlier in a staff meeting that he was a candidate, Warren summoned his staff to announce, "Contrary to what I told you—"

He was an unwilling candidate, the General told his staff. "I don't want to run. I like this job, but I'm forced, as a citizen of this state, to accept the decision of others that it's the only way we can defeat Olson, and I'm running."

The task was formidable. One survey taken for the Republican Finance Committee in late March, 1942, indicated that Olson had a 29 to 19 percent lead, with 52 percent of the voters undecided.

In that uncommitted 52 percent Warren saw opportunity. The large majority of the undecided had either a favorable impression of Warren, or an unfavorable opinion of Olson. "I'm going after them," Warren told his advisers.

The "smart money" was less impressed. In a meeting at the exclusive California Club in Los Angeles, a group of sixty-five corporation executives agreed to put their money into legislative campaigns rather than the governor's race. Expecting a Democratic victory, they preferred to beef up the "Economy Bloc" and once more thwart Olson's program.

The vote was 64 to 1, the lone dissenter Gordon Campbell, a junior partner in an insurance firm who was there merely to fill in for an absent senior partner. Campbell pledged to raise money for Warren without their help.

Warren accepted the Los Angeles decision calmly. "All right, we won't have any money, so we won't spend any money."

Afterward, Warren maintained the "Committee of Sixty-five" had done him a favor. "It relieved me after my election of any pressure based upon campaign contributions from powerful southland interests." He would owe the corporations nothing.

That independence was vital to the man, Deputy Attorney General Adrian Kragen recalled. Summoned once to Warren's office in the middle of the campaign, Kragen found himself confronting a group of lawyers representing newspaper chains.

They wanted Warren to drop a lawsuit to compel newspaper publishers to pay sales tax on newsprint.

Warren turned to Kragen. "Do you think it's an important case?"

"Yes, I think it's a very important case."

"Gentlemen," Warren said, turning to the publishers' representatives, "you have your answer." Kragen was to press on with the case whatever the political costs.

Still, his campaign needed funding, enough so that Warren solicited contributions personally.

In a move he would later regret, "Warren came to us with his hat in hand," said John A. "Black Jack" Smith, the Sacramento lobbyist for a group of independent oil companies. "He told me all the money he had was a thousand dollars which he had borrowed. He desperately needed money. I raised $7,500 for him and he gave me a receipt for the money."

Warren paid his $750 fee at the Alameda County courthouse, cross-filing for the Republican, Democratic, and Progressive nominations. Olson, true to his instincts, filed only on the Democratic ticket.

Warren's announcement of his candidacy on April 9, 1942, was calculated to appeal to the huge undecided vote, to cast himself as a man above partisanship in a time of crisis.

"I believe in the party system," Warren acknowledged in his statement, "and have been identified with the Republican Party in matters of party concern, but I have never found that the broad questions of national party policy have application to the problems of state and local government in California."

Warren's strategy depended on capturing a significant number of Democratic votes, in demonstrating a perverse kind of party loyalty. "I can and will support President Roosevelt better than Olson ever has or ever will," Warren claimed.

Democratic partisans sneered. The attorney general, scoffed Olson staff member Robert Clifton, "was a run-of-the-mill Republican." Clifton's wife, Florence, herself a dedicated Democratic Party worker, protested, "He was no more a nonpartisan than Olson was. It was a complete fraud."

Organized labor largely dismissed Warren as the conservative chip off Old Joe Knowland's block. "Warren had always been antilabor, antiunion," longtime organizer Lee Coe insisted. "He was hated by the labor movement."

For his part, Olson seethed with contempt for Warren. "Anyone who is so cowardly as to put on the cloak of nonpartisanship in an election like this, either . . . is a political eunuch and does not know what it is all about, or he is a political hypocrite." Warren, according to the speakers' manual for the Olson reelection campaign, was the product of "A Machine's Last Crank."

Despite the criticism, Warren's independence played well with voters, in large part because he convinced them "a man might be a nonpartisan governor," League of California Cities director Richard Graves commented. Warren "talked of the office as one where executive ability, not partisan philosophy, was needed. And he believed implicitly that a time of war forbade partisanship."

With the attack on Pearl Harbor, the new candidate insisted again and again, party differences had vanished. "We are not Republicans now; we are not Democrats now. We are Americans. And we want the type of government in California that puts America first and all other things second."

After all, "we are fighting for freedom now, not just for Party," he reminded the state convention of Republican Women. His single campaign theme over the next seven months would be "Leadership, Not Politics."

A small group of advisers had conceived the strategy: circumspect Steinhart, and Steinhart's outgoing law partner, Ed Feigenbaum; J. Ward and Kate Mailliard, San Francisco society figures and philanthropists; Joe and Bill Knowland; Charles Blyth; lawyer Eustace Cullinan, once an editorial writer for the Progressive *San Francisco Bulletin;* and, increasingly, Assistant Attorney General Bill Sweigert .

The advisers were just that, advisers. "Warren was his own campaign manager when it came to setting the tone and philosophy of his campaigns," a veteran newspaper reporter decided.

"It had to be a Warren-for-Governor campaign from start to finish."

Warren did yield on one point—to Joe Knowland, who feared his man was not getting sufficient attention in the press. Warren agreed to retain the San Francisco firm of Campaigns, Inc., to handle his publicity and promotion.

Founded in 1933, Campaigns, Inc., was created by the husband and wife team of Clem Whitaker, a onetime newspaperman, and Leone Baxter, the former director of the Redding Chamber of Commerce. They had managed the successful Merriam campaign, then had gone on to package complete election campaigns for Republican politicians.

Whitaker accepted, though he and his wife were to handle only the mechanics of publicity and promotion. They wanted the Warren campaign, for associated with a Warren victory, their firm would rank preeminent in California politics.

Whitaker and Baxter's first move was to humanize Warren, as the partisan critic Carey McWilliams put it. Gone were the round black-rimmed glasses that made earlier campaign fliers and window cards appear as if defaced by a child's pen. Gold-rimmed glasses added a genial touch to the broad smile.

On a campaign trip to Los Angeles planned by Whitaker and Baxter,

Warren visited the weathered two-story frame house at 457 Turner Street where he had been born fifty-one years before. The publicity still of Warren in suit and hat smiling at neighborhood urchins on the front walk ran in newspapers across the state.

Warren as a campaigner was a man conscious of his dignity. After the pictures on the steps of 457 Turner Street, he refused to pose for "gag" shots, those artificial pictures of the candidate kissing pretty girls, holding babies, or donning Indian war hats. His Plumas County chairman recalled that Warren might occasionally put on his American Legion cap, but "he always seemed a little self-conscious wearing the thing."

Leone Baxter and actor Leo Carrillo, Warren's friend from their days at Fort Lewis, persuaded Warren to permit use of a photograph of the family plucked from the *Oakland Tribune* morgue. Posed on the steps of Eighty-eight, the eight Warrens were to appear on hundreds of thousands of penny postcards mailed to Democratic women across the state.

The key decision in the campaign was, finally, Warren's. He would run independent of party label, under the banner of the Warren-for-Governor Non-Partisan Campaign Committee. He intended to campaign alone, endorsing no one, refusing even to appear with other Republican candidates.

Whitaker and Baxter soon had letterhead nonpartisan committees for occupational groups ranging from cosmetologists to insurance workers to pharmacists to women Realtors. A Loyal Democrats for Warren Committee, chaired by Carrillo, provided a haven for defectors; and a Railroad Men's Non-Partisan League for Warren proudly announced that four of its members had known the candidate as a boy in the Southern Pacific yards.

A campaign flier directed at union members trumpeted Warren's youthful membership in the musicians' union and his support of the right of unions to organize. The pamphlet also made virtue of what had once been a handicap. "His father was a union man, and was blacklisted for fighting for union rights."

In what would become a quadrennial ritual, Warren began his campaign in the Gold Country. Accompanied by Carrillo—celebrated as the Cisco Kid's motion picture companion, Pancho—Warren moved from Jamestown to Sonora, then on to Angels Camp, Jackson, Sutter Creek, Drytown, and Michigan Bar. "It was all very low key," Warren aide Merrell F. "Pop" Small remembered, an opening day intended to emphasize the General's California roots.

Warren ran a frugal primary, eventually reporting that he spent a mere $12,500. Carrillo's Loyal Democrats for Warren Committee reported additional expenditures of $24,000. (Other organizations may have spent closer to a quarter million unreported dollars on Warren's behalf, the Democratic candidate for lieutenant governor claimed.)

Secure in the knowledge of a registration advantage of 900,000 voters, Olson mounted a token primary campaign. He spent $72,804, gave only a few speeches, and ran on his staunchly Democratic record.

It was an inadequate effort, especially when Olson blundered. On June 30, Warren announced the attorney general's office would appear as a friend of the court to support the exclusion of the Japanese from the West Coast. A week later, Olson suggested that evacuees be used to bring in the vital San Joaquin harvest.

The "agriculturist" backing that Olson claimed for this proposal vanished under a press attack mounted by Whitaker and Baxter: ". . . [T]he vast majority of farmers as well as other citizens of California have no sympathy for the Governor's program and want the Japanese evacuated from the Pacific Coast area."

Through the exchange, Warren appeared resolute, even patriotic, and Olson weak-willed; Warren stood with the great majority, Olson with a tiny minority.

Three weeks later, Olson announced his opposition to an initiative to repeal the state income tax. Warren just as quickly endorsed the proposal. He appeared to be on the side of hard-pressed taxpayers while Olson seemingly ignored their plight.

Finally Warren accused Olson of pandering to "communist radicals" by releasing King, Conner, and Ramsay from prison. Olson weakly asserted the three had not personally killed George Alberts. Moreover, he had not pardoned them, but merely commuted their sentences to time served.

All the while, Warren stressed his nonpartisanship and independence. ". . . [I]f elected, it is my intention to represent all of the people of the state of California. In this primary I have no running mates and I am not part of any ticket of candidates."

The attorney general cautiously avoided troubling economic issues and made few political promises. He insisted the night before the primary election, "I would rather be overwhelmingly defeated at tomorrow's election than to win an easy victory on false promises."

Warren did issue a "pension pledge" intended to appeal to the swing voters of California's large and vocal senior citizens' lobby living on $40 per month state pension checks. Need should not be a requirement for a pension, he insisted. Neither should a senior citizen be compelled to sell his home to qualify for the pension, nor should the children shoulder the responsibility of caring for the aged parent.

"A system which arbitrarily freezes people out of industry and declares them to be obsolete, merely because they have lived a fixed number of years, must make honorable provision for their support during the years of their enforced idleness."

Warren's primary campaign was a grand success. On the night of August 25, 1942, Warren and Nina celebrated with Joe Knowland as the returns clattered on the news wires in the Tribune Building. As expected, Warren had easily captured the GOP nomination with 635,230 votes, handily defeating two feckless candidates.

The surprise came in the Democratic column. While Olson won his party's nomination with 514,144 votes, cross-filing Earl Warren polled 404,778 Democratic votes—and captured thirty-one counties on the Democratic ticket.

In the combined vote count, Warren had out-polled Olson two to one, despite the 900,000-vote Democratic registration bulge.

Now, with the primary results in, those Warren called "the moneybags" in Southern California offered to put together a finance committee "and give Olson a real licking."

Warren refused. He would stick with his finance chairman, Gordon Campbell, and if Campbell could not raise money "then we won't have any to spend."

Warren resumed the campaign with renewed energy, increasingly confident, replaying the same themes. According to a Whitaker and Baxter internal memorandum, he was to "make the attack on Olsonism and not the Democratic Party."

Olson played into Warren's hands. The governor attacked affable Earl Warren as the creature of "predatory interests," no more than a "bitter-end Republican partisan out of the most reactionary faction of his party."

Olson's attacks, Warren replied piously, only proved him driven by "bitterness, prejudices and hatreds"—even when unity was a wartime necessity.

Olson asked President Roosevelt to campaign in California on his behalf. The president declined. Warren, after all, had compelled the state GOP to incorporate into its platform a cessation of party politics "so that we may give President Roosevelt our unqualified support in prosecuting the war to a victorious conclusion no matter what the cost might be."

Olson had become a liability, unable to unite the Democratic Party, unwilling to temper his New Deal rhetoric. The governor was on his own.

As his opponent faltered, Warren reached for even the most loyal Democratic vote. Coached by the state's first black officeholder, Democratic Assemblyman Fred Roberts, Warren delivered a dinner talk in Los Angeles's black community addressed to "Fellow Americans."

The speech stressed that "equality of service should command and assure an equality of opportunity and of privileges. We of the United States will not have made good the principles of the Constitution until we have broken down the barriers of prejudice and ill will that separate any part of our people from their fellows. . . ."

These were not newly adopted principles, he continued, put on "like a new coat in which to show off before you. . . . They will continue to be my principles whether or not I am favored by the votes of your people."

Week by week, Warren's confidence grew. Shortly before the general election, he told the young capitol policeman Edgar "Pat" Patterson that he expected to be elected and would see that Patterson was detailed to the governor's mansion. "I want you to help take care of my kids."

"I'll take care of *you* and your kids," Patterson promised.

The general election campaign neared an end with Olson lagging badly.

Warren broadcast a last appeal for votes. "Just as I want no Democrat to vote for me who doubts the sincerity of my nonpartisan pledges, I want no Republican who doubts that pledge to mark his ballot in my favor."

Warren was as good as his word. While Warren's campaign surged, the GOP nominee for lieutenant governor faltered. Frederick F. Houser asked Warren to put their pictures on billboards as a slate. Warren refused, arguing that office seekers traditionally ran independent campaigns in California.

Houser was furious, threatening to withdraw and charge Warren had double-crossed him. The same people who had persuaded him to run had put Warren in, Houser insisted. That gave him the right to slate with Warren.

Three decades later, Warren's anger at Houser remained. "I told him that I did not know who put him in the campaign, but I did know that no one had put me into it, that I was a self-starter, and was going to remain independent not only through the campaign but throughout my administration as governor if elected."

On the last weekend before the general election, with Warren campaigning in Southern California, Clem Whitaker issued an unauthorized statement on campaign letterhead noting that Warren and Houser were both running on the Republican ticket. Republican Whitaker, faithful to party, had manufactured a slyly inferential endorsement for the lagging Houser.

Warren angrily telephoned Whitaker, instructing him to put out no more releases. He was suspended, Warren snapped, his services no longer desired.

The balloting on November 3 was almost anticlimactic. Warren piled up a total of 1,275,287 to 932,995, garnering 57 percent of the votes cast. Of the state's fifty-eight counties, he lost only mountainous, heavily Democratic Plumas.

Buoyed by the Warren tide, Houser squeaked past incumbent Lieutenant Governor Ellis Patterson by a mere thirteen thousand votes of 2.1 million cast. Democrat Robert Kenny comfortably defeated the Republican nominee for attorney general. Voters gave Warren Republican majorities in both houses of the state legislature.

Warren found himself cast as the Republican man of the hour, a new figure in national politics, welcomed by both wings of his party. Senator Robert A. Taft and newly elected New York Governor Thomas E. Dewey, the one a conservative, the other a moderate, joined the chorus of congratulations. Columnist Doris Fleeson of the conservative New York *Daily News* discovered in Warren an attractive national candidate, with "a Joe Kennedy family, with a wife like Rose Kennedy who has stayed young-looking and pretty."

Warren had run a comparatively inexpensive campaign. While disclosure laws were lax—gifts and donated services did not have to be reported—he estimated in his *Memoirs* that they spent $125,000 in Northern California and $175,000 in the southern portion of the state. Warren personally contributed $1,996, he reported to the secretary of state.

The Warren family looked to the move to Sacramento with mixed emotions. They were leaving Eighty-eight, the family home—or the five youngest children were.

Oldest son James, attending Harvard's Graduate School of Business Administration, would not live in Sacramento. "Jimbo" was to be married in May to Margaret Jessee, a Sacramento native he had met two years earlier at Berkeley. Jim would then join the marines, while Margaret stayed alone in the big house on Vernon Avenue—once the rest of the Warren family moved out.

The state-owned governor's mansion in Sacramento, built seventy-years before by hardware magnate Albert Gallatin, had slipped into moldering disrepair in the years since. Widower Culbert Olson had lived downstairs in unheeding solitude. Gas fumes periodically seeped through rooms daubed battleship gray; bats and rats left droppings on worn carpets.

"Mother was just broken hearted. It was just a mess. Mother wouldn't show it to any of us," daughter Honey Bear said.

The Warrens agreed that Nina and the children would stay in Oakland until the once-elegant Victorian edifice with its grand central tower could be refurbished. The restoration—for the patchwork repairs eventually became just that—fell to Nina, assisted by a local decorator. Oscar Jahnsen, "a get-things-done man," lent a hand, his task to scrounge scarce building materials in wartime Sacramento. The Warren family would not follow the new governor to the capital until April.

Warren rode in the family Lincoln to Sacramento for the January 3, 1943, inauguration with the newly elected attorney general, Democrat Robert W. Kenny. The two men, by now trusted friends, determined to avoid the rancor of the Olson-Warren relationship.

The governor-elect promised Kenny major changes. "Warren told me that none of the old Merriam officeholders could expect to make a comeback in his administration. They never did."

Warren redeemed all his pledges, as campaign insider Charles Blyth learned when he approached Warren to put in his private bid to sell a new state bond issue.

As Warren family members later told the story, the governor-elect refused. "They're going out to public bid."

"You can't do that," Blyth protested. "I've always had them."

"Charlie," Warren chided, "you told me you wanted honest, clean government. And that's what you're getting."

The inauguration was a restrained affair, in keeping with wartime austerity. The crowd was small and security absent. After the ceremony, polite spectators lined either side of the Capitol corridor as a tired Olson and a "blue-eyed, pink bear wearing steel-rimmed glasses walked by, on the balls of his feet, like a fresh young heavyweight taking the ring," United Press reporter Jack Smith recalled.

"Applause ran along the line of spectators as the governors passed by, but whether it was mostly for the old man or the young one it was hard to say."

Olson loyalist Florence Clifton guided the weary former governor into an elevator in the Capitol. Shaking hands with excited supporters, a beaming Warren crowded in, unaware of Olson standing at the rear of the car.

"From behind Warren," Clifton recalled, "Olson said, 'I hope you have a better administration than I did. It was four years of hell.'

"And Warren, without turning around and looking at him, and in a very stuffy way, said, 'Well, it depends on how one handles it.' "

Part II

THE GOVERNOR

CHAPTER 12

THE HAPPY GANG

GOVERNOR EARL WARREN CAME INTO OFFICE WITHOUT A LEGISlative program. The organization of civil defense was imperative; beyond that he had only a brief agenda.

His first problem was to create a staff. Culbert Olson's loyalists had scattered, taking with them their files. They left behind an all but empty corner office—and evidence of an extensive eavesdropping system throughout the executive suite.

Warren ordered the wiring ripped out. "I want to assure citizens of the state," he announced in righteous tones, "they can come into these offices at any time without feeling they are being spied upon or their conversations subject to eavesdropping."

The first appointments to Warren's informal cabinet included two women, Dora Shaw Hefner, a professional civil servant raised to director of institutions; and Helen MacGregor, nominally his confidential or private secretary, in actual fact, one of two chiefs of staff.

The efficient Helen MacGregor would be responsible for all matters requiring Warren's personal attention. She handled everything from official correspondence—with authority to sign his name—to payment of the governor's insurance premiums.

Loyal and tight-lipped both, MacGregor was protective of the governor and his family. The Warren children remembered her fondly, and MacGregor sometimes went to the mansion to have lunch with Mrs. Warren, "not to talk office talk but woman-talk, little things they could laugh about," a mansion guard recalled. In turn, Nina Warren would send jars of Swedish meatballs or slices of cake to MacGregor's apartment.

The other aide-de-camp was William T. Sweigert, the sometime campaign adviser and former chief deputy attorney general. Given to sober three-piece suits that covered his spreading waist, the forty-three-year-old Sweigert's stolid demeanor belied his innovative, venturesome liberalism.

Son of Progressive parents, a registered Democrat himself, Sweigert was a resolute advocate of governmental activism. As a campaign adviser, Sweigert had written a memorandum that effectively defended the New Deal Warren had once opposed:

> *There is no place today for the so-called reactionary—the person who still thinks that government exists only to protect the power of a successful few against the demands of plain people for a greater measure of health, comfort and security in their daily lives. . . .*
>
> *The primary obligation of government is to develop policies that will advance the welfare of the people as a whole in their efforts to live decently under modern conditions.*

In Sweigert's view, government was to step in "whenever the projects of the smart and the swift so selfishly develop in size or purpose as to endanger the welfare of the community as a whole." To do that, to be the impartial overseer, a Warren administration had to stand beyond "mere partisanship," beyond alliance with any one party, group, or clique.

Sweigert's memorandum, which Warren kept close in a drawer of his desk, would go far to shaping the new administration's program.

A good-humored man with a ready smile, Sweigert maintained an easy relationship with Warren. When they disagreed, Warren would challenge his deputy, "I'll bet you all the tea in China."

Sweigert had a ready retort, even as he gave way. "You'd lose. But what the hell would I do trying to drink all the tea in China?"

The third of Warren's key staff appointments went to Verne Scoggins, a forty-year-old reporter who would handle press and public relations. A dropout from the state agricultural college at Davis, the lantern-jawed Scoggins had since become a self-taught expert in state farm and water policy.

Scoggins, a reporter for the *Stockton Record,* was initially indifferent to the Warren candidacy. He joined the campaign only at the behest of his publisher, who saw in Warren a flicker of Progressivism. Over the next months candidate and press officer had proved themselves to each other.

Scoggins set up twice-weekly press conferences for the dozen men and, a year later, one woman who covered the state capital. Reporters were free to ask any questions; Warren rarely went off the record. Instead, he often delivered long answers explaining the issues "like a civics lesson," one reporter said.

"We got straight answers from him on any question. There was never a credibility gap between us, nor doubt about his integrity," an editor wrote. "If he didn't know the answer to a question, he'd say so."

Despite the openness, or because of it, there were few embarrassments and only rare leaks. Mutual trust fostered a relaxed, even joking familiarity between reporters and the governor.

Scoggins-nurtured press relations became vital. While the governor denied he had an ongoing political organization, he did insist on constant communication with the public—through the press, in weekly reports over the ABC radio network, in public appearances, even by letter. Over time, those repeated contacts fueled Warren's "machine" and reelection.

Scoggins also doubled as the governor's political listening post. When his contacts called using code names, "Verne went across the street to a little apartment to use the telephone to make partisan political phone calls," secretary Wilma Wagner insisted.

Scoggins was "a stickler for handling partisan political things out of the office. He didn't even make calls on the state office phone."

Sweigert, MacGregor, and Scoggins worked easily together, often sharing tasks. One former assemblyman who served in Warren's administration credited MacGregor with "tremendously good judgment in lots of affairs and on many occasions," but confessed he had no idea if she advised on policy. Similarly, reporters knew Scoggins was politically astute, but had no idea he actually directed day-to-day political affairs.

Together they managed an office notable for its indifference to politics. "Some pretty good Democrats worked for him," Verne Scoggins dryly remarked a half-century later. "Republicans would bawl him out for appointing Democrats."

Warren ignored the critics. "He was never beholden to anyone. He never owed anybody anything. There were no strings at all. That's why he could recruit from both parties and go after the best people," his son Earl explained. (Despite the governor's seeming nonpartisanship, Democrats later charged that of the thirty-two department heads Warren appointed from 1943 to 1953, only five were Democrats and one an independent.)

As Sweigert urged, nonpartisanship extended to policies. When a group of San Francisco bankers seeking to influence a decision reminded Warren how their prestige had helped elect him, he turned them aside. "There will be another election in four years and in the meantime I am governor of all the people of California, not just those who voted for me . . ."

The realities of coalition politics also dictated his choices of staff and cabinet officers, Warren acknowledged. "I had to get Democratic votes to win. I conducted a nonpartisan campaign and I am determined to give the State a nonpartisan administration."

At the end of a grueling eight-hour interview, Warren's choice for director of state welfare, Charles Schottland, noted, "Governor, you've asked me every possible question except two. You haven't brought up the subject of my religion or my politics. I am a Jew and a Democrat," he volunteered.

"I'm not interested in that," Warren snapped. "I am interested in one thing only, and that's whether you think you can do the job."

Seeking professional administrators, Warren opened the highest jobs in state agencies to civil servants rather than to political supporters. Even such a plum as director of public works went to the apolitical Charles H. Purcell, the builder of the Oakland–San Francisco Bay Bridge. Warren also held over an Olson appointee as director of agriculture on the grounds that economist William J. Cecil was best qualified.

Some associates did find their way to unpaid state appointments. Actor Leo Carrillo and Joe Knowland were named to the state parks commission, positions they used to create ever more state parklands. As Scoggins put it wryly, "J.R. gave Oakland a lot of parks."

When he wanted someone for a post, Warren could be persuasive. After campaign fund-raiser J. Ward Mailliard rejected a seat on the San Francisco harbor commission, Warren asked, rather casually, "How are your boys?" One son was then in the army, two in the navy, all three in the South Pacific.

"I just talked to the secretary of the army," Warren added, "and he said this port would have to double its capacity to meet the demands of war."

Mailliard served on the board until 1946.

Yet even in appointing trusted friends, he searched for qualifications. Frank Shay, edged out for district attorney eighteen years earlier and more recently head of the prune growers' association, became a member of the Farm Production Board. Warren's Berkeley classmate, Newton Drury, named chief of the Division of Beaches and Parks, was the former executive secretary of the Save-the-Redwoods League, then national parks director, a man counted "one of the highest-minded conservationists in the United States."

His onetime college sparring partner Walter A. Gordon—first a Berkeley policeman, subsequently a parole officer and an attorney—in 1944 became the first black named to the state Board of Prison Terms and Paroles.

Gordon's appointment, said one astute lobbyist, was a signal that Warren's thinking was changing. Once, ten years before, Warren had reportedly declined to appoint Gordon deputy district attorney in Alameda County on the grounds that the time was not ripe. No longer. Walt Gordon, a black man on the Adult Authority, was "passing judgment on white men in prison."

In one case Warren did yield to political pressure—to his chagrin.

Conservative Democrat Gordon Garland as speaker of the Assembly had been the key member of the "Economy Bloc" that crippled Olson's legislative program. Defeated in the 1942 primary for a seat on the state Board of Equalization, Garland then called in his political chits.

Oilman William M. Keck—who had contributed heavily to Warren's campaign fund—had been promised by "Black Jack" Smith that the pliant Garland would be named state director of natural resources.

Garland was simply the wrong man to manage natural resources. "He would have danced to the tune of the oil people," an aide cautioned.

Secondly, Garland's sponsor, William Keck, was "the most unscrupulous operator in the west," a man who "figured he could buy anyone."

Rather than set the fox among the hens, the governor instead appointed Garland director of the innocuous Department of Motor Vehicles. He would come to rue even this moment of generosity when he later dismissed Garland for inept management.

He made no such concessions in naming judicial appointments. There he took special pains. Bills might be amended or repealed altogether, but the judges a governor appointed would often serve twenty years or more after the governor himself had left office.

Though Warren did nominate a number of old chums and proven associates to the bench, most judicial nominations went to people Warren did not know personally. To screen the unfamiliar names, he solicited private comments about prospective jurists from local newspaper editors—usually through *The Sacramento Bee* editor Walter Jones.

Having passed local muster, potential nominees were then appraised by a State Bar committee. Finally, secretly, Warren also checked the background of prospective appointees against the FBI's files on subversives.

As early as November 22, 1943, Warren was screening appointees and, in some cases, organizations that had invited him to make personal appearances. Literally hundreds of Warren's prospective nominees—even to such benign agencies as the State Athletic Commission—as well as "suspect" civil servants and schoolteachers underwent FBI scrutiny; the exact number the agency had "no ready way to determine."

Briefed only orally, "Mr. Warren always treated the information in such a manner that no one was able to trace the source."

Many of the nominees were unaware they were under consideration, which prompted Warren to a small prank. He would telephone the successful candidate, booming "Hello, judge."

In one case, Helen MacGregor said, Warren's prank backfired. When the governor called a Sacramento lawyer to tell him he was to be appointed to the bench, the lawyer assumed it was a practical joke and hung up with a sarcastic comment. Warren summoned his driver, drove to the embarrassed attorney's home, and delivered the news in person.

Once nominated, Warren's appointees received no political marching orders. "He made the appointment," one recalled, "and then never spoke to me about how I should act."

The governor expected the nominee to know the correct path, another learned. "If you have good morals," Warren told him, "and a sense of fairness, if you understand government and politics and do a good job of getting the facts and then do what you think is right, you won't have any trouble with me."

In time, Warren did fashion a formal code of ethics for his administration.

As "a requirement of elementary fairness," state agencies were to be bound by their own rules, and "these rules should be applied uniformly to all . . ."

Those he appointed to office were to avoid even the appearance of a conflict of interest. They were expected "to be above reproach in every particular." They were not to use the office to advance a particular cause or personal ambition.

Cautious himself, Warren expected administrators confronted with a problem "to pick up the issue by its four corners" and examine it thoroughly. They were to remember that "no matter how thin you make a pancake, it always has two sides to it."

Warren wanted his administrators to "get the facts, know what you're going to do, and if you have public support, grab the ball and run like hell!"

Warren himself rarely ran that fast. Criticized for unhurried decision making, Warren retorted with Abraham Lincoln's quip: "I'm a slow walker, but I never walk backwards."

Once settled on a course or program, he was unswerving. "I've never heard Earl Warren admit a mistake," a friend conceded.

Confident in his path, "he can pronounce publicly a platitude with a reassuring tone of discovery as if here, with the help of God, he has stumbled upon a hitherto unsuspected but eternal verity," then—*San Francisco Chronicle* reporter Pierre Salinger wrote.

A Warren speech sounded "as if he's running for assistant God," sneered one critic.

He was *the governor,* set apart by his responsibilities, the only one among them elected to office by the voters. The line was not to be crossed. Relaxed with chums and family, the governor was formal in dealing with his staff. Even Helen MacGregor, his private secretary since 1935, remained "Miss MacGregor." The men he addressed by their first names, occasionally by a nickname. None called him "Earl."

Though Scoggins thought of them as "a happy gang," he acknowledged the work was stressful. They worked for a man "impatient with what we might call sloppiness or laziness or anything of that kind," Sweigert said later. Secretaries understood that no letter typed for the governor's signature might have even a single visible erasure.

Normally tightly controlled, the governor could flay senior staff members with harsh tongue-lashings.

"Sure, I'm a tough boss, hard to get along with," Warren once acknowledged. "But I *have* to get along with the public, so I take it out on you fellows."

Secretary Betty Henderson remembered watching the usually jovial Bill Sweigert, ashen-faced, return to his office after a dressing down from the governor. As Sweigert slumped into his swivel chair, his assistant Marguerite Magee loyally protested, "He has no right to do that to you!"

Sweigert turned in his chair, pondering a moment, then replied, "Oh,

Marguerite, think of all the pressure that man is under every minute of every day." As he spoke, the color returned to his face.

The worst days, the worst pressure came when executions loomed. As a district attorney, Warren saw himself as a law enforcement officer. His office had prosecuted more than 130 murder cases and often sought the death penalty.

He never got used to it. "There was never a sentence of death brought in that I didn't feel nauseated," he admitted later.

Now governor, Warren still considered himself sworn to uphold the law. "We did not make the law; we abided by it," a secretary in the clemency and extraditions section said later.

She recalled the mother and father of a death row inmate personally appearing in the governor's office to appeal on behalf of their son. "They appeared to be hardworking people, in their fifties, nice, ordinary people who tried to work hard and raise their son. We told them as gently as we could that we could not change the law. We just did what the court ordered."

On the mornings of scheduled executions, the hushed tension in the governor's office grew unbearable near ten o'clock.

"We'd all look at the clock but avoid looking at each other's faces," one secretary wrote, "knowing that the 'open line' to the gas chamber would soon ring to let it be known that the gas pellets would drop."

Eighty-two times in Warren's eleven years as governor, he secluded himself in his private office, waiting the call. In those same years, the governor granted seven reprieves and commuted nine others to life in prison. (While Warren was out of the state, his lieutenant governors also granted four commutations—to Warren's anger—and in one case against his express wishes.)

Despite such pressures, despite the demands on evenings and weekends, the governor's executive staff was not well paid. Their salaries ranged between $6,000 and $7,000 per year. (Warren himself made $10,000.)

"He was terribly stingy," a former travel secretary noted later. Those who asked for a raise would be passed over. "He was too stubborn to give it."

Demanding as he might be with senior staff members, he was considerate of clerks and stenographers in his office. When doctors told young Arlene Tomlinson that she must take six months off as a messenger to avert an attack of tuberculosis, she resisted. She did not want to lose her job, she told other clerks.

Not long after, the governor suddenly appeared in the mail room. Sitting on the edge of Tomlinson's desk, he told her about his niece, Dorothy Plank, once young and vivacious like her. Dorothy too had been losing weight, was warned of the risk of tuberculosis, and advised to take time off.

But Dorothy stubbornly insisted she wanted to finish high school first, the governor said, his eyes tearing. The disease had not waited. For six years

Dorothy had wasted away, beyond the help of doctors, until she died eighteen months ago.

"Your job will be here when you get back," he instructed, "but you must follow the doctor's orders and take a rest . . ." Persuaded by the governor, Tomlinson took the leave. Her job, as he promised, was waiting when she returned six months later.

Such kindnesses inspired a fierce esprit de corps within his staff. They saw themselves as a select group, recommended by the state Personnel Board as the most qualified for their jobs. "We all had the feeling we were working as a team. We felt if these problems could be solved, Earl Warren could do it. We were working for the cause of government," added another secretary.

While the war effort took precedence in the office, Warren deemed postwar planning vital. The scarcity of farmworkers and the conservation of natural resources needed legislative attention. Schools and prisons were in a "sorry state," he told the legislature. The state's fragmented mental health programs shrieked for correction, Warren insisted. "We must take California out of the asylum age and put it into the hospital age."

Warren's was a progressivism grappling with issues that Hiram Johnson never knew. Warren confronted the complexities of governing a burgeoning state with 8.5 million residents, suddenly weighted down with dozens of new defense plants, military bases, a vast influx of job seekers, and shortages, always shortages.

Shipyards and aircraft plants operated around the clock, seven days a week. Well-paying jobs once closed to women, to blacks, and, curse of old California, to the Chinese, opened.

Full employment and increased defense spending was to produce a state revenue surplus of $60 million in the first year of war. Even though he signed a bill that cut the sales tax, Warren managed to salt away a growing "Rainy Day Fund." California would need that money, once the war ended and scarce construction materials became plentiful.

Lured by promises of employment in California's mushrooming defense industry, hundreds of thousands of job seekers would increase the population almost 28 percent. All 2.1 million newcomers required some state services.

Nothing gave him more satisfaction, Warren said in later years, than providing for the residents of a state "growing at the rate of 10,000 people a week. Every Monday morning we had to find accommodations for a new town of 10,000 people . . . new sewers, schools, water supply and roads."

Physical facilities alone would not be enough to insure the quality of life, Sweigert continually insisted. In time, Warren came to accept Sweigert's contention that government must actively deal with the social and economic problems that the boom spun off. Government was not merely the impartial referee between management and labor, rich and poor, weak and strong.

Even as they planned for the future, they had to cope with new or inherited problems. Shortly after the inauguration, the state fire marshal reported that overcrowding at a Stockton mental hospital posed a threat to patient safety. Hospital officials, cramped by tight budgets, had fobbed him off, the marshal explained.

Warren's personal inspection left him shaken, appalled by the over-crowded conditions. He angrily ordered the top two floors of the hospital closed, waving aside protests of administrators who said they had no place to house the overflow. New mental hospital construction would take priority on his agenda.

To cope with such issues, he revitalized a strategy of the Progressive Era, the citizens' advisory group. A Warren investigating commission or advisory conference became a powerful tool for, first, exposure, then reform legislation. Just such a study committee during Warren's first year in office set the standard.

For nine years, the state legislature had ignored a report that called for progressive programs to deal with California's prison system. California's prisons ran "like country clubs" with guards and wardens susceptible to gratuities in exchange for lax treatment or even extralegal furloughs.

Warren himself had long complained that prisons did nothing to break the cycle of crime and punishment. "Caging men like animals, penning them within walls, then expecting them to become better men, is fallacious," he had insisted as early as 1931.

An unexpected opportunity launched his reforms. The chief of police of San Francisco telephoned to report that two of Folsom Prison's more notorious felons were dallying with women on weekends in the city.

"Arrest them and announce the arrest," Warren ordered.

In the blare of lurid headlines, the governor appointed a committee to investigate state prisons. Sixty days later, his Investigation Committee on Penal Affairs produced a scathing report.

Warren promptly called a special session of the legislature to implement the committee's recommendations for reform. Within four days, the legislators had passed Warren's package of bills and reorganized the entire state penal system.

A nationwide search turned up a new director, Richard McGee, from Washington State. McGee hesitated to hire other prison administrators who were not from California, explaining to Warren, "I don't want to get you into political trouble."

"Hire them," Warren ordered. "If I ever play politics with the California prison system, I want you to announce it immediately, and if I ever find you playing politics, I'm going to fire you immediately."

California's prison system would become a model copied across the country.

Prison reform might have been accomplishment enough, but Warren sought more. Fulfilling his campaign statement, he asked the legislature to eliminate "the requirement of pauperism" for old-age assistance. "I want it to be based upon social right," he advised.

Warren appointed a carefully nonpartisan investigating committee, thereby "removing the issue from the field of politics and propaganda." Unable to ignore the committee's final report, the legislature raised the pension ceiling from $40 to $50, and increased the amount relatives might contribute without penalty to senior citizens. By the end of 1943, California's average state pension of $47.15 led the nation.

The commission process usually moved slowly, allowing time for public opinion to generate impetus for reform. Sometimes, it could be deliberately hastened.

In early June, 1943, groups of sailors on shore leave took to roaming East Los Angeles's sprawling Mexican American barrios. While police looked on with casual disinterest, the sailors fell upon young men fitted out in the pegged pants, long jackets, and broad-brimmed hats known as zoot suits. Los Angeles's newspapers gleefully supported the "patriotic" servicemen.

At the urging of his personal friend Carey McWilliams, Attorney General Robert Kenny convinced the governor to appoint a commission to investigate the causes of the spreading riots. Unaware of the source of the names, Warren eventually appointed four of the five commission members McWilliams recommended; the governor added only Leo Carrillo to the panel.

Meanwhile, Kenny instructed McWilliams to prepare a report for the committee. "This has got to move very fast if it's going to have any quieting effect."

By June 16, the governor's committee had met and adopted a somewhat watered down version of McWilliams's report—without knowing its author. As planned, its release toned down the inflammatory press reports, reminded police of their duty, and dampened the violence.

With Warren's concurrence, Kenny also issued a manual for police on handling racial disturbances. The guide, written secretly by McWilliams, was the first such published in the nation. (Three years later, Kenny's Department of Justice brought out a comprehensive training bulletin dealing with race relations for police.)

The zoot suit riots notwithstanding, Warren's first year as governor had passed smoothly, with considerable accomplishment. The Republican-dominated legislature was cooperative, the Democratic minority demoralized. Even California's often clamorous pension lobby had quietly fallen into line. Labor, farm, industry, and business, all were harnessed to the war effort, momentarily distracted from selfish goals.

Warren's achievement came not merely because the governor was a good man, Bill Sweigert decided. "Good men can be eaten alive by the buzzards." A successful governor had to be a politician, "alert and knowing . . . and know where the bodies are buried," Sweigert added.

Beyond that, Warren had special qualities, travel secretary William Mailliard noted. "He listens to people. He learns. He has a terrific grasp of what's going on. He's stubborn. He doesn't forget a dirty trick."

Warren's years as lobbyist for the District Attorneys' Association had given him a special feeling for legislative politics—the north-south rivalry over scarce water and electricity; the urban-rural split; all the pullings and haulings of partisanship in the Golden State.

He also had an uncanny sense of public sentiment. "Warren's timing," said a former deputy, "was nearly always correct. He knew when the right psychological moment for decisive action had arrived, and then moved fast."

That sense of timing, what some dismissed as Warren's "luck," did not happen by accident, Verne Scoggins insisted. The governor "maintained personal contact with a surprising number of people in each county and was quick to sense a consensus." Old timers swore his popularity rivaled the fabled Hiram Johnson's.

With luck, intuition, or experience, Warren maneuvered passage of the bulk of his legislative program. He vetoed only a handful of the most egregious pork barrel measures, explaining with injured sincerity, "It's just not right."

His achievements as governor of a large and fast-growing state inevitably brought him further national attention. On the hunt for worthy presidential contenders, the conservative *Saturday Evening Post* in August, 1943, enthusiastically described the first-term governor as "a serious-minded Horatio Alger character in flesh and blood . . ."

Here was a political comer, the magazine enthused, a popular, proven vote-getter. Moreover, Warren was prudent, no radical. Best of all for a Republican Party in search of national leadership, he was "an ardent believer in states' rights and decentralized government."

Two months later, Warren's liberal critic, Carey McWilliams, weighed in with a contrary view. He scored the governor as "completely the creature of the Hearst-Chandler-Knowland clique in the Republican Party in California . . . the particular pet of the great shipping, financial, agricultural and industrial interests of California . . . the smoothest functioning 'big-business' machine in the nation."

Warren was "the front man for this machine . . . taught to mouth—and it must have been a bitter tutelage for this essentially grim and hard-boiled individual—such phrases as 'old-age security,' 'collective bargaining' and 'social planning.' "

If not seasoned enough for the presidential nomination, according to McWilliams, Warren nonetheless remained "*the* most plausible Republican vice-presidential nominee" in 1944.

GOP leaders took note.

CHAPTER 13

THE THIRD-FLOOR WIZARD

I T BECAME EARL WARREN'S CUSTOM TO LEAVE THE GOVERNOR'S MANSION about 8:00 A.M. and walk the ten blocks to the Capitol. This was the only exercise he got, and he enjoyed the amble through downtown Sacramento.

Two or three times a week he dropped in for a shoeshine and baseball talk at Bob Tinsley's stand at the corner of 10th and J Streets, then strolled across the Capitol grounds admiring the grand camellia trees and the dank rhododendron beds. Here and there along the way he stopped to chat with passersby or tourists who wanted to shake his hand.

For all his affability, Earl Warren remained a private man. Governor Warren liked meeting groups of people; Mister Warren stood aloof from individuals. He might laugh at others' jokes—provided they were not off-color—yet he told none of his own.

He exchanged pleasantries, yet revealed nothing of himself. To his staff, to lobbyists, to legislators, he was direct, humorless, and businesslike.

Warren saw Sacramento city manager Bartley Cavanaugh most often, the two of them sharing a passion for sports. (Warren acknowledged that each morning he first read the *Bee*'s sports page because "the sports pages report men's triumphs and the front pages seem always to report their failures.")

"If the governor was lost," his travel secretary William Mailliard said, "I'd always know where to find him. He'd be at a football game with Bart Cavanaugh. It might be a bunch of kids on an empty lot in Sacramento, playing touch football."

In public, Warren was "the Boss"; in private, Cavanaugh called him

"Earl." During baseball season, the two men stood in line with their children to buy tickets to Sacramento Solons home games. On Sunday, Warren and his longtime Oakland friend Oliver Hamlin sometimes played baseball on Cavanaugh's pickup team.

Similarly, Warren's circle of political advisers was small. He relied on a handful of friends from the Bay Area, particularly Joe Knowland and Jesse Steinhart, the one conservative, the other liberal.

In Sacramento, the governor had Bill Sweigert and Verne Scoggins close at hand. He also used *Bee* editor Walter Jones "as a sounding board," said Jones's assistant Thor Severson. "They thought almost as one in terms of human commitment."

Warren gravitated to such men, those who shared his zeal for public service. Two or three times a year the newly elected district attorney of San Francisco, Edmund G. "Pat" Brown, Sr., and the governor shared long, unhurried luncheon conversations at the Del Paseo Country Club. "I wanted to know the good things about the DA's office, and I wanted to know the mistakes I could avoid," Brown recalled fondly.

Gradually the relationship between the two men became more social. Warrens and Browns exchanged visits at each other's homes, but Earl and Nina Warren generally separated their family life from his public life. Pat and Bernice Brown, along with Jesse and Amy Steinhart, were exceptions.

The Warrens visited the Steinhart home in suburban Los Altos, where Nina and Amy swapped gardening tips. Not a hunter himself, Steinhart took young Earl and Bobby on camping trips to the High Sierra. At the same time, the governor drafted the Steinharts for public service. He appointed Jesse Steinhart a regent of the University of California, and Amy Steinhart to the State Board of Education.

The governor's mansion was home. He hosted few official functions there —an annual buffet dinner for the press, another for the 120 legislators when they were in session. For a handful of obligatory formal dinners at the mansion, Nina borrowed silver and dinnerware from Joe Knowland, picked up and delivered by a Capitol policeman.

Nina Warren knitted public and private lives together. "That social ease of theirs is not accidental," Mailliard insisted. "She's organized it. She's a very strong influence, not on policy or political questions, but on relations with people, the appearance they show to the world."

Nina was not merely the self-effacing housewife, still ironing her husband's size $17^{1}/_{2}$ dress shirts and fretting that his habit of tightly knotting his ties ruined them. "She's got a good mind, a very strong mind, with very positive ideas, and I think that almost no one ever sees this," Mailliard added.

By choice, Nina Warren's life revolved around her family. She made few public appearances, and fewer political.

"All I've ever said in public," she once said with self-deprecating humor, "is 'I christen thee so-and-so,' but nobody ever heard me above the smashing of the bottle and all the excitement." (She would send no fewer than eight bottoms down the ways of Bay Area shipyards during her husband's first term.)

Mother and father, said youngest daughter Honey Bear, shared "the most ideal relationship I could dream of. They didn't fight. Mother absolutely worshiped my father." And organized his life.

It was Nina who made sure comb, handkerchief, and pencil were in a breast pocket of every suit. It was Nina who saw to it that the worn shoes got to Randall Butler's repair shop on H Street. It was Nina who periodically assessed his wardrobe, then ordered a new suit from Stiegeler Brothers in San Francisco. Nina cooked the stews, lamb chops, steak, and leg of lamb her husband favored. And Nina ran the mansion as an official residence on the $500 per month provided by the Legislature.

"She made my father's life so perfect, so free, so he didn't worry about the trivia," James said.

In exchange, Warren gave his wife "everything a woman could ask: respect, love and total support," daughter Honey Bear said reflectively.

Oldest daughter Virginia shared that idealized portrait of her parents. "They adored one another; it was total devotion."

Warren's devotion to Nina, "the best thing that ever happened to me," was unswerving. There was simply no hint of personal or professional scandal about the man, even the most skeptical of reporters conceded.

His reputation was to be carefully guarded by family and staff alike. Warren—never socially comfortable in the presence of women unless Nina was by his side—strained to avoid even an accidental suggestion of impropriety, one secretary remembered.

Invited to ride with his wife in a parade in Los Angeles, the governor made his customary excuse for Nina. This visit to Southern California was her vacation. Besides, there were the children to mind.

Fine, the parade's sponsors replied; actress Ginger Rogers would be delighted to share the governor's automobile.

Moments later, as the amused secretaries predicted, the governor telephoned the parade sponsor to report that Nina had graciously reconsidered and would ride with him after all.

Their years came to follow a pattern. During the summers, the Warrens would decamp stifling Sacramento for a rented cabin in a private preserve blocks from the ocean in Los Angeles's wooded Rustic Canyon. There the boys learned to skin-dive—Bobby at one time holding a depth record for a free dive—and to spearfish.

For the family, the Los Angeles sojourn was a vacation. For Earl Warren, it was work. And politics. "Dad wanted to be sure he kept a strong political base in Southern California," Earl Junior commented.

Warren also fit in annual trips to the Santa Barbara Fair where, sombrero-topped, he rode horseback in a parade with Leo Carrillo playing the *vaquero*.

The California-Stanford football game, the East-West and Rose Bowl games were obligatory, partly pleasure, partly politics.

Together mother and father sought to provide their children as conventional a life as possible. Though their father was governor, oldest daughter Virginia said, "we just wanted to be like other kids." When they complained about the Capitol police officer driving them to school in the official limousine, their father arranged for them to be chauffeured in a less ostentatious Chevrolet. Still uncomfortable, they demanded they be dropped off a block from school,

"For the others," Honey Bear recalled somewhat ruefully, "it was easy, but I had to lug a cello a block to school."

First Virginia, then Dorothy, the oldest girls, dated. As the children began going out at night, one or the other parent lay awake until all were home. Earl Junior remembered tiptoeing past his father's bedroom late at night, suddenly brought to a stop by his father's jocular bellow, "Halt! Who goes there? Friend or foe?"

As they grew older, the rules loosened. "Somehow we knew what the guidelines were or what they should be for our behavior and we kept in line," daughter Virginia noted.

Discipline was firm. "He'd talk to them so they knew he meant business," Warren's sister, Ethel Plank, said.

The children were good but took liberties with their father that their mother would not have allowed. "The girls could always pull the wool over his eyes," Patricia Warren, Earl Junior's wife, later remarked.

He was more strict with the boys. Robert recalled his father angrily breaking up a fight between him and older brother Earl. "Earl was taking a swing at me, and I already had hit my brother. Because Earl was the bigger one, Earl was the one who got the discipline," Bobby said with a chuckle years afterward.

Father taught each of the boys to hunt and fish, even though their mother could never reconcile herself to the danger of guns. Better they learn early, their father countered, and then abide by the safety rules.

Warren made a point to take at least one son along on the five or six times a year he hunted deer, pheasant, ducks, or geese. Bobby, in particular, became a good shot, bagging a deer each season from the time he was twelve.

Ever after, Nina would think of these years in Sacramento, the years their five youngest grew up, as the best of her life. The children agreed, Robert said later. "It was a great time in our lives."

Virginia and Dorothy were swept up in the life of popular high school students. Their brother Earl planted a prodigious victory garden in the vacant lot adjacent to the mansion, his green thumb a neighborhood marvel. Fascinated by animals, Earl also took up taxidermy, then raised canaries and springer spaniels—and a Dalmatian that bit one of Virginia's dates.

Honey Bear and Bobby became interested in jumping horses. Their father's Oakland friend Oliver Hamlin gave them mounts of their own, which they boarded at a local stable. For six years the two rode virtually every day.

Honey Bear and Bobby trained their own jumpers, Porky and Peanuts, eventually traveling the state, winning ribbons and cups. Their father attended horse shows when he could fit them into his calendar; their mother never did. "She could not bear to see me jump," Honey Bear explained.

Despite all the activity, and the energy of five children growing up, "everything was kind of in a monotone," Robert recalled. "In our family, there wasn't room for emotions. There was no screaming or laughing. If you laughed out loud, you were silly.

" 'Don't be silly.' You were told that. My mother would say that and my dad would even say things like that. It was totally unacceptable to cry. It was not acceptable to be sad in our family. It was not acceptable to be mad, or to be moody."

The children were expected to behave, to be adult, the youngest son remembered. "If you weren't perfect, it wasn't acceptable."

Good grades, in good courses, were important too, "because that's what you needed to get to the next step."

Growing up the son of the governor was not always comfortable, Robert remembered. He had few hours alone with his father, in part because there were so many children, in part because "I was a shadow really."

If he went on a hunting trip with his father and his father's hunting companions, it was not because he was Bobby the good hunter but because he was Earl Warren's son.

He chose not to attend political affairs "because I didn't want to go to dinner and sit around and have fifteen people come up during the dinner and want to talk to Warren" while the lad sat mute.

"I never wrestled with my dad, never played catch with him," Bobby said. "We went hunting together, always in a crowd with other people. We went fishing together. Sometimes when we hunted ducks, it was nice 'cause we'd share a blind together. Other than that, it wasn't what I feel was a real good father–son relationship."

Either to attract attention or to mark himself an individual, older brother Earl mounted a stubborn rebellion. "I became very close to my father by 'knocking heads' with him, by being in certain respects a rebel at a very young age." Earl would raise questions, then doggedly hold his ground when his secretly delighted father took a contrary stand.

His mother also stood at arm's length. "The reason our family was close, but nobody ever said why we were close, is that my mom lost everybody that she ever got close to." Parents, brothers, her first husband, her father-in-law, a favored niece, "as fast as she could become connected to them they died."

Nina refused to talk about these losses. "If you didn't talk about it, it didn't exist," oldest grandson James explained.

The children were sure of their parents' love, Robert recalled, but did not express it. "You don't say, 'I love you.' That's not an emotion that you share with other people. That was something that was never said in my family."

Earl Junior agreed. As certain as they were of each other's love, he said, they were "not very demonstrative."

Father and son found it difficult even to express their love. Earl Junior would always remember that one time, three or four years before his father died, when he said, "I love you." Stunned, the son didn't know how to respond.

With the coming of grandchildren, Warren opened up. Doting grandparents Earl and Nina often dropped by 88 Vernon to play with the first grandchild, James Lee. "I always kissed him when I saw him," daughter-in-law Margaret said, "but I don't think he was terribly demonstrative."

The reserve existed between mother and father, son Robert said. "Very seldom can I remember ever seeing my father touch my mother, hold hands or hug. I'm sure that happened because there were a lot of children, but it wasn't something that happened in front of the children. Everything was very formal."

Some measure of the distance the boys felt may have come from their father's unavailability. Try as he might, Governor Warren could not always attend their school assemblies, football games, and horse shows.

The girls had more than adequate substitute in their mother. The boys, once they reached puberty, encountered an often distracted father.

He seemed to spend more and more time in his third-floor office, mastering the complex issues he confronted as governor. Even on holidays, grandson James Junior remembered, Warren spent hours there.

Told the third floor was off-limits, that grandpa was working, the little boy crept up the stairs, lured by the forbidden. On a couple of occasions, Warren caught him. "He was almost like a wizard, coming out from behind his desk."

He read, usually at night in bed, sometimes in the early morning before the children awoke, about population growth, expansion of the education system, the need for child care facilities, and power shortages. With time he came to understand each problem, to solicit solutions, and then craft a legislative response.

For all his diligence, Warren impressed no one with either blinding intellect or absolute mastery; he was, instead, credited as knowledgeable, hardworking, and determined to succeed.

By 1944, a presidential election year, Warren had also taken on a larger political responsibility. The Republican Party, his party, had suffered three successive defeats at the hands of the voters; it had to be redirected and provided new leadership.

In a speech calculated to bid for national attention, Warren argued that the nation, with California in the vanguard, might shape a postwar era of unequaled wealth.

"We can produce so abundantly that every man and woman and child in America can be supplied with all their needs," Warren told a group of sales executives meeting in Los Angeles in April, 1944.

"The curse," as he put it, was cyclic unemployment, a neat euphemism for the periodic panics and crashes of Wall Street. "Having sniffed our destiny and measured our native production ability, we still seek the remedy."

His speech, delivered just two months prior to the Republican National Convention, carried a partisan message. The government, he told the applauding executives, might continue after the war "through deficit financing, to buy for all of us an unlimited supply of both necessary and unnecessary public works. It wouldn't be the democratic American way of doing things, but it could be done."

This was dutiful Republican cant. He softened it with a leavening of California Progressivism. There would be a government role in the postwar world, to be sure: care of disabled veterans, better standards of roads and highways, new airports, and public works.

"We must buy, and pay for, a higher standard of health and safety, better controls of monopoly, more effective and equitable regulation of commerce, labor-management relations, and corporation practices."

With this address in January, 1944, Warren sought to moderate his once strident partisanship. A decade earlier he had scourged the New Deal as radical or worse. After a year in office—whether impelled by the burden of representing all the people or simply looking to his own reelection—he spoke of treating postwar problems "with a unity of purpose. . . . We can't advance by cultivating hatreds, prejudices, or engaging in needless controversy."

Such temperate language enhanced Warren's appeal to a wide swath of voters, from the conservative right across the broad middle of the fiscally cautious, to socially concerned liberals. He appeared reliable, safe, even fatherly to a majority of voters.

However much Warren tempered his rhetoric with platitudes, New Deal Democrats eyed him suspiciously. Warren was, after all, a creature of "black reaction," beholden to the hated Knowland family. The suspicion only grew when good, safe Earl Warren loomed as a potential presidential candidate.

The speculation had begun early—simply by virtue of his election as governor of a large state. Just two weeks into Warren's first term, *San Francisco News* columnist Arthur Caylor tabbed the governor as the Republican Party's vice presidential, perhaps even its presidential, nominee.

Despite Warren's denials, few paid any attention. On August 7, 1943, Hearst columnist Damon Runyon reported that Wendell L. Willkie, the putative front-runner for the nomination, wanted Warren as his vice president.

The national press weighed in. In a cover story that instantly transformed him into a serious candidate, conservative-minded *Time* magazine cited

Warren as one of a group of Republican governors who were the hope of the party. Though Warren's "record in public office fails to reveal much promise that he is a potential giant in U.S. history," the magazine noted, among party wheelhorses meeting in Chicago early in 1944 his was the name most often mentioned for the vice presidency.

The news stories about candidate Warren proliferated—despite his protests that he had been elected to a four-year term and felt obligated to stay put. He had a good record as a vote-getter. He was an attractive family man, a veteran himself, the father of a marine, and a newly made grandfather. Moreover, as governor, he represented the revitalized GOP in state government, rather than the Old Guard of discredited senators and congressmen in Washington.

Of such things were national tickets fashioned.

Warren was to write that he "maintained only mild interest in the Republican Party nationally" at the time. However mild that interest, he did seek to influence the party's direction.

As early as January, 1944, Verne Scoggins, Warren's adviser in matters political, wrote a potential supporter that "the program and platform upon which candidates will stand is going to be of major importance this year, and that he hopes all the western states can exert a definite influence in the determination of these policies."

California's national committeeman, William V. Reichel, was frank enough. "We have fifty convention delegates and we're going to get something. At the convention, our votes will get us a Western cabinet member, a Western Supreme Court justice, and a Western man on every high policy-making body in the government. That's what Warren will be bargaining for. We'll get them or they won't get our votes."

To assure his leadership, Warren announced he would file as a favorite son candidate for president on the California ballot. Unchallenged, the Warren slate piled up almost 600,000 votes in May. By then, New York governor Thomas E. Dewey had secured enough convention votes to claim the presidential nomination.

Firmly in control of the convention machinery, Dewey's managers asked Warren to serve as temporary chairman and give the keynote speech. It was a signal honor, it offered a great opportunity to shape the party's campaign, and it fueled anew talk that Warren would be the vice-presidential nominee.

On the eve of the convention, Warren once more announced, "I am not a candidate for any place on the national ticket."

Old pols nodded knowingly, and dismissed Warren's disavowal. After all, the governor was the ideal complement to Tom Dewey, a westerner to Dewey's easterner, a perfect running mate for the liberal New Yorker. In the folklore of national politics, the West produced conservatives, true men of independence who stood steadfast against government intrusion and regulation.

Furthermore, Warren was a party regular, aligned with the powerful men who controlled California's banks and industries. (It was no accident that Bill Reichel, the Republican national committeeman, was also *The Oakland Tribune*'s attorney. He was Joe Knowland's man, ready to stamp out the stray liberal heresy.)

Most important, Dewey wanted Warren on the ticket.

The two men first met in 1939 at a law enforcement convention, Warren the friendly Californian, Dewey the precise, even prissy, New Yorker. Their friendship grew slowly, but as early as March, 1942, Dewey had settled on the Californian as the perfect running mate.

Warren's keynote address on the night of June 26, 1944, in sweltering Chicago Stadium was long, tedious, and conventional. A rousing stem-winder might have pumped up the delegates. Instead, Warren delivered a flat speech—with prior approval from Dewey—that barely stirred the crowd.

The people, the fighting men, Warren claimed, had set the keynote for the 1944 convention:

> *To get our boys back home again—victorious and with all speed.*
> *To open the door for all Americans—to open it, not just to jobs but to opportunity!*
> *To make and guard the peace so wisely and so well that this time will be the last time that American homes are called to give their sons and daughters to the agony and tragedy of war.*

Warren advised the delegates that he had been chosen as keynoter because he came from the West, where "growth and change and adventure are still a part of our daily life." The GOP could not return to the status quo. "The future cannot be overtaken in reverse."

The Republican Party had rebounded from the depths of 1937–38, Warren claimed. In those states returned to Republican hands,

> *the record of public administration is progressive, enlightened and in the public interest. In those states you will find increased emphasis upon the public health, upon free education, upon care for orphaned and neglected children, upon support for the aged, for the victims of industrial accidents, for those handicapped by physical disabilities and for the victims of economic misfortune.*

It was a plea for a more liberal Republican Party, a Progressive Republican Party such as he had known as a young man.

Thirty-six hours later, prim Tom Dewey nominated, the New Yorker telephoned Warren to ask him to join the ticket. Warren declined.

He had a variety of reasons for rejecting the offer, he told Dewey. First and foremost, he would be ducking out on his implicit pledge to the people of California to complete his term as California's war governor. "I couldn't honorably do it to them," he insisted.

Beyond that, Warren enjoyed being governor. "Mine was a very happy situation, people were treating me well, and I felt I had a great feeling of independence out there that I didn't always have other places, and it was really a very attractive place to remain."

As Verne Scoggins plainly put it, "Warren thought his job as governor of California was more important at the moment than using his energy to campaign for the right to preside over the United States Senate."

There was also a practical consideration for Warren. He simply could not afford a pay cut with five children still at home. Neither did he fancy moving Nina and the children to a drab hotel in crowded wartime Washington.

Warren had private doubts as well. He sensed the widespread satisfaction among voters, the well-being fueled by billions in defense spending since 1939. Then too, the war was going well. As commander in chief, Roosevelt's chances for a fourth term had soared with the success of D-Day just three weeks before.

Warren considered Dewey's bid simply four years premature. The Californian would not play the sacrificial lamb.

Ever after, Warren would remember this as "the year they tried to force the vice-president nomination on me . . ." Dewey telephoned once more, spending an hour trying to persuade Warren to accept. The disbelieving California delegation urged its chairman to accept. Pennsylvania called to pledge its seventy votes. Only "some agility and fast footwork" at the last moment dissuaded the Oregon delegation from nominating Warren and setting off a stampede.

It was a narrow escape. While Warren would give six campaign speeches that fall, he was preoccupied with the threatened return of the exiled Japanese from relocation camps. Two years earlier, he had argued for their exclusion with great certainty. He would support their return with equal vigor.

Even a year after the decisive naval victory at Midway, rumors that the War Relocation Authority wanted to release selected internees provoked the governor's outrage. "The evacuation of the Japanese saved our state from terrible disorders and sabotage," Warren insisted at a press conference in Sacramento on June 11, 1943.

Nine days later, he again sounded the alarm—this time from the national platform provided by the annual Governors' Conference. Repatriation of even Japanese-American citizens, he asserted, "would be laying the groundwork for another Pearl Harbor."

Warren meanwhile approved California's joining Oregon and Washington in a friend-of-the-court brief arguing before the United States Supreme

Court that continued detention of evacuees was warranted as a military necessity.*

Disturbed by Warren's comments, a longtime political ally wrote in July, 1943, to urge him to "take a long view" of the relocation. Alfred J. Lundberg worried that the issue had become "so clouded by war-time emotions . . . with doubtless . . . emotions that have their root in economic jealousies."

Warren wrote a long, mulish reply to Lundberg, defending the internment as a necessary defense against fifth column activities. "[W]ho, I ask you, could tell the difference between a loyal Japanese on our coast line and a saboteur?"

The Japanese, "wherever born," were indoctrinated with the ambitions of the Japanese Empire, Warren continued. ". . . [W]e could not expect the *average* Japanese born in this country to give his loyalty to America in this war of survival. Again I hope that in saying this I am not giving vent to any feeling of race prejudice or hatred but rather to a recognition of loyalties that are born of home, family, race and religion. . . ."

There were many Japanese, Warren conceded, who had come to the United States seeking freedom. Many of their children "would have the same loyal sentiments that you and I have. . . . If there were any reasonable way of determining the loyalty of these individuals, I would be the first to insist upon their having the right to all the freedoms that we have. Unfortunately, I believe there is no way of determining this fact . . ."†

Early in 1944, with the war in the Pacific going well, Warren began to back away from exclusion of the Japanese. Throughout the war, Captain Earl Warren (United States Army, Ret.) had taken his cue from the military. Only as the military lost interest in excluding the Japanese from the West Coast did Warren change his mind.

On Monday, December 18, 1944, a unanimous United States Supreme Court found a compromise solution to the Japanese evacuation. Without challenging the military's right to order an evacuation in time of war, the Court held that indefinite detention had not been envisioned by President Roosevelt's Executive Order 9066. Therefore, the internees should be freed.

* The Earl Warren Papers in the California State Archives, Files 3655ff., contain anti-Japanese resolutions from, among other organizations, Rotary, Kiwanis, and Elks clubs; church groups; the Women's Republican Study Group of California; the Los Angeles County Peace Officers Association; as well as dozens of city councils and chambers of commerce north and south.

† Warren, uncharacteristically defensive, requested that John Weaver not quote this letter in Weaver's 1967 biography of the chief justice. Relations with the Japanese community, Warren wrote, were "so splendid [that he] would not like to see the matter reopened, especially piecemeal. . . . The situation is such that I would feel badly to see it disturbed, and to be the instrument for stirring up emotion and controversy would embarrass me and I am sure the Court." At the same time, Warren added, "I did write the letters, and I would not equivocate about it. Neither would I prohibit you or anyone else from publishing them if it is your belief that it is essential in order to tell the entire story." Warren's letter is in the JWP, Box 176, Warren correspondence file; and EWP/LC, Box 6, "Holiday Articles" file.

Apparently tipped off, War Department spokesmen the day before the decision was handed down announced that the release of loyal Issei and Nisei would begin immediately.

Warren was quietly relieved. He now regretted his advocacy of the removal order as "not in keeping with our American concept of freedom and the rights of citizens." He conceded that the removal had been brought about "without evidence of disloyalty." *

He did not mention his own role in bringing on the evacuation thirty-three months earlier.

---

* Until his 1974 memoirs, Warren never apologized publicly for advocating the evacuation. He regretted the evacuation, but told family members long afterward, "You have to put yourself in my place at the time." (Interview with Margaret Warren, October 1, 1992.) At the urging of Earl Junior, a retired Warren did publicly endorse repeal of Title II of the federal Internal Security Act which provided for summary detentions in times of national emergency. Warren wrote the Japanese American Citizens League, major proponent of the largely symbolic repeal, that "Title II is not in the American tradition" and should be repealed. "I express these views as the experience of one who as a state officer became involved in the harsh removal of the Japanese from the Pacific Coast in World War II, almost 30 years ago." (EW to Jerry Enamoto, March 18, 1970, in EWP/LC, Box 84, Personal File "J.")

CHAPTER 14

THE TURNING POINT

H IS COLD BEGAN ON A BLUSTERY SATURDAY IN OCTOBER, WHEN Earl Warren welcomed the Republican vice presidential nominee, John Bricker, to San Francisco. The following day, Warren was snuffling; by Monday morning, his doctor had hospitalized him in Sacramento. The diagnosis was influenza, Dr. Junius Brutus Harris told reporters.

A week later, the flu had become an infection in the right kidney. Harris reported his patient "much improved" after treatment with penicillin. "Another week in bed should see him a well man again."

The recovery took longer than June Harris anticipated. For a week Warren was too tired even to write acknowledgments for the flowers from Tom Dewey and the Capitol gardener or John Mullins's prayers to Saints Rita and Jude Thaddeus.

Discharged from the hospital, Warren fared poorly. Nina scrambled to care for him, mother, maid, and nurse, before a relapse sent him back to Sutter Memorial Hospital on October 31.

The recuperation went slowly; he returned to his desk, ten pounds lighter, on November 20, 1944, dutifully swallowing sulfa tablets. Ten days later, he was still under June Harris's orders, but working once more.

The long days he spent in bed gave him time to read and reflect, his daughter-in-law Margaret said. During one visit, he showed her a slim volume he had been reading about race in the United States, commenting that "a white man had so many more opportunities" than did blacks. Warren pondered whatever stroke of fate ordained one man black, the other white, and so profoundly changed their lives.

He was also a man troubled by the costs of his illness, he told daughter-in-law Margaret Warren. "One catastrophic illness could wipe out a man and his family."

As governor, his salary continued, but "what if I had no salary or income?" Warren wondered aloud.

Years before, his mother's illnesses had saddled the family with medical bills running into the thousands of dollars. If the comparatively secure Warren family had to sacrifice, how much more difficult it must be for others less well off.

Bill Sweigert stoked Warren's new-found concern about the costs of health care. The problem was widespread, Sweigert stated during a bedside visit at the mansion.

In 1944, Californians had borrowed $11 million at near usurious rates from small loan companies to pay for unbudgeted medical expenses. More loans were made to pay medical and dental costs than for any other reason, he added.

Borrowing a three-decades-old Progressive concept, Sweigert proposed adoption of some form of catastrophic health insurance.

"You know, by golly, maybe this is the time to do something about it," Warren agreed.

Sweigert arranged a luncheon meeting with a small group of California Medical Association leaders at the Family Club in San Francisco. To the doctors, including Ray Lyman Wilbur, president of Stanford University, Warren explained his idea for insurance against catastrophic illness. It was similar to a proposal for a tax-supported health insurance program advanced by then–Secretary of the Interior Wilbur in 1932.

Warren left the meeting late in the afternoon believing that he had secured the doctors' cooperation in shaping a health insurance program. The CMA people pledged to bring Warren's proposal before a special meeting of its House of Delegates in Los Angeles.

There, conservative opponents of medical insurance staged a floor revolt. Warren's people lost control of the meeting as the delegates erupted in bitter condemnation of the governor's proposal. At least one resolution tarred the concept as "communist."

The delegates insisted on "absolute freedom of choice," fee-for-service rather than capitation payments, and "unhampered" control of all professional services. Warren agreed with the first demand, preferred the second, and was firmly opposed to the third.

That was enough to assure the CMA's rigid opposition to what it now called "socialized medicine."

Warren was angry, convinced the CMA had reneged on its pledge. "If that's the way they feel about it, we'll just have to go ahead with it anyhow," he told Sweigert.

Warren expected substantial public support. Only one in ten Californians had any form of medical insurance, usually through an employer who grudgingly offered it as a fringe benefit in labor-short California. There was no free choice. Employers picked the plan, and the plan picked the doctors.

As drafted, Warren's 1945 bill was modest in scope. He proposed covering doctor's fees, laboratory and X-ray charges, medicine, some dental services, and twenty-one days of hospitalization. The plan would permit the public free choice of doctors and did not compel doctors to participate. The program was to be compulsory only in the sense that it would be financed by a mandatory payroll tax of 3 percent divided equally between employee and employer. It covered those earning $2,500 a year or less, about two-thirds of all workers, and their families.

The Warren plan was hardly revolutionary. In the United States, the Progressives had plugged for the concept; a commission appointed by California's then-governor Hiram Johnson in 1915 had recommended a voluntary health insurance program. In 1918, the voters had rejected a state constitutional amendment calling for a prepaid medical insurance program.

In the midst of the Depression, public agitation for compulsory medical insurance was so vehement that the California Medical Association endorsed the concept. The crisis of the Depression past, the CMA reversed itself.

On the eve of the 1945 legislative session, Warren presented his concept. He recognized that "a lot of people" might be startled by the notion of compulsory health insurance, but added, "Such things as workmen's compensation, unemployment insurance, social security benefits were 'startling' in contemplation but now are accepted and conceded to be essential to our system—not merely human but actually essential."

Warren's address to the legislature on January 8, 1945, called for bold initiatives. Medical insurance was the most controversial measure, but only a small piece of the wide-ranging legislative program Warren proposed that day. He also asked for modernization of the state's mental hospitals; expanded services for crippled children and the blind; establishment of an institute at the university to teach labor-management relations; creation of a state postwar reconstruction and retraining program; reduction of the 5 percent interest rate on veterans' housing and farm loans; and state licensure of all hospitals.

The *San Francisco Chronicle*'s respected political editor Earl Behrens decided, "The Governor's program was the most far-reaching of its kind since the days of the first administration of Hiram W. Johnson as Governor."

Republican state Senator George Hatfield, a canny floor leader, grumbled, "There sure is a lot of progressive talk going on around this place." A veteran Democratic assemblyman decided Warren was "trying to out–New Deal the New Deal" with his proposals. One quip passed about Sacramento had it that Olson had forgotten to clean out his desk when he left office.

Health insurance dominated the legislative session, the partisan rhetoric escalating week by week. With the announcement of details of the health insurance measure, a lobbyist blurted, "My God! And we called Olson a Red!"

Warren was accused of backing a "socialized medicine" measure inspired by communists. A vote against the bill was therefore "a vote against Stalin."

Few doctors supported Warren's bill. Even the governor's personal physician, Junius Harris, opposed the bill; Harris opened the CMA's lobbying office in the capital.

To manage its campaign, the medical association turned to the husband and wife team, Clem Whitaker and Leone Baxter, already estranged from Warren. For an annual fee of $25,000, Whitaker and Baxter would muster what seemed to legislators a massive outpouring of public sentiment.

The CMA succeeded in mobilizing doctors across the state. "They said, 'This is going to ruin you,' and the doctors were beginning to do very well . . ."

CMA President Lowell S. Goins released a shrill condemnation of the Warren proposal. Under the bill, he asserted, "doctors for all practical purposes will become state employees and the private practice of medicine will end."

Nine thousand alarmed doctors reciting speeches written by Whitaker and Baxter traveled the state, speaking out against "compulsory" health insurance. Prompted by Whitaker and Baxter, the doctors talked about *voluntary* medical insurance as "The American Way." By the end of the campaign, fifty-three of the fifty-eight counties in the state had officially proclaimed "Voluntary Health Insurance Week." More than 100 mayors and 600 city councilmen had endorsed the CMA program, along with hundreds of civic, patriotic, fraternal, and service organizations.

A puzzled Warren fought back. "I do not believe in socialized medicine. I do not believe in socializing anything. . . . Neither do I believe in calling every proposal to bring good medical care within the economic reach of families of modest incomes socialized medicine."

Warren looked to fashion a compromise. The foes, however, opposed "all suggestions for fear that any of them might be accepted by the people. It is a typical phase of the age-old contest waged for human betterment," Warren said in a statewide radio talk.

The CMA offered only an argument "designed to terrorize you, not convince you," Warren told his radio audience. "Was not the same argument made when the principle of industrial accident insurance was established in this state thirty years ago?"

The governor's usually cautious rhetoric grew more heated as the medical insurance battle wore on. He had reached a personal decision and he would not retreat.

His stand was costly. Warren's advocacy of health insurance first angered, then alienated men who had once been his strongest supporters, particularly in Southern California.

"It was not a terribly radical position," McIntyre Faries concluded, "but it hurt Warren with the monied people."

Invited to discuss mandatory health insurance with the influential Southland Committee in Los Angeles, Warren refused. To emissary Richard Graves, the governor explained, ". . . I'm not going because I have no way to persuade them, and they have no way to change me. So, what's the point of it? I've told them exactly that on the telephone."

"Well, there are other issues—"

"No, this is the end of the line with that group. It only takes one issue. This is the one. I must survive without them."

Meanwhile, Warren's bill ran into trouble.

At a hearing in the Public Health Committee on March 28, the man considered the nation's foremost medical economist, Nathan Sinai, gravely testified on behalf of the measure. Self-possessed, authoritative, and armed with telling graphs, the professor lectured his bored students. Doctors would make 20 percent more, not less, under the Warren plan. Hospitals too would benefit.

When Sinai finished, Democratic Assemblyman John Evans—a man who paid close attention to the wishes of lobbyists—pounced.

What were Sinai's credentials, Evans asked.

The witness was chairman of the School of Public Health at the University of Michigan, he stated.

"What is your degree?"

"I have a master's degree in public health and a master's degree in business."

"Yes, but you have another degree. What is that degree?" Evans bored in. What entitled Sinai to be called "doctor"?

There was a long, uncomfortable pause before Sinai replied: "Doctor of veterinary medicine."

Over the laughter, a wire service reporter standing in the rear turned to Verne Scoggins. "There goes your bill. Can't you see the headlines: 'Horse Doctor Backs Warren Medical Scheme'?"

The committee voted 7 to 3 to table the bill, but Warren refused to give up. At his behest the bill's author, Ways and Means Committee Chairman Albert Wollenberg, sought to circumvent the committee. Wollenberg moved a resolution to bring the measure out of committee.

By a single vote, 38–39, the Assembly voted against withdrawing the bill from committee. Only ten of twenty-nine Republicans in the house voted in favor of the resolution. Warren lost his bill because he could not keep a majority of his own party in line. He angrily chalked it up to "the power of the lobbies."

Throughout, the bitterest arguments had revolved around the question of doctors' fees. When the CMA charged that hospitals were the largest part of medical costs, Warren changed tack. He proposed new legislation in May, 1945, to provide only hospital insurance through payroll deductions.

CMA president-elect Phillip K. Gilman scored the hospital bill as "a subterfuge intended to permit the start of a system of government medicine in the hospitals, with the transparent intent of . . . bringing the medical profession under state regimentation at a subsequent legislative session."

The hospitals, suddenly alarmed about closer scrutiny and control, joined the medical association to have the new Warren measure killed in committee by an 8–5 vote. Once more Wollenberg forced the issue, this time losing a discharge motion, 45–32. Once more less than one-quarter of the GOP assemblymen voted with the governor.

Frustrated, Warren refused to give up his idea of compulsory medical and hospitalization insurance. If he could not do it by bold strokes, he would implement it by stages.

The following year he backed a labor-sponsored bill expanding the disability insurance program for workers. California became the first large state, and the second after Rhode Island, to extend medical coverage to off-the-job illness. The key to passage of the bill was support from the powerful insurance lobby. Under terms of the bill, private insurance companies could underwrite the medical coverage.

Two years later, Warren and labor secured additional legislation offering unemployed workers hospital benefits as part of unemployment compensation coverage. With that, the poorest were partially covered by insurance.

Warren's support of compulsory health insurance, and his Progressive legislative program in general, stirred opposition from the Republican right. Scoring the governor's advocacy of health insurance, Speaker Charles W. Lyon moved to snatch leadership of the Republican Party. "The governor has placed himself in the position of lobbying this bill, which he has no right to do. He has reduced himself to the position of a public relations man."

Warren bristled at the challenge. "In view of the accusation," he retorted, "it might be a good time to investigate the matter of lobbying thoroughly —a full and impartial investigation."

Similarly trolling for support, conservative San Francisco investment banker Earl Lee Kelly funded a mass mailing of 50,000 broadsides that reproduced a newspaper cartoon lampooning Warren for riding both donkey and elephant, in opposite directions. The governor's legislative program reeked of the New Deal, Kelly asserted. "Let's restore honest, sensible, *American* government," he urged.

Warren sailed on unfazed. Writing Tom Dewey after the end of the legislative session, Warren acknowledged that he might confront opposition in the Republican primary in 1946.

> It will come from those who believe I departed from orthodoxy in advocating the extension of social security and the solution of our race problems as proposed in our national platform and in following your campaign speech in Los Angeles on prepaid medical care. . . . I have no doubt that you

also encounter some reaction from that group in our Party which believes in turning the clock back. In my opinion, these people do more harm to our Party than twice their number among our opponents.

The battle to pass a compulsory health insurance bill became a political turning point for Warren. "I remember a lot of conservatives around here were absolutely flabbergasted that he would go along with 'socialized medicine,' and they just couldn't believe it," said *Sacramento Bee* political writer Richard Rodda.

"Most men," Attorney General Robert Kenny later commented, "have solidified their beliefs by the time they're in the mid-fifties. Earl Warren was an exception. His were just beginning to jell at a time when they could have been petrified. As his experience increased, his mind absorbed new concepts."

Carey McWilliams, no admirer of Warren, grudgingly acknowledged that the governor had proposed a liberal social program. That, and "the Governor's sudden, and total, reversal of attitude on the Japanese evacuee question . . . came as a distinct surprise to most factions, including apparently his own stand-pat Republican backers."

McWilliams attributed Warren's turnabout to ambition. The governor was angling for nothing less than the Republican presidential nomination in 1948, McWilliams concluded.

To achieve that, Warren first had to win reelection in a state increasingly Democratic in registration. He needed the votes of centrists of both parties, McWilliams argued. The legislative program was Warren's bid for that wider support.

Warren, however, could not go too far, too fast. It was essential he maintain leadership of the California Republican Party.

Though the Republican national platform of 1944 endorsed fair employment practices, Warren opposed creation of a state Fair Employment Practices Commission with power to enforce laws banning racial and religious discrimination in hiring. He proposed instead a panel, without enforcement power, to educate the public.

The model for an FEPC was a GOP-inspired commission in New York State, but "generally, all Republicans were against it in California," the bill's sponsor, Augustus Hawkins, recalled. "There was an attempt to brand an FEPC as a plot by communists and socialists. The only people supposed to be supporting it were Reds."

Warren eschewed the red-baiting, arguing "that you can't legislate change, but must educate the people, that you can't move too far ahead of the people."

"I got nowhere with *either* side," Warren complained. "The extremists" wanted to give an FEPC unprecedented powers; conservatives "against any form of FEPC thought this was just the camel's head in the tent . . ."

The Hawkins bill and Warren's alternative both died in committee. Warren would continue to seek, unsuccessfully, a fair employment commission, for the next six years.

In other racial matters, Warren moved deliberately. He publicly supported his director of corrections' decision to desegregate prisons, even after San Quentin guards quelled a threatened race riot. He aligned the state against an Orange County school district that sought to assign Hispanic pupils to separate grammar schools. He endorsed Attorney General Kenny's friend-of-the-court brief in the United States Supreme Court arguing that racially restrictive real estate covenants were unconstitutional.

Through the legislative session, Earl Warren cautiously zigzagged left, then right. "He had a businesslike, fiscally responsible administration that was free of corruption. He was still the prosecutor. On many issues—discrimination, capital punishment, job training, fair housing—we never counted on him," Hawkins said.

Once he had apparently occupied the political center, Earl Warren again confounded observers with a smart about-face and a bow to long friendship.

The death of Hiram Johnson a month short of his seventy-ninth birthday offered Warren a grand opportunity to repay a long-standing political debt. Once a fiery reformer, Johnson had subsided to cranky naysayer and overwhelmed isolationist. California needed someone with more vision, more energy.

Bill Knowland was Warren's choice. As J. R.'s son, young Bill had grown up in a home steeped in California politics. At twelve he campaigned for the Harding-Coolidge ticket. He was twenty-four when he survived the Roosevelt landslide of 1932 and was elected to the state Assembly. Two years later, he was the youngest member of the state Senate, then Republican national committeeman at age thirty, and three years later chairman of the party's executive committee.

Bill Knowland was steady, reliable, and conservative. Knowland's wartime letters to Warren also revealed a man, unlike Johnson, alert to the United States's new responsibilities as a world power.

Despite the debt he owed to the Knowlands—perhaps because of it—Warren debated with himself. He shuddered to be seen making a political payoff or be thought guilty of cronyism.

For a week Warren weighed the appointment of Knowland, then assigned to the Army of Occupation in Germany. Bill had great potential, and with the right kind of guidance, he might even become president, Warren told his son Earl Junior. Consulting no one, Warren settled upon his old friend to fill the unexpired term.

With that, Warren had repaid his political debt to the Knowland family, *Bee* reporter Richard Rodda said. "But there was nothing *wrong* about it."

The politically shrewd Robert Kenny agreed. "Of course it was a pay-off. Earl Warren would be an ingrate if he had done otherwise."

A similar old friendship played a role in what would be one of Earl Warren's proudest achievements.

Loyal alumnus Warren had long cherished his ties to the University of California. As governor, he was an ex officio member of the university's Board of Regents. Finally, his good friend and fellow clarinetist Robert Gordon Sproul was president of the university. Warren thus had motive, influence, and inspiration.

Warren had consistently advocated expanding and upgrading the university. He intended to build a public educational institution second to none, underwriting the costs from state funds. A tuition-free university would supply both a highly trained workforce and the ideas necessary for future state growth.

The expansion began in 1944. Anticipating that no fewer than 800,000 veterans would take up residence in California after the war, they would have to make space for the thousands who would want to attend the university. Those men and women were the guarantee of California's future prosperity, Warren and Sproul insisted.

The first phase of the expansion came at the urging of the *Santa Barbara News-Press* publisher, Thomas Storke, a prominent Democrat. Warren maneuvered through the legislature a bill bodily incorporating Santa Barbara College into the university system. On the day the bill came to his desk, Warren playfully telephoned Storke.

"Oh, Jesus, Tom. I've got that bill on my desk. And I wish you could see the letters I've got here explaining why I shouldn't sign it. The only person in California who seems to want it is you."

The governor paused while Storke fidgeted. "I've just signed it," Warren announced.

The university bill was a small part of an unprecedented expansion of state services that Warren was to oversee in the next years. California's population was not just growing, it was exploding. (The 1950 census would report a 53 percent increase in population.) Spurred by government contracts, civilian employment across the country had increased 14 percent, in California meanwhile, the workforce had ballooned 40 percent. Manufacturing was up more than 50 percent nationally; in California it had grown 200 percent.

The newcomers brought to California a heady optimism, a feeling that anything was possible here "on the coast." "I arrived on January 1, 1945," one of those newcomers recalled. "It was as if the bells were ringing. I was on the go eight days a week. It was just a wonderful place to live, a wonderful place to be."

Before the war, the migrants had largely been uneducated, with few job skills; many now were well trained or had college degrees, attracted by abundant opportunity and the climate. Further, they were young, healthy, and productive—the least likely to fall upon state assistance.

They—and the returning veterans eager to get on with their lives—

would need other facilities, particularly schools and highways.* Warren secured legislation creating a state Reconstruction and Reemployment Agency, then arranged the discharge of Army Colonel Alexander Heron, a former San Francisco business executive, to direct "R & R." That agency was to prepare plans for public agencies and set priorities.

Nothing had a greater priority in Warren's mind than planning for California's immediate future. "Just where do you think I got these gray hairs?" he exploded when a delegation charged he was not doing enough to provide jobs for the needy.

"I'll tell you. It was from lying awake at night trying to think of more things that might improve things in California, so that there might be jobs, money to support the poor, so that there could be new highway programs to make jobs, so that there could be opening and widening and lighting of streets, and making subdivisions and houses and factories, the building of new hospitals and water projects and sewage projects, and building of new schools, shopping centers—anything and everything that might create employment and help support our citizens."

Housing remained the state's number one problem, Warren told his staff. Dwellings remained so scarce that the thirty-six blocks of empty barracks, which had made up the Manzanar internment camp, were sold to returning veterans and trucked to other locations. Warren eventually called for a statewide rent control bill to prevent gouging and unfair evictions.

California's cities and counties were hard-pressed to meet the demands placed on them by the newcomers. With their real estate taxes frozen at prewar levels and investment in the infrastructure halted for the duration, the cities coped with a serious lack of sewers. Warren's own Alameda County "was one of the ones you could smell in those days," an attorney for the League of California Cities recalled.

The League's executive director, Richard Graves, informed Warren that the cities wanted to tap $100 million of the governor's hoarded "rainy day" fund to plan and build sewers.

Warren was opposed. He did not want mayors and county supervisors spending the money, he told Graves. "They're more interested in patronage than in preventing pollution." If the League managed to get such a "Christmas Tree" bill through the Legislature, Warren promised to veto it.

The governor had no specific plan to use the state surplus, Graves claimed. Keeping the hoard intact seemed motivated by Warren's presidential ambitions.

Though a longtime ally of the governor, Graves found his easy access to the corner office abruptly cut off. Graves managed to get his bill, but only

---

* Among the veterans was oldest son James, who did not feel he could come home since he had not seen combat in the Pacific. He weighed joining Chiang Kai-shek's battle against the Red Chinese until his father ordered: "The war is over. You come home and say, 'Here, sir,' " as he once did when calling from military school. (Interview with Margaret Warren, October 1, 1992.)

after securing the endorsement of the County Supervisors Association—which demanded half of the $100 million for its own members. Cities could use their share only for sewers; counties were free to spend their half as they wished.

Warren vetoed the bill, as promised. ". . . [I]t took everything we all had," Graves said later, to scrape together a two-thirds vote in the legislature to override the veto.

Graves, still banned from the governor's office, gained his satisfaction more than a year later. At a meeting with representatives of the United States Public Health Service, a spokesman for the agency asked how California, the only state in the union to do so, had met its sanitation needs.

Warren replied, looking directly at Graves, "I owe my friend, Dick Graves, an apology. The answer to your question is that he took fifty million dollars away from me, over my violent resistance, to spend on sewers. Now, Dick, I was right about those counties; but you were right about the cities."

It was an unusual admission for Warren. He was not often wrong about his native state—as the Democratic Party was about to discover.

CHAPTER 15

THE AFFABLE JUGGERNAUT

E ARL WARREN HAD DECIDED MORE THAN A YEAR EARLIER HE WOULD run for a second term. There were still unfinished tasks, and he was not a man to leave things half done.

Thirteen months before his formal announcement, a reporter casually asked Warren, "Will you be a candidate for President in 1948?"

The governor shook his head. "The answer is *no,* period."

Would he then run for reelection?

"Few die," the governor answered with a grin, "and none resign."

At any time, Warren would have made a formidable candidate. He was a popular incumbent with an unblemished record and broad appeal. In 1946, he would be even more difficult to defeat. Right-wing opposition from within his own party had failed to materialize, and the Democrats had only a token candidate. California attorney general Robert W. Kenny did not want to run. A practiced political observer, he appreciated Earl Warren's appeal better than most.

Further, he and Warren shared a vision of responsive government; as attorney general, Kenny took pride in describing himself as Warren's lawyer. Finally, Kenny—a jowly, rumpled former newspaperman fond of attractive women and good whiskey, a man tolerant of human frailty—simply lacked political ambition.

Once a reform-minded Progressive—as he put it, "a man who is afraid to be a Democrat and ashamed to be a Republican"—Kenny had joined the Democratic Party of Franklin D. Roosevelt only in 1931. The national party was badly divided; the state party floundered.

Beseeched by Democratic leaders, Kenny agonized for six weeks.* Kenny, they argued, was the only one who could carry the party past the primary. Without a candidate in the fall election, the California Democratic Party would implode, just two years before a presidential election.

Kenny understood the woeful odds his candidacy faced. He had long since told friends that anyone who took on Warren this year was "a fool or a martyr." Besides, he joked, the attorney general earned $14,000 per year, the governor only $10,000.

Better to wait his turn. Virtually assured of reelection as attorney general, he would be positioned to succeed Warren in 1950. Otherwise, he would have to run against Warren's record—trumpeted in a list of "60 Reasons for the Reelection of Governor Earl Warren" prepared by Verne Scoggins.

The California economy was booming, the state was debt-free—its taxes reduced $225 million per year—while plans were afoot to spend $350 million on public works. Warren had spent wisely.

He had helped to save the teachers' retirement fund from insolvency, had set $1,800 as a minimum teacher's salary, and begun a vast expansion of the university and state college system. He had increased the state's old-age pension payments and funneled money into social welfare, public health, and mental hygiene.

In California he had fashioned a program that could return the Republican Party to the White House in 1948, Warren argued. The GOP, he wrote in a letter to the Republican National Committee on February 19, 1946, needed "a definite program on social security, a program for improving the health of our people, and an anti-monopoly program. Unfortunately we are being held up to the public as the party that opposes legislation in these fields."

In addition to his record, Warren seemed to personify the state's robust vigor; his enthusiasm for the tasks ahead mirrored golden California's self-confidence.

A perplexed *San Francisco Examiner* reporter pondered the governor's undeniable aura, noting Warren was neither smooth nor particularly exciting. Warren was only a fair public speaker; his speech was deliberate and humorless. He struggled with his weight. He wore bifocals reluctantly, but increasingly.

"What was it then?" the *Examiner* asked rhetorically. "An obvious, almost rugged sincerity. A natural honesty. A cleanliness of mind and habit. A devotion to principle. An ability to get things done without shouting, without temper, without loss of friends. A wholesomeness in a world growing short of that commodity."

All these qualities were portrayed in oft-reprinted photographs of the

---

* Warren told reporter Mary Ellen Leary that "he had a strong impression that Kenny was pushed into it by either the Communist wing or the extreme left wing." (Interview with Leary, October 15, 1992.)

Warren family: father and mother friendly and smiling; the boys handsome, the girls growing into winsome beauties the entire nation would identify as California golden girls. "You can beat Earl Warren," ran the political saw, "but you can't beat that family."

The three Warren girls, Virginia, Dorothy, and Honey Bear, would join their mother and father on campaigns. "It was a wonderful opportunity to go to all these places and see these people," Virginia recalled fondly. Earl and brother Bobby shied away from photographs and campaigns alike.

In the face of this affable juggernaut, Democrat Robert Kenny reluctantly agreed to run, a sacrifice to political party. He was hamstrung, a candidate who found nothing to criticize in his opponent's, his friend's, program. On the very day Kenny announced his candidacy, a grinning Earl Warren signed a new Disability Insurance Act—praised by a labor spokesman as "the best legislation enacted for the welfare of the people of California in twenty years."

Warren and Kenny cross-filed, each man running for both the Republican and Democratic nominations. If either candidate won both—and each had managed that feat in the past—the race would be settled in the primary.

Kenny had no sooner announced he was a candidate for governor than he departed for Nuremberg, Germany, and the war crimes trial of the surviving Nazi hierarchy. For a month Warren tramped the state unchallenged, drumming up votes on both the Republican and Democratic tickets.

Kenny returned to California no more eager for the battle than when he left. He declined to raise campaign funds, expecting his long identification with the Democratic Party to carry him through the primary. He refused even to attack Warren.

The Congress of Industrial Organizations, through its militant Political Action Committee, scored "Oil" Warren as "a phony" who espoused liberal programs to broaden his appeal, knowing the Republican legislature would kill them. Kenny promptly disavowed that attack. At worst, Kenny could claim only that the governor was a "fake liberal" and a "pseudo-nonpartisan."

Warren shrugged; he had been more harshly abused by GOP conservatives, he told friends. Kenny "conducted a very restrained campaign. There was actually nothing in it to which I could take exception."

Warren mounted a modest campaign with the simple slogan: "Re-elect a Good Governor." He had no ongoing political organization, only a network of acquaintances scattered about the state.

"Every four years we brought the gang together," Verne Scoggins explained. "The gang" was an assortment of men Warren could call upon "to run a little campaign for me down there in your county."

The vital finance committees were equally informal—civic-minded men who quietly called a few friends for donations. Warren instructed that the fifty-three thousand state employees were not to be asked to contribute the traditional day's pay to his reelection fund.

He would run a campaign on the cheap, spending just $110,900. Warren himself reported raising $11,766 to run the state headquarters in Sacramento's Senator Hotel.*

Warren—the nominal head of the Republican ticket—once more ran as an independent. He endorsed no other candidates, shared no campaign headquarters, literature, or slate cards. He was once more playing the nonpartisan—a necessity for a Republican in a state where 61 percent of the state's 4.3 million voters were registered Democrats.

The state American Federation of Labor endorsed his candidacy, Secretary-Treasurer Cornelius J. Haggerty arguing, "A man of his stamp breeds confidence and respect even if you do not agree with him on every issue. Labor has nothing to fear from such a man." AFL leaders toured the state to drum up support for Warren, while Walter Gordon worked the state's growing black precincts with their high percentage of registered Democrats.

Even as Warren bid for Democratic votes, he held his own right flank. John Francis Neylan, most conservative of conservatives, endorsed the governor, praising him for ending "an era of crackpot and demagogic politics in California." The equally conservative men who managed the state's largest corporations—Pacific Gas and Electric, Standard Oil, Bank of America— "would get so damned mad at him, they'd be cursing, 'Damn Warren, he's too liberal.' " recalled a PG&E public relations executive. In fact, as Warren's travel secretary William Mailliard pointed out, the conservatives had no place else to go. They could support Warren or risk the even more liberal Kenny in the governor's office.

Warren's unassailable centrism provoked one frustrated Democrat to irritated lampoon:

> *What burning issues shall we use, the campaign fires to fan?*
> *Just tell the voters there is but one— "I am non-partisan."*

For all the endorsements, the 543 billboards across the state, the million lapel buttons, Warren himself remained his campaign's strongest asset. Supporters of old recalled the beaming governor walking over to shake hands, boom a welcome, and pick up a conversation broken off a year or two or even four years before.

Politics did not interfere with friendship. The governor's daughter-in-law, Margaret Warren, told of an acquaintance once greeting Warren on a San Francisco street, the two men pleasantly talking before the acquaintance offered, "Well, you know, Governor, we're out to get you this time."

"Yes, I know you are, Bill. That's what makes horse races. How's Marion?"

---

* Warren's finance committees did not file official reports since state law did not require it. The figure for costs of the 1946 primary is given in EWP/S 572.

"Oh, fine. How's the family?"

Throughout the campaign, Warren remained personally unassuming. When an overzealous aide asked a dining car steward on the overnight train to Los Angeles to seat the Warrens before other passengers, the governor instructed, "We'll take our turn." (When the legislature later purchased a surplus DC-3 for "executive use," Warren asked an aide, "Isn't this a helluva big airplane for just two fellows to be making a trip in?")

Warren was to sweep to a stunning victory in the June 4 primary, capturing both the Republican and the Democratic nominations. He won the GOP vote, 774,502 to Kenny's mere 70,000; and the Democratic, 593,180 to 530,968. One of every four registered Democrats had voted for the Republican governor.

Warren had demonstrated that the right candidate could hive out a large share of the Democratic vote by preempting the middle. There were simply not enough votes on the radical or liberal left to assure a Democratic victory.

The weight of the landslide again marked the reelected governor as a national political figure to be reckoned with in the 1948 presidential election. Right-of-center *Time* magazine determined Warren's bipartisan support "made politicians' eyes pop." The left-of-center *Nation* magazine concluded the election had "unquestionably made him a leading contender for the Republican nomination."

Once past the primary, Warren the nonpartisan was to relax his no-endorsement policy for two candidates. The political editor of the *San Francisco Chronicle,* Earl Behrens, relayed a request from "higher ups" asking Warren to put in a favorable word on behalf of the Republican candidate for lieutenant governor. Los Angeles Superior Court judge Goodwin F. Knight was caught up in a close race with San Francisco's state senator, Democrat John F. Shelley.

For Warren, the problem was that Democrat Shelley had been a reliable vote in a state senate where he could count on few such men. Knight meanwhile was a creation of the *Los Angeles Times,* plucked from the backwaters of the Los Angeles Superior Court by that paper's political editor, Kyle Palmer. Affable Goody Knight's sole credential was his party affiliation.

Under pressure from both the *Times* and the *Chronicle,* Warren acceded. After telephoning Shelley to warn him, Warren mildly praised Knight as a man "who had defended and supported his administration."

Warren also endorsed Bill Knowland in a difficult senatorial reelection campaign against Democrat Will Rogers, Jr., who had temporarily fused his party's factions. Former cabinet secretary Henry A. Wallace, a New Dealer, and conservative Kentucky Senator Alben W. Barkley both traveled to California to give speeches on Rogers's behalf.

It was some measure of Warren's friendship with Knowland that the governor uncharacteristically flayed the two visitors as "carpetbaggers" butting into California's affairs. It was proof, too, of Warren's influence. The endorsement was enough to bring home Knowland by a quarter-million votes in November.*

Warren himself faced only token opposition in the general election on November 5, Earl Warren became the first governor to win reelection since Hiram Johnson in 1914, and only the third in the history of the state. He polled 2.1 million votes more than the hapless Prohibition candidate.

Two months later Earl Warren took the governor's oath of office for a second time. The Earl Warren of this second term was politically stronger and therefore more independent than ever. He would take on more vested interests in pursuit of programs he deemed vital to a state with 2 million new residents and an additional 10 million expected in coming decades.

In his inaugural address he once more asked the legislature for a prepaid medical insurance program. The memory of his defeat in 1945 rankled still, he confessed, particularly because the need remained so urgent. California's hospitalization costs, an average of $12.84 per day, were the highest in the nation, "clearly beyond the ability of working people to pay."

His plan, *some* plan for prepaid medical insurance, "will relieve millions of our people from the specter of bankruptcy and indigence which are the present-day results of the cost of illness."

In all, Warren's inaugural address proposed legislation in twenty areas, from veterans' housing to forest conservation; from education—there were still 1,500 one- and two-room schoolhouses in the state—to the shortage of hospital beds.

The legislature eventually adopted a budget of $645 million, the largest in California's history. Flush with a wartime surplus of $300 million, the legislators fattened Warren's original budget by $3.6 million. They also increased state salaries; beginning clerks went from $80 to $140 per month. Warren's salary jumped from $10,000 to a welcome $25,000 annually.

Despite Republican control of both houses of the legislature, Warren still had to battle for key portions of his program. The new speaker of the Assembly, Sam L. Collins, offered a ready ear to the lobbyist's whispers, while the state Senate, dominated by rural legislators, had little interest in burgeoning urban problems.

Warren sought a scaled-back version of the prepaid health insurance program proposed two years before. Paid for by a 2 percent payroll tax, the insurance would cover only "catastrophic illnesses." Private, voluntary plans could compete with the state if they chose.

He anticipated opposition once more from the California Medical Asso-

---

* One of the Republican candidates whom Warren did not endorse was much put out when his Democratic rival circulated a letter from Warren thanking him for assistance in implementing the state disability insurance program. Warren ignored the demand by Richard M. Nixon's campaign staff that the governor withdraw the letter written to Congressman Jerry Voorhis two years before.

ciation, adding, "But I take the view that if a thing isn't worth fighting for it isn't worth having."

The CMA did not disappoint. Its president, Sam L. McClendon, charged, "This program is economically unsound, medically dangerous and cruelly misleading in that it holds out a promise of hospital care to the sick and injured which the State is wholly incapable of keeping. . . ."

Significantly, the CMA did not deny the need for more medical care. The organization's president-elect, John Cline, preferring not "to quibble about definitions," simply tarred the governor's proposal as "state medicine and socialized medicine."

While Warren once again scored the CMA for "trying to frighten people instead of appealing to their reason," reason would not settle this dispute. Dollars would.

Guided by Whitaker and Baxter, the CMA was spending $100,000 in newspaper advertising annually. That money, the CMA secretary frankly boasted, "has done something which we have never before been able to accomplish in the state. . . .

"Never before have we been able to get real support from the newspapers because the answer constantly came back, 'Why should we give the doctors any support when they don't advertise . . .' We have found the response from editors, in publicity, has been beyond anything we expected when we started the campaign."

The outpouring of editorials lent the appearance of massive public opposition to health insurance. That persuaded legislators; Warren could not even invoke party discipline.

The Senate Committee on Governmental Efficiency, with a Republican majority of 8–3, almost offhandedly killed the measure with a unanimous vote to table the bill. The Assembly Public Health Committee, composed of seven Republicans and four Democrats, similarly pigeonholed the legislation. The governor's health insurance program was dead for another two years.

Warren was more successful in a challenge to a second lobby, California's powerful oil industry. He proposed building 2,500 miles of new four-lane highways to keep up with traffic growth in the cities, and to widen narrow rural highways into divided roads that engineers had taken to calling "freeways." In all, it would cost an estimated $2.8 billion, money that Warren suggested come from increased gasoline and truck taxes.

To fund the new roads, Warren proposed to double the three-cents-per gallon tax. Furthermore, he argued, highway users should pay a fair share of the costs of maintenance and construction. Heavier commercial trucks and buses should pay higher license fees than private automobiles. That brought the trucking industry in on the side of the oil companies.

Warren had fought the CMA with only token support; this time he could muster influential supporters. The League of California Cities had influence in the urban-oriented Assembly, and the County Supervisors Association in the Senate. He also curried support from businesses that recognized a comprehensive highway system would spur growth, and from construction companies anticipating lucrative contracts.

The upper chamber, dominated by agricultural interests and rural counties, favored the Warren bill. New highways would speed produce to market, and make travel easier and safer. Warren's bill easily passed the Senate, providing for an $86-million-a-year highway construction program financed largely by an increase in the gasoline tax.

The legislation ran into powerful opposition in the lower house, particularly from a onetime oilfield roustabout and wildcatter who had built hugely successful Superior Oil Company.

William M. Keck, dark, animated, his face alternately a scowl or a smile, expected legislators to vote as he bid. Most lobbyists preferred to sit quietly during committee hearings, "then tend to their business privately one-on-one," as reporter Mary Ellen Leary put it. "Keck wasn't like this. He was conspicuous at hearings," a man who relished his power.

The Assembly's Committee on Revenue and Taxation "almost laughingly" gutted the Warren bill, *The Sacramento Bee*'s political editor fumed. The gasoline tax increase and the truck tax boost were eliminated; the committee let stand the increased auto registration fee.

Warren struck back. When California's oil companies arbitrarily hiked gasoline prices, he wrote U.S. Attorney General Tom C. Clark asking for an investigation of oil industry profits on the West Coast.

"This is a plain steal and an insolent disregard for the welfare of the people," the governor said in a prepared statement. "The oil companies have connived to siphon off all the loose change of the people . . ."

At Warren's behest, a state senator introduced a constitutional amendment to regulate oil companies. Then a sympathetic assemblyman proposed a severance tax on the oil industry, which would raise the $80 million stripped from Warren's highway bill.

Warren himself raked Speaker of the Assembly Sam Collins for permitting an oil lobbyist to use his office as a field headquarters in the fight against the highway bill. Warren also used his weekly radio address to flay the oil industry's "invisible government" and to woo the votes needed to secure the bill. "I refuse to believe that with people dying on our congested highways as they are today, the Legislature will go home from this session without taking proper steps to end the slaughter."

An infuriated Keck could not keep his people in line. Under pressure from other interests—industrialists and merchants, in particular—the assemblymen one by one reversed themselves. Warren was only one vote short when Democratic Assemblyman Don Allen, the onetime leader of the Economy Bloc, approached him.

The Los Angeles assemblyman explained he needed to appease a major supporter in his district, a dog food manufacturer. He offered to vote for the highway bill in exchange for Warren's signature on an Allen bill requiring that canned dog food containing horse meat be labeled as such.

Having already decided to sign the horse meat measure, Warren promptly accepted Allen's offer. "It's the only time I can remember when I traded an apple for an orchard," he said with a chuckle. The highway bill, with a tax on gasoline, passed out of committee and sailed through the legislature.

From then on, California's freeway and highway system would become the state's great badge of postwar progress.

Warren was playing politics with increasing verve in this second term. He rewarded legislators who carried his major bills with coveted judicial appointments. Supporters like Joe Knowland, who wanted to increase the size of the state's redwood parks, and Harry Lundberg of the Sailor's Union of the Pacific, who sought money for the California Maritime Academy, found their projects funded.

He could straddle issues with aplomb. He supported the lifting of the federal limitation on water deliveries to farms larger than 160 acres on the west side of the Central Valley, while retaining it on the east side. (California's huge corporate farms—including the *Los Angeles Times*–owned El Tejon Ranch Company—were largely on the west side.)*

When he thought it wise, he could duck an issue too. He deferred to the courts a decision on a "hot cargo" and secondary boycott bill, though as attorney general he had issued an advisory opinion stating such a ban was of dubious constitutionality.

Unions, swollen to record membership in the postwar boom, demanded he veto the measure. Business interests, including the state Chamber of Commerce and Asa Call's influential Southland Committee, pressed Warren to sign it.

Warren chose to allow the bill to become law without his signature, neither vetoing nor signing it. In a written statement he pointed to a constitutional challenge pending in state courts; Californians, he argued, were entitled to a ruling from the state Supreme Court instead of a gubernatorial veto.

Summarizing the 1947 legislative session, a statewide political magazine concluded Warren had confounded some observers with a series of measures that demonstrated a newfound "social consciousness." Furthermore, "his resounding slaps at the oil interests for their opposition to his highway program also came to many as a surprise."

He was a surprise indeed to those at both ends of the political spectrum. Warren, complained an editorial in the libertarian *Orange County Register*, was becoming the "California Roosevelt."

* He could also change his mind. In a 1964 letter to Paul S. Taylor, whom Governor Warren had removed from the state agricultural board, Chief Justice Earl Warren wrote, ". . . I hope the acreage limitation principle will not be abandoned, and that the west side will eventually develop as has the east side with its family-size farms." (See EW to Taylor, July 6, 1964, in EWP/LC, Box 120.)

At the same time, liberal Carey McWilliams begrudgingly moderated his sour opinion of Warren: "Essentially, he is a very able conservative politician, not a reactionary," who moved only as "a clear majority" dictated.

The Earl Warren of this second term was more politically independent than he had been, more sure of himself as governor. He was also more liberal, reporter Mary Ellen Leary discovered after a year-long absence from Sacramento.

The "moderate conservative" governor of old had moved leftward. To explain this shift, the political editor of *The Sacramento Bee,* "Pete" Phillips, decided Earl Warren learned by personal experience.

As governor he had learned that legislative politics hung on a willingness to compromise. There were no enemies, only issues; today's rival was tomorrow's partner.

There was but one exception to the rule. Warren could not compromise, nor accommodate the newly elected Attorney General Fred Napoleon Howser. Howser was tainted by longstanding links to gamblers.

Warren would have none of it. "Breach of the public trust was the one thing above all others that he would not tolerate," Helen MacGregor insisted.

Before the 1946 election, Warren had warned Republican Howser he would run without the governor's support. As district attorney of Los Angeles, Howser had permitted "Admiral" Tony Cornero to open another gambling ship off Long Beach. Howser's price was $35,000.

Cornero was only one of the smudges on Howser's dubious career. Howser's legal practice in Long Beach ran to local gamblers and the odd bar owner. With the support of liquor lobbyist Arthur H. Samish, he was elected to the state Assembly in 1940, considered a safe vote for Samish's beverage, racetrack, and trucking clients. When the incumbent district attorney died, Samish prevailed upon the Los Angeles County Board of Supervisors to select his boy Fred Howser in a hastily convened secret session.

Under Howser's benign watch, prostitution, numbers, and gambling had flourished in Los Angeles. The West Coast representative of the Chicago crime syndicate, Benjamin "Bugsy" Siegel, had organized bookmaking in Southern California while District Attorney Howser complacently looked the other way.

When Howser cast covetous eye on the vacant office of attorney general, he turned once more to Samish. Samish gave Howser his blessing and campaign funds. Well financed, Howser won the Republican nomination.

Warren kept his distance during the general election campaign, wary of Howser's debt to Samish. Despite that, the similarity of Howser's name to that of Frederick F. Houser, the outgoing lieutenant governor, and the Warren-Republican landslide itself assured Howser of victory in 1946.

Howser had no sooner moved into Bob Kenny's office than he moved to supplant Warren and Kenny veterans with his own men. The new attorney general intended to protect organized gambling in the state just as he had in Los Angeles.

"It was common knowledge around the state capitol that Howser and his lieutenants were in the numbers game," one Sacramento regular said. "His people were involved in gambling, not only in Long Beach where Howser came from, but in the mountain counties, in the hill towns around here."

It was immediately lucrative. Knowing deputies joked that Howser planned to hold office for just four years, then settle into a retirement made comfortable by several million dollars in payoffs.

Warren shortly had word that the monthly take on just punchboards was $500,000. When Warren braced Howser, the attorney general first dismissed the whispers as gossip, then told the governor to mind his own business.

Howser would not be easily curbed. He himself was well insulated by his bagmen from the actual extortion. Furthermore, he radiated sincerity in a manly, square-jawed fashion. "How can it be that anyone who is so persuasive and honest-appearing can be such a scoundrel?" one Sacramento veteran wondered.

Unable to persuade the attorney general to clean up his act, Warren moved instead to contain the corruption. He appointed a Study Commission on Organized Crime on November 1, 1947, and named as chairman Admiral William H. Standley, former chief of naval operations and ambassador to the Soviet Union. To fill the pivotal chief counsel position, Warren turned once more to Warren Olney III.

Strong ties bound Olney and Warren, feelings of affection and respect. Olney, said his son, "had almost a worshipful attitude towards Earl Warren [and] a self-conscious admiration for their shared sense of public service."

Warren turned to Olney often. "He was absolutely indispensable . . . a pro's pro," Earl Junior said.

A temporary assignment became a full-time job for the next two and one-half years as Olney pursued the elusive Howser. "Gumshoe," as Oscar Jahnsen teased the dapper Olney, began to accumulate evidence of Howser's agents skimming the take from slot machines in a half-dozen counties. At the same time Olney moved to close the wire service that furnished bookmakers prompt race results.

Trumpeting the first of Olney's reports for the Crime Commission, Warren prodded Howser to shut down the bookies. When Howser protested that he lacked funds, the governor retorted that the attorney general lacked the will. Furthermore, information turned over to Howser by the Crime Commission had found its way into the hands of the racketeers, Warren asserted.

Howser, in turn, claimed politics dictated Warren's every move. "Earl Warren has tried to dominate the Republican Party as long as I can recall in my public life." Warren was attacking him as "unworthy of his office," the attorney general continued, only because "he thinks I am a threat to his domination of the Republican Party."

Howser was brazenly defiant. "What drove Olney, [Special Prosecutor Arthur] Sherry and, behind them, Earl Warren, was the fear of organized crime getting control, and controlling a source of wealth that could be damaging to the whole state," Sherry's wife, reporter Mary Ellen Leary, said. "Other businesses—oil, telephone, retail—also feared organized crime would siphon off money from the state."

Howser's men finally stumbled in rural Mendocino when a onetime associate of "Admiral" Tony Cornero was arrested attempting to bribe the sheriff.

Facing a long and lonely jail term, Fred Grange identified his masters. The chief collector was Wiley "Buck" Caddel, appointed "coordinator of law enforcement" for the attorney general's office when Howser took office. According to Grange, Howser's monthly take was $100,000.

Grange gave them a partial victory. Caddel and two cohorts linked to bookmaking in Los Angeles were convicted of conspiracy to establish a slot machine protection racket in Mendocino County.

Implicated, but insulated from the actual payoffs, Howser hung on to his office. Nonetheless, Warren and Olney had isolated him from polite society.

With the Howser investigation and the Crime Commission reports, Warren had reaffirmed his own reputation for integrity. He was a man above scandal, apparently poised for national office.

Reviewing the governor's qualifications, best-selling journalist John Gunther decided that Warren had "the limitations of all Americans of his type with little intellectual background, little genuine depth or coherent political philosophy; a man who has probably never bothered with an abstract thought twice in his life. . . ."

With luck, Gunther concluded, the Californian "could make a tolerable president of the United States."

CHAPTER 16

LIGHTNING STRIKES

N ATTY IN HIS SUMMER SUIT AND STRAW HAT, THE PRESIDENT OF
the United States waved to the crowd of well-wishers gathered on the train platform. Harry S. Truman had not ex-
pected so friendly a reception in Sacramento. This was, after all, an election
year, and the Republicans were savoring victory.

Unable to resist, the president loosed a few barbs at Republican politicians. Then someone in the crowd yelled, "What about Earl Warren?"

Warren was different, the president promptly replied. "Your governor
pursues forward-looking, liberal policies. He's a man of sense and a man of
ability. The facts of the case are he is a real Democrat and doesn't know it."

When reporters told Warren of Truman's embrace, he demurred gracefully. "I am sure that if he were writing it, he would spell 'Democrat' with
a small *d*."

In fact, he was pleased. "He couldn't have said anything better for me,
talking to a Democratic crowd, and me being a Republican with our
cross-filing system out there, and my having a penchant for cross-filing."

Though the two men were in opposing political parties, they shared a
growing friendship. They had met first in August, 1945, when Warren
visited the White House to discuss the administration of employment services. The Californian, Truman later noted, was the only Republican governor to put aside partisanship and promote that Democratic-sponsored
employment effort.

Their cooperation, particularly to complete the vast Central Valley Water
Project, was typical of Warren. He avoided partisan labels, preferring instead

to describe politicians as reactionary, progressive, or radical. Warren personally favored the progressive, "not necessarily as a party label but as a concept.

"To me it represents true liberalism . . . distinguishable from both reaction and radicalism, because neither of these philosophies makes for real progress."

The "Progressive" tag fit Warren, in the opinion of reporter Mary Ellen Leary. His politics were rooted in the Bull Moose thundering of Theodore Roosevelt and Hiram Johnson, "when to be a Progressive was to be a proud, independent and good-government-minded Republican."

Like Roosevelt and Johnson in another respect, Earl Warren wanted to bring that progressive spirit to the White House.

Just when Earl Warren decided to run for the presidency he never quite made clear. From the moment of his surprising sweep in the 1946 California primary, his name had repeatedly come up when the 1948 presidential election was mentioned.

Warren had just as often denied he was a candidate. "I am making no effort in that direction and I wish my friends would not put me in the position of being a candidate."

He was less than candid. As early as May, 1947, he had at least toyed with a run for the presidency. Invited to appear at the Gridiron Dinner in Washington, Warren carefully prepared a speech, "fully aware," wrote his aide Merrell F. "Pop" Small, "that his performance would be useful to them in grading him as presidential timber."

He spent much of that year traveling the country, discreetly campaigning, surveying the field, weighing his chances. In June, he visited New York's Governor Thomas Dewey, "talking things in general [but] no personal politics."

By the end of 1947, he had made no fewer than nine "nonpolitical" trips out of state. His speeches now dealt more often with national and international issues, subjects that portrayed him as "presidential" in stature.

His travels attracted notice. Henry Wallace, about to declare himself an independent candidate for the presidency, sniped that Warren, a "rising political figure" in the GOP, "has all of the political ability but none of the vision and humanitarianism of Franklin Roosevelt."

Warren's political acumen told him he faced long odds. Out of office for sixteen years and sensing victory, the Grand Old Party boasted a sizable field of candidates: New York's Tom Dewey, the front-runner; Minnesota's Harold Stassen, now president of the University of Pennsylvania; Ohio's Robert A. Taft; Michigan Senator Arthur T. Vandenberg, who had made a name for himself in foreign affairs; and, for a small band of stubborn conservatives, General of the Army Douglas A. MacArthur.

Dewey had a political organization in place, seasoned and disciplined, internationalist by inclination, well funded by Winthrop Rockefeller and the Chase Manhattan Bank. Taft too had his supporters, men and women driven by conservative purpose. Stassen and Vandenberg were spoilers, capable of withholding support from the front-runners, bargaining for concessions from the leading candidates.

Warren's only real opportunity lay in a deadlocked convention, when tired delegates turned to the big, friendly Californian, everybody's second choice. As *The Sacramento Bee*'s Walter Jones put it, "Warren thought that . . . lightning might strike."

Warren's coy campaign was carefully orchestrated. *The New York Times* reporter Gladwin Hill noted that Warren preferred not to appear eager for higher office, but merely bowing to the entreaties of friends. He could not then be condemned as ambitious; instead, he appeared gracious when, only "at the solicitation of my friends, I entered a slate of delegates."

That appeal came in the form of a resolution from the Republican State Central Committee on October 19, 1947, urging him to run. Three weeks later, he consented once more to be a favorite son candidate. If he won the primary, the fifty-three votes of the California delegation would be pledged to him by law for the first ballot.

He would do nothing so crass as to solicit delegates' votes in other states and risk alienating any of the announced candidates. Neither would he attempt to raise money, a task for which he had little enthusiasm in any event.

"Sure, I'd like to be president," Warren conceded, but he had no great plan. "My strategy is no strategy."

If his presidential bid failed, would he accept the vice presidential nomination, a reporter asked. Warren firmly declined; he had "no interest in the vice presidential nomination whatsoever."

A Warren candidacy did not excite everyone. California oilman William Keck, stung by the increase in gasoline taxes during the legislative session, spent considerable sums publicizing among the convention delegates Warren's pro-socialist stands on prepaid health insurance and government housing. "It was a real vendetta," a Warren staff member commented.

The black press was decidedly cool. The *San Francisco Sun* advised Warren to "get an FEPC bill with some teeth in it passed by the Republican-controlled legislature." The paper also asked he "appoint qualified Negroes to important positions in the judiciary and executive branches of the state government."

The *Stockton Press* noted that easterners had asked about Warren's stand on racial issues. "The news going back east from California certainly isn't the kind to help the Governor." The widely read Baltimore *Afro-American* simply dismissed him: "Earl Warren for president? Are you kidding?"

For the first six months of 1948, Warren hung back. His one major address, an NBC radio broadcast a month before the Republican National Convention, urged adoption of a liberal platform. Noting the party had been out of power for sixteen years, Warren stated:

I am sure the American people want to know whether the Republican Party . . . has learned from the world-shaking events of recent years. Does it propose to turn the clock of government back to pre-war time, or does it propose to face the problems of this day in the light of changed and changing conditions? Does it understand the need for a higher concept of our government's duty to its people and to the world? Does the Republican Party nourish any secret longing to return to isolationism, or does it intend to dedicate itself wholeheartedly to the great strategy for world cooperation and lasting peace?

In posing the questions, Warren was declaring where he stood. He advocated foreign aid in the postwar world, and an end to isolationism. He also endorsed an emphatically progressive program at home.

So long as there are states or parts of states where impoverished schools deny a basic education to the children living there; so long as a large percentage of our hard-working, self-respecting Americans cannot afford medical care; so long as a large percentage of our housing is substandard or in slum condition; so long as workmen with years of life ahead of them are cast-off without the benefit of a broadened social security program; so long as our natural resources are being inexcusably wasted; just so long will America lack the strength to raise living standards here at home and fulfill at the same time the world obligations which we have assumed in recent years.

On the eve of the convention, Warren had positioned himself as a dark horse, a potential nominee for the presidency in the event of a deadlock. Inevitably, such men were also cast as vice presidential nominees.

The California delegation was not going to the Philadelphia convention "second class," he insisted. He had no interest in the vice presidency, he reiterated. Not with Dewey. Not with MacArthur. Not with anyone, he repeated.

Why was he running? CBS newsman Edward R. Murrow asked Warren ten days before the convention.

"My wife has asked me the same question about all the offices I have held through the years. I have answered her by saying, 'Why does a boy want to play quarterback when he knows that if the game is lost he probably will be blamed for it when he could as easily let someone else call the signals?'

"The answer," he continued, "is to be found in the American character, the desire to serve well in one's chosen field."

It was a lighthearted California delegation that assembled on the special campaign train on Thursday, June 17, 1948, united by no more sense of purpose than a feeling that the state's governor was a good and decent man.

"The plan of operation was simple," Helen MacGregor wrote a friend later. "We had no brass bands hired; no favors to hand out; the only supplement to California friendliness was to be orange juice served by a California senorita in Spanish costume."

They could count on only California's 53 votes—with 548 needed to nominate. Governor James Duff, the influential leader of the big Pennsylvania delegation, was friendly. So too were scattered delegates in half a dozen states. All were pledged to other candidates, but might become late-ballot votes for Warren. "It was thoroughly understood that Earl Warren's only chance would come if there were a deadlock," MacGregor agreed.

Warren had mounted a paltry effort compared to the slick floor operation laid on by Tom Dewey's handlers. Where California served a glass of orange juice to delegates, visitors to the Dewey headquarters received boxes of Cuban cigars or hard-to-get nylon stockings. Warren's campaign signs, daubed by Young Republicans on the train from California, were all but lost in tricolor rivers of ribbon and banners.

By Tuesday, the Californians were overwhelmed, their headquarters moved from the teeming Bellevue-Stratford to the quieter Warwick, two and one-half blocks away. Still communications broke down; the telephone lines were so jammed that it was easier to send a messenger on foot.

Tom Dewey was the acknowledged front-runner. Stiff and unbending, a man to whom social graces came with difficulty, he was denounced as "the only man who can strut while sitting down, someone you have to know to dislike." Despite that, he held 329 committed votes as the convention opened. His closest rival, Senator Taft, had 250, Harold Stassen 175.

The convention hotels floated on a sea of rumor as the delegates gathered. California, with 10 percent of the votes needed to nominate, appeared pivotal. If Dewey could get California's delegates, he would not have to cut deals with others. If California did not deliver, another report had it, Warren could expect no appointment in a Dewey administration. Dewey denied the report, "but in the process a message may have been delivered—the one Dewey wanted Warren to get."

Thursday morning, the roll call began. Dewey had 434 votes, Taft 224, Stassen 157 on the first ballot.

On the second, the New Yorker had jumped to 515 votes. Warren had 59. In the face of Dewey's momentum, his opponents opted for a recess.

Sitting in the damp heat of Suite 1619 at the Warwick with Pop Small and Verne Scoggins, Earl Warren conceded that Dewey could not be stopped. Warren telephoned Dewey to congratulate him, then drafted a statement throwing California's votes to the New Yorker.

When the convention reconvened on Thursday evening, Taft floor manager John Bricker shouldered his way through the sweltering delegates to gain the microphone just ahead of Bill Knowland. Bricker read a gracious concession on Taft's behalf.

For Tom Dewey, the next problem was persuading the man he had tapped months before to be his running mate.

Los Angeles Times political editor Kyle Palmer awakened Warren at 4:10 A.M. on Friday, June 25. Could Warren come to Dewey's quarters at the Bellevue-Stratford right away?

Alone with Warren and Palmer, Dewey was blunt. He had discussed the vice presidential nomination with his advisers. They agreed with him that Warren should be his running mate.*

Warren was just as frank. First of all, he couldn't afford it. As governor of California he made $25,000; he would take a pay cut to $20,000 if he became vice president. He had one daughter in college and four more children to educate.

Dewey promised to ask Congress to increase the salary and provide an official residence.

There was another condition. Warren had no wish to leave California merely to preside over the Senate, voting only when there was a tie. Dewey pledged to make the vice president a member of the Cabinet, with executive responsibilities, answerable to the president alone.

Warren asked for time to weigh Dewey's offer.

He walked the two blocks back to the Warwick just as dawn broke on Friday morning. In their suite he woke Nina to tell her of the offer.

"You could never be happy in that job," Nina advised her husband.

The governor was no more enthusiastic. "I sure don't want to do this, but I have to," he confessed later to Earl Junior.

If he rejected Dewey's offer, he would be a political suicide. To decline the vice presidential nomination a second time would end all hope of party support for national office. Lately he had been considering a seat on the United States Supreme Court, he had told friends.

Later that morning, Warren met with the California delegates to explain why he might do what he had pledged not to do—run for vice president.

Warren told his friend Philip Wilkins that "he felt an obligation to the party to do it, to run. He could help him [Dewey] in the West, help with California. He was doing the right thing on a so-called moral political basis."

Dewey was also leaning hard on Warren. "He demanded that he run," Wilkins said.

The California delegation took an advisory poll in a breakfast caucus, and split badly. "A lot of us still felt that he should be at the top of the ticket," one delegate said.

At 11:30 that morning, Warren surrendered. He telephoned Dewey to accept.

---

* An undated but early 1948 memorandum from a Philadelphia public relations firm in Warren's files noted, "Warren can be a terrific vote getter, not only for himself *but for Dewey* with the independent voting faction and the conservative Democrat." [Emphasis added.] Probably paid for by the Dewey campaign, the memo also advised, "The Governor's views on socialized medicine should not be mentioned as this would serve as a detriment to him." (See "Basic Easter Public Relations Campaign for Governor Warren," in EWP/S 619.)

"What made him change his mind?" a reporter asked one of Warren's staff members.

"They put a gun to his head."

An hour after Warren accepted, Dewey's men had arranged the vice presidential nomination. In his hotel room he and Pop Small silently watched the shadows on the television set. Warren displayed no elation, no pleasure, as he was nominated by acclamation. To Small he said only, "Pop, I had to take it this time, else they never would have considered me for anything again."

Warren had no prepared speech when he appeared on the rostrum that evening with Nina and their three beaming daughters. Accepting the vice presidential nomination, Warren told the restless delegates, "For the first time in my life, I know what it feels like to be hit by a streetcar. I had no idea, I assure you, that there was any such shock as this awaiting me today, and before you change your mind, I want to say that I accept the nomination."

However the nomination had been carpentered, the newly named national chairman, Hugh Scott, chirped, "We have a dreamboat of a ticket." The consensus among reporters and columnists was "only a miracle or a series of political blunders not to be expected of a man of Dewey's astuteness can save Truman . . . from overwhelming defeat."

According to Bill Sweigert, the first person the governor telephoned was former Alameda County supervisor John Mullins. Years before, Irish Johnny had told the new district attorney, Earl Warren, "One day you are going to be president of the United States."

Warren also telephoned Earl Junior and Bobby in California. When the youngest answered, his father asked, "Well, Bob, did you hear what happened today in Philadelphia?"

"No, Dad. What happened?"

"Well, I was nominated for vice president."

"Is that good?" the thirteen-year-old asked.

His mother would have answered no.

The problems began almost immediately. Watching their initial press conference, Kyle Palmer decided the two men were not well matched: "They struck fire every time they got close together."

Dewey's aides had laid out a tightly mapped campaign. His speeches were already drafted, each devoted to a particular issue, each to be delivered at a time already scheduled.

It was too rigid, Warren grumbled. If Dewey was to talk about conservation in Oklahoma City, he would not discuss it before that date. If the press questioned him about conservation, he would refer to the speech in Oklahoma City and say no more.

"I don't believe you can structure a campaign that way," Warren protested. "I believe you've got to meet things as they arise."

Furthermore, Dewey intended to make no campaign promises, to advance no specific programs. He would run merely on a pledge to unite all Americans.

In Warren's opinion, Dewey had erred by setting so rigid a schedule, then offering the voters only preplanned platitudes. With his advice unsolicited, Warren made few suggestions.

He did, however, make several attempts to open up the campaign, to get Dewey to take the offensive. Pop Small overheard one Warren telephone call in which he urged, "But Tom, we gotta say somethin' about somethin' some of the time!"

There were other calls, from both the summer cabin in Santa Monica and the governor's mansion, conversations between the two governors that lasted as long as ninety minutes, Earl Junior remembered. "There would be five- to ten-minute silences on this end, then you heard, 'Well, dammit, Tom, you've got to go to the people and tell it to 'em.'"

It was futile. Dewey insisted on a sober, dignified, and vaporous campaign.

Why run risks? They were far ahead in the polls and President Truman was besieged with problems. The new state of Israel was under attack from its well-armed Arab neighbors. The Soviet Union had blockaded Berlin, leaving open only air corridors to supply the former German capital with food. As tension mounted in this test of wills, President Truman confided in his intermittent diary that he feared "we are very close to war."

On the other side of the world, the corrupt Chiang Kai-shek continued to lose ground to disciplined Chinese Communist armies. Chiang's failure abroad raised ever greater fears of a Communist menace at home; only subversion from within could explain how the most powerful nation on the globe could be repeatedly thwarted in its foreign policies.

Domestically, Truman not only faced the "dream" Republican ticket of Dewey and Warren, but confronted dissidents within his own party. Bourbon southerners had organized a States' Rights Party to protest Truman's racial policies. Meanwhile, radicals and disaffected New Dealers had rallied behind Henry Wallace and a newly created Independent Progressive Party. Franklin Roosevelt's great coalition lay shattered.

Despite these problems, Truman remained buoyant. He mounted a slashing attack on the Republican Party as composed of "gluttons of privilege," as Wall Street "bloodsuckers" and "economic royalists" seeking to plunder the poor and middle class. The Republican Eightieth Congress was led by "your typical Republican reactionary . . . with a calculating machine where his heart ought to be."

Warren's task in the campaign was to blunt the Truman assault with a thirty-one-day rail tour. He would make fifty-two short speeches from the platform of the observation car *Aleutian,* address twenty-four major rallies, hold five formal press conferences, and receive local party mugwumps in twenty-nine states. In the hours between he read Winston Churchill's *The Gathering Storm.*

Throughout the tour, Warren wrote his own speeches, assisted by Sweigert and Knowland, then sent the texts off to Dewey headquarters for approval. It was wearying work.

Marguerite Gallagher, who typed and retyped the speeches on the train, noted that Warren's drafts were heavily edited. "And I know most of the time a lot of material got knocked out of there . . ."

The resulting speeches were bland, tepid stuff that tiptoed around the issues. Even the most incendiary of topics, the threat of communist subversion at home, provoked only the mildest of pledges.

Warren eschewed that traditional role for the vice presidential candidate, attacking the opposition ticket. The worst he would say about "well-intentioned" Harry Truman was that his administration was "a shambles—dispirited, chaotic, quarrelsome, and desperate." The Democratic nominee for vice president, Senator Alben Barkley, was "a fine American who has made many contributions to good government in his years of public service."

Ten days into the trip, Warren was straining at the leash. At a Detroit press conference, a reporter asked him, "What is your position on communism?"

"I am against it," Warren responded, grinning as the reporters broke out in laughter.

Speaking before a union audience that night, he endorsed the Taft-Hartley Labor Relations Act, passed by the Republican Congress over a Truman veto. But, he continued, "if any of its provisions are found to be oppressive, unnecessary or unworkable, they should be changed until the act fully guarantees democratic principles within labor organizations. . . .

"If I thought the Taft-Hartley law or any other law struck at the fundamental rights of workers to organize or to bargain collectively, or to use their full economic strength to improve their lot, I would fight it with every fiber in my body."

Dewey's people were immediately upset with Warren's comments. No matter that the Republican platform promised to enact needed reforms; Warren had committed Dewey to a policy. A round of telephone calls from Dewey headquarters harnessed a subdued Warren to the program once more.

Warren was an unhappy warrior. Fettered by Dewey's restrictions, forced to campaign before large crowds, the Californian was at his worst. "If Dewey was campaigning innocuously, which he was," said the assistant director for publicity of the Democratic National Committee, "Warren was campaigning twice as innocuously, and he wasn't really stirring anybody up."

Warren was frustrated; this was not the sort of campaign he wanted. "I'm so low in this campaign," he groused in a telephone call to Sacramento Bee editor Walter Jones. "I can't say what I want to say. I just wanted to tell it to someone and you're the only one I can tell it to."

The monthlong campaign trip ground to a close, brightened only by a visit from Dottie, Honey Bear, and Bobby, arranged by their father to surprise Nina on their wedding anniversary. The Warrens returned to California ten days before election day to discover the state Republican Party so confident of victory that the San Francisco headquarters had been closed.

The certainty of a Dewey triumph grew. Normally Democratic newspapers one after the other endorsed the New York governor. *Newsweek* magazine had asked fifty political experts who would win in November; all fifty predicted Dewey. Poll upon poll predicted an easy Dewey victory, even a landslide. Dewey's campaign manager was privately estimating a 4–1 margin in the all-important electoral college; Truman would be lucky to get four states outside the Democratic Deep South.

Why bother campaigning when the outlook was certain?

"The Democrats aren't making a fight out here," party officials explained to Warren. "People think there is just no contest."

Warren was disturbed. "They just thought it was in the bag and let it coast, and how people who have been through campaigns can *ever* get that idea, I don't know. . . ."

Back in California for the last weeks of the campaign, Nina—who had never taken part in politics, who had never solicited a vote—asked her husband, "Do you think you're going to win this election?"

"Well, I think so," Warren replied. "Everybody says so, and I don't see any reason why we shouldn't."

"Well, now, I don't want you to be shocked. You've never lost one before, but you're not going to win this one."

Uncertain himself, Warren asked the executive director of the League of California Cities his opinion.

"I think you're dead," Richard Graves replied. "I don't think there's any way to win a political campaign by not campaigning."

In these last two weeks of the campaign, in familiar California among people he had known all his life, Warren sensed the running of the tide. He told Pop Small that Truman would win. "He has reached the people and we haven't." It was as simple as that.

Warren stumped up to election day, doing what he could for the Republican ticket. He also issued a last-minute statement urging California voters to reject a ballot initiative that would reapportion the state Senate. (The measure proposed allocating twenty-one of the forty seats to the four largest urban centers, rather than the current system in which a scant 6 percent of the voters elected a majority of the Senate.)

Adoption of the initiative, sponsored by the state Federation of Labor, would invite boss rule by big city machines, Warren charged. Fifty of the state's agricultural counties would be transformed into "a mere tail to the kite," he argued.

Only in his *Memoirs* twenty-five years later did Warren acknowledge his opposition to reapportionment was a matter of political expediency. The opponents of the initiative included the most influential lobbies in the state, influential because they already guided the votes of a number of state senators. To preserve their influence, these vested interests entrusted a $300,000 campaign fund to Whitaker and Baxter, a sum sufficient to convince the public of the evils of approximately proportional representation.

Early on the morning of election day, the Warrens voted at their old Montecito Avenue precinct in Oakland. A testy governor barked at *Life* magazine photographer John Dominis who had snapped Warren as he marked his ballot. "Don't you know it is illegal to photograph a person while he is voting?" The chastened photographer promised to destroy the negative.

Nina Warren sweetly smiled for the photographers, then voted for Harry S. Truman. She had no desire to be the wife of the vice president, to uproot the children and leave the governor's mansion that had come to be home.

Later that day the Warrens crossed the bay to gather with their children and supporters in the St. Francis Hotel on San Francisco's Union Square. The evening ended early. Before 9:00 P.M., midnight on the East Coast, he suggested that Earl Junior drive his younger brother back to Sacramento; the young man took it as an indication they would lose.

Daughter-in-law Margaret passed him in the hallway later that night, aware that Republican candidates for Congress were falling, that GOP prospects had soured. "He didn't seem upset at all," she recalled.

Across the country, Tom and Frances Dewey awaited the election returns at the Hotel Roosevelt on East 45th Street. Through the night and early morning hours, Dewey watched as Truman's totals climbed; at 5:30 A.M. he finally muttered in disbelief, "What do you know? The son of a bitch won."

Amid the stunned aides on the eleventh floor of the St. Francis, Nina Warren sighed, "Thank God."

Her husband took his first electoral loss in six tries with good spirits. When a reporter asked if he had an explanation for Truman's victory, Warren replied, "Yes, I have. The President got too many votes for us."

The key to the Truman sweep—Republicans lost their majorities in both houses of Congress—lay in the farm vote. Three states thought to be safely in Dewey's column determined the outcome by narrowly going for onetime farmer Harry Truman: Ohio, Illinois, and, most surprising, California. A switch of 29,292 votes in those three states would have elected Thomas Dewey president of the United States.

Warren was unable to deliver California. Truman gained the state's twenty-five electoral college votes, 1,913,134 to 1,895,269, a margin of just 17,865. A switch of 8,933 votes, less than one in every two precincts, would have given the state to Dewey.

As Republican analysts weighed the vote, the race had been lost in the farm-rich Central Valley; there Truman ran up a lead of 180,000 votes. Had Dewey allowed Warren to campaign harder for the farm vote, as he had urged, the New Yorker might have won.

Warren took no blame for the loss. Vice presidential candidates did not ordinarily win or lose elections.

Some party leaders even assumed that Warren, unsullied, would contend for leadership of the national party. The other candidates were either too old or stood discredited. On the morning after the election, hastily penciled placards propped up in the lobby of the St. Francis Hotel proclaimed, "Warren in '52." Speaking on a not-for-attribution basis, Verne Scoggins crowed to a reporter, "It looks great for '52."

Still, some in the party were dissatisfied with Warren, particularly his instinct for the political center. Under Warren, the California GOP was no more than a "monstrous patchwork quilt of an organization which serves only one individual in the state," a group of Southern California Republican women complained in a resolution.

The national committeeman frankly agreed: "There is no Republican Party in California." Earl Warren had used the legal device of cross-filing to overcome the 60–40 registration bulge the Democrats boasted. He had fashioned personal election victories in 1942 and 1946, but had not built a disciplined party organization.

Another gubernatorial campaign loomed in 1950. For Republicans, the issue would come down to personality versus party.

CHAPTER 17

THE WEIGHTY FRIEND

EARL WARREN ANTICIPATED TROUBLE WITH THE OPENING OF THE 1949 session of the state legislature. After all, he told his staff, you could not be in politics without making *some* enemies.

Until now the hard-eyed men filling Sacramento's hotels had lacked opportunity. This year, they considered Warren a lame duck serving out a last term, his luster dimmed by running on a losing national ticket.

They misjudged their man. Earl Warren would not coast through the remainder of his term. With Bill Sweigert—whom he would shortly appoint to the bench—Warren had mapped out an extensive legislative program to deal with half a hundred growing problems. Water and air pollution, new highways, and a vastly expanded school construction program joined previously rejected fair employment practices and medical insurance on the agenda.

It was an ambitious program with a billion-dollar budget, the largest in the nation and 250 percent greater than Warren's first budget in 1943. Its growth was a result of the governor's expanded sense of responsibility for *all* the people, in the opinion of League of California Cities lobbyist Richard Graves. "He'd taken lessons from the slums, the crowded schools, and the inadequate hospitals."

Increasingly, Warren's bills drew opposition from within his own party, particularly a revived Economy Bloc. Northern California business interests bridled when Warren proposed a Central Valley water project that would "not let one drop of water go into the sea unused." Similarly, when the Department of Public Health proposed a statewide water treatment program, local industry up and down the state protested; let someone else pay for it.

Republican legislators, harkening to the California Medical Association for the third time, voted decisively in both houses to pigeonhole Warren's scaled-back prepaid health insurance legislation.

"It's quite a lobby, and it looks like they beat us again," Warren sighed.

That same lobby throttled a Warren bill creating a hospital insurance program paid entirely by employee payroll deductions. In the face of charges that this was "an entering wedge" for prepaid health insurance, Warren snorted, "I want to know why the worker should be denied the use of his own money for a hospital bill when he is in dire need."

When the Republican majority of an Assembly committee killed the governor's bill to create a commission to study racial discrimination in employment, Warren coldly took the members to task. That they could flout both state and national GOP platform planks at the behest of San Francisco's Chamber of Commerce and Los Angeles's Merchants and Manufacturers Association shocked him, he told reporters.

Warren was willing to challenge even those special interests considered his allies if the prize was important enough. When he proposed elevating Municipal Court Judge Edwin L. Jefferson to the Los Angeles Superior Court in 1949, the State Bar's Committee on Judicial Appointments balked at giving a black man "all that power."

The governor personally appeared at the next meeting of the bar's Committee on Judicial Qualifications in San Francisco. Warren reportedly informed the committee that unless Jefferson was approved, he would publicly condemn the committee as unfit to pass on further judicial nominations. Jefferson's nomination was ratified without further discussion.

There were some successes during the legislative session: passage of the $1 billion budget funded by an increase of sales, corporation, and income taxes; a school construction program to be underwritten by new state bonds; and a measure tightening regulation of usurious small loan companies.

Warren's biggest victory, however, came by accident, with the downfall of the most powerful lobbyist in Sacramento, the 300-pound Arthur H. Samish.

This self-described "King of the Lobby" had fashioned a new form of political organization in Sacramento, one founded not on party affiliation, but on economic self-interest. Tens of thousands of members of trade associations, respected businessmen, not ward heelers, served as Samish lieutenants across the state. It was "a nucleus of 500,000 people protecting their investment and the livelihood of their kiddies," Samish boasted to Lester Velie of *Collier's* magazine.

"I weld them together into the damnedest political machine you ever saw. Boy, we can exploit it when we need it!"

Never going beyond the seventh grade in public schools, Samish, coincidentally, took his first job as a runner in the law office of Warren Olney's father. In 1919, Samish met newly returned veteran Earl Warren when they both worked as clerks in the state Assembly. At the end of the session, Warren returned to Oakland; Samish stayed on in Sacramento, minutely studying the realities of government and the legislative process. In time he would brag, "There isn't a short cut around the place I don't know."

With the repeal of Prohibition, small-time lobbyist Artie Samish came into his own. Retained by the state Brewers Institute, he carefully built a nickel-a-barrel contingency fund. From 1935 to 1938, the fund disbursed $97,000 at Samish's discretion, at a time when a legislator's salary was $100 per month.

Over time, Samish's client list came to include brewers, bankers, truckers, and the Santa Anita Race Track. He had salted away his first million dollars by the age of thirty-two, he boasted.

Warren and Samish occasionally crossed paths during these years. Samish was creating his puissant political machine, and Warren was representing the District Attorneys' Association before legislative committees. Gregarious Artie Samish liked Warren, "a decent sort, with a pleasant smile and a hearty handshake. Earl was ambitious. But then show me the politician who isn't."

By 1939, Arthur H. Samish was the single most powerful figure in Sacramento, unelected and unchecked. He secretly funded legislative candidates. He picked the speaker of the Assembly, the single most powerful man in Sacramento after Samish himself. He was said to control thirty assemblymen and the key committees that reviewed his legislation.

"I'm the governor of the Legislature. To hell with the governor of the state," he boasted in a speech before the Commonweath Club of San Francisco.

Samish's power was not confined to the state legislature. He reached out to help sympathetic men running for local office. Most important, he dictated the decisions of the state Board of Equalization, which granted liquor licenses.

Other lobbyists were careful not to cross Samish. "The game was defense," former legislative analyst H. Alan Post commented.

By the time of Warren's election as governor in 1942, "Samish was a kind of fixture in Sacramento," *New York Times* correspondent Gladwin Hill said. "There wasn't a heck of a lot the governor could do about it."

Warren and Samish remained warily respectful. Warren conceded that "on matters that affect his clients, Artie unquestionably has more power than the governor."

As governor, Warren kept the lobbyists at arm's length. They complained that he refused to take their private telephone calls at the mansion. Instead, they were advised to call him at the Capitol—where all calls would be logged on a calendar reporters checked each morning. "They didn't want their names on the list, and they stayed away from me," Warren said later.

According to *Sacramento Bee* political reporter Richard Rodda, Warren "tried to keep out of Samish's way the best he could without letting it be revealed that he was afraid of Samish."

By the beginning of Warren's second term, Samish was a looming offstage presence. Other lobbyists stood in the back of the chambers, beckoning legislators from their desks when they wanted to offer guidance. Samish preferred to settle his 300-pound bulk in his suite at the Senator Hotel, dispatching aides to deliver summonses and instructions.

Then in 1949, Samish unexpectedly stumbled. Puffed with arrogance, he posed for an illustration of Velie's profile in *Collier's* with a ventriloquist's dummy propped on a knee.

"That's the way I lobby," Samish jested, pointing to the wooden doll painted as a clown and crowned with a top hat. "That's my legislature. That's Mr. Legislature."

The self-caricature, the open contempt for the legislature itself, abruptly undercut Samish's authority. Disclosure of his power destroyed that power. One by one, irritated clients began looking for someone less cocky, someone less uncouth, someone more discreet.

While Samish fought a rearguard action, Warren capitalized on the *Collier's* article. Agreeing that the majority of lobbyists were honest, Warren asked for legislation to control "the few who flout decency."

With the passage of corrective legislation in December, 1949, California became the twentieth state requiring lobbyists to register and file periodic financial reports. The bill lacked enforcement provisions; it did not ban the lucrative practice of legislators representing clients before state agencies, but it was a start toward reform.*

Samish's hour was fast running—and with it the career of the feral Fred Howser.

Howser had been politically wounded with the attempted bribery conviction of Wiley "Buck" Caddel, his "law enforcement coordinator," in the slot machine fix gone sour. The payoffs had not been traced back to Howser, but he was tainted by the association.

Expecting Warren, his nemesis, to be elected vice president in 1948, Howser waited until the presidential election passed. Then, believing Warren had been politically damaged, he sought to rally the Republican Party to himself.

Howser released a public statement, claiming his efforts to eradicate bookmaking had been hampered by the governor's cuts of his budget. Warren lashed back with the harshest political attack of his career. Responding to a question planted at his press conference on March 8, 1949, he pointed out that Howser's investigative budget was the same as in the

---

* Richard Carpenter, himself a lobbyist for the League of California Cities and a respected authority on state government, considered this legislation one of Warren's major accomplishments as governor.

previous two years. "The only amount cut was $25,000 he asked to investigate the newspapers because they hadn't been speaking kindly of him."

The problem was not budgetary, but Howser's unwillingness to investigate, Warren continued. Remnants of the Capone mob controlled bookmaking in California, and "any wide-awake law enforcement agency would demonstrate that fact to him."

Howser fired back before the day was out, charging Warren's motives were political. Warren intended to undercut what support Howser had within the party, and tag him as a Judas goat to potential campaign contributors.

Three days after the exchange, the Crime Commission released a hastily prepared "interim report" linking California's slot machine rackets to New York crime boss Frank Costello. In news stories headlined "Graft Here Tied to Murder, Inc.," commission counsel Warren Olney listed county after county where gambling—bookies, punchboards, slots, even gaming rooms —once more operated more or less openly. In each, from Los Angeles in the south to Mendocino in the north, Attorney General Howser was reportedly implicated.

Rattled, Howser turned for help to the man who had tapped him for the attorney general's office three years earlier. Howser wanted Samish to kill the appropriation for the bothersome Crime Commission.

Samish refused. He had no intention of squandering his accumulated chits on so tarnished a protégé. Howser's political career was effectively at an end.

With Samish's concurrence, the Assembly's Committee on Public Morals duly approved the appropriation for the Crime Commission. Samish decided that was his "first mistake," done only because he "felt sorry for Earl Warren."

In fact, Samish found himself outmaneuvered by Warren. With Howser discredited, legislators could not risk leaving unfunded the agency that had pointed out the corruption and identified the source of the evil: organized crime.

As Samish's grip loosened, Warren's tightened. The governor "could be very rough on someone who might not want to make any kind of trade or compromise," Assemblyman (later Congressman) John Moss said.

If he was tough with a legislator one day, he was charming the next. Watching Warren over a four-year period, Moss decided the governor was "a superb politician. There was a warmth there that no one could have quite matched." Whether or not they agreed with him politically, Moss decided, a majority of the 120 state legislators liked Warren personally.

Warren was to need both charm and political wiles to negotiate a bitter dispute that wracked his cherished University of California in the last months of the second term.

These were perilous times. The East-West amity of the war years had evaporated in Cold War rivalry. At every turn it appeared the Soviet Union was conspiring to undermine American influence abroad and security at home.

President Truman launched a government-wide loyalty program to root out suspected security risks, including not only communists but homosexuals and alcoholics. Three thousand would quit or be fired under a cloud of suspicion.

In July, 1948, the federal government indicted twelve ranking members of the Communist Party U.S.A. on charges of conspiring to overthrow the government. The following month, a *Time* magazine senior editor, Whittaker Chambers, named former Department of State attaché Alger Hiss as a member of a spy network that had infiltrated the government.

Overseas, the communist tide rolled on. In China, the People's Army captured Manchuria, then Peking; Hungary proclaimed itself a People's Republic on February 1, 1949. In March, the venerated Winston Churchill announced that only the West's sole possession of the A-bomb had kept the USSR from sweeping across all of Europe.

Daily the headlines shrieked of "the Communist menace." A federal grand jury returned an indictment against a Department of Justice analyst who allegedly spied for the Russians. For five weeks in June and July, federal prosecutors sought to prove in court that Alger Hiss had committed perjury in denying he had aided admitted communist spy Whittaker Chambers. Then on September 23, 1949, Truman announced the Soviet Union had secretly tested an atomic bomb—three years before scientists had predicted the Russians would have the weapon.

Confronting the apparent spread of communism at home and abroad, the chairman of California's own Un-American Activities Committee provoked the crisis that would threaten the university. For eight years state Senator Jack B. Tenney had pursued "subversives," increasingly irresponsible in naming those he deemed suspect. Tenney, whose biennial reports had repeatedly scored the university as a hotbed of radicalism, wanted to impose an oath requiring university personnel to declare themselves not to be members of "un-American" organizations.

The struggle over the imposition of a so-called negative oath began during the 1949 session of the state legislature. Tenney introduced seventeen pieces of anticommunist legislation, including a constitutional amendment shifting to the legislature authority to ensure the loyalty of university employees.

The university's vice president for business affairs, James Corley, returned from Sacramento to report, "It'll be easier to get the budget passed if there is an oath." Corley saw the loyalty oath as no more than a pacifying bone thrown to the dogs.

President Robert Gordon Sproul brought before the regents on March 25, 1949, a new affirmation to be tacked onto the constitutional oath required of all state officers. It required university employees from janitor to professor to swear he or she did not believe in, was not a member of, and did not support any group that believed in, advocated, or taught the over-throw of the United States government by illegal or unconstitutional means. Sproul's critics, led by regent John Francis Neylan, picked up the oath issue as a cudgel against the president.

Neylan, once a Progressive, had become in his later years a conservative. He had abandoned journalism first for accounting, then for the law, eventually to become an attorney for William Randolph Hearst. Widely credited with saving the press baron from bankruptcy in the Depression, hawk-beaked Jack Neylan filled "the Hearst seat" on the University of California Board of Regents. As a member of the regents' powerful Finance Committee, he saw himself as a paternal "owner."

Combative Jack Neylan and stolid Earl Warren, once friends and political allies, equally devoted to the university, locked in a power struggle.

The battle over a special loyalty oath for university employees was more than a debate about patriotism among the men and women who taught California's youth. That argument might stir those whom Harry Truman had taken to calling "the primitives," the single-minded rightists who saw communism as the source of all evil; it was a pretext for men like Jack Neylan.

Other issues were involved, most important, the question of who would govern the university: its Board of Regents, its president and faculty, or the state legislature through the budget process. Furthermore, regents from the southern portion of the state complained that Sproul, loyal son of Berkeley, treated the Los Angeles campus as a stepchild; seeking parity, they opportunistically weighed in. The oath controversy played out as a discordant obbligato over the struggle for governance and the north-south feud.

With the faculty north and south up in arms over any special oath requirement, Neylan made the proposed change even more offensive. He persuaded the regents on June 24, 1949, to insert in the proposed oath a specific disavowal of the Communist Party.

Warren delayed joining the battle. He sought instead to protect his right flank from conservatives for whom opposition to an oath would only be further proof of their governor's leftist leanings.

The caution was necessary. For the first time in a decade the Old Guard had a candidate, Lieutenant Governor Goodwin Knight.

"Goody" Knight made no secret of his desire to succeed Earl Warren as governor. Disappointed when the Dewey-Warren ticket fell to Harry Truman in 1948, Knight all but announced he was stumping for the 1950 Republican nomination for governor. By the spring of 1949 he was making as many as three political appearances a day.

Knight impatiently pecked at the governor and his programs. Lenin himself, the lieutenant governor asserted, had proclaimed socialized medicine the cornerstone of the socialist state. He seemed to be implying that the governor, by endorsing prepaid medical insurance, was laying the groundwork for a communist state in California.

By September, 1949, Knight was in full cry. Frankly seeking to represent disaffected Republicans, he contended there was no difference between the governor and the anticipated Democratic nominee, James Roosevelt.

The next month, ex officio member Knight attended his first Board of Regents meeting. He was there "apparently in order to vote against the governor and the faculty position," patently bidding for political support.

Warren held both temper and tongue while Knight stumped ever more boldly, ever more confident the governor would retire. Meanwhile, Warren quietly began to line up support for a third term, telephoning old friends around the state, pulling together his finance committee.

By late 1949, Warren had cut off Knight from all but the conservatives who would not support Warren in any case. That done, shortly after the first of the year he turned to the smoldering loyalty oath issue.

"Warren then came to take a position of leadership," said Clark Kerr, himself later to become president of the university. "Normally governors don't. But the controversy was tearing the university apart. The president was immobilized. Warren stepped in then, essentially against the oath or at least against the firing of the nonsigners, and took leadership of the more liberal elements of the board."

Warren, solid and thoughtful, was to be "what the Quakers would call 'a weighty friend,' " Kerr concluded. "The Warren position was clearly supported by at least 95 percent of the faculty."

The governor sought reason amid the rancor. Many of the advocates of a loyalty oath, men such as former Progressives Jack Neylan and Edward A. Dickson, he had known since the 1920s. Many he had appointed himself to the sixteen-year terms regents enjoyed.

"He didn't use pressure," Lieutenant Governor Goodwin Knight said. "He made his point that this was unfair to the university, that it cast a smear on the faculty. I didn't feel that way and said so. Yet the only time he ever tried to change my opinion was by indirection. We were going to a regents meeting one day, and he said, 'Fellow, you're on the wrong side of this question. Think it over.' "

Warren had stayed aloof from the anticommunist muddle of the postwar era. As early as September, 1947, he had publicly pooh-poohed the Red menace in California even as the Republican Party nationally took up the hunt for communists. Warren cautioned, "We must not permit the fear of Communism to dominate our lives, however despise it as we may. Our people are not Communists, and never will be, so long as we continue to advance human welfare under our system. Our vision of the future must be based upon faith in our institutions, not upon fear of others."

Asked by newsmen to comment on the Tenney Committee's 1948 report on un-American activities in California, Warren said mildly, "The Legislature has the right to conduct such investigations and it is up to the Legislature to determine its policies in that regard."

Earl Warren did not like oaths or special tests of loyalty. As early as 1945 he had vetoed a bill requiring conscientious objectors who sought public employment in California to answer the question: "If necessary, are you willing to take up arms in defense of the United States of America?" Such a question violated "the spirit if not the letter" of both state and federal constitutions, Warren announced.

The postwar excrescence of anticommunist oaths similarly troubled him as infringements upon the Bill of Rights. As a practical matter, the oaths were meaningless; a communist would sign one and laugh, Warren said repeatedly, and no oath would make a disloyal person loyal. Loyalty oaths rooted out no one other than the thoughtful man or woman who considered such a pledge an infringement upon the right to free association.

Warren objected to the regents' oath for other reasons too. University staff and faculty already took the oath administered to all government employees, including the governor and the regents themselves; imposing a second vow fingered them as a suspect group. Furthermore, the regents' oath was not statutory and therefore carried no punishment if a person committed perjury in signing it. Finally, the state constitution barred administering any oath other than the pledge to support and defend that constitution.

The University of California loyalty oath struggle would be played out against the backdrop of newspaper headlines that ratified the worst fears of the most militant anticommunists. Nation after nation went dark behind an Iron Curtain in eastern Europe; China fell to the communists. In January, 1950, Department of State attaché Alger Hiss was convicted of perjury; in Republican invective and the popular mind, here was the explanation for these foreign policy reverses. Two months later, British atomic scientist Klaus Fuchs confessed to spying at Los Alamos for the Soviet Union during World War II; even the most guarded of American institutions seemed wormed by subversives.

On February 24, 1950, Sproul read to the assembled regents a letter signed by forty-two deans and department chairmen objecting to the oath. This was no "small, willful minority," but a representative cross-section of the faculty, Warren insisted.

For the first time, Warren spoke out against the Regents' oath, recommending they adopt an oath the faculty could sign "without any thought of pride of opinion." He himself favored the oath taken by public officials from the president of the United States down to the rawest army recruit.

Regent Lawrence A. Giannini, a Warren appointee to the seat vacated by Giannini's father, the founder of Bank of America, would have none of it. The deans' letter was the work of "campus politicians," he countered. This was not a matter of pride but of principle, and principle was not to be compromised.

By a vote of 12 to 6, the regents voted to attach Neylan's communist disclaimer clause to the positive oath; those who did not sign were to be dismissed by June 30.

The "sign-or-get-out ultimatum" turned a parochial debate into a national news story. Faculty and students mounted rallies to protest the vote of the regents; a defense fund began raising money for a court case to challenge the oath.

On March 31, in Santa Barbara, the regents again were locked in four and a half hours of bitter, table-pounding debate. Again, as the leader of the anti-oath bloc, the governor took the floor near the end of the session to ask rhetorically why the university faculty should be singled out from all other state employees.

"I don't believe that the faculty of the University of California is Communist; I don't believe that it is soft on Communism, and neither am I," Warren stated. "The only thing the people of this state are interested in is our seeking to keep Communists out of the University and, believe me, I am interested in that too."

Once more Warren asserted that the simple oath he and other public officials swore, to support and defend the Constitutions of the United States and of California, was sufficient. But put to a vote, a motion to rescind the February ultimatum died in a 10–10 tie, and left standing the negative oath.

At the Board of Regents meeting three weeks later, Warren worked out a compromise. The language of the oath would be worked into the contract each university employee signed, and the oath itself rescinded. Nonsigners were to be permitted a hearing. The vote was 21–1; the lone dissenter, Lawrence Giannini, resigned from the board, claiming, "Flags will fly in the Kremlin."

The university's battle of the oath echoed for another year, but it was essentially lost when on June 26, 1950, tanks and infantry of the North Korean army crossed the 38th parallel and drove surprised South Korean forces into retreat. President Truman immediately ordered U.S. naval and air forces to support the fleeing South Koreans. Four days later, with the capital, Seoul, fallen to the invaders, the president committed American ground troops to the fight.

The loyalty oath fight was lost. No public figure could stand against a pledge of anticommunism when the nation literally was at war with communist troops. Eventually thirty-one university employees would refuse to sign for reasons of principle; none was ever identified as a communist. Only one known communist was ever discovered on the university payroll, a dance rehearsal pianist at UCLA. She was summarily fired.

Throughout the loyalty oath struggle, Warren portrayed himself as anticommunist, yet a staunch defender of civil liberties. He would remain one of the scant handful of Republican wheelhorses to stand their ground against Senator Joseph McCarthy and what Warren deemed McCarthy's "sadistic attacks upon the State Department, the Army, and even private citizens for any association with people of unorthodox or dissenting views."

At the June, 1950, Governor's Conference, Warren publicly rejected McCarthy's "blanket accusations" of communist infiltration of the State

Department. When a group of the most conservative Republican governors rounded on the guest speaker, Secretary of State Dean Acheson, as "an appeaser" or worse, Warren and Tom Dewey—the Republican Party's ticket just two years before—invited Acheson to lunch with them in the public dining room. The gesture was lost on the party's right wing.

Gestures were not enough at home, not if an incumbent politician was looking for reelection. Even as revitalized United Nations forces in Korea rolled northward on the attack, Warren summoned a special session of the legislature to create a state civil defense program.

As part of that program, Warren asked that the legislature define all state employees—including university personnel—as civil defense workers. They would be required to take an oath not to "advocate nor become a member of any political party or organization that advocates the overthrow of the Government of the United States or of this State by force or violence."

This was wartime, and wartime measures were required. ". . . I am of the opinion," Warren said in his address to the legislators, "that so long as we are in conflict with Soviet Russia, we are in imminent peril of sabotage." In Warren's mind, the Kremlin guided all communist actions around the world; communism was monolithic, subversive, and implacable.

The oath, embodied in a bill introduced by Assemblyman Harold K. Levering, sailed through the state legislature in hours. The Levering Oath was, if anything, more sweeping in its coverage and more stringent than the superseded regents' oath, legislative proponents claimed. Warren signed it as quickly with the explanation that "loyalty comes first—and hence this loyalty oath."

Just a month before the gubernatorial election, the Levering Act was no more, no less than a political prophylactic. It had dubious value as protection against communists, but it was a grand weapon against Democratic attacks.

CHAPTER 18

CRAFTY OPERATIONS

N O MAN WAS MORE EAGER THAN GOODWIN KNIGHT TO BECOME governor of California.

Gladhander Goody Knight, ever quick with a joke or a story, "had been running for governor throughout his entire term of office," Warren wrote in his later *Memoirs*. Knight intended to be so well funded and organized that he would dissuade the incumbent from filing for a third term.

Had Knight been less ambitious, had he bided his time as Warren once had, the governor might have stepped aside in his favor.

After all, Earl Warren had been in public service since 1920 and had held elective office since 1925. The jobs were satisfying, but the pay until the last few years was minimal.

From time to time, Warren's friends had put interesting business propositions in his way. Even more tantalizing, organized baseball had approached him about the soon-to-be vacant post of commissioner. He was fifty-eight; it was high time he put away some real money for Nina and the children.

Once he had considered sixty to be a good age to retire. A man sooner or later ran out of new ideas, he explained to Earl Junior. But as he approached that age himself, Warren grew less certain of the deadline. There was still much to accomplish.

He had weighed retirement from public life long and hard in the aftermath of the 1948 presidential campaign. As late as August 16, 1949, he had not decided he wanted another four years of "the political grind," he confided to newspaper columnist Drew Pearson.

After months of debate with himself, Warren discarded the notion of a career in business or finance. He knew little of those worlds and would be reduced to figurehead status, well paid but with little to do. The commissioner of baseball post would require too much traveling, too much time away from his family.

He was, after all, a public servant, an officeholder, and, it need be said, a politician. Any other life could not be as satisfying.

He could, if he wished, run for the United States Senate. Oil lobbyist "Black Jack" Smith, no friend of the governor after Warren raised gasoline taxes to build highways, talked of drafting Warren to run for the seat of retiring Democratic Senator Sheridan Downey in 1950. Smith wanted the governor removed from state affairs.

When a reporter asked about the Senate race, Warren spiked Smith's ploy. Stubborn Earl Warren simply would not back down in the face of a challenge.

Warren had another motive in running for a third term. Most of Knight's support came from conservatives like Smith who sought to undermine what Warren had built. Knight would repay them by opposing compulsory health insurance and by dismantling the workers' compensation and disability insurance programs. He would trim gasoline taxes, and with them the state's nascent freeway program. In the interests of economy, the model public health, juvenile delinquency, and mental health programs would be gutted.

Warren held off his decision until late in 1949. When asked if he intended to run for a third term, Warren merely smiled, then said he was too busy governing to play politics.

The longer Warren waited, the bolder Goody Knight became. At a press conference in September, 1949, Knight claimed a movement to draft him had reached "gigantic proportions." After all, "people tell me there is no difference between Governor Warren and Jimmy Roosevelt," the putative Democratic nominee.

As governor, Warren had steadily maintained his independence of political party; there would be no change in this year of pre-election maneuvering. "What I'm going to do is exactly what I've always done—exactly as I please," he told a group of Old Guard Republicans in Los Angeles.

With that, he alienated a fair number of Southern California's wealthiest political donors. They joined disaffected agricultural associations and the Hearst press—Jack Neylan had weighed in—to oppose a third term.

All the while, Knight's campaign gained momentum. Angered because the governor essentially ignored them, Old Guard–dominated Republican central committees of eight counties endorsed Knight's candidacy.

The Sacramento Bee was unimpressed when that county's central committee followed suit. Statewide, Democrats held a million-strong advantage in voter registration, political editor Herbert L. "Pete" Phillips noted. "The Republicans did not carry Warren to power in 1942 and 1946. Rather

Warren carried the GOP to power." Dropping Warren for Knight meant abandoning the vital middle.

Meanwhile, Warren used his status as the incumbent to cultivate those swing voters. Printers Union official Joseph W. Chaudet recalled the governor early on a Sunday morning at the Southern Pacific station in Santa Clara "standing out on the platform with a beautiful white mane of hair, bowing to everybody, welcoming the Santa Clara football team back from winning the Sugar Bowl in New Orleans.

"Here is Santa Clara, 99 percent Portuguese, 99 percent Catholic," Chaudet marveled. "Here is a past potentate of the Shrine. Look, by showing up he locked up every Catholic vote there for time immemorial."

All the while, Warren maintained his above-the-fray pose. He was stalling while other candidates, particularly Knight and Congressman Richard Nixon, running for the vacant United States Senate seat, organized their campaigns. Firmly independent himself, Warren wanted no one with divided loyalties in a position to claim favors.*

Near the end of 1949, Kyle Palmer privately delivered the verdict of the *Los Angeles Times:* Knight would be advised to wait his turn. Knight had a dedicated following, Palmer conceded, "not because of himself, but because of their blind hatred of Earl Warren."

Without vital newspaper support, Knight was in trouble. On January 10, 1950, he announced he would not be a candidate for governor—"for the good of the party." Three weeks later, Warren declared his intention to run for a third term.

The governor would be taking on a formidable candidate. By virtue of his name alone, James Roosevelt, oldest son of the late president, would present problems. Moreover, "after his father, he was the most personable Roosevelt," *New York Times* reporter Gladwin Hill declared.

But Roosevelt was more: a marine combat veteran in the Pacific, a good public speaker, a forceful man in his own right who enjoyed a 61 to 39 percent advantage in voter registration. He would also have the American Federation of Labor endorsement, though Warren had labor's private assurances, "We're endorsing Roosevelt, but you'll get our votes."

Roosevelt immediately lighted into Warren. "The Republican machine, with Governor Earl Warren at the controls, is trying in the same way to keep the people from realizing they are being fleeced by the power trust, the transportation trust, the oil monopoly, and a raft of other special interest

---

* Warren apparently was concerned most about the firm of Whitaker and Baxter, which managed Knight's campaign in 1942; and with Nixon's campaign manager, Murray Chotiner. Whitaker and Baxter had managed the campaigns against mandatory health insurance. Warren broke with Chotiner after the lawyer, expecting a favor in return for his political support in 1942, asked the governor not to extradite a Chotiner client to another state. Further, Warren wanted no part of a Chotiner-Nixon strategy that held a political candidate should not merely defeat, but should also destroy his opponent. (See the Mellon OH, p. 72; and the Hansen OH, p. 66.)

groups." It was time "to repudiate the crafty operations of Warren and his Republican machine . . ."

In contrast, Warren chose to stand serenely on the mountain top. He was running for reelection, he stated in his opening radio address, to continue his work on state problems, "beholden to no one but you who have elected me."

Warren came to judge this his best campaign, precisely because it was the most independent of large contributors. Trusted allies chaired the key regional committees and raised funds, men who would ask no favors for their aid. With Bill Sweigert appointed to the San Francisco Superior Court, the politically astute Verne Scoggins stepped in as campaign manager.

Warren's committees around the state raised and spent more than $293,000. Warren himself accepted additional contributions of $41,500. The campaign would be the best funded of his career.

Warren mounted only a token primary campaign. He played the role of the man of experience, the sober statesman compared to Roosevelt.

"I am going to make no grandiose promises that cannot be fulfilled," he promised. "There is no magic in government. It is a matter of training, experience, knowledge of the problems which face our state government—. and plenty of hard work."

Warren rolled up an easy victory in the Republican primary on June 6, with 1.1 million votes to a mere 120,000 for Roosevelt. On the Democratic side, Roosevelt topped Warren by a quarter-million votes. Even so, Warren's combined vote, a record, was 800,000 greater than Roosevelt's.

Chortling about Warren's total of more than two million votes, Verne Scoggins crowed to reporters, "No one is for Earl Warren except the people." Knight might have the Republican right, and Roosevelt the Democratic left; Warren had the great middle.

Warren too was in high spirits. On a balmy evening's stroll the night after the primary, he chanced upon the battered car of sixteen-year-old Robert Smith who had delivered campaign materials for Warren. Warren tucked a note under the windshield wiper, thanking Smith for his help, then adding, "But Sir, my machine always runs. Please, therefore, have yours in good order by November."

The primary behind him, the Warren family, as usual, moved to Rustic Canyon near the Santa Monica beach for the summer. The trip south in this campaign year was more important than ever, but Warren still felt uneasy in sprawling, vote-rich Los Angeles.

"I feel like a foreigner here," he confessed to Pop Small, yet it was here that he had to get enough Democratic votes to keep Roosevelt from winning.

Warren's feelings of estrangement were most apparent when he tried to deal with the candidacy of Richard M. Nixon. Nixon seemingly embodied all that Warren disliked about Los Angeles.

The second-term congressman from Whittier, his campaign bolstered by his success investigating Alger Hiss, had easily captured the Republican nomination for the open United States Senate seat. In the general election he would face Representative Helen Gahagan Douglas, an attractive motion picture actress, former opera singer, and ardent New Dealer.

Richard Nixon ran scared. No successful politician was ever so insecure as this World War II naval veteran who had grown up the eternal outsider in insular Whittier, California. A man of dark moods, he was a pragmatist who tempered his politics to the winds of public opinion, distrustful of others and distrusted in turn, "a two-fisted, four-square liar," one prominent Republican would decide later.

Four years before, Earl Warren had deliberately distanced himself from the mean-spirited attacks that Nixon had mounted against his first political opponent, incumbent Congressman Jerry Voorhis.

Warren had remained out of that race, thereby silently rebuking his fellow Republican. Despite requests, he refused to endorse Nixon—even though Democrat Voorhis was publicly quoting a letter that Republican Warren had written earlier in praise of Voorhis. That campaign, Nixon biographer Roger Morris concluded, "was the opening round in a historic antagonism."

In the four years since, Nixon had used his membership on the House Committee on Un-American Activities to advance his career. If the nation feared the communist menace, Richard Nixon would not hesitate to imply that those in the other party, even the president, were influenced or controlled by communists. His cunning anticommunism would gain him political supporters but rarely friends, while stirring an almost visceral hatred among Democrats.

This socially awkward loner found himself pitted against Douglas, a movie star married to leading man Melvin Douglas, a woman accomplished as he was not, well-liked as he was not. She had a huge advantage in party registration and would have White House support.

Earl Warren had another reason to be wary of Richard Nixon. The more conservative wing of the Republican Party saw in the thirty-seven-year-old Nixon more than an attractive candidate for the Senate. As a party loyalist, he could serve as a counterweight to the influence of the independent Earl Warren. (A small group of businessmen had already begun a secret slush fund for Nixon's political use, a fund that would later embarrass the party.)

Then there was Richard Nixon's political tutor, Murray Chotiner, "shrewd, pudgy, and unsavory." He ran the campaign on a day-to-day basis, stoking the anticommunism fires, determined not only to win, but to destroy Douglas as well.

Chotiner's scorched-earth strategy, he explained, was simple. To those who argued for a constructive campaign, "I say to you in all sincerity that if you do not deflate the opposition candidate before your own candidate gets started, the odds are that you are going to be doomed to defeat."

Warren disliked Chotiner's cynicism, *Sacramento Bee* reporter Hale Champion said. Chotiner notoriously used anything that came to hand or mind, true or not.

Earl Warren himself "was not a gentle politician," Champion added. Still, the governor was offended by the Chotiner-Nixon notion of win-at-any-cost, their repudiation of California football coach Andy Smith's long honored maxim: "It is better to lose than to win at the sacrifice of an ideal."

Warren and Nixon simply were different men, McIntyre Faries concluded. In Faries's mind, there are two types of politicians: those who worked for the people, and those who worked for themselves. Nixon worked for himself.

Shortly after the primary, Nixon traveled to Sacramento to meet with the governor. Nixon announced that the governor and would-be senator would run a joint campaign.*

"No, we're not," Warren snapped. "I never ran a campaign with anybody and I will not with you."

Nixon insisted. "You have to."

"Oh no, I don't have to."

In fact, Warren could not, without some embarrassment. A month before he had again claimed his usual nonpartisan label. "I have, to the best of my ability, tried to be governor for all of California, not for any particular group and not for any part of the state."

Nixon was demanding, in effect, that Warren, the senior man in service and office, repudiate his own policy and Republican Party practice dating to Hiram Johnson's day.

Warren was furious. He pointedly told reporters that the candidates would run independently, "as is the California custom."

California custom aside, Warren had a practical reason for refusing to endorse the congressman. Nixon had been a principal architect of the Taft-Hartley Act, which outlawed the closed shop and secondary boycotts, and curtailed union political donations. Warren enjoyed considerable support among rank-and-file union members, Democrats in the main; he risked losing this support if he suddenly backed the avowedly antiunion Nixon.

Over the five months of the campaign, Nixon and Chotiner tried repeatedly to induce Warren to endorse Nixon. Warren just as frequently declined.

Nixon was to give Warren good reason. Even as the campaign began, Warren told reporters at the national governor's conference, "None of the Republican candidates for office in California had adopted Senator McCarthy's techniques." He said he hoped none of them would.

---

* Warren's Northern California chairman maintained that prior to the primary Nixon had suggested that he and Warren run separately. It was only after Warren demonstrated his enduring popularity among the voters that Nixon sought to ride in on Warren's coattails. (See the Mellon OH, p. 23.)

Yet Richard Nixon was to do just that, in speech after speech, in a scabrous whispering campaign, and in a scurrilous flyer that came to be known in political circles as the "Pink Sheet."

Helen Gahagan Douglas was vulnerable to red-baiting. In the face of postwar anticommunist hysteria, the three-term congresswoman had voted against a succession of measures put forward as "anti-Red": Un-American Activities Committee appropriations; the Truman Doctrine; and contempt citations of the "Hollywood Ten," among other bills.

She disparaged the fear of communism in the United States, which "is being deliberately used in many quarters to blind us to our real problems . . ." By the end of summer, with American troops battling to retain a foothold in South Korea, Douglas's anticommunism appeared suspect.

At the end of August, Bernard Brennan, Nixon's campaign manager, and Chotiner compiled a sheet comparing Douglas's voting record with Vito Marcantonio of New York, the lone American Labor Party member of Congress and, in the words of the flyer, "a notorious Communist Party–liner." The two had voted together no less than 354 times in the past four years, while Nixon had voted "exactly opposite to the Douglas-Marcantonio axis."

The numbers on the broadside demonstrated Carl Sandburg's proposition that figures don't lie but liars can figure. On foreign policy and defense measures, the GOP's ultraconservative, isolationist wing similarly voted the Marcantonio "line." In fifty-three instances, Douglas and Marcantonio had joined either a House majority or a majority of Democrats voting. The Pink Sheet was tendentious by omission.

The flyer might have been just another piece of campaign abuse but for Chotiner's last-minute decision at Aldine Printing Company in Los Angeles to run it on a supply of cheap pink stock that the company wanted to get rid of. Eventually, a half-million copies of the Pink Sheet were distributed on street corners, at civic clubs, and even with paychecks across the state—the color of the paper as slyly suggestive of Douglas's politics as the purported facts were misleading.

The whispering campaign was even more pernicious, more careless with the facts, and laced with anti-Semitism. (Douglas's husband, born Hesselberg, had changed his name for professional reasons; Helen Gahagan was Scotch-Irish and Protestant by birth.)

Nixon himself drew laughs from all-male groups calling Douglas "pink right down to her underwear," or hinting with a wink and a smirk of a sexual relationship between his opponent and President Truman. In the end, Douglas was frustrated, tired, and defeated, capable only of tagging Nixon with the enduring label of "Tricky Dick."

Warren was offended by the tone of the Nixon campaign. Years later he would claim he had learned early in his career "that it is neither good politics nor good for one's own peace of mind . . . to develop hatreds merely because of political differences of opinion."

Through the fall Warren refused to endorse Nixon. As late as ten days before the election he publicly reaffirmed his independence. "I'm just interested in one campaign—my own."

At Nixon's request, *Los Angeles Times* political editor Kyle Palmer detailed Joe Holt, president of the Young Republicans and "a fellow with a considerable amount of fortitude," to dog Douglas's appearances. At each public appearance, he was to pass out copies of the Pink Sheet and heckle Douglas, demanding whether she supported Roosevelt or Warren.

Weary, her hopes fast fading, Douglas stepped into the snare. Five days before the election, she finally replied, "I hope and pray [Roosevelt] . . . will be the next governor, and he will be if Democrats vote the Democratic ticket."

The jubilant Chotiner quickly relayed Douglas's comment to Warren aboard his campaign plane. Warren stalled while an Associated Press reporter, at Palmer's instigation, continually pressed for a comment. Warren realized he was cornered. On Saturday, November 4, Scoggins released a carefully calculated statement: "The newspaper report from San Diego that Mrs. Douglas hopes and prays that Mr. Roosevelt will be the next Governor does not change my position. In view of her statement, however, I might ask her how she expects I will vote when I mark my ballot for United States Senator next Tuesday."

Warren had not actually endorsed Nixon, but Chotiner was quick to take advantage. At a hastily summoned press conference, Chotiner declared, "Every voter in California who reads his statement will realize that Earl Warren intends to mark his ballot for Dick Nixon on election day." *

Nixon made one more effort during the last weekend of the campaign. Phone banks placed an estimated one-half million anonymous telephone calls in Southern California. The caller asked, "Did you know Helen Douglas is a communist?" then abruptly hung up. It was precisely the last-minute smear that Nixon had pledged not to employ.

While Nixon ran scared, Warren campaigned serenely against Roosevelt, ahead in the polls throughout the summer and fall. Warren ignored his opponent, mentioning Roosevelt only after the Democratic candidate had charged Warren was a "labor-hater." In his last major address of the campaign, an appeal to the working men and women who formed the heart of Democratic Party registration, Warren summoned from wounded pride a righteous wrath.

He was himself the son of a workingman, Warren reminded his audience

---

* Warren may not have voted for Nixon; he never divulged that secret. At the family Christmas gathering that year, when oldest son James asked his father what he thought of Nixon, Warren replied, "Whenever he's dealing, be sure to cut the cards." (See the JWP, Box 169, File 37.)

at the Sailors' Union hall in San Francisco. "Both he and I have worked twelve hours a day, six days a week, at twenty-five cents an hour. I know what better wages mean to a home. I know what better hours mean to a family."

As governor, he had sought to improve working conditions and the lot of the workingman. "I defy him to name other states that have better labor laws concerning collective bargaining, workmen's compensation, industrial safety, social security or old age assistance. . . .

"I believe that every year in which some progress is not made for the working people of California is a poor year—a poor year for business, farming, industry, as well as labor."

Warren was closing his campaign with a clap of moral thunder.

On Tuesday, November 7, 1950, Warren and Nina met in Oakland to vote, then to have breakfast with Oliver Hamlin and his wife. They were confident about the election, but worried about their youngest daughter.

Honey Bear had been ill since Saturday morning, complaining of excruciating pain, unable to sleep at night for the agony in the muscles of her legs, arms, and back. The doctor had first suggested it was a virus, then perhaps the flu, then perhaps spinal meningitis. Only the doctor's assurance that Honey Bear's condition had improved persuaded her mother to leave on Monday night.

But the seventeen-year-old was not better. Her brother Earl discovered the next morning that a heating pad left on overnight had badly burned his sister's legs. She had felt nothing.

The family doctor, Junius Harris, examined the girl, then telephoned the Warrens in Oakland to suggest that they return immediately.

Mother and father arrived to find the hallway outside her second-floor bedroom crowded with doctors quietly talking among themselves. They had performed a spinal tap and settled upon a diagnosis: infantile paralysis.

Poliomyelitis, the summer scourge, reappeared annually, its cause never quite identified. The illness struck with high fevers, cramps, and torturous pains in the arms and legs before a lasting numbness set in. There was no cure, and recuperation was uncertain.

When her distraught parents sought to comfort her, Honey Bear whispered, "Oh, Daddy, I'm sorry I ruined your day."

Warren turned away. From her bed the frightened child could see her father standing alone in the hall. It was the first time she had ever seen him cry.

By midafternoon and her arrival at Sutter Hospital, the girl's paralysis extended from her toes to her diaphragm. It might creep higher, doctors advised, and there was always the risk of sudden death. June Harris had arranged for an experimental serum that might curb the spread of the paralysis to be flown from Chicago.

Moved into an isolation room with an iron lung ominously at the ready, Honey Bear was very frightened, but still attempting to soothe her shattered parents. It did not hurt any longer, not like it had the last few nights, she assured them. Her father withdrew to a corner of the isolation ward, slumped on the edge of a bed, weeping while doctors came and went.

Finally, late in the evening, Honey Bear urged, "Mother, take him home and make him rest."

Warren wearily returned to the mansion well after 11:00 P.M. on election night. Secretary Betty Foot Henderson was still fielding telephone calls from concerned friends in the third-floor library while listening to the radio.

Drawn by the light, Warren entered the room. He seemed pale and drawn, Henderson noted. "Betty, what are you doing here?" he asked, not surprised to see her, but almost indifferent to her reply.

"I was listening to the election returns."

"Oh," he said vaguely.

"You're winning."

"That's nice," he replied, his voice flat. It was the first election report he had heard.

"How is Honey Bear?" Henderson asked.

Warren's shoulders slumped. He gestured helplessly. The next three or four days would be crucial in determining the extent of the young woman's paralysis, he explained. Her legs were lifeless.

With his youngest daughter lying paralyzed in a hospital, his reelection seemed less than important. Still, the saddened man who made his way to bed that night had made history. He had been elected to an unprecedented third term, overwhelming Jimmy Roosevelt, 2,461,754 to 1,333,856. Warren had captured all fifty-eight counties in the state. Even in Los Angeles, where he felt so much the stranger, he rolled up 64 percent of the votes, just a fraction of a percentage point behind his statewide average.

At the same time, Richard Nixon defeated Helen Gahagan Douglas by 700,000 votes, the largest plurality for a senatorial candidate in the nation that year. Both Nixon and Warren had overcome a huge registration disparity.

San Francisco District Attorney Edmund G. Brown, a Democrat, would replace the discredited Fred Howser as attorney general. Following California custom, Warren had avoided making an endorsement in that race too, despite the fact that the Republican nominee, Edward Shattuck, was a longtime supporter. Warren assumed what he called "a benevolent neutrality" toward Brown, whom he liked personally.

On Thursday morning, a crowd of 4,000 supporters greeted Warren on the steps of the Capitol as he returned to work. He said nothing of his victory but soberly reported that Honey Bear had spent a "very satisfactory night. There has been no spread of the trouble and she has no aches, pains, and spasms." The fear of sudden death had abated.

Honey Bear's illness was to elicit an unprecedented outpouring of public affection. She was the golden girl, the fairest of three fair daughters; the newspaper photos and newsreels of her and her sisters during campaigns had made the effervescent, smiling athlete something of a celebrity.

Now she was stricken, and thousands of people wrote to offer their best wishes and encouragement. In Catholic schools around the state, children said daily prayers for her recovery.

More than twenty thousand cards, letters, and gifts from people who thought of her as a friend poured in. Those she considered special—a telegram from President Truman and a letter from singer Dinah Shore among them—Honey Bear kept under her pillow. Many more telegrams and letters were pinned to the walls of her bedroom. The bedridden girl spent hours each day reading the spidery handwriting of the elderly and the labored printing of schoolchildren. Some she answered herself. Secretaries hired with campaign funds sent thank-you notes to the balance because Warren considered this mail personal and not official business.*

For the first ten days, Betty Henderson said, the governor looked gaunt, a man burdened with grief and new responsibilities. Two weeks after Honey Bear was hospitalized, sister Dorothy suffered five cracked ribs and a punctured lung in an auto accident while coming home from a fraternity dance.

Nina and Earl shuttled between Honey Bear's bed at Sutter Hospital and Dorothy's at Mercy Hospital. Dorothy's injury was painful but not serious; her ribs would mend in time. Meanwhile, the father grieved for the once-vibrant Honey Bear, lying wan and uncomplaining in the isolation ward.

"It was just like he had been pole-axed," son Earl recalled of those frightening weeks. "He was ready to just chuck everything if it would do any good to save Honey Bear, to stay with her . . . It took my mother and other people, the doctors, close associates, to say, 'Look, you can't quit.' "

Earl Junior overheard his mother consoling an anxious father, insisting, "There's nothing that you can do that we can't do here, and you'll be moments away." There was nothing he could do that the doctors and Nina could not do better.

Honey Bear was to spend seven weeks in the hospital before doctors allowed her to return home. There her mother took charge of the young woman's care.

"She never left my side," Honey Bear recalled. "I didn't really sleep at night when I became sick. Mother stayed up with me," the two of them catnapping through the long nights of Honey Bear's convalescence.

The family would well remember Christmas, 1950. Honey Bear was strong enough to be carried downstairs to open gifts on Christmas Eve, and again the next day when the family gathered for dinner. For the Warrens, this was a year of special thanks.

Honey Bear was not only stronger each day, but her father was joyfully

* It was in connection with Honey Bear's illness that the only suggestion of Warren's taking advantage of his office turned up. A story circulated in Sacramento that the ailing girl had asked for a type of candy available only in Oakland. The governor reportedly called the highway patrol and asked that patrol officers pick up the box of candy in Oakland, then speed it by relay the eighty miles to Sacramento.

writing friends of her "almost miraculous recovery." Doctors now talked optimistically of her eventually walking again, with no permanent handicap.

Honey Bear faced eight more months of grueling physiotherapy. Her mother spent hours laying hot towels on the girl's lifeless legs—the doctors had opted for the methods developed by Sister Kenny—before Honey Bear took her first, tremulous step. As she improved, Honey Bear's room during the daylight hours became a swirl of energy. Brothers, sisters, and classmates visited each day after school, full of gossip and laughter.

The crisis receded. In off-the-record conversations with reporters, Warren acknowledged how costly was the medical care, and how burdensome the bills.

"What would the average family do if afflicted this way?" he asked. "They wouldn't have any resources to take care of it." He would make a fourth attempt to secure hospitalization insurance when the new legislature convened in January.

Governor Earl Warren could be doubly thankful that Christmas. Not only was Honey Bear on the mend, but his sweeping victory in November had reclaimed any prestige lost after the defeat two years before.

He was once again presidential timber.

CHAPTER 19

JOCKEYING THE DARK HORSE

T HIS WAS TO BE HIS YEAR. TWICE BEFORE, EARL WARREN HAD RUN
as a favorite son, less a true contender for the presidency than a
unifying figure whose candidacy would avert crippling intramural contests in California. This time out, he had his eye on the great prize.

He was sixty-one, vigorous, a proven vote-getter with a progressive record as governor. He was an attractive candidate, liberal on social issues, yet
fiscally conservative, a superior administrator with an unblemished personal
reputation. As a political moderate, he could cross party lines and appeal to
Democratic voters.

Further, in an age where television played an increasing role in political
campaigns, when the public *saw* presidential nominees for the first time, the
image of the candidate himself loomed larger perhaps than his policies,
program, or philosophy. And there, Earl Warren had an advantage over most
politicians: The governor of California exuded what a later generation
would call charisma.

On television or in person, Warren's aura seemingly magnified the man.
"Warren dominated any picture he was in," political ally Mildred Younger
said.

As youngest son Robert marveled, "People say he was a big man. He
wasn't a big man; he barely made it to six feet . . . but there was something
about him that was big."

There was a presence about the man when he walked into a room, the
son continued. "People recognized that he was the leader, but they didn't
feel intimidated by him."

As a presidential candidate, Warren had two weaknesses, one small, one large. He lacked significant experience in international affairs, a fault that could be papered over with a few speeches.

More critical, he had no national political organization or fund-raising apparatus. That would take some repair, for the resolute nonpartisanship that made Warren attractive to Democrats in California worked against him when seeking his party's nomination in Chicago.

Without any conscious plan, Warren had taken a greater interest in the world beyond California after 1945 when he formally welcomed the delegates to the founding session of the United Nations in San Francisco. He attended the inauguration of Miguel Alemán as president of Mexico the following year, then found excuses as the governor of a border state to visit that country.

An unflagging supporter of the United Nations since then, Warren went on to play a major role at successive governors' conferences in securing Republican backing for the Democratic president's foreign policy.

By August, 1951, when he traveled to Japan to meet the men of California's own National Guard division wounded in the Korean fighting, Warren's competence in the international arena at least equaled that of Ohio senator Robert A. Taft.

That all-but anointed candidate of the Republican Old Guard, however, boasted two formidable advantages over the Californian: a nationwide political organization manned by true believers and control of the party's apparatus. The Ohioan could count on large blocs of loyal delegates at the nominating convention, particularly from the South and the Midwest, where the yearning among businessmen for laissez-faire and small government was keen.

Taft's appeal ran deeply, but narrowly, too narrowly in the opinion of the more pragmatic politicians in a party out of office for twenty years.

As early as February, 1951, the new junior senator from California, Richard Nixon, was scouting for an alternative to the Ohioan. Taft was well in front, Nixon wrote the political editor of the *Los Angeles Times,* Kyle Palmer. "California, Pennsylvania and New York will probably have to get together on someone else if he is to be defeated."

The problem was to find an alternative candidate.

The former governor of Minnesota, more recently president of the University of Pennsylvania, Harold Stassen, was unabashedly eager to run. General Douglas MacArthur appealed to some, if only for his dashing image and status as a war hero; his policies beyond the Far East were unknown. Warren figured on many lists but remained silent about his plans.

Dewey personally declined a third try; he would not risk becoming a Republican William Jennings Bryan. He did, however, have a substitute in mind: General of the Army Dwight David Eisenhower, supreme commander in Europe during the war, currently commanding the North Atlantic Treaty Organization in Paris—a genial, authentic American hero.

Dewey and his former campaign manager, Herbert Brownell, had planted, then nurtured the concept of an Eisenhower candidacy. They met with the general in December, 1950, pledging their support, and with it the considerable backing of the GOP's international-minded Eastern Establishment.

The general hung back, though he was sorely disturbed by Taft's endorsement of an unrealistic "American Gibraltar" guarded by nuclear weapons. When Dewey and Brownell offered to continue their quiet exploration of a possible Eisenhower candidacy, the wary general gave tacit approval.

In search of a candidate who would represent their Eurocentric, international finance point of view, Dewey and his cohorts passed on Earl Warren. According to Brownell, Dewey rejected his former running mate for two reasons: Warren had not carried California for the ticket in 1948; and Eisenhower, who had no past political record to live down or explain away, was more popular among voters.

Sacramento Bee editor Walter P. Jones offered another reason. Warren, "pretty much of a lone wolf," would be hard to sell to the convention. "The national party bosses never did like Warren. They didn't like him in California; they didn't like him in Washington."

While kingmakers and candidates maneuvered, Earl Warren delayed his decision. A national political campaign would require a massive expenditure of time and money, and he could not devote himself to the task. As governor, he had to keep a wary eye on the state legislature; as a father he still was concerned about Dorothy and Honey Bear and for the third time in as many months, the Warren family confronted a severe illness.

Complaining of persistent shooting pains in his right arm, the governor himself was hospitalized in early February, 1951. His doctors offered a preliminary diagnosis of bursitis, an inflammation of the shoulder joint; they would later settle on the more vague "neuralgia," or convulsive pain along a neural path.

"It's a politician's problem," his doctor told reporters, brought on by "shaking so many hands."

Warren would be away from his desk for nineteen days, the agonizing pain finally subdued, though not eradicated for another two months. Typically, he was stoic, son Robert said. "I think he just felt it was his soreness and there was no need to pass it on to anyone else."

Meanwhile, Honey Bear continued her arduous physical therapy, equally uncomplaining and resolute. Despite a momentary alarm that the disease might have returned, the young woman was making "remarkable progress. She is swimming daily, and is able to walk a bit," her father wrote FBI director J. Edgar Hoover in mid-April.*

---

* By June, 1951, Honey Bear was well enough to walk across the stage and accept her high school diploma. In September she was able to travel by train to New York City with her mother and sisters for a vacation. She would gain nationwide attention for her pluck when she laughingly told reporters that getting her father to take her sightseeing in New York City was harder than beating polio.

Back at his desk, with his daughter recovering, Warren could once more focus on a possible presidential campaign. In the optimism of that spring, a year before the Republican national convention, Warren decided he would run.

He made no public announcement, but apparently dropped enough hints that party leaders and political reporters alike sniffed out his strategy. "Without any question," Lieutenant Governor Goodwin Knight advised the head of the FBI office in Los Angeles, "Governor Warren will seek the Republican nomination for the presidency as a compromise candidate."

Speculation about a Warren candidacy increased with a Gallup Poll in July, 1951, showing the governor easily besting President Truman in a "trial heat." Warren topped the president 52 to 29 percent, with the balance undecided.

More important to the political professionals, among independents—the swing voters who decide elections—Warren outpolled Truman by a 3 to 1 margin.

Anticipating a Warren candidacy, a group of Republican county chairmen gathered secretly in San Francisco in October, 1951, to weigh organizing an alternative slate for the June primary.

When the *Chronicle*'s Earl "Squire" Behrens broke the story of the Palace Hotel meeting on October 11, 1951, a spokesman for the insurgents denied that it was primarily an anti-Warren move. If elected, the unpledged delegation would cast its seventy votes for a true conservative yet to be chosen. The spokesman named Senator Taft, General MacArthur, and Illinois senator Everett Dirksen as alternatives.

The governor was, in the eyes of the conservatives, a traitor to Republican tenets. He favored big government, particularly on social issues, and expanding international entanglements, spokesmen for the insurgents argued. Warren might claim to be a moderate, but he pushed a liberal agenda.

Certainly by 1951, Warren's legislative program was predictable. He would propose measures to expand schools, parks, highways, and other public services necessary to serve a population doubling every twenty years. He would advocate a clutch of social welfare programs—health insurance, enhanced disability benefits, child care centers, fair employment laws, among others—not always expecting to get them but sometimes to educate the legislators.

Warren did advance bold proposals, but he was rarely the pioneer. Instead, the best ideas simmered for a while in the public prints or, like the highway program, were tested in other states before he adopted them.

Once settled on a program, Warren was unswerving. Old allies such as the state Chamber of Commerce, the Associated Farmers, and California's oil companies might by "strenuous and callous [lobbying] . . . wave back the tide," but their arguments that California was already too generous to the less fortunate were "as phony as any three-dollar bill you ever saw."

Warren the Progressive clung to no orthodoxy; no convenient political label quite fit. While Republicans such as Joseph McCarthy and Richard Nixon attacked Democrats as "soft on communism," Warren remained skeptical of both the claim and the menace. He was privately critical when Republican governors of Nebraska and Maine proposed that their states investigate "subversive" activities. He wanted no amateur witchhunters defaming the innocent.

When President Truman in April recalled General of the Army Douglas MacArthur for flouting orders, Republicans across the country leaped to the general's defense. On the floor of the Senate, Richard Nixon charged MacArthur's recall would make "the communists and the stooges for communists happy."

Earl Warren avoided such overheated rhetoric. Of MacArthur's recall he merely clucked, "It is a sad ending to the military career of the world's greatest soldier. I do not have sufficient details to comment further at this time."

However often he took the solitary path, Warren was also careful to maintain his credentials as leader of the Republican Party in California. This was his political base. He signed Republican-drafted redistricting bills that carved out congressional districts for seven new representatives and redrew lines to accommodate the state's population growth. The redistricting—Democrats preferred to label it gerrymandering—preserved Republican majorities in both the state legislature and the Congress, no small feat in a state where Democrats outnumbered Republicans six to four.

His credentials polished, Warren moved to isolate the alienated conservatives.

In mid-October, *Los Angeles Times* political editor Kyle Palmer reported from Washington that neither Senator Taft nor the still unannounced Dwight Eisenhower would enter the California primary. The carefully framed story quoted one "leading Eisenhower backer" who declared: "We haven't given a thought to wasting our time out there; Warren would beat Taft, Eisenhower and any others who might be unwise enough to tackle him."

Three weeks later, fourteen prominent California Republicans signed a letter urging Warren to become a candidate for president. The November 8 letter was signed by both United States senators, Knowland and Nixon, the national committeeman and -woman, the chairman and vice chairman of the California Republican Party, the leaders of both houses of the state legislature, six congressmen, and the constitutional officers—with the singular exception of Lieutenant Governor Knight. Within days forty-eight additional party leaders would sign what had become a Republican Party loyalty oath.

The letter was the "draft" that Earl Warren sought whenever he ran for statewide office, the summons that allowed him to mask his own ambition.

At the same time, the letter doubled as a preemptive strike against the anti-Warren right. It signaled that the "official" party had lined up behind the governor. By isolating the right wing, the GOP might avert a divisive primary.

In years past, such a move would have been sufficient to put down the rebellion. This year Warren and Verne Scoggins failed to appreciate the depth of the long-throttled rancor of the Republican right.

The November 8 draft and Warren's subsequent announcement came earlier than he intended. In a state where candidates preferred to delay throwing their hat in the ring "until the snow was on the Sierras," Warren's stomach had set its own timetable.

He first felt the ache in his gut in early November, each day the pain more insistent and each day less easily dismissed. After a week, the knot burned so fiercely that he abruptly broke off a meeting in his office to see a specialist in internal medicine.

Dr. Herzl Friedlander was comparatively new to Sacramento when the governor's office called for an appointment. Because of Friedlander's extensive experience treating infantile paralysis victims, June Harris had asked him to consult on Honey Bear's treatment. The grateful governor later attributed his daughter's recovery to Friedlander; now he wanted Friedlander to check him over.

The pain was on Warren's right side. His blood count was normal, all but ruling out an inflammatory disease or even appendicitis. Friedlander, who suspected something more grave, and Harris agreed that Warren should be examined at Sutter Hospital.

The barium X rays confirmed Friedlander's suspicion; Warren had a malignant growth in the right colon. With an immediate operation the prognosis was excellent.

Harris told Warren of the cancer diagnosis in a meeting at the governor's mansion, the doctor concerned with the urgency of medical treatment, the patient with maintaining secrecy.

Warren was poised to announce that he would be a candidate for president of the United States. In that age of fear, any hint of cancer would destroy his candidacy before it even began.

Warren and Harris devised a cover story. Because the appendix lies on the right side, appendicitis was "an opportune diagnosis" to use rather than state Warren had colon cancer, Dr. Friedlander explained later.

The true nature of the illness was closely held. "Harris supervised everything, down to what my people could say to the press," Verne Scoggins acknowledged. Even the children were not to be told their father was suffering from colon cancer.

On November 14, 1951, Warren announced at a press conference that he would be a candidate for the Republican presidential nomination. His statement, read before a bank of klieg lights and television cameras, was sober: "The presidency of the United States is a position of unlimited requirement. No man could have all the capabilities required by it. The best that can be expected is that the President, whoever he may be, will grow to required stature through the faithful assumption of his great responsibilities."

A favorite son for the moment, he told the reporters he would defer any decision about running in other states. Whatever he decided would "be done first in the interests of my country, second in the interests of my party, and lastly in my own interests."

The next day, the cover story now in effect, Warren announced that doctors had ordered him into the hospital for an immediate check-up. Appearing pale and drawn, he told reporters that for the past three weeks he had been suffering from intermittent and sometimes severe stomach pains.

To a handful of his staff and to Lieutenant Governor Knight, Warren confided that he expected to have his appendix removed. "The only time Earl Warren showed any emotion in my presence was the afternoon he was leaving for the hospital in San Francisco to have his appendectomy," Pop Small wrote later in his unpublished memoirs. "There were tears in his eyes as he wrung my hand and said good-bye."

Warren entered the University of California hospital in San Francisco on November 16, after recording a long-scheduled speech and radio broadcast before the Republican State Central Committee. That speech, a formal statement of his personal and political credo, staked out a wide range of liberal positions.

The country and the Republican Party could not stand still, Warren argued. The nation could confront its domestic problems or "try to go back to what is often called 'the good old days' by letting nature take its course. To do the latter would be fatal."

The international conflict with the Soviet Union, which "may last years or even a generation," was not an excuse to turn away from domestic reform, Warren said. "We must recognize the right of every segment of our society to a measure of security . . ." Among other programs, he endorsed slum clearance and public housing, universal medical care on reasonable terms, and public education from kindergarten through college.

In the international arena too, the Republican Party had to meet the challenges of a world still recovering from catastrophic war, the governor asserted. "We cannot afford to equivocate between world co-operation and isolation. We cannot believe or practice both at the same time. In our foreign policy we are committed to bipartisanship."

The San Diego speech reflected Earl Warren's political maturation, from Progressive Republican to Republican progressive. He was endorsing, indeed embracing, concepts given lip-service in the party platforms in 1944 and 1948 but scorned between times—all the while maintaining he represented the majority of Republicans.

The candidate listened to his recorded speech from his hospital bed in San Francisco. Five days after Warren was admitted, a team of surgeons removed two feet of his colon, and with it the cancerous tissue.

That afternoon, June Harris released a bulletin announcing that Warren had been operated on for "intra-abdominal adhesions caused by a series of appendix flareups. The adhesions as well as the appendix were removed."

Warren's recovery was uneventful, if slow. He left the hospital on November 30 to continue his recovery at the mansion, followed by a one-week trip to Hawaii with Nina and Honey Bear at the beginning of the year.

Warren's cover story began to fray almost immediately. Too many people —surgeons, radiologists, pathologists, and nurses—knew he had been operated on for colon cancer. Finally, a reporter at his first press conference upon returning to work asked bluntly, "Is it true your operation was for cancer?"

Warren exploded, suspecting that the leak had come from an opponent who wanted to hurt him politically, perhaps someone at the hospital who opposed his mandatory health insurance plan.

He neither affirmed nor denied the story. "I'll show the world during the next few weeks that I'm a long ways from dying," Warren barked.

The rumors persisted. Former President Herbert Hoover, no ally, assured forty leaders of the GOP at a private dinner party that Warren's candidacy could be written off. "They opened him up, took a look, and sewed him up again."

Warren suffered the gossip in silence. Ordered to go slowly by his doctors, he went for long drives into the foothills of the Sierra Nevada, chauffeured by Capitol Police Officer Edgar "Pat" Patterson.

One day, sitting under a tree in the mountains, Patterson mused, "You know, you and I, we would not be here if you were black."

"What do you mean?" Warren asked.

"Your life would have been different. You never would have been governor. You never would have been attorney general. Your whole life would have been different."

The black chauffeur and nominal bodyguard told him of black college graduates working on garbage trucks or as waitresses because there were no other jobs open to them; of white-only hotels; of how little had changed from Patterson's boyhood in New Orleans.

"We discussed how slow the country was in getting rid of discrimination. I told him that when I was a little boy I had to pass by a white school to get to the black school, and I knew I would have to fight or run . . .

"And we also talked about places I couldn't eat in when I was little, places that had a sign on the door, 'Whites Only,' and I . . . felt like tearing the sign down and going in there.

" 'Why didn't you do it?' he asked.

"I told him I didn't want to get beat up."

Jim Crow lived, even in California. Sacramento still had white-only neighborhoods, guarded by unconstitutional restrictive covenants and wink-of-the-eye real estate practice. There were still restaurants that refused to serve blacks, and stores where Patterson and his wife were not welcome to shop. There were still jobs closed to them because of the color of their skin.

Sometimes Warren would get angry, "very angry," Patterson recalled. "A lot of laws are being broken," Warren fumed, yet there was no enforcement.

The state needed a Fair Employment Practices Commission and fair housing laws, but bills to create these lay dormant in committee. However much Warren personally desired to end discrimination, Patterson agreed, the governor could not move too fast. He first had to bring public opinion around.

"You know, we have to be very careful who we fight and whether we are going to win," Warren cautioned.

It was good advice in the rough and tumble of this political year of 1952. Warren was to discover that he could not pick all of his fights; indeed, he would not learn, until it was too late, just who his enemies were.

On January 6, 1952, Eisenhower supporter Henry Cabot Lodge announced that he was asking the governor of New Hampshire to enter Eisenhower's name in the Republican primary. The heretofore apolitical general was in sympathy with "enlightened Republican doctrine" and would accept that party's nomination.

In Honolulu where he was recuperating, Warren graciously welcomed Eisenhower into the race. "The General will be a very powerful candidate," he told reporters, waving aside as "premature" a question about Eisenhower's chances.

Six time zones from New Hampshire, the vacationing Warren understood that the political equation had abruptly changed. The GOP's influential Eastern Establishment had persuaded Eisenhower to run for the presidency. They were sure to back Eisenhower with everything they could muster in delegate strength and dollars. With that backing, the centrist Eisenhower became the major challenger to Taft, the conservative. Warren could become the party's presidential nominee now only if the convention deadlocked between the front-runners, then turned to him as a compromise.

"My father realized," son Earl Junior said, "he's riding a dark horse, or at least a pretty gray one."

To keep slender hope alive, Warren first had to secure his base, California's seventy convention votes. In years past they had been his for the asking; this year he confronted a coalition of reactionaries led by an obscure congressman from Bakersfield, Thomas H. Werdel.

Werdel was a figurehead "favorite son," tapped only after Nixon, Hoover, and MacArthur declined to run. He was a spoiler, intended to deprive Earl Warren of California's convention votes. If he won the primary, Werdel promised, he would release his delegates upon their arrival at the convention.

Werdel had entered the list because "the candidacy of Earl Warren is neither genuine nor sincere." When other candidates declined to challenge Warren on his own turf, Werdel's backers argued, California Republicans were left without a meaningful primary vote. They could stay at home on election day or vote for the despised Warren delegation; they could not vote for their preferred candidate, whether it be Taft, MacArthur, Stassen, or Eisenhower.

Warren had no chance of winning the Republican nomination for president, Werdel's people claimed. "The voters are disenfranchised so that once again the governor may go horse-trading as a favorite son," John Francis Neylan charged. The governor's candidacy was no more than a bid for political leverage to assure himself appointment to the Supreme Court of the United States.

It was some measure of the conservatives' fury that the Werdel slate raised a reported $500,000 for the primary. Superior Oil president William Keck contributed $350,000 to the campaign, and San Diego banker-developer C. Arnholt Smith also kicked in large sums.

The California primary of June, 1952, was to be a test of ideologies. In an open letter to Warren, John A. "Black Jack" Smith—brother of C. Arnholt and lobbyist for Keck—charged the governor had "abandoned Republicanism and embraced the objectives of the New Deal." The governor had also "aided and abetted Communism" in opposing loyalty oaths, and he was attempting "to ram socialized medicine down the throats of the people."

In principle, Warren was tolerant of political opposition, but tolerance had its limits. Two days before the primary, the very conservative Reverend James Fifield of Los Angeles's affluent First Congregational Church devoted his sermon to flailing the Warren administration as corrupt.

Warren was stung. He devoted a portion of his campaign windup to savage the men behind the Werdel candidacy as "venomous and scurrilous." The "huge sums" they had lavished on billboards, direct mail, radio broadcasts, and newspaper advertisements were an attempt "to buy an election" and represented "a very serious menace to the free elective process itself," he declared.

Some of the anger stemmed from frustration. While Werdel and the men behind him had ample funds, a shortage of money hindered Warren throughout the campaign. With only a small bank account and no national organization to raise more, Warren could campaign in just two states beyond California: Oregon and Wisconsin.

Warren campaigned under another handicap. With the legislature in session, he could leave the state only three days a week. His travel schedule was grueling, and it left Dr. Friedlander treating the rundown candidate for a perpetual cold much of the spring.

In wintry Wisconsin, where he ran against Taft, Warren found himself an unwilling stand-in for the absent Eisenhower but without Eisenhower's resources. He nonetheless came in just 54,000 votes behind the well-funded Taft on April 3.

The Ohioan, with 42 percent of the vote, picked up twenty-four delegates. Because of a lopsided apportionment that favored rural districts, Warren's 35 percent of the vote netted just six delegates from urban Milwaukee and Madison.

In Oregon, meanwhile, Eisenhower's managers ran a well-financed, well-oiled operation. Crushed in the May 6 primary, 136,000 to 32,000, Warren gained no convention delegates. If he had hoped to demonstrate that his appeal to voters extended beyond the California state line, he had failed.

Warren stumped his home state only in the last two weeks before the June 3 primary. Almost disdainful, Warren raked the opposition as a gaggle of "disappointed office seekers, disgruntled legislators, and outsiders who want to run the government," all backed by "enormous sums of money spent in anger rather than reason."

Despite a token campaign in which he spent just $76,156, Warren scored an almost 2 to 1 victory. He tallied 994,220 votes to Werdel's 508,251.

The delegation was his, and with it seventy votes on the floor of the Republican National Convention.* He was off to Chicago to confront Richard Nixon's ambition.

---

* This campaign marked the political birth of the radical right in national politics. Werdel would run in 1956 for vice president on an Independent States' Rights ticket headed by T. Coleman Andrews. In 1962, Loyd Wright unsuccessfully challenged Warren's appointee to the United States Senate, Thomas Kuchel. Wright's campaign chairman was an actor who had recently taken up conservative causes, Ronald Reagan.

CHAPTER 20

HONORABLE MEN

T HE SEVENTEEN CARS OF THE WESTERN PACIFIC CONVENTION SPE-
cial lumbered from the Sacramento train yards, bound for
Chicago and the twenty-fifth national convention of the Republican Party. On board the "G.O.P.," the candidate, his wife and three daughters, delegates and alternates, reporters and staff members sweltered, cursing
an inadequate air-conditioning system.

With nightfall and the run through the Feather River gorge, the stifling
heat eased, and impromptu parties broke out up and down the train. In the
parlor of the observation car the laughing Warren girls danced to music from
a radio. Nearby a relaxed Earl Warren chatted with his political advisers. He
was going into the convention as a long shot, with the votes of seventy-six
delegates, a small number, but enough to give him credibility.

Their convention strategy was simple: hold those delegates as long as
Warren had "a reasonable chance," while Robert Taft and Dwight Eisenhower scrambled for votes among the remaining uncommitted. The Californians would wait, doing nothing, careful to alienate no one.

In the meantime, Warren had rejected all overtures, firmly and publicly.
As recently as the week before boarding the train, Warren issued a last
disavowal of any cabinet or Supreme Court appointment in exchange for
those seventy-six convention votes.

Warren's hang-back strategy depended upon a deadlock, with neither of
the leading candidates able to secure a majority on the first three roll calls.
With the fourth ballot, the dark horse would make his move.

Warren was traveling to Chicago on this third day of July, 1952, carrying a secret promise from Cornelius Haggerty, state chairman of the American Federation of Labor. More than one hundred delegates with ties to labor would shift to Warren if Eisenhower did not make it by the third ballot.

Erosion of that magnitude could trigger mass defections, and a landslide in Warren's favor. "He had a lot of support from the Midwest; the populist-minded were ready and wanted to jump," son Earl said later.

"He honestly believed a deadlock was possible and he would benefit. There was no place else anybody could go."

Warren's plan was simple—and flawed. He had failed to take into account the junior senator from California.

Richard Milhous Nixon was a man, in the words of writer Richard Rovere, whose political flexibility suggested "an almost total indifference to policy."

On domestic issues, Nixon voted as conservatively as Taft. He had opposed civil rights legislation in committee, and voted against conservation, flood control, and public power bills. On international questions, his views were conditioned by a posturing anticommunism and a belief that the United States must direct world affairs.

If any single characteristic marked the man, it was gnawing ambition. As early as June, 1951, just six months a United States senator, Richard Nixon had set his cap for the presidency. Nixon's closest advisers were convinced that their man would run for governor in 1954, then leap from Sacramento to the White House in 1960.

Instead, Nixon had another plan in mind, one that pitted him against Earl Warren for control of the seventy votes of the California delegation.

Warren and five trusted advisers had met early in 1952 to select his delegation, a delicate task of weighing each possible delegate's ego, obligations, and political clout.

As they began a marathon eleven-hour session, Mac Faries asked Warren, "Now, what do you want to get here? People who are definitely committed to you . . . or are they chosen as representatives of the Republicans in the area?"

They were to represent the local party, Warren instructed. But, he cautioned, "this is my delegation." If they agreed to be delegates, they were required by law to declare themselves for Warren and pledge to support him "as nominee of my party for President of the United States."

Faries was troubled with the names before them. "A lot of these people, while they'll sign up to support you, are not definitely *for* you. There is an increasing Eisenhower movement here," he warned.

"If they sign up, I will trust them on their support," the governor replied.

Congressional district by congressional district the committee discussed the best local representatives. It grew late, with delegates from Southern California still to be chosen. The group decided Bernard Brennan, former campaign manager for both Warren and Nixon, would fill out the slate.

In selecting the at-large delegates, Warren and his advisers had routinely enrolled Richard Nixon. The junior senator abruptly declined the appointment.

"This was a sign to Warren," Brennan told biographer Leo Katcher, "that Nixon had ideas of his own that had no relation to Warren. It would have been a slap in the face for Warren if Nixon was not on the slate."

Seeking the appearance of unity, Bill Knowland, in political philosophy a Taft man, undertook to bring Nixon back into the fold. Nixon acceded, but only after exacting a price.

"We permitted Brennan to name six or seven of Senator Nixon's stalwart supporters in addition to the senator himself," Warren acknowledged. They, like Nixon, were committed by their signed pledge until Warren released them.

Warren also reluctantly accepted Nixon's political adviser Murray Chotiner as nominal manager of the southern section of the convention train. Nixon agreed that Chotiner was merely to handle physical arrangements.

"The names in the southern half of the state, in terms of commitment to Warren, did not receive the scrutiny as the names in the top half of the state received," committee member Laughlin Waters acknowledged.

"The end result was that we had, in essence, a split delegation," about evenly divided among Warren, Eisenhower, and Taft supporters.

Though legally bound to Warren by virtue of his pledge filed with the California secretary of state on April 7, 1952, Nixon had long since written off Warren as a viable candidate. To Bill Knowland, who held Taft as his second choice, Nixon hinted that he too favored Taft's candidacy. Nixon promised that "once"—not "if"—Warren released his delegates they "would be free to look over the field and select the man best qualified to carry the Republican banner . . ."

Nixon had no doubt who that man was. Indeed, he was plumping for second place on an Eisenhower ticket.

Eisenhower's handlers had first weighed Nixon as vice presidential material early in 1952. Massachusetts senator Henry Cabot Lodge, a member of the Eisenhower inner council, approached Nixon on the Senate floor "well before the convention . . ."

Would he be interested in the vice presidency?

"Who wouldn't?" Nixon replied frankly.

They needed someone in California to "hold the line for the general," Lodge explained. Nixon was their choice.

"We had some very practical thoughts about Nixon," Lodge explained later. "We needed a counter to Taft in California, and Nixon was it. It was Nixon's role to keep California from going to Taft."

His reward would be the vice presidency.

Eisenhower's managers had settled on Nixon two months before the convention opened. They saw him as young, a navy veteran, and an effective public speaker with a superlative domestic record. All that made him the ideal complement to the older Eisenhower. Moreover, Nixon's friendly ties to the Taft wing would help to unite the party behind Eisenhower.

On May 8, 1952, at the Roosevelt Hotel in New York City, Tom Dewey offered Nixon second place on an Eisenhower ticket.* Nixon promptly accepted.

As the GOP convention neared, Taft and Eisenhower appeared in a dead heat, each with approximately 450 delegate votes. Nixon assured the *Los Angeles Times* that the state delegation with its seventy votes "is in a position to name the Republican nominee for President."

While Warren had personally disavowed any desire to be a kingmaker—to say anything else was to admit he was not a serious candidate—Nixon moved to lead the delegation into the Eisenhower camp.

To do that, he first had to loosen Warren's grip.

Under his United States Senate frank, Nixon mailed on June 11 a questionnaire to 23,000 Californians who had contributed to or worked in his senatorial race two years before.† Warren, the accompanying letter stated, had announced that if he could not win, he would release his delegates. Given that eventuality, Nixon asked his supporters to name "the strongest candidate the Republicans could nominate for President."

Word of the ostensibly secret poll promptly leaked, infuriating Warren's people. After all, argued Thomas Mellon, the Northern California campaign manager, "If you're going strongly for the head of the delegation who is the candidate for the presidency, you don't ask each member of the delegation who the second choice would be."

Then *Los Angeles Times* political editor Kyle Palmer learned, probably from Nixon himself, that the poll gave overwhelming support to Eisenhower. Palmer telephoned Warren.

The governor was furious. "I told Palmer," Warren recalled for his memoirs, "that was not consistent with the oath that all the delegates had taken to support my candidacy."

Warren dispatched Nixon ally Bernard Brennan to Washington to make certain the tallies were not released. Nixon agreed, but the poll results, ostensibly known to only a single secretary, leaked anyway. The Warren camp seethed.

---

* Former Congressman Patrick J. Hillings confirmed the date in a letter to the author dated August 5, 1991. "Nixon told me of Dewey's comments after the Al Smith dinner, and I heard about them from Dewey himself and another person who was present."

† Warren biographer John Weaver notes that Nixon, in his exculpatory "Checkers" speech of September 23, 1952, explaining an $18,000 slush fund, claimed "that the taxpayers have never paid one dime for expenses which I thought were political and shouldn't be charged to the taxpayers." (Weaver, p. 182, fn.; JWP, Box 120, File 175.) After the *San Francisco News* publicly broke the story on September 26, 1952, Murray Chotiner confirmed in *The New York Times* of October 3, 1952, that Nixon had used his franking privilege for this political poll. Nixon biographer Stephen E. Ambrose asserts that "Nixon's use of the franking privilege was illegal but commonplace." (Vol. I, p. 255.)

Palmer in his *Times* column on June 10 undertook to instruct the un-named Nixon: "Honorable men don't stab their friends—or enemies—in the back."

Chastised but not chastened, Richard Nixon waited for the next opportunity.

Three weeks later, the Warren convention special snaked through the night toward Chicago. In Denver, Nixon joined the train, fresh from platform hearings in the convention city, full of gossip, soundings, rumor, and sly maneuver.

What took place on that July 4 night, as the Convention Special raced across the prairies would be shrouded in conjecture for years to come. (Even those who were on the train, both Warren and Knowland later maintained, did not know for sure.)

Senator and governor met in Warren's private compartment with a small group of their closest aides. Over a late dinner, Warren asked, "Dick, what do you hear?"

They talked for an hour. In frank terms, said a Nixon partisan who was present, Nixon told Warren it had come down to Taft and Eisenhower.

"He didn't get into saying that Warren couldn't win," Congressman Patrick J. Hillings recalled many years later. "I don't know if anyone brought it up, but it was assumed that we were certainly not going to sabotage Warren in any way."

Nixon left Warren to make his way forward to Car 101 just behind the locomotive. Nixon stopped to speak with a handful of favored reporters while Bernard Brennan nervously hovered nearby. Nixon advised that an early nomination was possible, but if neither Taft nor Eisenhower emerged a winner, the convention could deadlock. "In the event of a deadlock, Governor Warren becomes immediately a forefront runner."

In the first car of the train, Nixon "gave his own followers a rundown on the latest preconvention developments. In essence, he reported that the Eisenhower drive was picking up and said it looked as though the General would win on the first ballot," according to Nixon's friendly biographer Earl Mazo.

The junior senator went further, much further, according to Nixon delegate John Dinkelspiel. Dinkelspiel entered the crowded compartment just as Nixon urged that California back Eisenhower. If California announced for Eisenhower, Nixon suggested, they could stop any Taft surge.

As Dinkelspiel recalled Nixon's briefing, the senator suggested "either that the delegation should not vote for Warren on the first ballot . . . or if he insisted that the delegation keep its pledge, that it be made known in advance that the delegation at least on the second ballot would vote for Eisenhower rather than Taft . . ."

Nixon argued repeatedly that this was "the only realistic position to insure [sic] that Eisenhower, rather than Taft, would be the candidate."

After a quarter-century out of office, Pat Hillings added, the Republican desire to win was so compelling that even party regulars who normally would have backed Taft were flocking to Eisenhower. This was not a matter of ideology, but "of who was most electable," the old pol or the war hero.

Unspoken, but threaded through the conversation in Car 101, was the question of Warren's abilities as a campaigner beyond the borders of California.

"Had he done enough, was he an addition to the ticket in '48? Was he really a saleable candidate nationwide? That as opposed to Eisenhower's popularity was the thing that festered," then-political newcomer Robert Finch said.

Those in the crowded compartment urged Nixon to speak out, to help them persuade the governor "it was going to be either Eisenhower or Taft," as Hillings put it.

Across the passageway, Warren supporter Tom Mellon lay awake in his darkened roomette, listening to the sometimes vehement conversation through the open doors. "I think he [Nixon] was making an effort to live up to his commitment to Warren, but they were really putting the heat on him."

In the end, Mellon decided, Nixon "really fell down. He didn't have quite the courage to meet the commitment he had made."

Hillings and Brennan left the ever more crowded compartment to talk with Warren delegates—"to try and get the people who were Warren friends to put pressure on the governor to see if he couldn't realize the facts of life."

It was either Taft or Eisenhower, they argued repeatedly. If Warren released his delegates, California could put Eisenhower over the top on the first ballot, Hillings stressed.

"As expected," Earl Mazo wrote in his authorized biography of Richard Nixon, "bits and pieces of the Nixon report filtered through the non-Nixon sections of the train. Warren men became furious."

"The chemistry on the train had changed," reporter Richard Bergholz said. Rumors raced from Pullman to Pullman.

Then-Assemblyman Laughlin Waters, a Warren delegate, recalled "there were kind of rumbles of what was going on." Waters was convinced that Nixon's emissaries were working the delegates, pressing them to renege on their signed pledge.

Nina Warren got wind of the whispering campaign, and passed the news to her husband.

Warren demurred. "Dick would never do anything like that." *

He would change his mind, however. By the morning of July 5, Warren "seemed gripped by an icy fury," reporter Carl Greenberg noted.

---

* Congressman Hillings commented in an interview on July 26, 1991: "The only thing that I resented is that word got out that we were sabotaging Warren, trying to stop Warren from being president. I don't think that was ever the case at all. He never had a chance in the first place."

The governor had learned that Nixon was suggesting that Bill Knowland would be a good man for vice president "and who heard of two men from the same state on the ticket?" Greenberg asked rhetorically.

Nixon had entered a stalking horse in the race. Bill Knowland's name, not Nixon's, would plant the notion of abandoning Warren for whatever advantage California could wrest.

With Chicago just hours away, the Californians were badly splintered. The Sacramento crowd, as Hillings called Warren's people, was angry; the frustrated Southern Californians were sullen and resentful.

Brennan protested that he had worked the delegates only to persuade them to switch to Eisenhower if Warren dropped out. "Warren was convinced otherwise," Pop Small wrote later.

At least some of Nixon's people were ready to bolt. Insurance man Frank Jorgensen, a Nixon stalwart, noted, "It became apparent that some of the delegates would desert Warren on the second ballot"—with or without Warren's release.

When the The Sacramento Bee's "Pete" Phillips, asked about the rampant rumors, Warren issued a pointed rephrasing of Kyle Palmer's column of three weeks earlier: "A delegate cannot break his pledge and still be a man of honor. People of honor keep their word; people of dishonor don't."

The paternal lecture infuriated those closest to Nixon. At least twenty-five delegates were "simmering with anger," reporter Carl Greenberg wrote authoritatively. The delegation was sundered.

Nixon and Hillings left the train at Englewood station, the last stop before Chicago, then took a cab to their hotel. Nixon wanted to avoid the press and questions about a Warren candidacy.

On Saturday, July 5, the "G.O.P." eased to a halt on a siding in the Chicago train yard. The welcoming committee consisted only of a half-dozen bus drivers hired by Murray Chotiner to transport the delegates. Banners draped on their buses incongruously urged "Eisenhower for President."

Oscar Jahnsen dashed around the buses, yanking down the Eisenhower banners and rigging Warren signs while a fourteen-piece brass band mindlessly blared "California, Here I Come" time after time.

It was a shabby welcome made worse when Warren learned that Brennan had persuaded the Knickerbocker to host a complimentary cocktail reception for Nixon. At Warren's instruction, Mac Faries persuaded Nixon that the reception should fete the entire delegation.

They were a restive group. Delegate Grant C. Ehrlich of Santa Barbara, friend of Nixon and dedicated Eisenhower man, told reporters he might ask Warren to release the delegation before the first roll call.

Knowland managed to suppress a revolt only by threatening to poll the California delegation on the convention floor. A roll call would force the rebels, one by one, to publicly declare themselves as oathbreakers.

The tired delegates, cranky and fractious, caucused an hour after arriving at the hotel. The governor spoke briefly, conciliatory, dismissing rumors of dissension. He was in it to stay, he assured them. "You trust me and I'll trust you."

Sunday evening the delegates caucused once more, this time to weigh a change of the convention rules. They gathered keenly aware that their decision on the so-called Fair Play Amendment could well determine the party's nominee.

In six southern states, rival delegations pledged to Taft and Eisenhower contended for eighty-five seats on the convention floor. Each faction claimed to be the legitimate delegation; each demanded to be seated.

With the delegates so evenly divided as the convention opened, whoever held those eighty-five votes would gain a big, perhaps decisive, advantage in the scramble for the presidential nomination. Taft had an edge; he controlled the Credentials Committee.

Eisenhower's advisers had fashioned a three-step strategy to bar the challenged Taft delegates. When the Credentials Committee delivered its expected report on the floor of the convention, the Eisenhower forces would move to reject it.

Under convention rules, however, the challenged pro-Taft delegates were permitted to vote on their own seating. If they voted, Taft would surely carry the day, and with it the nomination.

Eisenhower's managers proposed a "Fair Play Amendment" to change the convention rules before the Credentials Committee delivered its report. If adopted, the amendment would prevent the challenged delegates from voting on their own fate.

The vote on Monday, July 7, would be a close measure of the comparative floor strength of the Taft and Eisenhower forces. *The New York Times* projected that "the balance of power on the delegate contest issue will rest with the delegates now uncommitted or pledged to vote for favorite son candidates." California's seventy votes would count for much.

By the time the California delegation met on Sunday evening, the Credentials Committee had seated sixty-eight contested delegates from Texas, Georgia, and Louisiana. Fifty of these were Taft men, eighteen Eisenhower votes. Advantage: Taft.

As delegation chairman, Knowland proposed they divide their vote equally between the ayes and nays. They would thereby remain neutral, alienating neither Taft nor Eisenhower factions. In effect, he was backing the Credentials Committee's report and Taft—yet keeping Warren's hopes alive should a deadlock develop.

Nixon argued that supporting the Fair Play Amendment was a "moral issue." The Eisenhower delegates had won their seats in local caucuses, then had been jobbed out of them by Taft's old pols.

Citing press reports that Taft was leading in the delegate count by as many as one hundred votes, Nixon argued that the only realistic position was to support the amendment and, with it, Dwight Eisenhower. They would thwart Taft and keep Warren's compromise candidacy alive.

Presidential candidate Earl Warren, California's own, held the decisive vote. Under the unit rule, his one-third of the votes, thrown one way or the other, would determine how all seventy delegates from California voted on the issue.

Warren was the last to address the caucus. What he said in that crowded room would determine his political future.

As Tom Mellon remembered the governor's talk in the tense conference, Warren offered his own estimate of the Taft-Eisenhower race. Warren disagreed with Nixon's analysis; Eisenhower's campaign was gathering momentum, he stated.

Given that, Warren continued, "Well, of course I'd enjoy seeing the Taft delegation supported and seated. [But] you people have to go back to California. You have an obligation, and it seems to me that you have to discharge that obligation in a way that satisfies your conscience. . . .

"You have to go back to the State of California and face the people of California. You vote your conscience."

Warren's announcement was the convention's turning point, Mellon insisted. The governor had gone on record a week earlier, taking the "moral" position; his conscience impelled him to vote for the Fair Play Amendment. By freeing his people similarly to "vote their conscience," Earl Warren had undermined his own candidacy.

Warren was neither gull nor catspaw, as some Eisenhower backers later hinted. He "must have known that by going along with the Fair Play Amendment he was giving it to Eisenhower," Pat Hillings asserted. The Californians had reasonably accurate delegate counts.

Strategically, Warren's smartest move would have been to abstain, or to divide the seventy votes equally between aye and nay, as Knowland had proposed. "But," as he later explained, "I just couldn't go along with the way those Southern politicians manipulated the delegations." It was a matter of doing the right thing.

In the muggy caucus room atop the hotel, the tired delegates voted, aye and nay, on the Fair Play Amendment. The tally was 57–8 in support of the Fair Play Amendment and Eisenhower. By the unit rule, all seventy of California's convention votes would be cast in favor of the rules change.

Dwight Eisenhower and Richard Nixon had prevailed.

As the convention opened on Monday morning, July 7, Taft's managers publicly claimed 570 votes, with another 27 pledged on the second ballot. Senator Henry Cabot Lodge retorted that Taft had fewer than 500—with 604 needed to nominate. Associated Press, rather less biased, had Taft ahead of Eisenhower, 530–427.

That same day, however, a national poll reported that the general had edged out the Ohio senator among rank-and-file Republican voters 44 to 41 percent; just 5 percent named Warren their choice. Among independents, the general ran even stronger, 51 to 20 percent. The uncommitted delegates in Chicago, savoring a November victory, took note.

Warren paid a courtesy call on Dwight Eisenhower that morning. "Imagine my surprise," Warren wrote in his *Memoirs,* "when the doorkeeper who admitted me to the general's suite was Murray Chotiner, one of the managers of my train."

Governor and general spent forty minutes together in their first meeting. Warren told Eisenhower of the caucus vote. Then the two ranged over the issues, particularly water policy in the parched West and population growth.

Dwight Eisenhower, who knew nothing of national politics or issues had much to learn from Earl Warren. West Pointer Eisenhower had risen slowly in the small peacetime army between the wars, then rocketed to high command in the aftermath of Pearl Harbor. Guided by his mentor, the austere Army Chief of Staff George C. Marshall, Eisenhower had cemented together a vast Allied army that brought victory in Europe in little more than three years.

His critics, particularly the British, sneered that grinning, likable "Ike" Eisenhower was less a soldier than a political leader; but it was precisely those diplomatic skills that the Allies had needed and for which Marshall had chosen him.

After a postwar stint as army chief of staff, Eisenhower resigned to become president of Columbia University. President Truman had called him back into uniform to head the fledgling North Atlantic Treaty Organization.

Eisenhower had watched the political maneuverings of 1951–52 from his Paris headquarters. As a matter of habit, Eisenhower kept such close counsel that his political acumen was easily underestimated. He permitted his advisers to guide him only so far.

Like Warren, Eisenhower saw himself as a "liberal," that is, a man who believed in measured social progress. Like Warren in another regard, he eschewed overt partisanship. "There is no difference between the two great parties," he wrote in his diary on January 1, 1950. "I belong to neither."

Not until January, 1952, when he tacitly agreed to allow his name to be entered on the New Hampshire Republican primary ballot, was his political affiliation disclosed. A month after his victory there, Eisenhower asked to be relieved of his NATO command to return to the United States.

As Warren left the Eisenhower suite on the eleventh floor of the Conrad Hilton, newsmen cornered him. Though he and the general had met only for the first time, Warren told the reporters, "I know enough about him to know he is a great American."

For his part, Eisenhower symbolically embraced Warren as a centrist. "Neither Warren nor I is going to get involved with a lot of pinkos, but we're not going to get dragged back by a lot of old reactionaries either."

Later that day of July 7, Warren and Taft met. Once more Warren reported as a courtesy the results of the caucus vote on the Fair Play Amendment. Taft was wounded.

The son of a president and chief justice of the United States, Robert A. Taft was born into the secure and ordered world of 1889 Cincinnati, a recognized member of the American aristocracy.

At preparatory school, at Yale, at Harvard Law, Bob Taft had ranked first in his class. He returned to Ohio to practice law, to stand successfully for the state legislature, and to marry a woman whose privileged background was remarkably like his own.

Elected to the United States Senate in 1938, Taft earned a reputation there as an isolationist and fiscal conservative. Twice reelected, he was respected by his peers for unblinking integrity and intelligence, and resented for his self-righteousness and aloof distance.

Men who could not fault Taft's rectitude or his unwavering policies instead criticized Taft the man as personally shy, colorless, and insensitive to political niceties.

Warren himself faulted Taft's "sensitivity to human relations." Warren acknowledged he was "burned up" because Taft had failed to meet then–vice presidential nominee Earl Warren at the Cincinnati train depot in 1948.

So Taft clung to a politics rooted in turn-of-the-century Cincinnati, but out of joint in a world of intercontinental bombers and atomic bombs. At the very pinnacle of his powers in 1952, he "was on a collision course with political realities," David Halberstam wrote.

Taft was crushed by Warren's report of the vote in the California caucus. Not only had he lost, but the tally of 57–8 suggested an overwhelming number of Californians would bolt for Eisenhower once Warren freed them.

Taft hardly masked his desperation. This would be his last opportunity to run for the presidency, to match his father's career. A stubborn Californian with no real shot at the nomination stood in his way.

"Taft begged me. He said it was his last chance and I could have anything I wanted in his administration," Warren later told newspaperman Drew Pearson—off the record.

There was only one complication: Douglas MacArthur wanted to be vice president. "But Taft was sure he could rearrange this if I cooperated."

Warren turned a deaf ear. "I told him that I couldn't release the delegates, that I had been elected on a pledge to go to the first ballot, that I had been accused of being a stalking horse and not a serious candidate. Therefore, the delegates must at least cast their vote for me on the first ballot, after which I would release them."

(Warren would have been less than human had he failed to appreciate his ironic revenge. The Werdel people—Taft supporters to a man—had first raised the claim that the governor was not a serious candidate for the presidency. Now, to prove just that point, he was standing in the way of Taft's nomination.)

Later that day Knowland met privately with Taft and his handlers in a suite on the ninth floor of the Conrad Hilton. When Taft asked how many votes he had among the Californians, Knowland replied bluntly, "Twenty."

"That bad?"

"That bad."

That left Taft two options. If Warren held on to his delegates, he would deprive Eisenhower of fifty votes. Cast early and unexpectedly in the roll call, those fifty votes could start a bandwagon effect.

If, however, Knowland joined the ticket as Taft's running mate, that could swing California.

Knowland promptly cut Taft off. "I didn't feel that I could even discuss the subject without undermining the position of Governor Warren."

Warren would stay in the race, and California would go ahead on the first ballot as planned.

The Fair Play Amendment came to the floor on Monday morning. The roll call began, the secretary calling each of the states in turn.

Alabama: five aye, nine nay.

Arizona: three aye, eleven nay.

Arkansas: three aye, eight nay.

Bill Knowland stood waiting at the floor microphone near the California delegation.

"California."

"California casts seventy votes aye—" A great roar rolled from the Eisenhower delegations, drowning out Knowland and welcoming the Californians into the fold.

The convention secretary paused to let the cheers subside, then resumed the roll. State by state the Eisenhower cheers mounted and the Taft hurrahs faded. Minnesota, nominally supporting favorite son Harold Stassen, and uncommitted Pennsylvania shortly joined California to provide Eisenhower his winning margin, 658 to 548.

"I think," Knowland said later, "that a great many people thought that indicated that those 70 votes were going to soon be Eisenhower votes." The psychological lift the Fair Play victory gave Eisenhower was palpable, and the blow to Taft's hopes devastating.

The Fair Play Amendment, in effect, was to switch thirty-nine Texas, Georgia, and Louisiana delegates from Taft to Eisenhower, a shift of seventy-eight votes. Taft could not recover.

By noon on July 7, the senator's third bid for his party's presidential nomination was effectively dead.

Dwight Eisenhower could celebrate. "If anyone ever clinched the nomination for me, it was Earl Warren."

CHAPTER 21

THE BITTERSWEET

L ATER, MUCH LATER, WHEN THE FURIES HAD BURNED OUT, HE COULD be philosophical. But in the aftermath of the 1952 Republican Party convention, Earl Warren was angry.

A secretary in the governor's office recalled a pensive Warren staring out a window, then complaining to his staff that Richard Nixon had undermined the Warren candidacy.

Sitting at a nearby desk, Maryalice Lemmon vividly remembered the governor saying he no longer had a majority with him when he arrived in Chicago. "He was bitter, very bitter."

Later would come the rationalizations, the denials, the insistence that "I never felt there was any real chance of my being nominated." After all, he had been a long-shot candidate, a dark horse with admittedly "only an outside chance."

Whatever hopes Warren had nurtured evaporated with the Fair Play vote on Monday. But even as he stepped aside, another Californian had pushed forward. By Tuesday, the convention was awash with whispers that Nixon was the certain choice for second place on an Eisenhower ticket.

Warren too had picked up the rumors of Nixon's elevation. He asked Eisenhower's former vice president at Columbia University, Paul H. Davis, to relay a blunt message to the general.

"We have a traitor in our delegation," Warren grimly advised Davis. "It's Nixon." The senator had signed the delegates' oath, Warren explained, then worked assiduously for Eisenhower's nomination.

"I wish you would tell General Eisenhower that we resent his people infiltrating, through Nixon, into our delegation, and ask him to have it stopped."

Eisenhower tacitly confirmed Nixon's role. "I think it is highly desirable that for Vice President we have a young man such as Richard Nixon" on the ticket, he told Davis.

At the same time, Eisenhower added soothingly, if there was any further meddling with the California delegation, Davis or Warren was to call immediately. Eisenhower would put a stop to it.

Eisenhower could afford to be generous. By Tuesday, July 8, the Taft flood had crested and was ebbing. California was no longer crucial to an Eisenhower victory. There were enough uncommitted delegates to put the general over the top.

"All we wanted was for Governor Warren to stay in and not release his votes on the first ballot. We were more concerned about denying the California vote to Taft than getting it ourselves," Eisenhower strategist Lucius Clay explained.

If a second ballot was necessary, California's delegates would bolt, the *San Francisco Examiner* reported on Wednesday, July 9. "The delegation is likely to split wide open after the first ballot with the bulk going to Eisenhower if the present pro-Ike trend continues." Political writer Clint Mosher foresaw a 50–20 division in Eisenhower's favor.

Still Taft clutched some faint hope that California might resuscitate his faltering candidacy. On the Thursday morning of the presidential nominations, a Taft floor manager approached California's national committeeman, McIntyre Faries, to suggest that if Taft got the nomination, "he wants Knowland for vice president."

Knowland rejected the offer. "I'm pledged to Warren. I'm chairman of the delegation. I'm going to stay with him as long as he's in the race."

While Taft grasped at straws, the Eisenhower bandwagon heaved into motion. First Michigan announced it would go for Eisenhower, 34–12. Tom Dewey followed with a statement that New York would vote 92–4 for Eisenhower. Finally, Pennsylvania weighed in with a similar big majority for the general.

That evening, in the tumultuous rites of such events, Bill Knowland nominated his old friend Earl Warren as the Republican presidential candidate. Knowland urged the delegates to give the nation "an administration of honor."

The eighteen-minute demonstration that followed was raucous and good natured. The organist thundered "California, Here I Come" again and again, occasionally substituting the University of Southern California's fight song, while the state's delegation snaked along the crowded aisles, pumping blue and orange "Warren in '52" picket signs up and down in time to the music. High above the floor of the amphitheater, nervous spotlights danced back and forth, then settled on Nina Warren and her three smiling daughters in their box, waving in the smoky air to the delegates far below.

The demonstration swayed no one.

The presidential balloting finally began at 11:30 on Friday morning. Shaking off a weariness brought on by too many late nights, the delegates grew increasingly excited and increasingly tense as the secretary opened the roll call:

Alabama: Taft 9, Eisenhower 5.

Arizona: Taft 10, Eisenhower 4.

Arkansas: Taft 6, Eisenhower 4, MacArthur 1.

California: Warren 70.

State by state, Eisenhower picked up votes as the uncommitted delegates weighed in.

State by state, Warren held firm. In their suite at the Conrad Hilton, Herbert Brownell and Lucius Clay huddled, worried that they would not make it on the first ballot, ready to order Nixon on the floor to raid California during the second round.

Texas: Taft 5, Eisenhower 33. Especially loud cheers for these votes, once so safely Taft's, pried loose by the Fair Play Amendment.

Vermont: Ike 12.

Washington: Taft 4, Ike 20.

At the end of the roll, Eisenhower had 590, just 14 short of nomination. The convention secretary turned to the overseas possessions.

The amphitheater churned with excitement. The roll concluded, Eisenhower had 595 votes, Taft 500, Warren 81, Stassen 20.

Sitting in the California delegation, Knowland turned to Frank Jorgensen, a Nixon man, and said California should get to the platform, prepared to switch at the end of the roll call. Twice Knowland attempted to reach Warren at the Conrad Hilton headquarters for instructions, and twice he reported, "I can't get Earl, can't find him, can't get hold of him."

Dwight Eisenhower stood just 9 votes short of the 604 needed to nominate. He was not to be denied. Any of a dozen states might clamor for the honor of changing its vote and putting Eisenhower over the top. It had been so close, Knowland muttered, closer than the delegates realized, closer than Eisenhower's men acknowledged. "The Eisenhower and Taft forces were so evenly divided that had Michigan held to its favorite son and had Minnesota held to Stassen, until the second ballot, there might have been a substantial movement toward Warren on the second or third ballot. . . ."

Now it was over. Eisenhower delegates on the floor joined the packed galleries to chant, "Minnesota, Minnesota," as that state's chairman Edward Thye and Eisenhower floor manager Warren Burger worked over favorite son Harold Stassen. The game was up; Stassen, with less than ten percent of the ballots, could legally no longer bind his delegates.

At the podium, convention chairman Joseph Martin almost grudgingly recognized Minnesota. Drowned out by the cheers, hidden behind the bobbing signs, Ed Thye announced that Minnesota wished to change its vote.

The dam burst. Delegation chairmen around the hall shouted for recognition as one after the other sought to throw his state behind Eisenhower. The bandwagon rolled on while the California delegation seethed restlessly, silent amid the bedlam.*

Bill Knowland forced his way through the packed aisles to the podium. Though California withheld its votes, Warren ironically had made Eisenhower's victory possible, *San Francisco Chronicle* political editor Earl Behrens noted. When Warren defeated Tom Werdel in the June 1 primary, he deprived Taft of the delegates necessary for victory on the Fair Play Amendment vote. Weeks later, Eisenhower reaped the harvest.†

Even as the convention approved a motion to make the vote unanimous, Eisenhower adviser Henry Cabot Lodge approached Nixon in the California delegation. "I'm authorized to tell you General Eisenhower has picked you for vice-president," Lodge told Nixon.

Warren masked his disappointment. To reporters, the governor said only that his party had put together "a great ticket. . . . I will do everything I personally can to make it win." Nixon's nomination was "a great honor to our state."

Faint praise could not paper over the rift; the antipathy was deep and enduring. As Warren's traveling secretary noted, "He never forgets and rarely forgives." ‡

In his own defense, Nixon protested, he had done nothing to hurt Warren. "The California delegation was pledged to Governor Earl Warren and stayed with him to the finish."

Nixon supporters argued that friction between the two men ran back further and was only exacerbated by the convention. "There was always a feeling," said Pat Hillings, "that the governor of the state should have endorsed the Republican nominee for the Senate. It was awkward, but, of course that was Warren. He'd always run his own independent show." Hillings's explanation effectively blamed Nixon for the break.

---

* Warren received seventy votes from California, six from Wisconsin, and one each from Georgia, Nebraska, North Dakota, Rhode Island, and Hawaii. After switches, he was left officially with seventy-seven from California, Wisconsin, and North Dakota.

† Knowland explained cryptically in the *San Francisco Chronicle* of July 12, 1952, that he did not change California's votes because "in the interest of healing wounds, it was best to do it this way." California had more than enough Eisenhower votes to put the general over the top, but Nixon, as Ike's spokesman in the state, would have received the political credit. As it played out, Warren temporarily reaffirmed his control of the delegation and, by extension, the California Republican Party. Meantime, Knowland was asserting *his* authority, both in California and in the United States Senate. He demonstrated that his rival, Nixon, could not dictate state politics. Furthermore, even as vice president, Nixon would have to respect Knowland's clout as majority leader in the upper house.

‡ Knowland too never forgave Nixon for his maneuvering, according to Frank Mankiewicz. In 1972, Bill Knowland called Mankiewicz on election day to report, "I just want you to know that I just voted for your candidate. I went for George McGovern and I just wanted to tell you that I had." Knowland explained "he would never, ever vote for Richard Nixon under any circumstances," Mankiewicz said in an interview on July 20, 1992.

Despite misgivings about Nixon, Warren soldiered on during the campaign. He officiated at a send-off rally in Pomona for Nixon's first campaign tour, then presided at a Whittier College homecoming when the vice presidential candidate returned.

When reporters sniffed out an $18,000 secret "slush" fund pooled by wealthy supporters for Nixon's private use, Warren said nothing publicly. Speaking privately to a small group of law enforcement officers, however, Warren acknowledged he was disturbed.

The slush fund "was particularly bad because some of the contributors were government contractors, others had participated in building the highway to Alaska at government expense and it was a most embarrassing situation."

For days Nixon twisted in the wind while Eisenhower's closest advisers debated retaining him on the ticket. Attorney Dana Smith, who had set up the fund to underwrite Nixon's personal expenses, explained, "The whole idea was to enable Dick to do a selling job to the American people in behalf of private enterprise."

The beleaguered senator was to rescue his political career with a brilliant, half-hour television address. Nixon weaved between counterattack and bathos—his wife owned only a "respectable Republican cloth coat," and he would not make his girls return the gift of their pet cocker spaniel, Checkers.

The nation's emotional outpouring was the first proof of the power of television to sway voters instantly. Some 150,000 telegrams rained down on Republican headquarters, the overwhelming majority in support of Nixon. The men who had questioned the wisdom of retaining him on the ticket abruptly reversed themselves. Nixon the redeemed would stay.

Warren loyally fell into line. He was to campaign in fourteen states, from Washington to Georgia, making no less than forty-seven appearances on behalf of the Republican ticket. His particular assignment was to appeal to independents and Democrats, Eisenhower's press secretary, James Hagerty, explained.

Warren's tours helped both the top of the ticket and men running for House and Senate seats, *San Francisco Chronicle* political editor Earl Behrens noted. "He was asked to talk to groups who hadn't voted Republican in twenty-five years and were openly antagonistic to him. Before he finished, he might not have converted them, but he'd destroyed a lot of the antagonism."

The Democratic Party's presidential nominee, Illinois governor Adlai Stevenson, somewhat ruefully recognized his friend's appeal to Democrats. On a whistle-stop tour of California, Stevenson told a Fresno audience, "I don't know how in the world the Republicans keep him."

Harry Truman also praised Warren after the governor welcomed the president's whistle-stop tour to California in October. When photographers asked Republican Warren to pose with Democrat Truman on the platform of the observation car, Truman waved them off. He did not want to embarrass Warren.

"Well, Mr. President, there's no embarrasment to a Governor greeting the President of the United States. Of course, I'll go out there with you and if you want, I'll introduce you."

The following day at a San Francisco fund-raiser, Truman returned the courtesy. "At the Republican Convention last July, it seemed that the dinosaur wing of the Republican Party had suffered a real defeat. . . . But they turned away from your liberal Governor and chose another Californian who is not worthy to lace his shoes."

On Tuesday, November 4, Dwight Eisenhower swept to easy victory, compiling 55.1 percent of the national vote and a 442–89 triumph in the electoral college. In California, he did even better, overcoming a Democratic registration lead of 900,000 to take 56.8 percent of the 5,000,000 votes cast.

The ballot count was not yet complete when the speculation about a Warren cabinet position began.

Eisenhower had good reason to reward Warren. Though the two were not cronies, they shared a similar political sensibility.

Then there were the political debts incurred. Warren's position on the Fair Play Amendment vote had been vital, perhaps decisive. Further, Warren had campaigned hard for the ticket, particularly in the unpredictable West. Of such things were high-level federal appointments fashioned.

Precisely when Eisenhower settled upon Warren, the president-elect never made clear.* Precisely when Warren decided he would even accept an offer of a federal appointment, he did not say.

It *was* time for a change, Warren believed. He was sixty-two, and he had long held that age should give way to younger men with fresh ideas.

Warren's alternatives were limited, however. He felt no urge to enter the business world, the private practice of law held little interest after his years in public life. A federal apppointment seemed the best course. And he had a promise.

At the convention, Lucius Clay had guaranteed Warren the federal office of his choosing if he would stay in the race for the nomination. It was "the only commitment we ever made," Clay claimed.

Extended without Eisenhower's knowledge, Clay's offer was not necessarily binding on the candidate. Still, Clay was Eisenhower's oldest and most trusted adviser; Warren had stayed in, for his own reasons; and the debt remained unpaid.

Brownell and Clay discussed the Interior Department for Warren—nor-

---

* In an interview on August 12, 1991, McIntyre Faries said that shortly *before* the November election, Bill Knowland returned from a whistle-stop tour with Eisenhower to announce, "I have an understanding with Eisenhower that if a vacancy occurs on the Supreme Court, Warren will have it."

mally given to a westerner—but the Californian declined. It was again a matter of economics.

As governor, Warren earned an annual salary of $25,000 and received an additional $1,000 per month allowance to maintain the governor's mansion. They lived modestly enough, saving something each month while also helping to support Warren's widowed sister.

But life in Washington was expensive. On a Cabinet officer's $22,500 per year and his projected monthly state pension of $1,008.49, they would not be able to help the children through college and buy a home. A Cabinet post simply would not pay enough.

When Eisenhower announced his Cabinet on November 21, 1952, speculation about the Warren prize immediately turned to the federal bench. The following day, Associated Press moved a knowledgeable story suggesting Warren was "in line for the first vacancy on the Supreme Court." *The New York Times* carried a Sacramento story reporting similar speculation.*

The stories were apparently planted, trial balloons lofted to gauge the reaction. If there was any protest, it was not enough to dissuade Eisenhower from repaying his political debt.

Within the week, the president-elect telephoned from his temporary New York office to inform Warren, "I want you to know that I intend to offer you the first vacancy on the Supreme Court."

"That is very generous of you," Warren replied.

"That is my personal commitment to you," Eisenhower confirmed.

Warren apparently gave no thought to the financial implications if he accepted appointment to the high court. A justice's salary was $25,000, and with his state pension he and Nina would make do. The honor, the sense of fulfillment was too great to pass up.

Warren had only to wait. The age of the justices, particularly Felix Frankfurter at seventy, suggested that Eisenhower would be the first Republican president to appoint a high court judge since Hoover's nomination of Benjamin Cardozo in 1932. Only one Republican now sat on the court—Harold Burton, ironically, a Truman appointee.

There it remained. The first nine months of 1953 were for Warren "a silly time," according to *Bee* political editor Herbert Phillips, a time of rumored conjectures about his future. He was said to be in line for an ambassadorship to an unnamed Scandinavian country, to Spain, even—the silliest of all to a man of limited means—to London and the Court of Saint James.

---

* Warren had been considered earlier for a federal appointment—by the Democrat Harry S. Truman. Warren had been mentioned after the death in July, 1949, of Associate Justice Frank Murphy. President Truman had instead named his attorney general, Tom Clark, to the court. In March, 1950, State Department officials anxious to present a bipartisan front had weighed the appointment of the California governor as a roving ambassador. Ultimately the idea was scotched.

Late in February, the *San Francisco Call-Bulletin* reported that Warren was to replace Frankfurter on the Supreme Court. That rumor would surface repeatedly for the next six months.

Warren publicly denied the rumors. Privately, he advised Asa Call, who had been pulling together a Southern California campaign committee for 1954, that there would be no fourth term.

Despite his disavowals, Warren's very actions stoked speculation he would soon be leaving. As if he were setting his affairs in order, one by one he appointed the people closest to him to choice public office.

First he tapped the liberal state controller, Thomas Kuchel, to fill the Senate seat vacated by newly elected Vice President Nixon. Then he chose another supporter, Assemblyman Robert C. Kirkwood, to be the new controller.

Warren's clemency secretary, James Welch, went to the state Industrial Accident Commission. Merrell "Pop" Small was to leave Sacramento to join the staff of newly appointed Senator Kuchel.

Most telling, Helen MacGregor, Warren's private secretary since his days as district attorney, departed for the California Youth Authority with a quip: "I had been his secretary for twenty years and had done forty years of work."

The persistent rumors of Warren's departure eroded his influence in California. In the name of party unity, Warren accepted former vaudevillian and M-G-M contract player George Murphy as party chairman. "A party wheelhorse in campaign season and out," Murphy was a conservative closer in thought to the Old Guard than to Warren.

Three days later, Assembly Majority Leader Harold K. Levering obliquely attacked the governor by raking an official in the Warren administration. Despite another plea for party unity, Levering insisted he would continue to attack the governor and his departments whenever he chose. A majority of the Republican assemblymen in the closed meeting reportedly applauded Levering's challenge.

And Warren waited. Sometime in the spring of 1953, Attorney General Herbert Brownell advised Eisenhower that he was having difficulty filling the position of solicitor general. Shortly after, Eisenhower proposed Warren for the post.

"I've been thinking some fresh legal experience for him, if he is to go on the Court, would be a good thing."

They delayed a decision, instead appointing Warren to be one of four American representatives at the coronation of Queen Elizabeth II. The assignment provided Warren, his wife, and their three daughters an excuse to visit Europe for the first time. For Warren, the additional pleasure of the appointment was to meet another of the American delegation, former Secretary of State George C. Marshall.

The spectacle of the June 2 coronation over, Nina and the three girls set off on a tour of England while Warren returned alone to Sacramento. A stack of bills passed by the Legislature awaited his signature or veto; Lieutenant Governor Goodwin Knight was not to be trusted.

Warren was preparing to rejoin Nina and the girls in Europe when Herb Brownell telephoned on July 13. Brownell asked Warren to stop in Washington before resuming his vacation.

Meeting at the Statler Hotel to avoid press scrutiny, Brownell formally offered Warren the post of solicitor general—with the understanding that the first vacancy on the high court was still to be his.

Warren told Brownell that he had decided against running for a fourth term, but was undecided about his future. Warren explained his financial responsibilities—the solicitor general's salary was the same as a Cabinet officer—then asked for time to weigh the offer.

He would also need some time to close out his administration gracefully. There were still loyalists to reward with appointments to state agencies or to the bench. There were any number of longtime supporters who deserved the courtesy of a personal telephone call.

Brownell needed an answer soon. The Supreme Court term would open, as usual, on the first Monday in October, and it was imperative that the solicitor general be prepared to represent the United States government before the high court. If he accepted, Warren would have to move to Washington promptly.

Traveling through Scandinavia, Warren pondered the appointment. The solicitor general was the primary advocate in court of the United States government; Warren considered the post the most prestigious in the American practice of law. It would clear away any possible objection to his fitness for the Supreme Court.

For three weeks, the Warrens visited the small towns their forebears had left in the mid-nineteenth century. Finally, on August 3, 1953, from Stockholm, Warren wired to Brownell his prearranged, coded acceptance: THANKS FOR MESSAGE STOP HAVE BEEN REFRESHED BY TRIP STOP LOOKING FORWARD TO MY RETURN TO WORK.

Brownell promptly replied for the president and himself. WE ARE BOTH GRATIFIED TO RECEIVE YOUR CABLE.

The president made no public announcement. Instead, at an informal White House breakfast late in August, Eisenhower feigned innocence to ask former Warren travel secretary and now Congressman William Mailliard about Warren. "Herb Brownell tells me that he should be on the list of first consideration for any vacancies on the Supreme Court." Did Mailliard think Warren would want to be an associate justice?

After Warren's years as attorney general and governor, Mailliard responded, "he'd be very likely to be bored to death."

However, Mailliard continued, Warren was by nature a public servant, and if the job were important enough, it would appeal. Under Fred M. Vinson the Supreme Court was "in shambles. And what you really need is a Chief Justice. . . . My answer would be emphatically different if we were talking about the chief justiceship. . . . The court would have decorum and dignity and it would be well-managed."

Eisenhower said nothing further.

The Warrens returned to Sacramento at the end of August, in time for Nina to help with arrangements for Earl Junior's wedding to a young woman he had first met at McClatchy High School.

On September 3, his unannounced move to Washington still in the offing, the governor announced he would not be a candidate for reelection. He gave a solitary reason: "My firm and long-standing belief that periodic change in administration is essential to the continued health of our representative system of government."

Five days later, Warren's world abruptly turned on its head.

In the early morning hours of Tuesday, September 8, 1953, Chief Justice of the United States Fred Vinson, corpulent, a three-pack-per-day smoker, suffered a heart attack in his apartment in the Wardman-Park Hotel. A doctor summoned at 1:30 A.M. could do nothing to help; Vinson died, age sixty-three, forty-five minutes later.

Vinson's death came at an awkward moment for the Eisenhower administration. A month before the term began, the high court's docket was crowded with important cases, particularly a clutch of vexing school segregation suits. The Court needed a chief justice.

Promised the first vacancy on the Court, Warren was anxious for the appointment, "wearing a path in the carpet, pacing up and down," Joe Knowland told Mac Faries by telephone. Yet neither Clay's commitment nor Eisenhower's offer had envisioned that the first vacancy on the Supreme Court would be the chief justice's.

Warren wanted that seat.

Eisenhower apparently did not feel himself bound by his pledge in this case. ". . . [N]either he nor I was thinking of the special post of chief justice, nor was I definitely committed to any appointment," Eisenhower maintained. Furthermore, "the truth was that I owed Governor Warren nothing."

Rather than appoint a chief justice from the outside, Eisenhower might shift an incumbent associate justice to the center seat on the court. The vacant chair then would be Warren's.

But the president had no viable candidates for promotion. The only Republican on the court was the less than towering figure of former senator Harold Hitz Burton—who lacked both the personal authority and the legal scholarship to lead the fractious justices.

Far better was Associate Justice Robert H. Jackson, but Jackson's drawbacks were grave. Though firmly conservative, he was a Democrat, and fifteen years earlier he had backed Franklin Roosevelt's "court-packing" scheme. Moreover, Jackson and Associate Justice Hugo Black were feuding again.

Eisenhower preferred to appoint a Republican to fill the empty seat, allow Warren his refresher course in the law as solicitor general, then give him the next vacancy. Determined "not to make any mistakes in a hurry," the president stalled while Brownell pulled together a list of possible nominees.

Believing he lacked the temperament for the job, Tom Dewey excused himself from consideration. That eliminated the one man for whom Warren might have stepped aside, on the grounds that Dewey was the party's elder statesman.

John Foster Dulles also removed himself. He was happily ensconced as secretary of state, a post he had coveted all his life. Eisenhower needed him there.

The president toyed with the notion of appointing John W. Davis, a true conservative but a Democrat—in fact, that party's nominee for the presidency in 1924. Further, Davis was in his eighties. Eisenhower wanted men who were vigorous and would serve long after he himself had retired.

Three others figured on Brownell's list: John J. Parker of the Fourth Circuit Court of Appeals, Orie Phillips of the Tenth Circuit, and Arthur T. Vanderbilt, chief justice of the New Jersey Supreme Court. For reasons of health or age, all three were disqualified.

While Eisenhower pondered, Warren chose to go hunting with Earl and Bobby, joining Ventura County Supervisor Edwin Carty on remote Santa Rosa Island off the coast. There he could hide out, hunting mule deer; the only communication with the mainland was by ship-to-shore radio.

Their hunting vacation was interrupted on Friday, September 25. A navy PT boat standing offshore radioed, "You are needed back in Ventura," a prearranged code indicating that the White House was calling.

They hastily gathered their gear for the bumpy trip across the Santa Barbara Channel to the Carty home at Rincon Beach. Once there, Warren returned Brownell's call.

Earl Junior listened as his father insisted that Eisenhower keep his pledge: "Yes, the agreement was for the first vacancy."

Pause. "No, the first vacancy means just that."

Pause. "No, Herb, no. The first vacancy means the first vacancy."

In the face of Warren's insistence, Brownell proposed that they meet personally. The attorney general would use the president's own plane to fly to McClellan Air Force Base outside Sacramento on Sunday morning.

No one was quite frank about the purpose of the meeting. Eisenhower wrote that he dispatched Brownell to California "to gain a more definite opinion on the governor's record of attainments as a lawyer, as district attorney, and as attorney general of California . . ."

But Brownell had known Warren for a decade. By 1953, Brownell concluded, "my relationship with Warren was one of long standing duration, and one which eliminated necessity for formalities."

In truth, Brownell was flying to California because Eisenhower, imbued with the West Point honor code, had given his word. He could not renege on that pledge without Warren's consent. "The main reason," Brownell later conceded, "was to ask Warren to accept the next opening."

Eisenhower's hesitation was based solely on Warren's lack of recent experience at the bar, Brownell explained. The attorney general knew of no other candidates for the office. "I think he would have continued the search for someone to appoint."

The president's plane, with Brownell as its solitary passenger, landed at McClellan at eight o'clock on Sunday morning, September 27. Warren and Brownell chatted aimlessly for an hour until airmen had serviced the plane and they could speak frankly.

Finally left alone, Brownell explained his mission. As the attorney general reconstructed the "low-key" meeting of these "two old friends," Warren stated that he had been highly gratified when President Eisenhower originally had called him about the 'first vacancy' on the Court, and now that the vacancy had occurred, he would be extremely honored to be nominated to the Chief Justiceship. It had been, he said, a lifelong ambition of his, to be appointed to the Supreme Court." *

Brownell found himself uncomfortably squeezed between his president and his "old friend." The president, he explained, "did not feel that his prior discussions with Governor Warren had related to a vacancy in the post of Chief Justice, but that he had had in mind an associate justiceship in his original call to Governor Warren about a 'first vacancy.' "

Warren insisted on his claim. "He was very firm," Brownell said. "He thought that the next appointment meant the next appointment."

If the president chose to raise an associate justice to chief, Warren would take the associate's chair left vacant, he told Brownell. That then would be the "first opening." (Warren the politician, of course, understood that Eisenhower had no viable option there and understood too why Brownell had flown to California.)

As he recalled the confidential conversation, Brownell asked Warren no questions about his stand on issues pending before the high court. The closest he came to probing Warren's possible votes came when Brownell asked, "Are you generally in sympathy with the policies of the Eisenhower administration?" He was, Warren assured Brownell.

The final decision was Eisenhower's, Brownell cautioned, but there was one condition: Warren had to be in Washington within the week, to be sworn in on the day the Court began its October term. Warren agreed.

Three hours after he landed, Brownell was once more airborne. As Warren rejoined Pat Patterson, waiting beside the limousine parked on the tarmac, the governor was broadly smiling.

---

* When magazine writer Jack Harrison Pollack later wrote in a draft that "the Supreme Court has always been the dream of lawyer Earl Warren," the chief justice struck out the sentence, asserting, "It simply wasn't true." See Pollack, p. 13.

The Warren family
in 1894, the year Methias
(top right) found work in
the Southern Pacific car
shops in Bakersfield.
From left: Methias's wife,
Chrystal; Earl, age three;
Ethel, age seven.

(California State Archives)

One of the few
early photographs of Earl
Warren, taken when he was
about eight years old.

(California History Section, California State Library)

Earl Warren *(left)* and Ezra Decoto, the outgoing district attorney of Alameda County, on January 12, 1925, the day Warren assumed his first elected office as the new DA.

(California History Section, California State Library)

Then-California Attorney General Warren advocated the evacuation of 110,000 Japanese and Japanese-Americans from the West Coast in March and April, 1942. Not until late in his life did Warren finally make amends.

(Hearst Newspaper Collection, University of Southern California Library)

Thomas Dewey *(left)* and Earl Warren, the Republican presidential and vice presidential nominees, met at the New Yorker's upstate farm to discuss the 1948 campaign. Warren came away from the meeting, despite this optimistic pose for press photographers, concerned about Dewey's passivity.

(Hearst Newspaper Collection, University of Southern California Library)

The Warren family in a 1948 campaign photograph.
From left: Robert, Dorothy, Nina, Jr. ("Honey Bear"), Earl, Jr.,
Virginia, James, Nina, and Warren.

(Courtesy of Betty Henderson and the Governor's Mansion, California State Parks)

The Warrens scan early election returns at AP's San Francisco bureau
on election night, June 8, 1950. From left: Virginia; the governor,
elected to a third term that night; Nina; Bobby; and the news service's
Sacramento reporter, Morrie Landsberg.

(Courtesy of Morrie Landsberg)

The Supreme Court in 1953.
In front row, from left: Felix Frankfurter, Hugo Black, Warren, Stanley Reed, and William O. Douglas. Standing, from left: Tom Clark, Robert Jackson, Harold Burton, and Sherman Minton.

(Photograph by Fabian Bachrach, Collection of the Supreme Court of the United States)

Felix Frankfurter.

(Photograph by Harris and Ewing, Collection of the Supreme Court of the United States)

William O. Douglas.

(Photograph by Harris and Ewing, Collection of the Supreme Court of the United States)

Hugo Black.

(Photograph by Harris and Ewing, Collection of the Supreme Court of the United States)

William Brennan.

(Photograph by Harris and Ewing, Collection of the Supreme Court of the United States)

Earl Warren's last court. Seated, from left: John Harlan, Hugo Black, Warren, William Douglas, and William Brennan. Standing, from left: Abe Fortas, Potter Stewart, Byron White, and Thurgood Marshall.

(Photograph by Hessler Studio, Collection of the Supreme Court of the United States)

At the height of the most serious constitutional crisis since the Civil War, President Eisenhower reluctantly called upon federal troops to enforce Supreme Court orders to integrate Little Rock's Central High School in 1957 over the opposition of Arkansas Governor Orval Faubus.

(Hearst Newspaper Collection, University of Southern California Library)

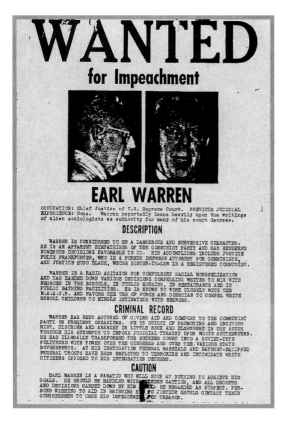

The first call for Warren's impeachment—later to be futilely promoted by the John Birch Society—came with this "wanted" notice taped to a bulletin board in the 7th and Mission branch post office in San Francisco, and reported to the FBI on October 14, 1958. The original is in Warren's FBI file.

In bitterly cold weather, with almost a foot of snow blanketing Washington,
Warren swore in John F. Kennedy on January 20, 1961.

(U.S. Army Signal Corps Collection, John Fitzgerald Kennedy Library)

Warren presents President Johnson with the report of the
Commission on the Assassination of President Kennedy on September 24,
1964. From left: John McCloy, General Counsel J. Lee Rankin,
Richard Russell, Gerald Ford, Warren, Johnson, Allen Dulles,
John Sherman Cooper, and Hale Boggs.

(Photograph by Cecil Stoughton, Lyndon Baines Johnson Presidential Library Collection)

This was reportedly
Nina Warren's favorite photograph
of her husband in later years.

(Hearst Newspaper Collection,
University of Southern California Library)

Puliter Prize–winning
editorial cartoonist
Paul Conrad of the
Los Angeles Times
drew this tribute
cartoon to Warren
when the former
chief justice died.

(Courtesy Paul Conrad.
© 1974, Los Angeles Times.
Reprinted with permission.)

Earl Warren
1891-1974

Returned to Washington, Brownell immediately reported to Eisenhower: Warren was immovable. The president might elevate an associate justice; otherwise, the "first vacancy" was the chief's position.

Eisenhower pondered his decision overnight, then settled on Warren. To pass over the Californian was to risk being tagged as politically unreliable and, personally, as a man whose word meant nothing.

With Eisenhower's permission, Brownell summoned a small group of reporters to his home on Monday night to loft a trial balloon. Brownell leaked a not-for-attribution story that the president was considering Warren's appointment.

In talking to reporters, Brownell was more definite than he had intended. The stories in Tuesday's papers specifically named Warren as Eisenhower's choice for chief justice.

The reaction was overwhelmingly favorable. Warren appeared a safe choice, moderate and respected, though one San Francisco attorney who acknowledged that he was not fond of the governor grumbled, "I can guarantee that every one of Earl Warren's decisions will sound as if he's running for president or assistant God."

More formal notice of his appointment came by telephone on Wednesday, September 30, at 10:00 A.M. Because Warren had not yet arrived at the office, secretary Maryalice Lemmon routed the call to the mansion, where Nina Warren answered the telephone.

"The White House is calling, Mrs. Warren."

"He couldn't possibly come to the phone, Maryalice. He's in the shower."

With some asperity, Lemmon asked Mrs. Warren, "Well, what do you want me to tell the president?"

Nina Warren took charge. "Maryalice, you send that call over here. I'll take care of it."

Ever after, Lemmon would hold the mental image of Earl Warren, dripping from his shower, accepting the president's offer to be the chief justice of the United States.

Warren himself was so excited he could not recall if it was the president himself or the attorney general who spoke to him. He celebrated by taking his first political sponsor, onetime Alameda County supervisor John Mullins, to lunch that day.

California was losing, according to Kyle Palmer, "the smartest politician this state has ever seen." In an era of weak political parties, Warren had prospered, coming to dominate state politics by virtue of his leadership abilities and evolving nonpartisan appeal. His was a personal triumph, often in the face of conservative resistance from within his own party.

Had California a strong two-party system, wrote Warren booster Raymond Moley, 'Warren would now be a useful, prosperous but little-known lawyer in San Francisco or Oakland. His firm independence, vital conscience, and tendency toward independent judgments would have been difficult, perhaps indigestible materials in a disciplined party."

When Warren stepped aside, Moley had predicted in 1949, the governor would leave a record of solid achievements, "and a potent lesson in personal integrity and intelligent leadership."

Warren's first budget of $464 million had grown to $1.3 billion this year. (John Francis Neylan would grouse Californians were the "most tax-ridden" of all American citizens.) During the Warren years, California had swollen in population by 5 million people. At the same time, the workforce had increased from 3 million to 5 million while public school enrollment jumped from 1.2 million to 2 million.

Meeting their needs and planning for the future took most of Warren's time. California annually was building 15 percent of all new housing in the nation; new subdivisions covered acreage amounting to a dozen cities the size of San Francisco.

In 1943 state programs for physically handicapped children served just 2,500. A decade later, 48,283 were protected. During the same period, the number of counties with local health clinics funded by state aid doubled; all 58 counties were now served. Warren's new Department of Mental Hygiene had spent $126 million and had created 8,113 more beds and four new hospitals "to take California out of the asylum age."

Aid to the blind, to dependent children, to the elderly had all increased. Warren had organized statewide conferences, sometimes more than one, on water, traffic safety, sex crimes against children, youth and child welfare, educational television, employment, industrial safety, mental health, and aging. All had produced major reforms in California, and often model legislation other states emulated.

In meeting these responsibilities Warren grew, first as an administrator, then as a man. Over time, said League of California Cities lobbyist Richard Graves, the governor slowly came to understand that "government was not merely the organization of society, but service to society."

Robert Kenny, Warren's friend and political rival, agreed the governor's sense of social responsibility grew. "If Hiram Johnson altered the political structure of the state, then Warren altered its social structure."

Oddly, Earl Warren, a Republican, brought the New Deal of Franklin D. Roosevelt to California.

As governor, Warren had signed into law more than 10,000 bills, and vetoed more than 850. In his ten years and ten months as governor, he had issued fifty-two commutations of sentences, twenty-one in his last three days in office, and signed 517 pardons at the recommendation of state courts. Among the last nineteen pardons he signed just hours before re-signing on October 2, 1953, was one for paroled *Point Lobos* defendant Ernest G. Ramsay, whose civil rights were to be restored, and three for men convicted long before by then–District Attorney Warren.

The Warrens were leaving Sacramento with both excitement and sadness. This city was familiar, always welcoming. Washington was far away, even forbidding. Yet there lay the new challenge, the reward for his years of service, and the honors of high office.

"My mind has sort of been a racetrack these last few days for conflicting emotions," Warren confessed.

Having decided to accept the appointment, he had a private concern, he acknowledged to Earl Junior. "I will not accept this unless you promise to tell me when I start to slip." He had seen other men stay in harness too long, dulling the luster of fine careers with failing performance at the end of their lives.

Finally there were the farewells. He spent an hour with Herzl Friedlander, thanking the doctor who had diagnosed the colon cancer two years earlier. "I want you to realize that if it weren't for you," the governor told him, "someone else would be making this trip to Washington."

On his last morning in Sacramento, Warren said good-bye to his staff. "Without your loyalty, integrity, efficiency—"

He paused to clear his throat, started to speak once more, and stopped a second time. In the awkward silence he stood gripping the edge of his desk, staring at the blotter for a long moment, unable to continue.

Finally he regained his composure. "I believe we are having lunch together," he managed, abruptly ending the meeting.

Warren attended a good-bye party hosted by the reporters who had covered his administration for the past ten years. For the first time, said one of those in the upstairs dining room of Bedell's Restaurant, Warren "let his hair down and spoke very candidly."

As former Associated Press reporter Joe Lipper remembered Warren's comments, the resigning governor acknowledged the men in the room, fondly recalling shared moments during the past ten years. Then Warren added in farewell, "I am glad to be going to the Supreme Court because now I can help the less fortunate, the people in our society who suffer, the disadvantaged."

On Friday afternoon, October 2, 1953, Warren rode for the last time with Capitol Police Officer Pat Patterson at the wheel of the governor's limousine. While they drove, Warren edited his final radio address as governor, scribbling in the margin a farewell to the people of California.

"Here I was born. Here Mrs. Warren and I have reared our family. Here our children have attended public schools. Here three of them are now attending the university. They will remain here.

"Here our fondest memories and our greatest hopes are. Here my home will always be . . . where my children are and where my heart is."

Part III

THIS HONORABLE COURT

CHAPTER 22

AGREEABLE TO THE
CONSTITUTION

OMENTS BEFORE NOON ON MONDAY MORNING, OCTOBER 5, 1953, Earl Warren turned to face Associate Justice Hugo Black, the senior member of the Supreme Court of the United States. His wife at his side, Warren raised his right hand and placed his left on a Bible.

"I, Earl Warren, do solemnly swear," he repeated after Black, "that I will support and defend the Constitution of the United States . . ."

The seven other associate justices lined one side of their oak-paneled conference room. Facing them stood President Dwight Eisenhower, Mrs. Eisenhower, Vice President Richard Nixon, and a handful of invited guests.

"That I will bear true faith and allegiance . . ." If Warren was nervous, he showed no sign of it. He was sober, even grave, every inch the chief justice. "And that I will well and faithfully discharge the duties of the office on which I am about to enter. So help me God."

Ushers guided the president into the crowded courtroom as Warren shook hands with the men he would now call "brethren": Black and William O. Douglas, New Deal liberals; Robert H. Jackson, Stanley Reed, and Felix Frankfurter, Roosevelt appointees as well but more conservative in their view of the law; and three Truman appointees, Tom Clark whom Warren had met in the frightened months of 1942 prior to the Japanese evacuation; Ohio Republican Harold H. Burton whom Warren knew from political life; and former Indiana senator Sherman Minton.

Moments after midday, the dark red velour curtains parted behind the raised mahogany bench in the three-story-high courtroom. The associate justices filed to their swivel chairs for the first time in this, the October term, 1953. The center seat remained vacant.

Clad in a silken robe on loan from the Ralph Macias Tailor Shop in Washington, Warren sat unsmiling at the desk below the bench normally occupied by Clerk of the Court Harold B. Willey.

The bailiff sounded the traditional summons: "Oyez! Oyez! Oyez! All persons having business before the Honorable, the Supreme Court of the United States, are admonished to draw near—"

Justice Black began the proceedings with a tribute to the late Chief Justice Fred Vinson read in the soft drawl of the Alabama hill country. When Black concluded the Court's eulogy to "this capable and loyal public servant," he nodded to Willey.

Clerk and chief justice together rose. Willey read the presidential commission: "Know ye: That reposing special trust and confidence in the Wisdom, Uprightness, and Learning of Earl Warren of California, I do appoint him Chief Justice of the United States." His right hand again raised, Warren pledged to administer justice without respect to persons, to do equal right to the poor and to the rich, and to perform his duty as chief justice "agreeably to the Constitution and laws of the United States."

Willey escorted the new chief justice to his chair at the center of the high bench. Beaming, Warren shook hands with the senior men at his right and left, Black and Reed. Together, the nine men took their seats.

Earl Warren was once again "Chief," for so colleagues and clerks addressed all chief justices. He had left California, setting aside one career, to take up another within the quiet confines of the Court. Here he intended to conclude his public career, in this place encrusted with majestic symbol and ancient ritual.

The bailiff announced the Court was in session with a cry first used in fifteenth-century England. The clerk of the court still wrote his formal docket entries in a flowing ink script more of the eighteenth than the twentieth century. Spittoons stood at the ready behind each justice's chair; sharpened goose quills lay on counsel's table. Even the traditional robes of justice were relics of medieval scholars' gowns.

Life here was orderly, outwardly serene, removed from the hurly-burly of official Washington, most of the work done in secret. There was no jostling for position or pride of place. On the bench or in their weekly conference, the justices sat according to seniority at the chief justice's left and right hand. Under the stern portrait of the third chief justice, John Marshall, they shook hands all around, a practice according to Court legend that had begun sixty years earlier. In conference, the chief spoke first, then the most senior justice, finally the newest member, always, in just that order. The junior justice voted first, the chief last—just why, no one could say for sure. So it had been. So it remained.

When the children of justices married, each received shortly thereafter a silver serving tray from Martin's Inc., the tray engraved on the bottom with the signatures of the father's colleagues. The death of a parent prompted flowers to the grieving justice or his wife. A justice's birthday was recognized at the luncheon break during the Saturday conference before the date. When a justice retired, his colleagues gave him as a gift the leather covered chair upon which he sat in the courtroom. When he died, the senior justice would deliver a sober memorial from the bench, with handsomely printed copies provided to the family.

Thus it was, and thus it would be, ordained by hallowed tradition.

Men served a contented lifetime in these chambers. The careers of just seven justices spanned the entire history of the Court from its first session in the Royal Exchange Building in New York City in 1790 to the day Earl Warren was sworn in 160 years later. Only thirteen men had presided as chief justice in that span—while thirty-four were elected president.*

Except for those who held menial jobs, this was an all-white, virtually all-male institution. Indeed, aside from John Jay, whose antecedents were French, every chief justice prior to Warren had British forebears.

Blacks might serve as messengers, custodians, or garage attendants, but there had never been a black law clerk or page. The first Jew to sit on the Court, Louis D. Brandeis, took his seat only in 1916; just three Jews and five Catholics had served on the Court by the time Warren took the oath. The first woman had yet to sit, though William O. Douglas had appointed in 1944 the first, and nine years later still the only, female clerk.

Even the clothing was prescribed. Officers of the Court, government attorneys, and older members of the bar wore swallowtail coats. The marshal passed small, discreet cards to attorneys so careless as to unbutton the jackets of their two-piece suits to reveal they were not wearing vests.

To this august temple came Earl Warren, the third Californian to serve on the high court.

Warren was sixty-two, far better known nationally as a politician than as a lawyer. Still, he brought to the Court useful attributes. He had served ten years as governor of his native California, longer than any other man. During that time, he had earned high marks as an administrator; those skills would be necessary in the chief justice's task of overseeing the entire federal court system.

He was personable, gregarious, and widely respected both in political and law enforcement circles. He had spent four years as attorney general and almost fourteen as district attorney before that. Critics might concede Warren's knowledge of criminal law was sound.

They faulted him, however, for lack of experience with the sweep of civil

---

* Warren was the fourteenth chief justice to serve, the thirteenth to be confirmed. John Rutledge, appointed in 1795 by George Washington, sat for five months, but held only a recess appointment and was refused confirmation by the Senate. Additionally, Warren was just the seventh formally nominated, confirmed, and commissioned to be chief justice of the United States; until 1888 the incumbent was known variously as chief justice of the Supreme Court of the United States or chief justice of the Supreme Court.

law. That assertion overlooked Warren's responsibility for acting as legal counsel to Alameda County on all civil matters when he was district attorney, not to mention similar experience as attorney general. He was better prepared as a practicing attorney than many gave him credit for.

The most frequent criticism stemmed from Warren's choice of public service four decades earlier: Academics carped that he was not a legal scholar, and the conservative attorneys who dominated the American Bar Association crabbed that he had no judicial experience.

In a letter to his brother Milton, whom he counted a trusted adviser, President Eisenhower disputed the assumption that a lifetime on the bench or practicing law was the best training for the Court. He defended Warren's appointment, arguing:

> *I believe that we need statesmanship on the Supreme Court. Statesmanship is developed in the hard knocks of a general experience, private and public. Naturally, a man occupying the post must be competent in the law—and Warren has had seventeen years of practice in public law, during which his record was one of remarkable accomplishment and success, to say nothing of dedication. He has been very definitely a liberal-conservative; he represents the kind of political, economic, and social thinking that I believe we need on the Supreme Court. Finally, he has a national name for integrity, uprightness, and courage that, again, I believe we need on the Court.*

Warren was the seventh to take the seat without prior experience on the bench, his supporters pointed out. Further the two men generally rated as the greatest chief justices in the court's history, John Marshall and Charles Evans Hughes, had never sat as a judge before they went to the Supreme Court.

Indeed, only two of the thirteen chief justices before Warren had even spent their working lives as lawyers. Most had been politicians or political activists who graduated to the president's cabinet.

Whatever Warren might have lacked in a legal sense, he made up for with his badly needed political skills. The Court he now led had been badly administered and sorely divided since the days of FDR. Harry Truman, fretting about the Court's disarray, promised to name a consensus builder as chief justice when Harlan F. Stone died in 1946. But Truman's appointment, Secretary of the Treasury Fred M. Vinson, lacked the stature necessary to unite his eight brethren.

Vinson faltered while Associate Justices Hugo Black and Robert Jackson escalated their philosophical differences into visceral antagonism.

In that sour atmosphere, dissenting opinions and bad feeling proliferated; the Court split sharply into two philosophical wings. Loosely tagged in the press as conservative and liberal, more accurately the rivals were precedent-minded and activist-oriented.

Black and Douglas composed the "liberal" or activist minority. Black was a gracious Alabaman—a onetime member of the Ku Klux Klan in the 1920's when social membership was important to a young politician—and a former senator who had served Franklin Roosevelt well and loyally.

The young man from rural Clay County graduated from the University of Alabama School of Law at age twenty, opened a Birmingham law practice, and eventually rose to political prominence. Elected to the United States Senate, Black had in early 1937 sponsored FDR's "court-packing" bill, an effort to shatter the anti–New Deal bloc on the high court.

Like most Republicans at the time, Earl Warren had opposed the court-packing bill. It died in the Senate, but not before one associate justice began shifting his votes to the liberal side, and a second of the "Nine Old Men" announced his retirement. Black filled the vacancy in 1937, giving Roosevelt and the New Deal a tenuous majority on the court.

By the time of Warren's appointment, Black had evolved into a judicial activist, a populist and an absolutist, particularly in reading the First Amendment. The Constitution, argued Black, who carried a dog-eared copy in his pocket, was to be taken literally. If the First Amendment said that Congress shall make no law abridging freedom of speech, in Black's interpretation, that meant *no* law.

Black's courtly manners masked a fierce competitiveness, some of which he vented on the tennis courts of his Arlington, Virginia, home. The balance he poured into defending his position on a Supreme Court that tended to heed the arguments of government lawyers. By 1945, it was said, Black's "vehemence" and "ruthlessness" in the Saturday conferences had propelled Associate Justice Owen Roberts into bitter retirement.

Black's closest ally, at least in philosophy, was crusty William Orville Douglas. Perhaps the most brilliant of the justices, Douglas had a reputation as a quick but careless worker.

Born in Washington State, Douglas had overcome childhood polio to graduate from tiny Whitman College in Walla Walla. He hoboed across the country the summer before enrolling in Columbia Law, then eventually made his way to the Yale Law School faculty.

Widely praised as a law professor, Douglas had accepted appointment to the New Deal's Securities and Exchange Commission. The weathered Douglas looked every inch the outdoorsman he was; paradoxically, he knew as much about corporate law as any Wall Street lawyer.

Douglas was wary of Warren, Black welcoming. A week after administering the oath to Warren, Black wrote his sons that the Chief "is a very attractive, fine man. Just a short acquaintance with him explains why it was possible for him to get votes in both parties in California.

"He is a novice here, of course, but a man with his intelligence should be able to give good service. I am by no means sure that an intelligent man with practical, hard common sense and integrity like he has is not as good a type to select as could be found in the country."

For his part, Warren saw in Black's rise a model for himself. "Warren thought Black had been cruelly criticized when he came on the court," said Warren friend Phil Wilkins. Black "had vowed to make himself, and had made himself, a profoundly able lawyer by sheer hard work." Warren intended to do the same.

Paired against Black and Douglas stood the equally formidable Robert H. Jackson and Felix Frankfurter, the one a churn of suppressed fury, the other a legal gamecock.

Born in 1892 in tiny Spring Creek, Pennsylvania, Jackson had studied for a year at a second-rate law school. He chose instead to read for the law in the law firm of a cousin active in local Democratic politics. For the next twenty years Jackson's legal and political careers flourished apace in Jamestown, New York.

When New York governor Franklin D. Roosevelt was elected president, he summoned his loyal political supporter Robert Jackson to Washington as counsel to the Bureau of Internal Revenue. Jackson moved successively to the Department of Justice, then to the post of solicitor general, and finally to the Supreme Court in 1941.

Jackson was considered a prime candidate to succeed Chief Justice Harlan Fiske Stone in 1946. But President Truman had his doubts, the more so after *Washington Star* columnist Doris Fleeson reported that were Jackson appointed, Black and Douglas would resign.

With that, the disarray on the Supreme Court, the smallest and once the most collegial of Washington's offices, became public knowledge. Seeking comity, Truman nominated his friend and poker-playing buddy Fred Vinson, the secretary of the treasury.

Vinson was overmatched in his new post, particularly by the irrepressible, brilliant, ever-manipulative Felix Frankfurter. Frankfurter was, in the Yiddish that he heard as a boy, a *kochleffl,* a pot-stirrer.

Born in Vienna, Austria, Frankfurter migrated with his parents to the United States and the teeming Lower East Side of New York City in 1894. By dint of sheer brilliance—it may be that there has never been so widely read, so truly intellectual a Supreme Court justice—he made his way out of the ghetto, first through City College of New York, then through Harvard Law, always first in his class.

Frankfurter defied the odds in a legal world still deeply anti-Semitic. He spent eight years as an assistant United States attorney in New York City, then from 1914 to 1939, Frankfurter served on the faculty of Harvard's School of Law, counted both a brilliant teacher and legal scholar. Harvard and teaching were ever Frankfurter's haven; no man ever loved that New England institution more than the slight professor from the Lower East Side.

Aided by an annual stipend from Supreme Court Associate Justice Louis Brandeis, he took up the liberal causes from which Brandeis was barred by his judicial post: advocate of Zionism at the Versailles Conference; adviser to the National Association for the Advancement of Colored People and the newly established American Civil Liberties Union; and a constant consultant to government agencies.

The election of Franklin D. Roosevelt brought Frankfurter new influence. He dispatched dozens of former students to positions in the new adminstration, launching the careers of Frankfurter's "Hot Dogs" in virtually every department of the federal government. He offered FDR advice on everything from legislation to speeches.

In January, 1939, Roosevelt rewarded the Harvard Law School professor with the "Jewish seat" on the court, to replace Benjamin Cardozo who had died.

For all his talk of the high court as a monastery, Associate Justice Felix Frankfurter continued to made his presence known. He still telephoned the White House to recommend appointments. He still talked politics with his "boys," now risen to positions of power in a dozen government agencies.

He was vital, witty, and, when he wished to be, charming. He stalked the halls of the Supreme Court, whistling the melody from the slow movement of Mozart's clarinet concerto, a short man, barely five feet three inches tall and seemingly smaller because of his slight build. He would buttonhole clerks, ever eager to expound a legal theory, happy in debate with even the greenest of them, the teacher still, but an unrelenting advocate for his deeply held theory of judicial restraint.

Liberal Felix Frankfurter had become the Court's, perhaps the nation's, leading proponent of the argument that the judiciary must refrain from policy making. That was the role of the legislative branch; the courts were to defer to Congress so long as its acts squared with the Constitution.

Had the Nine Old Men of the Hughes Court followed that rule rather than imposing their economic views on New Deal legislation, Frankfurter argued, there would have been no court-packing furor in 1937. The Court would also have avoided even the appearance of political partisanship and not have tarnished its reputation as the impartial arbiter of disputes.

In practical effect, Frankfurter's sense of restraint often left him voting against causes he had once advocated, either by declining to review cases at all or refusing to overrule even the most ill-considered acts of Congress.

If it troubled him, he gave no public sign. A judge was not to impose *his* personal views on the Constitution; he was to interpret the law. Paradoxically, sometimes painfully, Frankfurter's philosophy hobbled his instincts to do justice.

Philosophically, this put him at odds with Hugo Black, more than willing to look behind the face of a legislative act to see the unintended consequences. Frankfurter and Black would argue their respective positions for two decades, neither moving the other, but polarizing the Court.

Black and Douglas, for their part, enjoyed provoking Frankfurter, a man whose voice screeched in proportion to his irritation. While Black sought to maintain a semblance of civility with Frankfurter, Douglas made no pretense.

The four other members of the Warren Court were hardly the intellectual equal of a Frankfurter or Douglas, though all were men of broad experience. They were certainly more convivial.

Harold Hitz Burton was the only Republican ever to be appointed to the Supreme Court by a Democrat. He had earned that badge by serving loyally with then-Senator Harry Truman on the Missourian's War Investigating Committee during World War II.

Square-jawed, handsome, every bit the public image of a United States senator, Harvard graduate Burton had practiced law; had served in the state legislature; and had been elected mayor of Cleveland, Ohio. He served four years in the Senate before joining the high court.

A meticulous, even obsessive man, each morning he strolled around the Capitol building, noting in his daily diary the weather and those flowers in bloom, frequently with their Latin names. Twice weekly he marked the number of yards he swam in the gym and his weight; he periodically noted the pressure of the tires on his 1952 Model 72 Roadmaster Buick, and always recorded motor, serial, and key numbers of that machine on the front page of his diary.

Now sixty-five, Burton sat on the Supreme Court, a conscientious journeyman who tended to follow the Jackson-Frankfurter lead. So pleased with friend Earl Warren's appointment Burton thanked President Eisenhower for the choice. ". . . I shall consider it a privilege to work with him."

Like Burton, Sherman Minton had also served in the Senate with Harry Truman—he was Truman's seatmate—and like Burton, he too was deemed a member of the conservative wing.

A multisport letterman as an undergraduate at Indiana University, Minton at sixty-three still had an athlete's burly physique and the salty vocabulary of the locker room. "Shay" Minton—whose tobacco chewing was a habit acquired during his days as a baseball player—was probably the last justice to actually use the spittoons for their intended purpose.

A Yale Law graduate, Minton practiced law in tiny New Albany, Indiana, until elected to the Senate as an ardent New Dealer. He served one term as an assistant whip plumping for Roosevelt's legislative program, then was defeated by the isolationist vote in 1940 because he advocated rearmament and a peacetime draft.

Such men merited political reward. His was appointment to the United States Court of Appeals for the Seventh Circuit, where he sat for more than eight years. Thus he and Black—who had served for eighteen months as part-time police court judge early in his career—were the only members of the high court with judicial experience at the time of their appointment.

Like Black too, Minton had defended Roosevelt's court-packing plan. Unlike Black, once on the court, Minton cleaved to the conservative position. In the four years since his appointment, he had consistently voted to allow the executive and legislative branches wide lattitude, particularly in matters of national security and criminal law.

Shay was well-liked among the brethren. Had he been more assertive, more willing to break with judicial precedent, he might have evolved as a leader on the court. It was not to be.

Similarly, Associate Justice Stanley Reed could have stepped forward, but did not. Born in Kentucky in 1884, he had studied law at the University of Virginia, at Columbia, and at the Sorbonne. He had the legal experience from a successful private practice, then a stint as general counsel to the Reconstruction Finance Corporation in the Republican administration of Herbert Hoover.

Franklin Roosevelt named Reed solicitor general in 1935, then promoted him to the high court in 1938 as the Nine Old Men began to fall away.

On the court, Reed was a careful draftsman of opinions, but a man of neither great imagination nor daring. A connoisseur of fine bourbon and horseflesh, he remained a southerner—refusing even to attend a Christmas party at the Court to which black staff members had been invited. He was a courtly man, but not one to lead the brethren in battle.

Instead, he plodded at the side of the scintillating Frankfurter and the fiery Jackson, quick to vote for the government in civil liberties cases and on matters of internal security.

The third of Truman's appointees was Texan Tom Clark, far better known for his jaunty bow ties than for his legal opinions. A graduate of the University of Texas, Clark practiced law in Dallas from 1922 to 1937, in the middle of that period spending six years as civil district attorney for Dallas County.

A protégé of Speaker of the House Sam Rayburn, Clark moved to New Deal Washington in 1937. Over the next dozen years, he held a succession of posts in the Department of Justice, eventually serving four years as Truman's attorney general.

As AG, Clark had compiled in 1947 the "attorney general's list," the names of eighty-two allegedly subversive organizations, membership in which was a virtual bar to federal employment. With that list, Clark began a nationwide witchhunt, rooting out alleged Communists from government.

Clark joined the Supreme Court in 1949, a man deemed insensitive to civil liberties by liberals and legally deficient by conservatives. On the high court, Clark tended to support the government position, critics on the left charged. The criticism, said one Texas lawyer who knew the man, was "not inaccurate enough to be wrong."

Earl Warren, the ninety-second to take the oath as a member of this Court, was to preside over these men who commanded the halls of the seeming ageless "Marble Palace" on the east side of First Street facing the Capitol.

It *was* a grand building, though actually less than thirty years old. White Vermont marble sheathed the four-story structure inspired by the Greek temples of antiquity; sixteen Corinthian columns supported the commanding west portico, and massive bronze doors, each weighing 6.5 tons, opened on the sanctum inside. Carved on the triangular tympanum over that entrance, the tableau "Liberty Enthroned" by Robert Aitken displayed Liberty holding the scales of justice, guarded on either side by Order and Authority. High overhead, the architrave promised, "Equal Justice Under Law."

Here Earl Warren would be *primus inter pares,* the first among equals. As chief justice, he received a token salary differential of $500, as well as precedence in public ceremonies, even though he might be the most junior of justices. Associate Justice Felix Frankfurter, a man supremely sensitive to the niceties of office, referred to these as mere "ceremonial rosettes." *

A chief justice could issue no orders; he led by persuasion, by brokering compromise, by the consent of his colleagues. His greatest power lay in the assignment of opinions.

The chief, as long as he was in the majority, could pick a man who would seek to broaden the impact of a decision, or one who would narrow it. He could tap the justice whose opinions were closest to his own. He could pick a man given to compromise, or to unbending doctrine. He could give a case to a man expert in an area, or one whom the chief hoped might become expert. He could cultivate alliances or drive a wedge into the philosophical opposition with a desired assignment. He could assign the most important cases to the favored few, including himself, or he could give each an opportunity for judicial fame.

The wise chief justice also watched for political implications when making assignments—for the Court could never be far from the political. So it was that Kentuckian Stanley Reed rather than Felix Frankfurter, a Jewish New Englander, wrote the 1944 decision banning the white primary so beloved of southern states.

Despite his seemingly free hand, even in the assignment function, the chief justice's power hung by the most slender of threads. The responsibility for assigning opinions could be taken away by a simple vote of the brethren.

In short, one judicial commentator wrote, "A Chief must get his real eminence not from the office but from the qualities he brings to it. He must possess the mysterious quality of leadership."

The job was awesome. Even the most confident of men—and Earl Warren knew his own strengths—would pause at the responsibility he suddenly faced virtually alone.

"I've always thought that perhaps the most lonesome day I ever had in my life was the day I arrived at the Supreme Court," he acknowledged in an interview years later.

---

* Among the rosettes was a limousine, the story of which Warren enjoyed telling. Invited for the first time to a White House dinner, the chief justice and his wife rented a limousine. The driver apologized, but they were short of limousines that night. So it was that the Warrens tooled through the White House gate and up to the portico in a black Cadillac with a sign on the side: "Airport Limousine." Newspaper columnist Drew Pearson wrote of the incident, shaming Congress into appropriating funds for a limousine for the chief justice of the United States.

As governor, he had commanded a staff of fifty, "available for many services that one accustomed to them would be lost without." He had drivers, guards, a limousine, even a DC-3 with pilots at the ready.

In Washington, Warren discovered, the chief justice's staff consisted of a single secretary, three law clerks, and two aging messengers—one of whom died within six months. The younger messenger, past seventy, spent his afternoons dozing in an unused conference room; he retired the next year.

His secretary was Margaret McHugh, a veteran of Washington bureaucracy who had worked as secretary to New Deal Treasury Secretary Henry Morgenthau, Junior. When Roosevelt loyalist Morgenthau resigned, to be replaced by Truman crony Fred Vinson, McHugh stayed on as Vinson's secretary. She followed Vinson to the Supreme Court, an efficient, close-mouthed aide as well as secretary to her boss.

After seven years with Vinson, she knew the routines of the chief justice's office. She was familiar too with the unwritten policies of the Court, the hallowed functions of the clerk, the librarian, and the reporter. Warren promptly asked her to stay.

As chief justice, Warren had three law clerks, one more than the other justices, except for Douglas, who insisted he could get along nicely with just one. The clerks were recent law school graduates, chosen competitively from class rankings at the nation's most prestigious law schools. A Supreme Court clerkship was a distinct honor, prelude and stepping-stone to a distinguished legal career.

Warren elected to retain the three clerks Vinson had selected for the 1953–54 year. Replacing them at this late date would be unfair to them, and the families they had moved to Washington; it would also take time, which he did not have.

Warren went to Washington on less than a week's notice, with no preparation and no knowledge of the docket. He had to familiarize himself with the cases accepted for oral argument, and some 400 petitions that had come in during the summer months when the Court was not in session. The Chief thus began his first term depending on strangers, three of them terribly new to the law.

His senior law clerk, William Oliver, introduced him to the legal routines Vinson had followed, particularly in the preparation of advisory memos on each petition. Clerks in each justice's office read the Appellate Docket petitions filed with the Court by private counsel. The clerk then prepared a memo summarizing the facts and the legal issue presented, and recommending whether the case be taken up.

Each justice independently decided whether to grant a petition for certiorari, that is, actually to review the case on its merits. Some justices tended to rely on the recommendation of their clerks, particularly if the clerk was especially well informed on a subject. Others ignored them.

In that sense, each of the associate justices operated as if he were the sole partner in a small, independent law firm. By long-held rule, four votes were needed to grant cert, and bring the case to the Supreme Court for briefing and argument.

The chief justice's office had an additional responsibility: summarizing for all nine justices the often illiterate and confused petitions that flowed from those unable to afford attorneys. These *in forma pauperis* petitions, largely from prisoners, consumed a considerable amount of the clerks' time. If they were frequently baseless, they did inspire enough petitions for certiorari to have an impact on the Court's caseload.

The two dockets were, in fact, misnamed, Warren law clerk Larry Simon noted. The difference between the Appellate Docket and the Miscellaneous Docket was no more than the difference between the affluent and the poor.

Each of the prisoners' petitions received about the same amount of time as the appeals filed by attorneys, one or two pages of summary, but only the chief's copy of the nine flimsies prepared bore the clerk's recommendation to grant or deny. Thus each of the associate justices or his clerk made his own decision before the *in forma pauperis* or Miscellaneous Docket cases came up in the Court's Saturday conferences. On any given Saturday, the brethren might dispose of as many as 100 petitions for certiorari, relying only on the flimsies prepared by Warren's clerks.

While Earl Warren was finding his way about the Supreme Court, he also confronted an awkward personal adjustment. For his first two months in Washington, Warren lived alone, "perfectly miserable" without Nina. She had remained in Sacramento to sort and pack their belongings, some destined for storage, some to be shipped to Washington.

There were also the children to get settled. Jim, of course, was married and prospering in the advertising business in San Francisco. Younger daughters Dorothy and Honey Bear, fully recovered from polio, were attending UCLA. Sons Earl and Bobby were enrolled at the University of California Davis. Oldest daughter Virginia, a Berkeley graduate, was to move with Nina to Washington.*

It all took time. "It's a job to move out of the mansion after living there for eleven years with six children on five floors." Nina told friends.

She was inundated. "She could have a million maids," said Earl Junior's new wife, Patty, "and she would still do all the work. She was very busy, boxing and labeling, boxing and labeling."

While he waited for Nina to join him, the new chief justice filled his evenings reading clerks' memoranda and briefs for cases already scheduled for argument this term.

He visited Warren and Margaret Olney often in those two months, eating dinner with these California friends. Olney, now the assistant attorney

---

* It was Virginia who finally found an apartment for the Warrens at the Wardman-Park, a comfortable residential hotel in northwest Washington not far from the National Zoo.

general in charge of the criminal division, and the man Olney had called "Chief" since 1939 pleasantly idled the evenings with conversation.

Mrs. Olney recalled their discussions, particularly one about "the Japanese situation at the time of Pearl Harbor." The decision to evacuate the Japanese living on the West Coast troubled both men, Mrs. Olney realized; ten years later they had nagging doubts about their part in the removal.

"I think they were trying to decide whether the right thing had been done or not. I don't think they came to any conclusions."

Olney, grandson of a Civil War veteran, twice convinced Warren to accompany him on Sunday tours of the grassy battlefields spotted about the nearby countryside. The Chief seemed barely to pay attention, Mrs. Olney decided; he was more interested in their company than the history.

He seemed to prefer the present to the past, she recalled. He perked up only momentarily as they scouted out the site of an engagement of a California regiment, but the War of Rebellion as a subject disturbed him. "I think it was kind of painful to him. He was always glad when we started back home."

There his reading awaited him, as always.

More than 125 cases crowded the calendar, and there was one particularly big file to be read, the appeal of the Reverend Oliver Brown, a father critical of his daughter's education in the all-black schools of Topeka, Kansas.

CHAPTER 23

A NEW DAY

EARL WARREN, AS THE BRETHREN QUICKLY DISCOVERED, WAS NOT Fred Vinson.

The new chief justice brought to the Supreme Court a sense of assured command. A politician popular with California voters of both parties, he had mastered the jobs of district attorney, then attorney general, and governor. He was confident he would similarly grasp the work and the symbolic role of chief justice of the United States.

Most important, Earl Warren was to be the *Chief* as Vinson was not. Warren had the vision and sure hand of the leader that Fred Vinson had lacked.

Warren had other gifts as well. Not by nature an intellectual, Warren compensated by hard work; Vinson, with similar handicaps, had preferred poker with Harry Truman or bridge with Dwight Eisenhower.

A month after Warren joined the Court, Felix Frankfurter concluded the new chief justice showed great promise, despite the lack of an eminent legal career. "He brings to his work that largeness of experience and breadth of outlook which may well make him a very good Chief Justice provided he has some other qualities which, from what I have seen, I believe he has."

Those qualities, Frankfurter continued, included a focus on the work of the Court; a willingness to work hard; an ability to grow in the job, to learn; and a capacity to truly listen to others. Frankfurter was certain Warren had that "to a rare degree."

The new chief justice easily fitted himself to the Court's routine. He was genial, quick to introduce himself to elevator operators and secretaries.

Within days, law clerks joked, he knew all 200 people working in the building and was running for office.

Warren effortlessly established "an air of amity in the Court to the extent it had not existed immediately before his appointment," said Warren law clerk Richard Flynn. "He helped eliminate some internal hostilities and bring people together through his personality. . . ."

In his first days as chief justice, Warren relied on the brethren for guidance. At his request, the senior associate justice, Hugo Black, led the conferences during the first three weeks of the term. Warren watched but did not vote on the backlog of certiorari petitions that had accumulated since June.

Not long after, he asked Black to recommend a book on opinion writing. Black suggested Aristotle's treatise, *Rhetoric,* which Warren read before drafting his first opinion for the Court in November. (That was a case of "no notoriety" granting compensation to an injured longshoreman who had failed to file a timely claim. Warren's opinion for the unanimous Court held, "This Act must be liberally construed in conformance with its purpose.")

Felix Frankfurter too was quick to offer advice. Within days of Warren's arrival, the former Harvard law professor, unbidden, had loaned the new chief justice a two-volume study of the work of the Court. Ever the professor, Frankfurter pulled from his files two memoranda on procedural matters, offering them as guidance for the newest justice.

Warren settled in, guided by Vinson's former secretary, Margaret McHugh; no one knew the Court's arcane procedures better than she or understood the $1.5 million budget so well.

"I ran the office," the firm-handed McHugh explained. "I did most of his work, all of his work as far as chief justice was concerned." It was her responsibility to see that the office functioned smoothly, that the clerks were meeting deadlines, that opinions from other chambers were logged in.

Warren was demanding, but "Mrs. McHugh," as he invariably referred to her, "found him very easy to work for. He was a fair-minded person. He did like things done right. I liked to do things right, so we had no problem there."

Warren also asked Margaret Bryan, his former appointments secretary in Sacramento, to join him in Washington. At age thirty-three, Bryan was tested, reliable, and ever affable.

With nothing to tie her to Sacramento, Bryan agreed to come to Washington. "I just thought if he could do it, I could do it."

For the next sixteen years, Bryan was to handle Warren's personal correspondence, type his speeches, pay his bills and keep his calendar. She also scanned *The Sacramento Bee* daily for news of California and Californians; the obituary of an acquaintance invariably prompted a Warren letter of condolence.

When the Court's work was heaviest, Maggie Bryan and Peggy McHugh shared the typing. Bryan also helped McHugh type the original and ten flimsies of the memoranda that clerks wrote to advise the justices on the merits of *in forma pauperis* petitions.

Once comfortable with the Court's grave pace, on Monday, December 7, 1953, the new chief justice effectively assumed leadership of the Court. That morning lawyers would begin three days of oral argument in five cases as important practically and symbolically as any in the history of the Supreme Court.

The Reverend Oliver Brown had come to Washington seeking to overturn more than a half a century's judicial precedent.

The end of the Civil War in 1865 ushered in the Reconstruction Era, and brought forth three constitutional amendments. The Thirteenth abolished slavery, the Fourteenth declared the former slaves to be citizens, and the Fifteenth assured them the vote.

But Reconstruction also fostered a harsh reaction. Within a decade the constitutional rights seemingly assured by the amendments had been undercut or nullified by legislatures and courts.

In 1873, the United States Supreme Court held, 5–4, that the Fourteenth Amendment's guarantee that "no State shall make or enforce any law which shall abridge the privileges or immunities of citizens of the United States" applied only to the federal government.

In subsequent years the Court struck down a public accommodations act passed by Congress in 1875. Subsequent decisions would effectively take away the black man's right to vote, the right to a jury of peers, even the right to be free of a lynch mob.

With that, the Louisiana legislature in 1890 adopted an "Act to promote the comfort of passengers" which required that "all railway companies carrying passengers in their coaches in the State, shall provide equal but separate accomodations for the white, and colored, races." Passengers were to sit only in the section designated for their race under penalty of a $25 fine or not more than twenty days in jail.

In what appears to have been a carefully arranged test of the law, authorities arrested Homer Adolph Plessy, just one-eighth black, for taking a seat in the white-only section of a Louisiana Railway train bound from New Orleans to Covington, thirty miles away. Judge John H. Ferguson rejected Plessy's contention that the segregation statute violated his rights under the Fourteenth Amendment.

The case of Homer Plessy made its way to the United States Supreme Court in 1896. There Justice Henry Billings Brown, as lackluster a man as ever sat on that bench, wrote the 7–1 majority opinion, with one justice recusing himself without explanation.

It fell to Justice Brown to determine the scope of the Fourteenth Amendment and "the exact rights it was intended to secure to the colored race." Brown rested his argument on an unproved assumption that Congress had not intended "to abolish distinctions based upon color, or to enforce social, as distinguished from political equality, or a commingling of the two races upon terms unsatisfactory to either."

As Richard Kluger argued in his comprehensive history of the school desegregation cases, nowhere in the congressional debates nor in the amendment itself was any distinction made between "political" and "social" equality. This was a court-made distinction that would result in a court-made law. (The amendment itself spoke only of equal protection of the law.)

Justice Brown's tortured opinion continued:

> *Laws permitting, and even requiring, their separation in places where they are liable to be brought into contact do not necessarily imply the inferiority of either race to the other, and have been generally, if not universally, recognized as within the competency of the state legislatures in the exercise of their police power. The most common instance of this is connected with the establishment of separate schools for white and colored children, which has been held to be a valid exercise of the legislative power even by courts of States where the politial rights of the colored race have been longest and most earnestly enforced.*

Louisiana was free, Brown rumbled on, to adopt a law in accordance with the "established usages, customs and traditions of the people, and with a view to the promotion of the comfort, and the preservation of the public peace and good order."

Plessy's lawyers erred, according to the majority opinion, by assuming that social prejudices might be overcome by legislation. "If one race be inferior to the other socially, the Constitution of the United States cannot put them on the same plane."

There was a single, brave dissent, written by a former slave owner, John Marshall Harlan. A Kentuckian who had supported the Union cause, Harlan poked at the sophistry of the majority opinion. If blacks and whites could be separated by law, why not require separate coaches for naturalized and native citizens, for Protestants and Roman Catholics?

"Our Constitution is color-blind, and neither knows nor tolerates classes among citizens . . . ," Harlan argued. "In respect of civil rights, all citizens are equal before the law."

Under the guise of "separate but equal," Jim Crow laid firm hand on the institutions of the Old South. State after state of the former Confederacy enacted laws requiring separate restrooms and drinking fountains, and segregated seating on public streetcars and buses. Others prohibited mixing of the races in hotels, barbershops, poolrooms, restaurants, even at domino and checker contests.

Through the first four decades of the century, the legal plight of American blacks remained essentially unchanged. They might take heart with an occasional victory—the Scottsboro Case of 1932 held seven blacks had been denied due process when they were not given counsel in a capital case. Then in 1935 the Supreme Court returned to the Scottsboro case to find that blacks had been systematically excluded from Alabama grand juries.

With the end of World War II, the pace of litigation, and victory, picked up, spurred by a zealous National Association for the Advancement of Colored People and fostered by a sea change that had come over the United States. The war had been waged, at least in terms of propaganda, against the scourge of Nazi racism; blacks had performed creditably, sometimes heroically, in that struggle.

The Cold War rivalry with international communism made it increasingly difficult to maintain Jim Crow at home when the nation postured as leader of the "Free World" abroad. New allies, particularly in what would become known as the Third World, looked askance at the gap between promise and achievement in the United States.

Racism thus became unpatriotic.

The first major case to reach the Supreme Court after the war involved covenants in property deeds that prohibited sales to, or occupancy by, non-whites. The issue was simple: Could private parties rely on a state's legal system to deprive blacks of the right to live where they chose?

Four times before, the Supreme Court had denied review of cases that raised this question. This fifth time Chief Justice Vinson wrote for a 6–0 court—three justices disqualified themselves—that enforcement of such private agreements by state courts violated the Fourteenth Amendment's guarantee of equal protection of the law. The covenants were not void, merely unenforceable; voluntary adherence to the ubiquitous covenants would still be permitted.

In 1948 too, the Supreme Court unanimously ordered the prompt admission of Ada Sipuel, a black woman, to a state law school, but ducked the *Plessy* question of separate but equal. If the state of Oklahoma wanted to set up a second law school for blacks, it could direct Ada Sipuel to enroll there.

Two years later, the court held unanimously that George W. McLaurin could not be confined to a graduate school classroom seat set aside for "colored." Such restrictions, as well as segregated eating and studying tables, "impair and inhibit his ability to study, to engage in discussions and exchange of views with other students and, in general, to learn his profession."

On the same day the Supreme Court unanimously ordered that Herman Marion Sweatt be admitted to the University of Texas School of Law. Without overruling the tattered doctrine of separate but equal, Chief Justice Vinson held that a newly opened black law school with a small faculty and no reputation was in fact separate and not equal.

Encouraged by these incremental successes, the NAACP took up public school segregation cases across the country. But as eager as the organization was to take on *Plessy,* the Supreme Court was reluctant.

The Court granted review of the first of the school cases, from South Carolina, in June, 1951. Six months later, the justices sent it back to the

Circuit Court of Appeals for a report on the progress made toward equalizing black and white schools.

The Vinson Court was stalling.

In that atmosphere the Reverend Oliver Brown's suit against the Topeka, Kansas, Board of Education came to the Supreme Court. The Reverend Brown, a black man, sought to send his eight-year-old daughter Linda to a school closer to home, a school designated by the board for whites only.

Granted certiorari, or review of the record in the courts below, the Reverend Brown's appeal was to become the lead school integration case. It would be joined by similar suits from Virginia and Delaware; the back-and-forth South Carolina case back once again; and another from the District of Columbia, a federal jurisdiction.*

The justices took up the school desegregation cases four days after oral argument at their regular Saturday conference on December 13, 1952. As chief, Vinson spoke first, opening the discussion with a defense of precedent and *Plessy*.

At that moment, Fred Vinson missed his opportunity for judicial greatness. With his court split into three camps on the issue of school desegregation, Vinson lacked the vision to unite this pack of individualists.

Two justices more or less agreed with Vinson, though for different reasons. Stanley Reed, a Kentuckian, wanted to uphold *Plessy*. Tom Clark, from Texas, preferred to allow the states to find their own solution.

Hugo Black, William Douglas, Harold Burton, and Sherman Minton stated their willingness to reverse *Plessy*.

The outcome lay with Felix Frankfurter and Robert Jackson. Jackson instinctively wanted to strike down segregation, but could see no way legally. The NAACP briefs, he complained, offered no more rationale than "sociology," poor stuff for his lawyer's soul. If a vote were taken now, he would reluctantly uphold the precedent.

At some deeply felt level, Frankfurter recognized the inequity of Jim Crow and the separate-but-equal justification. Getting a decision on grounds he could support intellectually was another thing. Frankfurter was ever loath to overrule hallowed precedent. Above all, he wanted a narrow holding when the Court ruled, one that would be politically palatable to the nation.

Frankfurter favored delay for now. As it stood, a mere 5–4 vote in such a major case "would have been catastrophic."

Frankfurter in the next months would play a shrewd game, seeking time to change minds, hoping a narrowly drawn decision might sway at least Jackson. His strategy was to discuss the cases, avoid a vote, and put the cases over to the following term.

---

* Seventeen states required segregation in the public schools by 1954: Alabama, Arkansas, Delaware, Florida, Georgia, Kentucky, Louisiana, Maryland, Mississippi, Missouri, North Carolina, Oklahoma, South Carolina, Tennessee, Texas, Virginia, and West Virginia. Four others permitted segregation by local option: Kansas, New Mexico, Arizona, and Wyoming, where the law went unused.

To divert suspicion that the Court was stalling, Frankfurter posed five new questions for attorneys to address at a new round of arguments.

The questions asked what evidence there was that the Fourteenth Amendment was intended to cover school desegregation; whether Congress might abolish school segregation on its initiative; what was the Court's power to do likewise; whether the remedy, if ordered, should be gradually imposed or delayed; and, finally, what form the decree might take if the Court elected the gradual approach.

But before the fall term began and the cases could be reargued, the corpulent Vinson was dead and Earl Warren was chief justice. "This is the first indication that I have ever had that there is a God," a relieved Frankfurter told two former law clerks.

The issue in the school segregation cases was no longer a legal one, but political. In successive decisions the Supreme Court had knocked most of the props from under *Plessy v. Ferguson.*

The looming question came down to whether the nine justices were finally ready to pronounce the coup de grâce.

The new chief justice knew where justice lay. He had come of age in a state with a long history of discrimination against Asians. In ignorance, in fear, in obedience to his perceived patriotic duty, he himself had urged the wartime confinement of those of Japanese descent.

Since then, he had championed civil rights.

When the army decided to release the Japanese evacuees, Warren defended their right to live where they chose. When the National Guard's 40th Infantry Division returned to state control at war's end, he had desegregated the unit. (Proudly he claimed to be the first governor to desegregate the Guard.)

Not long after, Warren's Department of Justice chose not to appeal a federal court order that prohibited California school districts from maintaining segregated schools for "Indian children, or children of Chinese, Japanese or Mongolian parentage."

Warren had gone to public schools with blacks, but knew few. He had no loyal black constituency. "Most Negroes voted against me," he once commented to newspaper columnist Drew Pearson.

He had, however, seen something of segregation during the 1948 presidential campaign. From the observation car of his campaign train he had spotted the little knots of blacks on one side of the track, separated as if by a fence from the whites who had also turned out for his whistle-stop tour.

In Savannah, Georgia, he refused to speak to a segregated audience. The local sponsors then recruited a handful of blacks to sit on the stage while the majority were confined to the balcony of the auditorium. "I can see their eyes to this day, a searching look, as I told them there should be one law for all men," he told a law clerk many years later.

Four years later, as a dark horse candidate for the presidency, he publicly endorsed a federal fair employment act, anti-lynching laws, and an end to the poll tax. "I insist upon one law for all men," he told a reporter for a black newspaper.

By the middle of the century, Warren well understood the sorry lessons Edgar Patterson had discussed during their automobile trips through the Gold Country so long before.

"*Plessy* was a disastrous opinion for the blacks," Warren had come to believe. "Restrictive measures were implemented on the heels of that decision," so severe that by the time Warren took up the segregation cases "a near condition of apartheid existed."

Blacks in the American South, "could not use the same rest rooms, drinking fountains or telephone booths; they could not eat in the same restaurants, sleep in the same hotel, be treated in the same hospitals; or be transported to a hospital in an ambulance which, on other occasions, was used for whites."

In motion picture houses, black patrons entered by separate entrances and were confined to the balcony. "They could not use the same public parks, playgrounds, beaches, golf courses or athletic stadiums, even though the facilities were supported by public funds. They could not use the same reading room or even the same books in a public library."

Their children attended segregated schools, and were offered only "substandard school facilities and inferior teaching provided at grossly less cost than at white schools." They rode buses for hours to crowded schools, while nearby schools for whites had empty desks.

And if they prospered against all odds, they were denied admission to any university attended by whites, public or private. They would not be permitted to vote or to sit on juries. No matter what their education, they were, forever, addressed as "boy," or "Joe," or "Mary," never as "Mister" or "Miss."

From birth to burial—even the cemeteries were segregated—black people in the former states of the Confederacy and the border states beyond lived separate and unequal lives.

When his son Earl spoke generally about the pending case, Warren replied, "You know how I feel about segregation. It isn't a question of what I'd *like* to say, but what the Constitution permits me to say."

Jim Crow might fall. The issue was how, and when.

To the marble courtroom on Monday, December 7, 1953, came the attorneys, in themselves embodying the clash of old and new.

Lead counsel for the school boards was courtly John W. Davis, at age eighty senior partner in a prestigious New York firm, once solicitor general of the United States, ambassador to the Court of Saint James, and presidential candidate in 1924 on the Democratic ticket.

No private lawyer had argued more cases before the Supreme Court, 140, than had Davis, or was as polished. At ease in the Court—these judges were his peers, after all—Davis in swallowtail coat represented the comfortable, settled ways of the past.

Born in West Virginia, Davis shared the prejudices of his times. If he thought of blacks at all, it was likely in the paternalistic sense of responsibility for the less fortunate. Here in this court, he was defending not the social practice of segregation, but the legal custom of honoring precedent.

"Sometime to every principle comes a moment of repose when it has been so often announced, so confidently relied upon, so long continued, that it passes the limits of judicial discretion and disturbance," he argued.

Ranged against this distinguished and assured defender of the accepted order was Thurgood Marshall, with each passing case increasingly recognized by the press as the spokesman for black America in the courts.

Unlike Davis, Marshall had known no privileges of high office and wealth. As counsel for the NAACP Legal Defense and Education Fund, he had appeared in dozens of steamy southern courts, scorned as the "nigger lawyer," suffering the abuse to shape cases for appeal to higher courts, where reason might prevail.

The descendant of slaves—Marshall bragged that one forebear was "the baddest nigger in the whole state of Maryland"—the NAACP attorney had been born in 1908, and christened Thoroughgood after a grandfather. He attended tiny Lincoln College across the Mason-Dixon Line in Pennsylvania, then matriculated to Howard University Law School.

In 1936, Marshall became a staff attorney in the national office of the NAACP. With the head of the legal staff, Charles Houston, and William H. Hastie, a Harvard Law School graduate, Marshall would spend two years shaping a legal challenge to the embedded principle of separate but equal.

Almost two decades later, their challenge was once more before the Supreme Court of the United States, and Thurgood Marshall was now the NAACP's lead attorney.

The courtroom on the first day of the argument was electric with excitement as Davis, counsel for the state of South Carolina, argued his last case before the high court.

"He handled it in a very commendable way based on prior decisions and the weaknessess of some of the arguments being made for abandoning some of the earlier precedents," Warren's clerk Earl Pollock said. "It was a very lawyer-like job."

At the end of his argument and his career before the court, Davis's eyes welled with tears. He recognized his time and his cause had passed.

For Thurgood Marshall, this was less a legal case than a righteous crusade. After a fumbling start on the first day, struggling through sharp interrogation by Frankfurter, he recovered with a passionate plea the next.

Black and white children, Marshall told the court, "in Virginia and South Carolina—and I have seen them do it—they play in the streets together, they play on their farms together, they go down the road together, they separate to go to school, they come out of school and play ball together. They have to be separated in school. . . . If they go to elementary and high school [together], the world will fall apart."

The Court heard the last of the arguments on Wednesday, December 9, and adjourned. Three days later, the brethren met in their oak-paneled conference room at the rear of the Supreme Court building to take up the cases numbered 1, 2, 4, 8, and 10 of the October term, 1953.

Warren spoke first. He proposed they not rush to judgment this day. Instead, they would merely discuss the cases and the underlying issues.

Postponement to permit a consensus to develop was a political device unusual in the Court's deliberations. It was also crucial. *Brown,* said Frank-furter, a veteran of fourteen years on the Supreme Court, was the first case in memory that the justices had put off a vote promptly after argument.

With Black absent because of a family illness, troubled Stanley Reed spoke next. He also favored postponing a vote; discussion would help them frame the issues.

The others concurred, though Burton warned they had to reach a decision this term.

Warren agreed. "The Court has finally arrived at the place where it *must* determine whether segregation is allowable in public schools."

For his part, Warren told historian Richard Kluger two decades later, he had no doubt which way it should go. Once shorn of emotion, "it seemed to me a comparatively simple case."

The Court had chipped away at the separate-but-equal doctrine for years, Warren stated. "Only the *fact* of segregation itself remained unconsidered. On the merits, the natural, the logical, and practically the only way the case could be decided was clear."

As for himself, "the more I've read and heard and thought, the more I've come to conclude that the basis of segregation and 'separate but equal' rests upon a concept of the inherent inferiority of the colored race."

Earl Warren's America would not abide such a thought. "I don't see how in this day and age we can set any group apart from the rest and say that they are not entitled to exactly the same treatment as all others. To do so would be contrary to the Thirteenth, Fourteenth, and Fifteenth Amendments.

Earl Warren had his court. Black, Douglas, Minton, and Burton had stated they would vote to overturn *Plessy* the year before. But the Chief wanted more than a narrow decision; he wanted an overwhelming majority, even a unanimous Court.

"It would be unfortunate," he continued, "if we had to take precipitous action that would inflame more than necessary." Some states would resist any implementation, particularly in the Deep South, but border states like Delaware and Kansas—not unlike his own state of California in racial makeup—would be more likely to accept the court order.

"My instincts and feelings lead me to say that, in these cases, we should abolish the practice of segregation in the public schools—but in a tolerant way."

Warren had neatly framed the argument in moral terms rather than legal. He looked to the root issue, brushing aside as unimportant the legal questions that had ensnared the Vinson court.

Reed followed, a troubled man uncomfortably defending a legal doctrine he acknowledged had resulted in unequal treatment of blacks and whites. He agreed, too, that the Constitution was changing, and what might have been within judicial reason in 1896 was no longer justifiable.

In the drawl of his Kentucky boyhood, Reed sought to counter the Chief's moral argument. "Of course there was no inferior race," he agreed with Warren, adding the very real concession, "though they may be handicapped by lack of opportunity."

Felix Frankfurter hung back. Usually bound by precedent, the former law professor told the conference he disliked reinventing the Fourteenth Amendment, but they could not avoid the issue.

In a memo written for his files the year before, Frankfurter the political liberal warred with Frankfurter the judicial conservative. "However passionately any of us may hold egalitarian views," he wrote, "however fiercely any of us may believe that such a policy of segregation . . . [is] both unjust and short-sighted, he travels outside his judicial authority if for this private reason alone he declares unconstitutional the policy of segregation."

But, replied the liberal within him, if it were desirable to mold one nation of different peoples, then they were to rely on the Fourteenth Amendment which guaranteed equal protection of the law.

In their turn, Douglas and Jackson, philosophical antagonists, disagreed on strategy. Douglas favored striking down *Plessy* now, while leaving for another day what remedies they might propose.

Jackson disdained that approach as *political*. It was merely intended to give the southern states a chance to absorb the concept of integration before black students actually sat beside white in previously segregated classrooms. If they struck down *Plessy,* he for one did not intend to postpone the question of enforcement.

Jackson was, in effect, warning that he would write a separate opinion if the court did not acknowledge this was "new law for a new day." He began drafting a concurrence.

Texan Tom Clark had also softened his position since Vinson's death. He recognized they had implicitly overruled *Plessy v. Ferguson* in the earlier college cases, and he was troubled. If segregation existed, there was some connotation of inferiority, of political inequality.

Clark said he could go along with the majority if its remedial decree permitted flexibility by local officials. Without saying so directly, he was conceding their decision rested on a political, not a legal footing.

Warren proposed they continue to discuss the segregation cases. The brethren agreed "to talk it over, from week to week, dealing with different aspects of it—in groups, over lunches, in conference. It was too important to hurry it," Warren stressed.

Week after week, Warren set aside time in the Saturday conference to discuss the school desegregation cases. "Each justice would pick out a point that he thought was debatable . . . and we would discuss it in that light without anybody announcing that he felt this way or felt that way."

The chief's proposal that they delay a vote was vital. "I think it was the fact that we did not polarize ourselves at the beginning of it that gave us more of an opportunity to come out unanimously on it than if we had done otherwise," Warren said later.

The delay gave Warren time to negotiate, to search for common ground. He was to use the politician's tool of compromise in a temple where acts were ostensibly measured against the inflexible yardsticks of The Law.

The Court held a second full conference on *Brown* on January 16, 1954. The Chief directed this session to remedies—tacitly assuming the Court would strike down *Plessy.*

The brethren split over what they called "the decree," the remedial instructions they would issue once *Plessey* fell. The southerners, Black, Clark, and Reed, feared an order that implemented desegregation too quickly. It would be best to let each state find its way to acceptance of the new social order, they insisted.

Warren wanted the Supreme Court involved as little as possible in the implementation of the remedies. Better to hand that responsibility over to the federal courts below with some guidelines.

Black sought flexibility, agreeing with Warren that the lower federal courts could fit enforcement to local conditions. Douglas, normally the first to enforce civil liberties, also spoke in favor of flexibility.

Jackson was troubled by the fact that he was acceding to his better angels and signing onto what he deemed a political or sociological decision. He would yield that much, but he wanted time to consider enforcement.

"Let's have a reargument on terms of a decree," Jackson suggested, according to Frankfurter's notes. They would rule on *Plessy,* but delay enforcement.

Over the next weeks, Warren talked to other justices, particularly the reluctant Reed. "He followed a precept that . . . if you want to talk to somebody, don't ask them to come to your office. . . . [G]o to theirs," law clerk Richard Flynn noted.

In his meetings Warren pressed for two results: a unanimous decision that would demonstate that the court was unshakable; and a ruling unencumbered by concurring opinions that might dilute the legal authority upon which they were overturning *Plessy.*

One by one the associate justices fell in behind the Chief. They agreed to hand down a decision declaring segregation unconstitutional, yet avoid immediate imposition of a single rule for ending segregation.

There was finally just one holdout, the troubled Stanley Reed. Despite frequent lunches with Warren and Associate Justice Burton from January to April, Reed remained torn between long-held belief in blacks as a race apart, and the knowledge that his dissent could detract from the moral authority of the Court.

Near the end of April, Warren walked down the hall to confront the Kentuckian one last time.

"Stan, you're all by yourself in this now," Warren reported. "You've got to decide whether it's really the best thing for the country."

As Reed's law clerk George Mickum recalled the conversation, "the Chief Justice was quite low-key and very sensitive to the problems that the decision would present to the South. He empathized with Justice Reed's concern. But he was quite firm on the Court's need for unanimity on a matter of this sensitivity."

Reed eventually yielded. A southerner dissenting would only provide excuses for the irreconcilables to cause trouble, Reed realized. He dropped all thought of filing the dissent he had written. In exchange, he asked only that they implement the decision gradually.

Sometime that month, Warren suggested to the brethren that the decision might be more palatable in the Old South if one of the southerners on the Court wrote it.

Several of the justices protested. From the early days of the Republic, when John Marshall wrote decisions that literally defined the meaning of the Constitution, the chief justice had always assumed the politically important cases. Warren agreed to draft the opinion.

The formal vote on the cases now massed under the title *Brown v. Board of Education* came apparently at the regular Saturday conference on Saturday, May 1, 1954. Robert Jackson was not present; stricken with a heart attack two weeks before, he was recuperating at Bethesda Naval Hospital.

Immediately after the 2:30 P.M. adjournment, Warren handed to law clerk Earl Pollock a handwritten memorandum on lined yellow paper. The eight-page document outlined the general approach that Warren wanted the opinion to take.

Only Warren's clerks were to work on the opinion, he instructed Pollock. He assumed they would not discuss it beyond their chambers.

Further, he told his clerk, he wanted the language simple, easily understood, and the opinion itself succinct. He wanted it read.

From the tenor of the Chief's instructions, Pollock inferred that Warren wanted a draft opinion immediately. "He didn't want to wait around and lose somebody."

Pollock worked for thirty-six hours without interruption that weekend, refining the broad legal arguments the Chief had laid out in his memorandum. Pollock decided that they would need two opinions, one for the four state cases, the other for the the federal District of Columbia case. The state cases would rest on the Fourteenth Amendment's guarantee of equal protection, the District case on the Fifth Amendment's assurance of due process of law.

On Monday, May 3, Warren concurred with Pollock's recommendation. The District of Columbia would be handled in a separate decision.

Unusual secrecy surrounded the drafting of the opinions. Not even Nina knew how the brethren had voted, Warren cautioned Margaret Bryan and Peggy McHugh. At Warren's instructions, the two women divided the typing of Pollock's draft between them as a precaution. Each night Miss Bryan and Mrs. McHugh gathered up the papers and stowed them in the big walk-in safe in the outer office. (If at times the chief justice seemed to have disappeared, they might find him sitting in the six-foot-square foyer of the safe, reading a draft opinion.)

In a conference with his three clerks, Warren reported the outcome. The only surprise was the unanimous vote, clerk William Oliver said later.

Warren assigned the District case to Richard Flynn, with Oliver to help him on the draft. They had no more than Pollock's covering memorandum to guide them. Pollock, meanwhile, turned to the legal citations and footnotes for the state cases. Oddly, much of the later criticism of the opinion fell upon one of those footnotes. Pollock cited in note 11 seven works by sociologists and educators "to say that, whatever the situation was in the 1890s, we know a lot more about law in society than we did then."

The rationale seemed sensible. "It wasn't anything anybody thought about, and nobody raised any question about it at the Court. But Gunnar Myrdal was the source, a Swedish socialist, and people opposed to the opinion seized on that," Flynn said later. The only change in the footnote came when Tom Clark asked that the initials of one writer cited, Kenneth B. Clark, be inserted to distinguish the two men.*

The three clerks had final drafts of both decisions ready on Friday, May 7. In a covering memorandum to the brethren, Warren explained he had separated the District of Columbia case from the state cases. He also suggested the cases be restored to the calendar for argument on the questions of whether integration of public schools could, constitutionally, be done gradually, and whether the high court should retain jurisdiction or pass questions of enforcement back to the lower courts.

Finally, he advised his colleagues that the drafts "were prepared on the theory that the opinions should be short, readable by the lay public, non-rhetorical, unemotional and, above all, non-accusatory." He hoped that newspapers across the country would reprint the decision.

On Saturday, May 8, the Chief personally delivered copies of the revised opinion to the justices in the building. His clerks carried copies to Black on the tennis court of his home in Alexandria, Virginia, and to Minton at his residential hotel in the District.

---

* Warren thought the footnote so unimportant, he did not read it from the bench, though he did incorporate a quotation from a lower court decision contained in footnote 10. Warren's edited text of the reading copy is in the State Segregation Cases file, Box 571, EWP/LC.

In the next days, each of the brethren signaled his concurrence. One by one, all but Jackson, still recuperating from his heart attack a month earlier, signed on. Douglas went so far as to send a note praising Warren for "a beautiful job."

This was Warren's victory. Though Frankfurter had conceived the strategy of delay a year earlier, Frankfurter could not have predicted Vinson's death and Warren's appointment. Though Burton had labored to convince the holdouts, the unanimous opinion was, finally, Warren's achievement.

He had chaired the extended discussions. He had negotiated with each of the brethren. He had diplomatically tamed the most passionate, and coaxed along the reluctant, concession by concession.

In his diary entry for Saturday the eighth, Burton praised Warren's "magnificent job," then added, "This would have been impossible a year ago—probably 6–3 with the Chief Justice at that time one of the dissenters."

The justices formally approved the two opinions at their May 15 conference. They agreed the decisions would be read the following Monday without notice, again to preserve secrecy.

The Court's printing plant worked through the weekend to produce the opinions. On Monday morning, May 17, Warren personally took a copy of the printed opinion to the hospital where Robert Jackson lay recuperating.

Jackson approved the final wording. Then, over Warren's protests, the feeble justice insisted on being present when the Court convened at noon that day, "in order to demonstrate our solidarity."

Despite the agreement to secrecy, some of the justices could not resist suggesting that their wives attend what would be a historic session. Warren also alerted Attorney General Herbert Brownell that *Brown v. Board* would come down that day, without telling him what it would hold.

When the visibly slowed Justice Jackson unexpectedly arrived in the robing room, word spread quickly among the law clerks that something important was afoot. Just two weeks before the end of the term, it could only be the segregation cases.

The courtroom was crowded at noon as the bailiff bawled the traditional cry, "Oyez! Oyez! Oyez!" and the justices filed through the scarlet drapes to take their seats on the high mahogany bench. Warren looked out to see not only Nina in the family section, but surprise visitors Helen MacGregor and Warren Olney seated beside her.

With Nina's cooperation these old friends had plotted their own surprise that day. Fearing they were there to witness a historic event, Warren was irritated—an irritation that evaporated shortly after the beginning of the session when Olney, as assistant attorney general, moved the admission of MacGregor to the Supreme Court bar.

The session began routinely. Clark read an antitrust opinion, then Douglas two decisions; all three cases would be quickly forgotten.

Warren followed with an unsigned decision by the Court in a simple matter, then announced, "I am authorized to report the decisions of the Court in cases Numbers 1, 2, 4, and 10 on the docket—"

It was 12:52 P.M. There was no hint in the first pages of the opinion just how the Court would rule. Warren read on, steadily, the tension in the marble courtroom growing.

"We come then to the question presented," Warren read. "Does segregation of children in public schools solely on the basis of race, even though the physical facilities and other tangible factors may be equal, deprive the children of the minority group of equal educational opportunities?"

He barely paused. "We unanimously believe that it does."

Warren sensed more than heard a collective gasp from the people in the courtroom, "a wave of emotion" without sound or movement, "yet a distinct emotional manifestation that defies description."

It was that, and more, others who were there that day recalled. There was a feeling of surprise, even shock, that Warren had pulled a unanimous decision from a court once so badly split.

With *Brown,* the chief justice had transformed the brethren into "The Warren Court."

CHAPTER 24

ALL DELIBERATE SPEED

T HEY HAD MADE HISTORY THIS DAY.

Normally so self-possessed, even reserved, the brethren were almost giddy in their excitement.

Harold Burton quickly shucked his robe to return to his chambers and write Warren a note of warm praise. "Today I believe has been a great day for America and the Court," the Ohioan enthused.

"I expect there will be no more significant decision made during our service on the Court. I cherish the privilege of sharing in this.

"To you goes the credit for the character of the opinions which produced the all-important unanimity. Congratulations."

An almost euphoric Felix Frankfurter agreed. "*This* is a day that will live in glory," he too wrote in a note dashed off to Warren that afternoon. "It is also a great day in the history of the Court," Frankfurter continued, "and not in the least for the course of deliberation which brought about the result. I congratulate you."

Jim Crow, age fifty-eight, was dead as a legal doctrine, felled by a single blow.

In a letter to his close friend Learned Hand, Frankfurter wrote that the new chief justice had demonstrated qualities of leadership not seen on the Court since Charles Evans Hughes's retirement in 1941. The unanimous opinion in *Brown* "could not possibly have come to pass with Vinson."

In one term, Warren had surpassed his two immediate predecessors, Harlan F. Stone and Fred M. Vinson. "What a pleasure to do business with him," Frankfurter wrote the failing Robert Jackson.

Warren's achievement ended what had been an agreeable first term on the bench. Only a remote political power struggle marred his tranquility.

Dwight Eisenhower had named Warren chief justice during a congressional recess. While Warren took the oath of office prior to the opening of the October 1953 term, he still needed Senate confirmation.

There it ran afoul of a onetime plains Progressive, William "Wild Bill" Langer, chairman of the Judiciary Committee. Unhappy with the lack of patronage accorded to him and his state of North Dakota, Langer sought to send a pointed message to the White House.

For seven weeks Langer deliberately put off committee consideration of the Warren appointment while dawdling through 133 lower court appointments. Warren continued to preside across the street while the committee's staff picked through some 200 letters for allegations of Warren's unfitness for the post.

A longtime Warren critic, Loyd Wright, wrote to call "the president's attention to the fact that Warren is not a Republican, he is not a lawyer nor an executive in the sense of the judiciary." Hearst newspaper columnist Westbrook Pegler objected on the grounds that Warren would receive his California pension while drawing a Supreme Court salary. Neither could rally an opposition.

Nor could Langer. On February 19 he announced that critics of the appointment had raised questions about Warren's fitness. The Langer charges perversely alleged that Warren, among other things, had been "under the domination and control" of liquor lobbyist Artie Samish; that, as both attorney general and governor, he had permitted organized crime to flourish in California; and that he had condoned corruption in his administration.

Southern senators, fearful Warren would vote to overturn *Plessy v. Ferguson,* asserted that the charges were serious enough to merit investigation by the FBI. Turning the screws on the White House, Langer agreed; Earl Warren would be the first nominee as chief justice whose background would undergo bureau inquiry.*

Others were quick to Warren's defense. President Eisenhower reiterated his support for "one of the finest public servants this country has produced." A member of Langer's committee, Arthur Watkins of Utah, dismissed the accusations as "the biggest lot of tommyrot ever brought before a Senate committee." Majority Leader William Knowland and Vice President Richard Nixon issued similar statements.

Satisfied that the White House was finally paying attention to him, Langer called up the Warren nomination. It passed, and on March 1, 1954,

---

* Eight FBI agents interviewed more than fifty people about Warren. Only one criticized the appointment, on the ground that Warren lacked judicial temperament. The FBI did learn that Warren's credit was good. The Retail Credit Association of Sacramento reported the Warren file was inactive since there had been no use of credit by Warren in the past three years. The FBI file is document 77-61323-41.

with no more than forty senators present, the Senate by a voice vote approved Warren's appointment. There was no dissent.

Earl Warren was now confirmed as chief justice. In a handwritten note of gratitude to President Eisenhower, the new chief justice wrote, "No greater honor, responsibility or opportunity in life could possibly come to me, and I want to say to you that the remaining useful years of my life will be dedicated to serving the cause of justice in a manner justifying the confidence you have reposed in me."

The first cause he confronted was the scope of *Brown*.

The immediate impact of *Brown* was to fall upon the seventeen states still maintaining segregated public schools and upon the 11 million children attending those schools. Still, the logical, the inevitable consequences of the decision were clear—to the justices, to the press, and especially to southern politicians.

Separate-but-equal public accommodations, from rest rooms to city parks, must also fall. The Court's decision was to father "a social upheaval the extent and consequences of which cannot even now be measured with certainty," one of the lawyers for the National Association for the Advancement of Colored People marveled fifteen years later.

But if Jim Crow was dead, decent burial would take time. Opposition to *Brown* ran deep and bitter in the South.*

"The decision won't affect us at all," one Mississippi school superintendent blustered. "That's because we're not going to observe it in our county."

In Alabama, state Representative Sam Englehardt pledged, "We are going to keep every brick in our segregation wall intact."

Campaigning for the governorship, Georgia's lieutenant governor, Marvin Griffin, pledged, "I will maintain segregation in the schools and the races will not be mixed, come hell or high water."

Even South Carolina governor James F. Byrnes, himself a former associate justice of the Supreme Court, promised, "South Carolina will not now nor for some years to come mix white and colored children in our schools."

Georgia's Richard Russell, deemed the most influential of southerners in the Senate, raked the decision as a "flagrant abuse of judicial power." He insisted, without explanation, that "ways must be found to check the tendency of the Court to disregard the Constitution."

The public reaction in some states was, if anything, even more hostile. Associate Justice Tom Clark conceded that mail on the segregation case "was pretty bad."

Margaret Bryan recalled that "after *Brown versus Board of Education* we got

---

* Not all southerners stood in opposition. Among others, Harry Ashmore, executive editor of the *Arkansas Gazette,* supported the decision. Kentucky's most influential newspaper, the *Louisville Courier-Journal,* editorially noted: "The Supreme Court's ruling is not itself a revolution. It is rather acceptance of a process that has been going on a long time—people everywhere could well match the Court's moderation and caution." The paper is quoted in *The New York Times,* May 18, 1954.

boxes of hate mail. Some of it went to the FBI. It was vitriolic and nasty. Some envelopes enclosed excrement."

Warren dismissed the personal attacks on himself. He was far more concerned for the three southerners on the Court. "I think Justice Black was not welcomed in Alabama for a good many years after the *Brown* decision," the Chief said in a later interview.

Similarly some folks in east Texas were upset with Tom Clark's vote. "And Stanley Reed, the gentle soul that he is, I know it was a great strain on him," Warren noted.

Those three, turning their backs on a lifetime of segregation, "were the men who were really entitled to the credit for making that [decision] unanimous."

If Warren felt anything, he would later tell his clerks, it was disappointment. He had hoped the opinion, written in plain English, would be understood and persuasive. Instead, it had ignited a firestorm of criticism—and not only from southerners.

"It doesn't matter what God damn reasons we give, they react depending on whether they like the result or not," Warren grumbled. "No matter how carefully we work on it, state our most basic reasons as clearly and simply as we can, it doesn't make any headway against the opposition we run into."

Political and social conservatives were particularly alarmed. Georgia's governor, Herman Talmadge, asserted the decision had discarded eighty-six years of "sound judicial precedent, repudiated the greatest legal minds of our age and lowered itself to the level of common politics."

L. Brent Bozell, later senior editor of *National Review,* argued there was only one justification for abandoning the principle of following precedent on a constitutional issue: "If today's judges are convinced that the past judges had misinterpreted the design of the Constitution's framers, they have the right and duty to reverse the current line of decisions and put the law into accord with the framers' intentions."

Warren's opinion, however, had specifically disavowed turning the clock back. "We must consider public education in the light of its full development and its present place in American life throughout the Nation," he had written.

Brown then was an "explicit repudiation of the underlying assumptions of constitutional government," Bozell and his intellectual colleagues asserted.

Fastening on Pollock's footnote number eleven, some critics also complained the decision was bottomed on sociological theory, not judicial precedent. The justices "had abandoned their role as judges of the law and organized themselves into a group of social engineers," Mississippi Senator John Stennis snapped.

His fellow senator, James Eastland, protested, "The Court took the writings and teachings of pro-Communist agitators and people who are part and parcel of the Red conspiracy and substituted them for the law of the land."

The most prominent of the critics, and necessarily the quietest, was Dwight Eisenhower. No less than "Segs" like Stennis and Eastland, the president had lived most of his life in a segregated society, the United States Army. He knew of black troops as a young officer—the all-black Tenth Cavalry had earned an enviable record in the American West. As supreme commander in Europe, he had black units in his vast army. Some, like the 761st Tank Battalion, had fought well, and the largely black "Red Ball Express" had performed prodigious feats supplying Eisenhower's advancing armies. But they had been men and units set apart. Not until July, 1948, with Eisenhower as president of Columbia, did Harry Truman order the integration of the military.

In what was at least a breach of decorum if not an outright attempt to influence the pending *Brown* decision, the president had invited both Warren and counsel for the southern states, John W. Davis, to a White House stag dinner. "During the dinner," Warren wrote in his *Memoirs*, "the President went to considerable lengths to tell me what a great man Mr. Davis was."

As they left the dining room, the president took the Chief's arm and urged, "These are not bad people. All they are concerned about is to see that their sweet little girls are not required to sit in school alongside some big overgrown bucks."

From that moment on, said a young attorney who discussed the incident with the chief justice, the relationship between the two men was very cool. "It isn't what the president said, but it is the fact that he did say something that really upset Warren."

Within a few weeks, the Court delivered its unanimous opinion, "and with it went our cordial relations," Warren added. The two men would maintain the formal relationship required of their offices, but they were personally estranged.

"Dwight Eisenhower was just completely opposed to the segregation decision and the chief justice knew that," Warren's secretary Margaret McHugh said later.

If there was criticism in the United States, the overseas reception was friendly. Within an hour of the decision, the Voice of America broadcast news of the opinion. Before nightfall, reports of *Brown* in thirty-four languages proclaimed the ruling a victory in the diplomatic war between East and West for the allegiance of unaligned nations.

As the *San Francisco Chronicle* editorialized, "To the vast majority of the peoples of the world who have colored skins, it will come as a blinding flash of light and hope."

Brown unexpectedly raised the man who made that possible into a world figure. He and Nina in the summers to come would travel widely, often at the invitation of foreign governments, acting as quasi-official ambassadors of the American promise of racial equality.

"When you travel," Solicitor General J. Lee Rankin later commented, "you realize this is the best-known American in the world. The new nations of Asia and Africa call him a saint—the greatest humanitarian in the Western Hemisphere since Abraham Lincoln." Jurists around the world proudly hung photographs of themselves with the chief justice on office walls, noted former American Bar Association President Charles Rhyne.

Praise and criticism alike would continue as Warren and the brethren turned to the remaining task: implementing the school desegregation decision.

The Chief's strategy had been to strike down *Plessy,* but to refrain from implementation of the decision. Instead, they had set the case down for argument on that single issue during the October, 1954, term. The delay, they hoped, would give the irreconcilables time to come to terms with a new reality.

The arguments on April 11, 1955, in what would come to be known as *Brown II,* supposedly were to deal with the matter of implementation: by whom and how soon.

Nonetheless, "the argument in Brown II," one of Warren's clerks that year recalled, "was, in effect, an occasion for a bunch of stump speeches by attorneys general of the southern states who were playing to the hometown newspapers and heaping scorn and hatred on blacks."

In the face of that, Warren interrupted the attorney for Clarendon County, South Carolina, to ask if the Court could assume the states would immediately comply with the decree, "whatever it may be."

S. Emory Rogers hedged, asking that the lower federal courts decide the specifics. He wanted an "open decree," one without a deadline.

"Is your request for an open decree predicated upon the assumption that your school district will immediately undertake to conform to the opinion of this Court of last year, to the decree, or is it on the basis—"

Rogers interrupted, almost defiant, "Mr. Chief Justice, to say we will conform depends on the decree handed down. I am frank to tell you, right now in our district I do not think that we will send, the white people of the district will send their children to the Negro schools."

Rogers added, "But I do think that something can be worked out. We hope so."

Warren flared. Justice was not a matter of bargains to be "worked out."

Compliance should be left in the hands of federal district court judges, Rogers stressed.

"But you are not willing to say here that there would be an honest attempt to conform to this decree, if we did leave it to the district court?" Warren asked, his irritation growing.

"No, I am not. Let us get the word 'honest' out of there," Rogers snapped, poking a finger at Warren.

Warren was livid. "No, leave it in," he barked.

"No," Rogers insisted, defiant in a failing cause, "because I would have to tell you right now we would not conform. We would not send our white children to the Negro schools."

Those in the courtroom shifted uncomfortably. Virginia's attorney general, J. Lindsay Almond, thought for a moment that Warren might cite the red-faced Rogers for contempt.

There was a stunned pause. Warren stared down at the pugnacious Rogers, then visibly collected himself to mutter through clenched teeth, "Thank you." His rage subsided, and with it the tension in the courtroom.

On Saturday morning, April 16, the brethren met in their weekly conference to take up the implementation order. They shook hands, as custom demanded, arranged themselves in their usual seats, and waited for robing room attendant Alvin Wright to close the tall doors.

As chief justice, Warren led these conferences, relying on his clerks' bench memoranda in each case, laying out the issues simply, without legal cavils. He ran the meetings briskly, preferring not to argue when one of the brethren disagreed with him, but framing the issues so as to lead the brethren to the outcome he wanted.

His collegial style promoted a sense of harmony among the brethren. The number of dissents fell from ninety during Fred Vinson's last term as chief justice to fifty-four in Warren's first year, and forty-five in the 1954 term.

Warren opened this conference proposing that they first reiterate the desegregation holding. The justices would, in effect, show they were firm in their conviction.

At the same time, they could be fair-minded. Warren opposed setting a fixed date for desegregation to be completed; some states would move faster than others. Instead, they would allow the lower federal courts—local institutions, after all—to fulfill the promise of *Brown I*. Warren would trust to reason and the rule of law.

The Chief also suggested that they provide minimal guidelines to the lower courts. It would "be rather cruel to shift it back to them and let them flounder without instruction."

As the senior associate justice, Hugo Black spoke next. More than most, Black recognized the reality of southern resistance. He anticipated a "deliberate effort to circumvent the decree." Even as they spoke, the state of Florida was still resisting in court the integration of the law school at the university five years after the Supreme Court had settled the issue.

Black agreed with the Chief. They should issue a spare decree and leave enforcement to the lower federal courts. The judges below better understood how to shape orders in the face of local opposition.

"The less we say, the better off we all are." If they maintained jurisdiction, they would only provoke "a storm over this Court." Most important, Black wanted their decision to be unanimous.

One by one, the brethren agreed.

Reed: "Short opinion—asserting the Const[itution] and some guides. Fix no definite time," Warren's notes quoted him.

Frankfurter: School integration would be "a slow process and something should be said about it."

Douglas: "Would not suggest a date but [include] words to show we must get along with this matter."

Burton: "Vital that it be unanimous."

Minton suggested the court "be careful [not] to issue a decree it cannot enforce."

Based on his conference notes, Warren drafted a handwritten opinion on May 18, 1955, then turned it over to law clerk Gerald Gunther for polishing. As the brethren returned their copies with comments, Warren either accepted the changes or personally convinced the justices to accept the draft as proposed.

Announced on the last day of the term, May 31, 1955, *Brown II* ran just seven paragraphs. The decree was mild in tone, firm in intent; nowhere did it mention the words "segregation" or "desegregation."

Warren began by reiterating the principle announced in *Brown I* that "racial discrimination in public education is unconstitutional. All provisions of federal, state, or local law requiring or permitting such discrimination must yield to this principle."

"Good faith" efforts to provide equal education for black and white children were to be administered by local federal courts, Warren continued. Those courts might take cognizance of local conditions, but, Warren added, "the validity of these constitutional principles cannot be allowed to yield simply because of disagreement with them."

Finally, Warren concluded, the district courts were promptly to "enter such orders and decrees consistent with this opinion as are necessary and proper to admit to public schools on a racially nondiscriminatory basis with all deliberate speed the parties to these cases."

"With all deliberate speed." While the decision was essentially the work of Warren and Gunther, its most celebrated phrase, condemned by supporters and opponents of school integration alike, was not Warren's at all.

The justices had agreed their decree would set no firm deadline. At the same time, they realized that intransigent southern politicians could stave off integration for years. The Court needed to impart some urgency to its decree.

Felix Frankfurter proposed the phrase "all deliberate speed," borrowed from a 1918 decision by Oliver Wendell Holmes, "Felix's favorite source on anything." Frankfurter suggested incorporating the phrase to point out that they were "at the beginning of a process of enforcement and not concluding it." Warren agreed.

With that, the Supreme Court had ordered southern states to make haste slowly, in the phrase of *Brown* historian Richard Kluger. They were temporizing, with the understanding, in Frankfurter's phrase, that "the harvest of today's planting won't be fully assessed for many a day."

Warren too was prepared to take the long view. In a brief letter to a circuit court judge, he stressed, " 'Good faith' and 'deliberate speed' combined with understanding, patience and perseverance on the part of the courts are the basic factors in the program."

If Warren was satisfied, the president of the United States was not. "Eisenhower was annoyed at *Brown II*," then-Attorney General Herbert Brownell agreed, "as I was, which left 'all deliberate speed' without limitations. Ike felt he had been left out on a limb." *

Eisenhower said nothing publicly, even though, as he acknowledged in his memoirs, ". . . there can be no question that the judgment of the Court was right." His silence while critics flailed *Brown*, his refusal to put the prestige of the presidency behind a judgment he said he believed to be correct, vexed Warren. Were he president, the Chief privately told his clerks, he would have taken steps to implement the school decision within a year.

The growing gap between president and chief justice only confirmed Warren in his feeling that the Court was a lofty but lonely place. Normally gregarious, he felt obliged to isolate himself "to eliminate every influence from personal contacts that could be brought to bear upon me."

In an excess of caution, he even limited his visits with Warren Olney, now an assistant attorney general; Warren wanted no one to infer he was partial to the government when federal cases came before the Court.

The isolation was difficult, Warren acknowledged, "almost a traumatic thing for me." He held on to a few friends from California—particularly non-lawyers, men he had known for years and who had no special interest in the law or a political position to advance.

He no longer spoke with the press. He stopped reading the mail from the public, favorable or critical. "I led pretty much of a monastic life on the Court, contrary to what I had been before. . . ."

Despite his vows, Warren could not quite still his politician's soul. He agreed to crown the queen of the Louisiana Mardi Gras ball in February, 1954; he attended a stag dinner for the Friendly Sons of Saint Patrick in March; and he spun the wheel to pick the queen of the Cherry Blossom Ball in April.

He and Nina entertained infrequently, both preferring small dinner parties with other members of the Court, their wives, and daughter Virginia. When Virginia married in 1960, their circle expanded to include her husband, television newsman and game show host John Charles Daly.

Beyond official functions, they went out rarely. William Mailliard, once Warren's traveling secretary in California, now a congressman representing

---

* Unhappy with the desegregation opinions, the president instructed that the Republican platform of 1956 be amended to remove any statement that the party or administration supported the Supreme Court "in the desegregation business." (See "Telephone Calls, August 19, 1956," in Ann Whitman Diary, Eisenhower Library.)

San Francisco's Silk Stocking District, recalled the Warrens' first visit to the Mailliard home in an unfamiliar and largely black neighborhood just two blocks from the Supreme Court building.

Virginia Warren tentatively knocked on the door while her parents waited in the taxi out front. "Daddy wasn't sure it was the right house," she explained.

As he ushered the Warrens in, Mailliard joked, "Earl, if anybody ought to feel at home in this neighborhood, it's you."

Why had they used a taxi though?

The chief justice of the United States had to wait his turn to use the Court's sole limousine, Warren explained.

Mailliard and Bill Knowland arranged to slip funds for a vehicle for the Chief into the 1955 Justice Department budget. As a courtesy to Warren, J. Edgar Hoover instructed the Federal Bureau of Investigation to find a suitable chauffeur for the chief justice.

The Warrens did feel comfortable accepting a dinner invitation during the 1954 term from law clerk Payson Wolff and his wife Helen. The Wolffs were older—he a thirty-three-year-old veteran of World War II, she the holder of a master's degree in public health and a particular favorite of Warren's.

Nina that evening brought her homemade divinity candy, a treat for the two Wolff boys, ages six and four. Four decades later, Payson and Helen Wolff well remembered the relaxed visit: their sons climbing on and off the chief justice's lap, Nina and her husband chatting easily with the parents, the conversation ranging from children to family to life in Southern California, where the Wolffs intended to move after his clerkship ended.

Evenings the Warrens generally spent at home in their spacious first-floor apartment at the Wardman-Park with its views of the tree-shaded lawn. As chief justice he read late into the night in his bedroom; as "Papa" Warren, he wrote fond letters to the growing number of grandchildren. (A five-dollar bill was the promised reward for a good report card.)

The Warrens rarely ate in restaurants; Nina shopped at the Calvert Market on Columbia Road Northwest, then cooked the solid American foods her husband preferred. When they did eat in neighborhood restaurants, Nina favored spare ribs and Coca-Cola, her husband roasts and steaks.

Even attempting to be selective, they found their social calendar crowded: a White House reception and dinner for the king and queen of Greece; a stag dinner at the Peruvian embassy in honor of the chief justice of Peru; the de rigueur Gridiron Dinner; the German ambassador's dinner in honor of the chief justice—at least one black-tie event a week.

Sports fan Earl Warren attended Washington Senators baseball games with friends or, if he could find no one else, with his driver. He himself had stopped driving, to Nina's relief, "because he had so much on his mind, he became distracted."

Beginning in 1954, he managed to attend at least a portion of each World

Series for the next twelve years; he shared a hotel suite with three old chums from Sacramento—city manager Bart Cavanaugh, attorney Phil Wilkins, and tilesetter Jack McDermott.

McDermott, a part-time football referee, would constantly bait Warren, futilely attempting to catch him in errors on rule interpretation. "Argue, argue, argue over sports, who did this and that and when. Earl Warren's mind was so good as to memory that it was weird," McDermott wrote later.

When McDermott in 1954 spontaneously invited former major league outfielder Jo-Jo White to stay with them, it was Warren who arranged for a roll-away bed, then stayed up until the early morning talking baseball.

Warren and Nina also began the practice that year of hosting the brethren and their wives in a junket to Philadelphia and the Army-Navy football game. They left Washington Station in a private railroad car at 9:00 A.M. and returned in the evening with dinner aboard the train. (Tickets for the justices, as government officials, were free; Warren bought tickets for the wives and paid rental costs on the railcar—including a $30 tip for the stewards.) That first year Felix Frankfurter caught a cold in the windy and damp stadium, confirming him in his dislike for things athletic.

Family became all the more important to Earl and Nina as the boundaries of their world closed in. As time went on, he began to look more and more upon his law clerks as surrogates for his three sons in California.

Warren and Frankfurter agreed to be godfathers to the firstborn son of Gerald Gunther in January 1955. After the ceremonial bris in the Gunthers' apartment—the baby had been circumcised at the hospital—Warren enthusiastically gave Gunther a bear hug, clasped his hand, and boomed, "This has been a great experience, what with all the family spirit and the religious feeling! You know, this is the first bar mitzvah I've ever attended."

These men who clerked for Warren were carefully chosen. In his first term on the Court, he had retained the three young men whom Vinson earlier selected. From then on he took men whom friends recommended —one from the East, one from the Midwest, and one from the West. As chief justice of the United States, he insisted that his clerks come from beyond the Ivy League.

He gave little guidance to those who made the selections. When Adrian Kragen, onetime Warren deputy attorney general and Berkeley law professor, asked what qualifications Warren had in mind, "his answer was that he wanted a top-flight student who would be able to think for himself and who was not biased either toward the right or the left."

Over the next years, depending on the expected caseload of the Court, "sometimes Warren would say, 'I think the Court is going to have quite a bit to do with criminal law, and we need somebody who is interested.' Usually, he just talked about quality."

Twice a year Nina and Earl returned to California for visits with friends and family—in the summer after the Court adjourned and over the Christmas–New Year break.

During the summer trip, Nina visited the children and grandchildren, while her husband attended the two-week-long Bohemian Grove gathering of industrialists and government figures. They also returned to Sacramento, where Warren would pay a visit to the governor's office, shaking hands with the secretaries of old, asking after the families, meeting new members of Governor Knight's staff one year—and recalling their names the next.

The Sacramento visit was stuffed with nostalgia for both Earl and Nina. "The best years of our lives were there," Nina said. She revisited the governor's mansion just once after moving to Washington; the place was too full of sweet memories. "I cried in every room."

At Christmas the family gathered at San Francisco's Fairmont Hotel; friend and financial adviser Benjamin Swig provided Earl and Nina with a suite high above the city. On the day before Christmas, they would assemble for dinner at son James's home in suburban Piedmont, then later in St. Helena—Warren invariably insisting he knew the route and invariably getting them lost on the way. Christmas Day the growing family migrated to Earl Junior's home in Sacramento, then drove on to Bobby's home in nearby Davis for Christmas dinner.

One or two days Warren set aside to go duck hunting with his sons and a few friends on Wallace Lynn's ranch north of Sacramento. Though Warren could not hunt regularly, he remained a good shot. To son Bobby's surprise, his father frequently bagged the limit when others failed.

On New Year's Eve, Earl and Nina stayed with Honey Bear and her new husband, pediatrician Stuart Brien, at their Beverly Hills home.* Up at four in the morning they first watched the Rose Parade from the reviewing stand, then attended the annual Rose Bowl football game, and finally capped the long day at the VIP reception in the evening.

On January 1, 1955, Warren served as grand marshal of the Rose Bowl parade. It was a dismal day. Just as the first band stepped off, the Warrens in their open convertible felt raindrops. They sat undaunted through parade and football game as the rain continued, the field turned to mud, and Ohio State beat Southern California, 20–7.

Their lives fell into welcome routine. Despite the isolation he felt from day to day, Warren discovered pleasure in his new job. "I've found the quiet of my chambers and of the library a very soothing thing after the hectic years I've put in as an executive," he told the *San Francisco Chronicle* in July, 1954.

"The work here is intensely interesting, and I am enjoying it immensely," he wrote a former campaign contributor at the end of his second year in Washington.

---

* Honey Bear met her future husband when she went to work for him as a receptionist. "Mother thought he was just wonderful," Honey Bear said in an interview. That Brien was Jewish never came up. "When we meet someone, we don't think about their religion or ethnic background," she said. It was a quality learned from her parents, she added.

Just as Warren took to Washington, so that city took to him. Official Washington's benediction on the chief justice at the end of Warren's first term was delivered by *New York Times* columnist James "Scotty" Reston. The capital's arbiter on all things political, Reston concluded that the chief justice was a rare fellow in a town of talkers: He was a good listener on the bench. He also asked penetrating questions of attorneys arguing cases in the courtroom.

Obviously relying on a not-for-attribution conversation with one of the associate justices, Reston reported that Warren "has certain qualities of character and mind that have impressed his associates, especially in the court conference—an ability to concentrate on the concrete; a capacity to do his homework; a sensible, friendly manner, wholly devoid of pretense; and a self-command and natural dignity so useful in presiding over the Court."

The chief justice also had a nagging conscience.

CHAPTER 25

MOON AND STAR

T HROUGHOUT HIS FIRST TWO TERMS ON THE COURT, EARL WARREN trod a careful legal path. However bold the two *Brown* decisions seemed, the Court was a new experience for Warren and the responsibilities of the office unfamiliar. His instinctive reaction was to move cautiously.

Warren the chief justice was like Warren the governor. "I don't believe you ever got any answers off the top of his head," his personal secretary, Margaret Bryan, noted.

Moreover, the new chief had not personally practiced law since his days as district attorney in Oakland. His clerks sensed "it took some time for him to mentally feel comfortable with what he was doing," one recalled. "It was simply that he hadn't done it for a long time."

Justice William O. Douglas maintained that a new justice spent three years adjusting to the work of the Court. Until "he had considered the variety of issues it brought, the philosophical content of a Justice's opinions could rarely be predicted with any assurance."

Felix Frankfurter would not wait. He began, as one Warren law clerk viewed it, "a fight for Warren's soul the very first year."

After a lifetime of teaching, Associate Justice Frankfurter remained at heart the law professor. For much of the chief's first two years on the Court, Earl Warren would be his most important student.

The new chief justice, law clerk Gerald Gunther decided, "was a very decent guy, with very good instincts, who had very little idea of the difference between being a judge and a governor or a president.

"When he first came to the court, he heard a lot of noise from Frankfurter and others; you don't vote 'no' on everything you don't like." Not everything one disliked was unconstitutional.

He also heard a great deal of praise. "Frankfurter spent a lot of time calling on Warren," law clerk William Oliver noted with some sarcasm, "and he was, oh, so generous in his praise before everyone about how great Warren was and what a great chief justice he was going to make and such."

Meanwhile, a barrage of memoranda on matters great and small flowed from Frankfurter's fussy pen. Unbidden, he dispatched to Warren copies of former Chief Justice Hughes's reports at the end of each term; comments on conflict of interest as determined by previous justices; the text of Abraham Lincoln's "Farewell to the People of Springfield"; and all manner of items from English judges' jury instructions to Tom Dewey's message explaining why he had signed a bill that banned cameras from the courtroom.

With truckling note and brilliant memorandum, helpful Felix Frankfurter pressed his legal philosophy of judicial restraint on the new chief justice.

The young Frankfurter, a Progressive in spirit and intellect, had agitated for political and legal reforms. He had taken up many a liberal cause and watched as a conservative Supreme Court successively gutted progressive legislation from Roosevelt to Roosevelt.

In Frankfurter's mind, the answer was to restrict the Court's jurisdiction solely to matters of law. Today's liberal Court, pressing social policy decisions to the left, could easily become conservative, pushing social policy in the opposite direction.

According to Frankfurter's jurisprudence, the Supreme Court was to move slowly, preferring precedent to innovation, the narrow decision to the sweeping. Frankfurter's arguments appealed to Warren's natural sense of caution.

In these first terms, Warren felt his legal way. "He wanted everything to be thought out very carefully, to move slowly and not go public until he was perfectly satisfied that the work that was in the office was first rate and satisfactory to him," said law clerk Payson Wolff.

Warren was sensitive to criticism of his judicial performance, first-year law clerk Richard Flynn noted. "I think he could be hurt in his feelings."

Even two years later, clerk Samuel Stern came away with the same impression that the Chief "did not have a tough hide at all, considering all his years in public life, the rough and tumble of politics. He was quite a sensitive human being."

Often enough during his first term, Warren relied on instinct. In law enforcement cases, the chief justice voted personal views shaped years before as district attorney of Alameda County and as California attorney general.

Former clerk Gerald Gunther recalled a petition for certiorari filed by attorneys for Chicago bootlegger Roger "The Terrible" Touhy during Warren's second year on the Court. Convicted twenty years before of kidnapping, Touhy had steadfastly maintained he had been framed.

Touhy's petition raised serious search and seizure questions. Gunther wrote a cert memo, arguing that Touhy had made a substantial claim and the issue was new to the Court. He recommended the Court accept the case.

Warren agreed, Gunther said. "I am willing to go along with Jerry's recommendation and grant." He initialed the docket sheet.

When Margaret McHugh saw the Chief's approval, she knocked on Warren's door. "Chief, do you know you voted to grant in number 452?"

"Yeah," Warren replied. "That's an important search and seizure issue, I'm told."

"Do you know who Touhy is? That's Roger 'The Terrible' Touhy! You'd vote to spring Roger 'The Terrible' Touhy?"

Warren turned to Gunther. Had he ever heard of Touhy?

No, Gunther admitted. He just took the case as a legal issue, well presented.

"I'm not going to vote for him," Warren stated firmly. "Record me as saying no," he instructed Mrs. McHugh.

No bad guy was going to get help from Earl Warren, Gunther concluded.

Similarly, the Chief relied on deeply held personal values rather than legal principles in obscenity and white slavery cases. "I've got three daughters, and Virginia is still at home. As long as I sit, I'm never going to vote for any of those pimps."

As far as Gunther was concerned, Warren's unwillingness to help criminals was "a very human blind spot, but a blind spot nevertheless."

At the same time, Californian Earl Warren was quick to defend California law and criminal practice in the weekly conferences. These predilections to aid police and protect California criminal law fused in a 1954 police case in which Warren later decided he voted wrong.

The question raised in the cert petition of Patrick Irvine, a convicted bookmaker, was simple: could prosecutors use tainted evidence in court?

Long Beach, California, police three times sneaked into Irvine's home to plant eavesdropping equipment. In their third try, they repaired bugs planted in a bedroom closet and under the bed itself, then spent a month listening for incriminating evidence. Well before they decided they had sufficient proof to secure a conviction, the eavesdropping officers apparently overheard the suspect and his wife repeatedly enjoying the marriage bed.

"I was shocked by the Irvine case," Warren explained later. "I thought it was a terrible abuse of power on the part of the police, a shocking invasion of privacy."

It was not illegal under California law, however, nor was police use of eavesdropping equipment. Furthermore, Irvine was a gambler, and Earl Warren disliked gamblers.

Against that was the simple fact that police three times had broken the law in order to enforce it. Three times they had committed trespasses by surreptitiously entering the bookmaker's apartment to plant and maintain the bug.

The justices' vote in conference fell not along liberal–conservative lines but on personal estimates whether the police had overstepped permissible behavior. Black, Frankfurter, Douglas, and Burton voted to overturn, Jackson, Clark, Minton, and Reed to sustain.

Warren cast the deciding vote. Just five years before, the Court had held state police practices were to be left to state remedy. If a state sanctioned the practice, even illegally seized evidence could be used to secure a conviction.

Four of the brethren maintained that view, "and I being a new Justice on the Court still groping around in the field of due process, I went along with that opinion, shocked as I was at the conduct of the police." To assuage his sense of outrage, he joined Robert Jackson in a concurring opinion that recommended the FBI investigate the police break-ins as violations of the bookmaker's civil rights.

Short weeks later, the appeal of New York physician Edward K. Barsky came before the Court. Barsky had refused to produce for the House of Representatives' Committee on Un-American Activities records of the Joint Anti-Fascist Committee, of which he was chairman.

Suspended for six months by medical authorities, Barsky had argued that his suspension was based on grounds unrelated to his fitness to practice medicine. Warren voted with a six-man majority to uphold the suspension.

Similarly, he voted to uphold the deportation of an alien who had joined the Communist Party between 1944 and 1946. The party was legal at the time, but the federal Immigration and Nationality Act of 1950 later held that membership at any time was grounds for deportation.

Hugo Black and William O. Douglas dissented, arguing that Robert Norbert Galvan was being punished for exercising a right guaranteed by the First Amendment. Warren signed onto Felix Frankfurter's majority opinion which held that judicial precedent gave Congress the power to regulate aliens.

But even as the Chief hewed to the Frankfurter position, the Warren–Frankfurter relationship was going sour. Near the end of the term, Warren's clerks became aware of a rift, conscious too that both the Chief and Frankfurter were "trying not to let this explode" in conference.

Law clerks Gerald Gunther and Payson Wolff were sitting in their office adjacent to the justices' conference room one Saturday, Gunther recalled. Through the heavy oak doors, they could make out Frankfurter's shrill voice raised in squeaky outrage.

Shortly after the conference ended, the two clerks asked the chief justice what had provoked Frankfurter.

"Well," Warren replied, "he was going off on some basic jurisdictional problem of taking a particular state case."

At that moment, Mrs. McHugh knocked on the door and stuck her head in. "There's a page from the library here with an armful of books for you. Did you order any books?" she asked.

"No. But show him in."

The page deposited a half-dozen volumes on the Chief's desk. Sticking out of the top volume was a yellow sheet of paper.

The Chief pulled out the paper and read it. His face turned pale, and his jaw clenched tightly. Without a word, he handed the note to Gunther.

Chief:
You said in conference you never heard of Martin v. Hunter's Leasee.
You really have to read up on it. Here are some useful places to start. I suggest you read—

Warren was livid, Gunther said. Frankfurter, the law professor, "was treating the chief like a student, and giving him an assignment."

According to Gunther, Frankfurter thought this just kindly advice. However, "it sure as hell didn't come across as a courteous gesture to the Chief."

Frankfurter might have retained some measure of influence over the chief justice had he not lost an effective ally with the death of Robert Jackson. To everyone but Hugo Black, Jackson could be soothing or persuasive when Frankfurter was abrasive or lecturing.

In Jackson's seat was another New Yorker, John Marshall Harlan, a conservative who came to the Supreme Court with a reputation as "a lawyer's lawyer." Grandson and namesake of the first John Harlan to sit on the high court—across the vest of his Savile Row suit hung the gold chain and pocket watch of his grandfather—this second Harlan was a man bred to the law.

Son of privilege, son of Princeton, and a Rhodes scholar, Harlan had made his way naturally to Wall Street. There he had distinguished himself by workmanlike preparation prior to trial and a restrained demeanor in court. A lifelong Republican, he gained a reputation among lawyers by representing corporations, particularly in antitrust cases brought by the government.

For twenty-five years Harlan practiced in the most prestigious of arenas until he accepted an appointment to the federal Second Circuit Court of Appeals. Harlan had served just seven months on the appellate court before Dwight Eisenhower named him to fill the Jackson vacancy on November 8, 1954.

Like Jackson before him, Harlan at age fifty-five was a proponent of judicial restraint; to his mind, the president and the Congress might be the activist branches of government, the Court was the brake.

Unlike the contentious Frankfurter, who was closest to him philosophically, Harlan was the quiet patrician, secure in his place in the community, in the law, and on the Court. He had no need to proselytize.

Harlan easily struck up friendships among the brethren, even among those who stood against him philosophically. Legal scholar Herman Schwartz recalled Harlan and Black, the one a strict constructionist, the other a judicial activist, standing in the line at the Court's public cafeteria, the elegant conservative and the rumpled liberal chatting and laughing.

With Warren growing more secure as time went on and Bob Jackson no longer there to reinforce him, Felix Frankfurter lost sway. As Frankfurter's moon waned, Hugo Black's star rose.

Black provided the intellectual leadership of the "liberal" wing of the Court. A judicial activist who saw the Court's duty as expanding constitutional rights, he frequently clashed with Frankfurter in conference and opinion.

The two men were dissimilar in more than philosophies. Black had come to the Court as a political appointee, tapped by Franklin Roosevelt to repay Black's support of the so-called court-packing plan in 1937. Black, in Frankfurter's view, was indelibly "the Senator."

Frankfurter the Harvard scholar preferred to think *his* appointment was based solely on intellectual attainment. He tended to disregard both his own political activities as confidential adviser to Roosevelt, and the fact that national politics demanded there be a "Jewish seat" on the court.

Frankfurter the Jewish immigrant had spent his entire life striving to become a member of what a later generation would label the Establishment. Black, in the words of his biographer Roger Newman "was in constant intellectual rebellion, questioning fundamental assumptions most people cheerfully swallowed." Now sixty-nine, he still sang a defiant post–Civil War song learned in his youth, "I Am a Good Old Rebel," sardonically proclaiming,

> *"I'm just a dirty rebel, and that is what I am.*
> *For this fair land of freedom, I just don't give a damn. . . ."*

Frankfurter was deemed master of the "Harvard School" of jurisprudence. In an unguarded moment, he insisted, "The Supreme Court exists to establish rules of law, not to provide justice." To buttress that position, Frankfurter had mastered federal rules and procedures, the better to narrow scope or deny certiorari.

Black, in turn, disdained the Harvard School as mechanical. "It takes all heart out of the law," he contended. The threat was not from liberal judges usurping the prerogatives of president and Congress, but of judges abdicating their responsibility.

The man Supreme Court employees called "Judge Black"—in recognition of his eighteen months as a police court judge thirty years before—carried in his suit pocket a dog-eared copy of the United States Constitution, as if to proclaim his first principle.

Privately, Frankfurter scored both Black's concept of the law and his hornbook scholarship. "I've never known anyone who more steadily reads for confirmation of his views and not for disinterested enlightenment," Frankfurter sneered.

Black was not intimidated; he yielded nothing to Frankfurter in conference or on the bench. The Alabaman, said *New York Times* reporter Anthony Lewis, "may have been the most relentless person I ever met in my life about getting his way. He did it with much more casualness, friendliness, easiness [than Frankfurter], and, I'm sure was a more pleasant companion."

Such a man would be more to Earl Warren's liking. If Warren followed Black "leftward" in the next year, it was because he found the Alabaman and his expansive concept of the law more agreeable.

Warren took to visiting Black's corner office during the 1955–56 term, law clerk Graham Moody recalled. The two men talked, "and things came out the way the Chief wanted them to, and the way Black wanted them to a great deal that year." When they could not prevail, "there were three dissenting justices: Black, Warren and Douglas," he added.

The shift from Frankfurter's camp required no compromises on Warren's part. As clerk Gerald Gunther put it, the Chief reverted to his natural instincts.

His fellow clerk Payson Wolff agreed. "I don't think that Warren's own basic notions of justice and fairness and propriety and morality and so on changed at all." Warren simply found a way to express them.

Warren's sympathy for the underdog, or a sense of fair play surfaced—as a later member of the brethren, Potter Stewart, explained. "I often thought to myself, if the Chief Justice can see some issue that involves widows or orphans or the underprivileged, that he's going to come down on that side."

That sensitivity pried open the rift between Warren and Frankfurter. Appeals under the Federal Employers' Liability Act (FELA) covering railroad workers poured into the court during 1955–56, clerk Graham Moody said. Most questioned whether lower courts had erred in ordering new trials after employers had been found liable by a federal jury.

Though these cases rarely involved luminous legal matters, Warren invariably voted to add them to the Court's docket. In doing so, Frankfurter complained bitterly, the Chief was turning the Supreme Court into "a Court for the correction of errors."

The railroad call boy of long-ago Bakersfield could hardly have done anything else. He told a clerk that he felt "the jobs used the men and, when they were no longer valuable, cast them aside."

Warren had no difficulty looking beyond the legal questions to the principle of justice embodied in the FELA cases. Arguing the facts, he generally pulled the Court with him to reverse in favor of the worker; they relied on Hugo Black's legal argument that jury verdicts in the trial court were not to be lightly overturned.

The turning point in Warren's relations with Frankfurter came in a civil suit for damages brought by the widow of a Korean War soldier against a private cemetery in Sioux City, Iowa.

The case came to the Court without fanfare. The cemetery had refused burial in August, 1951, to Sergeant First Class John Rice, a Winnebago

Indian killed in the battle to hold the Naktong River bridge. The Catholic graveside ceremony concluded, cemetery workers had refused to lower Sergeant Rice's casket into the ground when they realized the mourners were virtually all Indians. Widow Evelyn Rice had overlooked a clause in the sales contract that specifically restricted burial privileges "to members of the Caucasian race." Eleven-sixteenths Winnebago, Sergeant Rice did not qualify for admission.

The denial rankled Warren twice over. In the first place, Rice had died fighting for his country. In the second, the cemetery's refusal to bury a non-Caucasian simply offended his sense of fairness.*

Six years earlier, the high court had ruled in *Shelley v. Kraemer* that private parties could not rely on the state to enforce a discrimination clause in a private real estate contract. The clause might remain in effect by private agreement, but it was unenforceable by law.

The widow sued for monetary damages and the cemetery asked a state court to throw the case out. Mrs. Rice's attorney, relying on *Shelley,* argued in his petition that the state could not throw out a suit for damages merely because the contract had been made between private parties.

When the matter came to the Supreme Court on a petition for certiorari, the clerks looked at it as "a next step following *Brown* for dealing with race relations," Payson Wolff explained.

The brethren took up Mrs. Rice's petition in conference on November 13, 1954. The eight justices—Robert Jackson had died of a second heart attack just days after the October term began—were sharply divided.

In presenting the case, Warren argued, "This woman who makes this contract does not have to go give up this contract if a clause is illegal." He would vote to grant certiorari and to reverse the lower court. Hugo Black, William Douglas, and Tom Clark agreed. The cemetery could not use the courts to enforce a private agreement to bar the body of a non-Caucasian.

Four justices disagreed.

Frankfurter saw, and shied from, the larger issue. To reverse the lower courts would mean that any act of discrimination, public or private, would be a violation of the Fourteenth Amendment's guarantee of equal protection. Frankfurter feared to take that next step with the clamor raised by *Brown* still ringing in their ears.

For Stanley Reed, the question was simple: Could a private cemetery select whom it would bury? Reed said it could.

Sherman Minton and Harold Burton joined Reed and Frankfurter, leaving the Court evenly divided. In such instances, the justices automatically

---

* Warren's response was similar to Harry Truman's. News accounts of the aborted burial so angered the president, he immediately and personally ordered that Sergeant First Class Rice be buried with full military honors at Arlington National Cemetery. He also sent an Air Force plane to ferry the Rice family to Washington for the service.

MOON AND STAR | 309

affirmed the lower court decision. On November 15, 1954, the United States Supreme Court sustained the earlier denial by the Iowa courts.

With the appointment of a ninth justice, John M. Harlan, Mrs. Rice returned to Washington with a petition for rehearing. But by now, southern anger at the *Brown* decision was, if anything, rising.

Politically, ran Felix Frankfurter's unspoken argument, this was not the time to plow ahead on civil rights. He wanted to avert a narrow decision that might inflame southern resistance to *Brown*.

He sought to make Mrs. Rice's suit vanish by invoking his academic specialty, judicial jurisdiction.

Frankfurter produced successive memoranda for the brethren, arguing that the record of the case was unclear. Equally unclear was Frankfurter's legal research when he cited no less than twenty-four cases as precedent for declining the petition. At Warren's instruction, law clerk Gerald Gunther researched a rebuttal which argued that not one of Frankfurter's twenty-four cases was directly applicable to the Rice case.

Blocked there, Frankfurter caromed off in another direction. He noted the Iowa legislature had subsequently passed a law barring the denial of burial rights because of race or religion. (The law did not cover cases then in litigation—in practical effect, only Mrs. Rice's.)

Furthermore, Frankfurter argued, Rice's cold remains were already buried elsewhere. "It's moot, for God's sake," he insisted.

Eventually Frankfurter was to prevail upon Tom Clark to switch his vote. With new justice Harlan not taking part in the case, Warren, Black, and Douglas lacked the fourth vote necessary to grant a review.

Rather than confront the underlying constitutional question, the Court dismissed the petition for a rehearing. At Frankfurter's suggestion, the one-paragraph statement said only that the original writ had been "improvidently granted."

What might have been the successor to *Brown* thus became "the biggest flop."

The little noted *Rice* case was more than a flop, argued Frankfurter protégé and Warren clerk Gerald Gunther. "The Chief was on to the fact why Frankfurter wanted to back off."

Fearing a hostile reaction from an old Confederacy already resistant to *Brown*, Felix Frankfurter had bent the very legal doctrine he had helped establish. Felix Frankfurter could turn it on and turn it off, as it suited his purpose.

"This was the justice's fatal flaw." Gunther added.

Frankfurter was to raise questions of jurisdiction repeatedly in efforts to block appeals in other cases. Three times from 1954 to 1956, the Court at Frankfurter's urging denied certiorari to cases that challenged state laws prohibiting mixed marriages.

As Gunther noted, "The Court decided that to take on the gut issue of miscegenation while implementation of *Brown* was up in the air was doing a disservice to *Brown*."

Striking down miscegenation laws would only trigger the deepest fears of those who feared "mixing the races." But by denying review of the miscegenation laws, the justices were stunting the scope of *Brown*. How was it possible to prevent the states from discriminating in public schools yet allow them to discriminate in regulating marriage?

Frankfurter played the jurisdiction card once more. Over Warren's protest, he persuaded a majority to return the first of these mixed-marriage cases to the Virginia Supreme Court for clarification of several questions.

The Virginia court overtrumped Frankfurter. The state tribunal denied it had further jurisdiction, having heard the case; and thus could not respond to the questions posed. The United States Supreme Court was impotent.

Warren was furious. They had ducked their responsibility and the state court had rubbed their face in it.

"That's what you get when you turn your ass to the grandstand," he snapped.

Frankfurter's elastic interpretations "turned the Chief into a great skeptic, if not a cynic, about the alleged binding nature of jurisdictional rules," Gunther concluded.

Those rules, Warren scoffed, were "only binding because Felix says so."

The Chief struck out on his own, no longer intimidated by Frankfurter's erudition and his own inexperience. "I think he learned from the reaction to *Brown* and the subtle and not so subtle maneuverings of Felix Frankfurter that a judge could do whatever he damn pleased," Gunther explained. "At least it didn't turn much on whether he had a legal basis for it.

"And so he didn't give so much of a damn about the legal grounds."

In the years to come, the chief justice would become ever more results oriented, less concerned with the legal arguments than the outcome. Felix Frankfurter saw the Supreme Court as a seat of law. Earl Warren saw it as a seat of justice.

As he grew more comfortable, Warren modified his work habits. "Sometimes he would ask the guy who wrote the bench memo to outline two paragraphs to give him a start," Payson Wolff recalled. "Sometimes without the bench memo he would write a few pages and say, 'Here, fellas,' and we'd polish or substantiate."

Over time, Warren's drafts of his opinions were to grow increasingly sketchy. He took pains to write out the initial statement of facts, but the legal support for the conclusion that he proffered to his clerks grew ever more skimpy. He left it to them to fill in the arguments.

Warren did not ignore the law, "but he was strongly grounded in fact, and how he felt things ought to be," clerk Graham Moody explained. "I wouldn't say he was 'unjudicial' in any significant sense, but if you got down to any very technical, jurisdictional questions . . . he got a little impatient with the law."

Also over time, his attitude toward his clerks shifted. During his first term, Warren was somewhat standoffish, feeling his way. With the second, he unbent slightly.

Payson Wolff recalled one Saturday afternoon during the fall of 1954 when Warren invited the three clerks to his apartment to watch a California Golden Bears football game on television.

The clerks thought the visit an invitation to sit around and talk legal philosophy or the nuances of particular cases—as other justices did with their clerks. Instead, Warren rolled out a metal tea cart with a bottle of whiskey, ginger ale, and ice, and instructed, "Help yourselves."

He then turned on the television, sank into the couch, drink in hand, and proceeded to talk football.

As his second term wore on, the Chief seemed to open up gradually. During informal discussions, Warren spoke frankly, underscoring his points with thumps on the desk. He evaded nothing, trusting in their discretion.

"He disliked heartily Vice President Nixon," Payson Wolff remembered. "Even though he was further away politically from Senator Knowland than he was from Nixon, nevertheless he liked and trusted Knowland much more."

He defended past decisions, particularly the internment of the Japanese a decade before. "He simply said that it was right. It troubled him, but he still thought he was right" to have urged the evacuation at the time, Richard Flynn said.

Warren's growing confidence in his ability to carry off the role of chief justice could be measured in the incremental changes he brought about in the administration of the Court. Though change came slowly to this temple where the brethren collectively decided issues of management as petty as the planting of greenery, Warren proposed a series of modifications in Court procedures. Once ratified by the conference, those changes subtly affirmed Warren's leadership of the Court.

In July, 1954, the Court selected the first black youth to serve as a page, an appointment noted with approval by the press. Shortly after, the pages switched to long pants from the traditional knickers, which were increasingly unavailable in clothing stores.

At the beginning of the October, 1954, term, Warren's second, he simplified the introduction of new attorneys to the Supreme Court bar. With the change, as many as 125 lawyers might be enrolled in what was, for the majority of them, a largely ceremonial office. (For a fee of $25 they received a handsomely engraved certificate sure to impress clients; few would ever appeal, let alone argue a case before the high court.)

In May, 1955, the justices agreed to a Warren proposal that they no longer hear cases on Friday. Instead, they shifted the weekly conference from Saturday and freed the weekends. If additional days were needed for argument, they would extend the term into June.

The October, 1955, term began with the most startling of innovations: a loudspeaker system with microphones before each of the justices and counsels' tables. The amplifier made it possible to hear plainly in the cavernous courtroom. Equally important, a tape recorder set down the first historical record of oral arguments.

At the suggestion of *New York Times* Supreme Court reporter Anthony Lewis, Warren eventually persuaded the conference to abandon "Decision Mondays." Opinions were to be delivered when they were ready rather than held for the following Monday.

The shift, as Lewis suggested, promoted fuller press coverage of each decision. Reporters covering the Court no longer crammed brief notices of four or five cases into a single day's hastily written story. With fewer decisions coming down at any one time, there was more time to read, digest, and write intelligently.

Warren's influence ran well beyond the building. He recognized that "the Court system generally was fifty years behind," former Supreme Court Chief Clerk James R. Browning said. The entrenched staff "clung to the way things had been done and didn't want to change anything." Even the shift from a handwritten docket to typewritten seemed revolutionary.

As Browning put it, "Warren dislocated that." He reorganized the Court's police force, arranged for its officers to be trained at the FBI academy, and soon discovered that smaller police departments were quick to hire away his men as chiefs of police.

As chief administrative officer of the entire federal court system, Warren eventually undertook to create an office that would handle day-to-day problems of the judiciary. Eventually, he appointed a small committee to draft legislation creating a federal judicial center.

Approved by Congress, that center would be responsible for the continuing education of judges, for research and training, and for administration of the court system. Warren saw to it that his longtime aide Warren Olney III was named the first director.

By the beginning of 1955, Warren had settled into the Court, standing as first among equals. Traditionally, his Supreme Court appointment would have removed him from the political arena. Supreme Court justices were, in Felix Frankfurter's phrase, "to live and die true to the vow of political celibacy that we, everyone of us, should take when we come to this place." (If any justice violated that vow, it was Frankfurter, a constant adviser to the Roosevelt White House.)

Once confirmed, those who took the vow sank into political obscurity. The puissant became the powerless; the celebrated lion was quickly forgotten.

Earl Warren was the exception. Because of *Brown*, his stature had grown rather than shrunk.

Gerald Gunther recalled that he and Payson Wolff slipped off to a New York Yankees–Washington Senators night game in the spring of 1955. The two had no sooner found their seats in the stands when they noticed a milling crowd, and what looked like a fight. It was Warren, standing on a chair, signing autographs for clamoring fans.

As early as May 18, 1954, just one day after the first *Brown* opinion, *The Sacramento Bee* eagerly picked him out of the crowd. "There is small doubt the Republican Party will consider him among the very eligible persons when the time comes to nominate a successor to President Eisenhower."

Washington, a city driven by such speculation, continually whispered of a Warren candidacy as the presidential year of 1956 approached. Repeated soundings by the respected Gallup Poll fueled the gossip; the poll showed Warren the most popular of potential candidates among Republicans and independents—if Eisenhower chose not to run.

The political speculation provoked Warren at a dinner party to complain, "Do people have so low a regard for the Supreme Court that they think all they need do is tap a justice on the shoulder and he will run for the presidency? If so, it's time they learned better."

Another guest at the dinner chided him. "Chief, maybe you shouldn't have foreclosed your future like that."

"I want to. I'm fed up with politics."

The Gallup Poll of April 12, 1955, forced Warren's hand. The results gave Warren the edge over Richard Nixon, 25 percent to 19 percent, among Republicans, and he topped Nixon almost three to one as the choice of independents.

Such polls could take on a life of their own. Warren moved to stop the speculation in April with a statement disavowing any further interest in the White House:

> *This has been a matter of some embarrassment to me because it reflects upon the performance of my duties as Chief Justice of the United States.*
>
> *When I accepted that position, it was with the fixed purpose of leaving politics permanently for service on the Court. That is still my purpose. It is irrevocable. I will not change it under any circumstances or conditions.*
>
> *Be they many or few, the remaining useful years of my life are dedicated to the service of the Supreme Court of the United States, in which work I am increasingly happy.*

Warren's announcement received a mixed greeting. Associate Justice Harold Burton sent a note by messenger applauding Warren. "You not only have added to your stature but have raised the prestige of the Court and rendered a major public service to the country."

A *New York Times* editorial lauded him for a statement "typical of the straightforwardness and candor which the country has long since learned to expect of him. . . . The promptness with which he has met an issue that might involve the court in politics will add to the already high respect in which the Chief Justice is held."

The internationalist wing of the GOP groaned. With Warren removing himself from consideration, the red-hunting, parochial vice president, Richard Nixon, became the front-runner. He was followed by a fellow Californian, William Knowland, now the nominal leader of the Taft Old Guard. Neither could beat the likely Democratic nominee, former Illinois governor Adlai Stevenson.

Warren's April statement thus laid no ghosts.

His name shot to the top of the list on September 24, 1955, when Dwight Eisenhower, vacationing in Denver, suffered a heart attack. While the president lay recuperating, his closest White House advisers jockeyed to keep control of the party from Nixon and the right wing.

Once more the potent name of Earl Warren wafted in rumor. The October Gallup Poll reported that if Eisenhower did not run, only Warren could best Stevenson. Two months later, Gallup announced that Republicans and independents alike still favored Warren as the GOP nominee, though narrowly over Nixon.

Unsure of his own future, the president personally discounted a Warren candidacy. "I know the Chief Justice is very happy right where he is," he told his press secretary and political adviser, Jim Hagerty. "He wants to go down in history as a great Chief Justice."

According to Hagerty, the president continued, "Earl is one of those fellows who needs time to make decisions, and his present spot is the best spot in the world for him. He is perfectly happy where he is. He has a lifelong job and I think he means it when he says he will not enter political life again."

The president misjudged his man. With Eisenhower mending but undecided about a second term, and Richard Nixon savoring the prospect of his party's nomination, Earl Warren had reluctantly reconsidered. Visiting California in late December, 1955, the chief justice reportedly told his longtime aide Oscar Jahnsen, "I will run for President rather than see Nixon in the White House."

Near the end of January, 1956, Warren sent a discreet message to the president. The chief justice pulled Hagerty aside at a party to confide he was disturbed that the president had days earlier told reporters he agreed with Warren's statement of April "that the Supreme Court and politics should not be mixed."

Despite his disagreement with the *Brown* decisions, Eisenhower apparently welcomed Warren's hinted availability. If Warren was serious about running, the president noted in his diary, "it would be a great relief to me." Eisenhower dreaded the prospect of the Republican Party abandoning world leadership in a spasm of neo-isolationism. After himself, Eisenhower thought Warren the best man to keep the party to its internationalist course.

Warren's best strategy would be to hold himself aloof. "I think it would be possibly feasible and ethical for him to say nothing until the time of the Convention," Eisenhower wrote in his diary.

"At that time, if literally drafted, he could submit his resignation and accept the nomination. The difficulty with this solution is that unless I could have personal assurances in advance that he would respond to a draft, my own problem remains more difficult to solve."

Eisenhower's problem was whether to run for a second term in the face of his heart attack. Through the fall and winter he had debated the question within himself, with his supportive wife and dubious son, with bridge-playing friends and political advisers. He remained undecided.

A week after Warren hinted of his availability, Eisenhower signaled his endorsement. To a planted question at a February 8 press conference—did he oppose a Warren candidacy—the president replied, "Opposed? For goodness sake, I appointed him as Chief Justice of the United States; and there is no office in all the world that I respect more. I admire and respect and have a very deep affection for Mr. Warren."

In effect, Eisenhower had advised Warren to wait until summoned.

That call was not to come. Cleared by his doctors, Eisenhower announced on February 29, 1956, he would be a candidate for a second term.

Warren was frankly relieved. As if to scotch any thought that he had even contemplated making himself available for a draft, Warren adopted a rhetorical defense. When questioned about a possible campaign, he would ask in reply, "Why on earth should I want to run to save the country from my friend Adlai Stevenson?"

Why indeed? Next to the president himself, public opinion polls marked him the most respected public figure in the country. And his was a job for life.

CHAPTER 26

THE JESUS QUARTET

W HILE IT HAD TAKEN HIM ALMOST THREE YEARS TO ADJUST to the Supreme Court and the awesome responsibility, by mid-1956 and the end of his third term, the chief justice had found his way.

If Earl Warren had any self-doubts, he kept them private. In public, the Chief radiated confidence. "He had one of the most powerful personalities I ever encountered," law clerk Curtis Reitz remembered. "When he came into the room, it was just a commanding presence. He was totally comfortable with himself."

Commissioned to draw Warren's portrait for a *Fortune* magazine article, artist Miriam Troop four decades later easily recalled Warren: "Tall, broad-shouldered, fair, with silver-grey hair neatly brushed, and smiling broadly, he was a highly attractive man."

The pleasant man who sat for Troop's portrait was increasingly confident as a jurist, relying on instinct to find the right legal course. "He had a compass. He didn't know where he was going to, I don't think, but he knew where we could go from here," a clerk in a later term observed. "He had that tactical, pragmatic sense of what was feasible, what he could politically get away with."

With each passing year, he had voted increasingly with liberals Hugo Black and William O. Douglas. In Warren's first term, as he cautiously followed Felix Frankfurter, Warren and Black had differed twenty-two times. In the second, they voted on opposite sides twelve times.

By this, Warren's third term, the chief justice and Black disagreed but twice; in eighty-nine of the ninety-one cases decided that year by full opinions, the two voted together.

Eleven times during the Court term that ended in June, 1956, Warren, Douglas, and Black joined in dissents. They objected in cases holding that the states could ban mass picketing by strikers; that civilians accompanying military personnel overseas were subject to courts-martial for crimes committed abroad; that a private employer could fire an employee alleged to be a communist; and that the Du Pont company had not monopolized the cellophane business.

Hugo Black, finding himself aligned with a chief justice growing in confidence, wrote a friend, "My own belief is that he will stand out as a great head of this Court."

As chief justice Warren was shaping a personal judicial philosophy. He had come to understand that the law had to meet the changing needs of society.

Each decision of the Court in Warren's judgment was to be "evaluated in terms of practical application. Everything we do must include the human equation, for what we do with our legal system will determine what American life will be—not only now but in the years ahead," he explained to a law school audience.

Law was by nature conservative and honored the past, Warren agreed. At the same time, the "law must not be placed in a straitjacket of historical precedent." In the law, as in governing, he sought flexibility.

"He wasn't tied down by doctrine. He wasn't into the piddling kinds of distinctions that so box the lawyer," clerk Curtis Reitz said.

Warren's great strength was his sensitivity to people, Reitz continued. "His understanding of human beings, and his understanding of social conditions, and the way society and government worked, was absolutely extraordinary."

Amid closely reasoned oral arguments, frequently interrupted by the justices' questions, Warren sat silent, only to lean forward at the end of an argument to ask, "Yes, but is it fair?"

No single question could more quickly deflate a government prosecutor or corporation lawyer swollen with legal precedent. Fairness, simple justice was fundamental and was learned as early as the child's protest, "That isn't fair."

Law in all its panoply, Warren wrote in *Fortune* magazine about this time, "is simply a mature and sophisticated attempt, never perfected, to institutionalize this sense of justice and to free men from the terror and unpredictability of arbitrary force."

A series of cases involving the jurisdiction of military courts-martial marked Warren's evolution as a jurist, and his shifts from judicial restraint to judicial activism.

In February, 1955, halfway through his second term on the Court, the brethren took up the case of an honorably discharged airman arrested for a murder committed while serving in South Korea. Could the Air Force try a civilian?

At the post-argument conference Warren maintained that Congress had reasonably chosen to make the airman subject to military justice for crimes committed on active duty. Speaking next, Hugo Black argued that courts-martial were "not in high regard. I would not extend court-martial power any further than we have to."

Warren tactfully agreed to set the case for reargument in the fall. With the vacant seat of Robert Jackson filled, they would be firmer in their decision.

The reargument came during the second week of the 1956–57 term, Warren's third. In the eight months since February's initial arguments, the chief justice had changed his mind.

"Courts-martial were for discipline, and that is all," Warren told the conference on October 15, 1955. The man who had acceded to the arguments of military necessity when advocating the evacuation of the Japanese in 1942 no longer bought in.

Trying an ex-serviceman by court-martial violated the Sixth Amendment's guarantee of trial by jury. Warren's argument carried the day, 6–3.

Seven months later the justices once more took up the matter of the jurisdiction of courts-martial. Two women were convicted by military tribunals of murdering their serviceman husbands in separate incidents overseas. Sentenced to life imprisonment, they appealed.

At the May 4, 1956, conference Warren again argued in favor of jury trials. This time he was in the minority.

Normally Tom Clark's opinion for the court on June 11, 1956, would have settled the matter. But the dissenters prevailed upon an uncertain majority to have the case reargued. By the time of the reargument, February 27, 1957, the majority to sustain was gone.

Warren pressed hard at the reargument for an explanation of the scope of military jurisdiction over dependents: Were juveniles who committed serious crimes to be court-martialed? Were dependents living on military bases in the United States?

"The simple question is whether Congress has the right to declare these dependents a part of the armed forces of the U.S. and subject to court-martial."

Warren prevailed in the outcome, but not in remaking the law. Six of the eight justices who participated in the case agreed the two women should not be tried by military courts. But only three justices would agree to a broadly stated rule.

Though Warren and Frankfurter had agreed to trim military jurisdiction, the differences between the newly made judicial activist and the advocate of judicial restraint grew as the 1956–57 term wore on. In temperament, in his emerging judicial understanding, Warren had moved to polar opposition.

The chief justice found himself more and more offended by legalities that resulted in unfair results. In contrast, the onetime Harvard professor favored logical process over subjective concepts of justice. "I do not conceive that it is my function to decide cases on my notions of justice and, if it were, I wouldn't be confident as some others are that I knew exactly what justice required in a particular case," he explained in a personal letter.

Inevitably, "they were bound to clash," one clerk concluded.

When they did, Frankfurter would flare in shrill anger, then muster sincere apologies. "Such clashes," he wrote to "Dear Chief," "are part of the process of truth-speaking."

His apologies, however sincere, would not paste over their differences. As the rift grew, Warren turned increasingly to Hugo Black for counsel. "The Chief talked with the Judge about cases, the Court's calendar, Eisenhower, politics, anything at all," a Black clerk during the 1955 term recalled.

For the remaining dozen years they would serve together, Warren solicited the Alabaman's advice on assignments. "If anyone complained," Associate Justice William Brennan, Jr., said later, "I didn't hear about it. It was just accepted as a fact of life here."

Whatever advice he sought, Warren drafted his own opinions, relying on the bench memoranda and his conference notes to shape opinions that would hold a majority together. The clerk who had written the bench memo generally would add the legal citations.

The concepts in Warren's twelve majority and dissenting opinions that year were Warren's own, clerk Samuel Stern insisted. "He would very strongly decide, and frequently in disagreement with the clerk who was assigned the argument. I don't remember a case in which he allowed himself to be swayed against his own instincts."

On the Miscellaneous Docket, composed largely of prisoners' appeals, the clerks might have a slight influence, clerk William Allen added. "Whether one saw anything [in these often unlettered appeals] depended on the imagination, creativity, and willingness to look at it.

"I was always sort of proud they took a very significant number of cases off the Miscellaneous Docket that were heard in that term and the succeeding term. The three of us, our record was pretty good," Allen said with some pleasure. They had helped to make sure the highest court in the land was not closed to the poor.

Finally settled in the routines of the court, Warren acknowledged his adjustment to the sequestered life of a Supreme Court justice had been difficult. As governor, he met daily with legislators, bureaucrats, and constituents, "learning from actual contact with people before I made a decision."

Now he dealt with an arid printed record, cold abstracts of legal debates. These he leavened with an hour of oral argument delivered by attorneys who often knew nothing more of the case than the legal citations offered in defense of a cause. It was all so bloodless.

The change from Sacramento to Washington, Warren said, was "really a shock for me and it took a long time to overcome it. But I did it just by dropping everything else and paying no attention to the politics or current events and just sticking to our legal work."

Warren was something less than forthright. He and his Court were only too aware of cold political winds breezing up from a southerly direction.

Eighteen months after the first *Brown v. Board* decision, a weary seamstress returning from work at the Montgomery Fair department store in Montgomery, Alabama, refused to relinquish her seat on a city bus to a white man. Arrested on a charge of violating the state's bus segregation law, Rosa Parks was summarily convicted on December 5, 1955, and fined $14.

That day Montgomery's long-suffering black population invoked a boycott of the city bus line led reluctantly by a young minister, Martin Luther King, Jr. The guerrilla war of civil rights demonstrations in the streets of the Deep South had begun.

On February 1, 1956, two days after a bomb shattered the King home, the local National Association for the Advancement of Colored People challenged Alabama's bus segregation law. The NAACP's federal suit sought to expand the *Brown* rule that separate was not equal from public schools to publicly regulated buses.

Fearing the end of a lifeway, 19 senators and 82 representatives—virtually the entire congressional delegation from states that had formed the Confederacy—issued a "Southern Manifesto" condemning the Supreme Court and its decision in *Brown v. Board.*

The mid-March statement asserted the justices had ignored 100 years of precedent, and, "with no legal basis for such action, undertook to exercise their naked judicial power and substituted their personal political and social ideas for the established law of the land."

No more restrained, South Carolina's governor, James Byrnes, insisted, "The Supreme Court must be curbed." As a former secretary of state and associate justice himself, Byrnes laid a patina of respectability over racist screed.

The segregationists' worst fears were confirmed: *Brown* was only the beginning. On June 4, 1956, the federal circuit court voted 2–1 to hold Alabama's bus segregation unconstitutional.

When city and state attorneys appealed, the Supreme Court summarily disposed of the case on the initial pleadings filed with the clerk. The terse, unsigned opinion on November 13, 1956, granted the NAACP's motion to affirm the lower court decision. The very fact that there had been no oral argument, no written opinion suggested just how firmly the Court stood behind *Brown.*

Tainted as bigots, southern critics of the Court might have remained on the political fringe had the brethren in April, 1956, not taken up the case of Steve Mesarosh, secretary of the Communist Party in Pennsylvania.

Under his party name of Steve Nelson, Mesarosh had been convicted in a Pennsylvania state court for advocating the overthrow of the United States government. On appeal, the Pennsylvania Supreme Court reversed

Mesarosh-Nelson's conviction. The court reasoned that the federal government had passed the similar Smith Act in 1940, and thereby preempted enforcement of state sedition laws. State prosecutors appealed to the United States Supreme Court.

The issue was simple. Given the federal law, did the forty-two states as well as the territories of Alaska and Hawaii that had similar sedition statutes need the additional protection?

Warren, the former governor who had once signed a bill imposing a loyalty oath on state employees, argued in conference there would be "no loss to the U.S. if these acts are stricken."

This onetime deputy DA, who decades earlier had helped convict Wobblies under a similar state criminal syndicalism law, now moved to end such local prosecutions. "My general impression is that for him, the witch-hunt was worse than whatever danger there was [from communists]," clerk Samuel Stern explained.

Sober reason might prevail among the brethren but to some the Supreme Court appeared to be freeing an acknowledged communist. Worse, the court was preventing the states from defending themselves from the Red Menace.

Aware of the political sensitivity of the case, Warren assigned the opinion to himself. As chief justice of the United States, he would take responsibility for the work of *his* Court.

In drafting the 6–3 *Nelson* opinion, Warren relied heavily on the Pennsylvania Supreme Court's earlier decision. "Sedition against the United States is not a local offense," he wrote. "It is a crime against the Nation. As such it should be prosecuted and punished in the Federal courts where this defendant has in fact been prosecuted and convicted and is now under sentence."

A week later, the Court compounded its problem. A majority held that the New York City Board of Regents could not dismiss a Brooklyn College faculty member merely because he invoked his Fifth Amendment right against self-incrimination while testifying before the House Committee on Un-American Activities. Tom Clark, for a 7–2 majority, wrote that due process required Professor Harry Slochower be granted a hearing before he could be fired.

With *Nelson* and *Slowchower,* the already angry southerners took up anti-communist cudgels to bash the Warren Court. "Something has got to be done to stop the Supreme Court," thundered Congressman Mendel Rivers of South Carolina. "They are a greater threat to this Union than the entire confines of Soviet Russia."

The Supreme Court was made up of "politicians instead of lawyers," raged the chairman of the Senate Judiciary Committee, Mississippi's James Eastland.

Surfacing momentarily from his alcoholic fog, Joe McCarthy agreed. "We made a mistake in confirming as Chief Justice a man who had no judicial experience, who had practically no legal experience except as a district attorney for a short time and whose entire experience was as a politician."

In Senate Judiciary hearings a month later, Eastland and McCarthy reaffirmed the expedient pact between southerners and conservative anticommunists.

"You have heard one communist after another come before this committee and take the position that the Communist Party was just another political party; in fact, that is the Communist line, is it not?" Eastland asked rhetorically.

"That is strictly the Communist line," McCarthy replied.

"Is not that the line that the Chief Justice of the United States takes?"

"Unfortunately, yes, Mr. Chairman," McCarthy agreed. "And I may say that I follow what is said in communist publications, to follow their line, rather closely. And the communist *Daily Worker* applauded this decision, the *Nelson* decision, and other decisions of the Supreme Court. In their book Earl Warren is a hero."

Warren could say nothing. As he wrote a sympathetic California acquaintance, "Members of the Court can neither resent nor refute criticisms no matter how far-fetched they may be." Within his chambers, however, he dismissed the Wisconsin senator as a "querulous, disreputable liar."

Concern about an increasingly liberal Supreme Court spread well beyond segregationists and red-hunters. Conservative business organizations such as the National Association of Manufacturers and the National Chamber of Commerce, fearing severe antitrust and pro-labor decisions, lent weight to the anti-Court hue and cry.

Segregationists, business interests, and anticommunists fell in behind a bill introduced by Virginia congressman Howard W. Smith, the powerful chairman of the House Rules Committee. The Smith bill proposed that no act of Congress be construed as preempting a field of legislation unless the act contained a provision to that effect. Had that been the federal law at the time *Nelson* was argued, the Court could not have struck down the state statute.

Only a series of adroit parliamentary moves by the House leadership kept Smith's bill from coming to the floor. Any vote would have been a victory in itself, even if the bill was defeated. A roll call registering the depth of anti-Court disaffection among congressmen would legitimate the denunciation.

The public furor diminished over the summer of 1956, with both the Court and Congress in recess. Warren and Nina spent much of that summer traveling in Denmark and Switzerland with Santa Barbara newspaper publisher Thomas Storke and his wife, Marion. The Warrens broke off the vacation at the request of Secretary of State John Foster Dulles to accept an unexpected invitation from the government of India to visit that country.

Warren's visit to India turned into a personal and diplomatic triumph.

He was celebrated from Bombay to Calcutta to New Delhi as the man who had lifted America's color bar. At the University of Delhi ceremony in which Warren received an honorary L.L.D., the audience broke into sustained cheers at the mention of the *Brown* decision.

The widespread publicity that American newspapers devoted to the Warrens' triumphal sojourn, coupled with the congressional recess, helped mute criticism of the Court. Earl and Nina returned in quiet triumph to a humid, somnolent Washington after Labor Day, 1956—and to a new justice.

On October 15, 1956, the conservative Sherman Minton, weakened by chronic anemia, retired on his doctor's orders. Warren was losing a friend in Minton, a dedicated Chicago White Sox fan with whom the Chief talked baseball.

At the same time he was gaining a legal ally. In Minton's place, President Eisenhower named William Brennan, who was to shape many of the intellectual arguments that defined *the* Warren Court.

Bill Brennan was born in 1906 in Newark, New Jersey, the son of immigrant parents from Roscommon, Ireland. His father worked as a coal heaver in Newark's Ballantine Brewery, before becoming a union organizer, then city commissioner.

Money was tight in the home where the Brennans raised their eight children. Brennan senior was an honest politician in a city not noted for such. Young William's family and the working-class neighborhood in which he grew up left a lasting impression on the young man; he was to be a lifelong Democrat.

Brennan attended the University of Pennsylvania, then Harvard, where he took classes from the legendary Felix Frankfurter. After graduation in 1931, Brennan built a thriving practice representing large corporations, sometimes in labor-management relations.

After service as a labor negotiator for the army during World War II, Brennan accepted appointment from New Jersey's Republican Governor Alfred Driscoll to the state trial court. While it meant a sizable loss of income, the new job would leave him more time for his family.

Three years later, at the suggestion of Chief Justice Arthur Vanderbilt, Driscoll named Brennan to a vacancy on the state supreme court. Brennan might have remained there, a respected justice with a capacity for court reform, but for Vanderbilt's uncertain health. In May, 1956, the ailing Vanderbilt asked Bill Brennan to fill in for him at a national meeting devoted to the administration of justice.

There gregarious Bill Brennan met and impressed the attorney general of the United States, Herbert Brownell. Five months later, Shay Minton informed the White House that he intended to retire.

Discussing the vacancy with the president, Brownell learned that two groups had Eisenhower's ear: the Conference of Chief Justices of the State Courts asserted the Supreme Court needed someone with state judicial experience to balance the federal-state relationship; and the Conference of Catholic Bishops, dominated by New York's Francis Cardinal Spellman, pointed out that no Catholic had sat on the high court since 1949.

Brennan had an additional advantage: Eisenhower was running for reelection. "We were glad that he was both a Democrat and a Catholic," Deputy Attorney General William Rogers acknowledged. The appointment of Brennan, from vote-heavy New Jersey, would underscore Eisenhower's nonpartisan approach to government.

His court opinions, which Brownell read, cast Brennan as a moderate with a particular interest in state taxation policies. That was in keeping with Eisenhower's own posture of moderation.

On September 29, 1956, the president announced he was appointing the unabashedly delighted Brennan to the Court. Characteristically self-deprecating, Brennan told a reporter he compared himself to a mule entered in the Kentucky Derby: "I don't expect to distinguish myself, but I do expect to benefit from the association."

At Earl Warren's invitation, Brennan visited the Supreme Court a week later. As Brennan retold the story, Warren led the newest justice from his chambers to a darkened third-floor room where the brethren had gathered to watch the opening game of the World Series. "I was introduced by the Chief to each of them, and someone said, 'Put out the light.' They put out the light and went on watching the game."

He and Warren, "a couple of gregarious, bear-like folk," formed an immediate friendship. Nina and Marjorie Brennan too hit it off.

Friendship aside, Brennan promptly aligned himself with Warren, Black, and Douglas—to Frankfurter's irritation. Frankfurter—who might have taken secret pleasure that a former student had done so well—reportedly quipped, "I always encouraged my students to think for themselves, but Brennan goes too far!"

Circuit court judge Learned Hand, anything but a judicial activist, came to scorn Warren, Black, Douglas, and Brennan as "the Jesus Quartet." The scholarly Hand, himself often mentioned for a seat on the high court, was particularly irritated that Warren lacked the polished legal skills of Hand's beloved Oliver Wendell Holmes.

"The more I get of your Chief," Hand wrote Frankfurter, "the less do I admire him." Some of Hand's associates on the circuit court had taken to calling Warren "that Dumb Swede," Hand added.

Frankfurter was equally unhappy. Now the discarded suitor, Frankfurter fumed that the Chief had joined the " 'hard-core liberal' wing of the Court" composed of men whose "common denominator is a self-willed self-righteous power-lust." They voted out of prejudice and their own experiences, he complained, rather than from the disinterested study of the law.

No power lust but righteous indignation drove the Court majority when communist Steve Nelson and four party comrades returned to the high court at the beginning of the 1956–57 term. The state case against him nullified, Nelson sought to overturn his conviction under the *federal* Smith Act prohibiting advocacy of the overthrow of the United States government by force and violence.

In theory, Nelson's appeal centered on First Amendment issues of freedom of association and of speech. But two weeks before the scheduled oral argument, the new solicitor general, J. Lee Rankin, informed the Supreme Court that some of the principal witness' trial testimony against the five might have been perjured. Rankin asked that the case be remanded to the trial court to determine if the suspect testimony of that paid informer had influenced the outcome.

Whatever Nelson's political opinions, Warren saw his appeal as no more than a straightforward question of criminal procedure. In a scathing opinion released on November 5, 1956, Warren raked the prosecutors. "The dignity of the United States Government," he thundered, "will not permit the conviction of any person on tainted testimony."

An acknowledged perjurer could not testify in a federal prosecution, he held for the 6–3 majority; the case was to be retried without the perjurer, or the prosecution dropped.

A second case hinging on a government witness' admitted perjury—with only Tom Clark dissenting—was to reignite a brushfire of congressional criticism.

Clinton E. Jencks had also come under federal scrutiny because of his political beliefs. An organizer for the decidedly left-wing Mine, Mill and Smelter Workers Union, Jencks was convicted of falsely signing a non-communist affidavit required by law of all union officers.

The case against Jencks rested on testimony by Harvey Matusow, a professional informant paid $70 per week by the FBI. Matusow testified in April, 1953, that Jencks had privately acknowledged he was a member of the Communist Party three years before.

Seeking to discredit testimony by Matusow and a second witness, Jencks's attorneys asked the trial judge to order the FBI to produce copies of their earlier confidential reports. The judge was to screen them for material pertinent to the witnesses' testimony and turn over copies for use during cross-examination. The judge refused and thereby provided grounds for Jencks's appeal of his conviction.

(Complicating matters for the government, Matusow, in a stunning about-face, had meanwhile confessed he had perjured himself repeatedly. He had lied not only in Jencks's trial, but before credulous congressional committees.)

The Jencks case seemingly posed problems for the Court—at least the brethren discussed it five times between October 1956, and March, 1957. The chief justice had no doubts; from his opening comments at the first conference, he insisted that Jencks and his attorneys had the right to see all statements. Because Jencks was denied the right to inspect the documents, his conviction could not stand.

Brennan's opinion for the majority followed the Chief's argument. Black, Douglas, and Frankfurter signed on; Harold Burton and John Harlan concurred in the reversal, but preferred to have the judge first screen the documents for relevance.

Clark, who as attorney general in the Truman administration had issued the first list of subversive organizations, was the sole dissenter. The majority, he complained in uncharacteristically strong language, had opened a "veritable Pandora's box of troubles."

Unless Congress stepped in, Clark warned, "those intelligence agencies of our Government engaged in law enforcement may as well close up shop, for the Court has opened their files to the criminal and thus afforded him a Roman holiday for rummaging through confidential information as well as vital national secrets."

Fearing his agency's files would be laid open, the secretive J. Edgar Hoover prodded allies in Congress to attack the *Jencks* decision. For a season of discontent, they would fasten on Clark's dissent to argue that naive justices had jeopardized national security.

Paradoxically, a second Brennan opinion dealing with First Amendment issues that term would have far greater impact on the nation, yet produced almost no comment when it came down.

Samuel Roth had spent a lifetime dodging the protectors of public morals, publishing spicy, bawdy, and patently obscene books and magazines for almost three decades under an array of imprints. He had been convicted four times for selling material deemed obscene—at least some of which had been written by major figures in twentieth century literature.

Roth fought his legal battles alone. He might have enlisted greater support from literary and artistic figures except for his penchant for stealthily pirating their "unprintable" works.

Roth found himself convicted in 1955 of violating postal laws, attempting to advertise and sell obscene literature through the mails. When his conviction was sustained by the circuit court, 3–0, he appealed to the Supreme Court.*

Obscenity more than troubled Earl Warren, a man born in 1891 and come of age prior to World War I and the sexual revolution it wrought. According to Brennan, "Warren was a terrible prude. . . . If Warren was revolted by something, it was obscene. He would not read any of the books. Or watch the movies. I'd read the book or see the movie and he'd go along with my views."

Sexually graphic material not only offended Warren's sense of propriety, it struck at values he cherished. "If anyone showed that book to my daugh-

---

* Federal circuit court judge Jerome Frank concurred in the result reluctantly, in the belief that it was not appropriate for a circuit court jurist such as himself to hold a law unconstitutional. His concurrence was, in fact, an eloquent plea for intellectual freedom; it would be quoted in the Supreme Court briefs of those seeking to overturn the conviction. See 237 F. 2d 796.

ters," he told a clerk when discussing one appeal to the court, "I'd have strangled him with my own hands."

At the same time, Warren realized that censorship was pernicious to a democracy, "a withering function," as he put it. History demonstrated it "to be dangerously oppressive."

He tried to balance intellect and upbringing. His draft concurrence in the *Roth* case argued that obscenity since the founding of the Republic had been considered "an abuse of freedom of expression, rather than a protected right.

"Essential as it is that the term be not expanded so as to abridge free expression either in the discussion of public affairs, the freedom of the press, or in the arts and sciences, we should not deprive the states of the right to protect their people from this form of depravity."

William Brennan's decision for the majority on June 24, 1957, held that obscenity might be restrained, but for the first time laid out a gauge of the obscene: "whether to the average person, applying contemporary community standards, the dominant theme of the material taken as a whole appeals to prurient interest."

But, Brennan's opinion continued, if the challenged work had even the slightest redeeming social value—"unorthodox ideas, controversial ideas, even ideas hateful to the prevailing climate of opinion"—it was protected by the First Amendment.

The 7–2 *Roth* decision and companion *Alberts*, 6–3, stirred little comment beyond the law reviews, apparently because the Supreme Court had upheld the convictions of the two "pornographers." Sam Roth, then sixty-two, would spend most of the five years remaining to him in the federal penitentiary at Lewisburg, Pennsylvania.

But the decision bearing his name was to open the way for filmmakers, novelists, and magazine editors to explore human sexuality for fun and profit. As the adventurous pushed the boundaries outward, the reluctant brethren would progressively narrow the definition of pornography and the scope of obscenity laws. In the end, virtually any work with a modicum of artistic, literary, or scholarly pretension—no matter how sexually offensive to some—might be safely published.

If *Roth* was difficult and excited no comment, one of the least problematical, and the easiest to decide based on precedent, would become the most notorious.

Washington, D.C., police arrested Andrew Mallory shortly after 2:00 P.M. on April 8, 1954, for the rape of a woman in the building where he lived. Police interrogated him for two hours, gave him a lie detector test after a delay of six hours, arranged to have the victim identify him, and finally secured oral and written confessions.

He was not arraigned until the following morning, some eighteen hours after his arrest, and ten hours after his confession. Tried and convicted a year later, he was sentenced to death.

On a petition for certiorari, Mallory's case came to the Supreme Court, which has direct jurisdiction over criminal cases in the District of Columbia. The justices deemed it a simple case: the long-standing Federal Rules of Criminal Procedure required arrestees be arraigned "without unnecessary delay" and informed of their rights.

In 1943, the Supreme Court had held that confessions secured while suspects were deliberately detained without arraignment could not be used in court. Under that *"McNabb* Rule," Mallory's confession was invalid, Warren stated in opening the conference discussion of the case.

Earl Warren had devoted eighteen years of his life to the Alameda District Attorney's Office. He demanded his men follow the law rather than cut corners to secure convictions.

"And that's all I'm asking of these police forces," he explained later. "I think they are a bunch of lazy people who aren't getting their work done because they are too lazy to do it right." *

His confession tossed out, Mallory's conviction had to be reversed. The brethren agreed in a unanimous opinion written by Frankfurter and handed down on June 24, 1957.

Mallory was to be momentarily overshadowed in the closing days of the 1956–57 term, but the brethren would hear of him again.

---

* In the Shipboard Murder Case, however, Warren's agents interrogated Frank Conner for twenty-one hours before obtaining a confession. Hospitalized, Conner would not be formally booked and arraigned until eight days after his arrest. If California had a *NcNabb* Rule in effect at the time, Warren could not have introduced Conner's confession in court.

CHAPTER 27

RED MONDAY'S SPAWN

A
S THE END OF THE 1956 TERM APPROACHED, THE LAW CLERKS kidded each other half-facetiously. Here they were, just out of school, and they faced a sudden end to their law careers, damned as communist sympathizers. Four internal security cases remained to be announced, and in each the appellants had won.

"It was a uniform success for all the Communists in the country," a clerk during that term joked. The four cases raised both legal issues and symbolic questions. All involved political dissent, First and Fifth Amendment rights to be weighed against the demands of national security. However narrowly the Court ruled, the decisions would provoke some members of Congress.

The Supreme Court, as Warren had discovered, "was anything but serene, particularly throughout the [Joseph] McCarthy days when he was complaining that so many cases were in favor of Communism, you know, and things of that kind. And there was great disturbance in the Congress over the segregation cases."

In the four years since Fred Vinson's death, the Supreme Court had shifted its stance in dealing with the "Red Menace." The brethren no longer dutifully ratified congressional efforts to suppress communism.

Vinson was gone, replaced by Warren, and William Brennan sat in place of Sherman Minton. The two newcomers generally joined Hugo Black and William O. Douglas to form the court's "liberal" wing. To prevail in these loyalty cases, the four needed only an additional vote, and that from a Court less doctrinaire, less reflexively "anticommunist."

Stanley Reed, weary of the unremitting stress at age seventy-two, had abruptly elected to retire in February, 1957. In place of that invariably conservative vote was Charles Whittaker, as malleable as Reed was rigid.

Whittaker lacked the older man's sureness. The son of a Kansas farmer, Charlie Whittaker had attended public school only through the tenth grade. He had gone to work as a youth, eventually to pay his way through night law school. Dogged rather than brilliant, Whittaker had prospered, dealing with a largely corporate clientele in Kansas City.

At the urging of Dwight Eisenhower's brother Arthur, the president appointed Whittaker first to the federal district court in 1954 and then to the Eighth Circuit Court of Appeals. Whittaker had served less than three years as a judge when Eisenhower tapped him in March, 1957, to fill the Reed seat.

To Washington and the Supreme Court came Charlie Whittaker, awed by his unexpected ascendancy. As the warning buzzer summoned him to his first oral arguments, a shaken Whittaker confessed to two of Warren's clerks, "Boys, I have never felt so inadequate in my entire life."

Those feelings of doubt were to hound him all of his days on the Court. Yet, paradoxically, the least certain of them would for a time be the most important of justices. "The Whittaker vote was often decisive because he weighed in with his vote later on some of these more troublesome matters," Warren clerk Jon Newman said.

Inclined to follow the authoritative voice, Whittaker was a possible fifth vote for the liberals as the brethren turned to the four national security cases that remained to be announced by mid-June, 1957.

As revolutionaries, the fourteen California communists whose case was before the high court were an unprepossessing bunch. Their lives had been divided between spasms of dialectic debate and idealistic efforts to organize labor unions in the face of police and strikebreakers. They came to the Supreme Court convicted of membership in an organization that advocated the overthrow of the United States government.

If the Communist Party ever posed a threat to domestic tranquility, the menace had long since dissipated in internal politics and disillusion. As defendant Ben Dobbs put it, "At our trial, we used to say we should plead not guilty on the basis of incompetence. Not only did we not know how to run a country, we didn't know how to run ourselves."

By 1950, there were no more than 10,000 dues-paying members, and party leaders guessed that as many as a third of these were paid informers for the Federal Bureau of Investigation. The Californians joked that without the FBI's dues the party would have died.

However impotent the communists truly were by the beginning of their Smith Act trial in February, 1952, overwhelming public opinion thought otherwise. What threat could be greater than an organization ostensibly part of an international conspiracy to conquer the United States?

In Korea, Chinese communists had reinforced faltering North Koreans and denied United States troops their rightful victory. Even as the trial in Los Angeles ground on, Julius and Ethel Rosenberg awaited execution in New York, convicted of atomic espionage on behalf of the Soviet Union. Most Americans believed these were parlous times.

After six years—from arrest in August, 1951, to trial and then appeal—the Californians clung to a faint hope: The once despised "Oil" Warren was chief justice.

Defendant Ben Dobbs recalled a handwritten letter to "Dear Bob" that Robert Kenny, newly retained for the appeal, pulled from a cluttered drawer of his desk. As Dobbs paraphrased the letter, Warren had written his former attorney general:

"I've just received an appointment to the Supreme Court of the United States. I want to pledge to you my firm, loyal support of the Constitution of the United States in its broadest, most humanistic interpretation."

Still the California communists faced long odds. Courts, including the Supreme Court of the United States, tended to follow precedent. And, in 1950, the Vinson Court had affirmed the convictions of eleven national Communist Party leaders for advocating the violent overthrow of the government.

Hugo Black, dissenting from the majority opinion, could only hope that in "calmer times, when present pressures, passions, and fears subside, this or some later Court will restore the First Amendment liberties to the high preferred place where they belong in a free society."

Seven years later, Black's time had come. If calm had not settled upon the Supreme Court, reason had. The very mood of the courtroom had changed.*

So too had Earl Warren. Sixteen years before, as California attorney general, Warren had urged that those who "advocate the overthrow of our government by force and violence . . . should not be permitted to invoke the right of free speech or assembly. We have seen other democracies crumble and their people subjugated because they permitted such treacherous conspiracies under a broadminded but uncritical adherence to old concepts of their bills of rights."

By mid-1955, he was more willing to honor those old concepts. "We must test all of our public actions by dissent," he said that year in a speech honoring Progressive Robert LaFollette, Sr. "The majority does not always discover the right answer until it is so tested."

In taking up the California communists's appeal, Warren relied on a pragmatic jurisprudence. The defendants were openly members of the Communist Party, and therefore useless as spies or saboteurs for a foreign power. Whatever threat of revolution these "garden variety Communists"

---

* Arguing on behalf of one of the California communists on October 8, 1956, Robert Kenny noted that a messenger continually fed slips of paper to the Chief. Warren would look at the notes, then pass them along to the brethren; Warren later told Kenny they were following the course of Yankee pitcher Don Larsen's no-hit game against the Dodgers in the World Series.

might have posed during the desperate days of the Depression had been obliterated by postwar prosperity.

That settled, he could ask himself, as a later law clerk put it, "Who is getting picked on here?"

His arguments in chambers made no allusions to lofty constitutional theory. "He was a real underdog-protector. He would say, 'They're picking on this guy. This guy is no more a threat than my aunt is.' "

The Chief opened the October 12, 1956, conference on the appeal arguing the government had a weak case. They "have proved only membership in the Communist Party, not unlawful conduct. The only overt acts were attendance at public meetings and nothing was shown there to prove advocacy of force and violence." Furthermore, teaching and advocacy of communist doctrine did not pose the necessary "clear and present danger."

The first vote in conference had Warren, Black, and Douglas for reversal. Burton, Clark, Reed, and Minton voted to affirm. Frankfurter and Harlan were undecided. With the brethren split, Warren suggested they put the matter over for another time.

Three weeks later, Shay Minton retired. In his place was William Brennan, who would not participate because he had not heard oral arguments.

At the end of the second conference on the case, the vote was 5–3 to reverse the convictions. Both Frankfurter and Harlan had decided that active rather than theoretical incitement was required to convict.

Shortly after, the weary Stanley Reed resigned. Whittaker too would not take part in the case, leaving Burton and Clark to stand alone.

Warren assigned the California communist case to John Harlan, probably for two reasons: Felix Frankfurter had commended a Harlan opinion from the second circuit upholding the Smith Act conviction of a communist, and to make certain that Harlan did not change his vote.

Harlan was unenthusiastic about the Smith Act prosecutions. At worst he thought the law unconstitutional, at best he dismissed it as "dumb."

Yet he was a man who believed in lawful order and governmental authority. He could never go so far as to strike down the Smith Act on constitutional grounds, but he could narrow its application. Harlan—"once a preeminent advocate for American capitalists"—was to craft a closely reasoned opinion that effectively gutted the anticommunist Smith Act.

The essential issue was the matter of advocacy, Harlan wrote. A Smith Act defendant could be convicted only for advocating and teaching "concrete action for the forcible overthrow of the Government, and not of principles divorced from action."

There was the scant evidence of those actual acts. The government had relied on simple membership in the Communist Party to establish a plot to conspire. Indeed, some of those acts committed as members might have been otherwise legal.

Harlan's majority opinion on June 17, 1957, "Red Monday," ordered that five of the fourteen be acquitted outright, and nine receive new trials.

Under Harlan's finely drawn opinion, the Smith Act still stood, providing the government could meet the burden of proof.

Warren, Frankfurter, and Burton—who had changed his mind with Reed's retirement—joined Harlan. Black and Douglas concurred in the result in a separate opinion, arguing that the Smith Act itself offended the First Amendment and should be struck down. Clark was the only dissenter; Brennan and Whittaker, who also had not heard oral arguments, did not take part in the case.*

If Warren was dubious about the risk of subversion, he was even more wary of federal and state legislative efforts to expose "the Red menace." As early as 1939, he publicly charged that the House Un-American Activities Committee "starts with preconceived notions and its investigators go out to find supporting evidence. They bring that kind of evidence to the committee and suppress the evidence which will not support their theses."

Functioning as a virtual court, HUAC relied on two kinds of witnesses to generate newspaper headlines and airtime for itself: accusers and victims.

The accusers Warren had scorned since his days as attorney general, calling them "irresponsible professional red-baiter[s]." Their victims were men and women who relied on the Bill of Rights' guarantee that no person would be compelled to testify against himself. They escaped prosecution, but were damned in the community as "Fifth Amendment Communists."

Those who claimed a First Amendment right of free association, or of free speech ran greater risks. Inevitably, the committee would hold them in contempt of Congress, and just as inevitably, courts found them guilty.

Two of the four cases handed down on what became known as "Red Monday" involved such legislative investigations.

Summoned in 1954 before HUAC, John T. Watkins had testified freely about his own activities as a labor organizer years before when he had openly cooperated with the Communist Party. Watkins refused, however, to give the committee the names of those long-ago party members.

That refusal to bring down others led to his indictment for contempt of Congress. Convicted of not answering "any question pertinent to the question under inquiry," he appealed, contending the committee's questions were intended to expose for exposure's sake alone.

At the March 8 conference, Warren framed two issues in the Watkins case. First, he argued, the investigating committee had to demonstrate why Watkins's testimony was relevant to the inquiry. Second, the committee had no right to expose merely to expose.

---

* Government prosecutors six months later moved to dismiss the remaining indictments because they could not meet the new evidentiary requirements. (Among them was Dorothy Healey, who, as a girl of fifteen, had been arrested in a May Day, 1930, demonstration in Earl Warren's Oakland for disturbing the peace.) Meanwhile, more than one hundred cases brought by government prosecutors against party members in Baltimore, Honolulu, Seattle, Detroit, Philadelphia, and Cleveland ground to a halt. In retrospect, Warren's clerk Curtis Reitz said, Red Monday marked the end of the witch-hunt.

Again, all but Clark agreed, with Burton, whose nephew had prosecuted the government's case, and Whittaker who had missed the oral arguments, not participating. Both Frankfurter and Harlan, though, argued for a narrowly written decision, one that placed the burden on the committee to show the relevance of its questions.

Warren assigned *Watkins* to himself because the decision would attack the practices of a coequal branch of government. The chief justice was the most appropriate spokesman.

For Earl Warren, this was a case of first principles, of rules learned as a boy in the schoolyard: You did not tattle on your friends.

Watkins had testified fully about his own membership in the party, the government conceded. He had also testified about those still in the party—and well known to the FBI. He had refused only to identify those who had since "removed themselves from the Communist movement."

Congress was free to investigate for clearly defined legislative purposes, the Chief wrote in his opinion. But "there is no congressional power to expose for the sake of exposure," Warren added.

The legitimate need of Congress to investigate "cannot be inflated into a general power to expose where the predominant result can only be an invasion of the private rights of individuals."

Despite his broad condemnation of HUAC's practices, Warren was to rest his opinion on narrow legal grounds. Because the committee had not carefully defined the scope of its investigation, Watkins could not know if the questions asked of him were pertinent. Thus he did not have sufficient legal notice.

The vote was 6–1, with Frankfurter concurring and Clark again dissenting.

The third decision on this Red Monday involved an appeal by former university professor Paul M. Sweezy, who twice refused on First Amendment grounds to answer questions put to him by New Hampshire attorney general Louis C. Wyman. Wyman had subpoenaed Sweezy, a classical Marxist, to testify about lectures he had given at the University of New Hampshire in 1954, and about his organizing activities on behalf of the Independent Progressive Party in the 1948 presidential election.

Warren, the former ex officio regent of the University of California who had once opposed loyalty oaths for professors, assigned the Sweezy case to himself.

The issue seemed clear to him. It was "unthinkable" for a legislature to create an investigative agency with unrestricted power such as New Hampshire's had. Wyman, like HUAC, had subsequently abused that power to conduct a "personal vendetta" against Sweezy unrelated to any legislative purpose.

Warren's opinion swatted down Wyman's investigation of the Progressive Party in New Hampshire:

Our form of government is built on the premise that every citizen shall have the right to engage in political expression and association. This right was enshrined in the First Amendment of the Bill of Rights. Exercise of these basic freedoms in America has traditionally been through the media of political associations. Any interference with the freedom of a party is simultaneously an interference with the freedom of its adherents.

Similarly, academic freedom was so important, Warren wrote, "we do not now conceive of any circumstance wherein a state interest would justify its infringement."

But having staked out the broad constitutional position, Warren's opinion once more retreated to narrow legal grounds. The state had not proved that the information the legislature sought had been wanted for legislative purposes. Without that, Sweezy's conviction could not stand.

Warren's opinion, in the words of even a sympathetic observer, *New York Times* reporter Anthony Lewis, could "only be called opaque." As in the *Watkins* opinion, Warren had surrounded "a kernel of legal accomplishment with a large quantity of moralizing."

The vote on Sweezy's behalf was 6–2. Black, Douglas, and Brennan signed onto the Warren opinion. Frankfurter, ever the college professor, wrote a stronger concurrence flatly stating that New Hampshire had not justified its invasion of academic freedom. Harlan joined. Only Burton and Clark dissented, with Whittaker not taking part.

The fourth of the day's decisions involved John Stewart Service, one of the State Department's "Old China Hands" scapegoated by supporters of Chiang Kai-shek for the fall of China.

The State Department investigated Service's fitness and loyalty no less than five times. Four times a Loyalty Review Board cleared him. On the fifth, the board succumbed to political pressure from the pro-Chiang "China Lobby," and ruled against him. Fired on the last day of 1951 for alleged communist sympathies, Service had filed suit to reclaim his job.

Again the decision was narrowly cast. For an 8–0 court, John Harlan wrote that then–Secretary of State Dean Acheson had ignored the department's own procedural rules when he summarily fired Service. Service was to be reinstated.

The *Service* decision was no more than a reproof, but coupled with the other three opinions of Red Monday, it took on a larger, symbolic importance.

The American Civil Liberties Union issued a jubilant statement proclaiming that the Court had set a national mood "in sharp contrast to the hysteria and near-terror of only a few years ago."

With his *Watkins* opinion, said *Time* magazine, "Warren read the riot act to the same UnAmerican Activities Committee whose contempt charge against Barsky had been allowed to stand" just three years earlier.

Reviewing the day, *The New York Times*'s "Scotty" Reston, concluded that the high court was "reasserting its ancient role as a defender of the Constitution and the Bill of Rights . . ."

The *Christian Science Monitor*'s respected Joseph C. Harsch saw in the four opinions a larger vision: "There is implicit in these decisions a judgment . . . that communism has ceased to be such an active menace to the state in the United States that measures at the expense of the individual are necessary to the survival of the state."

Not everyone agreed.

The *Richmond (Virginia) News Leader,* already infuriated by the school desegregation opinions, railed against the "arrogant incompetence" of the justices and their "flagrant and willful disregard of the judicial function."

The *Chicago Tribune,* staunchly conservative, editorialized, "The boys in the Kremlin may wonder why they need a 5th column in the United States so long as the Supreme Court is determined to be so helpful." In New York City, the Hearst *Daily Mirror* claimed the Court had made "Communists superior to every other citizen in the country."

Right-of-center magazines ginned a steady flow of critical articles after Red Monday. *U.S. News & World Report* founder-editor David Lawrence was particularly incensed that a Supreme Court once safely conservative was now stocked with men "selected from a cult that believes the Constitution can be rewritten at will by the judiciary."

A succession of articles in Lawrence's magazine scored the Court's direction and urged that it be curbed. Another article, by former law clerk William H. Rehnquist, argued that politically liberal clerks exerted undue influence on their justices.

According to Rehnquist, the clerks displayed "extreme solicitude for the claims of Communists and other criminal defendants, expansion of federal power at the expense of state power, great sympathy toward any government regulation of business—in short, the political philosophy now espoused by the Court under Chief Justice Earl Warren."

The *National Review* took up curbs on the Court as a holy cause. Warren was no more than "a partisan agent of a fashionable ideology" who wallowed in "juridical sloth and political tendentiousness," Associate Editor L. Brent Bozell insisted. The court's jurisdiction must be curtailed.

Meanwhile, Dwight Eisenhower fumed.

By Warren's own account, the president was angry with the decisions of Red Monday. In private, Eisenhower told the chief justice that "he had been disappointed in Justice Brennan and me."

When Warren asked why, Eisenhower complained about "those Communist cases."

Had he read the decisions? Warren asked. No, he had not, Eisenhower acknowledged, but he knew what was in them.

Their relations, already at arm's length, markedly cooled. Correspondence once addressed to "Dear Earl" now went invariably to "Dear Mr. Chief Justice."

For his part, Warren also found fault. Law clerk Graham Moody recalled a cold Saturday during the winter of 1955–56, when the Chief and his clerks were discussing southern conformance with the school desegregation opinions.

Warren was unhappy with the pace of integration in the face of massive resistance. The president had not spoken out to support the desegregation decision, to Warren's irritation, and apparently did not intend to.

Eisenhower's "clear lack of enthusiasm for the decision contributed to the massive resistance," he told law clerk Benno Schmidt in a later term. "Warren was, I would say, very, very disappointed with Eisenhower in this area," Schmidt concluded.

The president had said nothing, while resistance to the Supreme Court's "all deliberate speed" mandate grew in the South. In the three years after *Brown I,* the eleven states of the old Confederacy had adopted 141 pieces of legislation designed to thwart school integration, while segregationist White Citizens Councils gained members daily.

The schools of the Old South essentially remained segregated. "If I were president," the Chief told his clerks, "I would send the U.S. Marshal in there."

By Red Monday, June 17, 1957, Eisenhower had thrown his hands up. The appointment of Warren as chief justice "was the biggest damn fool thing I ever did," he reportedly exclaimed.

Asked who first had recommended Warren's appointment as chief justice, Eisenhower allegedly grumbled, "I wish I could remember, because I'd like to shoot him." *

The two men were far apart, with little expectation they could come together. "I'm satisfied that Eisenhower never understood Warren," the president's chief of staff, Sherman Adams, said. "Nor do I think he ever took personal time to discover how Warren's mind worked. . . . I doubt if Eisenhower at any time ever understood the intricate mechanisms of the Warren mind."

In the interests of protocol, president and chief justice remained punctilious in observing the courtesies of office. Nonetheless, the two men had long memories.

When in 1961, CBS news producer Fred Friendly asked the retired Eisenhower if he had made any great mistakes as president, Eisenhower snapped, "Yes, two, and they are both sitting on the Supreme Court."

---

* Tom Dewey was equally distressed with Warren's emerging liberalism. According to Dewey's biographer, the New Yorker "came to regard Warren as Eisenhower's greatest error, a judicial wrecker who pulled out the very underpinning of what was designed to be a conservative-to-moderate administration. See Smith, *Thomas E. Dewey,* p. 608.

Even later, Warren told his law clerks "he felt that Eisenhower had betrayed his responsibilities as the president and failed to support the Court" on *Brown*. In a conversation with his grandson Jeffrey, Warren sadly shook his head and deplored the lost opportunity. "How much more we could have done had we had the president behind us." *

No such questions of protocol or courtesy restrained the Congress— where segregationists lined up with anticommunists to fulminate against the court. Earl Warren became, in the oratory of the influential Virginia Democratic senator Harry Byrd, "the modern Thaddeus Stevens." (The comparison suggested Byrd's fears sprang not from a Red but from a black "menace.")†

Mississippi Democrat James Eastland, chairman of the Senate Internal Security Subcommittee, claimed that from October, 1953, when Warren took the oath, through the 1957 terms, the Supreme Court had sustained the communist position thirty of thirty-nine times. (In fact, there had been only thirty-one cases involving communists or leftists during that period; nine had favored the government position.)

No matter the truth. From January, 1957, through the end of the congressional session in August, conservative legislators introduced 101 anti-Court measures, historian David Caute noted. The denunciations flashed like a contagion through the Congress, spreading from the Court's unanimous rulings in the school cases to its decisions in internal security matters and on to issues of criminal law.

South Carolina's Senator Strom Thurmond took up *Mallory,* decided a week after Red Monday, and flailed the justices. In its decision reaffirming that suspects were to be promptly arraigned, Thurmond asserted, the Court had confronted the nation with a choice between "judicial limitation or judicial tyranny. Congress must take action to limit the power of the Court," he thundered.

The *Jencks* decision permitting defendants to see witnesses' statements prior to trial upset the formidable J. Edgar Hoover. At Hoover's covert prompting, his allies in Congress overnight introduced eleven bills to nullify the decision, and halt "rummaging" by criminals in law enforcement files.

Congressional action would restore a sense of balance to a decision by naive or duped justices who had put the FBI "out of business," as North Dakota's Representative Usher Burdick put it. "This decision encourages crimes. It encourages the underworld, and it is a blow to law enforcement."

Jencks and *Watkins,* charged California Republican congressman Donald

---

* Perhaps their relationship eventually warmed. Long out of office, Eisenhower gave the Warrens a gift of an oil, which Eisenhower, a Sunday dauber, had painted.

† The same suspicion lurks in the adoption of a resolution by the state of Georgia's General Assembly on February 22, 1957, fully four months before Red Monday. That august body called for the impeachment of Warren, Black, Douglas, Frankfurter, Clark and Reed (!) for "undertaking by judicial decrees to carry out communist policies . . . [their] high crimes and misdemeanors too numerous to mention." Coincidentally, Reed resigned on February 23.

Jackson, represented "a victory greater than any achieved by the Soviet on any battlefield since World War II."

Amid the soaring hyperbole—Brennan's *Jencks* ruling granted defendants only pretrial statements of those called as witnesses—Senate Majority Leader Lyndon Baines Johnson guided Congress to a face-saving solution. First Johnson adopted as his own a modest bill written by Assistant Attorney General Warren Olney III for the Eisenhower Department of Justice. Then Johnson saw to it that Olney's measure—which did little more than codify as law the *Jencks* majority and concurring opinions—was treated with denaturing amendments.*

With the passage of that diluted measure on September 2, 1957, the storm abated. But the unreasoned criticism had stung Warren.

Criticism from lawyers particularly smarted. When Horace Albright, fellow member of the Class of 1912, grumbled about the *Watkins* decision, Warren chided him. "Horace, you never read the decision. You only read the stuff in the newspapers."

Similarly, to friends who complained that the Court was going too fast, Warren mildly scolded, "There should be no delay in correcting a mistake."

Only by implication could Warren openly reply to critics. In a speech before the National Conference of Christians and Jews, he quoted his predecessor as chief justice, Charles Evans Hughes: "Democracy has its own capacity for tyranny. Some of the most menacing encroachments upon liberty invoke the democratic principle and assert the right of the majority to rule—freedom is in danger of being slain at her own altars if the passion for uniformity and control of opinion gathers head . . ."

The Court term ended, the summer offered momentary relief. Warren traveled to Independence, Missouri, to speak at the dedication of the Harry S Truman Presidential Library. The former president's invitation was calculated; it represented Harry Truman's endorsement of Earl Warren, of *Brown,* and the direction of the Court.

In temperatures that rose well above 100 degrees, before a sweltering audience of 5,000 that included former presidents Truman and Hoover, Eleanor Roosevelt, former Secretary of State Dean Acheson, and a dozen other Washington figures, Warren praised the man from Missouri as "tireless, fearless, and decisive."

In a wry aside, Warren added, "Let me say that I personally came to appreciate his dynamic fighting qualities, perhaps earlier and more fully than some other people, in the fall of 1948."

Warren could escape Washington in this summer of 1957; he could not escape his critics.

---

* A significant group of liberals in both parties supported the Court, some openly, some discreetly. In addition to Johnson, they included Democrats Richard Neuberger (Oregon), Hubert H. Humphrey, (Minnesota), Paul Douglas (Illinois), Thomas Hennings (Missouri), and Joseph Clark (Pennsylvania), in addition to Republicans Wayne Morse (Oregon), Jacob Javits (New York), John Sherman Cooper (Kentucky), and Thomas Kuchel (California).

The Warrens had planned on spending a leisurely month abroad, beginning their summer vacation with a transatlantic voyage on the *Queen Mary.* He was to attend the second half of the annual meeting of the American Bar Association to be held this year in London.

Reluctant to attend the London meetings, he had agreed to attend only after Felix Frankfurter argued that this convocation was a celebration of English common law, from which American jurisprudence descended. Such a tribute would not be complete without the presence of the chief justice.

When Warren learned that Richard Nixon had also been invited, he balked. "I had understood this was to be a meeting to emphasize the law, a tribute to English law from which our law derives." he reportedly told bar association officers.

"If Nixon comes, it will change the emphasis completely, to the political. If he comes, you can count me out."

Nixon was disinvited. Warren noted with satisfaction, "Was he sore!"

Even so, Warren embarked for London with real misgivings. The ABA had stood silent amid the criticism of *Brown v. Board of Education.* "They're always worried about their Southern members," Warren sneered.*

The ABA had publicly scored Supreme Court decisions dealing with alleged communists, and, earlier that month, the ABA's assembly had voted down a resolution condemning unreasonable criticism of the Supreme Court.

More abuse followed. In London, the report of the ABA's standing Committee on Communism served up a plate of gratuitous advice: "If the courts lean too far backward in the maintenance of theoretical individual rights, it may be that we have tied the hands of our country and have rendered it incapable of carrying out the first law of mankind—the right of self-preservation."

The Committee on Communism's ten members, including New Hampshire's attorney general, Louis Wyman, recommended legislation to negate the decisions of Red Monday, as well as rulings that limited the deportation of suspected communists.

Finally the committee urged congress to pass a bill to "permit schools, universities, bar associations and other organizations to set standards of membership high enough to exclude those who refuse to testify frankly and fully about their past activities in furtherance of Communist plans to conquer the free world by subversion."

The ABA's House of Delegates accepted the report without comment. Warren's supporters chose not to challenge the committee; a debate would only stir more publicity.

"The report," said the cautious Associated Press, "was a direct slap at

---

* A decade later, former Warren law clerk Michael Smith said, Warren was still bitter. Reviewing an ABA petition to appear as a friend of the court in an upcoming case, Warren remarked, "Those bastards! Where were they when we needed them on *Brown v. Board?*"

United States Chief Justice Earl Warren, under whose leadership the Court has taken a 'liberal' trend . . ."

Warren attributed the attacks to the machinations of conservative Californian Loyd Wright, a prominent figure in ABA politics. Wright, who held no affection for Warren either as a politician or a jurist, had joined with Wyman, loser in the Sweezy case, to take revenge.*

In addition to the committee's report, Warren suffered an indignity at the ABA convention, one deeply resented and long remembered. Through an unexplained mix-up, the chief justice did not receive notice of the formal dress expected of those on the dais at one of the functions. Amid peers and pontiffs of the law, decked in morning coats and striped trousers, Warren sat uncomfortably in bright chocolate brown suit and brown shoes.

What he termed "snide" press notices of his dress the next day did not improve his temper.

Combined with the committee report, "a disservice the American Bar Association did to the Supreme Court," the dress gaffe left the chief justice livid by the end of the London meeting.

He had had enough. Warren resigned from the bar association on September 3.†

The balance of the overseas trip was more pleasant. Warren and Attorney General Brownell traveled on to Dublin where the two men were invested with honorary degrees from the university. They spent four days at the Lakes of Killarney, then went on to that eternal tourist attraction, the stone set high in the wall of Blarney Castle, County Cork.

For a month, the Warrens toured the British Isles in unusually pleasant weather. With Helen MacGregor they visited Scotland, a happy moment of "girlish giggles" for Nina and the governor's former aide-de-camp. The Warrens returned to Washington at the end of August—in time to confront a constitutional crisis unparalleled since the days of the Confederacy.

---

* In fact, some of the more conservative leaders of the bar association had opposed Warren's nomination as chief justice. See Robert G. Storey OH, Columbia University, p. 9.

† President-elect Charles Rhyne held on to the letter of resignation, with the hope he could convince Warren to withdraw it. (The original, Rhyne said in an interview on August 5, 1993, was stolen in a later burglary of his office.) When the ABA membership office routinely sent the chief justice a bill for membership in 1958, Warren ignored it. The ABA then announced he had been dropped from the rolls for nonpayment of his dues. Had there been any remote chance of reconciliation, that bungle ended it. See Stanley Barnes OH, p. 68.

CHAPTER 28

THE STORM

THE ANGRY CROWDS CHURNED ALONG PARK AVENUE, STALKING prey in the sweltering heat. Before them stood a line of raw Arkansas Air National Guard troops, drawn up before the entrance of Little Rock's Central High School.

Arkansas governor Orval E. Faubus had "prayerfully" mustered the Guard on September 2, 1957, the night before the fall semester began. The nervous troops were "to protect the lives and property of citizens"—by barring nine handpicked black students from enrolling at Central under a federal court order.

Faubus had reached back in time to resurrect the discredited antebellum doctrine of interposition. At Faubus's direction, the state of Arkansas would stand between a federal government mandating the schools be integrated and Little Rock's resisting citizens. Faubus was both defying a federal court order to integrate the public schools and placating Arkansas's unyielding segregationists at the same time.

The muster of the guard had been unnecessary, the mayor of Little Rock protested. City police had not recorded a single instance of interracial violence in the previous week.

"If any racial trouble does develop, the blame rests squarely on the doorstep of the Governor's Mansion," Woodrow W. Mann insisted.

The guardsmen stood uneasy watch through Tuesday, September 3. Raucous groups of white protesters roved Park between 13th and 16th streets, but no black children appeared to demand admittance to the school grounds.

After a five-minute hearing that night, federal district court judge Ronald

Norwood Davies reaffirmed the order that Central High admit its first black students. Faubus refused to remove the Guard.

The following morning, 400 protesters filled the streets near the school. They shouted racial epithets as an escort of white and black ministers convoyed eight black students to the line of troops.

The students and their escort halted, impassive, in front of the guardsmen. Before a battery of newspaper and television cameras, each side played out its role in the staged drama. A Guard officer ordered the children to move away.

Moments later, another of the black students, fifteen-year-old Elizabeth Eckford, showed up at the school without an escort. Twice the frightened girl edged her way through the roiling crowd to come face-to-face with a guardsman's unyielding bayonet. The crowd catcalled its triumph.

"Go back where you came from!" shrieked one of the youths.

"Lynch her! Lynch her!" ordered another, hidden in the rear.

"Go home, you bastard of a black bitch!"

Surrounded and alone, the terrified young woman in her stiffly starched dress hugged her schoolbooks closer to her chest. Newspaper and television pictures captured the unsettling image of a bewildered teenager lost amid a mob of howling whites, their faces contorted by hatred.

Whatever sympathy the segregationists might have aroused beyond the South vanished with those photographs. No longer were the protesters victims of a faceless federal judiciary rending local customs; they themselves became the bullies. Preserving a traditional southern way of life stood revealed as no more than naked bigotry.

On Thursday, September 5, the school board asked Judge Davies for a stay in carrying out the gradual integration plan approved in August by the federal court. (The schools would not be fully integrated for six years, according to the plan.)

That day too President Eisenhower spoke out for the first time. He had waited, as he often did, and evaded crises by denying that a crisis even existed.

The president could wait no longer, Attorney General Herbert Brownell cautioned. Faubus was, in effect, challenging Eisenhower's oath to support and defend the Constitution.

In a telegram to Governor Faubus, the president warned that he would uphold the Constitution "with every means at my command."

Faubus, unyielding, asked to meet the president. In effect, he was playing to the president's known sympathy for the plight of the white southerner.

The governor accepted Eisenhower's invitation to meet on Sunday, September 15, at Newport, Rhode Island, near the president's summer retreat. During their two-hour talk, Eisenhower warned Faubus that the federal courts must be obeyed. Whatever his personal feelings about the speed of integration, Eisenhower hinted, a test of his will was unwise. The governor could not win.

As expected, on Friday, September 20, Judge Davies enjoined Faubus from interfering with the integration plan. Faubus immediately withdrew the Guard, leaving Central High bared to the protesters Faubus himself had inspired. City police assumed reluctant patrol of a high school perched atop a racial tinderbox.

The following Monday, eight black students stoically attempted once more to attend classes at Central High. Once more the crowds swirled along Park Avenue, chanting, "Two, four, six, eight, we ain't going to integrate."

The crowd dissolved into a mob. Knots of angry men assaulted four black reporters while others jeered white newsmen. In the turmoil, the black students slipped into the school by a side door.

When rowdy students swept through the hallways, alarmed school authorities decided to withdraw the eight blacks. The youngsters had managed to integrate Central High for less than three hours.

Orval Faubus had left the president with no alternatives. Whatever his personal sympathies, Dwight David Eisenhower, West Point 1915, understood his duty under the Constitution he had sworn to uphold.

According to Attorney General Brownell, Eisenhower "abhorred the idea of using troops, but he never contemplated that a governor of a state would defy the law and his oath."

At noon the next day, the president ordered units of the United States Army's 101st Airborne to Little Rock. Their task, he wrote in a note to himself, was *"not* to enforce integration, but to prevent opposition by violence to orders of a court." At the same time, he called into federal service the Arkansas National Guard, neatly removing them from Little Rock and Faubus's control.

By nightfall, 1,000 members of the Airborne's 327th Battle Group under Major General Edwin Walker—himself an ardent segregationist—were bivouacked on the playground of Central High. For the first time since Reconstruction, federal troops had been dispatched to the South to maintain civil order.

Central would remain integrated as a school board suit to delay worked its way to the Supreme Court and the constitutional crisis eased. The protesters lost interest, once the black students were inside, and the paratroops began a gradual withdrawal. On October 23, 1957, the nine black students entered quiet Central High without guards for the first time.

The fight was not gone from Arkansas officials, however, nor was the crisis ended. Rather than continue its already slow pace, the Little Rock School Board asked the federal district court for permission to delay further integration until tempers cooled.

The board's strategy, as Little Rock's school superintendent Virgil Blossom explained, was "to get as little integration over as long a period of time as is legally possible."

Public resistance, stirred by the governor and state legislature, made compliance with *Brown* impossible, attorneys for the board argued in federal court. They asked to halt the current integration at Central High School and to delay further desegregation for two years.

Sympathetic district court judge Harry Lemley on June 20, 1958, granted the delay, and gave the board until the opening of school in September, 1960, to implement its plan. The NAACP immediately appealed.

A three-judge panel of the circuit court of appeals on August 18, 1958, agreed with the arguments of the NAACP's chief counsel, Thurgood Marshall, and reversed Lemley's order. "The time has not yet come in these United States," the court held, "when an order of a federal court must be whittled away, watered down, or shamefully withdrawn in the face of violent and unlawful acts of individual citizens."

With the opening of the fall semester just a week away, the school board hastily appealed to the Supreme Court. Time was short and the brethren were scattered; the chief justice himself was in Los Angeles for the annual convention of the American Bar Association at the invitation of his friend, ABA president Charles Rhyne.*

Throughout a long reception for the chief justice at the Biltmore Hotel, Warren continually ducked from the receiving line to take telephone calls from Solicitor General J. Lee Rankin and Associate Justice William Brennan in Washington. They were arranging an unusual special session, only the third in the Court's history, to decide whether to hear the Little Rock appeal before school began on Tuesday, September 2, 1958.

Even as the justices gathered in humid Washington, the Arkansas legislature rallied behind Faubus and passed a clutch of bills to shore up his position. One measure compelled the governor to close any school facing integration; another ostensibly would permit the transfer of funds from integrated public schools to white-only private academies.

Technically, school board attorneys had brought their suit on behalf of William Cooper, president of the Little Rock School Board. The respondents were the black parents who had sued the board to force the school's reopening, led alphabetically by John Aaron. They would be represented by the NAACP's Thurgood Marshall.

In fact, the real parties in the Supreme Court of the United States on August 28, 1958, were the president of the United States and the governor of the state of Arkansas. *Cooper v. Aaron* had become a great test of the Constitution and the meaning of federalism in twentieth-century America.

Despite the importance of the case, then newly arrived law clerk "Mike" Heyman recalled, "there was a sense of summer lethargy" in the Supreme Court building. That august institution admitted to no sense of either urgency or crisis.

---

* In contrast to his cool reception the year before, Warren was a great hit in Los Angeles, Rhyne later recalled. Friendly members of the bar association, joined by enthusiastic lawyers from Warren's home state, clamored for tickets to hear him speak. When Rhyne sought a larger auditorium, Warren told him not to bother. "Nothing makes a speaker feel as good as to fight his way into a crowded hall." (Charles Rhyne int.)

Little Rock attorney Richard C. Butler was to represent the school board before the high court, his task to challenge a bedrock constitutional principle that dated to 1803 and *Marbury v. Madison*. A man of serene dignity polished by years as an unchallenged civic leader, Butler personally blamed the confrontation not on the governor, but on "some bad law created by the judiciary . . ."

Butler found himself in difficulty from the very start of his argument for a temporary stay of the circuit court order until the case could be argued on its merits. "May it please the Court," he began with the traditional introduction, "The people of Little Rock—"

He got no further before the chief justice interrupted. "What people? Which people of Little Rock are you talking about?"

The implication that Butler spoke only for white Arkansas hung in the marble courtroom, unanswered and damning.

Butler recovered to remind the justices that the two *Brown* decisions had "recognized that time was required for certain cultural patterns to change. . . . 'Deliberate speed,' as used by this Court, is certainly not just a phrase coined on the spur of the moment or developed as a philosophy of opportunism . . ."

When Butler urged that Judge Lemley's two-year stay be approved, Warren quietly asked if the school board had made plans to desegregate if the stay were not granted.

"No, sir; it has not decided," Butler responded, "because it is almost compelled to see what statutes are passed by the General Assembly now in session . . ."

"Well, as to these specific children, have they been assigned to any school?"

"Yes, sir; they have now been assigned," Butler said. "To the all-Negro school, the new high school there, Horace Mann."

"Well, isn't that action toward segregating them again?"

"Oh, yes, sir. It is, it is, and that was done under the order of Judge Lemley's decision."

"Yes." Warren seemed to sigh. And if the Supreme Court affirmed the integration order "then the School Board will proceed to segregate these pupils who are plaintiffs in this case?"

"Yes, sir," Butler conceded. Little Rock would defy the Supreme Court of the United States.

Throughout his life, Warren dimly recollected the boyhood memory of an angry Los Angeles mob that had hung an effigy from the schoolyard flagpole in the light of a great bonfire. "It gave me a horror of mob action which has remained with me to this day," he recalled seven decades later.

Once more the mob was in the streets.

"Mr. Butler," Warren said with some sympathy, "I think there's no member of this Court who fails to recognize the very great problem which your school board has. But, can we defer a program of this kind merely because there are those elements in the community that will commit violence to prevent it from going into effect?"

Butler sought to argue that Faubus's very act of defiance had so clouded the legal issue that the school board was correct to delay. "Mr. Chief Justice, you have been the Governor of a great state, and if you—"

"I never tried to resolve any legal problem of this kind as Governor of my state," Warren broke in. As governor, he had abided by the decisions of the courts, state and federal.

"We all realize that, sir. The point I am making is this: That if the Governor of any state says that a United States Supreme Court decision is not the law of the land, the people of that state, until it is really resolved, have a doubt in their mind and a right to have a doubt."

Warren's voice was laced with cold fury. "But I have never heard such an argument made in a court of justice before, and I have tried many a case over many a year. I never heard a lawyer say that a statement of a governor as to what was legal or illegal should control the action of any court."

Butler withered in the face of the stern lecture. There would be no stay of the integration order. While he would return on September 11 to argue the case on the merits, the school board had no hope of winning.

Immediately after the September 11 argument, the brethren met in conference. They were unanimous. They were unbending. Under the Constitution, there was a single rule of law, and governors no less than judges were bound to it.

"We knew the kind of opinion we wanted," William Brennan told legal historian James F. Simon. "I remember Justice Harlan saying that this was the biggest crisis in Court history, since we were told that governors and other courts were not bound by our decision."

Warren assigned to Harlan and Frankfurter the responsibility for a brief unsigned order affirming the appellate court. Brennan was later to write the full opinion, laying out the Court's reasoning.

Noting that three of their number—Harlan, Brennan, and Whittaker—had not taken part in both *Brown* decisions, Frankfurter on September 19 suggested that each of the brethren sign the Brennan opinion when it was ready. It was unprecedented, but it would make clear the Court was as one. With the "notoriety given Governor Faubus's obstructive conduct in the case, we thought well of the suggestion," Warren commented dryly.

Frankfurter remained concerned about the tenor of Brennan's decision. Frankfurter hoped to be conciliatory, but feared Warren.

"His attitude toward the kind of problems that confront us is more like that of a fighting politician than that of a judicial statesman," Frankfurter complained.

Brennan's final opinion, which the chief announced on September 29, 1958, was largely a narrative of the aborted integration of Central High. In a single, uncompromising paragraph, the brethren made clear they would not acquiesce:

> *The constitutional rights of the respondents are not to be sacrificed or yielded to the violence and disorder which have followed upon the actions of the Governor and Legislature. . . . [L]aw and order are not here to be preserved by depriving the Negro children of their constitutional rights.*

At the last conference before Warren announced the opinion, Frankfurter without warning moved to seize leadership of the Court. He told the brethren he would sign the Brennan opinion, but was also going to write a personal concurrence.

His proposal "caused quite a sensation on the Court," Warren noted with some understatement. A Frankfurter concurrence would inevitably take something from the appearance of unanimity.

Frankfurter's explanation was less than convincing. As a law professor, he had taught many of the leading lawyers of the South, men to whom he could appeal with his concurrence. Though they might not like desegregation, "the lawyers of the South will gradually realize the transcending issue, namely respect for the law."

The brethren were more than angry; Frankfurter was shattering the image of a Supreme Court that spoke as one on the subject of school integration. "Felix was a pariah around here for days," Brennan later recalled.

To another interviewer Brennan acknowledged, "There was havoc around here, just hell to pay. The Chief, Black and I were furious. We almost cut his throat." Black and Brennan momentarily weighed their own concurrence, then decided to remain silent rather than reveal the friction within.

The Frankfurter stratagem raised no demonstrable support for the Court, nor did it persuade anyone that Frankfurter led the conference. Richard Butler, the counsel for the Little Rock School Board, laid his failure to gain the two-year delay he sought squarely on the chief justice.

"I think that Mr. Earl Warren was a strong enough personality to persuade one way or another men who probably did not have the tendency toward that end.

"I think Mr. Warren had qualities of persuasion and even domination in some areas that perhaps other justices either did not have, or did not desire to have."

Had another man been chief justice, Butler told an interviewer, the Court would have granted the delay.

Revisiting the case, Warren's clerk Marc Franklin agreed. "When the institutional integrity of the Court was in question, or its role, he [Warren] behaved as Chief, and he corralled people, and the Court spoke as one."

With *Cooper v. Aaron,* the Warren Court had reaffirmed that the Supreme Court was the ultimate interpreter of the Constitution.*

The crisis that came to be called simply "Little Rock" loosed a flood of vituperative mail condemning the Court in general and the chief justice in particular.

The anti-Court sentiment was both personal and vitriolic. Archconservative newspaper columnist Westbrook Pegler produced a series of five columns protesting that Warren drew a state pension of "more than $1,000 per month" while earning $35,000 per year as chief justice.

Warren told friends he read few of the screeds addressed to him. Documents in his FBI file suggest he paid no heed to repeated assassination threats; in any event, he declined J. Edgar Hoover's offers of bodyguards.

Out of some perverse sense of humor, Hugo Black did retain a number of letters from self-professed "good Christians" averring solemnly that "God does not want integration." Amid the hysterical pamphlets printed in blue ink and the shabby mimeographed epistles that Black saved, the Reverend George W. Cheek's "Pending Tragedy in the South" lasciviously asserted:

> It is crystal clear that the native and naive longing of the ordinary negro is to enter the bedroom door of white women. It is the avowed purpose of the NAACP to intermarry and mongrelize the races. . . . Just wait till one of them, possessing a veneer of civilization, asks you for the hand of your daughter in marriage, or from lurking in the dark corner suddenly seizes your wife or daughter, pulls her into the dark and brutally assaults her. Then you will wake up from your unseemly lethargy!

The brethren could brush aside such grotesque scattershot from the public with small jokes among themselves. They could not so easily ignore the escalating debate that spewed from Capitol Hill.

The criticism had begun with the first *Brown* decision in 1954. It flowed from aggrieved Southerners, and thus could be dismissed as the protests of racists. Red Monday and *Jencks*—"treason's biggest victory," according to conservative columnist David Lawrence—added an anticommunist treble to the critical chorus.

Just as the outcry seemed to dwindle, Senator William E. Jenner ratcheted up the attack. Never one to speak in moderate tones—he had once defamed Secretary of State George C. Marshall as a willing "front man for traitors" —Jenner fired a broadside into the court on July 26, 1957.

"By a process of attrition and accession, the extreme liberal wing of the

* The drama in the streets of Little Rock would eventually peter out, overtaken by the stunning news of the Soviet Union's Sputnik satellite beeping a signal as it orbited the earth. Under authority of the state legislature, the school board closed Central High School for the 1958–59 academic year. The school would not reopen until yet another NAACP appeal to the United States Supreme Court resulted in orders to reopen an integrated Central.

Court has become a majority; and we witness today the spectacle of a Court constantly changing the law, and even changing the meaning of the Constitution . . ."

In particular, Jenner was alarmed that "the Supreme Court has dealt a succession of blows at key points of the legislative structure erected by Congress for the protection of the internal security of the United States."

Jenner proposed Congress pass legislation to bar Supreme Court review of five legal issues: contempt of Congress; the federal loyalty program; state subversion laws; limiting subversive activity in public schools; and admission to state bar associations.*

In February, 1958, Jenner and the chairman of the Senate Judiciary Committee, Mississippi's James Eastland, staged a public hearing at which a succession of witnesses flailed the court's "pro-Communist" decisions. Whatever these spokesmen for a dozen patriotic and genealogical organizations lacked in credentials as constitutional scholars, they made up with passionate conviction.†

The high court's decisions of Red Monday, said a spokesman for the rightist newsletter *Human Events,* "have brought glee to the mortal enemies of our Republic—both domestic and foreign."

The rot ran deep within the high court, the executive vice chairman of the Illinois Right-to-Work Committee warned the subcommittee. "I have seen other quotations besides that from the Chief Justice of the Supreme Court, which tell me that others on the bench are humanists, and I am telling you, humanism leads to paganism which leads to communism."

Not all the witnesses appearing before the subcommittee stood bootless.

South Carolina Senator Strom Thurmond, who had walked out of the 1948 Democratic Convention to run for president on the States Rights ticket, raked the court for boldly seizing power. "The choice we face in this country today is judicial limitation or judicial tyranny," he thundered.

"Judicial limitation will strengthen the ramparts over which patriots have watched through the generations since 1776. Judicial tyranny will destroy constitutional government . . . "

L. Brent Bozell, Washington editor of the conservative opinion magazine *National Review,* argued the court had overreached itself. "Therefore, the Court needs to be disciplined quite aside from the impact of its decisions on our constitutional system. . . . We must teach the Court judicial responsibility."

The dean of the University of Notre Dame's law school, Clarence Manion, argued that the justices were plainly unaware of the communist menace.

---

* Article III, Section 2 of the Constitution grants the Supreme Court appellate jurisdiction "with such exceptions and under such regulations as the Congress shall make."

† These included representatives of Defenders of the American Constitution, Inc.; The American Coalition of Patriotic Societies; Sons of the American Revolution; the Ladies of the Grand Army of the Republic; the Women's Patriotic Conference; and American Legion Departments of Wisconsin and Maryland.

"They fail to recognize that the Communist who operates in Washington operates under the same directives that the Communist operates under in Moscow. . . . *"Salus populi suprema lex,"* he continued. "The safety of the community is the highest law."

Earl Warren himself "did not hesitate to approve the order putting thousands of American citizens of Japanese ancestry into concentration camps in 1942 when he thought this was necessary to protect his native State of California from subversive activities."

The hapless Japanese were unable to commit espionage, Manion continued, "but the Communists have stolen many of our military secrets, including all the secrets of our atomic and hydrogen bombs . . . "

The Jenner bill was to receive a considerable if unanticipated boost in early February with the presentation of three lectures at Harvard Law School by federal circuit court of appeals judge Learned Hand. Deemed "the most revered of living American judges," Hand at age eighty-seven represented the soul of the legal Establishment. In him was embodied the very concept of judicial restraint.

In his Harvard addresses, this longtime friend of Felix Frankfurter lashed out at the Warren Court for acting as a "third legislative chamber." The more the Court strove to do justice, the more Hand recoiled. He viewed the law not as a tool to right wrongs, but as intellectual process, the search for precedent and with it judicial truth.

Even *Brown,* especially *Brown,* was suspect, in Hand's finely stropped intellect. The courts were not fit places to decide such questions of public policy. The Warren Court had overreached itself.

At another time, Hand's pointed comments might have passed with no more public notice than any other set of academic lectures on the Cambridge campus. Coming as they did amid the Jenner onslaught, however, they lent credibility to the gaggle of frightened critics.

Friends of the Court mounted a counteroffensive. The ABA's House of Delegates, prodded by President Charles Rhyne, voted on February 25, 1958, to oppose the Jenner bill as "contrary to the maintenance of the balance of powers set up in the Constitution between the executive, legislative and judicial branches of our Government."

In the Senate, Missouri Democrat Thomas C. Hennings, Jr., moved to counter the Hand lectures on two fronts. He polled the deans of the nation's leading law schools as well as managing partners of some of the most influential of law firms. The result was a scathing set of criticisms tagging the Jenner bill as "unwise," "dangerous," "utterly lacking in merit," "unfortunate," and "ill-advised."

To trump Court critics' use of the Hand lectures, Hennings also solicited Hand's opinion of the Jenner bill. The old man replied "that such a statute if enacted would be detrimental to the best interests of the United States."

His disagreement with the direction of the Warren Court notwithstanding, Hand wrote, "It seems to me desirable that the Court should have the last word on questions of the character involved. . . . Some final authority is better than unsettled conflict."

As the Eighty-fifth Congress neared adjournment, the Senate took up three measures to reverse court rulings. A bill to overturn the 1957 *Mallory* decision, which barred federal prosecutors from using confessions obtained during unwarranted delays before arraignment, failed on a technicality.

A second measure that would have reversed the *Nelson* ruling, and permitted the states to enforce anticommunist laws, failed by a single vote, 41–40.

Then, on August 20, 1958, just four days before the end of the session, the Senate finally turned to the sweeping Jenner bill. During the debate, northern and western senators mustered by Hennings managed to show that the "reverse the Court campaign" stemmed in large part from anti-*Brown* segregationist sentiment.

With Democratic majority leader Lyndon Johnson craftily maneuvering against the Jenner bill, the Senate voted 49–41 to table the measure. Thirty Senate Democrats and 19 Republicans voted to table. Forty-one—25 Republicans and 16 southern Democrats—voted in favor.

Anti-Court sentiment in the Congress had reached high tide.* Critics of the Supreme Court, tagged with the onerous label of "segregationist," would be unable to muster another serious challenge. At the same time, the critics had managed to permanently politicize the Court's rulings; from this moment on, the opinions of nominees to the Court, especially those of the chief justice designate, would undergo close congressional scrutiny.

The criticism of the Warren Court continued. Too late to influence the 1958 debate in Congress, the unofficial Conference of (State) Chief Justices voted 36–8 to endorse a report critical of the trend in Supreme Court decisions. Complaining that the high court had progressively shifted power from the states to the federal government, the state justices warned of a perceived Supreme Court tendency to make policy.

Frequent differences between state and federal courts over interpretation of constitutional questions, the justices wrote, "cause us grave concern as to whether individual views of the members of the court . . . do not unconsciously override a more dispassionate consideration of what is or is not constitutionally warranted."

In a sharp rebuke to the Warren Court, the state jurists lectured, "It has long been an American boast that we have a government of laws and not of men. We believe that any study of recent decisions of the Supreme Court will raise at least considerable doubt as the validity of that boast."

In February, 1959, the American Bar Association's Committee on Communist Strategy, Tactics and Objectives rose up once more to snipe at the Supreme Court. The committee's report again asserted that various Su-

---

* The forty-one votes Jenner rounded up represented at least ten more than Franklin D. Roosevelt had been able to enlist for his 1937 "court-packing" plan.

preme Court decisions encouraged communist activities in the United States.

The document was hardly judicious; indeed, its anti-Warren bias was clear. Two of the more forceful members of the committee, chairman Peter C. Brown and New Hampshire attorney general Louis Wyman, still smarted from losses of loyalty cases in the Supreme Court. And among the influential delegates supporting the committee report on the floor, Earl Warren's long-time foe, Loyd Wright, rhetorically demanded, "Isn't it time we told the Court to read the law and stop writing ideological opinions?"

As before, the delegates voted to accept the committee report, without further notice. Having achieved its intended publicity effect, the report would sit forgotten on library shelves. Meanwhile, the chief justice of the United States would be transformed.

CHAPTER 29

SIMPLE PRINCIPLES

L ITTLE ROCK ANNEALED *Brown v. Board of Education* and with it Earl
Warren as chief justice of the United States. The confrontation
transformed Warren into a figure of righteous idealism, of silent
dignity resolute against the mob, of Good standing against Evil.

For millions of Americans, the chief justice had come to embody the
promise of a nation of truly equal peoples. At the same time, he had led the
Court to reestablish itself as a coequal branch of government, to reassert
the authority of the judiciary under the Constitution.

Little Rock had changed Warren as well. Warned by a predecessor that
Warren stood aloof and seldom commented on their work, incoming law
clerks Dallin Oaks and Jon Newman discovered a different man.

Warren was not only accessible, but he began to reach out to these young
men. From time to time, late in the day, the Chief would wander from his
office through the dark-paneled conference room into Newman's office
simply to chat.

The subjects of their talks ranged widely, from the work of the Court to
sports. A criminal case on the docket would remind him of another he had
prosecuted three decades earlier. The Chief reminisced about his boyhood,
or his father. The stories were "absolutely fascinating," said Mike Heyman,
a clerk during the following term.

These conversational interludes never lasted long. Almost inevitably, War-
ren's disappearance "would precipitate a call from a slightly perturbed Mrs.
McHugh who wanted to know if he was there. She had lost track of him,"
Newman said.

The chief justice was momentarily playing hooky, relieving some of the tension that as governor he had expelled by meeting constituents. Confined to his chambers by a crowded docket and a judge's traditional isolation, he missed the human contact. He welcomed the rare moments of freedom.

On a visit to Chicago, law clerk Dallin Oaks watched the Warren of old work his way through the *Chicago Sun-Times's* new building, meeting department heads from composing room to fashion pages.

"The Chief," Oaks wrote in his journal, "would exchange a few pleasantries with these people, and then he'd be off around the department shaking hands with the common folk. An old grease monkey down in the pressroom sheepishly wiped off his hands before grasping the Chief's; a startled young secretary almost tipped her desk over rising to meet him, etc.

"For each person he had some comment that put them at ease. 'How do you like your new building?' 'How do you like this lovely air conditioning?' "

"It was something to see," Oaks marveled.

When Oaks's wife, June, stopped by the Court one afternoon with their three young children, one-year-old Lloyd toddled across the carpet to the welcoming chief justice, signaling he wanted to be picked up. In Warren's arms he alternately squirmed and nestled for ten minutes, then pulled off the Chief's glasses and tossed them to the carpet.

Unperturbed, Warren assured the parents, "Don't worry. I've had my glasses thrown in a corner dozens of times."

Decades later, Oaks could only marvel. "Imagine, the chief justice of the United States coming and sitting there, bouncing kids on his knee."

Warren also took more interest in the personal lives of his clerks. When Oaks told the Chief he was weighing a return to Chicago to practice law at the end of the 1957 term, Warren counseled against it.

"Chicago was a terrible place to live due to the crookedness of the government (including judiciary), the hoodlumism and racketeering which is prevalent, and the generally low moral tone prevailing," Oaks quoted the Chief in a journal of the term.

"The West was the place for a young man to go," Warren urged for the next half-hour. There was vigor and growth, and opportunities for a young man with Oaks's character and ability.

A year later, when clerk Michael Heyman announced he was weighing an offer of a teaching position at Boalt Hall, Warren "put the screws to him." Heyman accepted the Berkeley teaching post.

Warren—who favored his clerks taking up public service or teaching—applauded when Oaks eventually abandoned private practice to teach law. "Oh, that's great. You'll be able to influence these young lawyers. That's a wonderful thing to do."

The chief justice brought the same expansive vision of social responsibility to the business of the Court. In relaxed conversations with his clerks, one recalled, "he would talk about simple principles, about what government should do—the whole package of middle-American, 1940s idealism sort of stuff. That's what he believed, right down to the core of who he was."

Weighing cases, he reacted to personal experience rather than philosophical abstraction or contemplation. Relying on well-understood personal values, he reached decisions quickly, more rapidly than most of the brethren, Heyman noted.

The facts governed Warren's jurisprudence. "He went for a decision that would be right," said Oaks, who often disagreed with the Chief's indifference to the legal niceties. "And right for him was what was morally based, what was good for the individual, and in the larger sense good for the country to have a fair society."

Finely wrought arguments and legal procedure—even the most obvious to the clerks—left him cold. "What he cared about—almost exclusively, not completely—was the bottom line: who won and who lost. That gives you a lot to negotiate with," said Larry Simon, another clerk turned law professor.

A skillful politician within the court, Warren led by indirection, noted a third who became a legal scholar. "Most of these justices are very strong-willed, and nobody is going to push them to do anything they don't want to do," Jesse Choper noted. "You don't twist arms on the Court. You have no patronage."

Warren took pains to assign opinions to those who most cared about an issue. He assigned each of the justices important cases and took his share of the less important. He willingly accepted criticism of his own opinions and cut offending passages. He cared only for the outcome.

"He seizes on facts (something he understands) to decide his cases, and on facts his judgment is good. I am sure he makes a valuable contribution to the Court," Oaks wrote in his journal on November 22, 1957, "but he's exasperating to law clerks."

The clerks, after all, had reached this lofty place precisely by parsing such subtleties in law school. Once installed in the Chief's office, they discovered their training and honed intelligence were less important to Warren than their humanity.

More important, Warren's sense of jurisprudence also riled Felix Frankfurter. During one conference late in the 1957 term, Frankfurter exploded at the Chief. "God damn it, you're a judge! You don't decide cases by your sense of justice or your personal predilections."

"Thank heaven, I *haven't* lost my sense of justice," Warren roared back.

That overriding sense of justice led the Chief to instruct his clerks when they were reviewing petitions for certiorari not to keep off petitioners "where personal rights are concerned. With property cases, we may be more severe and deny cert."

He expected the clerks—his staff, after all—to think for themselves. He wanted no "yes-men," but reliable advisers.

"There were some really good arguments we had over cases," Mike Heyman recalled. "He wanted a very independent view of a case from his clerks."

Warren often disagreed with the clerk's recommendation on the bench memoranda, and the arguments might go on for twenty minutes, Heyman said. When he reached a decision on his vote, Warren would lean forward and announce, "Fellas, this is where I am." From that moment on he demanded "absolute loyalty."

On the rare occasion, the Chief could be persuaded to change his mind. Jesse Choper, a clerk during the 1960 term of the Court, recalled discussion of a Maryland statute requiring notaries public to take an oath to God. Choper had recommended the Chief vote to hold it unconstitutional.

"I'm just troubled by this," Warren told him. "You know, we administer an oath which invokes God when we admit people to the Supreme Court bar. How can we strike this down?"

Choper parried. "What would happen," he asked, "if one of those lawyers, who satisfied all the other qualifications, felt it was against his religious scruples to take an oath to God? Would you not admit him?"

Warren looked at Choper and sighed. "You know, you're right."

Warren began the conference discussion of the Maryland case insisting, "The fact that we are a religious people can't mean that public office constitutionally must depend upon belief in God." Once more his comments guided the Court; the vote to overturn the statute was unanimous.

Virtually impotent in deciding cases, the clerks did exert "a lot of influence on the doctrinal rationale of the opinions" Warren signed. The Chief outlined what he wanted in the decision, "and we'd just go to work on it. He gave us a good deal of leeway."

The guidance to the clerks could be scant. In a case dealing with technicalities in the tax code, the chief simply told clerk Henry Steinman, "This is the result. Write it up."

Warren then read the draft "very carefully, very carefully," Choper said. In one instance he struck the word "arguendo," with the explanation, "I don't use that word."

More concerned with the results than the rationale, still Warren did not disdain "the received law," Heyman cautioned. Lawyer Warren understood that "you didn't just decide a case because that was how you felt about it."

There had to be "respectable authority for getting where you want to be. At the same time, the chief justice understood they could make a legitimate legal argument for whatever position he took. As far as I know, an opinion never emanated from that office that was a silly opinion, that couldn't be argued with a respectable face," Heyman said.*

Though he was careful not to assign to himself all the choicest cases,

---

* As a graduate of Yale Law, Heyman thought himself "well prepared . . . for seeing the judicial world in that way." Yale law scholars were drilled as legal realists; they held that a good legal scholar could always find precedent for his position. "The realists posited that regardless of what a judge thought he was doing, in fact, he was coming to a conclusion on the basis of facts and his own values, and then dressing up the conclusion with a legal analysis." This was especially true in the Supreme Court, where the issues were thorny, the outcomes rarely evident, and the briefs for each side persuasive. The legal realist argued that Frankfurter no less than Warren was driven to support the legal argument he found sympathetic to his personal philosophy.

when he felt strongly about an issue, he did write. "And when he wrote, his writing reflected conviction," clerk Jon Newman stated. "The opinions are not dry. They have life and vitality to them."

Newman was to take the lead oar in drafting Warren's opinions in the Expatriation Cases, the most important decided in 1958 after *Cooper v. Aaron.* The two cases had been argued the year before, leaving the justices so narrowly divided that they set them for a reargument of the issues.

For Warren, the question was the lack of due process afforded the petitioners. Clemente Perez, a railroad laborer born in the United States, had lived in Mexico most of his life, and voted in a Mexican election. Albert L. Trop, a twenty-year-old immigrant serving in the army, had broken out of a military stockade in North Africa, wandered about for a day, then turned himself in to the first officer he met. Both had been stripped of their citizenship by administrative fiat, without trials.

Those rulings offended Warren's sense of justice. "There is no power in Congress to make an American citizen stateless for the commission of a crime. It can punish him by imprisonment, or even death for certain crimes, but it cannot take his birthright."

Over the summer, Warren had hardened his stand. He opened the conference after the October 28, 1957, reargument with the broad assertion that Congress had no constitutional right to make the loss of citizenship a punishment. "It makes no difference whether it's by a jury or administrative procedure."

But if Warren was more firm, John Harlan, William Brennan, and Charles Whittaker were not. They switched votes in conference, Whittaker repeatedly, making it 5–4 to reverse in *Trop,* and 5–4 to affirm in *Perez.*

The Expatriation Cases sorely tested the Court. By examining the power of Congress and of the military, in effect, they probed the very meaning of the Constitution itself. Now in the minority, Warren dissented in *Perez,* maintaining that "the power to denationalize is not within the letter or the spirit of the powers with which our Government was endowed."

The second of the denationalization cases, *Trop,* posed special problems for Whittaker. An indecisive man, Whittaker frequently changed his votes, sometimes more than once on a case; he froze, unable to write, when he was assigned an opinion; and he distrusted his own clerks because he distrusted himself.

In a closely divided Supreme Court, Whittaker's vote became vital. This weakest of judges, oddly, could markedly influence decisions. To bring Whittaker back into the fold, Warren struck from his *Trop* draft an admonition based on sorry experience with military authorities:

If the priceless right of citizenship is ever to be forfeited in a trial, it should be in a civilian court of justice, where all Bill of Rights protections guard the fairness of the outcome. Military courts are to try soldiers for military crimes and impose punishments that do not encroach on purely civilian rights. Who is worthy of continued enjoyment of citizenship is not the constitutional concern of the Army. Its business is to fight wars.

To Newman's draft opinion, Warren inserted strong language. "The basic concept underlying the Eighth Amendment is nothing less than the dignity of man. While the State has the power to punish, the Amendment stands to assure that this power be exercised within the limits of civilized standards."

Recognizing that those standards changed over time, Warren then added a paragraph that effectively defined his personal sense of jurisprudence. "The Amendment must draw its meaning from the evolving standards of decency that mark the progress of a maturing society . . . The provisions of the Constitution are not time-worn adages or hollow shibboleths. They are vital, living principles that authorize and limit governmental powers in our Nation."

Society changed; the meaning of the Constitution necessarily changed too.

Warren's understanding of the interlocked obligations of the citizen and the government had shifted over the years. The man who fifteen years before had endorsed the Japanese evacuation stressed to his clerks, "The Court must not allow the government too much power lest we degenerate into a police state."

That would be a defining principle.

When the State Department's passport office declined to issue a passport on the basis of a file the applicant was not permitted to view, Warren was upset. It was unconscionable to deny travel privileges on the basis of confidential information, he argued.

Similarly, the former California attorney general who had once supported a state legislative committee's effort to obtain lists of union members joined an opinion in 1958 holding that Alabama was not entitled to a list of NAACP members in that state.

Warren did not always prevail. His court was closely divided, with Warren, Black, and Douglas on the left, and Brennan usually joining to form a bloc that Frankfurter sarcastically called "The Four." Frankfurter, Harlan, Clark, and Burton stood on the right, with Whittaker tentatively signing on.

The retirement in October, 1958, of Harold Burton and the appointment of fellow Ohioan Potter Stewart shifted the balance on the Court. Stricken with Parkinson's disease, the conservative Burton was giving way to a centrist in politics and philosophy.

At forty-three, Stewart was the youngest man to be appointed to the Court since Bill Douglas in 1939. The son of a successful lawyer, Stewart had enjoyed a privileged education: Hotchkiss School, Yale—where he briefly considered a career in journalism—and a year's study at Cambridge before entering Yale Law.

World War II interrupted Stewart's climb up the Wall Street pecking order. He spent the war in what he called "the dungaree Navy," on an oil tanker in the submarine-infested Atlantic, "floating around on a sea of 100 octane gas, bored to death 99 percent of the time and scared to death 1 percent.

His wartime service lent Stewart a broader perspective, and some respect for men whose lives were less privileged than his. He came to Washington "interested in people and talking to people, and getting to know people," according to a Warren clerk who befriended the newest justice.

Frankfurter was optimistic that Stewart would "turn out to be a judge," as the former professor wrote his confidant Learned Hand. In a snide reference to the chief justice, Frankfurter added, "I do not believe that he [Stewart] will convince himself that the mere fact that he sits on this bench calls for arrogant confidence in his own wisdom and learning."

A moderate, the handsome Stewart resisted easy classification. When newsmen asked him if he were a liberal or conservative, Stewart replied simply, "I am a lawyer."

Warren and the junior justice were to get along well. Stewart and his wife, Harriet, spoke often of Warren's gesture on the day they arrived in Washington, when the Chief met their train "at the crack of dawn. You seemed not officially there but rather you were the personification of understanding, sympathy and warmth," Harriet Stewart wrote in a thank-you note.

Warren and Stewart attended Washington Redskins football games together, and shared stories about their children. Both were fishermen; Stewart even gave the Chief a gift of well-worn fishing flies, proven lures if somewhat moth-eaten, he apologized.

Stewart joined a court in momentary pause, as if waiting for the congressional storm stirred by William Jenner to pass. With *Cooper v. Aaron* decided in September, 1958, the session was over before it began, one of Warren's law clerks of that year stated.

There were few major cases, and the chief justice was "in dissent frequently, finding it hard to occasionally tear away a fifth vote from a newly installed Stewart or frightened Whittaker."

Jenner's accusations that the Court had laid the nation defenseless against communist infiltration seemingly had some effect too. In monitoring the government's pursuit of Reds, the Supreme Court this year would take one step forward and two back.

Willard Uphaus was, at sixty-seven, perhaps an innocent abroad, perhaps misguided in his quest for world peace. If so, the outspoken Methodist layman was also stubbornly principled.

Steadfast, he refused to identify either guests or staff at his annual World Fellowship summer camp when questioned by New Hampshire attorney general Louis C. Wyman. The obstinate Uphaus received an indefinite jail term for contempt.

The decision two years before in *Sweezy v. Wyman* might have governed the *Uphaus* appeal when it came before the Supreme Court. Further, just five months earlier, the brethren had touched a similar issue and ruled unanimously that the NAACP did not have to turn over its membership lists when the state of Alabama demanded them.

The Chief began the discussion of *Uphaus* in conference arguing for reversal of the contempt citation. Wyman had conducted his one-man investigation "without the state showing an interest endangered or being subverted. It would deter people from freely speaking."

But two years of political criticism had chastened the brethren. Warren could line up only Black, Douglas, and Brennan to reverse Uphaus's citation.

Once more the philosophical difference between Warren and Frankfurter, who led the arguments against reversal, was clear. Warren would find a way to do justice; Frankfurter could not, despite his almost plaintive assertion in a letter to Bill Brennan: "There isn't a man on the Court who personally disapproves more than I do of the activities of all the Un-American Committees, of all the Smith Act prosecutions, of the Attorney General's list, etc., etc."

In a "dazzling high-wire act," the Court produced a 5–4 decision that argued the academic and political freedoms so apparent in Paul Sweezy's case were not present here. Uphaus's World Fellowship was neither a university nor a political party. Thus, Tom Clark wrote for the majority, Willard Uphaus did not deserve the same rights that guest lecturer Paul Sweezy did.

The anticommunists of New Hampshire could do what the racists of Alabama could not.* Gentle Willard Uphaus, still resisting, would spend a year in a six-by-eight-foot jail cell in Merrimack, writing pleas for an end to the Cold War.

The second step backward came in the appeal of former Vassar College psychology instructor Lloyd Barenblatt. For reasons of principle, Barenblatt had refused on First Amendment grounds to tell the House Committee on Un-American Activities whether he was now or had ever been a communist.

Had he "taken the Fifth"—that is, rested his refusal on the privilege against self-incrimination—Barenblatt would have avoided legal trouble. Instead, he insisted on asserting his right to speak freely and assemble without congressional scrutiny. He was convicted of contempt of Congress.

Barenblatt eventually appealed to the Supreme Court on the narrow grounds of the 1957 *Watkins* decision. Warren agreed with Barenblatt's position in conference: The pertinence of the questions asked of Barenblatt to any legislative intent had not been made clear.

---

* In *Scull v. Virginia*, decided that term, the Supreme Court once again differentiated between communism and racism. The court unanimously ruled that the state could not investigate a group organized to support school integration. Harlan's decision was narrowly based on the pertinency of the questions, but the justices apparently agreed with the Chief that the state law was unconstitutional and intended solely to intimidate.

Once more the vote was 5–4 to sustain the contempt charge, Warren again in the minority. With lawyerly precision John Harlan retreated from *Watkins* to hold for the majority that an individual's First Amendment rights were to be balanced against the public interest by the courts.

HUAC's authority rested, finally, on the right of self-preservation, Harlan continued. Barenblatt's right to freely associate with whomever he chose did not outweigh that "ultimate value in any society." Lloyd Barenblatt would serve a six-month jail sentence in Lewisburg Penitentiary and pay a $250 fine for his principles.

On occasion the four liberals managed to pick up a vote from Stewart or Whittaker, but the victories in this year of caution were few and narrowly drawn.

Warren prevailed in the appeal of an aeronautical engineer, William L. Greene, fired by a navy contractor on the basis of confidential information in government files. While his decision for the 8–1 majority held only that Congress had not authorized such a procedure, Warren's findings were broad and his tone angry. "I think he saw this in terms of some poor slob losing his clearance and being unable to work," clerk Mike Heyman explained.

But if the defeats rankled, Warren did not reveal it. When he was in the minority, he didn't assume "that the country was going to hell. I don't think he took his losses worse for being Chief." In all, Warren dissented twenty-four times during the October, 1958, term, but wrote just three dissenting opinions in cases about which he felt most strongly.

Critics were pleased with the redirection of the Court. *U.S. News & World Report* decided "a five-year trend toward limiting the powers of states and Congress is to be halted and reversed." New Hampshire's Louis Wyman crowed, "The Court is returning to the middle of the road."

Though 1958 would be "a very spotty year for Warren," the court was firmly in his hands. He set the tone. He guided debate in conference. He led the brethren.

The Chief did so, not so much by intellect than by sheer force of personality. "He was an instinctive leader whom you respected and for whom you had affection," newcomer Potter Stewart recognized.

His leadership stemmed from personal vision coupled with political acumen. "He had an incredible sense of timing, and knew when to seize the moment," law clerk Peter Taft decided. "He probably understood better than anyone else on the court what a decision's impact would be on society."

In conference, the Chief made no attempt to stifle debate, said another of the brethren. "At the same time he stops acrimony. He keeps the personal bitterness out."

Warren maintained cordial relations with each of the brethren. He was punctilious with solicitous notes when someone lost a parent, sometimes noting how much he missed his own mother, "taken too soon from us." He sent congratulatory notes on birthdays, usually adding a quip, such as this to

Hugo Black on his seventy-second birthday: "I hope you agree, as I do, with the fellow who said, 'Never object to growing older because that privilege is denied to so many people.' "

As chief justice, Warren believed it his responsibility to shield these friends and colleagues from unwarranted criticism. He was particularly concerned that their sometimes sharp internal disputes not leak beyond the Court and damage its institutional reputation. Briefing his new clerks, he invariably cautioned them about passing on "Court gossip and intrigue"; personal memoranda, too, were privileged. He himself would sometimes reply orally to certain justices rather than leave a caustic note in their files where future historians might see it, he explained.

When Tom Clark wrote harsh language in a dissent to a Warren opinion, the chief justice opted to do "a little private horse-trading." After all, they were old friends. Over the years, the Clarks had shared "quite a few" social evenings and had traveled with Earl and Nina, Mary Clark recalled. Her husband had cherished a great deal of respect for the Chief. "Everything he said about Earl Warren was complimentary," Mrs. Clark recalled.

Negotiation among friends came easily. Warren offered to delete a paragraph in his majority opinion that irritated Clark if Clark would strike the passages that might be deemed critical of the Court. "Here the Chief was exercising the leadership that he did so well in behalf of the public image of the Court," law clerk Dallin Oaks commented.

Again, when a Clark dissent would have scored a Douglas majority opinion as sounding "wondrously like the pitch of tyranny to me," Warren persuaded the Texan to drop the scalding language.

Careful as he was to shield the public image of the Court, Warren did let slip some hint of the friction between himself and Frankfurter, recalled *New York Times*'s Supreme Court correspondent Anthony Lewis. After the Chief delivered a one-paragraph *per curiam* opinion rejecting a capital punishment case from California, Frankfurter began to read his dissent.

Frankfurter "went on at great length about how terrible this was. And when he finished, Chief Justice Warren leaned forward and, obviously very disturbed, said, 'And none of what Justice Frankfurter has just said is actually in his written dissent.

" 'He is just speaking to the people in the courtroom, and I want you all to know that the criminal justice process in California is not as savage as he said.' "

Such outbursts were rare. Warren kept a tight control on his emotions, hiding more or less successfully behind the politician's mask.

That pose cracked in public on June 28, 1959, at a party celebrating the twenty-fifth wedding anniversary of friends Barnet and Naomi Nover. In this gathering of Washington insiders—Nover was bureau chief for the *Denver Post*—*Minneapolis Tribune* correspondent Clark Mollenhoff introduced Warren to Earl Mazo, the author of a new biography of Richard Nixon.

The chief justice rounded on Mazo. "You are a damned liar." The glowing book, released as Nixon mounted a campaign for the Republican presidential nomination, "is a dishonest account to promote Nixon."

Mazo, Washington correspondent of the emphatically Republican *New York Herald-Tribune,* had touched a still raw nerve in the chief justice. Warren was particularly angered by portions that implied Nixon had outwitted Warren in securing an endorsement in the 1950 California senatorial campaign.

"I don't like it when you use me, when you use this book to step on my head—to go over my body to promote Nixon," he raged. His arms out, his wrists pressed together as if handcuffed, Warren stormed on. "You people are persecuting me because you know I can't strike back."

The following morning at breakfast with law clerk Mike Heyman, Warren was still livid. Meanwhile, Mollenhoff, a friend of Nixon, violated one of the understood rules of life in official Washington: The events at private parties were off the record. Mollenhoff wrote a story about the tirade at the bar.

Warren was keenly embarrassed. Publicly he denied the account, claiming in his autobiography, "I was taught better manners than that." Privately, Warren equivocated. To retired justice Shay Minton, Warren acknowledged, "I don't know Mazo, either, and while I didn't call him a 'damned liar,' that is the interpretation he put on what I said, and maybe he is right."

Mollenhoff, in fact, was correct; Warren had lost his temper. Naomi Nover, "heartsick about the unfortunate publicity," could only write an apology to the Chief for Mollenhoff's breach of her hospitality.

Weeks later, the incident still rankled. Once more Warren called Mazo a "son of a bitch" when former California assemblyman Laughlin Waters teased the chief justice about being in the book-huckstering business.

In effect, Warren had confirmed his dislike of Nixon. The chief justice's feeble denial was discounted as the usual papering over of rivalries in politics.*

That much of himself Earl Warren revealed—briefly. Otherwise, he remained a private man.

Parting from Warren at the end of his year-long clerkship, Dallin Oaks found their farewell strained. The Chief, Oaks noted in his journal, might have wanted "to say something endearing, but it was suppressed by the business-like front he always maintains. As he shook my hand though, I could see genuine affection in his eyes."

After a year at Warren's side, Oaks remained a critic of Warren's "faulty

---

* Richard Mosk, a longtime family friend, recalled attending the Rose Bowl game with the chief justice in 1960, the year Vice President Nixon was grand marshal of the pageant. When Nixon changed his seat to the other of the field at halftime to demonstrate his impartiality, Mosk asked, "You're the chief justice. Shouldn't you do that too?" Warren growled, "If that guy can't even pick a side in a football game, we're in trouble." Interview with Mosk, August 14, 1992.

notion of how a judge should reach decisions." But over that year, he wrote in his journal, "I have developed a profound affection and respect for him. I believe him completely honest, sincere, and utterly without guile. He has wonderfully mature judgment about many matters, and he is the most kind and considerate employer one could ask for.

"I will miss him."

CHAPTER 30

THE WASP AND THE

ELEPHANT

URING THE SUMMER MONTHS THE SUPREME COURT DOZED. THE staff shuffled the cool marble corridors unhurried by deadlines or the whims of justices. Custodians slowly rubbed already lustrous brass rails, paused to admire their work, then rubbed some more. Even the overworked law clerks droned through the days, reading the accumulated stacks of certiorari petitions and drafting summaries.

Then late in the summer, after the worst of Washington's humidity had drained away, the atmosphere in the building changed. Librarians and messengers suddenly perked up, newly arrived law clerk Henry Steinman noticed.

The building seemed galvanized. "Word went out: 'The Chief is coming back.'"

Police officers on duty buffed their shoes, and self-consciously pulled at uniform jackets a shade too tight for expanding stomachs. Secretaries made appointments to have their hair done, and weighed bringing out their new fall outfits after Labor Day.

When his limousine did eventually pull into the basement garage, the guard on duty saluted and telephoned an alert to the chief clerk's office: "He's in."

The Chief was back.

If some complained that Earl Warren was a demanding boss, most of those who worked for him did so happily. How else when the chief justice of the United States boomed hellos to elevator operators and asked after their children by name? How else when he took such obvious pleasure in

the confirmation of a cafeteria worker's daughter or the high school graduation of the son of an electrician? What other chief justice would have hosted
a reception for onetime secretary Helen Lally when she was admitted to the
Supreme Court bar?

The Chief was back.

In the summers the Warrens traveled, he dashing off enthusiastic postcards
to the brethren or to friends while Nina bought souvenir spoons for Mrs.
Randall Butler, wife of the Sacramento shoemaker who had kept the children well shod during the war.

In 1961 with the Drew Pearsons and Agnes Meyer, an old acquaintance
and widow of the owner of *The Washington Post,* Warren and Nina cruised
the fjords of Norway and visited Haugesund, his father's birthplace. Joined
the following year by Adlai Stevenson and Alicia Patterson, editor of Long
Island's *Newsday,* they cruised the Mediterranean and paid a visit to Yugosla-
via's Marshal Tito. (Told of Warren's twice daily swims off the Dalmatian
coast, Tito pointed meaningfully to a shark net in front of his beach home.
Agnes Meyer immediately put her foot down on swimming in the Adriatic.)

In 1963 the Warrens, Pearsons, and Meyer family sailed the Black Sea,
stopping so that Pearson could interview Soviet Premier Nikita Khrushchev.
(Warren declined to meet Khrushchev lest his visit be seen as a piece of
American-Russian diplomatic relations.)

The Chief was back, settling into familiar routine. He woke about 7:00
A.M., then read clerks' memoranda and draft opinions in bed for as long as
two hours. A bit before 9:00, he rose, did what he called "stretching exercises," and ate a light breakfast prepared by Nina.

His limousine trailing, Warren walked on pleasant days from the Wardman-Park to meet Tom Clark in front of his residential hotel on Connecticut Avenue. Sometimes joined by former Secretary of State Dean Acheson,
they marched down Connecticut as far as the old State, War and Navy
Building, old friends talking politics or foreign affairs.

The two justices had no end of subjects to discuss, particularly when a
new president occupied the White House, Warren assured reporters. Any
change of administration was exciting for a man like himself "who has been
concerned with government all his life."

These two former politicians had quietly arranged in 1959 to secure the
old age of the widows of Supreme Court justices. At Warren's request,
Clark hosted a small dinner party at his home, inviting Speaker of the House
of Representatives Sam Rayburn and Senate Majority Leader Lyndon Johnson, both fellow Texans and longtime friends. There Warren quietly expressed his fear that the widows of retired justices—particularly those like
the failing Harold Burton—who had devoted themselves to public service
rather than business affairs, might be left in difficult circumstances. Two
weeks later a bill providing pensions for the widows was signed by President
Eisenhower.

In fair weather, these two-mile walks began the day. In foul, Warren's driver, Jean Clemencia, would drive the two jurists to the Court. Warren worked there until 6:15, until rush-hour traffic had dwindled, then returned to the newly renamed Sheraton Park.

Evenings, Warren and Nina spent at home, eating dinner in the kitchen. "I just can't be out a number of nights a week at social affairs," he confessed to reporters in a seventieth birthday interview. It was too tiring. Furthermore, by staying home, sometimes to watch television with Nina or to read, he avoided potentially embarrassing questions innocently posed by friendly party-goers.

On rare occasions, they had friends from California in for drinks, then ate dinner in the hotel dining room. Rarer still, they went to a favored restaurant in Georgetown, where Nina ordered her usual spare ribs and Coca-Cola.

The Warrens were hardly withdrawn from society, however. They had a circle of friends as well as daughters Virginia and Dorothy living nearby. Furthermore, the election of John F. Kennedy had restored Warren to a favored place on the White House guest list.

Despite the difference in their ages—Warren was just shy of seventy when the forty-three-year-old Kennedy was inaugurated—the two men hit it off. Both relished politics and politicians, and both profoundly disliked Richard Nixon whom Kennedy had narrowly defeated in November, 1960.

Prior to the election, the chief justice had doubts about the younger man. But Nixon's nomination left Warren with no choice but to look to the Democratic Party for a candidate. (The Chief had sentimentally favored his old friend Adlai Stevenson for the presidential nomination. Texan Lyndon Johnson he deemed a "prisoner of the cozy southern bloc.")

Whatever his initial doubts, Warren was charmed by the new president. At first he had considered Jack Kennedy "too young for the job," he acknowledged, "but he's growing and he'll keep on growing. That's the most important thing in this business, the capacity for growth."

Like so many Americans, Warren eventually came to idealize the young president. "No American during my rather long life," he wrote later in profound grief to Jacqueline Kennedy, "ever set his sights higher for a better America or centered his attack more accurately on the evils and shortcomings of our society than did he."

Kennedy returned the affection. Long before his election, he held Warren in high regard, Jacqueline Kennedy assured the chief justice.

"I remember him saying one night when he was quite upset about what was happening in Congress, 'The Republicans, how can you hope for anything from them. They nominated Dewey and Nixon when they could have had Earl Warren.' "

The new president recalled with admiration that in the bitter cold of his inauguration day, Warren had remained on the reviewing stand while others sheltered from the chill winds. The chief justice and Nina, following protocol, declined to leave before their newly inaugurated president.

Jack Kennedy repaid the gesture. When Warren's clerks, past and present, staged a surprise seventieth birthday party for the Chief at the Metropolitan Club, the president dropped by on his way to another event.

According to White House staff member Fred Dutton, "Warren was always trying to help, both at a personal level and because he believed in government. Warren had far larger horizons than his rather stolid and cautious, patient personality has been publicly pictured."

The chief justice spoke fondly of Kennedy, son Robert Warren recalled. "They both had a vision, not so much a political vision as they had a vision of what life should be for Americans in regard to their human rights. I think that's where they connected."

White House invitations aside, Warren's days on the Court became days of habitual routine. In the first weeks of the term, the justices met in conference to vote on the petitions that had backed up since the Court's adjournment the previous June.

They confronted a huge task, particularly in dealing with the mountain of often unintelligible petitions sent by convicts representing themselves. The 618 *in forma pauperis* petitions of Warren's first year on the high court had grown to 1,005 by the 1959 term; 1,302 total cases filed had increased to 1,862 in the same span.

At the beginning of a new term, Warren scheduled as many as 175 petitions to be called up each week. Only those presenting an issue in which a justice had already expressed an interest were actually considered in conference. Most Warren consigned to an "X list" to be declined without comment.

Perhaps twenty-five sparked some interest and so came to a vote in conference. Warren relied on his clerks' memoranda briefing these cases to summarize the facts and the legal questions presented for the brethren.

Led by the Chief, the justices moved briskly through the conference agenda, in practical terms, determining the Court calendar and the legal issues that would rivet the country for the next year. If four justices agreed to hear a case, Warren set it down for argument.

Increased filings generated more cases on the calendar. Gradually the number of cases argued rose from 113 in Warren's first year to 131 in 1959, and 148 the following year. (Contrary to assertions by some critics, the Court was not more sympathetic to pleas of the poor; the justices continued to grant so-called paid petitions at a rate three or four times greater than the *in forma pauperis* petitions.)

All the while, the Court remained divided into liberal and conservative wings. The Warren-Frankfurter disagreements hardened into "polar positions" and the clashes grew more frequent. Frankfurter was peppery and argumentative by nature; Warren was acutely sensitive when he thought either his good name or the Court's reputation was under attack.

Arthur Rosett, the first clerk to be formally assigned to the retired Stanley Reed, Sherman Minton, and Harold Burton, found himself caught between

Warren and Frankfurter. Rosett had little to do for his three justices; instead, he helped the Warren clerks winnow the Miscellaneous Docket, cases filed mostly by prisoners representing themselves.

The Columbia Law School graduate sensed that Warren was initially suspicious of him, in part because Columbia closely followed the Harvard doctrine, in part because he drove to work each morning with a Frankfurter clerk. In the evenings, Rosett was often in Frankfurter's chambers, waiting for his ride, and therefore susceptible to the justice's considerable wiles.

Gradually, week by week, Rosett was "brought into the fold" for practical reasons. "I suspect that maybe both the Chief and Mrs. McHugh were interested in getting more help," Rosett decided.

Practicalities played a role, but so did Warren's increasingly comfortable relationship with his clerks. The thaw came in 1958, with the selection of Michael Heyman, a later clerk suggested. Heyman was confident and easy to get along with, a young man not unlike Warren's three sons living 3,000 miles from Washington. From then on, the Chief seemed annually to adopt one of two of the young men as surrogates for his absent sons.

The Chief took clerks into his confidence. After the justices' weekly conference, they would gather in Warren's office. There he briefed them on the decisions made in conference, and recounted the discussions. "He had a fantastic memory," clerk Murray Bring said, both for the details of arguments and the cases themselves.

On Saturdays, Warren and the four law clerks adjourned to the University Club. They sat in a favorite banquette where they could keep an eye on the television set and the college football game of the week.

And there Warren would reminisce. About politics, about personalities, about Warren's years as district attorney. He was frank, and unflinching in the face of their questions, but still defended the Japanese internment of 1942–45 as "the right thing to do," Bring recalled.

"There was this large Japanese community," clerk Murray Bring quoted Warren. "Most of them, I'm sure, were loyal, but all of whom had cultural and heritage ties to Japan. I could not be sure how many of them would be loyal and how many of them would be disloyal."

In the end, the chief justice shrugged. "We had to do everything necessary to protect the country."

Warren's relations with the brethren were equally cordial and equally open—except for Felix Frankfurter. As his influence waned, Frankfurter grew ever more peevish.

In the spring of 1961, he twice ad-libbed censures of decisions in the form of dissents from the bench. Concluding the second, he scolded the five-man majority opinion by Hugo Black as "an indefensible example of judicial nit-picking . . . turning a judicial appeal into a quest for error."

Warren barely choked back his anger at what he deemed Frankfurter's injudicious comment. "I must say . . . that was not the dissenting opinion that was filed. This is a lecture. This is a closing argument by the prosecutor to the jury. It is properly made perhaps in the conference room, but not in the courtroom.

"As I understand it," he continued, "the purpose of reporting an opinion in the courtroom is to inform the public and is not for the purpose of degrading this Court."

Had Frankfurter included such comments in his written dissent, Warren continued, then he would have written a concurrence that replied to Frankfurter. "I would have much to say," he added ominously.

Time magazine noted the two had crossed swords, explaining in its omniscient fashion, "Chief Justice Earl Warren has a notably thin skin, and waspish Justice Felix Frankfurter can get under an elephant's hide."

Moments later, the tempest had passed and Warren was chatting amiably with Frankfurter. Still, William O. Douglas, no ally of Frankfurter, grumbled in a letter to the retired Sherman Minton that it was Warren who by speaking out had "degraded the court. . . . It's a nasty spectacle. Perhaps the old boy is off his rocker."

Douglas, as cranky as he was opinionated, had privately decided Warren, "in his personal relations, is a very petty man, but he has at the professional level stood up extremely well."

Warren and Frankfurter would clash often in the next years, in conference and in written opinions, the chief justice seeking solutions to new problems, the onetime academic defending a judicial past. "A lot of the old legal doctrine was being challenged, or hanging like a six-year-old's loose tooth," law clerk and later law professor Arthur Rosett said.

The loosest tooth was criminal law and particularly the widely varying police practices of local jurisdictions. Fifty states operated under fifty different criminal codes—which might or might not agree with the federal rules.

The first debate centered around the Fourth Amendment's guarantee of freedom from illegal searches and seizures. How was it to be enforced?

The Supreme Court had held in 1914 that federal prosecutors could not use in court evidence illegally seized by federal agents. In handing down what became known as "the exclusionary rule," the Court relied on its authority to make rules governing the administration of federal courts.

State prosecutors, meanwhile, remained free to use evidence taken in illegal searches. To do otherwise meant "the criminal is to go free because the constable has blundered," argued Benjamin Cardozo, then on the New York Court of Appeals.

Thirty-five years later, the United States Supreme Court effectively reaffirmed Cardozo's position. The Court specifically held that the Fourteenth Amendment's due process clause did not prevent states from using illegally seized evidence in court.

Frankfurter's long discourse for an 8–1 majority was rooted in his bedrock belief that federalism permitted the states free rein. Each state could decide if it wished to adopt the exclusionary rule.

As in so many of Frankfurter's opinions, he could state a grand philosophical principle rooted in the passions of his youth, then negate that principle with a hasty retreat to the legalisms of his later years. In this case, *Wolf v. Colorado,* Frankfurter argued that "the security of one's privacy against arbitrary intrusion by the police—which is at the core of the Fourth Amendment—is basic to a free society." But having said that, he refused to give it meaning by imposing penalties for its violation with an exclusionary rule.

Providing the states did not actually authorize invasions of privacy, Frankfurter wrote, local police were free to do as they wished. By 1960, thirty states continued to use illegally seized evidence; seventeen rejected Cardozo and invoked the exclusionary rule. (Three states had no rule.)

That year the Court granted certiorari in a case challenging what had come to be called the "Silver Platter Doctrine." Because evidence illegally seized by state authorities was permitted in federal criminal trials, state police, sometimes by prior agreement, would seize the evidence necessary for a conviction, then turn it over to federal prosecutors.

Over the years, then–District Attorney Earl Warren's investigators had made good use of the Silver Platter Doctrine to aid enforcement of federal prohibition laws. Oscar Jahnsen and Lloyd Jester had raided secret stills, then handed over the incriminating copper coils to the United States attorney. They viewed the practice more or less as a game, with bootleggers the invariable losers.

The doctrine still prevailed when James Butler Elkins appealed his federal wiretapping conviction to the Supreme Court in 1960. Elkins sought reversal on the grounds his conviction was based entirely on tape recordings taken from his home by Portland police who were ostensibly looking for obscene pictures.

When a state court judge threw out Elkins's indictment on the ground that the incriminating tapes had been illegally seized, prosecutors turned over the evidence to the United States attorney. Convicted in federal court, Elkins received a twenty-month sentence and a fine of $2,000.

Warren opened the post-argument conference on *Elkins* stating he would abolish the Silver Platter Doctrine, and reverse. They could do so and avoid reaching a constitutional issue merely by asserting the Court's responsibility to supervise all federal judicial procedures.

Additionally, the chief justice continued, he personally did not want the state standard to govern the admissibility of evidence in a federal court. He carefully left unspoken the contrary proposition: Could the federal standard govern the admissibility of evidence in state courts?

Potter Stewart's vote, the first cast, decided the matter, 5–4. He agreed with the Chief. Since this was a federal prosecution, he explained, the federal exclusionary rule established in the *Weeks* case more than four decades before should govern.

Black, Douglas, Brennan, and Warren concurred; Frankfurter, Clark, Harlan, and Whittaker disagreed. The chief justice assigned the *Elkins* opinion to Stewart.

Frankfurter was distressed; Stewart's narrow opinion in *Elkins* was a fore-warning that one of Frankfurter's most cherished judicial theories was in danger. With the right case, a majority of the Court might overturn precedents by the score, and scrap Frankfurter's concept of federalism in criminal law.

One year later, a sometime numbers operator from Cleveland, Ohio, was to do just that—without even trying.

Purportedly seeking information about the bombing of an automobile owned by a rival numbers racketeer, Cleveland police paid a visit to Dollree Mapp's apartment on May 23, 1957. When she refused to let them in without a search warrant, they staked out the building. Three hours later they knocked once more with what they claimed was a warrant based on the word of "a confidential source."

When police forced their way in, Mapp snatched the supposed warrant from the officers and stuffed it down the front of her dress. One of the officers reached into her bosom to retrieve it before they went on to ransack her home.

The officers failed to find either evidence of the bombing or of betting markers reputedly in the flat. Instead, they rummaged about until they found in a locked suitcase under a bed a smutty comic book featuring the sexual exploits of Popeye the Sailor and a handful of racy photographs.

Despite Mapp's protests that the suitcase belonged to a former boarder, she was convicted of possession of obscene literature. Sentenced to state prison for one to seven years, she appealed.

The case of Dollree Mapp came to the United States Supreme Court as an obscenity matter. Only a single throwaway paragraph in a friend-of-the-court brief by the American Civil Liberties Union urged reversal on the grounds that the evidence was ill gotten.

With the brethren poised to rule that the Ohio obscenity statute was too vaguely drawn, Douglas raised the Fourth Amendment as grounds for reversal. If there had ever been a warrant in the case, it had disappeared, he pointed out.

Furthermore, a warrant had to describe the evidence to be seized; not in their wildest imaginings could Cleveland police have guessed that Dollree Mapp had in her possession a "Tijuana bible" and some smutty pictures.

Douglas was prepared to overrule precedent, the opinion by Felix Frankfurter in 1949's *Wolf v. Colorado*. To overturn *Wolf* was to argue that the Fourteenth Amendment incorporated within the meaning of due process a requirement that the states hew to criminal law standards enunciated by the United States Supreme Court.

The concept of incorporation was not new. By the 1930s, the Supreme Court had held that federal guarantees of freedom of speech and religion stipulated in the First Amendment did apply to the states. At the same time, Fourth, Fifth, and Sixth Amendment rights were not uniformly applied.

Any questioning of his deeply felt *Wolf* opinion provoked Frankfurter. In a letter to his colleagues, he explained, "I care deeply about our federalism fundamentally because it is, in my view, indispensable for the protection of civil liberties to avoid concentration of government powers in one central government."

According to Frankfurter, a criminal conviction might be reversed under the Fourteenth Amendment's guarantee of due process only if it "shocks the conscience." But there was no guarantee, and no definition of that vague term.

The court in 1952 had unanimously reversed a drug conviction because a doctor had pumped an arrestee's stomach for two swallowed morphine capsules. Such behavior shocked the conscience. But two years later, an eavesdropping bug planted in a bedroom did not—with Warren, just two months on the high court, agreeing.

By 1956 the Chief was finding his own way. That year he sharply dissented when the brethren, by a 6–3 vote, affirmed a drunk driver's manslaughter conviction based on a blood sample drawn by a doctor while the suspect was unconscious. Warren saw no distinction between a stomach pump and a hypodermic needle; in each instance, the suspect had been compelled to testify against himself.

As a district attorney, Warren prided himself that he had hewed to the letter of the law. At that, his investigators enjoyed freedoms he would later deny law enforcement officers. So long as the Supreme Court held that wiretaps were not searches within the meaning of the Fourth Amendment, Oscar Jahnsen recalled, "I never thought anything of tapping a telephone line."

In the Shipboard Murder Case, Jahnsen had burglarized a hotel room, copied letters in a bureau, then planted a bug, he told Warren biographer John Weaver. Similarly, in the effort to shut down "Admiral" Tony Cornero's gambling vessels, Jahnsen had placed fruitless taps on Cornero's telephone.

Two decades later, Warren had come full circle. The laws could be enforced and the community protected even if police were held to a higher standard, Warren told his son Earl.

Aware that poorly trained local police willfully violated the law in the name of law enforcement, "he thought the exclusionary rule was the only way. He said there is no other way that you can control governmental misadventure."

When Douglas in conference floated the concept of reversing Mapp's conviction on search and seizure grounds, Bill Brennan and the chief quickly agreed. They dropped the matter when no one else supported their stand. The vote in conference was unanimous; they would reverse on First Amendment grounds.

The conference over, Clark had a change of heart. As he, Brennan, and Black boarded the elevator to take them to their automobiles in the basement, Clark asked mildly, "Wouldn't this be a good case to apply the exclusionary rule and do what *Wolf* didn't do?"

Pressed by the others, Clark confirmed he would reverse on search and seizure grounds—and apply the exclusionary rule to the states. They had four votes for a revolution.

That evening, law clerk Jesse Choper drove the chief justice home. Recapitulating the conference, Warren confided, "Well, we're just all over the lot, but I'll tell you, I think there are five votes there to overturn *Wolf v. Colorado.*"

They still needed a fifth vote. Hugo Black, a former prosecutor himself, held the Fourth Amendment's guarantees in somewhat less honorable state than the First, Fifth, and Sixth Amendments. The great advocate of incorporation, of applying the Bill of Rights to the states, was skittish about giving the Fourth Amendment such sweep solely on the grounds of privacy.

Together Warren, Douglas, and Brennan visited Black in his chambers, and persuaded him in an unrecorded conversation to sign on. Black agreed to join, though he wrote a long concurrence to explain why he had changed his mind since the earlier *Wolf* decision.

Warren assigned the case to Tom Clark. Bill Brennan was going to work with Clark, Warren told clerk Jesse Choper.

Clark's draft opinion came as a surprise to the four members of the Court who thought *Mapp* would be decided as an obscenity case. "Frankfurter was livid," Choper recalled.

"At the next conference he raised the roof. This was early April already, and this issue was not argued, considered, and he could not prepare a proper dissent in time before the end of the term, and he insisted it be put over and the case be reargued."

According to the chief justice, Douglas teased Frankfurter: "You've had that dissent written all your life."

Harlan and Stewart sought to persuade Clark to narrow his opinion so as not to reach the larger question of excluding from trial illegally seized evidence. Clark politely declined.

"There is no war between the Constitution and common sense," he would argue in his opinion. To affirm the conviction would be to permit local police to do what federal police could not. "Thus the State, by admitting evidence unlawfully seized, serves to encourage disobedience to the Federal Constitution which it is bound to uphold."

Dollree Mapp was to begin a revolution in criminal justice, and fuel the ongoing controversy surrounding the Warren Court. *Mapp* was "so terribly important," Warren told his son, so important, Earl Junior decided that "it's hard to say it's a case. It's like a huge cloud from which a lot of things are raining." *

Felix Frankfurter took the decision hard. Not only did *Mapp* reverse a

* Mapp moved to Queens, New York, where she prospered selling heroin. She was convicted in 1974 and sentenced to a jail term of twenty years to life for running a heroin factory in her home.

Supreme Court ruling of just twenty-one years earlier, but it discarded one of his most cherished tenets.

The former Harvard professor had spent much of his adult life constructing a judicial philosophy widely praised among his intellectual peers. At an age when he might have enjoyed the respect due his achievement, he found instead this simple-minded politician from California undermining the edifice.

Frankfurter's irritation knew no bounds. How was he to deal with a man who held to no overarching judicial principle, but molded his decisions by instinct, one after the other?

The two also clashed, for similar reasons, in the most politically sensitive case of the term.

In January, 1961, Warren held for a 6–3 majority that a private power company was not entitled to damages when the government canceled a contract fashioned by a government employee who had an indirect financial interest in the enterprise.

"Dixon-Yates," as the press dubbed the case, had grown out of an Eisenhower campaign promise to curtail the growth of the government's Tennessee Valley Authority in favor of private power companies. A so-called dollar-a-year adviser to the Bureau of the Budget consulted on a federal contract for a private consortium organized by Edgar H. Dixon and Eugene A. Yates to build a power plant in the Tennessee Valley. The consortium of Dixon's Middle South Utilities and Yates's Southern Company would then sell power to the Atomic Energy Commission's Oak Ridge facility in competition with the TVA.

After the contract was signed, word leaked that Adolphe H. Wenzell, the part-time Bureau of the Budget consultant, was a vice president and director of First Boston Corporation, which was to finance construction. In addition, Wenzell had also secretly advised Dixon on the financing arrangements.

An embarrassed Eisenhower administration summarily canceled the contract on July 11, 1955, with the lame assertion that the $100 million plant was no longer needed. The Dixon-Yates consortium sued to recover its $1.8 million in costs.

The case came to the Supreme Court in the October term, 1960, redolent with favoritism and insider dealings. Even the president was implicated. Eisenhower had written a letter praising the contract.

"Pepsi-Cola took over the White House," Warren told law clerk Markham Ball, a sarcastic reference to Eisenhower's close tie with the president of the soft drink company. Warren himself had no doubts. Dixon-Yates represented "one of the worst conflicts of interest in history," he later told Drew Pearson.

The Chief particularly resented, and even took personal offense at the consortium. After Solicitor General J. Lee Rankin argued on behalf of the government that the contract was invalid because of the conflict of interest, lawyers for the company read into the Supreme Court record the Eisenhower letter proclaiming the project's merit.

That sort of legal red herring angered the Chief. Warren was himself direct, virtually guileless. He expected that of others.

"If he has any notion that a lawyer is trying to flim-flam the Court, he is not inclined to be generous. Stupidity in the Court doesn't bother him, but artfulness or duplicity does," clerk William Dempsey said.

In conference, Warren argued the contract was rendered invalid by a Civil War statute prohibiting direct or indirect benefit to a government employee negotiating the contract. Five of the brethren, including Frankfurter, agreed with him. Harlan, Whittaker, and Stewart dissented.

In view of the president's involvement, Warren took responsibility personally for the 6–3 majority opinion. His holding resonated with the ethical lessons learned in boyhood and reinforced by a lifetime of government service.

The federal law, Warren wrote, was intended to prevent conflicts of interest. "The moral principle upon which the statute is based has its foundation in the biblical admonition that no man may serve two masters, Matt. 6:24, a maxim which is especially pertinent if one of the masters happens to be economic self-interest."

The law, Warren continued, made no mention of corruption, or government loss because of the conflict of interest. "The statute is thus directed not only at dishonor, but also at conduct that tempts dishonor."

Frankfurter sneered at Warren's draft opinion. The chief justice's "crude, heavy-handed, repetitive moralizing makes me feel like eating rancid butter, and there are things in it now that I will not swallow," he wrote in a note to John Harlan.

Warren, Frankfurter continued, had the "bias of a sans-cullotte," the most poor of the French revolutionaries, the most radical, and the quickest to use the guillotine.

Warren's draft opinion was full of gratuitous criticism of the "whole 'business' community," Frankfurter asserted. Warren would have to remove "his excessive moral (and some 'legal') baggage before I can join his opinion."

Though Warren complied to gain Frankfurter's vote, the January 9, 1961, "decision did not endear us to the electric power industry," Warren dryly noted. His opinion thundered a morality almost quaint in the boom years of this affluent decade.

Similar moral values rather than legal doctrine might have governed Warren's votes in the growing number of obscenity cases coming to the Court, but for William Brennan.

Brennan's 1957 opinion in *Roth v. United States* had established a new definition of the obscene, and therefore what was prohibited. To be banned, a publication had to be without redeeming social, literary, or educational value; its predominant appeal had to be to the prurient; and it had to be measured against contemporary community standards.

The effect of *Roth* was to give writers and publishers greater liberty to deal with the sexual. The more they tasted the heady freedom, the more they ran afoul of local authorities.

As strong as he felt about alleged pornography, Warren could put aside his personal feelings, former clerk Jesse Choper recalled. "He hated obscenity. He hated it. He rose above that, most of the time."

In October, 1960, the brethren voted 5–4 to evade ruling on a Chicago municipal ordinance that required all motion pictures be licensed before they were exhibited. Warren, in the minority, was upset enough to ask Choper to prepare a dissent.

Choper had compiled an "indeed astonishing" list of films denied licenses by the Chicago film panel and the reasons for the denial. They included newsreels showing Chicago policemen shooting at labor pickets; Walt Disney's *The Vanishing Prairie,* which depicted the birth of a buffalo; a pre–World War II *March of Time* documentary critical of Nazi Germany; and a motion picture based on the best-selling novel *Anatomy of a Murder,* because it used the words "rape" and "contraceptive."

The issue, in Warren's mind, was censorship, and it was not to be ducked. "It is axiomatic that the stroke of the censor's pen or the cut of his scissors will be a less contemplated decision than will be the prosecutor's determination to prepare a criminal indictment."

Still, he confessed he was reluctant to issue the dissent. "I really hate to do it for these people [in the motion picture industry]," he told Choper. "I really don't like these people or this business. But it's the right thing."

Warren released the dissent, joined by Black, Douglas, and Brennan. Increasingly, the right thing, the fair thing determined the Chief's jurisprudence.

CHAPTER 31

INTO THE THICKET

T HE DISPARITIES WERE STARK. MEMPHIS, TENNESSEE, ACCORDING to the 1950 census, had 312,000 voters; the city had seven representatives in the legislature. At the same time, the twenty-four counties surrounding that city had an identical population, and twenty-six representatives.

Rural interests controlled Tennessee. The state legislature's failure to reapportion since 1901 had left the state to be governed "by the hog lot and the cow pasture," the mayor of Nashville complained.

Seeking to end the malapportionment, Charles W. Baker and nine other residents of Tennessee's underrepresented cities brought suit in 1959 against Secretary of State Joe C. Carr. Their case was to alter profoundly the course of American politics.

Baker v. Carr was by any measure one of the most influential the Warren Court would decide, more far-reaching than even *Brown v. Board,* an about-face more abrupt than the previous term's *Mapp* ruling. Historians and legal scholars alike would come to rank the case among the most crucial ever taken up by the Supreme Court of the United States.

Earl Warren himself would state repeatedly that it was "the most important decision" of his tenure as chief justice. He believed it would eventually remake the rotten boroughs and satrapies that effectively governed the country.

On the facts alone, Baker and his colleagues would have been easy winners. Their problem was overcoming the Court's traditional reluctance to meddle in an area the Constitution seemingly set aside to the legislature.

When the liberal bloc of Warren, Black, Douglas, and Brennan voted to grant certiorari on November 21, 1960, Felix Frankfurter girded for battle.

No issue could have been more at the core of Frankfurter's philosophical view of the Constitution. In 1946, the justices had refused to halt an election in Illinois's congressional districts where the population disparities ran as high as nine to one. Only Congress could determine the qualifications of its members.

Frankfurter, writing for the plurality in that case, *Colegrove v. Green,* had declared that "the petitioners ask of this Court what is beyond its competence to grant. . . . It is hostile to the democratic system to involve the judiciary in the politics of the people . . ."

In a statement that would become a shibboleth, Frankfurter insisted, "Courts ought not to enter this political thicket."

In sum, *Colegrove v. Green* held there was no judicial remedy for even willful malapportionment. "The remedy for unfairness in districting," Frankfurter advised, "is to secure state legislatures that will apportion properly, or to invoke the ample powers of Congress."

By the time Baker's case reached the Supreme Court in April, 1961, inequities as great as two to one in state legislative districts were common. A few were bizarre; in Vermont, one member of the legislature represented just 49 people while a colleague served 33,000.

A University of Virginia study released in October, 1961, showed that nationally "big city voters have less than one-half the representation of people in open-country areas." Rural areas continually shrank in terms of relative population, but gained in representation. The big losers were urban areas, particularly the suburbs.

Frankfurter's proposed solution was no solution at all, a Warren law clerk of that term later commented. In Florida, probably the most malapportioned of state legislatures, an estimated 19 percent of the population determined the majority of the legislature.

"So it really didn't matter how informed the 81 percent were; their votes didn't count," James Adler said. "Now where Frankfurter or Harlan could write that and not find it nauseating or inconsistent with reality, Warren would know that's bullshit. He would know that. He had been there."

Been there and gone.

The chief justice had made an unvarnished about-face in the reapportionment case. As early as 1926, he had endorsed a modified "federal plan" on the California ballot that effectively handed to the agricultural, mining, and forestry interests dominant in rural counties veto power in the state senate.

Fourteen years later, in an address to the Associated Farmers organization —the biggest beneficiaries of the federal plan—Governor Warren reaffirmed his admittedly "politically expedient" support for rural California. It would be "a sorry day," Warren stated, if the federal plan were amended and "the farmers of California lose their present representation in the legislative halls of our State."

Population growth magnified the inequities. California was so badly apportioned after the 1950 census that the 15,000 residents of three northern California rural counties had equal weight in the state senate as the 7 million in Los Angeles County.

A decade later, Warren had come to realize that redistricting was often racial gerrymandering—and not only in the South. Blacks found themselves in segregated districts, particularly at the city council and school board level.

The year before they took up Baker's petition, the justices had struck down, on grounds of racial discrimination, the tortured redistricting of Tuskegee, Alabama's city council districts. Four hundred black residents found themselves summarily redistricted out of the city, leaving but five black voters in a town that was home to one of the nation's foremost black colleges.

To protect his *Colegrove* opinion holding redistricting beyond the Court's power, Frankfurter had deftly defined the Tuskegee gerrymander as a racial rather than a political issue. His decision for a Court unanimous in the outcome rested on the Fifteenth Amendment's guarantee that the right to vote might not be abridged by the state.

In effect, the Court was holding that malapportionment was unconstitutional if based on race, but acceptable under any other rationale.

The Tuskegee case apparently opened Warren's eyes. After the April, 1961, oral argument in the Tennessee appeal, Warren not only wanted to rule that reapportionment was a matter for the courts, but favored determining a remedy. Black, Douglas, and Brennan agreed.

"Frankfurter unleashed a brilliant tour de force," Brennan told law professor Herman Schwartz, "speaking at considerable length, pulling down reports and reading from them, and powerfully arguing the correctness of *Colegrove.*"

Clark and Harlan joined Frankfurter. Whittaker, for once decisive, explained he thought the Court had jurisdiction, but would vote with Frankfurter to deny, believing that a precedent should not be overruled by a single vote. "I'll be the sixth vote for jurisdiction but not the fifth," he told the brethren.

They were knotted at 4–4 when the junior justice, Potter Stewart, spoke last. He was undecided, and asked that the case be put over to the following term for reargument. The brethren agreed.

By Monday, October 9, 1961, and the reargument, Frankfurter sensed he had lost ground. Both Whittaker and Stewart were plainly vexed by the riddle of so fundamental a constitutional right as equal representation so pervasively denied.

During the oral argument, Warren summarized the dilemma with a question to Tennessee's assistant attorney general, Jack Wilson:

"Mr. Wilson, is there any remedy in the courts of Tennessee for these people—if they are, as they say now, at the end of the road—if we don't take this case?"

"I would say, may it please the Court, that on the present status of the case law in Tennessee and of the views held as to the constitutional law in Tennessee, that this right, alleged right, is not enforceable in *any* of the courts of Tennessee to *any* degree whatsoever."

Warren opened the conference on Friday, October 13, with the assertion that Tennessee's failure to redistrict was a violation of equal protection. In this case at least, he could not accept Felix Frankfurter's oft-stated argument that there was not a remedy for every wrong.

Narrowing his April stand, Warren added, "I don't think we have to decide the merits. . . . All we have to decide is that there is jurisdiction."

The chief justice had borrowed his two-step strategy of *Brown* eight years earlier. He suggested their opinion assert the Court's purview, "and leave the rest of the case and the form of the decree to the district court."

Once more the vote was 4–4 as they turned to Potter Stewart. He began by stating "he was most troubled with the court interfering in this area."

Frankfurter sat back in his chair, sighing in relief.

"However—" Stewart continued. Tennessee's failure to redistrict had left the state so malapportioned that he believed "the district court did have jurisdiction."

Attorney General Wilson's honest response had decided Stewart. What good was a right if it was not enforceable? Stewart would join in the narrow decision the Chief had suggested.

A downcast Frankfurter returned to his chambers to tell his clerks, "This is the darkest day in the history of the Court."

Warren might have assigned to himself such a major case that sharply departed from past rulings. Instead, he weighed giving the case to Stewart, and thereby cementing him to the majority. In the end, Bill Douglas persuaded Warren to hand it to Brennan.

Brennan was a judicial craftsman. Furthermore, Warren "had the utmost respect for Brennan, and Brennan's sense, his political approaches to matters of this sort," said William Dempsey, a former Warren law clerk.

While Brennan was to write the opinion, the Chief played a significant role in keeping a majority in line. The justices were uneasy with the case, its political impact, and the possible repercussions.

Wounded, ranging between petulance and anger, Frankfurter shaped his dissent into a reaffirmation of his discarded judicial philosophy, a statement of his love of the institution he had so faithfully served, and a warning.

"The Court's authority—possessed of neither the purse nor the sword—ultimately rests on sustained public confidence in its moral sanction. Such feeling must be nourished by the Court's complete detachment . . . from political entanglements and by abstention from injecting itself into the clash of political forces in political settlements."

Meanwhile, Tom Clark and Charles Whittaker, both of whom had signed Frankfurter's sixty-page dissent, were having second thoughts.

Realizing the people of Tennessee had no effective relief, Clark reversed his stand on March 7. Brennan suddenly had a sixth vote.

Then a seventh. Early in March, Whittaker told the brethren he was rethinking his position. "And Frankfurter went berserk about that, and became quite abusive to Whittaker."

Whittaker buckled under the pressure.

On a court split 4–4, Whittaker felt overwhelmed. As one of his former clerks put it, "Whittaker sort of found himself the guy who had to decide all these important questions. . . . His vote was going to decide what the Constitution said."

As a practicing lawyer, Whittaker had given little thought to the constitutional issues that came to the high court. He told his clerks, "You know, I don't really have a philosophy. I don't come to these cases with a preconceived notion. I come to them trying to figure out basically as a lawyer, as a judge, who's right."

The lack of background left Whittaker adrift, tending to fall in with the conservatives since that seemed to be the safest course. But the stress—particularly Frankfurter's scornful lectures in conference—told on Whittaker. He missed days of work, then weeks.

Warren cautioned Whittaker, "You know, Charley, you can't let this injure your health." He recommended Whittaker make decisions, put them behind him, and move on to the next case.

Whittaker could not. On March 6, 1962, he entered Walter Reed Hospital, pleading exhaustion. Ten days later he formally notified Warren that doctors "advise me that my return to the Court would unduly jeopardize my future health." After five years on the high court, he was retiring.

In his place, President Kennedy nominated Deputy Attorney General Byron White. A former All-America halfback at the University of Colorado, "Whizzer" White had met the president while a Rhodes scholar at Oxford before World War II. White returned to the United States to play professional football and attend Yale Law School. He and Jack Kennedy crossed paths again during the war, when they served in the same torpedo boat squadron in the South Pacific.

White had been tested first as cochairman of Citizens for Kennedy in the 1960 campaign. As a deputy attorney general, he had directed the federal marshals defending the Freedom Riders risking their lives to integrate public transportation in the South during the summer of 1961.

White "was a great force in the Department of Justice," respected among Kennedy's closest advisers as "wise and kind," said Edwin Guthman, then special assistant for public information at the Department of Justice.

Attorney General Robert Kennedy, the president's brother, had first proposed federal appellate court judge William H. Hastie. "I thought it would mean so much overseas and abroad that we had a Negro on the Supreme Court."

Robert Kennedy met with the chief justice in Warren's chambers to test his opinion. "He was violently opposed to having Hastie on the Court," Kennedy recalled.

According to Kennedy, Warren protested, "He's not a liberal, and he'll be opposed to all the measures that we are interested in, and he just would be completely unsatisfactory." *

Similarly, Warren objected to the appointment of Paul Freund, a Harvard law professor. Close in legal philosophy to Frankfurter, Freund would bring to the conservative wing intellectual powers that Whittaker lacked.

William O. Douglas, once an associate of the president's father on the New Deal Securities and Exchange Commission, also scored Hastie and Freund. Twice rebuffed, the attorney general looked elsewhere.

The president personally selected Byron White from a list of potential nominees. White, who had clerked for Chief Justice Fred Vinson in 1946–1947, was the first law clerk to return to the Supreme Court as a justice. At forty-four, still near his playing weight, White would be a fierce competitor in half-court basketball games in the fourth-floor gym against the much younger law clerks.

Sworn in on April 16, White did not take part in *Baker v. Carr*. But even without Whittaker's vote, Brennan had a 6–2 majority when the opinion was announced on March 26. Only John Harlan and Felix Frankfurter were left to dissent.

Brennan's ruling was cautious in its wording, and far-reaching in its impact. The opinion held only that the courts had jurisdiction in reapportionment matters, and that Baker and his associates had stated a grievance for which they were entitled to relief. The brethren would leave it to the federal district court to fashion relief if the judge found that Tennessee's failure to reapportion was a violation of Baker's constitutional rights.

Warren was jubilant. "Bill," the Chief wrote in a note as Brennan finished reading his majority opinion from the bench, "It is a great day for the Irish." Then he drew a single line through "Irish," and scrawled, "country."

Baker v. Carr was "inevitable," said one legal watchman, adding, "But twenty years ago, or even ten, it would have been inconceivable." Through the political wisdom of the chief justice the inconceivable had become the inevitable.

Rarely did a Supreme Court case produce such prompt action. Within hours of the decision, attorneys in Georgia had filed a suit asking that that state be redistricted. Within days, another was in federal court in Alabama.

---

* Warren was not entirely candid when on September 17, 1964, he wrote the retired Felix Frankfurter: "While I have never pressed my opinion on judges at the White House, I agree with you thoroughly that he [Phillip Elman, a former Frankfurter clerk who had helped to draft the government's influential brief in *Brown v. Board*] would be a very capable Court of Appeals judge." Apparently Warren did not want to help Elman, a critic of the Warren Court's activism, secure a federal judgeship. EW's letter is in Box 354, EWP/LC.

Three months later, the Maryland legislature, under court order, redistricted its lower house for the first time in forty years. In two dozen other states, Anthony Lewis reported in *The New York Times,* similar moves were afoot.

Baker would shortly claim a second casualty. Ten days after Brennan announced the opinion from the bench, Felix Frankfurter suffered a stroke.

It struck the justice, a man of such spirit, without warning. While sitting at his desk, he suffered a massive stroke that left his left side paralyzed.

The exertion of the last weeks was too much for him, Frankfurter's secretary said. Others attributed the crippling stroke to the tension Frankfurter felt; the redistricting decision had simply been the last and greatest blow.

"There was dismay and a sense of loss," Frankfurter clerk Roland Homet, Jr., remembered. "Frankfurter was a vibrant figure no matter what you thought of his positions. To be anywhere near him was to be near a field of force."

Partially paralyzed and unable to talk, Frankfurter retreated from the Court to a closely guarded hospital room, then to his Georgetown home, wounded in spirit as well as body. Medical bulletins minimized the illness, even when he suffered what Warren termed "a second seizure."

Reluctant to surrender his life's work, Frankfurter clutched the hope that he might return to the Court when the October term began. Only after his doctors, his friend Dean Acheson, and his colleague on the Court, John Harlan, beseeched him to step down and save his health did Frankfurter yield.

On August 28, 1962, after twenty-three years and seven months of service on the Supreme Court, Felix Frankfurter, partially paralyzed, submitted his letter of resignation to President Kennedy. "To retain my seat on the basis of a diminished work schedule would not comport with my own philosophy," he wrote.

Frankfurter's resignation marked the end of an era. Brilliant, prickly, combative Frankfurter had upheld a judicial tradition slipping into disfavor. He lent balance to the Court, generally at odds with the liberals, not in desired result but in the means to that end.

The day after Frankfurter resigned, the White House announced the appointment of Arthur Goldberg, onetime counsel to the United Steelworkers of America and now secretary of labor, to fill the vacancy.

The son of Russian immigrants, Goldberg had grown up on Chicago's poverty-ridden South Side, where his father sold vegetables to hotels and restaurants from a horse-drawn wagon. The young man had raced through school, eventually graduating Northwestern University Law School so early he had needed a waiver of the bar's minimum age requirement.

Goldberg set aside his thriving practice in labor law to serve during World War II in the Washington headquarters of the Office of Strategic Services. Released from service, he played a major role first in purging alleged communists from the Congress of Industrial Organizations and then negotiating a merger of the CIO with the rival American Federation of Labor.

Newly elected Jack Kennedy tapped Goldberg as secretary of labor to recognize the contribution of organized labor to Kennedy's victory. Goldberg had been on the short list for the Whittaker vacancy, but was still needed in the Cabinet. Presidential special counsel Theodore Sorensen recommended they "save Goldberg for the vacancy of Chief Justice."

Three months later, they tapped Goldberg to fill the so-called Jewish seat.

Earl Warren was especially pleased. Goldberg, a liberal shaped by family and religion, and tempered by the Great Depression, readily acknowledged that he shared the chief justice's social values. "There is nobody I felt closer to than Warren."

Though Arthur Goldberg would be a fifth vote for judicial activism, neither he nor White would take part in the most controversial of the cases the Court took up in the 1961 term.

Less than three months after *Baker v. Carr,* the seven justices who had heard arguments in the appeal handed down the decision in a case even more inflammatory than *Baker.* In part because it had no easily understood defense such as *Baker's* "one-man-one-vote" principle, the School Prayer Case would lodge as a thorn in the side of the Court.

In 1951, the New York Board of Regents adopted a twenty-two-word prayer with the recommendation that it be offered at the beginning of each day in the state's public schools: "Almighty God, we acknowledge our dependence upon Thee, and we beg Thy blessings upon us, our parents, our teachers, and our country. Amen."

Seven years later, the Herricks school board on suburban Long Island voted to begin the class day with the prayer. It was not compulsory; if a parent objected, the child was to be excused.

Nonetheless, the American Civil Liberties Union sued the school board on behalf of five parents, two of them Jewish, one a Unitarian, one a member of the Ethical Culture Union, and the fifth a nonbeliever. They contended that the adoption of an official prayer, no matter how nonsectarian, for use in a compulsory setting violated the First Amendment's Establishment Clause. Congress and, through the Fourteenth Amendment's due process clause, the states were barred from imposing any official prayer.

The parents' request fell upon deaf ears. The federal court of appeals in July, 1961, decided that the Founding Fathers meant only to prohibit the imposition of an official religion. The regents' prayer was so nonsectarian as to be harmless.

Seven of the justices of the Supreme Court voted on December 4, 1961, to grant certiorari. Only Whittaker and Stewart opposed.

Seven would decide the case. By the time *Engel v. Vitale* was argued on April 3, 1962, the Whittaker seat was vacant. Then Felix Frankfurter was suddenly gone. Three days after the argument in the prayer case, ambulance attendants carried the stricken Frankfurter from the Court for the last time. He would not participate in another case.

The justices settled the matter easily, too easily, perhaps. With only Stewart dissenting, five voted to ban the regents' prayer on First Amendment grounds; Douglas concurred in the result, but argued that the case should be decided on the grounds of an unconstitutional expenditure of public funds.

At best a nominal Baptist, Warren was nonetheless profoundly religious. "A person who has no religion of any kind is almost a lost soul," he said in a candid interview published only after his death. "If one has guidelines such as one gets from religion, it is not difficult for him to find his way."

He and Nina had sent the children to Sunday school, confident they would acquire a religious sensibility, but unconcerned about its sectarian nature. A Bible rested on the nightstand beside his bed, and he had lately taken an interest in the Talmud as a guide to morality and the law that followed it.

Warren brushed aside the one objection raised from an unexpected quarter, William O. Douglas. How could they strike down the regents' prayer when the Supreme Court itself opened its proceedings with the cry, "God save the United States and this honorable Court."

The chief justice had, in effect, answered that during the oral argument, borrowing clerk Jesse Choper's rationale in the previous term's notary public oath: "I wonder whether it would make a difference if we were to require every litigant and lawyer who comes in here to say the same prayer your school district requires." In Warren's mind, it was one thing to invoke God's benevolence, and another to compel that prayer.

Because he assumed religion to be a function of the home, a parental responsibility, Warren uncharacteristically missed the political implications of the Herrick school board's prayer. Certainly the brethren were unprepared for the public outcry that the School Prayer Case provoked.

Southern members of Congress, already fuming about the Court's civil rights rulings since *Brown,* rose in frenzy. Alabama Representative George Grant raged, "They put the Negroes in the schools and now they've driven God out of them."

South Carolina Representative Mendel Rivers saw an even greater threat. "I know of nothing in my lifetime that could give more aid and comfort to Moscow than this bold, malicious, atheistic and sacrilegious twist by this unpredictable group of uncontrolled despots."

Beyond the South, the reaction to the School Prayer decision was hardly less shrill. "This is not the first tragic decision of the Supreme Court, but I would say it was the most tragic decision in the history of the United States," charged Congressman Frank Becker of Long Island, New York.

Clerics both liberal and conservative denounced the opinion. New York's Francis Cardinal Spellman—a Warren acquaintance—described himself as "shocked and frightened" by a decision that struck "at the very heart of the Godly tradition in which America's children have for so long been raised."

In Los Angeles, James Cardinal McIntyre dismissed *Engel* as "shocking and scandalizing to one of American blood and principles."

Even the liberal Episcopalian Bishop James A. Pike of San Francisco joined in the criticism. The court had "deconsecrated the nation," he claimed.

While the director of the Baptist Joint Committee on Public Affairs endorsed the decision, the most celebrated of Baptist ministers in the country, evangelist Billy Graham, scorned it as "another step toward the secularization of the United States."

Former President Herbert Hoover proposed a constitutional amendment to prevent further "disintegration of a sacred American heritage." Various members of Congress would make futile attempts over the next years to comply.

Newspaper editorial writers were equally apopleptic. Warren himself wrote, "I vividly remember one bold newspaper headline, 'Court Outlaws God.'"

The decision prompted a flood of mail condemning the opinion—enough so that Hugo Black took to answering those who wrote critical letters, and Tom Clark felt impelled to publicly defend the ruling in a San Francisco speech.

Warren chose to hold his silence on the assumption that "the hysteria concerning the decision will subside." In a letter to an old friend in California, he noted somewhat ruefully, "It is strange how many people, including a number of the clergy, have forgotten the essentials of American history and particularly the reason for the Bill of Rights. It bears out the statement of one writer to the effect that the only thing we learn from history is that we do not learn."

Of the few who spoke up for the Court, the most important was President Kennedy. To a planted question at his press conference, the president slyly proposed "a very easy remedy" for the absence of prayer in the schools: more prayer at home and more frequent church attendance.

Through the furor, Warren managed to retain some sense of humor. A year after the decision, he told California congressman James Corman, his favorite magazine cartoon depicted two children on the way to school. One said to the other: "It might be unconstitutional, but I always pray before a test."

Warren was wrong; the hysteria did not subside. Like rivulets merging to form a stream, the outcry against the School Prayer Case flowed with protests over the redistricting decision of the same term, and earlier holdings in *Mallory, Jencks, Watkins, Mapp,* and, especially, *Brown.*

Reasonable people might disagree with the Court's opinions; the brethren themselves were often sharply divided. Legal scholars many times found fault with outcome, or reasoning, or both.

The Supreme Court had known controversy before, particularly with *Dred Scott,* that terrible self-inflicted wound of 1855 requiring that escaped slaves captured in free states be returned to their owners; later with the decision striking down the first income tax; then with the "Sick Chicken" case of 1935 gutting Franklin Roosevelt's National Industrial Recovery Act.

In all those instances, however, the Court had struck, then retreated to noncontroversial issues, allowing the outcry to fade away. This was different. With each decision of the Warren Court, the din from the right rose, fell, then rose higher still. If constitutional scholars and politicians saw *Baker* as most vital, the lay public fastened on the School Prayer ruling.

The criticism became clamor. The clamor became frenzy.

The first call to impeach Earl Warren came early in September, 1957, from an obscure organization with a scant, even invisible membership and a Hollywood, California, mailing address. The Cinema Educational Guild was run by the even more obscure Myron C. Fagin, who had tenuous links to the notorious anti-Semite Gerald L. K. Smith.

Fagin's blue-ink-on-white brochure proclaimed, "WANTED! FOR IMPEACHMENT" over a picture of the chief justice. Fagin listed two reasons: the " 'Desegregation Decision,' which aids and abets the plans of the Communist conspiracy to . . . mongrelize the American White Race"; and the Jencks and Watkins rulings which "shatter the FBI as a barrier to the security of our nation . . . freed convicted traitors . . . [and] nullify *all* our protective laws against the Communist Conspiracy."

The impeachment cry echoed next from Chicago, at the end of the two-day convention of We, the People, a local right-wing organization claiming to favor "limited government." A spokesman said the resolution calling for impeachment was prompted by the *Jencks* decision, which bared the FBI's most secret files.

It was from We, the People that Massachusetts candy maker Robert H. W. Welch got the idea of impeaching the chief justice. However futile the effort, however marginal its advocates, Welch and his well-financed John Birch Society would bring the campaign national attention.

Welch and the John Birch Society were consumed by anticommunist fervor. In keeping with that passion, Welch and his Birch Society advocated not only the impeachment of Earl Warren, but the repeal of the federal income tax, opposition to the North Atlantic Treaty Organization, and an end to United States membership in the United Nations.

The Birch Society was hardly the first "Americanist" or super-patriotic organization to see subversion rotting the nation's morality, its military strength, and its political sinew. But it was easily the most prominent, in part because it was the best funded of the right-wing organizations. At its height, it boasted an $8 million annual budget and a membership approaching 100,000.

Its leader, Robert Welch, lived in a closed world darkened by suspicion and dread. His twisted fears led him to bizarre judgments.

President Eisenhower, Welch intuited, had spent his adult life "knowingly accepting and abiding by Communist orders, and consciously serving the

Communist conspiracy." Nor was the president alone in the hidden conspiracy Welch had spied out. Central Intelligence Agency director Allen Dulles and former Secretary of State John Foster Dulles were caught up in the conspiracy. The president's brother Milton, a trusted adviser, was "actually Dwight Eisenhower's superior and boss within the Communist Party."

By January, 1961, and the inauguration of John F. Kennedy, Welch had concluded that "Communist influences are now in almost complete control of our Federal government. Nor was the judiciary free of the plague. The entire Supreme Court, Welch wrote, "is now so strongly and almost completely under Communist influence that it shatters its own precedents and rips gaping holes in our Constitution in order to favor Communist purposes."

To promote his impeachment campaign, Welch sponsored a national essay writing contest. He would donate $1,000 to the undergraduate college student who best answered the question, "Why Chief Justice Warren should be impeached."

Birch Society allies picked up the cry. In Dallas, former FBI agent Dan Smoot attacked Warren in a series of syndicated radio broadcasts as lacking the background to be justice of the peace. Dan Smoot called for Warren's impeachment, claiming that thirty-six state supreme court justices, various members of Congress, and members of the American Bar Association's Committee on Communist Tactics, Strategy and Objectives would testify against Warren.*

Warren came to believe that western oil and gas interests, in particular his nemesis of old, William Keck of Superior Oil, underwrote the attacks on the Court. "They talk about the need for law and order, protection against Communism, and anything else that has popular appeal," but "nothing about the poor, downtrodden oil and gas industry and its tendency toward monopolistic practices," he wrote.

The anti-Court infection seeped from the fringes of the radical right toward the political center. Panicked by the unreasoning clamor or craftily taking advantage of it to preserve their positions, state legislators across the country hastily approved a series of constitutional amendments ostensibly designed to protect "states' rights."

The first of the proposed changes, drafted by the Council of State Governments, would have rewritten the amendment clause of the federal Constitution. Under the proposal, approval by two-thirds of the state legislatures would be enough to amend the Constitution—without the requirement that Congress initiate the amendment with its own two-thirds vote.

The second and third proposals were directed at the Supreme Court. Again on the ground of states' rights, one would have reversed *Baker v. Carr*

---

* In 1959, the ABA committee had claimed that "the paralysis of our internal security grows largely from construction and interpretation centering around technicalities emanating from our judicial process." See the ABA *Journal* (1959), p. 406.

and its threat to rural legislators; the other would have created a Court of the Union, made up of the chief justices of the fifty states, with power to overrule Supreme Court decisions. Those purporting to be conservatives were promoting the most radical of solutions.

The suggested super Supreme Court appeared to Warren the gravest of all threats, particularly as state legislatures continued to endorse the idea. The prestige of the Court had suffered from these proposals, Warren claimed in a post-retirement interview with *New York Times* Supreme Court reporter Anthony Lewis.

"Those things went through Legislature after Legislature till almost two-thirds of them passed some kind of resolution on them, and there was no debate of any kind on the part of the bar in the country. To think of coming that close to a constitutional amendment on important issues of that kind without the bar taking an interest is almost a frightening thing."

These were constitutional changes—and they posed a threat to the Republic in Warren's mind. Of the campaign against himself he gave no public notice, even as the calls for impeachment grew more shrill.

In November, 1961, conservative Hearst newspaper columnist Fulton Lewis, Jr., announced, "I wouldn't impeach him. I'd lynch him." Three weeks later, *Newsweek* magazine quoted right-wing spokesman J. Everts Haley complaining of Birch Society board member Tom Anderson, "All he wants to do is impeach Warren. I'm for hanging him."

Retired Marine Colonel Mitchell Paige on December 13, 1961, joined the lynch mob, and inadvertently dealt the political right a grievous blow.

Speaking at a road show anticommunist "school" entitled Project Alert, Paige told an applauding audience of 700 in Los Angeles that he felt impeachment was "not the proper penalty" for Warren's votes. Paige said he had read sixteen or seventeen court decisions in which "Warren seemed to stand with our enemies," and had decided "a more deserving punishment would be hanging."

With that, Paige had peeled the patriotic skin from even respected anti-communist organizations and revealed the worm of hysteria burrowing within. Tagged as extremists, the right lost ground.

For the next five years, these organizations would futilely seek to impeach Earl Warren—with picket lines, posters, and billboards. Leaflets urging Warren be impeached turned up three times in a single year at the Downey, California, high school bearing his name. An otherwise unknown organization, the Committee to Restore God and Prayer in Our Schools, picketed the White House, carrying signs blaring "The Flag Is Next," and "Remove Warren, Restore God."

The campaign against Warren grew ludicrous. By mid-decade, the radical right was whispering that Warren had murdered his father, and then covered it up; or that whenever the investigation got close to the real killer, Warren shut it down. (At one point, the Liberty Lobby was reportedly underwriting a book that would name Warren as the murderer. FBI assistant director

Cartha DeLoach intervened, bringing back word "that they had reason to believe that the book was not going to be published.")

Through the din, Warren managed to retain a sense of humor. Informed of the Birch Society's essay competition, Warren joked, "I'll have to get Mrs. Warren to enter the contest. She knows more of my faults than anyone else."

On the wall of his apartment he hung a framed cartoon from *The New Yorker* magazine depicting Whistler's mother embroidering a pillow cover with "Impeach Earl Warren."

Nina was initially troubled as the painted "Impeach Earl Warren" billboards sprouted across the country. Her husband shrugged them off.

"Signboards such as this are not pleasant," he wrote a television station manager who had editorialized against the billboards, "but they do make evident that we have freedom of speech in our country."

When former California assemblyman Ralph M. Brown wrote a sympathetic letter, Warren replied with philosophical resignation. He had become accustomed to criticism from the right on "the theory of Mark Twain that a few fleas are good for any dog."

For his own part, he said in a later oral history for the Lyndon Johnson library, "I can understand why they were against me, because I was against everything they were for."

The Birch Society reached its peak of national influence as the GOP's far right captured the 1964 Republican National Convention. In an elliptical defense of Robert Welch's passionate screeds, its presidential nominee, Barry Goldwater, argued that "extremism in the defense of liberty is no vice" and "moderation in the pursuit of justice is no virtue."

Goldwater went on to campaign with the promise, among others, to appoint as judges "only seasoned men who will support the Constitution," men who would be tough on criminals.

An enduring political issue had been born. Four years later, an opponent of old would use it to club the Court.

Part IV

THE
WARREN COURT

CHAPTER 32

HIGH MORAL GROUND

NOW, PAST THE AGE OF SEVENTY, ROBUST IN HEALTH AND COM-
fortable in his work, his life had settled into a familiar routine.
The first Monday in October and the opening of the Su-
preme Court term marked the beginning of the year. By then the law clerks
had prepared the first certiorari memoranda, and begun the process of
whittling the docket to size.

Of 2,373 cases filed in this, the 1962 term, the justices would set just 151
for argument and decide 129 with signed opinions. (They would dispose of
nineteen with short court orders, and reset three for reargument.)

During the eight months the Court was in session, each of the justices
would write approximately fourteen majority opinions. They were free to
write as many concurring or dissenting opinions as they chose; in the
interests of cohesiveness and workload, Warren personally tended to write
fewer dissents than any of the brethren.

In addition to his work as one among equals, the chief justice had two
other, often time-consuming duties: he was responsible for the administration of the court and its 200 employees; and, because protocol dictated, he
was a frequent host to foreign dignitaries. (In one instance, informed by
Mrs. McHugh that the Indian delegation had arrived, Warren looked up to
ask innocently, "Californian?")

Any number of visitors claimed his time, and only the firm hand of
Margaret McHugh kept the work flowing. "He felt that was part of his job,
to show the human side of the federal government," said law clerk Gordon
Gooch.

"He was very good, even in talking to high school students," Gooch added. "He did it all willingly. He didn't seem to resent it."

He particularly welcomed visitors from California, those with whom he could talk about programs he had put in place as governor. Years after he was sworn in as chief justice, he still asked guests about the University of California or day care centers or preservation of the stately redwood groves in Mendocino County.*

Favored visitors—Pat and Marge Patterson; the daughter and grand-daughters of *Sacramento Bee* editor Walter Jones; Pacific Gas and Electric public relations executive Robert Gros; or Warren's World War I army buddy Tatsu Ogawa—received tours of the building, enthusiastically guided by the chief justice himself.

Beyond the Court, Warren had a coterie of friends, a number of them newsmen. He sometimes invited to apartment I-140 at the Sheraton Park CBS television commentator Eric Sevareid, ABC news director William Lawrence, and ABC radio commentator Edward P. Morgan. With such trusted men as these—professionally nonpartisan and publicly circumspect —the chief justice could tap into the political gossip upon which Washington thrived.†

Trial lawyer Edward Bennett Williams was a frequent guest, spinning tales of clients as diverse as organized crime figure Frank Costello, Teamsters' president James Hoffa, and Senator Joseph McCarthy. Williams, as celebrated as his clients, held the chief justice in awe. "Warren had an Olympian appearance in his eyes," according to Williams's wife Agnes.

The Warrens' circle expanded when oldest daughter Virginia married former ABC vice president for news John Charles Daly on December 22, 1960. The urbane moderator of the long-running television game show *What's My Line,* Daly was a staunch conservative. Over the next years, father- and son-in-law enjoyed the sharp discussions one or another Court decision fostered. The intellectual sparring continued with his law clerks at their Saturday lunches, Texan Gordon Gooch said. "When we got into

---

* The fate of the redwoods was of enduring concern to Warren. Shortly after becoming chief justice, he wrote to John D. Rockefeller, Jr., a thank-you note for the contribution of $1 million to the $2.8 million purchase price of the Calaveras South Grove of Big Trees. The project had begun when Warren was governor. On March 23, 1964, he wrote Newton Drury, a classmate from 1912, and now secretary of the Save-the-Redwoods League, "I have been greatly disturbed recently by the proposal to desecrate the great redwood forests in the Coast Range. I do hope that sanity will prevail, and that another route for the speedway will be found, if one is necessary." A week later, Governor Brown vowed that not a single redwood would be cut to build the freeway. Warren also met with Lyndon Johnson at the White House in an off-the-record "meeting on California Redwoods," according to index cards at the LBJ Library.

† Warren also felt at ease with such out-of-town journalists as Irving Dilliard, editorial writer for the *St. Louis Post-Dispatch,* and editors Ralph McGill of the *Atlanta Constitution* and Harry Ashmore of the *Arkansas Gazette,* both of whom supported *Brown v. Board of Education* at considerable risk to their newspapers.

political disagreements—because I am more politically conservative than he was—he encouraged you. He enjoyed the debate.

"In those days they had the 'Impeach Earl Warren' billboards around. So when we would get in an argument and there would be an impasse, I would say, 'Sir, you know, if you would just fire me, I could go back to Texas and run for governor unopposed on both tickets.' "

Walter Jones's occasional visits to Washington invariably offered an excuse for a small group of California legislators from both parties to gather with Warren in a private home and swap stories over glasses of scotch.

The circle of intimates expanded but slowly. Out of a courtesy call by newly elected Congressman James Corman—whose first vote in 1942 was for Culbert Olson—grew a lasting friendship. The Cormans were repeatedly to host Earl and Nina at informal dinners in the Cormans' modest Alexandria, Virginia, home.

"He was always so gracious, and it was such a thrill, particularly for young people, for anybody, to get to spend an evening with him," Corman said.

Warren at ease was disarming. At one of these parties, California Superior Court judge Harry Pregerson told the Chief he was weighing a federal court appointment. While he had a lot of experience in state courts, Pregerson fretted, he had very little in the federal.

"Well, Harry, don't worry about it," Warren reassured him. "I hadn't that much experience either when I went on the Supreme Court."

As time went on, Warren's friendships on Capitol Hill began to tilt from the Republican to the Democratic side. Then-Representative Augustus Hawkins recalled that "Republicans soured on him. We wanted to give Warren a banquet in his honor and couldn't get the Republicans to agree."

Nationally, the GOP found ever more fault with Warren, his court, and its direction. California's Republicans at the same time were less progressive than pragmatic, then less pragmatic than conservative—and hostile to the Warren philosophy.

Paradoxically, Democrat Edmund G. Brown's policies as governor seemed an extension of Warren's. "I instinctively followed Warren's political philosophy as governor," Brown acknowledged. "I tried to pattern my administration after his."

From the beginning of Brown's first term in 1959, Warren had quietly advised the new governor, in language "more forthcoming and candid than I sort of anticipated the chief justice would be," said Brown's chief of staff Fred Dutton. "I always thought they stopped short of overt politics. At the same time, Warren was being very fatherly, and frank, and helpful to Pat."

When it became clear that Richard Nixon, defeated for the presidency in 1960 by John F. Kennedy, intended to run against Brown in 1962, Warren made it a point to drop in on Brown when in California. News photos pictured the two men together, beaming, obviously friendly; the endorsement was unspoken, but clear.

"It was a very conscious show," said Hale Champion, Brown's finance director and campaign adviser. Friendship may have played a part, but "these two guys were very wily politically, and the political implications of this could not have been unknown to either of them."

Lest the message be lost on anyone, Earl Warren, Jr., changed his party registration from Republican to Democrat. He switched, he announced with some publicity, "for one reason only—to do everything I could to insure California's future as my father visualized it. Richard Nixon does not have that vision."

Brown would go on to beat Nixon by 300,000 votes, of 5.8 million cast in the general election. It was a stinging defeat for the former vice president, who bitterly announced his retirement from politics the morning after the balloting. (The value of Warren's "endorsement" of Brown lay in the fact that Republican Senator Thomas Kuchel swept every county in the state, and won reelection by 700,000 votes. Brown—with Warren's subtle endorsement—had managed a million-vote turnaround.)

Three days after the California election, reporters on Air Force One spied a chortling Earl Warren and Jack Kennedy relishing once more the news stories of Nixon's defeat. "It would have been hard to say, watching their faces, who had enjoyed the downfall more, the Chief Justice or the President of the United States," newswoman Mary McGrory commented. "They had their heads together over the clipping and were laughing like schoolboys over the contents."

Warren's pleasure in the Nixon defeat was twofold. He considered Nixon "a bad man," according to Merrell "Pop" Small. Equally, the state he loved was preserved from ignorant mismanagement.

Twice a year, summer and winter, the Warrens flew to California. Invariably they returned to Sacramento, visiting the governor's office and shaking hands with former staff members. Afterwards he dropped by Bob Tinsley's stand on J Street for a shoe shine and some baseball talk, while Nina visited shoemaker Randall Butler to drop off yet another harvest of silver demitasse spoons. The Christmas stay was crowded with family, football, and a drive to Wallace Lynn's Colusa ranch to go duck hunting.

The very air of the Golden State seemed to restore him. "This is home," he joyously announced with every return. (The Warrens paid California income taxes until the state Franchise Tax Board in 1960 ruled the chief justice was no longer a resident for tax purposes. From then on, they paid District of Columbia income taxes.)

California was an emotional lodestone ever drawing them back. Any recollection of the governor's mansion brought fond tears to Nina's eyes. For both the primary and general each election year, husband and wife dutifully wrote Alameda County clerk-recorder Jack G. Blue for absentee ballots.

In California too, four of the Warren children lived. James had left the advertising business and with his wife Margaret and three sons moved to St.

Helena, at the northern end of the Napa Valley. He was settled and prospering as a real estate agent. So too was Honey Bear in Beverly Hills, married to her doctor and the mother of three.

After a conversation with his father, Earl Junior had decided to leave his job as a farm adviser to attend law school at Boalt. He and wife Patty were back in Sacramento with their children where Earl was to practice.

Warren Senior also prodded son Robert, an athletic coach in the California prison system, to seek broader horizons. Bobby also secured a real estate license, then opened an office in Davis.

In California too were the chief justice's closest companions—Bart Cavanaugh, Wally Lynn, and, more recently, hotelman Ben Swig.

Swig had met Warren by accident shortly after World War II when Swig blundered into then-Governor Warren's Pullman compartment on a cross-country train. The two struck up a conversation, and ended up talking about investment opportunities in California.

Persuaded by the governor, Swig left Boston for California. He eventually purchased the swank Fairmont Hotel atop San Francisco's Nob Hill, and became a major contributor to the Democratic Party.

Swig and Warren drew close. For two weeks each Christmas, the hotelman turned over to the Warrens a suite at the Fairmont, first on the fifth floor, later the lavish penthouse with its glorious views of the Golden Gate, the bay, and the city far below. In the summer, they spent three weeks together on a 115-foot yacht that Swig rented to cruise the Mediterranean with his family.

The cruises were singular. On the first one, Swig and Warren were present for the dedication of a forest planted in Israel. On another voyage, Swig arranged for the party to be presented to Pope Paul VI—which sent Nina and Swig's two granddaughters scurrying about Rome for the proper dresses.

"Uncle Chiefy and Auntie Nina were just up for everything," said Swig's granddaughter, Caroline Zecca. "We'd go into ports and they would be off seeing whatever they could—they were not young then—and swimming in the Mediterranean with all the ship's hands standing around in case they had to dive in quickly . . ."

The Warrens were undemanding guests, unassuming and unpretentious. On one water-short voyage Nina offered to do everyone's laundry as long as she was washing Earl's underwear and socks daily.

If his wife looked after him still, Warren in turn treated Nina, "the best thing that ever happened to me," with an endearing respect. He invariably stood up when she entered the room. He held doors open for her, and seated her at the dinner table. Though they were not publicly demonstrative, Warren's love for his wife was unquestioned.

A *New York Times* "story of human priorities" in the midst of the October, 1962, Cuban missile crisis revealed some measure of Warren's affection for his wife. With the United States and the Soviet Union poised on the brink of nuclear war, government officials issued laminated passes which would admit key government figures to an ultra-secret "alternative seat of government" dug deep into a mountain in Appalachia.

When the earnest young man brought the chief justice his pass to this cavernous nuclear bomb shelter, Warren said he did not notice a pass for Mrs. Warren.

There was no room for wives, the courier informed him.

Well, in that case, Warren replied, now you have room for another VIP. Smiling, he handed his pass back.

If Nina made his life run smoothly, in return, Warren assumed his obligation was to protect her financially. At the chief justice's request, Swig recommended a series of real estate investments intended to supplement Nina's pension in the event of Warren's death.

He was not wealthy. After a lifetime of public service, he had accumulated just the proceeds of 88 Vernon when they sold it, and interest on that money since. It amounted to barely $50,000, he wrote Swig in 1957.*

It troubled him, daughter-in-law Margaret recalled. One Christmas, the man she called "Papa" came out to the kitchen, near to tears.

"You know, Jim," he confessed, "I lie awake at nights just thinking all the time. I've had many offers where I could have been a millionaire, and as it turned out, I always felt that I was a public servant and this was my life. And now I have nothing to leave my family."

It weighed on him, particularly with that family growing. By 1962, the Warrens had no less than fourteen grandchildren, the oldest of them eighteen. In an effort to know something of these youngsters, Earl and Nina decided to bring one grandchild to Washington each summer for two or three weeks.

The first visitor, in 1960, was sixteen-year-old James Junior. With a guide to lead them, Warren and his oldest grandson toured the Gettysburg battlefield on July 4, a brilliant, sunny day. Standing at the battle line that marked the high tide of the Confederacy, looking down at the green fields below, Warren spoke in wonderment:

"Just think, Jimmy, you are standing at *the* point in *the* war, that turned *the* tide, that created *the* nation that is now the United States of America."

Grandfather and grandson also visited the Lincoln Memorial, walking slowly up the steep stairs in the front of the building, the great seated figure of the sixteenth president looming up as they neared the top. Warren solemnly told the youth that the memorial was a continual inspiration.

"He said he would come down there from time to time, and look at it

---

* To avoid any possible conflict of interest, Jesse Steinhart had advised then-Governor Warren to invest his $50,000 in tax-free municipal bonds. Swig was to shift some of the funds into various real estate ventures, including the development of Cannery Row in Monterey; an office building in Portland, Oregon; and the landmark Mills Building at the corner of Montgomery and Bush in downtown San Francisco. Most were sold; the Warren family did retain a fractional interest in that Daniel Burnham–designed building.

because he was moved by Lincoln. He had seen people walk into that memorial with the same reverence they had when walking into a cathedral. He said it always struck him that way."

With the grandchildren Warren-the-solemn as easily became Warren-the-playful. During the pilgrimage of James's sports-minded younger brother in 1961, the chief justice took him off to a Washington Senators baseball game.

Invited to sit on the Kansas City Athletics' bench by manager Hank Bauer, Warren accepted. "It was quite a thrill for me," Jeffrey Warren recalled.

As game time neared, the umpire waved them from the dugout; major league rules stated only those in uniform were allowed. The two Warrens meekly retreated to their box as Bauer mounted the dugout steps to yell, "Good goin', ump! You just threw out the chief justice of the United States."

Sporting events remained a release from the burdens of the Court. Warren not only attended Senators baseball games, but traveled to the Penn Relays, and law clerk Murray Bring introduced him to hockey.

Seven Sundays each fall, Warren was a guest of Ed Williams at Washington Redskins football games, crowded into Williams's presidential box with John and Virginia Daly, Robert and Ethel Kennedy, *Washington Post* editor Ben Bradlee, columnist Art Buchwald, diplomat Averell Harriman, and Tom Clark, all there to cheer a team of indifferent talent and mediocre record.

In such company, the chief justice ranked among Washington's royalty, yet Warren never confused the office with the man. Though a stadium functionary stood ready to usher the chief justice of the United States through a VIP gate, Warren invariably refused. "No, no, I'll wait my turn in line with everyone else."

Beyond his limousine, Warren did not take advantage of the perquisites of office. "He knew how important he was when he was governor and chief justice," explained longtime family friend Robert Gros, "but he didn't go around playing the role."

When the Smithsonian Institution commissioned the celebrated modernist Gardner Cox to paint a portrait of its honorary chairman, Warren sat repeatedly in the morning before the Court day began.

"It took forever," the chief justice told Frankfurter law clerk Roland Homet, Jr. "At the end I showed it to my wife, and she still didn't like it."

Warren was similarly unimpressed when approached in 1958 about publication of a collection of his speeches. Despite his reservations about their worth, Warren turned over a box of materials. He would neither select those speeches he thought his best, nor even write an introduction.

When the book came out as *The Public Papers of Chief Justice Earl Warren,* he shrugged it off. In a letter to Bill Brennan, he confessed "wonderment as to why the book was published."

Because the chief justice would not presume on his office, Warren summarily put an end to a "hobby" law clerks Gordon Gooch and Henry Steinman took up as a joke. Once mistaken as Warren's bodyguard at a baseball game, Gooch and Steinman secretly started posing as Secret Service agents guarding the chief justice.

"He'd be walking down the street, talking to whomever he was walking with, and Steinman and I would drop back, and drop back. Then we'd move out on the flanks a little bit, and whenever someone would approach, we would put our hands in our pocket like we were putting it on the butt of a pistol. People would just clear the path."

The two clerks enjoyed their private charade "something fierce," until one afternoon the chief justice marched off to the Washington Hotel to get a haircut. Steinman and Gooch fell into their Secret Service roles just as a derelict lugging two suitcases approached.

"He looked up and saw Steinman and me with our hands on our [imaginary] pistols . . . and the man dropped his suitcases, went over and put his hands up against the wall."

Warren took one look at the derelict leaning against the wall, looked back at Steinman and Gooch, and realized what they had been doing. "Cut that stuff out!" he ordered.

"And we couldn't be police officers anymore," Gooch lamented. "He said he's never had a bodyguard in his life, and he wasn't going to start now."

Unassuming as he might be, the chief justice of the United States was about to take on even greater leadership, spurring the legal revolution already begun, secure in a solid liberal majority for the first time since joining the Court nine years earlier.

The replacement of Felix Frankfurter with Arthur Goldberg in August, 1962, dealt a double loss to the conservatives on the court. Frankfurter had provided both scholarly justification for their position, and an anchor to windward for the entire Court. No one could fill that role.

Moreover, Goldberg was an enthusiastic judicial activist, a wholly different man than Frankfurter. Within weeks of Goldberg's arrival, he was to make his vote felt in the cases reargued from the 1961 term.

The first was an appeal to bar enforcement of a Virginia law making it illegal for any organization to retain a lawyer in a cause in which it had no financial interest.

Warren had argued in conference during the previous term that the state law was intended to thwart implementation of *Brown v. Board of Education.* In effect, it would put the NAACP out of the legal business in Virginia.

Despite his arguments, the brethren had voted in conference 5–4 to uphold the statute. But before Frankfurter's majority opinion could be issued, Whittaker had resigned and Frankfurter himself was felled by a stroke. With the vote now 4–3 to strike down the legislation, the Court set the case for reargument.

That fall Byron White and Arthur Goldberg sat in the seats once occupied by Charles Whittaker and Felix Frankfurter. Goldberg voted to reverse, willing to go even further than Bill Brennan's opinion for the majority. White concurred in part and dissented in part. Clark, Harlan, and Stewart dissented.

Similarly, Goldberg was the critical fifth vote in a case challenging the Florida legislature's investigation of the Miami chapter of the NAACP for communist influence. Branch president Reverend Theodore S. Gibson refused to provide the committee with a membership list and financial records. He was held to be in contempt, then sentenced to six months in jail and a $1,200 fine.

Argued first in 1961, this case might also have been decided by a 5–4 vote to uphold the contempt conviction. Once again Warren, Black, Douglas, and Brennan were in the minority.

The illnesses of Frankfurter and Whittaker forced reargument of the case. Goldberg voted with the chief justice to reverse, and turned around the result, 5–4.

A third time Goldberg provided the deciding vote, and with it changed the outcome in a search and seizure case from San Francisco. Deadlocked at 4–4, with the hospitalized Whittaker not participating, the brethren in April, 1962, put the case over for reargument.

By October and the new term, White and Goldberg were installed. They split, White voting with what had been the Frankfurter wing, while Goldberg gave the activists a majority in favor of reversal.

Seven more times in that 1962 term, the junior justice would join Warren, Black, Douglas, and Brennan to form majorities in civil rights or civil liberties cases. With Goldberg's coming, Earl Warren had his Court.

No case better demonstrated the Court's new sensitivity to simple matters of justice than did the *in forma pauperis* petition of Clarence Earl Gideon penciled in neat block letters on the lined paper provided by Florida's state prisons.

Gideon, a sometime drifter, sometime convict, had been found guilty on August 4, 1961, of breaking and entering a Panama City poolroom with the intent to commit a misdemeanor. He had broken into a cigarette machine for the change, then snatched up a bottle of cheap wine and a six-pack of beer.

Denied an attorney by the trial court judge, Gideon's felony trial was short, the result predictable. He was sentenced to the maximum, five years in Raiford State Prison. The Florida Supreme Court summarily rejected his appeal.

"The question is very simple," Clarence Gideon argued in his awkward petition to the Supreme Court of the United States. "I requested the court to appoint me attorney and the court refused." Florida did not provide counsel for indigents except in capital cases.

Logged in by the court clerk's office, Gideon's five-page petition made its way to the *in forma pauperis* pile in the chief justice's chambers. When it eventually rose to the top of the pile, law clerk Henry Steinman picked it up.

The Sixth Amendment to the Constitution assured a right to counsel in criminal cases only in federal courts. Twenty years earlier in *Betts v. Brady,* the Supreme Court had ruled that the Due Process Clause of the Fourteenth Amendment did not require that criminal defendants be represented by counsel in state courts. An attorney was required only if the absence of counsel constituted "a denial of fundamental fairness."

The Court in *Betts* had refused to set "hard and fast rules" stipulating in which cases the states had to provide counsel. Instead, in subsequent decisions, the Court said the defendant had to be the victim of "special circumstances"—his own illiteracy, youth, or mental illness, or the conduct of the prosecutor or judge at the trial.

As he read Clarence Gideon's letter, Steinman became excited. "It was obvious to me. The guy had been denied counsel. In almost every case the Court had up to that time, the Court sent it back down because they [the justices] found there was some special circumstance—he had grown up poor, he was mentally unbalanced. They found something they could rely on without saying there was an absolute right to counsel."

This one was clean, Steinman exulted.

Steinman's typed IFP memo to the justices was terse: "Right to counsel case. There appear to be no extenuating circumstances."

To the chief justice, he wrote on the bottom of the typed flimsy his recommendation to grant certiorari. "This may be it!" he added.

When Clarence Gideon's petition came up in conference on June 1, 1962, eight justices voted to take up the case. Only Tom Clark voted to deny cert.

Three weeks later—after Gideon had requested counsel be appointed to argue his case in the high court—Warren proposed that Washington attorney Abe Fortas be asked to represent Gideon, without fee.

Pro bono appointments in the Supreme Court are considered great honors by lawyers. At the same time, the cases can be costly, not only in the unbillable hours devoted to them, but in out-of-pocket investigative, printing, and travel costs. It may be a great honor, but it is not one all can afford.

Abe Fortas could. He was one of the most influential attorneys in Washington, a veteran New Dealer with enduring connections to the Democratic Party. More important, he was an experienced courtroom advocate.

By the time the redoubtable Fortas argued the case on January 15, 1963, *Betts* hung by the thinnest of threads. The legal profession had long held it in faint regard, the law journals in even lower repute. The attorneys general of twenty-three states had prepared a friend-of-the-court brief asking that *Betts* be abandoned.

Thirteen states still had no legal requirement that counsel be provided in all felonies; in eight of these, however, the indigent found attorneys through informal systems. Only five states did not provide counsel for the poor except in capital cases: Alabama, Florida, Mississippi, North Carolina, and South Carolina. (Gideon, unfortunately, was not tried in one of Florida's three largest counties. These three did have countywide public defenders.)

In practical effect, the case would have comparatively small impact. Symbolically, it towered above the balance of the cases decided in the October, 1962, term.

Fortas's legal argument, the best Bill Douglas claimed to have heard in his thirty-six years on the Court, was more than enough. The brethren voted unanimously to reverse *Betts.*

The question to be answered was whether the Fourteenth Amendment embodied a right to counsel in *state* trials. As Steinman later pointed out, "There is nowhere in the Constitution where it says you are entitled to legal counsel" in a state case.

"But if that is what you believe, you go to the Due Process or Equal Protection Clauses and find it."

Warren, his eye on producing a unanimous Court, led off the conference discussion with a canny suggestion. They did not need to lay out exactly how far the decision went. He proposed they leave to another day and other decisions whether the states were required to provide counsel in misdemeanor trials or for appeals, or when the right to counsel applied. The fewer the extraneous issues, the less likelihood Clark, Harlan, Stewart, or White would dissent.

The brethren agreed with his terms but rejected his additional suggestion that the decision be made retroactive. After all, the deputy attorney general arguing Florida's doomed case as best he could stated that 65 percent of all inmates in state prisons were convicted without representation by lawyers at their trials.

In a gesture to Black, a dissenter twenty years earlier in *Betts,* Warren assigned *Gideon* to the senior justice. Black's opinion in one sense was narrow; to hold on to his unanimous court, he "incorporated" only the right of counsel when defendants faced felony charges.

While there would be three concurring opinions—Douglas embraced incorporation of the entire Bill of Rights rather than the piecemeal approach they were taking—once more the Warren Court was unanimous in the outcome of a major case.

Clarence Gideon's journey to the Supreme Court of the United States was a piece of storybook Americana: the luckless drifter, in and out of prisons since he was fourteen, the least among men, could appeal to the highest, the most august court of the land. And once there, not only would he be heard, but he would triumph.

No tale so affirmed the American democracy. No story broadcast around the world so clearly proclaimed that not just the rich received justice in American courts.*

Gideon came down on March 18, 1963, the last in a series of decisions that critics of the Court claimed had marked this as a "black Monday for states' rights."

That day, the Court also ruled in a case challenging Georgia's peculiar unit system in Democratic primary elections. With it, rural voters firmly controlled the state legislature, but also determined party nominees for governor.

A winner-take-all primary system made it possible for as few as 11 percent of those voting statewide to elect the Democratic gubernatorial nominee—providing they cast their ballots in a handful of key rural counties. The apportionment was so skewed that 6,980 residents of the state's three smallest counties had as much voting strength in primary elections as Atlanta's 556,326 citizens.

Four times before, disgruntled Atlantans had challenged the primary system, the last when an incumbent congressman won renomination despite losing the popular vote. Four times courts had rejected the suits on the grounds they lacked jurisdiction to enter that political thicket. The fifth attack came to the Supreme Court on an appeal by the state, after a three-member federal panel struck down the malapportionment as unconstitutional.

Warren again set the direction of their discussion in conference. The Georgia unit system was defective, he maintained, because it disproportionately favored some voters over others. So too were similar primaries in other states.

The vote was 8–1, with John Harlan the lone dissenter. Warren assigned the decision to Douglas.

Two weeks later, Douglas had a draft opinion. He argued that "once a geographical unit for which a representative is to be chosen is designated, all who participate in the election are to have an equal vote. . . . The conception of political equality from the Declaration of Independence, to Lincoln's Gettysburg Address, to the Fifteenth, Seventeenth and Nineteenth Amendments can mean only one thing—one person, one vote."

Warren immediately signed on, with a terse, "I agree. EW, 2/5/63." He asked for no changes as Douglas went through six revisions, making changes in each to accommodate the brethren.

---

* Represented by an attorney, Clarence Gideon was acquitted after a second trial on August 5, 1963, and faded from sight. While hoboing across the country, he was later arrested in Jefferson, Indiana, but released when authorities learned his identity. A local radio station raised enough cash to send Gideon on his way. By 1966 he was living in Miami. Meanwhile, *The New York Times*'s Anthony Lewis would write a successful book about the case, *Gideon's Trumpet*. That book served as the basis for a well-regarded television movie shown to the justices and their wives at a dinner hosted by Tom and Mary Clark. There was a second screening in the East Conference Room on February 20, 1967. The film was apparently well received.

This would be a recurring pattern in the next years. If he was in the majority, as chief justice Warren would make the assignment. When the drafts circulated, he quickly signed on, requesting few if any changes.

He left to others the nuances; he preferred to lead in conference, to find common ground and direct a majority to it. Rarely did he seem to change his mind because of the reshaping of a decision or the line or argument taken. He was interested only in the result, in the underlying principle.

Privately, Warren acknowledged that some decisions of the Court "will be a little rough, or go too far. We know that, and we know future generations will tame it down."

At times, the Warren Court did not wait for those future generations, but chose to polish its own work. The clamor had hardly died down on *Engel* when the high court took up two more school prayer cases.

One appeal came from the Supreme Court of Maryland, which had approved a Baltimore city schools order that the day begin with the recitation of the Lord's Prayer and the reading of a selected Bible passage. In the second, a federal appellate panel had struck down a state law mandating that the school day begin with a reading of ten biblical verses.

The court might have disposed of this volatile issue quietly. A brief *per curiam* decision citing the previous year's School Prayer decision would have whisked away the Maryland matter. The justices might have rejected the appeal of the losing school board in the Pennsylvania case.

Instead, the brethren granted certiorari. The misunderstood School Prayer opinion had not been well received a year earlier; this was an opportunity to reiterate the ruling, and perhaps educate the public at the same time.

Once more Earl Warren's political judgment played a hand in shaping the opinion. Normally, the writing assignment would have gone to Hugo Black; he had, after all, written the first School Prayer ruling. Instead, Warren assigned the majority opinion to Tom Clark, whom critics of the Court considered a conservative, one of their own.

Bill Brennan, either by prearrangement with the Chief but certainly with Warren's agreement, informed the brethren he would write a concurrence in the Pennsylvania case. It would be a historical review of the Supreme Court's church-state decisions, a reminder that this Court was not out of step with its predecessors.

Brennan, the sole Catholic on the court, asked that no one else join him. He was, in effect, appealing as a communicant to the hierarchy of the Catholic Church in America and to influential laymen for their support.

Arthur Goldberg, with John Harlan joining, and William Douglas would also write concurring opinions. Only Potter Stewart dissented.

On the last day of the term, June 17, 1963, Tom Clark began reading the 8–1 majority opinion, soundly affirming *Engel v. Vitale* of the previous year. His holding also extended the prohibition from the more or less nonsectarian Christian prayer once recited in the Long Island school district to passages from the King James Bible.

School District of Abington Township v. Schempp was also a reaffirmation that the Warren Court would countenance no breach of the wall between Church and State. Public funds were not to be expended to support even token, voluntary religious activities.

The protest was subdued. News stories and press commentators made a point of noting that Clark, a Methodist by upbringing; Brennan, a Catholic; and Goldberg, a Jew, had affirmed the decision in separate opinions. Forewarned by the outcry triggered by *Engel* the year before, sympathetic churchmen were ready with supportive statements when the second prayer decision came down.

Far more difficult for the brethren was a cluster of cases arising out of sit-in demonstrations throughout the states of the old Confederacy. The sit-in cases presented "a legal Gordian Knot because competing interests were at stake," as Court historian Bernard Schwartz put it.

Could the state prosecute trespasses committed in the course of civil rights demonstrations against discrimination by private citizens? Or, put another way, could merchants expect the state to enforce their personal preference not to serve blacks?

The sit-ins had begun on February 1, 1960, when four nervous freshmen at North Carolina Agricultural and Technical College sat down at the "white-only" lunch counter of the F. W. Woolworth store in Greensboro, North Carolina.

"They sell us merchandise from other counters," one of the four explained to a local reporter. "If they sell us other merchandise, we say they should serve us at the lunch counter."

Denied that service, the students returned in growing numbers each day for a week. They quietly filled the seats at the lunch counter, one by one, and peacefully ended sales for the day. The sit-in movement had been born.

As the sit-ins spread across the South, the convictions multiplied. By the beginning of the 1962 term, the brethren had agreed to review six different sit-in cases involving scores of demonstrators.

The lead case was to be *Peterson v. Greenville,* the appeal of ten black youths in Greenville, South Carolina, arrested for unlawful trespass for sitting in at the lunch counter of the local S. H. Kress dime store. Their convictions for violating a city ordinance prohibiting the races from eating together were upheld in the state supreme court.

Warren opened the November 9, 1962, conference on the cases with the cautious suggestion that they avoid the fundamental constitutional question of property rights versus civil rights. Instead, he proposed they reverse the convictions on the basis of unlawful state action.

In three of the cases, the cities had ordinances requiring separate seating of the races in restaurants.

The fourth, involving the Reverend F. L. Shuttlesworth, had two clergymen convicted of inciting a violation of a similar ordinance in Birmingham, Alabama.

A fifth, from New Orleans, had no such local law, but did involve a mayor and police chief pledging any sit-in would not be permitted.

In the sixth, a security guard deputized by a county sheriff in suburban Maryland had arrested two black youths for entering a white-only amusement park and boarding the carousel.

Warren prevailed as one by one the brethren came to agree with the Chief. According to notes Warren made at the conference, Hugo Black "believes a store owner as [does] a home owner has a right to say who can come in his premises, and how long they can stay. If he has that right he cannot be helpless to call the police."

Private parties might discriminate. If, however, the *state* made "it illegal for the races to eat together, it is unconstitutional." On those grounds he could reverse.

Bill Douglas emphatically disagreed with any defense of property rights. To accept Black's position meant "we will have a new *Plessy v. Ferguson,*" he insisted.

Douglas proposed they step boldly into the uncharted. He wanted not only to reverse, but to "make the store owner a public utility" by overturning the 1883 court decision, which held the Fourteenth Amendment did not apply to public accommodations. Failing that, he would simply go along with the Chief.

Clark, Harlan, Stewart, and Goldberg fell in with Black's position. Brennan suggested they rely on the fact that local ordinances were coercive; they did not give private property owners the right to integrate their lunch counters, if they chose. Byron White seconded Brennan's position.

Keenly aware they were undermining not just law, but social custom in the South, Warren assigned the sit-in cases to himself. Over the next seven months he sought "as nearly a unanimous conclusion as possible," striving, as Stewart and Goldberg pointed out in a final two-hour conference on May 16, for "the great benefit that flowed from the unanimous decisions in the first school cases . . ."

To achieve that, Warren accepted a series of editorial changes in his personally drafted opinions from Brennan, White, Goldberg, and Harlan. At the last moment, Clark nearly bolted, only to be brought back in line by Warren and Brennan.

In the end, only John Harlan dissented. He concurred in the result, but disagreed with the reasoning.

Warren delivered the simply written, easily understood majority opinion on May 21, 1963. His conclusion in disposing of cases from Greenville, South Carolina; Birmingham, Alabama; and Durham, North Carolina, was unequivocal:

When a state agency passes a law compelling persons to discriminate against other persons because of race, and the State's criminal processes are employed in a way that enforces the discrimination mandated by that law, such a palpable violation of the Fourteenth Amendment cannot be saved by attempting to separate the mental urges of the discriminators.

In the fourth case, from New Orleans, neither city nor state had a law barring the races from eating together. Nevertheless, the mayor and the police chief had pledged they would not permit integration of lunch counters.

Warren's opinion made short work of their extralegal conduct. The convictions of one white and three black college students for breach of the peace at a McCrory five-and-ten were reversed.

The outspoken mayor and police chief were adamantly opposed to desegregation; in effect, their orders were as law, Warren wrote. Consequently, the city was to be treated as if it *had* adopted an ordinance prohibiting the races from eating together.

Finally, the chief justice magically whisked away the convictions of the Reverends Fred L. Shuttlesworth and Charles Billups for inciting two young men to commit a criminal trespass at a Birmingham lunch counter.

The Alabama city had a segregation ordinance. That ordinance was this day ruled unconstitutional. The convictions of the two youths for trespass under that ordinance were reversed. Since the two had therefore not committed a crime, Warren reasoned, the two clergymen could not be convicted of inducing them to break the law.

With that decision, the brethren were able to postpone for another year the underlying question: Could a private property owner summon the police powers of the state to enforce his personal bigotry? Could a merchant invoke seemingly race-neutral trespass or disturbing the peace laws to discriminate?

Because the Maryland amusement park case squarely presented that issue, Warren agreed with Clark to put the matter over for reargument in the following term.

And with that Earl Warren concluded his tenth term as chief justice of the United States.

Such anniversaries are, for journalists, moments of assessment. Left or right, they agreed the Court had had profound impact on the nation. Their appreciation of that impact divided along political lines.

Conservative *U.S. News & World Report* noted with barely throttled alarm that "the trend of the Warren Court in using its judicial authority to promote change in more and more fields shows no sign of abating." The magazine quoted California Democratic congressman Charles H. Wilson complaining, "Our entire way of life in this country is being revised and remolded by the nine Justices of the Supreme Court."

The *Milwaukee Journal,* still laced with Progressive vigor, applauded Warren editorially. ". . . Court historians are already according him future rank as 'one of the great Chief Justices.'" With his vote and leadership, the editorial continued, the Supreme Court "has more profoundly influenced and shaped the course of individual human affairs than in any equal period of time before."

The court's decisions over the ten-year span had fundamentally changed the nation—while leaving the institution mired in controversy. A Gallup Poll that year reported 10 percent of the public rated the court as doing an excellent job, 33 percent a good job, and 26 percent a fair job. Fifteen percent told interviewers they believed the court was doing a poor job.

In September, 1963, shortly before the opening of the new term, the chief justice broke his decade-long silence with an elliptical response to critics of the Court. Speaking to the annual convention of the California Bar Association, Warren acknowledged that the Court's docket had shifted. A quarter century before, hardly more than 1 percent of the Court's opinions dealt with civil rights or civil liberties; now almost half did.

But those who complained the Court was going too fast, he continued, overlooked the fact that the Court merely reviewed cases decided by lower courts. "But really, where the supreme court of a state is vigilant in its protection of constitutional rights, as is the Supreme Court of California, few differences arise between it and the Supreme Court of the United States."

Left unstated, but surely not lost on the delegates, was the implication that the high court "moved so fast" only because the state courts moved so slowly in protecting constitutional rights.

A week after Warren's speech, *The Washington Post,* partially owned by the Warrens' summertime traveling companion Agnes Meyer, rallied to the defense. According to the paper, four towering cases—*Brown, Baker, Mapp,* and *Engel*—marked the Warren decade, cases that came to the Court "tragically late" and so "ran counter to settled convictions and rooted practices among many Americans."

Led by Earl Warren, the Supreme Court had met its responsibilities, the editorial continued. "It was a piece of magnificent good fortune that the chief justiceship was held during this trying period by a man of exceptional poise and strength and understanding."

Poise. Strength. Understanding. Earl Warren would need all that and more in the next term.

CHAPTER 33

FACTS SO SIMPLE

MARGARET BRYAN HEARD IT FIRST, FROM A COWORKER IN THE Supreme Court cafeteria who had a reputation as "a terrible kidder," she recalled later. "I thought it was in bad taste."

And then she realized the story was true, so terribly, terribly true.

Bryan made her way upstairs to the chief justice's offices and told Margaret McHugh. Steeling herself, Mrs. McHugh typed a brief note to the Chief: "It was reported the President has been shot while riding in a motorcade in Dallas, Texas."

Alvin Wright, the robing room attendant who guarded the great oak doors of the conference room, knocked softly. He handed the folded note to Arthur Goldberg, who as junior justice answered the door.

Warren read the note, suddenly numb, then tearfully adjourned the conference. The justices scattered to their chambers, some to drift with their law clerks to Bill Brennan's office with its fair-sized television set.

They stared at the television, subdued, waiting. "It was a bizarre, and ultimately sad scene," Warren law clerk Frank Beytagh recalled. "There were people there who knew Jack Kennedy quite well, like Byron White and Arthur Goldberg."

Warren retreated to listen alone to the radio bulletins. Texas governor John Connolly had also been gravely wounded. Both he and the president were at Parkland Hospital, Dallas's finest emergency facility. A half-hour later came the news flash: The president had died in the emergency room of Parkland Hospital shortly after 1:00 P.M.

Shocked, wanting to deny the truth, the chief justice wandered from his office. With tears in his eyes, he talked quietly to his small staff in the reception area.

He spoke of the young president whom he had seen just two days before at a White House dinner honoring the Supreme Court. The members of the Court were teasing the president about his upcoming political trip. "We were joshing and laughing. We told him to watch out for those Texans; they were a wild bunch. All in fun, you know."

And now that vibrant young man was gone, his great promise obliterated by a sniper's bullet. "The days and nights following were more like a nightmare than anything I had ever lived through," the chief justice wrote later.

Warren grieved. He had looked upon Jack Kennedy as more than the president. "It was like losing one of my own sons," he acknowledged later. "You know, he was just a little older than my oldest boy."

The chief justice was somber throughout the afternoon, Mrs. McHugh recalled. "He was very, very upset." The prompt arrest of a suspect by Dallas police offered no consolation.

Washington was a stricken city that afternoon. One by one, people drifted away from their offices, often to drive about aimlessly. Warren's chauffeur, in suburban Maryland with Nina, called to report he was stuck helplessly in traffic.

Warren turned to law clerk Frank Beytagh and requested he stay. Later that afternoon, the Chief asked Beytagh to drive him to Andrews Air Force Base. The president's plane was to land there. Warren felt it was his duty to be on hand, to demonstrate that the government, the nation lived still.

When Air Force One landed, the sight of Jacqueline Kennedy still wearing the pink suit stained with her husband's blood unsettled Warren once more. On Wednesday night, she had been his dinner partner, exchanging pleasantries, a glittering hostess in formal gown. Less than forty-eight hours later, they watched helplessly as her husband's casket was loaded into a hearse.

Saturday evening around nine o'clock, Jacqueline Kennedy telephoned the Warren apartment. Gathering her composure as she made funeral arrangements, Mrs. Kennedy asked if Warren would deliver one of the eulogies during memorial services in the Capitol the next day.

Warren agreed, then struggled futilely that night to write something meaningful. Distraught, he put off the task until Sunday morning.

He was writing the eulogy when a television reporter broke in on the regular programming to report that the suspected assassin, Lee Harvey Oswald, had himself been shot dead in the basement of police headquarters in Dallas. The madness reeled beyond comprehension.

Warren's eulogy, delivered before the coffin resting on the Lincoln catafalque in the Capitol rotunda, was laced with the shock felt across the nation. John Fitzgerald Kennedy, "a great and good President," was dead, "snatched from our midst by the bullet of an assassin."

What moved some misguided wretch to do this horrible deed may never be known to us, but we do know that such acts are commonly stimulated by forces of hatred and malevolence, such as today are eating their way into the bloodstream of American life.

What a price we pay for this fanaticism.

Without saying so specifically, Warren personally blamed the radical right and Texas's extremely conservative oil millionaires. He had known their allies in California, the William Kecks and Tom Werdels, bitter men who preached a form of politics based on fear and hatred.

Warren could only close his eulogy to a fallen leader with a plea to

abjure the hatred that consumes people, the false accusations that divide us, and the bitterness that begets violence.

Is it too much to hope that the martyrdom of our beloved President might even soften the hearts of those who would themselves recoil from assassination, but who do not shrink from spreading the venom which kindles thoughts of it in others?

The implicit accusation in the eulogy was a measure of his grief and the haste with which he finally wrote. While others also leaped to similar conclusions in those first days after the assassination, it was unlike Warren to point a finger of guilt.

Long after, said his son Earl, Warren would alternate between sadness and anger. "He told me, at the height of his anger, 'I don't know who or what caused this or did the deed, but I sure know where the blame is.'"

The day after, a heavyhearted Earl Warren walked behind the caisson that carried the body of the dead president, first to the funeral service, then to the burial at Arlington National Cemetery. He returned to the Court on Tuesday a different man, Mrs. McHugh remembered. "He just wasn't like himself."

On a gray, rainy Friday, November 29, after the justices' weekly conference, Warren received a telephone call from Solicitor General Archibald Cox and Acting Attorney General Nicholas Katzenbach. They requested an immediate appointment.

Behind closed doors, Cox and Katzenbach explained that they had been sent by President Lyndon Johnson. "They told me that because of the rumors and worldwide excitement about the assassination, the President wanted to appoint a commission to investigate and report on the entire matter. The President wanted me to serve as chairman of the commission."

In the conversation, either Cox or Katzenbach indicated that the Kennedy family had specifically approved his nomination.

The newly sworn-in president had been mulling just such a commission since the previous Sunday. Katzenbach, a Kennedy appointee, had suggested to two of Johnson's closest advisers that there were already doubts in the press about the successive deaths of the president and his suspected assassin.*

In the days that followed, the United States Information Agency had culled widespread reports from overseas expressing doubt about Oswald's guilt, and hinting at a larger conspiracy. The communist press, meanwhile, was "making a determined effort to attribute the assassination of President Kennedy to a rightist conspiracy, and the killing of Lee Oswald by Jack Ruby has given them new ammunition."

Domestically, Johnson confronted a differing interpretation, an aide explained. It was "far more incredible for the American people to believe that one nut killed the president of the United States than if this was some plot masterminded in the Kremlin."

On Friday morning, Johnson made up his mind. He dispatched Cox and Katzenbach, men close to the Kennedys and known to the chief justice.

The envoys returned empty-handed. Warren told the two that the brethren had often discussed extra-Court activities by justices in the past, and had condemned them as being either political or perilously close.

Most recently, in December, 1941, Associate Justice Owen Roberts had agreed to investigate the Pearl Harbor attack. Roberts's report to President Franklin Roosevelt resulted only in further investigations and led the justice himself to decide his service had been a mistake.

After the war, Robert Jackson had accepted assignment as a prosecutor at the Nuremberg war crimes trial. That too had ended in a swirl of public controversy about a justice's involvement in extrajudicial activity, and bitterness among the brethren.

In earlier discussions of a proposed constitutional amendment on presidential disability, Warren had publicly stated he did not believe the chief justice should be one of those to determine if a sitting president was incapacitated and unable to fulfill his duties.

Explaining all this to Katzenbach and Cox, Warren declined. "And I thought that settled it."

Lyndon Johnson was not so easily put off. About ninety minutes later, the president himself was on the telephone. He asked the chief justice to come to the White House.

The two men met privately at 4:30 that afternoon for approximately twenty minutes in the Oval Office. The president personally asked Warren to serve as chairman. "I told him that I had to have someone of his stature to head this commission," Johnson explained.

---

* Others apparently had the same idea, among them Walt W. Rostow, then dean of the Yale Law School, and House whip Hale Boggs, who would serve on the commission. Katzenbach seems to have been the first, with a telephone call to Johnson friend Homer Thornberry, who relayed the message to White House adviser Walter Jenkins. Jenkins's resulting memorandum to the president of November 24, 1963, is in "Original Warren Commission Material" folder in the LBJ Library.

The problem was far larger than Warren imagined, Johnson confided. The FBI had turned up a Cuban who claimed to have offered Oswald $6,500 on behalf of Cuban Premier Fidel Castro to kill John Kennedy.

As Warren recounted the conversation, "The President told me that he felt that the assassination was such a torrid event that it could lead us into a war, and that if it did it would be with another world power." As many as 60 million would die in a nuclear war. "We don't know what this thing will bring forth."

Warren remained adamant. The brethren agreed it was wrong for them to take presidential assignments. It blurred the lines between their separate branches. Furthermore, they had enough work to do as it was, without taking on more.

But Lyndon Johnson was not to be denied. Cunning and manipulative both, he resorted to the guilt-laden pressure tactic he called "jawboning," turning on Warren all the persuasive power and authority of his office.

"You're a man who occupies one of the most important positions in this country and this country has been good to you. And it's recognized you, and I know it hasn't made any mistake. I know that the merit that the country feels you have is justified."

Once launched, Johnson soared. "I remember somewhere seeing a picture of you in an Army uniform when this country was under— involved in war, where you went out and offered your life to save your country.

"And now your services are more necessary at this moment than they were then to save this country."

Johnson jawboning was an irresistible force. He had lined up the six other members of the committee, he said: Senators Richard Russell and John Sherman Cooper; Congressmen Hale Boggs and Gerald Ford; banker and frequent presidential counselor John McCloy; and former Central Intelligence Agency director Allen Dulles. All had agreed to serve on condition that Warren chair the commission, the president fibbed.

"And I'm not going to take no for an answer. And you're not going to tell me that if the president of the United States says to you that you must do this for your country so that we can resolve once and for all without any peradventure of a doubt what happened here, that you're going to say no, are you?"

Under the pummeling, Warren gave way. As the president retold the story—and embellished freely—tears came to Warren's eyes.

"Well, Mr. President, if, in your opinion, it is that bad, surely my personal views don't, shouldn't count. If you wish me to do it, I will do it."

A worried chief justice returned to the Supreme Court that evening, law clerk Frank Beytagh remembered. "It took a lot to shake him, but he was pretty shaken that evening."

As Beytagh recalled the Chief's explanation, he confessed, "I just don't want to do this thing."

Johnson's flattery had not seduced Warren. "I was told I am the only person who could do this, and I've lived long enough to know that's probably not true."

Instead, the Chief's own sense of patriotic responsibility had led him to consent. "I don't think it's the right thing to do, but I don't feel I had the right to tell the President, 'No.' "

The president, in turn, had given his own commitments. Warren would remain on the Supreme Court and would handle both Court and commission simultaneously. He would have full cooperation from other government agencies and whatever funding he needed to produce a report.

Johnson wanted a quick investigation by the commission, one based on the FBI report that Director J. Edgar Hoover had promised to complete no later than the first of the week. Not only were there international implications, but the new president wanted to scotch any rumors that he was involved in any fashion.

That concern helped to shape the commission. Five of its members were registered Republicans, only two were Democrats. That would negate any rumors of political influence on the report.

Each of the commissioners was there for a purpose, sometimes more than one, Johnson explained in the series of telephone calls he made on November 29 while lining up the panel.

Warren as chief justice lent the prestige of his office to the commission. Even Georgia senator Richard Russell, who disliked Warren, acknowledged, "I don't have much confidence in him though I realize he's a much greater man in the United States than almost anyone."

Russell had stubbornly refused to serve with Warren. "I just don't like that man," he insisted. (Warren was aware of Russell's harsh feelings, and attributed them to the Court's racial decisions, he told a commission staff member.)

The Democratic senator—once Lyndon Johnson's mentor in the Senate —weakened when the president appealed to his patriotism. "You can serve with anybody for the good of America," Johnson insisted. "Now, by God, I want a man on that Commission and I've got one." Russell consented reluctantly.

John Sherman Cooper, the liberal Republican who had defended Warren and the Court from William Jenner's attacks in 1957, readily signed on. Once ambassador to India, Cooper would be sensitive to foreign policy implications, an important consideration when ambassadors at 125 stations overseas were clamoring to know if a new president meant a new foreign policy.

From the House of Representatives, Johnson selected Hale Boggs and Gerald Ford. Boggs was the first in Congress to propose an investigation; smart politics suggested his foresight be acknowledged. Gerald Ford, eyeing the leadership of the GOP in the lower house, was on good terms with

J. Edgar Hoover. Ford could be counted on to keep the FBI's shoulder to the wheel while protecting the bureau's interests.

The "civilians," both recommended by the slain president's brother, were Allen Dulles and John McCloy. Dulles, for eight years director of the Central Intelligence Agency under Eisenhower, would ostensibly assure CIA cooperation. Former U.S. High Commissioner of Germany John McCloy was the least entangled, a representative only of the GOP-leaning Establishment that had guided presidents since the Civil War.

Still wary of plots or "copycat" assassins, Lyndon Johnson ordered the Secret Service to protect various government officials, including the chief justice. Nina and Earl Warren dismissed it all as unnecessary, particularly the armed agents with walkie-talkies who tramped the grounds of the Sheraton Park at night. Somewhere between annoyed and amused by the security force, the Chief and his law clerks took to ducking into restaurants, abruptly leaving by the back door, and shaking the ubiquitous guards.

Warren's first task was to build a staff. His immediate choice as the staff director, almost as a reflex, was Warren Olney.

Olney, however, had enemies. As assistant attorney general in charge of the criminal division, he had come to hold a less than enthusiastic opinion of J. Edgar Hoover. Olney was "the only guy who had balls enough to stand up to Hoover," one FBI agent reportedly congratulated him.

Furthermore, Olney had helped push through Congress the Civil Rights Act of 1957; however mild it was, it angered southern Democrats, Richard Russell among them.

Russell and Hoover, through Gerald Ford, lobbied against Olney's appointment. Ford, in turn, complained that Warren was "attempting to establish a 'one-man commission' by appointing a chief counsel, Warren Olney, that [sic] was his own protégé."

Fighting for Olney's appointment might sunder the commission even before it met. And John McCloy had another man in mind.

Warren had known J. Lee Rankin as a former assistant attorney general in the Eisenhower administration, then as solicitor general from 1956 to 1961. Warren particularly respected Rankin's principled stand against the cronyism and influence-peddling in the Dixon-Yates case.

Now practicing law in New York City, Rankin agreed to take on the pivotal responsibility of the commission's general counsel. Rankin proposed the organization of the investigative team, and the assignment of a senior and junior counsel to each of five research areas: the basic facts of the assassination; the identity of the assassin; Oswald's background; possible conspiracies; and Oswald's death. (A sixth, on presidential protection, would be added shortly after.) Relying on the FBI investigation, they would be able to finish their work in three or four months, Rankin estimated.

Based on recommendations from friends and associates, Rankin selected the staff. Of the eleven practicing attorneys he chose, just two had ties to the chief justice: Joseph Ball, senior counsel charged with determining the identity of the assassin; and former law clerk Samuel Stern, who volunteered his services shortly after the commission was named. Stern was given responsibility for the subject of presidential protection.*

A prominent trial lawyer in California, Joe Ball had known Warren the governor slightly, largely through common membership in the American College of Trial Lawyers. Their relationship deepened during Warren's first years on the Court. Ball's outspoken defense of "liberal" Warren Court decisions led to social meetings when the chief justice visited California. In 1960, the chief justice asked Ball to serve on a committee revising the federal rules of criminal procedure. Over time, they drew close, sharing dinner and a ball game when Ball was in Washington. Ball would also handle daughter Dorothy Warren's divorce.

For the ten months of the Kennedy Commission's life, Ball was to play a pivotal role on the staff. "He *was* my father's right arm on that commission. Nothing would have come of that commission without Joe Ball," Earl Junior stressed.

Ball's responsibilities broadened when the senior counsel charged with investigating the basic facts of the assassination failed to appear regularly. Ball and his junior counsel, David Belin, joined forces with the orphaned Arlen Specter.

Warren as chairman of the commission met with the assembled staff for the first time early in January. His charge to them was straightforward: "Truth is our only goal."

Because they would handle classified documents, each of the men appointed had to be cleared by the FBI. A bureau report that one of Rankin's assistants, Norman Redlich, had once signed an ad opposing the House Committee on Un-American Activities prompted Ford to demand that Redlich be fired.†

Warren dismissed the accusations as "nonsense," Ball said. "What do you think those files show on me," Warren joked privately.

When Ford persisted, Warren countered, "Then we will have a public trial and give Redlich the same opportunity as anyone else to be heard in his own defense." Ford's motion to hold a hearing died for lack of a second.

The commission waived the necessary clearances for Redlich and Ball, who similarly opposed the committee, Ball said later.

From January to October, 1964, Warren held two full-time jobs. He arrived at the commission's second-floor offices in the new Veterans of Foreign Wars building diagonally across the street from the Supreme Court

---

* The senior counsel received $100 per day, junior $75. Both received a $25-per-day expense allowance. Over the next ten months, staff salaries would amount to $239,000 and the commission's total cost $1.2 million. (Of that sum, $608,000 paid for printing the final report and its twenty-six volumes of supplementary material.)

† Californian Joseph Ball privately told the chief justice that he had campaigned up and down the state against the loyalty oath, and in public lectures had often spoken out against the Un-American Activities Committee. Apparently the FBI had no record of Ball's activities.

at 8:00 A.M. Shortly before the 10:00 A.M. opening of the court, he left to hear the day's arguments, then returned around 3:00 P.M. to work once more on the assassination investigation.

At the commission offices, the chief justice spent much of the time closeted with Rankin or with Joe Ball. Together they reviewed the staff work, Warren approving it or suggesting follow-up investigations.

The chief justice devoted himself to the commission. Despite his responsibilities on the Court, despite a bronchial infection through the winter that Sam Stern described as "a major strain on his health," Warren missed only one commission hearing, and part of a second.

It was grueling, and doubly a burden for Warren, Stern noted. "The assassination was a terrible loss to him personally. He was terribly solicitous to Mrs. Kennedy and the family. It was a constant emotional drain on him."

Warren aside, the commissioners did not play major roles in the investigation. When commissioners made suggestions, Rankin implemented them, but the staff went where instincts and judgment led. Rarely did Warren balk.

Initially, the commission had intended to rely on the FBI's report, a narrative of the assassination reconstructed from hundreds of interviews. But Warren found the report a summary, "in more or less skeleton form," of the evidence against Lee Harvey Oswald.

At Warren's urging, the commission adopted a resolution on December 16 asking all government agencies to produce the raw material on which the summary report was based. Concerned with what the commission might find—the FBI had its own secrets to protect—J. Edgar Hoover alternately fumed and fretted.

Within the first week, staff counsel had turned up problems with the supporting field investigations, and thereby justified Hoover's fears.

First, a page was discovered to be missing from Oswald's notebook. "We checked back and, sure enough, it was ripped out by FBI Special Agent James Hosty because it had Hosty's name and phone number," commission counsel W. David Slawson stated.

"Hosty was afraid of his future career in the FBI if it came out that he had such close contact with Oswald and he [Hosty] had not warned the FBI that Oswald was such a dangerous person."

The approximately 25,400 pages of FBI reports proved frustrating to the commission staff. Frequently, questions that should have been asked were not "because the agents didn't have any flexibility," Slawson decided. David Belin, working with Joe Ball on the identity of the assassin, found "a lot of inaccuracies, a lot of inconsistencies" in the 2,300 FBI documents.

By the end of January, Ball said, he and Belin had concluded the "FBI reports were insufficient to our minds. They were contradictory, and things that should have been explained in them weren't."

Faced with that, Ball recommended first to Warren and then the commission that they investigate anew the identity of the assassin. "All we got back was, 'Go ahead.' "

Ball, Belin, and Specter were independently to reinvestigate the case against Oswald. They considered the FBI reports no more than a preliminary inquiry, an aid to their own autonomous work.

Once he realized his bureau's report would not go unquestioned, J. Edgar Hoover fell into sullen uncooperation. He refused to permit informal access to FBI agents and laboratory technicians. If staff members wanted to speak with them, Hoover insisted, call them before the commission. They were called.

Far more important, Hoover withheld from the commission an internal FBI document of December 10, 1963, summarizing the censure of seventeen agents in the wake of the assassination. The seventeen, field agents and supervisors in Dallas, New York, New Orleans, and Washington, had failed to put Oswald on a security watch list. Thus the Secret Service was not informed of Oswald's presence in Dallas on the day of the Kennedy motorcade.*

Other members of the commission staff confronted problems as well. The Central Intelligence Agency was tight-lipped, never to reveal that it had launched repeated efforts to assassinate Fidel Castro. As long as the commission did not ask—and the CIA's involvement in such intrigues was not yet public knowledge—CIA representatives did not tell.

The commission itself was embarrassed by a series of leaks. The Dallas Police Department was a sieve; ranking officers often talked on a not-for-attribution basis with favored local reporters. At least one member sold a portion of Oswald's "diary" for publication.

Hoover slipped copies of the FBI's initial narrative report to friendly journalists—and then hinted that Warren was responsible for the leak. Finality, in late spring, *Life* magazine published an illustrated "inside account" of the assassination by Congressman Ford. The unauthorized story—for which Ford reputedly received $1 million—"was a real breach of confidentiality clearly done for personal profit and political motive," one staff member complained.

Despite these distractions, Warren pressed the investigation. Attendance at commission hearings by the commissioners was spotty. Warren, as presiding officer, and McCloy were there for every session. Dulles came almost as often, though at age seventy he grumbled that he had only two good hours a day. Senator Cooper and Congressmen Boggs and Ford were constantly

---

* A text of the document is in *Investigation of the Assassination of President John F. Kennedy,* Hearings Before the Select Committee on Assassinations of the U.S. House of Representatives, 95th Congress, 2nd Session, September 18–21, 1978, vol. III, pp. 531–33. Hoover apparently sought to compel Special Agent James P. Hosty, Jr., to resign. (Hosty was monitoring Oswald's pro-Castro activities.) Hosty doggedly stayed on to retire at age fifty-five in 1979.

leaving hearings to answer quorum calls on the Hill. Russell simply did not attend but at Warren's invitation sent a monitor.

Early on, Warren decided "a surface case was established" against Oswald. Ex-marine Oswald had worked at the book depository. He had disappeared immediately after the shooting, the only depository employee to do so. An Italian rifle had been found, with spent cartridges, on the sixth floor where Oswald worked.

"These circumstances, followed by his trip from the building, getting on a bus and getting a transfer, then getting a cab, killing [Dallas policeman J. D.] Tippit, and running into a theater where he tried to shoot the policemen who came to get him, these made a case."

Within days, law enforcement officers would tie the Mannlicher-Carcano rifle to a mail-order house, and from there to Oswald through handwriting analysis. FBI ballistic tests linked the rifle and spent cartridges to the bullets and lead fragments found in the president's body and on Governor John Connally's stretcher. With that, onetime prosecutor Earl Warren had his case.

"The facts of the assassination itself are simple, so simple that many people believe it must be more complicated and conspiratorial to be true," Warren wrote in his posthumously published *Memoirs*.

Warren personally had no doubts. "If I were still a district attorney and the Oswald case came into my jurisdiction, given the same amount of evidence I could have gotten a conviction in two days and never heard about the case again."

In the face of immediate polls indicating that more than half of all Americans believed a conspiracy was afoot, Warren stood firm. "One person and the truth is a majority," Warren repeatedly told the staff.

Warren never doubted that Lee Harvey Oswald, the disaffected outsider, was the lone assassin. While others argued that a second rifleman was posted in Dealey Plaza, the chief justice said firmly, "No one could have fired from the knoll or the overpass without having been seen."

He put no faith "in a conspiracy of any kind," Warren told the commission's historian. "The only thing that gave me any pause about a conspiracy theory was that Oswald had been a defector to Russia at one time." *

Still, a conspiracy was possible, he conceded. But Warren the former prosecutor relied on hard evidence, not supposition in building a case.

"I don't doubt there were hundreds of people in the South who talked about killing President Kennedy," he told newspaper columnist Drew Pearson in the summer of 1967.

---

* In 1979, a select committee of the House of Representatives criticized the Kennedy Commission for not adequately investigating the possibility of a conspiracy, then added, "In large measure, the Warren Commission's inadequacies in investigating important aspects of the President's assassination was [sic] a result of failures by the C.I.A. and F.B.I. to provide it with all relevant evidence and information." See *The New York Times*, November 29, 1985.

"But the question is—were they in on the assassination in Dallas? We know what Oswald did, and I am satisfied that there is no evidence that anyone else did."

If not domestic, the conspiracy might have had its roots in foreign intrigue. "I am quite prepared to believe that Castro wanted to kill Kennedy, and may have sent some teams here to do it. But there is no evidence that he did," Warren added.

For the next ten months, Warren took a direct hand in the inquiry out of exasperation with the pace of the investigation, according to Earl Junior. A self-imposed deadline of July 1 was fast approaching; only Ball, Belin, and Specter had their draft reports completed.

So as not to miss a single session of the Court in the crowded closing days of the term, Warren compressed what Rankin estimated would be a week's work in Dallas into a single crowded day.

In the quiet of Sunday morning, June 7, 1964, Warren walked Dealey Plaza, talked to police officers and witnesses who had been in the School Book Depository Building, then retraced Oswald's movements from his boardinghouse to the sixth-floor sniper's nest. From there, he peered down through the trees to Elm Street below. He squinted through the four-power telescope on the same 6.5-millimeter Mannlicher-Carcano rifle Oswald had used while staff lawyer Arlen Specter detailed his theory of the shooting.

As Specter had reconstructed the shooting, Oswald's first shot struck the president in the back of the neck, hitting no bone, sliced the trachea, and exited the front, nicking the tie he was wearing.

Hardly slowed, the bullet struck Governor Connally, sitting on a jump seat in front of Kennedy, just to the left of the right armpit, sliced a rib, tumbled out leaving a four-inch hole in Connally's chest below the right nipple, and continued on to pass through his wrist and lodge superficially in his left thigh.

Though scorned as far-fetched by later critics, this "single bullet" theory was supported by laboratory tests.

The second was the fatal shot, striking the president in the back of the skull, spraying a mist of blood, bone fragments, and brain tissue over the limousine's interior.

A third shot seemingly missed the automobile entirely, struck a curb, and sent a concrete chip off to nick a spectator's cheek. From first to last shot, slightly less than eight seconds had elapsed.*

---

* The commission was unable to determine conclusively which of the three shots missed. In point of fact, it made no difference in the findings. Warren personally was inclined to believe the first bullet struck Kennedy and Connally, and the second was the fatal shot. Connally maintained he heard the first shot, turned, and was wounded by the second, leaving the third shot the fatal one. However, in a statement released in Austin, Texas, on November 23, 1966, Connally stressed, " . . . [S]imply because I disagree with the Warren Commission on this one detail does NOT mean that I disagree with the substance of their overall findings."

When Specter finished, Warren silently turned from the window. The distance from the rifle's muzzle to the president's limousine ranged from 175 to approximately 270 feet. Divided by four, the power of the telescopic gunsight, the range was effectively less than 70 feet; it was a simple shot for a practiced Marine Corps marksman—as hunter Warren realized.

That completed, Warren, Ford, Rankin, and Specter interviewed Jack Ruby, convicted of Oswald's murder, in the basement of the Dallas city jail. Ruby had consented to talk to Warren, on condition he be given a lie detector examination. The test, he believed, would prove he was not involved in a conspiracy.*

Warren only reluctantly agreed to the polygraph test. He had no faith in unreliable gadgetry he dismissed as "Big Brother paraphernalia."

The jailhouse meeting with Ruby was disjointed, Ruby at one point demanding that someone Jewish be in the room with him. According to Earl Junior his father "felt that he and Ruby got along well together, that Ruby talked to him honestly, as best he could under his mental condition. But he felt that Ruby's mental condition was very fragile . . ."

Warren came away convinced that Ruby had not known Oswald before shooting him, that Ruby had acted alone, and that his decision to kill Oswald was made on the spur of the moment.

"But the fellow was clearly delusional when I talked to him," the chief justice commented. "He took me aside and he said, 'Hear those voices? Hear those voices?' He thought they were Jewish children and Jewish women who were being put to death in the building there." †

That afternoon, the men from Washington retraced Oswald's attempted escape route from the book depository to the Texas Theater on West Jefferson Boulevard where he was captured. By nightfall, they were on their way home, Warren still reading witnesses' depositions.

In Washington, Warren also took the lead in questioning both widows, Jacqueline Kennedy and Marina Oswald. They would receive considerate attention from the courtly, solicitous Earl Warren.

The chief justice and Rankin took Mrs. Kennedy's statement privately on Thursday, June 4, at her Georgetown home. Seeking to protect her from any renewed horror, Warren convinced his fellow commissioners to accept her statement without further questioning.

Compassionate he was, but not fawning. When "little Mrs. Kennedy"

---

* The lie detector test was suggested to Ruby's rabbi, Hille Silverman, by David Belin. Belin was sidestepping a commission decision not to employ inconclusive polygraph examinations. "I just circumvented the Warren Commission and [became] a committee of one to do it. I didn't tell Joe Ball. I didn't tell anyone. I just did it," Belin explained in an interview on June 11, 1992. Examined on July 18, 1964, Ruby persuaded the polygraph operator that he was telling the truth when Ruby denied knowing Oswald or having any involvement in a conspiracy.

† Treated by Dallas jailers with Pepto-Bismol for an upset stomach, Jack Ruby died of metastasized cancer at Parkland Hospital on January 3, 1967.

later asked Warren for the president's bloody clothing, he declined. He suspected she wanted to destroy it, and "we couldn't be in the position of suppressing or destroying any evidence."

Members of the staff were unhappy that Mrs. Kennedy did not testify before the entire commission. Many were even more unhappy when the chief justice acceded to Attorney General Robert Kennedy's wishes to keep secret the X rays and photographs of the autopsy conducted at Bethesda Naval Hospital.

David Belin contemplated resigning in protest. If Officer Tippet's widow could not withhold evidence from the commission, why could the Kennedy family?

Warren explained that he feared souvenir hunters would turn the assassination into a ghoulish yard sale. Scavengers had offered $10,000 for the Mannlicher-Carcano, and had asked to buy Oswald's clothes and the pistol with which he killed Dallas patrolman J. D. Tippit. Others had inquired about the president's bloody shirt.

The chief justice alone reviewed the autopsy photographs taken at Bethesda, color enlargements "so horrible that I could not sleep well for nights." He did not want these exhibited in some touring Grand Guignol devoted to the assassination.*

He took responsibility for the decision—affirmed by the commission— not to make these part of the public record. Instead, the commission would rely on the testimony and sketches of the pathologists who performed the autopsy. "The public was given the best evidence available—the personal testimony of the doctors who performed the autopsy," Warren insisted.

The fifty-two autopsy photographs, the fourteen X rays, and the president's bloodstained clothes were turned over to the Department of Justice for permanent archiving; they would not be shown to anyone without the consent of the Kennedy family. "I am certain it was the proper thing to do," Warren wrote in his *Memoirs*. That would be his final word.

Marina Oswald also received special consideration from the Chief. The staff attorneys who had investigated Oswald's life and his disillusioning stay in the Soviet Union wanted to question her closely about inconsistencies in her statements to the FBI.

Instead, Warren assigned that task to Rankin, who lacked the detailed knowledge others had. "So Marina Oswald was not questioned as thoroughly as she should have been," David Belin insisted. "In part, this was because Earl Warren was a compassionate person and I believe somewhat naive when it came to Marina Oswald."

Marina Oswald, "a little spitfire" newly widowed with two small chil-

---

* More grisly still, the president's personal physician, Admiral George Burkley, took the metal box containing the brain of the late president from Bethesda. While Burkley said the family wished to have the brain interred with the body, various investigators concluded that the Kennedys feared it might somehow be displayed in a public exhibition.

dren, impressed Warren. "I was convinced she was telling the truth," he told Drew Pearson off the record.

The evening after Marina Oswald testified before the commission, Warren met briefly with reporters. In response to a question, he explained all of the evidence gathered would be turned over to the National Archives. Some of it "might not be published in your lifetime," he added in an unguarded aside.

When reporters pressed him, Warren sought to explain. "I am not referring to anything especially, but there may be some things that would involve security. These would be preserved but not made public."

Though he was referring to classified files from the FBI, the CIA, and the Department of State, Warren's bald statement provoked the first doubts about the commission's work. "I have never cussed myself so much for saying anything as I did that evening," Warren confessed to Drew Pearson. "I couldn't correct it. A denial never catches up."

The commissioners and the staff were aware of the possibility that Oswald might be the point man in an international conspiracy. On June 24, the deputy director of the Central Intelligence Agency, Richard Helms, privately informed Warren that the agency had custody of a defector who claimed to have knowledge of Oswald's activities in Russia. Yuri Nosenko, a former lieutenant colonel in the KGB, insisted that Oswald had acted without Soviet knowledge.

Nosenko, Helms continued, was not a reliable source. To base any part of the commission's report on him was to risk the credibility of the entire document.

Warren simply accepted Helms's explanation. The commission concurred. Rankin made the final decision not to interrogate Nosenko on the grounds that the commission staff lacked someone with the expertise to do what a cadre of CIA interrogators could not.

The irony was that the foreign conspiracy to kill a national leader had been formulated in the United States, by the Central Intelligence Agency, with Fidel Castro as its intended target. Prodded by Attorney General Robert Kennedy, the CIA had set in motion a number of schemes, one of which involved the use of organized crime figures, to assassinate the premier.

While the CIA volunteered nothing of this, Warren apparently got wind of the plot. Near the end of the investigation, Warren wrote a letter to Robert F. Kennedy asking if he had "any additional information relating to the assassination" of the president. The carefully drafted letter asked specifically about information bearing on a conspiracy, foreign or domestic.

Kennedy returned a guarded reply. All information *in the possession of the Department of Justice* had already been turned over to the commission. His reply thus carefully excluded the CIA and FBI, which did have information, as Kennedy knew, about plots on the life of Fidel Castro.

The attorney general in effect signed off on the commission's investiga-tion, with the assertion that he had "no suggestions to make at this time regarding any additional investigation which should be undertaken by the Commission prior to the publication of its report." *

Self-imposed deadlines came and went. In the last two weeks of August and in September, some twenty men sat down to finish the commission report—including two of Warren's law clerks from the 1963 term who stayed on for a week to help check footnotes and two incoming clerks.

Everyone wrote, law clerk John Hart Ely recalled. Rankin and two assistants edited the incoming drafts.

After nine months of work, Warren, "relentless as a taskmaster," was tired, putting in fifteen- and sixteen-hour days. "It was taking ten pints of blood a day from him," Earl Junior said. "It was tearing him up; he was so emotionally involved."

The draft report written by the staff raised additional difficulties for the Chief. Gerald Ford and Richard Russell refused to approve the document.

Warren invoked his diplomatic skills. "It would have been disastrous if we hadn't been unanimous," he explained.

"Ford wanted to go off on a tangent following a communist plot," Warren explained to Drew Pearson. Castro was responsible, Ford insisted.

Ford also objected to the report's sharp criticism of the FBI for failing to report Oswald's presence in Dallas to the Secret Service. Warren tempered that language, but enough criticism remained in the report to leave Hoover "furious about it."

At Warren's request, Hale Boggs negotiated with Richard Russell, whose personal animosity to the chief justice barred an agreeable meeting. Like Ford, Russell balked at the draft report's conclusion that Oswald was not part of a conspiracy. The Georgian threatened to write a minority report on the grounds that there were "far too many unresolved questions for him to accept that as an incontrovertible fact . . ."

For the sake of unanimity, Warren personally drafted alternative language which left open a possibility that there might have been an as-yet-undiscovered conspiracy: "The Commission has found no evidence that either Lee Harvey Oswald or Jack Ruby was part of any conspiracy, domes-tic or foreign, to assassinate President Kennedy."

With these changes to accommodate Russell and Ford, the commission

* Members of the Warren family claim that the chief justice developed covert sources of information: a small group of FBI agents, concerned about the quality of the investigation and desiring the true story be told; Edward Bennett Williams, who had represented Mafia figures; and Warren Olney, who had accumulated extensive law enforcement contacts from his days as a deputy attorney general. "As far as Warren was concerned," asserted grandson Jeffrey Warren, the family's acknowledged expert on the Kennedy Commission, "the FBI was Inspector Clouseau," a reference to a bumbling detective in a popular film series. (Interviews with Jeff Warren, March 3, 1994 and Earl Warren, Jr., July 29, 1991.)

was unanimous. "It was remarkable that the Commissioners all agreed on anything," Warren marveled later, perhaps with some pride. "Politically, we had as many opposites as the number of people would permit."

Essentially, the commission came to three conclusions:

First, Lee Harvey Oswald was a lone assassin. He had fired three shots from the sixth floor of the School Book Depository Building in Dallas, Texas, killing the president of the United States and wounding the governor of Texas.

Second, the commission found no evidence of a conspiracy to assassinate President Kennedy.

Third, the commission found no evidence that Oswald had assistance in planning or carrying out the assassination.

Beyond those basic conclusions, the commission dealt a mildly worded rebuke of both the Secret Service and the FBI. The Secret Service had not developed adequate criteria to define persons who might pose a threat to the president. Though the FBI had "considerable information" about Oswald, it "took an unduly restrictive view of its role in preventive intelligence work prior to the assassination." *

The commission delivered to President Lyndon Johnson its 888-page report on September 24, 1964, barely ten days before the beginning of the Supreme Court's October term. The immediate press reaction to the report was favorable, based in large part on the unquestioned reputations of the commissioners themselves, and on the apparent thoroughness of their investigation.

Spread over twenty-six supplemental volumes, the commission published the testimony, depositions, and statements of the 552 witnesses it had reviewed. These were supplemented with numerous photographs, sketches, maps, and illustrations.

The seventeen appendices to the report went so far as to include an analysis of Oswald's budget for the eighteen months prior to the assassination. Another took thirty pages to deal with rumors ranging from the source of the shots to the claim that the army burial party had practiced for the Kennedy funeral a week before the assassination.

The report was a best-seller. The Government Printing Office sold more than 140,000 copies of the one-volume report, and 1,500 copies of the supporting twenty-six volumes. Together, sales produced a profit of $191,400. A mass-market paperback edition sold hundreds of thousands of additional copies.

Warren, said a former law clerk who discussed with the chief justice the commission's work, believed "they had done as good a job as they could

---

* Smarting from the report's criticism of the FBI, J. Edgar Hoover in December, 1964, ordered Warren's name deleted from the FBI's "Special Correspondents List," an index of favored friends of the agency or its director.

have under the circumstances." Still, "he was frustrated by the pressure to wrap it up as fast as he could."

In a private conversation a year later, Warren conceded that the report "was probably done too quickly," but he affirmed his belief in the evidence pointing to Oswald's guilt. "There was great pressure on us to show, first, that President Johnson was not involved, and, second, that the Russians were not involved. These aspects were posed to us as the most important issues. And I do think our report conclusively proved these points."

It was a tired man who delivered the commission report to the White House on September 24. In the final weeks, the commission had met daily, for hours at a time, reviewing successive drafts, with Warren at each session.

"One can't say too much about the Chief's sacrifice," commission Assistant Counsel Howard P. Willens said. "The work was a drain on his physical well-being."

Warren's youngest son, Robert, judged it worse still. "That commission did more to age him than anything I've ever seen." (The report eventually completed, Warren and Bart Cavanaugh went off to attend two World Series games in New York with Secret Service agents in tow.)

Normally a man of great energy, this time Warren himself acknowledged the strain. "This has been a tough thing, living with this thing for ten months—along with my other work. Certainly I'm glad it is over."

If Warren thought the commission was behind him, he was wrong. The critics were just beginning.

The conspiracy-minded insisted on fixing blame, either on a communist plot somehow involving Fidel Castro, or on a rightist conspiracy funded by Texas oil millionaires. No whisper, no rumor, no coincidence was too outlandish to be woven into ever more elaborate scenarios.

Arrant speculation combined with procedural errors by the commission itself—the taking of Mrs. Kennedy's testimony in private, the refusal to release the autopsy photographs and X rays. Conjecture run amuck became conspiracy.

When Joe Ball telephoned Warren from California to ask what he might do in the face of growing skepticism, Warren coolly advised, "Nothing. We'll let history answer."

His position was simple. "The report is going to stand or fall on what's in it. We did an accurate job," he insisted.

Again, when David Belin asked the chief's advice about replying to critics, Warren advised against it. "Warren's position was the report spoke for itself," Belin explained.

Warren would reaffirm that view until his death. "I don't think there is much left to be desired from the report," he told an interviewer. "We reported every bit of evidence we took in the case. . . . We got everything we wanted. We achieved as much proof as could be achieved."

In 1966, the conspiracy theorists, still largely marginalized, received a major boost with the publication by major New York publishing houses of two books critical of commission procedures and findings.

Edward J. Epstein's moderate-in-tone *Inquest* was based in part on sketchy interviews with five commissioners and twelve staff members. Written originally as a master's thesis at Cornell University, *Inquest* faulted the commission's work.

Epstein claimed the commission was inherently a political agency, faced with "the problem of trying to have an autonomous investigation, free from political interference." What he termed a part-time staff and commissioners detached from the day-to-day work hampered the investigation. Finally, he found fault with the evidence itself, particularly an FBI observer's account of the autopsy he believed negated the official report by doctors.

The second book, by former New York state assemblyman Mark Lane, was no more or less than the author's attempt to act, after the fact, as Lee Harvey Oswald's defense attorney. A commission "gadfly" or "journalistic scavenger," Lane promoted his *Rush to Judgment* with the fervor of the true believer.

Ultimately, Lane's critics found him willing to distort the evidence, to use material out of context, even to charge a conspiracy at the highest levels of government to frame his "client" for the murder of President Kennedy.

The two books disturbed Warren, said law clerk Kenneth Ziffren, less for their contents than for what the chief justice considered the "underhandedness" of the critics themselves.

Wesley Liebeler, the junior counsel assigned to investigate Lee Harvey Oswald's background, had provided copies of commission working papers and a chronological file to Epstein. "These were of particular importance in understanding the mechanics of the Commission," Epstein acknowledged in his book.

For the Chief, this was "the ultimate act of disloyalty," said Ziffren. At their last meeting, Warren had specifically reminded staff counsel that their relationship to the commission was similar to that of attorney and client.

He blamed Liebeler for Epstein's *Inquest* and scored Epstein for exaggerating both his access and his sources. (In his book, Epstein sometimes inflated brief conversations with staff members such as Joe Ball into "interviews.")

Of Mark Lane and his *Rush to Judgment,* Warren had only contempt. He deemed Lane no more than a publicity seeker who played "fast and loose with the subject."

Under fire, with no one to speak in its defense, the commission report fell into disfavor.

As presidential press secretary George Reedy put it, Lyndon Johnson hoped to use the report "to do something that was impossible. The public can't believe a lone assassin with a mail-order rifle was capable of killing the president of the United States, no matter how easy it is, in fact, to do and how easy was the shot for Oswald. . . . The sheer banality of it makes for disbelief."

By 1967, a Gallup Poll reported that six of every ten Americans doubted Oswald was the lone gunman at Dealey Plaza that day. Seven of ten concluded that there were still important unanswered questions about the assassination, a Harris Poll revealed.

Charges of a cover-up irritated Warren. "What possible set of circumstances could get Jerry Ford and me to conspire on *anything?*" he asked in exasperation.

That the chief justice would be party to a cover-up amused or angered the men who had served on the commission staff. Staff counsel David Belin, who would eventually become the most vigorous defender of the commission's work and its report, recalled Warren's charge to them. Truth was to be their only goal.

"I took him at his word," Belin said. "I think the other people who were the lawyers on the staff also took him at his word. And I don't know of any single lawyer on the staff who at any time tried to bend the truth for any preconceived notion."

In the end, the speculation of serpentine intrigues that reached even to the White House frustrated Warren.

"I have read everything that has come to my notice in the press and I read some of the documents that have criticized the Commission very severely, but I have never found that they have discovered any evidence of any kind that we didn't discover and use in determining the case as we did."

Just three months before his death, Warren still maintained the commission had left nothing uncovered, and no witness unheard. "There were no loose ends."

Nor was there resolution.

CHAPTER 34

BARE BONES

I T WOULD BE THE MOST INFLUENTIAL OF THE 170 MAJORITY OPINIONS
he would write, more important than *Brown,* more important than
the communist cases that so angered his critics, more important than
the criminal law decisions that purportedly had loosed a crime wave upon
the nation.

Baker v. Carr, the Tennessee redistricting case of 1962, had plunged the
brethren into the political thicket. A year later, Earl Warren was to guide
them out.

Within hours of the *Baker* decision, civil rights lawyers in Atlanta had
filed suit challenging Georgia's rural-weighted representation. By the end
of the October, 1962 term, the court confronted no less than twelve appeals
and petitions for certiorari attacking apportionments by state legislatures.
Another eighteen cases trailed behind in the lower courts.

The issues were simple enough: legislatures had either refused to redistrict
or had allowed the population of some districts to bloat while others remained small.

As governor of California, Earl Warren had supported the "federal plan"
of apportioning one legislative house by population and the other by geographical boundary. That provision assured rural California perpetual control of the legislative process.

After five years on the Court, Warren had changed his mind. As early as
1958 he had hinted to the brethren that he no longer believed the federal
plan was appropriate for the states, but the brethren had rejected a petition

challenging Georgia's apportionment. In 1964, he was to make good on the implicit promise.

Two different apportionment issues confronted the justices as the October, 1963, term began: the disparate sizes of federal congressional districts within each state; and the fitness of the federal plan in state legislatures.

The federal case, from Georgia, posed no problem for the brethren. That state's ten House of Representatives districts ranged in population from 272,000 to 823,000 in 1960. Given the mandate of *Baker v. Carr* in 1962, that congressional districts be of similar population, the state legislature was compelled to redraw the boundaries.

Only John Harlan would dissent in the Georgia case, here a lone defender of Felix Frankfurter's argument that there was not a judicial remedy for every injustice.

Warren assigned the majority opinion in the congressional case to Hugo Black. Eighteen years earlier the Alabaman had strongly dissented when the Supreme Court refused to correct a malapportioned Illinois congressional delegation. Black had written that Article I of the Constitution guaranteed the right to vote and to have that vote effectively counted.

Black's opinion in the Georgia case, *Wesberry v. Sanders,* on February 17, 1964, effectively recast his 1946 dissent into the majority opinion.

The state cases were another matter entirely. To abandon the federal plan and instead apportion both houses of the state legislature on the basis of population would provoke an outcry, particularly from state legislators who discovered their once-safe seats in jeopardy.

In conference on November 22, 1963, a majority of the brethren indicated they favored applying the mandate of *Baker v. Carr* to state legislatures. Just moments before learning of John Kennedy's assassination, Warren had assigned the opinion to himself.

The justices understood that whatever they held would have a sweeping impact on American politics. In such cases, particularly if he anticipated public criticism, Warren felt it was his responsibility to speak for the court. It meant too he would assume the brunt of that criticism.

Despite chairing the concurrent Kennedy Commission investigation, Warren spent an unusual amount of time on the state cases, eventually handed down as *Reynolds v. Sims* on June 15, 1964. Even before the oral arguments, he drafted "a lengthy memorandum outlining his thoughts on the legal analysis," according to the law clerk who worked with him on the opinion.

"Then it was up to mostly me to work with him from there," Frank Beytagh explained. Beytagh wrote; Warren corrected. "He would call me at home because he had been over at the commission all day, and I might have done a paragraph or section that he was reading." Warren was driven by "the desire to right something that was wrong," said law clerk Kenneth Ziffren. "In dealing with southern politicians, he thought he knew what they were up to, and it upset him."

Through a succession of drafts, Warren was at his diplomatic best, seeking to round up more than a bare majority of the brethren. "He took all the comments of all the justices seriously and continued to talk with those who raised different questions because he thought it was important to have as many votes as he could get for what he thought was an important principle," Beytagh said.

Eventually the core of the opinion lay in three sentences drafted by Beytagh:

> *Legislators represent people, not trees or acres. Legislators are elected by voters, not farms or cities or economic interests. As long as ours is a representative form of government, and our legislatures are those instruments of government elected directly by, and directly representative of the people, the right to elect legislators in a free and unimpaired fashion is a bedrock of our political system.*

In drawing legislative districts, the states could not favor some voters more than others merely because of residence. "Diluting the weight of votes because of place of residence impairs basic constitutional rights under the Fourteenth Amendment just as much as invidious discriminations based upon factors such as race, or economic status."

The Fourteenth Amendment's Equal Protection Clause, Warren concluded, required "that the seats of both houses of a bicameral state legislature must be apportioned on a population basis."

Warren's opinion dismissed arguments that the states bore an analogous relationship to the federal government. It was often "little more than an after-the-fact rationalization offered in defense of maladjusted state apportionment arrangements."

The political subdivisions of states—counties, cities, school districts—had never been independent principalities. "The relationship of the States to the Federal Government could hardly be less analogous."

Based on his own experience in state government, Warren endorsed bicameral legislatures "to insure mature and deliberate consideration of, and prevent precipitate action on, proposed legislative measures." Though both were apportioned by population, the two houses could be distinguished by the length of terms, the number of members, and the geographical size of districts, he wrote.

One by one, what the justices called "the returns" came in. Arthur Goldberg wrote an enthusiastic note: "My congratulations on an [sic] historic opinion which will take its place with Brown 'as a revelation of the great purposes which were intended to be achieved by the Constitution as a continuing instrument of government.'"

Hugo Black too had praise for "your very fine treatment of this difficult case." William Douglas deemed it "a splendid opinion." Bill Brennan and Byron White joined.

Tom Clark and Potter Stewart concurred in striking down the six state apportionments then before the Court; they refused, however, to go along with the Chief's argument that both houses in a state legislature be apportioned on the basis of population.

Only John Harlan resisted. He had dissented in *Baker;* he would dissent here, on the ground "that these adventures of the Court in the realm of political science are beyond its constitutional powers." For practical purposes, Warren had a 6–3 majority.

As William Brennan saw it, Warren's decision in *Reynolds* stemmed from his abiding sense of fairness. "Possessed of an equal right to vote, the least of us, he thought, would be armed with an effective weapon needed to achieve a fair share of the benefits of our free society."

On June 15, 1964, Warren read his opinion holding the basic requirement of representative government was that each person's vote be weighted equally. One man, one vote. No more, no less.*

The outcry was immediate and pained. The Court with *Reynolds* had "finished its work of completely devastating one of the most basic and one of the most revered concepts of American constitutional government," the separation of powers, Missouri Democrat Richard Ichord asserted on the floor of the House.

Campaigning for the presidency, Arizona Republican Senator Barry Goldwater seized on the Supreme Court as a political issue. "I would be very, very worried about who is president the next four or eight years, thinking of only one thing—the makeup of the Supreme Court," he reminded the conservative faithful.

In speech after speech, the Republican candidate flailed the Court, scoring the school prayer ban and claiming law and order had been subverted by successive court decisions. If he was elected, square-jawed Barry Goldwater promised to "redress constitutional interpretations in favor of the public."

From the White House, Lyndon Johnson disdained the battle. "There is nothing to be gained by involving another independent branch of government in a political campaign."

Surrogates would defend the Court for Johnson. Forty-seven nationally known attorneys from both parties, including five former ABA presidents and a dozen law school deans, chastised Goldwater. "All who are devoted to our constitutional heritage, whatever their party, must share our concern at this attack upon the ultimate guardian of American liberty."

Warren recoiled from Goldwater's politics. Shortly before election day, the chief justice assured Santa Barbara publisher Tom Storke, "Nina and I

---

* Apparently the first person to use that phrase in the Supreme Court was Attorney General Robert F. Kennedy. In oral argument of another apportionment case from Georgia, *Gray v. Sanders,* on January 17, 1963, Kennedy said, "We think it is clear that the ideal is 'one man, one vote . . .'" Justice Douglas changed that to "one person, one vote" in his opinion.

have just voted, and those are two votes that Barry won't get anyway. He would be dangerous . . ."

More than 61 percent of the voters agreed. Lyndon Johnson scored a landslide victory for liberalism in November. Despite that, Goldwater's conservative attacks had transformed the Supreme Court into an enduring political issue.

For the next two years conservatives of both parties futilely sought to amend the Constitution to permit the states to employ a federal plan in redistricting. Though supported by such influential lobbies as the National Association of Manufacturers and the American Farm Bureau, the proposals had little popular support. The politicians might rail, but they had no slogan, no argument to counter the simple principle of one man, one vote.

Similarly, by *Newsweek* magazine's count, no less than 147 bills to permit school prayer rattled about Congress. Most represented grandstanding, introduced to appease constituents. Cooler members assured that nothing would come of them.

The criticism of the activist Court spread well beyond the halls of Congress. Thirty-two state legislatures, just two less than the required minimum, passed resolutions calling for a constitutional convention. Apportionment was to be just one of the agenda items.*

According to *Newsweek* magazine, critics of the Warren Court viewed it as "too doctrinaire, too eager to right what it takes to be wrong, too much concerned with grand abstractions of liberty at the expense of the orderly growth and continuity of the law."

One unidentified "scholar" groused to *Life* magazine, "All in all, the justices are acting less like judges than like members of a[nother] branch of government. Every time they see a situation where they think the President or Congress should have acted, they step right in."

The dean of Harvard Law School, Erwin Griswold, similarly expressed doubts. "The Supreme Court is as good a way as man has ever invented to resolve judicial problems—but I very much doubt that it's a good way to resolve political problems."

Throughout the debate, legislators continually reprinted in the *Congressional Record* Warren's earlier remarks endorsing the federal plan in California. Warren was unembarrassed. "I was just wrong as governor."

He had not started on the state cases with one-man-one-vote in mind, he explained to former law clerk Jesse Choper, now teaching constitutional law at Boalt Hall. "After a while I just couldn't see any other way, any other principle that would handle the situation."

---

* There were serious legal questions about the validity of the call. The resolutions varied markedly in language from state to state; did that invalidate them? Did a convention call open the entire Constitution to wholesale amendment or just the question of apportionment? Had either question reached the Supreme Court, it would have precipitated the greatest constitutional crisis in American history.

More directly, he told grandson Jeffrey Warren, "You don't give votes to rocks and trees."

Given Warren's previous stance, his longtime friend and political ally Thomas Storke asked, "Why in the hell didn't you get somebody else to write that decision? Why did you do it yourself?"

"Because I didn't want some son of a bitch to say I didn't have the guts to write it myself," Warren snapped.

Despite its impact, the Chief tended to minimize the *Reynolds* decision as "merely the application" of the principles laid down earlier in *Baker v. Carr.* That opinion, he would steadily maintain, "was the most important case that we decided in my time . . ."

Had there been a *Baker v. Carr* decision shortly after the adoption of the Fourteenth Amendment, "most of those problems that are confronting us today, particularly the racial problems, would have been solved by the political process where they should have been decided, rather than through the courts acting only under the bare bones of the Constitution."

Reynolds "ultimately had an enormous impact on the political face of the United States." In Georgia, court-ordered redistricting carved out a seat in the state Senate for Leroy Johnson, the first black in almost half a century to serve in a southern legislature. A generation later, an estimated 3,000 black men and women held elective office in the United States.

In the states of the old Confederacy, where the Democratic Party had held sway since Reconstruction, newly redrawn suburban districts began to vote Republican. Within five years of *Reynolds,* the GOP could claim the two-party system had returned to Dixie.

By 1970, William Douglas noted with satisfaction in his autobiography, thirty-six states had passed reapportionment bills substantially in keeping with *Reynolds*'s mandate. The changes would be permanent, for legislative power, once won, was not likely to be returned to trees, rocks, or cows.

Reynolds, coupled with the Voting Rights Act of 1965, had redrawn the political landscape. In Congress and state legislatures alike, long-tenured incumbents found their safe rural districts redrawn to accommodate urban and suburban growth. Many chose to announce their retirement.*

The redistricting case was just one of three rulings that made this term "one of extraordinary importance for Court and country," Anthony Lewis concluded on the eve of its last decisions.

Reynolds was politically the most important. Equally momentous was the appeal of *The New York Times* in a libel suit that most Court watchers would count among the most important of Warren Court holdings.

As a young prosecutor and later district attorney, Earl Warren had dem-

---

* The court would eventually extend the Baker and Reynolds principle to local levels with its later decision *Avery v. Midland County,* 390 U.S. 474. In that case, four county commissioners represented districts with, respectively, 67,906; 852; 414; and 828 residents.

onstrated no keen sensitivity to freedom of the press. At the instruction of Alameda's district attorney, Ezra Decoto, Warren had three times unsuccessfully prosecuted an unusual criminal libel case against the editor-publisher of a local weekly that took wild, roundhouse swipes at local politicians.

Somewhat later, when Warren himself was district attorney, he found another way to deal with libel matters. Twice he dispatched investigator Oscar Jahnsen to squelch books that allegedly defamed press lord William Randolph Hearst and his mistress, actress Marion Davies.

With Jahnsen in the van, police and firemen raided the printers, and snatched up the offending books. "We took them out and burned them, destroyed them all . . ." Jahnsen recounted in a later oral history. "There wasn't any arrest made; it wasn't done with the intent to make any arrests."

But the summary judgment invoked by the district attorney in 1930's Alameda County could not work for the chief justice of the United States three decades later when the Court took up the *Times*'s appeal of a $500,000 libel judgment awarded to L. B. Sullivan, a Montgomery, Alabama, city commissioner.

The judgment flowed from a full-page advertisement placed in the newspaper on March 29, 1960, by a committee of New York religious leaders and entertainers. The ad sought to raise a legal defense fund for embattled civil rights leader Martin Luther King, Jr.

Under the banner "Heed Their Rising Voices," the ad stated:

> *In Montgomery, Alabama, after students sang "My Country, 'Tis of Thee" on the State Capitol steps, their leaders were expelled from school, and truckloads of police armed with shotguns and tear-gas ringed the Alabama State College Campus. When the entire student body protested to state authorities by refusing to re-register, their dining hall was padlocked in an attempt to starve them into submission.*

Though the advertisement mentioned no Alabama authorities by name, Sullivan sued. The ad contained factual errors.

A month later, four more public officials, including Alabama governor John Patterson, joined in the lawsuit. Patterson asked for $1 million, his three fellows $500,000 each.

A state court ruled the advertisement libelous and awarded the plaintiffs $3 million, though none of them had shown any financial loss because of the libel. When state appellate courts upheld the verdict, the *Times* appealed "this monstrous judgment" to the Supreme Court.

The justices had no doubt the cases had been brought in an effort to retaliate for press coverage of the civil rights movement. As noted by Hugo Black—no stranger to Alabama politics—the record in the case lent "support to an inference that instead of being damaged Commissioner Sullivan's political, social, and financial prestige has likely been enhanced by the *Times*'s publication."

Counsel for the *Times,* Herbert Wechsler, argued on January 6, 1964, that the newspaper had an absolute privilege under the First Amendment to print whatever it wished about the public acts of public officials. Elected or appointed officeholders could not use libel laws to suppress critical media attention, even if the coverage was factually inaccurate.

For Sullivan—and, indirectly, for the state of Alabama—M. Roland Nachman, Jr., argued that libelous material, like obscenity, lay beyond the protection of the First Amendment. Under the concept of federalism, it fell to the states to decide what was libelous and what was not.

Warren began the January 10 conference discussion of *Times v. Sullivan* with the recommendation that they reverse on narrow, factual grounds. Then he suggested they might also examine the concept of libel itself to see if the advertisement's criticisms were covered by the concept of "fair comment."

At the other end of the conference table, the senior associate justice, Hugo Black, pressed his long-held belief that "at least in the area of public affairs, the First Amendment permits any type of discussions, including false." A public official could not be libeled, in his view.

More conservative by nature, John Harlan argued the First Amendment did not prohibit libel. He urged instead they impose constitutional standards on state libel actions, including proof of actual malice.

One after the other, the brethren agreed the libel judgments could not stand. The First Amendment required convincing evidence of libel, evidence lacking here.

A few days after the conference, the chief justice wrote Bill Brennan a note requesting he take on *Times v. Sullivan.* Though Hugo Black had made the First Amendment his special cause over the years, Brennan, with his knack for conciliatory, carefully negotiated language, was the better choice here.

Brennan's first circulated draft in early February, 1954, was to stake out a broader position than the justices had taken in conference. He borrowed a concept, used in a handful of states, that a public official could not claim he had been libeled unless he could prove his critic had spoken out of malice. (Technically, "malice" meant that the critic had made the statement with the knowledge it was false or with a reckless disregard for the truth.)

Warren signed on six days after receiving the draft, the first of the brethren to do so. Through five more printed drafts he never wavered, despite quibbles among the brethren over language or sharp disagreement as to whether the case should be remanded to the Alabama courts for retrial.

The usual practice was to remand a case reversed by the high court for retrial in accordance with the new interpretation. In this case, Brennan preferred not to.

The chief justice had little regard for the will of state courts and politicians in the South. During concurrent discussions of *Reynolds,* he was rejecting suggestions they put into that opinion temporizing language that gave the states time to reapportion. He had seen how wily bureaucrats with court approval too often used Frankfurter's "all deliberate speed" as an excuse to do nothing. He wanted no more of it.

In *Times,* Warren was Brennan's bulwark. The case should not be sent back for retrial, the Chief wrote in a short note on March 3. "Otherwise, we will merely be going through a meaningless exercise. The case would be remanded, another improvisation would be devised and it would be back to us in a more difficult posture."

The Chief prevailed. One by one, the brethren signed, the last, John Harlan, on Sunday night, March 8, the day before the decision was read from the bench.

With *Times v. Sullivan,* Brennan had crafted "one of the enduring landmarks of constitutional law." The nine justices had agreed that the judgment of the Alabama court must be reversed, and the case immediately settled without remand.

The brethren had reaffirmed "a profound national commitment to the principle that debate on public issues should be uninhibited, robust, and wide-open." The Court dramatically rewrote the law of libel, and expanded the scope of the First Amendment. Short of knowingly lying, or refusing to check the facts when time permitted, the press and private citizen alike were free to speak freely about public officials.

The chief justice had grown skeptical toward state courts in the South, a skepticism reflected in his handling of both *Reynolds* and *Times v. Sullivan.* His feelings had been shaped by a succession of appeals involving what he deemed blatant racial discrimination, even in the courtroom.

"We get two or three petitions a week from prisoners, particularly from some states," Warren once said, implying the states were those of the former Confederacy. "And we do question whether he had as fair a trial as a white man would have gotten.

"There was one from North or South Carolina, where the judge said from the bench, 'An hour and one-half is enough trial for a nigger.' " In cases like that, he added, "we're going to come out with a pretty strong opinion a lot of people won't like."

If the Supreme Court tended to deal with great issues and constitutional principles, Earl Warren never forgot that people, individuals, stood behind each case appealed to the Court, and each appeal granted certiorari.

In his posthumously published *Memoirs,* Warren left unmentioned the landmark case of *New York Times v. Sullivan,* while he devoted half a page to Mary Hamilton's search for simple respect in an Alabama courtroom.

Called to testify in a local case, Miss Hamilton, a black woman, sat silently as the attorneys addressed white witnesses by honorific titles, Mr., Mrs., Miss. When the white lawyer addressed her by her first name, she insisted, "My name is *Miss* Mary Hamilton."

"Mary, answer my question," the lawyer commanded.

"Judge," she asked, "do I have to answer the question unless he addresses me properly?"

"Answer the question," the judge ordered.

When she continued to refuse, the judge summarily decided, "You are in contempt of court. I sentence you to five days in jail and fine you fifty dollars." *

She would suffer the further indignity of the jail term before appealing her fine through the courts of Alabama to the United States Supreme Court. Once there, she finally found her scant measure of respect. The chief justice wrote a terse per curiam decision summarily reversing Miss Mary Hamilton's contempt citation.

A similar concern for human dignity, albeit on a larger scale, led the brethren to affirm the constitutionality of the most sweeping piece of social legislation since the Social Security Act of 1935.

Lyndon Johnson had "shoved his stack of chips in the pot" early in 1964 to secure passage of a stalled civil rights bill. Among other things, the measure banned racial segregation in all places of public accommodation.†

Warren was frankly delighted when the president signed the Civil Rights Act on July 2, 1964. As far as he was concerned, it was long overdue.

In 1875, under the authority of the Fourteenth Amendment, Congress had adopted a public accommodations act, only to have it struck down eight years later by the Supreme Court. The void had remained unfilled since. Had the Congress acted sooner, Warren said, the Supreme Court would not have been forced into the civil rights breach so often. The failure was political, not judicial.

At the same time, the Court had helped pave the way for the bill. "I'm not sure we would have gotten civil rights legislation in the sixties without *Brown*," retired Representative James Corman said.

Heart of Atlanta Motel promptly challenged the public accommodations section of the 1964 act. Located on Courtland Street, just two blocks from the main thoroughfare of Peachtree Street, the motor inn advertised widely, soliciting tourist trade. Fifty billboards scattered along interstate highways snared those who had missed the motel's magazine advertisements. Three out of four guests in the motel's 216 rooms were from out of state.

They were all white. And Heart of Atlanta intended to continue its white-only rental policy.

---

* In his "Letter from Birmingham Jail" of the previous year, Martin Luther King, Jr., raged, ". . . when your first name becomes 'nigger' and your middle name becomes 'boy' (no matter how old you are) and your last name becomes 'John,' and when your wife and mother are never given the respected title 'Mrs.' . . . then you will understand why we find it difficult to wait."

† After he signed the bill on July 2, Johnson told aide Bill Moyers, "I think we delivered the South to the Republican Party for your lifetime and mine." In fact, he lost five southern states in the November, 1964, election, four of which had voted Democratic since 1880.

In an expedited test case, the motel challenged Title II of the Civil Rights Act, which had relied on the power granted by the Constitution "to regulate commerce with foreign nations, and among the several states . . ."

Counsel for the motel, Moreton Rolleston, Jr., presented a clutch of oral arguments on the first day of the Supreme Court's 1964 term. The motel, he argued, was entitled to select its guests under the Court's 1883 decision. Furthermore, nothing in the Constitution prohibited private acts of discrimination. Third, the commerce clause dealt with goods, not people.

"The fundamental question . . . I submit, is whether or not Congress has the power to take away the liberty of an individual to run his business as he sees fit in the selection and choice of his customers." That these customers were blacks was incidental, he argued.

For Earl Warren, *Heart of Atlanta* was no more than the case of Mary Hamilton writ large. During oral argument, Solicitor General Archibald Cox had cited testimony from a frustrated black parent before a House committee considering the original legislation.

"How far do you drive each day? Where can your family eat? Where can they use a rest room?"

Such indignities were simply not acceptable in Earl Warren's America.

The brethren made short work of Rolleston at the October 9 conference. Warren began the discussion with the assertion that the commerce clause did cover services sold to interstate travelers.

One by one, each of the brethren agreed. In hardly more than ten minutes, they had strengthened the commerce clause and scrapped the precedent of the Civil Rights Cases of 1883.

The Chief assigned the opinion to Tom Clark, Texas born and raised, a man who had seen firsthand the personal inconvenience and social embarrassment of segregated public accommodations. Clark's ruling was as plainspoken as the man himself.

". . . [T]he Act as applied here to a motel which concededly serves interstate travelers is within the power granted it by the Commerce Clause of the Constitution, as interpreted by this Court for 140 years." Clark proposed they use that 140-year-old lever to overturn another precedent just 81 years old.

In a terse note to Clark, the chief justice wrote, "I agree," then added a suggestion of his true feelings: "*Bueno.*" Both statements were emphatically underscored with a heavy wavy line.

Tom Clark would understand the high praise.

CHAPTER 35

THE ROVING COMMISSION

T HESE WERE TO BE YEARS OF ACHIEVEMENT, YEARS OF SATISFACTION for Earl and Nina Warren. Their children were well settled, and the sixteen grandchildren provided diversions and well-remembered family anecdotes when Grandma Nina and Grandfather visited.

But if there were the satisfactions of these late years, there were losses as well, painful ones for the Chief.

Shay Minton, crippled with circulatory problems, died in New Albany, Indiana, on April 9, 1965. Warren and Minton had rarely agreed on legal matters, but found baseball and politics the cement that bound a fast friendship. Minton's widow, Gertrude, wrote to thank Warren for attending the funeral, noting, "He loved you dearly and appreciated so much your telephone calls during the years he was unable to visit Washington."

Minton's was the third death of a retired justice in six months. First, Harold Burton, his back bowed taut by Parkinson's disease, yet still meticulously noting in his diary the blooming flowers, succumbed in October, 1964.

Then Felix Frankfurter, increasingly bitter as the Warren Court turned from his ideal of judicial restraint, died on February 22, 1965. While they had personally grown apart, Warren recognized Frankfurter's achievements.

In a statement released on behalf of the Court, Warren praised Frankfurter as "a great man of the law . . . a scholar, teacher, man of letters, confidant of presidents, and as a justice of the Supreme Court for almost a quarter of a century . . ." Whatever Frankfurter had thought of him, Warren could respect those with whom he disagreed.

Far more personal, far more painful, the Warrens lost a close friend with the sudden death of Adlai Stevenson.

As United States ambassador to the United Nations, Stevenson had joined the Warrens in San Francisco for the commemoration of the twentieth anniversary of the founding of the organization. Warren, Stevenson, California governor Pat Brown, and Ben Swig had spent the morning fishing the choppy waters of San Francisco Bay on Sunday, July 11, 1965. Tuesday, Stevenson flew to London; the following day, he collapsed and died on a city street.

The death of Adlai Stevenson—which left the Warrens heartsick, Nina wrote—reverberated in the Supreme Court. To fill Stevenson's vacant post, Lyndon Johnson turned to Arthur Goldberg, former union attorney and secretary of labor, now an associate justice of the Supreme Court.

On July 19, moments after the funeral of Adlai Stevenson, Goldberg informed the Chief that "there was talk of his going to the United Nations but that he was rather inclined against it."

Warren agreed with Goldberg, adding a personal note, "I would hate to see [you] leave the Court."

According to the chief justice, Goldberg "had the misfortune" to return to Washington with the president on Air Force One. During the flight, Johnson focused his considerable powers of persuasion on the justice.

Goldberg reluctantly accepted what he described as "the most compelling call to duty." In the expectation he might blunt the increasing involvement of the country in Southeast Asia—what he deemed the "wrong war, wrong place"—Goldberg agreed to accept the UN post.

Once a similarly unwilling recruit himself, the chief justice was sympathetic to "poor Arthur, bushwacked by Johnson." The president had assured Goldberg he "would play a key role in determining what we ought to do about Vietnam." As quickly as that promise was made, it was forgotten, Goldberg later acknowledged.*

To replace Goldberg on the high court, Johnson dragooned his longtime friend and adviser Abe Fortas.

One of the most powerful of Washington's insiders, this son of a Tennessee cabinetmaker had excelled at Yale Law School, then joined the faculty there. Imbued with the Yale concept of legal realism, he rejected the contrary notion taught at Harvard of the law flowing, like a science, from a handful of unchanging principles. Instead, Fortas argued that judges too often cited legal rules only as "camouflage with which to rationalize a decision grounded in private prejudice."

---

* Johnson biographer Robert Dallek suggests that the president was intent on placing his own man, Abe Fortas, on the Supreme Court. Even before Stevenson's death the president had asked Goldberg to the White House, where presidential aide Jack Valenti "mentioned something about HEW," that is, secretary of the Department of Health, Education and Welfare. Goldberg declined. See Califano, *Triumph*, p. 39; and Goldberg's interview at the LBJ Library, Part I, p. 3.

Following his former teachers, William O. Douglas and Thurman Arnold, Fortas gravitated to government service. An ardent New Dealer, he eventually spent four years as undersecretary of the interior.

In 1946, Arnold, Fortas, and Paul Porter opened a law firm, soon to be one of the more influential in the capital. Two years later, Fortas headed a combine of New Deal lawyers who managed the legal battle to preserve Lyndon Johnson's eighty-seven-vote victory in the Texas senatorial race.

From then on, Fortas was Johnson's closest adviser. And all the while, the Fortas law practice flourished.

If corporations concerned with tax and antitrust problems made up the bulk of its clients, Arnold, Fortas, and Porter also took on civil liberties cases. Fortas himself handled the Clarence Gideon case on appointment by the Supreme Court, and in an echo of past causes would represent the daughter of Max Radin in a First Amendment case.

Gregarious and social—on "sacrosanct" Sunday evenings he played violin in the 3025 N Street Strictly No Refund String Quartet—Fortas did not want to go to the high court. There he would be removed from the hurly-burly of political Washington. Further, he was not convinced he had the philosophical assurance necessary to be a judge.

His wife and law partner, tax lawyer Carol Agger, also opposed the appointment. There were such practical considerations as a huge cut in income, and the fact that their expanding law firm needed the large fees Fortas commanded.

Fortas was twice to turn down Johnson, the second time blurting out, "God almighty, Mr. President, you can't do that!"

But Johnson could, and would. He not only wheedled and cajoled his friend, he prodded others to persuade Fortas. Hugo Black reported in a handwritten note to "Dear Chief" on August 3: "Immediately after our telephone conversation a few days ago I called and talked to Abe Fortas, telling him that both of us hoped he would agree to come to the Court. He seemed much gratified, and I was glad we gave him the message."

Fortas held out until July 28 when the president announced he had appointed Fortas to the Supreme Court vacancy. Fortas too had been overwhelmed. "To the best of my knowledge and belief, I never said yes," he confessed ruefully.

While Warren was disappointed that Goldberg was leaving the Court, he welcomed the replacement, Fortas. "He's a good man," Warren assured his oldest son, James.

Fortas's appointment merely confirmed the voting alignment. If anything, Fortas was even more a judicial activist than Goldberg.

The new justice saw the Chief as "a great and powerful leader," Warren's leadership indefinable but accepted. In the Friday judicial conferences, Fortas learned, the chief justice "made no apparent effort to impress his views on his brethren. He was no more emphatic than some of them in stating his conclusions."

Warren instead led by asserting the "simple view that the imperatives of truth and justice and fairness could not, and should not be avoided," Fortas concluded.

He was indefatigable in that pursuit. On major cases, one clerk recalled, Warren would visit the brethren, seeking compromise and consensus.

"We'd sit down. We'd have a cup of coffee, and the Chief would say, 'Bill, I think it's really important that we try to get five justices on this opinion because this is an important area.'

"And they would give and take in a very friendly way. It was a very friendly court. They liked each other, so it was a very civil discussion."

Warren could be persuasive in these informal settings. Law clerk Scott Bice recalled a clerk from another office muttering over his lunch in the cafeteria, "God damn it! I saw Warren out walking the halls today. I know we are going to lose our Court. I know we are." They did.

Friendly persuasion and force of personality could produce dramatic results, Warren law clerk Tyrone Brown said. In working through the ever-increasing stack of petitions on the Miscellaneous Docket, Brown noticed a number trickling in from Raiford State Prison in Florida.

Over a period of months, Brown pieced together a coherent story of a May 27, 1965, riot at the prison, of prisoners stripped to the skin and held in a barren, windowless cell for as long as thirty-five days. Then, one by one, the filthy prisoners had been led naked, past snapping guard dogs, to an interrogation room where they numbly signed confessions to mayhem and rioting.

Those confessions served to convict them in new trials; judges tacked additional time onto the terms the prisoners were already serving.

Brown gathered the prisoners' letters and sent a covering memorandum to the Chief. Warren agreed there was an issue here.

There was also a problem. Normally, the Court did not like to interfere with internal prison discipline.

Warren and Brown drafted an argument that this was not solely a question of prison discipline. State authorities had brought the convicts back into the criminal justice system, and had used coerced confessions to convict them.

The first vote in conference produced one, Warren, for granting certiorari and eight opposed. "The Chief was livid," Brown said, so upset he would break a personal rule, and write a dissent to the denial of cert.

Warren sketched his dissent, then handed it to Brown to be filled in. With each draft, Warren told the young man, "That's not strong enough. That's not strong enough. You're trying to be too polite."

Finally Warren was pleased with the dissent. The confession, Brown wrote, was neither voluntary nor uncoerced.

For two weeks this man's home was a barren cage fitted only with a hole in one corner into which he and his cell mates could defecate. For two weeks he subsisted on a daily fare of 12 ounces of thin soup and 8 ounces of water. For two full weeks he saw not one friendly face from outside the prison, but was completely under the control and domination of his jailers. These stark facts belie any contention that the confession extracted from him within minutes after he was brought from the cell was not tainted by the 14 days he spent in such an oppressive hole.

The Chief nodded. "We'll put that in the *U.S. Reports* and let posterity decide who was right."

One by one, the brethren read the terrible facts Brown had laid out in Warren's dissent and, one by one, they switched their vote. From 1–8, the tally grew to 9–0 for summary reversals of the convictions for rioting, without oral argument.

Warren's leadership, his aggressive defense of human rights, and his judicial activism suffused the Court. First with Goldberg, then with Fortas, the Warren Court in the middle years of the 1960s was to hand down successive decisions that redefined American liberties.

The great departure came in the 1964 appeal by Estelle Griswold, executive director of the Planned Parenthood League of Connecticut; and Charles Lee Buxton, a member of the Yale Medical School faculty, and the medical director of the league's center in New Haven. In a deliberate test case, Griswold and Buxton had been amicably arrested ten days after opening a birth control clinic. They were charged with violating an 1879 state law that prohibited the use of contraceptive devices.

The case that would be known as *Griswold v. Connecticut* was the second attack on the state law in three years, and it would show just how much the Court had changed with Felix Frankfurter's departure.

In June, 1961, Frankfurter had whisked away a challenge to the state law by Dr. Buxton and three others on the grounds that their case was not "justiciable." Writing for a five-man majority in *Poe v. Ullman,* Frankfurter noted the state law had been enforced just three times in the eighty-three years since its passage, and each time the prosecution had dropped charges after the constitutionality of the law was upheld.

Frankfurter's decision was novel, unprecedented, and clever, Warren's law clerk that term, Jesse Choper, said later. "It got rid of the case."

Warren thought the state law bad, he told Choper. But he agreed with Frankfurter that *Poe* was a test case "for an abstract principle. We don't want to decide a contrived litigation."

The division on the vote followed no pattern of liberal or activist versus conservative. Warren and William Brennan joined Frankfurter, Charles Whittaker and Tom Clark to form the majority for dismissal.

Black, Douglas, Potter Stewart, and John Harlan dissented. Douglas and Harlan contributed long dissents, Douglas predictably since he had been propounding a constitutional right of privacy for two decades.

Harlan's thirty-three-page dissent was not only unexpected, but uncharacteristically vehement. The state law, Harlan wrote, breached "a most fundamental aspect of 'liberty,' the privacy of the home in its most basic sense."

The patrician justice, one of his clerks commented, "was outraged at . . . government going into places it simply shouldn't."

Three years after *Poe,* Dr. Buxton was back before the Supreme Court, convicted with Ms. Griswold for giving a married couple advice about, and selling a birth control device. No sleight-of-law device would make this disappear; all nine justices voted to grant certiorari.

By April 2, 1965, and the brethren's conference on *Griswold,* the chief justice had shifted his stance from *Poe.* The convictions of Griswold and Buxton changed everything in his mind; this was no longer a lawsuit man-qué, but a real case with real people. He favored reversing the convictions and striking down the law.

Warren was unsure of the grounds, suggesting that three or four approaches might work to overturn the law. For the moment he favored reversal on the grounds that the state law was overbroad. "This is the most confidential relationship in our society. It [the law] has to be clear-cut and it isn't."

The justices tended to agree that the state law should fall. They could not agree on the grounds.

Bill Douglas favored a First Amendment, freedom of association, argument put forward in Yale law professor Thomas Emerson's brief.* Hugo Black scoffed. "The right of a husband and wife to assemble in bed is a new right of assembly for me."

The vote in conference was 7–2 to overturn the state law, with only Black and Stewart dissenting. In recognition of Douglas's oft-stated arguments favoring a right to privacy, Warren assigned the opinion to him.

Douglas's first draft of the opinion rested on First Amendment grounds. Bill Brennan intervened, urging instead that Douglas rely on the Ninth Amendment's statement that the people retained rights not enumerated or guaranteed in the Constitution.

Five days later, Douglas delivered a greatly expanded opinion. Through six revisions, he labored to hold his majority, fashioning as he went a startling new concept of constitutional law, and an equally unprecedented right of privacy.

The guarantees of the Bill of Rights, Douglas wrote in his decision delivered on June 7, 1965, had "penumbras, formed by emanations from those guarantees." Together various guarantees combined to create zones of privacy.

Douglas summoned the First Amendment freedom of association clause,

---

* Emerson, affectionately nicknamed "Tommie the Commie" by his law school colleagues, had had long experience in the high court; he had written a pivotal-friend-of-the-court brief for the ACLU in 1948 when the court struck down segregated law schools, and he successfully appealed one of the "Red Monday" cases, Paul Sweezy's contempt conviction for refusing to testify about subversive activies before a state committee.

the Third Amendment's prohibition against the quartering of soldiers "in any house" in time of peace, Fourth and Fifth Amendment protections against illegal searches and self-incrimination, and, Brennan's contribution, the Ninth Amendment—all to create a new right.*

To secure Warren's vote, Douglas noted that the Court had often held in the past that governments might direct or even bar activities as long as they did not overreach into "protected freedoms." (A city, for example, might regulate the timing and route of a parade, but could not ban a parade outright.)

Douglas had offered something for everybody. In Warren's case it was just enough. The Chief concurred in the result.

Black, ever the constitutional literalist, and Potter Stewart were the sole dissenters. Black, who found the law "just viciously evil," judged his dissent "the most difficult I have ever had to write." Nowhere in the Constitution did he find a right of privacy.

Griswold boldly defined a new civil liberty, a new field of law, and set in motion a political and social movement. Spurred by *Griswold,* public opinion dramatically shifted, from a scant 20 percent favoring a woman's right to choose to have an abortion, to 60 percent. Out of *Griswold* would flow seven years later *Roe v. Wade,* striking down a Texas anti-abortion statute.

Well before *Roe,* the Warren Court would twice return to the question of unnecessary state intrusion into family life. The first appeal provided the chief justice the sweet taste of victory, and completion of unfinished business.

After a long courtship, Richard Loving and Mildred Jeter were married on June 2, 1958, in Washington, D.C. Five weeks after returning to their home in rural Caroline County, Virginia, they were rousted from their bed and arrested on charges of violating the state's miscegenation law. Loving was white, his wife part American Indian and part black. The law had been on the books since 1691.

To escape a jail sentence, the Lovings pleaded guilty. The trial judge sentenced the pair to a year in prison, but suspended the sentence on condition they leave the state for twenty-five years.

The Lovings moved to the District of Columbia, but were unhappy in the city. Secretly, they returned to Caroline County where, sheltered by friends and family for five years, they raised three children. Still a fugitive, Richard Loving wrote a letter to Attorney General Robert F. Kennedy, seeking his help.

Kennedy forwarded the letter to the American Civil Liberties Union, which provided counsel for the couple. They appealed unsuccessfully through the state courts, then to the Supreme Court.

Fourteen states had repealed similar miscegenation statutes since the Sec-

---

* The legendary Justice Louis D. Brandeis, dissenting in a 1928 wiretap case, argued "the right to be let alone [was] the most comprehensive of rights." No one was listening. See *Olmstead v. United States,* 277 U.S. 438.

ond World War, including Earl Warren's California. Sixteen still had miscegenation laws at the time the Lovings' attorney Philip Hirshkop stood to argue their appeal before the Supreme Court on April 10, 1967.*

Virginia's miscegenation laws, Hirshkop argued, "are slavery laws, were incepted to keep the slaves in their place, were prolonged to keep the slaves in their place, and in truth the Virginia laws still view the Negro as a slave race."

These "are the most odious laws to come before the Court. They rob the Negro race of its dignity," he charged.

R. D. McIlwaine III had the thankless task of defending the state law. The best argument he could summon was based on sociological studies demonstrating that "intermarried families are subjected to much greater pressures and problems than are those that of the intramarried . . ."

The chief justice, whose youngest daughter had been married for twelve years to a Jew, was dubious. "There are people who have the same feeling about interreligious marriages. But because that may be true, would you think that the state could prohibit people from having interreligious marriages?"

"I think that the evidence in support of the prohibition of interracial marriages is stronger," McIlwaine replied.

"How can you say that?"

"Well, we say that principally—"

"Because you believe that?"

McIlwaine, in effect, confessed he did not accept his own argument. "No, sir," he answered lamely.

There was no doubt in the courtroom that the last of the slave laws must fall. The brethren intended to right past wrongs—including their own. Twice before they had ducked the very question the Lovings brought to the Supreme Court.

In 1954, just months after the thundering decision in *Brown v. Board of Education,* the justices had declined to take up an appeal of a black woman sentenced to five years in an Alabama jail for marrying a white man. "The denial of cert," said Gerald Gunther, a Warren law clerk that term and later a constitutional scholar, "was totally prudential, totally based on a high-level political judgment."

Intermarriage remained the ultimate southern fear. As one Alabaman, leaning on the cafe's counter, bluntly put it, "How do we know, if we shove kids in schools together, our white girls won't get so used to being around nigras that after a while they won't pay no attention to color? Then pretty

---

* As attorney general, Warren was earlier obliged to render a formal opinion to a district attorney informing him that, according to United States Supreme Court rulings, as little as one-eighth "Mongolian, Negro or Malayan" defined an individual as non-white and barred by law from marrying a Caucasian. See the *San Francisco Examiner,* May 28, 1939.

soon they will be socializing together, dancing all hugged up, and the next thing they'll be at the altar."

In 1955, the issue was again thrust under their noses. This time an Asian man opposed the annulment granted to his Caucasian wife solely on the ground that their marriage violated Virginia's miscegenation law.

Naim v. Naim came at an awkward time. Still hoping the South would rally behind the school desegregation decisions, the justices were reluctant to provoke resistance by striking down miscegenation laws.

At the November 4, 1955, conference, Warren, Black, Douglas, and Reed voted to grant review. Clark, however, requested a week's delay, so that he might mull it.

When they reconvened on November 11, Frankfurter was ready with a prepared statement arguing that a ruling here would "very seriously embarrass the carrying-out of the Court's decree of last May."

He and Clark meanwhile had crafted a per curiam opinion that remanded the Naims' domestic dispute to the Virginia Supreme Court of Appeals. The remand asked the state court to consider the fact that the couple had deliberately married in North Carolina where marriages between Asians and whites were not barred.

Warren and Black disagreed. The chief justice, according to one of his clerks, "was furious. He thought that the failure to take the case was an evasion of the Court's responsibility." *

For its part, the Virginia Supreme Court of Appeals delivered a stinging rebuff. The record was adequate and state law did not provide a way to send the case back to the trial court for new findings, the court held. As far as Virginia was concerned, the Naims were divorced.

Back to Washington came Mr. Naim's appeal for a last, brief moment. Warren and Black were still short the necessary four votes. This time Frankfurter bootstrapped a terse per curiam decision rejecting the petition on the ground that the state court's refusal to act "leaves the case devoid of a properly presented federal question."

The two *Naim* rulings were uncomfortable expedients. Frankfurter acknowledged as much to his close friend Learned Hand. "We twice shunted it away and I pray we may be able to do it again, without being too brazenly evasive."

Earl Warren considered *Naim,* in the blunt words of his law clerk Gerald Gunther, "total bullshit." But for a decade that blot on the Warren Court remained unscrubbed.

---

* Black had changed his stand since his days as an Alabama politician. In 1929, he wrote a constituent deploring a marriage between a black and a white in New York, adding, "New York State should have a law prohibiting this sort of thing." He predicted with increased migration of blacks northward, "the intelligent Northern and Eastern people will, in all probability, come to realize the merit in our Southern legislation along this line." See Newman, pp. 128–29.

It was only a question of time. In December, 1964, the justices unanimously struck down a remnant of Florida's "black code" which made it a crime for an unmarried white and black to "habitually" occupy the same room at night.

The justices quickly reversed the couple's conviction as a denial of equal protection. Potter Stewart's concurring opinion went to the heart of the matter, stating, "I think it is simply not possible for a state law to be valid under our Constitution which makes the criminality of an act depend upon the race of the actor . . ." *

Ten years after ducking the once volatile issue of interracial marriage, the Lovings had raised the question again before the Court. This time, the brethren made short work of the matter; the vote to reverse was unanimous.

This was a sweet moment for the chief justice. He was wiping clean the record of his Court. He was eradicating the last vestige of legal segregation. And he was vindicating his stand ten years before in *Naim*.

Warren assigned *Loving* to himself.

As Benno Schmidt, the law clerk who was to draft the opinion, put it, the Chief believed the state law unconstitutional on two grounds: Virginia had discriminated on racial grounds, and had unreasonably interfered with the right to marry.

To make these points, Warren instructed Schmidt to include the patently racist language of the trial judge in sentencing the Lovings:

"Almighty God created the races white, black, yellow, malay, and red, and he placed them on separate continents. . . . The fact that he separated the races shows that he did not intend for the races to mix."

On the right to marry, Schmidt was to cite a 1923 case, *Meyer v. Nebraska*, which held that there were freedoms so fundamental to family life protected by the Fourteenth Amendment's due process clause that the courts could not restrict them.

The citation was "like a red flag" to Black, Schmidt recalled. Black vehemently rejected any reference to a "right" to marry—a right not specified in the Constitution, and, thus, in his opinion, not a right at all.

The Alabaman had come to the court in 1937 as the first of Franklin Roosevelt's appointees, opposed to the Nine Old Men who had used the selfsame concept of "substantive due process" to enshrine their conservative economic theories as law. Under that doctrine, the Supreme Court had created rights for corporations that struck down labor and work regulations, and successively gutted Roosevelt's New Deal legislation.

Substantive due process gave judges "a kind of roving commission" to

---

* *McLaughlin v. Florida* reversed an 1882 Supreme Court decision upholding an Alabama law that punished adultery between blacks and whites more severely than between people of the same race. The 1882 opinion reasoned that such a law was not discriminatory since it punished both white and blacks equally.

find in their attic of prejudices preferred constitutional rights. Black held if a right was not stipulated in the Constitution, it was not to be shoehorned in by the due process clause.

Due process, of course, could cut two ways. "Warren was quite sympathetic to the idea of substantive due process where it dealt with what he thought were basic human rights," Schmidt explained.

Not Hugo Black. "If Black had a view about something thirty years ago and it came up again, he'd never recant it," Schmidt said. "Warren, of course, took a broader view . . ."

Seeking a unanimous decision, Warren trimmed the offending passages, and Black then surrendered his objection.

The opinion that the chief justice read from the bench on June 12, 1967, resonated with convictions imbued in the son of Methias and Chrystal Warren seven decades earlier.

> *The freedom to marry has long been recognized as one of the vital personal rights essential to the orderly pursuit of happiness of free men.*
>
> *Marriage is one of the "basic civil rights of man," fundamental to our very existence and survival. . . . Under our Constitution, the freedom to marry, or not marry, a person of another race resides with the individual and cannot be infringed by the State.*

The chief justice would prevail again the following year in yet another instance of states arbitrarily defining the meaning of a family.

The five children of Louise Levy, all born out of wedlock, sued for damages as a result of the death of their mother after treatment by a New Orleans hospital. The suit was thrown out by a Louisiana court on the ground that, under state law, the legal definition of "child" did not include the illegitimate.

Warren had no problem with the case. "I can't see any interest that the state can have to exclude illegitimate children for the loss of their mother by a tortious act." He recommended they reverse on the ground of equal protection.

Once again the Chief prevailed. The vote was 6–3 to reverse. As Douglas wrote in a draft of the opinion, they were granting a civil liberty to a class of people responsible neither for their conception nor their birth.

The Douglas opinion handed down on May 20, 1968, was characteristically blunt:

"Why should the illegitimate child be denied rights merely because of his birth out of wedlock? He certainly is subject to all the responsibilities of a citizen. . . . How under our constitutional regime can he be denied correlative rights which other citizens enjoy?" Merely to ask the question was to expose the evil of the discrimination.

Harlan dissented, joined by Black and Stewart, basing their objection upon the majority's reliance on concepts of substantive due process, natural law, and the evolving nature of society. "These decisions can only be classed as constitutional curiosities," the dissent insisted.

The opinions were constitutional curiosities, but in one sense not intended by Harlan. In each of the "family" cases, the Court had stepped in to protect rights of the powerless because state legislatures had not.

While the states tolerated what lawyers called "invidious distinctions"—defining differences between children born in wedlock and out, or between all-white and mixed marriages—Earl Warren's Court would not condone such raw discrimination.

If the lack of any protest was any indication, the family and privacy decisions fell in line with public opinion. Not so the Court's rulings in the field of law enforcement.

CHAPTER 36

DEEP-ROOTED FEELINGS

T HE THREE YOUNG MEN, NEW TO WASHINGTON AND THEIR JOBS clerking for the chief justice of the United States, listened quietly on this midsummer day in 1965 as he explained their responsibilities.

Petitions for certiorari, bench memos, opinions, all that they understood. Their days would be long and crowded.

The Chief had one added instruction. "I think we are going to end up taking an *Escobedo* case this year." They were to be on the lookout for such appeals, he ordered. The court was once more going to consider the use of confessions in criminal cases.

Since 1936 and the first Supreme Court decision upsetting a state conviction founded on a coerced confession, the justices had repeatedly grappled with the issue. In dozens of cases since, the high court had successively applied to state prosecutions rights granted by the Fifth and Sixth Amendments.

Court rulings and increased police professionalism in more recent years had curtailed the once-common "third degree." But the psychological pressures of the police station itself still generated questionable confessions.

In Warren's first term on the Court, he was one of five members who voted to throw out a New Yorker's murder confession secured only after three days of intensive questioning, and after the suspect began complaining of a painful sinus condition.

Police produced a "doctor," in reality a state-employed psychiatrist, to "help him." With leading questions, the psychiatrist managed to elicit a confession from the exhausted prisoner.

Detectives had simply worn their subject to "trance-like submission." Such station house interrogations were unfair, Warren argued.

The confession cases continued. The Chief himself would write a 1957 opinion for the six-member majority holding that a mentally retarded man had been deprived of due process when he was subjected to intermittent interrogation over a long period by police in Alabama.

The following year, the brethren heard a similar appeal from Arkansas. An arrestee had confessed after being held incommunicado for three days, denied food, and threatened with lynching.

Two years later, Warren again wrote the majority opinion throwing out a confession obtained from a suspect by a policeman who had played on their boyhood friendship.

With unusual eloquence, the chief justice wrote for a unanimous court in that case:

> The abhorrence of society to the use of involuntary confessions does not turn alone on their inherent untrustworthiness. It also turns on the deep-rooted feeling that the police must obey the law while enforcing the law; that in the end life and liberty can be as much endangered from illegal methods used to convict those thought to be criminals as from the actual criminals themselves.

Earl Warren continued to ponder the issue of confessions. In 1961, he began to slip into a file occasional newspaper stories about police interrogations. Almost five years later, Chicago laborer Danny Escobedo gave Warren his opportunity.

Police had arrested the twenty-two-year-old Escobedo on January 19, 1960, as a suspect in the shooting death of his brother-in-law. Escobedo's attorney finally managed to spring him on a writ of habeas corpus only after his client had been interrogated for fourteen hours.

Eleven days later, police rearrested Escobedo. For three and one-half hours, he demanded repeatedly to see his attorney.

The frustrated lawyer meanwhile stood outside the interrogation room, insisting he be permitted to speak with Escobedo. The attorney even recited to unyielding police a section of the Illinois penal code that required they allow him to see his client.

Handcuffed in a standing position, agitated by lack of sleep since his first arrest, Escobedo wilted. He admitted he had offered an accomplice $500 to kill the brother-in-law who was beating his wife, Escobedo's sister.

Under Illinois law, the statement made each of the conspirators equally guilty. Escobedo was convicted of murder and sentenced to a twenty-year prison term.

Four years later, Escobedo's appeal made its way to the United States Supreme Court. Writing for a scant 5–4 majority, Arthur Goldberg wrote a narrow decision reversing Escobedo's conviction on grounds that his interrogation violated his Fifth Amendment right not to be compelled to testify against himself, and his Sixth Amendment right to counsel.

Goldberg laid out a two-part test of a confession's validity: Had police interrogated a suspect after he requested and was refused an attorney; *and,* had the officers advised the suspect of his constitutional right to remain silent?

The decision provoked an outcry from law enforcement. Los Angeles Chief of Police William H. Parker, a lawyer himself, snapped, "It will do nothing to enhance the security of America against crime." Translated into populist rhetoric, Parker's assertion became "the Court is handcuffing the police."

In practice, *Escobedo* applied to only the few arrestees who had an attorney at the time of the arrest, and asked to see him. *Escobedo* was, in effect, an appeal to the fifty states to go beyond this minimum and to devise their own rules—to practice the federalism that critics claimed the Supreme Court was taking from the states.

As an appeal, it failed. The shrill denunciation of the decision apparently froze both state courts and legislatures fearful of being seen as "soft on crime." The highest courts in just three states, California, Oregon, and Rhode Island, responded.

Confession cases continued to crowd the Supreme Court docket. As law clerk Michael Smith recalled from his briefing, "They realized they couldn't leave things the way they left it with *Escobedo,* that more needed to be said."

By November, 1965, Earl Warren's clerks had identified 170 appeals from state prisoners who raised the unanswered issues of the previous year's *Escobedo* decision: When was the arrestee to be advised of his rights? If he did not already have a lawyer, was the government obligated to provide one for him?

From the 170, they winnowed twenty of "the good ones"; the brethren granted certiorari to four. The lead case was from Phoenix, Arizona, an appeal by twenty-three-year-old Ernesto A. Miranda, then serving two concurrent twenty-to-thirty-year prison terms.

Police had located a 1953 Packard, stolen from a woman kidnapped and raped eleven days earlier, parked in front of Miranda's home. Because Miranda fit the description offered by the victim, Officers Carroll Cooley and Wilfred Young arrested him.

At a police station lineup, the victim immediately identified Miranda as her assailant. Interrogated, Miranda protested his innocence, then two hours later confessed.

At no time was he advised of his right to remain silent or his right to an attorney. In Miranda's case, this was pivotal.

His English was limited. He had attended school only through the eighth grade. Beginning at an early age, he suffered from what a psychiatrist described as a sociopathic personality disorder stemming from rampant sexual fantasies. He had a prior arrest for rape, a half dozen arrests as a Peeping

Tom, military courts-martial for peeping and for being absent without leave, a dishonorable discharge and a "bizarre" marital relationship.

There had been no coercion in Interrogation Room Number 2, his attorney conceded at the oral argument. But Miranda "was called upon to surrender a right that he didn't fully realize and appreciate that he had."

In cases like this, continued attorney John Flynn, the Constitution "certainly does protect the rich, the educated, and the strong—those rich enough to hire counsel, those who are educated enough to know what their rights are, and those who are strong enough to withstand police interrogation and assert those rights."

Ernesto Miranda was poor, uneducated, and unprotected at the time of his arrest. In addition, Arizona Assistant Attorney General Gary Nelson conceded, Miranda had only a limited mental capacity. If anyone needed his constitutional rights protected, it was Ernesto Miranda.*

At the March 4, 1966, conference, the chief justice began the discussion of the confession cases proposing a major reform in criminal procedure. At the moment that police focused on a particular suspect, he suggested, law enforcement officials were obligated to issue a four-part warning.

The suspect had a right to remain silent. Anything he said could be used against him.

He had a right to an attorney. If he did not have an attorney, the court would appoint one.

Warren dismissed arguments that such warnings would hamper police. Most states already required arrestees be brought "promptly" before magistrates so the suspects might be informed of those very rights. Few states enforced those statutes, however, as the Supreme Court had for federal courts in the 1957 *Mallory* decision.

There was ample evidence that warning suspects would not free the obviously guilty or send crime rates soaring. As district attorney of Alameda County, Warren told the brethren, he had ordered his deputies to warn suspects of their right against self-incrimination. Federal police, including those in the District of Columbia, had long given that warning. The FBI used it routinely.

That assertion, one of the brethren told Warren Court historian Bernard Schwartz, was telling. "I believe that was a tremendously important factor, perhaps the critical factor in the *Miranda* vote."

The brethren divided 5–4. Black, Douglas, Brennan, and newly seated Abe Fortas joined the chief justice. Harlan, Stewart, White, and Clark voted against. Surely aware of the incendiary nature of the confession case, Warren assigned the opinion to himself.

---

* Ironically, prosecutors did not need the confession at all. Given Miranda's possession of the victim's automobile, and her firm identification of Miranda as her assailant, prosecutors had enough to secure a conviction. Police in Arizona and elsewhere routinely sought confessions since they tended to assure that defendants would plead guilty without demanding costly jury trials.

He was to take special pains with *Miranda* over the next ten weeks. First he drafted a six-page outline of the opinion to guide the three clerks. Then he edited and reedited their drafts of various sections.

On May 9, Warren sent a copy to Brennan asking for his comments. Brennan replied two days later with a detailed memorandum. "I feel guilty about the extent of the suggestions," he wrote, "but this will be one of the most important opinions of our time and I know that you will want the fullest expression of my views."

Brennan recommended a number of changes, particularly one that shifted the focus from civil rights to civil liberties.

Warren's draft had referred to prior Supreme Court cases in which "Negro defendants were subjected to physical brutality—beatings, hanging, whipping—employed to extort confessions."

Brennan instead wondered "if it is appropriate in this context to turn police brutality into a racial problem. If anything characterizes the group this opinion concerns, it is poverty more than race."

In effect, the well-to-do, those who had an attorney, were protected by *Escobedo*. The poor, like Ernesto Miranda, were not.

Warren understood two systems of justice were at work in the United States. Noting the shoplifting arrest of actress Hedy Lamarr earlier that year, columnist Drew Pearson had sympathized, "It's a disease with which some people are afflicted."

"When poor people are afflicted with the disease, they are jailed," Warren retorted. "Richer people are given a chance to return the property."

Warren adopted Brennan's suggestion that differential treatment was more a factor of social class than of race. He dropped the passage, and thereby cast the issue in a broader light.

Brennan also recommended relaxing the stringent rules that Warren had proposed, and give the fifty state legislatures some room in which to fashion responses.

Warren, usually quick to adopt Brennan's suggestions, declined to soften the mandate. The specific warnings were necessary to protect the privilege against self-incrimination. These were the minimum.

No one on the Court—and probably few in the entire judiciary—had had his experience, as a prosecutor and as a governor, with the vagaries of police and legislatures. He sought compliance, not evasion; the states could go beyond, but adopt nothing less.

With that, as Abe Fortas said, *Miranda* "was entirely his."

The final opinion was a sixty-one-page interrogation manual that began with the sort of plain-language statement that Earl Warren favored.

[T]he prosecution may not use statements, whether exculpatory or inculpatory, stemming from custodial interrogation of the defendant unless it demonstrates the use of procedural safeguards effective to secure the privilege against self-incrimination. . . . Prior to any questioning, the person must

be warned that he has a right to remain silent, that any statement he does make may be used as evidence against him, and that he has a right to the presence of an attorney, either retained or appointed. The defendant [sic] may waive effectuation of these rights, provided the waiver is made voluntarily, knowingly, and intelligently.

As the chief justice read the majority opinion from the bench on June 13, 1966, he interpolated additional clarification plainly intended for police and public.

"One. We do not outlaw confessions, but permit their use when they are in fact voluntary.

"Two. We do not outlaw police interrogations. We do require proper warnings and full opportunity for assistance of counsel if it is desired.

"Three. We do not restrict the activities of the police in making on-the-scene investigations of crime and in interrogating the witnesses in the vicinity."

Reviewing police interrogation manuals, Warren's opinion emphasized that deceit and psychological pressure in hostile, unfamiliar police stations was the lauded norm:

It is obvious that such an interrogation environment is created for no purpose other than to subjugate the individual to the will of his examiner. This atmosphere carries its own badge of intimidation. To be sure, this is not physical intimidation, but it is equally destructive of human dignity.

If the Warren Court's prior criminal law decisions had been bold, *Miranda* was brazen, lawyer and Supreme Court reporter Fred Graham decided. "*Gideon v. Wainwright* had created a constitutional right to counsel in felony cases at a time when all but five states already provided it; *Mapp v. Ohio* had extended the exclusionary rule to illegal searches after roughly one-half of the states had adopted the same rule; *Miranda* was to impose limits on police interrogation that no state had even approached prior to the *Escobedo* decision."

The outcry from police was immediate, and predictable. Speaking for departments large and small, Henry C. Ashley, chief of the Garland, Texas, police department, grumbled, "We might as well close up shop." William C. Ransdell, the public prosecutor in Raleigh, North Carolina, scored the high court as "so detached from reality that they cannot possibly make a decision in the matter." The *California Highway Patrolman* tagged *Miranda* as one of "the judicial rules that are making the law a shield for the criminal . . ."

Conservative politicans took up the cry. Ignoring the fact that his own police department was warning arrestees of their Fifth Amendment rights, Los Angeles Mayor Sam Yorty raked *Miranda* as "another set of handcuffs on the police department."

With notes for his speech covertly provided by FBI Director J. Edgar Hoover, Senator Robert C. Byrd lashed out at the court's "decisions which hamper effective law enforcement, elevate individual rights out of perspective, and relegate the over-all rights of society to a secondary position." (Hoover was stroking both sides in the nondebate. He expressed his appreciation that Abe Fortas had worked into the *Miranda* opinion a glowing reference to the FBI's professionalism and the fact that special agents routinely advised arrestees of their rights.)

North Carolina Democrat Sam J. Ervin, who had fourteen years' experience as a judge in that state, attributed *Miranda* to an "excessive and visionary solicitude for the accused." Ervin predicted that "multitudes of guilty suspects will escape conviction and punishment and be turned loose upon society to repeat their crimes . . ." *

Almost defiantly, prosecutors began releasing prisoners arrested prior to the *Miranda* decision, but whose trials started after the decision came down. In fact, there were relatively few, but they made for sensational headlines: "Bronx Man Who Admitted Rape Set Free Under Miranda Ruling; Confessed Slayer of Wife and 5 Children Freed; Two Who Confessed Go Free in Slaying." (That they were released at all suggests how little investigation police routinely performed, and how much they preferred to sweat a confession.)

While there was nothing to prevent prosecutors from reinvestigating and retrying these cases, the public relations damage had been done. The publicity seemed to paint a picture of nine unworldly judges flinging wide the jailhouse doors in a burst of softhearted compassion.†

Those who knew Earl Warren the tough prosecutor of old were frankly surprised by *Miranda*. Oscar Jahnsen, for years an investigator in both the district attorney's and attorney general's offices, complained that the Supreme Court was "now making unreasonable demands" on police.

The confession instrumental in the Shipboard Murder Case, which more than any other cast District Attorney Warren as a political comer, would not be admissible under Chief Justice Earl Warren's *Miranda* opinion.

To get that confession, Jahnsen had squirreled away Frank Conner in the Hotel Whitecotton for a full week. They interrogated Conner for as long as five and one-half hours at a time, denied him access to his attorney, and

---

* There remained the accumulated cases the brethren had rejected for one or another reason in singling out the four they would decide by full opinion. Shortly after announcing *Miranda,* Warren recommended that fifty-three other right-to-silence or right-to-counsel appeals be remanded for new trials; that nineteen convictions be affirmed; and that twenty-nine be denied on grounds of retroactivity. No prisoners were freed.

† Ernesto Miranda himself would not benefit from the decision bearing his name. He was tried a second time, without the confession, convicted, and again sentenced from twenty to thirty years in prison. Four years after he was paroled, Miranda was stabbed to death in a Phoenix bar. In making arrests for Miranda's death, police read suspects their rights—in English and Spanish. See Irons and Guitton, p. 222.

kept him awake over one stretch for twenty-one hours before obtaining his confession and arraigning him.

Chief Justice Warren knew what District Attorney Warren's men had done in those long-ago days, former Inspector Lloyd Jester maintained. "Deliver me from a reformed drunkard!" (For his part, Warren preferred to remember "we were really clean," he told a law clerk.)

If not reformed, Warren had grown. He was no longer the tough prosecutor who had served as legislative lobbyist throughout the 1930s for the California District Attorneys Association. He was, instead, chief justice of the United States, with greater responsibilities.

Warren took special pride in the *Miranda* decision. He forwarded to Arthur Goldberg at the United Nations a copy of the opinion. Goldberg, in turn, praised the ruling. "This opinion will go down in history books as another great contribution by you to liberty under law."

Miranda capped a series of reforms in criminal procedure invoked by the Warren Court. First *Mallory,* tentatively, then *Mapp,* more assertively, had launched what would amount to a revolution in the law by putting teeth in existing statutes or constitutional mandates.

The later *Gideon* and *Escobedo* decisions had reinforced the right to an attorney as guaranteed by the Sixth Amendment. Meanwhile, the Court was steadily overturning confessions the brethren deemed extracted by physical or mental coercion; that so many of these were appeals from southern courts, and so many of the defendants powerless blacks cast them as de facto civil rights cases.

Those two lines of cases vectored with *Miranda.* The ensuing protest contributed to a public perception of a Supreme Court of the United States indifferent to the needs of police or to society's insistence upon law and order.

To those who charged the Court was moving too fast and thereby "throwing society in a turmoil," Warren mildly replied the criticism assumes "that the Court looks about for sore spots in the society and proceeds to operate upon them. That is not how we work."

The Court waited, until issues came before it. "[T]he times we are living in determine the kind of cases we hear. We reflect the burning issues of our society; we do not manufacture them."

To those who claimed the Supreme Court was responsible for the rise in crime, Warren replied, belatedly and in speeches that only generally dealt with legal questions:

"Thinking persons and especially lawyers know that this is not the fact. They know that crime is inseparably connected with factors such as poverty, degradation, sordid social conditions, and weakening of home ties, low standards of law enforcement and the lack of education."

The charge that his Court was "coddling criminals" angered Warren. Why would he do that? he asked friends rhetorically. Had not his father been murdered, the slaying unsolved these three decades?

Had not Nina suddenly awakened in the middle of a July night two years before to see the silhouette of a man on the balcony? Had they not discovered the screens slit on the doors of their first-floor apartment while other apartments at the newly renamed Sheraton Park had been burglarized? That incident and a rape in the Catholic church across the street had prompted the Warrens to move to a more secure sixth-floor apartment.

To those whom he trusted not to repeat his remarks, Warren argued, ". . . [N]one of us want to injure law enforcement in any way, but I am sure that if the police will play the game according to the rules and in the spirit of our Bill of Rights, the public will have great respect for the law, enforcement will be better, and the dignity of the police themselves will be greatly enhanced."

To police and politicians who complained about *Miranda* and its predecessors, Warren directly replied only years later, after he had retired: "It is always easier to obtain a conviction if you are permitted to use excesses that are prohibited by the Constitution, and thereby avoid the necessity of going out and convicting a man on independent evidence."

Giving an arrestee an attorney, he said in a second post-retirement interview, "is just so much a question of common humanity that nobody should want to avoid it."

With *Miranda,* Warren's past had overtaken him three times in two years. Twice he avoided embarrassment by declining to take part in cases from California, the first of which challenged a state constitutional amendment Warren had himself advocated in 1934.

By a 6–2 margin, the Supreme Court on April 28, 1965, ruled that a judge's and prosecutor's remarks about a murder defendant's failure to testify infringed on the Fifth Amendment's Self-Incrimination Clause.

Three weeks later, the Court decided the knotty question of ownership of the oil-rich California tidelands. While awarding in-shore tidelands to the state, the brethren held that Santa Monica Bay was entirely within state waters. "Admiral" Tony Cornero had been right after all.

Amid the cascade of reforms he had brought down, the chief justice stood against change in one area of criminal procedure: television coverage of criminal trials. Warren felt strongly that cameras had no place in the courtroom, so strongly, said law clerk James Gaither, that "he spent hours and hours working that one," more than any case argued during the 1964 term.

The issue arose in the appeal of Texas-sized confidence man Billie Sol Estes, convicted in a courtroom that, as *Time* magazine put it, had been turned into a broadcast studio.

Normally a case like Estes's, involving the alleged sale of nonexistent fertilizer tanks and spraying equipment, would have attracted minimal press attention. But Estes had tenuous ties to Bobby Baker, secretary to the Senate majority leader, and through him to Baker's former boss, Lyndon Johnson.

Fame-by-association spurred extensive media attention. Reporters took up three-quarters of the seats in the courtroom, while as many as thirty more stood along the walls.

Estes had objected to the bank of television cameras, the klieg lights, and the sound booth in the rear of the courtroom with its cables snaking out through the door. The trial judge rejected the motion by Estes's attorney to bar the broadcasters and news photographers after a two-day hearing that was itself televised.

Thirty years before, District Attorney Warren had taken advantage of every opportunity to appear in the press. He had enjoyed his share of celebrated cases—from the death of Bessie Ferguson, to the graft trials, to the Shipboard Murder Case—and had posed with more than a few comely witnesses during court recesses.

He had not, however, succumbed to such excesses as the trial of Bruno Hauptmann, accused of the kidnap-murder of the infant son of Charles and Anne Morrow Lindbergh. Seven hundred aggressive, competitive reporters descended on the tiny town of Flemington, New Jersey—"more correspondents, sob-sisters, sportswriters, psychiatrists, cameramen, etc., etc. . . . than represented American papers in France during the World War." They transformed the trial into a public spectacle while a feckless judge looked on helplessly.

As a member of the American Bar Association's Section on Criminal Law, District Attorney Warren had reviewed a report of a special committee that condemned the "commercialization of the administration of justice" in the Hauptmann case.

To curb such circuses in the future, the special committee had specifically recommended, among other things, that no cameras or "photographic appliances" and no "sound registering devices" be permitted in the courtroom when the trial was in progress.

Three decades later, Chief Justice Earl Warren clung to the same position. "I think this violates due process," he said when the brethren on April 2, 1965, took up Estes's appeal. "To stage a trial this way violates the decorum of the courtroom, and TV is not entitled to special treatment."

The initial vote was 5–4 to uphold Estes's conviction, and thus sustain the presence of cameras in the courtroom. Harlan, Goldberg, and Douglas joined Warren in the minority.

Disturbed, the chief justice, said clerk James Gaither, went to work. He reviewed tapes of the trial "over and over again, to see if the judge and jurors were primping for the cameras." He visited the brethren, seeking a fifth vote, then once he had convinced Tom Clark to switch, making sure the opinion was strong enough.

"Not only was he involved emotionally in the decision, he was involved emotionally in the opinion," Gaither continued. *Estes* "represented how hard it was for him to get up before a jury, and his sense of how jurors decided cases. It was quite clearly a product of his earlier career."

Warren had written a heated dissent when it appeared he would be in the minority. With little effort he might have transformed it into a majority opinion. Instead, he asked Clark to write the decision, and thus assured that Clark would hold firm for reversal.

Clark's ruling, issued on June 1, 1965, was moderate in tone. The Chief's concurrence, by contrast, was unusually impassioned.

Televised trials, he wrote, influenced the conduct of trial participants. They became vehicles for entertainment and "the commercial objectives of the television industry." Broadcasters transformed the trial participants into dramatic characters in a continuing drama.

Were the Supreme Court to sanction television coverage,

> *trials would be selected for television coverage for reasons having nothing to do with the purpose of trial. . . . [T]he most important factor would be the nature of the case. The alleged perpetrator of the sensational murder, the fallen idol, or some other person who, like petitioner, has attracted the public interest would find his trial turned into a vehicle for television.* *

The constitutional right to a public trial, Warren continued, conferred no special privilege on the press or broadcasters. A trial was "public" if there was a reasonable number of seats for members of the press and public.

A year after *Estes,* the court returned to the issue of fair trial versus free press, this time to lay out definitive rules to sanitize criminal proceedings from infection by publicity.

Osteopath Sam Sheppard had been convicted of the 1954 murder of his pregnant wife, Marilyn, at their home in the Cleveland suburb of Bay Village, Ohio. In statements to police, Sheppard claimed a "bushy-haired" intruder had killed his wife, then attacked him, and fled.

As police focused their investigation on Sheppard, newspapers editorially speculated about the evidence, trumpeted reports of "Dr. Sam's" extramarital affairs, and carped about the creeping course of justice.

The mounting frenzy climaxed on July 30, 1954, with an editorial stripped across the eight columns of the front page of *The Cleveland Press* that ordered: "Quit Stalling and Bring Him In!" The following day, Dr. Sam was arrested.

Sheppard went on trial amid a firestorm of nationwide publicity. Out-of-town reporters joined the locals to fill the courtroom and commandeer the courthouse. It was, *Time* magazine concluded, "the biggest murder story in the U.S. press since the trial of Bruno Hauptmann in 1935."

---

* The United States Supreme Court in 1981 would effectively overrule *Estes v. Texas,* permitting television coverage in the courtroom. The 1995 trial of O. J. Simpson in a Los Angeles courtroom given over to the national media offered proof enough of the public spectacle, the hucksterism, and the soap-opera entertainment aspects that Earl Warren had feared thirty years earlier.

Potential jurors read about the case against Dr. Sheppard and, once seated in the jury box, followed the day's proceedings in newspapers and on broadcasts. A helicopter with a photographer aboard tracked the jury on its visit to the murder scene. "Bombshell witnesses" promised in the press never appeared in court. Police investigators commented on the trial testimony— and not to Sheppard's favor.

Convicted, Sheppard spent ten years in state prison before the Supreme Court took up his appeal in 1966. Citing "increasingly prevalent" instances of prejudicial news coverage, Tom Clark wrote the 8–1 opinion reversing Sheppard's conviction and remanding the case for a new trial.

Due process required that Sheppard be tried before an impartial jury, Clark noted in his June 6, 1966, decision. The opinion went on to lay guidelines for trial court judges intended to insulate juries from undue publicity.

"The carnival atmosphere" could easily have been avoided had the judge better regulated press behavior in the courtroom, Clark suggested. Additionally, witnesses, police, and lawyers might be prohibited from speaking to reporters about the case—a gag rule that infuriated newsmen seeking easy stories.

If the pretrial publicity continued, Clark recommended that the judge transfer the trial to another county or even delay its start until the press clamor had quieted. Once the trial began, the judge could sequester the jury to keep prejudicial news accounts from tainting the proceedings.

Because of careful drafting, nothing in Clark's opinion reached the news media. The press was free to print whatever it obtained; the brethren sought only to limit what the press received from those connected to the case. *Sheppard* stood as a landmark in due process, not a First Amendment case.

Despite its decisions from *Mallory* to *Sheppard* according rights to the accused, the Warren Court was not insensitive to the needs of law enforcement, particularly the safety of police on the streets. Ironically, when the high court turned to that question in 1968, both Warren and his critics would claim *Terry v. Ohio* as a victory.

The issue was simple: Did a police officer have a right to stop and frisk a suspect on the street, then make an arrest for carrying any concealed weapon he found?

For ten minutes on the afternoon of October 31, 1963, Cleveland Detective Martin McFadden watched the two men slowly walk back and forth past Zucker's clothing store, eyeing the building. "They didn't look right to me," McFadden testified.

It appeared the two were casing the store, planning a stickup. When MacFadden asked their names, they mumbled answers.

McFadden grabbed the nearest man, John Terry, spun him around, and patted him down. He discovered a gun in the pocket of Terry's topcoat. Moments later he discovered another weapon in the pocket of the second man, Richard Chilton.

Terry and Chilton were each convicted of carrying a concealed weapon. They appealed, contending that McFadden had not met the legal requirement of probable cause, that is, that a crime had been committed and they could reasonably be suspects.

Until he frisked the two men, McFadden had no evidence of a crime; finding the guns gave him evidence both of the commission of a crime and the evidence of guilt.

Through the state courts, then to the United States Supreme Court, Terry's attorneys contended that the common police procedure of "stop and frisk" was an illegal search. Under *Mapp,* the guns could not be used as evidence; without the guns, there was no case.

In the midst of the December 12, 1967, oral argument, Warren indicated a concern for the safety of law enforcement officers. "Police officers are very often in a position where they might not be able to make an actual arrest, but they are in a position of danger," he reminded Terry's attorney.

It was a cue to his position when the Chief opened the *Terry* discussion at the weekly conference three days later. The issue was not whether McFadden had probable cause to arrest, he suggested, but the lower threshhold of probable cause to fear harm. If so, then McFadden had a right to protect himself with a "pat-down" search or "frisk" for weapons; if, as had McFadden, he felt a hidden gun, he could conduct a more thorough search.

From senior to junior justice, the brethren concurred. Viewing *Terry* as a major case in which the Court should speak as one, Warren assigned the opinion to himself.

It took six months to fashion that decision. The justices were concerned that whatever they wrote would be construed by police as a hunting license, particularly in minority communities where hostility to police ran high.

Any stop-and-frisk license, moreover, ran up against the Fourth Amendment. Police were required to have specific justification for any search.

With Brennan's considerable aid—he was to write the majority of the opinion—Warren would find the necessary justification not in the behavior of the suspect but in the realities of police work.

The Chief's opinion noted that fifty-five law enforcement officers were killed by gunshots in 1966 alone, then continued:

"In view of these facts, we cannot blind ourselves to the need for law enforcement officers to protect themselves and other prospective victims of violence in situations where they may lack probable cause for an arrest."

As he had in *Miranda* two years before, the Chief turned his decision into a practical police manual. He laid out specific conditions that had to be met before a patrolman was justified in patting down a suspect.

The police officer was required to identify himself, and he could search only the outer clothing, where a hidden weapon might be accessible to a suspect. With those conditions met, any weapon discovered could be introduced as evidence against the arrestee.

Warren's opinion—a Douglas change of heart led to the only dissent—

found a compromise between constitutional mandate and the needs of law enforcement in a society with ever more guns. The *Terry* ruling was practical.

And too late to defang the Court's critics.

CHAPTER 37

SQUARING THE CORNERS

L EGAL ISSUES COME TO THE COURTS IN CYCLES, OR GREAT WAVES raised by a landmark court decision, a piece of legislation, or even the very temper of the times.

So Earl Warren's Supreme Court busied itself in the later years of the 1960s, mopping up behind its own precedent-setting decisions.

On March 7, 1966, with surprising ease, the high court upheld the constitutionality of the federal Voting Rights Act of 1965. Enacted under the authority of the Fifteenth Amendment, the sweeping legislation was intended "to banish the blight of racial discrimination in voting . . ."

The legislation took life in the wake of a demonstration for voting rights in Selma, Alabama, on March 7, 1965. Mounted state troopers and a sheriff's posse had set upon 600 marchers in a fury of billy clubs, dogs, tear gas, and bullwhips. Grainy news footage of the bloody assault captured intransigent southern officials brutally suppressing a peaceful protest by citizens asking only the right to vote.

Lyndon Johnson seized on those images to ask Congress for legislation to enforce that right. Eight days later, Johnson told a joint session of Congress in a crowded House of Representatives:

"What happened in Selma is part of a far larger movement which reaches into every section and state of America. It is the effort of American Negroes to secure for themselves the full blessings of American life. Their cause must be our cause too. Because it is not just Negroes, but really it is all of us who must overcome the crippling legacy of bigotry and injustice."

Johnson paused, his arms raised high, and proclaimed the triumphant pledge of the civil rights hymn, "We shall overcome."

The hall erupted in cheers and applause. Men and women, including Earl Warren among the brethren sitting in quiet dignity, wept at that moment.

By August 8, the bill was law.

The key provision of the act permitted the attorney general of the United States to replace state officials with federal overseers if he found a pervasive pattern of discrimination in elections. South Carolina promptly challenged the act in federal court, its arguments quickly supported in a friend-of-the-court brief by Alabama, Georgia, Louisiana, Mississippi, and Virginia.

To render a decision prior to the 1966 congressional elections, the Supreme Court assumed original jurisdiction—for just the fifteenth time since 1789.

Warren's opinion, delivered on March 7, 1966, for a unanimous Court —with Hugo Black dissenting in part—took note of "nearly a century of widespread resistance to the Fifteenth Amendment." With the Court's decision, Warren wrote, "hopefully, millions of non-white Americans will now be able to participate for the first time on an equal basis in the government under which they live."

The reference to "non-whites" rather than to "blacks" was acknowledgment that voting discrimination extended to others, particularly Spanish-speaking people in the Southwest. (The Court had already struck down, 7–2, New York State's English literacy tests as applied to Puerto Ricans.)

Two weeks after sustaining the constitutionality of the Voting Rights Act, the court took up a third voting case, and ruled that poll taxes were unconstitutional.

The Warren Court had first reviewed the issue in 1965 when a petition for certiorari challenged Virginia's $1.50 poll tax. The Chief in conference had spoken strongly against the levy and for granting review, but found only Douglas and Goldberg agreed.

Six of the brethren instead preferred to let stand a 1937 Supreme Court opinion upholding the constitutionality of state poll taxes. The majority would have whisked away the appeal with a one-sentence per curiam decision.

In the face of that, Goldberg wrote a passionate dissent to the denial of certiorari. Both Warren, contrary to his usual policy, and Douglas joined. Goldberg's strongly worded dissent persuaded first Black, then Brennan and White, to reverse their positions and vote on March 8, 1965, to grant a review.

The poll tax appeal argued before the Court, the brethren took up the issue during their January 28, 1966, conference. Warren argued the poll tax demonstrably operated against the poor—whites and blacks alike. He would strike it down on equal protection grounds.

Black, speaking next, again had had a change of heart. "This is a tax and not necessarily a discrimination," he insisted. Congress might pass a law to end poll taxes, but the court could not use an equal protection argument to rule them unconstitutional.

This time Warren had the votes. Clark, Brennan, and White switched to reversal, making the vote 6–3 to strike down the poll tax.

Black was a sorely troubled man. A southern politician himself, he understood how poll taxes worked to keep the poor from voting. In his first campaign for the United States Senate in 1926, the Ku Klux Klan had paid the $1.50 poll tax for thousands of poor whites ready to vote for populist Hugo Black. Those votes had set him on the road to Washington as the junior senator from Alabama.

Now the senior associate justice, Black waffled. He drafted a concurrence, then changed his mind and shifted to a dissent. Through five tortured drafts, Black struggled with the issue.

He finally concluded on the fifth version that the Equal Protection Clause of the Fourteenth Amendment was not to be used as a conservative Court had employed the amendment's Due Process Clause during the early years of the New Deal. It was not "a blank check to alter the meaning of the Constitution as written."

A gap had opened between the Warren-led liberals and the justice who so long ago had stood at their philosophical center. When the Court overturned a clutch of sit-in convictions in February, 1966, Black's dissent denied that "mistreated [groups] have a constitutional right to use the public's streets, buildings, and property to protest whatever, wherever, whenever they want . . ."

Warren could only shake his head sadly. To first-term justice Abe Fortas, Warren explained that Black's dissent "does not represent the better part of his nature."

Black was eighty-one on February 27, 1967. Though he ignored a cataract problem to play tennis daily, he was slowing physically and was increasingly more resistant to changes he might once have encouraged.

The sit-in cases became a perennial irritant. The chief justice viewed peaceful sit-ins as symbolic speech, protests of discrimination. For Warren, they were First Amendment activities that could not be infringed by local breach of the peace or trespassing laws.

Black, on the other hand, found it difficult to bring these protests under the protection of the First Amendment. They were not specifically enumerated, and he would make no effort to spread that mantle. The protesters, he complained to his wife, "all seem to want a 'government by demonstrations and marching.'"

The question of sit-ins returned in October, 1966, to the Supreme Court with the appeal of Harriett Louise Adderley and thirty-one fellow black students from Florida A. & M. University. The young people had peacefully gathered in front of the county jail three years before to protest continuing arrests of students seeking to integrate local theaters.

Ordered to disperse, Adderley and her fellow protesters stood fast. Tallahassee police arrested them on trespass charges.

On appeal, Warren, Douglas, Brennan, and Fortas voted to grant certiorari. Those four would also dissent.

For the five-member majority, Black came down firmly on the side of public order. "The State, no less than a private owner of property, has power to preserve the property under its control for the use to which it is lawfully dedicated," he wrote. By the terms of Black's ruling, the public could be barred from public property if officials chose to do so.

The visionary liberal grew increasingly conservative. "In the history of the Supreme Court," *New York Times* Supreme Court reporter Anthony Lewis wrote on the occasion of Black's seventy-fifth birthday in 1961, "there has been no more zealous, no more single-minded advocate of individual liberty than Justice Black."

Five years later, he seemed wary of the very First Amendment freedoms he had so vigorously defended. The activists on the Court had lost their automatic fifth vote.

"Hugo changed, the man changed, right in front of us," lamented William Brennan. "It was so evident. We talked about it much, the Chief and Bill Douglas probably more than anyone else."

In the span of the 1965 and 1966 Court terms, Black was to air a variety of grievances, yet never acknowledge that he had retreated from the activism of earlier years.

Law and order had been cast aside in favor of protest, he complained. The brethren were relying on the Due Process Clause to create civil rights and liberties not mentioned in the Constitution. The court, he took to lecturing the brethren, "is not allowed to write laws. We are here to interpret only!"

Some of Black's petulance stemmed from a sense that the public gave the chief justice too much of the credit for the judicial revolution wrought by the Court. An advocate of liberal reforms since first taking his seat in 1937, the Alabaman thought himself deprived of his rightful place.

For his part, Warren was dismayed. One evening as he watched Black enter the banquet room of the Statler Hotel, Warren confided to *New York Times* reporter Anthony Lewis, "He's going to stay too long."

"What do you mean?" Lewis asked.

"You know what's happening, don't you?"

"I don't know what you're talking about, Chief."

"Oh, he is trying to break the record for the number of years anyone has served on the Court."

The implication hung there. Black was past his prime, yet holding on, in an effort to best the thirty-four years and nine months that Stephen J. Field had served from 1863 to 1897. Black's decisions in these declining years, both Warren and Brennan feared, would unfairly cloud the older man's reputation among lawyers and academics.

Black's criticism grew more pointed. In March, 1968, the justice elected to give three lectures at Columbia University in which he attacked the Court's use of the Due Process Clause to upset precedents.

His vision of the law, he told his audience, "is based on my belief that the Founders wrote into our Constitution their unending fear of granting too much power to judges. Such a fear is not so prevalent today in certain intellectual circles where the judiciary is generally held in high esteem for changes which it has made in our society which these people believe to be desirable."

In a paragraph widely inferred to be a criticism of the chief justice, Black cautioned, "Judges may also abuse power, of course, not because they are corrupt, but because of a completely honest belief that unless they do act the nation will suffer disaster. . . . Other judges, with an equally honest belief that changes are absolutely imperative, take it upon themselves to make changes which Congress alone has legislative power to make."

News reports of the Black speeches stung. When Warren asked about the lectures, Black sought to blame the press for misinterpreting his statements.

Warren would accept no excuse. "Look, Hugo, you can't unring a bell."

Despite a widening philosophical difference, the two men continued to join in those appeals Black could fit squarely within the bounds of the First Amendment.

Warren led a five-member majority including Black in June, 1965, to rule unconstitutional a federal law that made it a crime for a communist to hold office in a labor union. The Chief's majority opinion quoted Alexander Hamilton's reminder: "Nothing is more common than for a free people, in time of heat and violence, to gratify momentary passions, by letting into the government principles and precedents which afterwards prove fatal to themselves."

Such momentary passions had instigated endless anticommunist legislation from 1940 through the McCarthy years. The flotsam continued to fetch up in the years after.

In November, 1965, the Supreme Court unanimously struck down one of the remaining provisions of the Subversive Activities Control Act of 1950 requiring members of the Communist Party to register with the attorney general.

The law was flawed, Warren asserted. It compelled party members to incriminate themselves as members of a "subversive" organization despite the Fifth Amendment prohibition on self-incrimination.

Warren again found vindication in May, 1967, when the Court held 5–4 that Congress had no right to strip an American of his citizenship for voting in a foreign election. Temporarily reunited, the liberal bloc of Warren, Black, Douglas, Brennan, and Fortas voted to overturn Frankfurter's decision in the futile appeal of Clemente Perez in 1958.

Seven months after that decision in *Afroyim v. Rusk,* Warren crafted a majority in the appeal of a communist barred from working in a defense plant under authority of the Subversive Activities Control Act. Once more Black joined Warren; Douglas, Fortas and Stewart signed the majority opinion and Brennan concurred in the outcome.

For Warren, there was even greater satisfaction with the April 18, 1966, decision in favor of Tucson junior high school teachers Barbara and Vern Elfbrandt. Out of conscience and conviction, they had refused to sign a loyalty oath.

The Elfbrandts were descended from what western history books proudly referred to as "pioneer stock," homesteaders on the Snake River, a Wobbly steelworker, and Finnish immigrants to Grays Harbor, Washington. With teaching degrees in hand, the couple had moved to the Tucson, Arizona, region, where they eventually found teaching jobs.

In 1961, the state legislature adopted an "Arizona Communist Control Act" including a new loyalty oath. Barbara Elfbrandt, the first to object, found no problem in the oath to defend both federal and state constitutions. She disliked the long tail on the oath, which made it an act of perjury to belong to any "successors or subordinate organizations" of subversive groups.

Soft-spoken Barbara Elfbrandt bridled. "The law said, to me, the McCarthy Era isn't really over."

This was state control of their lives far into the future, she insisted. The Elfbrandts were active in a number of socially conscious organizations—the local NAACP, a small ban-the-bomb group, and others that sprang from their association with the Friends meetinghouse. Who could know what was a "successor organization"?

There *was* a loophole in the law, an attorney for the state helpfully pointed out to the Elfbrandts. Rather than mandating that nonsigners be fired, the new law simply said they could not be paid.

The Elfbrandts and a third nonsigner, Clyde Appleton, could continue to teach if they chose as long as they did so without pay.

They chose. For five years the Elfbrandts lived on the charity of the Friends, a small mailing list that periodically yielded a few dollars to live on, a fixed rota of dining invitations, and a landlady who deferred their $70 per month rent. Their attorney, W. Edward Morgan, took the case on a contingency basis.

For five years they scraped along while their appeal made its way to the high court on February 24, 1966. There they and Chief Justice Earl Warren found vindication.

As governor of California, Warren had vigorously opposed the imposition of a loyalty oath on University of California faculty—a disclaimer or negative oath similar to that which the Elfbrandts declined to sign. He had lost that fight.

In the post-argument conference, Warren weighed into the state law. The legislature had singled out a single class of people, state employees, for the oath, he asserted.

In addition, he deemed the law too vague. It did not require a specific intent to further the illegal aims of the successor organization. On a practical level, there was no provision for a hearing if a teacher or applicant did not sign. A nonsigner ought to have that right, he insisted.

There were simply too many defects. "They can't limit the right of association without turning square corners, procedurally and substantively," Warren maintained.

The conference vote once again was 5–4, the liberals holding against Clark, Harlan, Stewart, and White. They would wipe away this vestige of McCarthyism with Bill Douglas's opinion on April 18, 1966.

Warren and Black would again part company in three other First Amendment cases the court took up in the 1965–1966 term. In each the chief justice was responsible for the split.

Earl Warren loathed what he called smut. It gnawed at his sense of morality even as he understood intellectually that serious works of art were frequently suppressed as obscene.

His dilemma was finding a standard against which to measure the socially valuable against the simply pornographic. The brethren had no desire to scrutinize banned material on a book-by-book basis. "This Court is about the most inappropriate Supreme Board of Censors that could be found," Black snapped.

Yet lower courts were groping for guidance, and the cases continued to come up on appeal. In the wake of the precedent-setting *Roth* decision in 1957, authorities had prosecuted erratically, even quixotically. Cases often arose because of political pressure rather than any belief that a book or film was truly offensive.

Ralph Ginzburg might have avoided prosecution but for his "uncanny ability to go straight for the vulgar," as one former associate put it. Coupled with his bold marketing capabilities, that sense had brought Ginzburg considerable national publicity and the attention of post office inspectors.

Ginzburg was eventually convicted of violating federal obscenity laws by selling through the mail *Eros,* a handsome quarterly he published given over to subjects inspired by the title; a newsletter, *Liaison,* devoted to similar matter; and a purported sexual autobiography, *The Housewife's Handbook on Selective Promiscuity.* Facing a five-year prison term, Ginzburg appealed to the Supreme Court.

Ginzburg sought to reach a mass audience; Edward Mishkin did not. Mishkin appealed to a specialty market; his paperback books like *Dance of the Dominant Whip, Mistress of Leather, Cult of the Spankers,* and *Screaming Flesh* were devoted to sado-masochistic themes. Mishkin's stable of authors hewed to strict guidelines—"the sex had to be strong, it had to be rough, it had to be clearly spelled out"—and the fifty books in his catalogue boasted little literary distinction.

The Housewife's Handbook and *Screaming Flesh* were joined in the Supreme Court by a book of quite another stripe.

The almost legendary *Memoirs of a Woman of Pleasure* had considerable literary merit, both for its own sake and for its place in the history of the English novel. When a Massachusetts court judged as obscene the eighteenth-century book, more often known as *Fanny Hill,* its twentieth-century New York publisher, G. P. Putnam's Sons, appealed.

In all three cases, the chief justice had voted against granting certiorari. Once cert was granted, however, he could not avoid the uncomfortable presence of obscenity in his courtroom and in American life.

There were five votes in conference to sustain the Massachusetts court in its determination that *Fanny Hill* was utterly without redeeming merit: Warren, Clark, Harlan, Brennan, and White. The same five agreed to sustain the Ginzburg and Mishkin convictions.

Warren was particularly anxious to secure a solid majority, something more than 5–4, in the Ginzburg and Mishkin appeals. Those two had crossed some moral boundary in his mind and turned protected bookselling into unprotected pandering to prurient interest.

He had just one option if he was to change a vote. Black and Douglas, as First Amendment absolutists, were not to be moved. Potter Stewart was weary of the books and films they had to review, and appeared to favor greater freedom.

That left Fortas, who had voted to reverse the lower court findings in all three cases. In the midst of his first term on the Court, he was perhaps more malleable, more willing to accede to the chief justice's lead than more veteran men.

Fortas, a skilled and sophisticated litigator, offered to cut a deal. The junior justice feared that sustaining the Massachusetts decision in *Memoirs* would ignite a "book burning." The novel had at least some merit, "a modicum of social value," even the state court conceded. Thus it should fall under the protection of the 1957 *Roth* decision.

Fortas offered Warren a trade. He would cast his vote to affirm the Ginzburg and Mishkin convictions on pandering grounds, provided Warren changed his vote in favor of *Memoirs.*

Warren agreed, and Brennan promptly fell in with the pact. The 5–4 vote against *Fanny Hill* became 6–3 in its favor. Still in the majority, Warren, though now on the other side of the issue, assigned the three opinions to Brennan.

Brennan's decision in *Memoirs* was based in part upon a 1957 Warren dissent that argued the courts should not place books on trial. To do so, Warren had written, was to remove the personal element basic to the criminal law and create a book burning.

Obscenity should be determined not by the content of the work, Warren believed, but the use to which it was put. The individual's conduct should be judged, "not the quality of art or literature."

That dissent of ten years before offered a tidy solution to their problem. A majority of the Court agreed that the handsomely printed, well-edited

Eros, whatever they thought of the way it was advertised and promoted, was simply not obscene. They would look not to the book, but to its promotion.

First Brennan was to use the opinion in *Fanny Hill* to reaffirm the three criteria announced a decade before in *Roth.* For a work to be judged obscene,

> *three elements must coalesce: it must be established that (a) the dominant theme of the material taken as a whole appeals to a prurient interest in sex; (b) the material is patently offensive because it affronts contemporary community standards relating to the description or representation of sexual matters; and (c) the material is utterly without redeeming social value.*

Brennan's was only a plurality opinion. Black and Douglas, dedicated First Amendment absolutists, would countenance no act infringing on freedom of the press. Their votes to concur with Brennan, Warren, and Fortas, however, were enough to free *Memoirs* for sale.*

Ralph Ginzburg and Edward Mishkin were not so fortunate. Adopting Warren's suggestion that the bookseller's conduct might be the determining factor in these cases, Brennan's majority opinion, handed down on March 21, 1966, raked Ginzburg for the "leer of the sensualist" that permeated his advertising.

Ginzburg's ads had broadly hinted his publications were as bold as the law permitted. He mailed promotion pieces from two small towns in Pennsylvania, Intercourse and Blue Ball, and from Middlesex, New Jersey, just for the postal cancellation.

As Court historians Bernard Schwartz and Stephen Lesher put it, "Ginzburg stood convicted and subsequently went to jail—not because he published and distributed obscene materials (though a majority of the Court agreed that *some* of his materials were obscene), but because he committed a bad joke."

Similarly, Mishkin had catered to the desires of his special audience of bondage devotees. In doing so, he had deliberately pandered to their prurient interest, and thus he too was guilty of selling obscene matter. He too would serve time for offending the chief justice.

Black was outraged. Ginzburg, he wrote in his dissent, "is now finally and authoritatively condemned to serve five years in prison for distributing printed matter about sex which neither Ginzburg nor anyone else could possibly have known to be criminal."

* Warren was not an absolutist. He believed that in adopting the First Amendment, the members of the constitutional convention "were concerned with assuring the right of the people to speak about their government. . . . At the time of the adoption of the amendment, thirteen of the fourteen states provided for the prosecution of libel, and all of the states prohibited blasphemy and profanity by statute." Warren's statement is in the unpublished concurring opinion in *Redrup v. New York,* dated February 3, 1967, in Box 620, EWP/LC.

The *Ginzburg* opinion—which especially pleased Warren—capped a season of triumph for the chief justice. The three obscenity decisions came down as something of a belated present two days after Warren celebrated his seventy-fifth birthday.

In honor of the birthday, the National Lawyers Club unveiled a bronze figure of the chief justice. Tom Clark as master of ceremonies assured the audience this was Warren's first "bust."

Clark's jibe prompted a Warren anecdote from his years as governor of California. He recalled that when his official portrait was to be presented to the state Capitol, a reproduction appeared in the local newspaper under the cut line, "To Be Hung Today."

The birthday triggered a host of newspaper editorials in praise of Warren and his leadership on the Court. *The New York Times Magazine* described him as "the greatest Chief Justice in the nation's history." *The Washington Post* concluded that "not since the formative days of the Republic when John Marshall presided over its deliberations has the Supreme Court played so dynamic a part in American affairs as during the dozen years since Earl Warren became Chief Justice of the United States."

The St. Louis Post-Dispatch, a liberal voice in the Midwest, concluded, "More and more, Justice Warren is being hailed as one of the great Chief Justices in history, a towering figure ranking with John Marshall and Charles Evans Hughes . . ."

Across the country, *The Sacramento Bee* and *San Francisco Chronicle* agreed. The Court under Warren, wrote the *Chronicle,* had "undoubtedly done more to strengthen the rights of the individual than it ever did in all the years up to his appointment." The *Bee* marked him "the strongest and most influential Chief Justice in American history, with the possible exception of John Marshall." *

If Warren at seventy-five had any complaint, it was an unwanted eight pounds, enough to make him mad, Nina told friends, enough also to prod him to summon law clerk Ken Ziffren for walks at the end of the day. As often as three times a week in good weather, they would leave the court and walk down Constitution Avenue toward the Circuit Court Building, talking politics as Warren's new Cadillac limousine trailed behind.

In less pleasant weather Warren went swimming, though he complained of the heavy chlorine in the plunge at the University Club, and the Senate swimming pool was off limits even to the chief justice of the United States.

---

* His seventy-fifth birthday was also to inspire two biographies. Warren nominally cooperated with a California writer, John Weaver, who in the course of his research grew to become a friend of the family. He gave no aid to former New York newspaperman Leo Katcher; without Warren's approval, close friends including Harry Truman refused to speak with Katcher. Both books would be published in 1967. At that point, columnist Drew Pearson proposed he write a biography of Warren entitled *The Chief,* and began taking extensive notes of their conversations. Pearson did not go forward with the project and died two years later.

Lyndon Johnson solved that problem by inviting Warren to use the White House pool—with or without bathing suit.*

To celebrate Warren's milestone birthday, John and Virginia Daly hosted a black-tie dinner at a local country club. The guest list was to include not only the family and friends, but the brethren and their wives, Warren's clerks and former clerks.

When the Dalys suggested inviting the president, Warren demurred. "The president is a very busy man. If asked, he'd feel obliged to come, and the family shouldn't impose on him."

On the night of the party, as they were dressing for the dinner, Warren received an unexpected call from the White House. The president was on his way to pay his respects.

Short moments later, Lyndon Johnson swept in, his arms laden with gifts: a copy of Samuel Eliot Morison's *Oxford History of the American People;* a photograph of the Johnson family inscribed, "To the greatest Chief Justice of them all—with great respect and affection"; and a bottle of thirty-three-year-old King's Favorite scotch.†

The president sat chatting with the Warrens and members of the family, the men in black ties, the women in evening gowns. He stood up to leave and said, "I can see you all are going out somewhere."

For an embarrassing moment, the family turned to Papa Warren. The chief justice explained as best he could the Dalys' suggestion and why the president had not been invited.

Johnson smiled, nodded, chatted for a bit more, then walked to the door. He shook hands with Warren, offered his congratulations, then added, "And next time let your daughter and her husband pick their own guest list."

Johnson's affection and respect for the chief justice was genuine. Warren at seventy-five had achieved not only a national, but an international reputation far greater than any of his predecessors.

Overseas, particularly in developing nations, he had become an icon. *Washington Post* columnist John P. Mackenzie decided, "He has emerged as a world figure and symbol of an American commitment to equal justice to all races and income levels." (As if to underscore that reputation, in Geneva, Switzerland, the newly organized World Association of Judges later in the month named Warren its first chairman.)

The decisions of the Warren Court since *Brown v. Board of Education* in 1954 had become a pillar of foreign policy, Arthur Goldberg wrote from

---

* Warren would use the White House pool at least once with the president and Abe Fortas. Johnson's presidential calendar does not indicate whether they wore swimming suits.

† Warren wrote a note to the President on April 6, 1966, thanking him for the gifts and adding that the scotch was untouched "and will remain so until the election night of 1968, when I will drink it to your health and continued success." The note is in Box 105, EWP/LC.

the United Nations. "Whatever doubts there may be in anybody's mind about aspects of that policy, there is no doubt in anyone's mind of America's commitment to equal justice for all . . ."

Lyndon Johnson took advantage of both Warren's reputation and his sense of duty to draft the chief justice as a temporary goodwill ambassador.

So long as his participation in these overseas trips was symbolic, Warren saw no conflict with his role of chief justice. Indeed, he explained to his biographer John Weaver in 1966, "We must offer a worthy example by stressing the theme of equality abroad as well as at home."

The president designated Warren as one of four American representatives to the funeral of Winston Churchill in February, 1965; sent him to Barbados a year later at the founding of that nation's independence; and dispatched him as a goodwill ambassador on Air Force One to Bolivia, Ecuador, and Colombia in March, 1967.

No matter how well regarded Warren was overseas, there was no end of criticism at home. According to a Lou Harris poll taken later that year, just 48 percent of the public felt the Supreme Court was doing a good or excellent job.

On specific issues, three out of four approved the reapportionment decisions; almost two out of three approved desegregation of schools and of public accommodations. Meanwhile, just 35 percent favored the *Miranda* decision, barring confessions given without counsel, and 30 percent agreed with the School Prayer decision.

Congress found its own way to express displeasure with the Court.

Though a presidential commission had recommended that salaries of Supreme Court justices be raised from $35,000 to $60,000, annoyed House and Senate members refused. In what amounted to a referendum on the Court, the Congress voted to boost the $35,000 annual salary only by $4,500.

Lest their displeasure with the high court be missed, they raised salaries of judges on the lower federal courts by almost twice that sum. The justices of the Supreme Court would continue to earn a junior law partner's salary.

A month after Warren's birthday, southern Democrats and Republicans in the Senate joined to vote, 55–38, in favor of a constitutional amendment that would have reversed the one-man-one-vote rulings. The measure, introduced by minority leader Everett Dirksen of Illinois, failed for lack of a two-thirds vote. (Had it passed the House, the proposed amendment still would have needed approval by thirty-four state legislatures, an impossible task since twenty-eight had already redistricted themselves in the wake of *Reynolds v. Sims*.)

Congress was sending a message.

CHAPTER 38

SIMPLE VIRTUES

I T IS AXIOMATIC. SOONER OR LATER, THE GREAT ISSUES OF THE DAY WILL make their way to the Marble Palace atop Capitol Hill, in one form or another.

The very organization of the republic, the banking system, slavery and states' rights, civil and world war, economic justice, one after the other, were argued in the Supreme Court of the United States.

So too the conflict in Vietnam.

The first of the Vietnam era cases began in 1957 when twenty-one-year-old Daniel Seeger, a physics major at Queens College in New York, sent a polite letter to his draft board stating he intended to refuse induction if called up.

In a carefully typed, seven-page statement, Seeger based his conscientious objection upon "a purely ethical creed," derived from philosophers ranging from Aristotle to Mahatma Gandhi. With that declaration, sincere and thoughtful though he was, Seeger had run up against the 1948 Universal Military Training and Service Act.

Conscientious objection, according to the law, was to rest upon a "belief in a relation to a Supreme Being involving duties superior to those arising from any human relation." An ethical or moral imperative did not rise to that threshold.

Eventually reclassified 1-A and drafted, the young man formally refused induction in Manhattan on October 20, 1960. Two years later, the wheels of bureaucracy grinding fine, he was indicted by a federal grand jury, convicted, and sentenced to a year and a day in federal prison.

On appeal, a three-judge panel from the court of appeals reversed Seeger's conviction. Judge Irving Kaufman, who had sentenced convicted atom spies Julius and Ethel Rosenberg to death in 1950, wrote the surprisingly compassionate decision.

This time the government appealed, to the Supreme Court of the United States. The brethren voted unanimously to grant certiorari.

The oral argument was civil, with Solicitor General Archibald Cox even agreeing that Seeger was sincere in his beliefs. For his part, Seeger later described himself as "very pleased at the quality of the justices' grappling with the issues . . ."

Warren began the November 20, 1964, conference on the Seeger case arguing that belief in an organized religion was not necessary to claim conscientious objector status. The language of the draft act could be stretched to cover Seeger's obviously sincere belief "in a guiding spirit."

"I don't know how to define 'Supreme Being' and judges perhaps ought not to do so," Warren asserted.

The chief's argument to the brethren was nothing more than the lessons he had imparted to his six children a generation before. "People ought to be free to practice their religions as long as they weren't hurting other people," Earl Junior explained.

"I know he had a strong belief in a Supreme Being and he probably felt that everybody's Supreme Being is personal to that person."

The brethren agreed with Warren to duck the larger constitutional issue. Rather than striking down the conscientious objector clause on equal protection grounds—the failure to grant conscientious objector status to the ethically as well as religiously motivated—they would simply redefine the language of the statute to include men like Daniel Seeger.

(If they struck down the clause, Congress might not enact a new, more comprehensive section. That would leave the nation without *any* draft exemption for conscientious objectors—something none of the justices wanted.)

The proper test of an objector's faith, Tom Clark was to write for a unanimous court, "is whether a given belief that is sincere and meaningful occupies a place in the life of its possessor parallel to that filled by the orthodox belief in God of one who clearly qualifies for the exemption. Where such beliefs have parallel positions in the lives of their respective holders we cannot say that one is 'in relation to a Supreme Being' and the other is not."

Seeger, thereby defined as a religious man by the Supreme Court, saw himself as "the beneficiary of the American justice system in its most pristine and beautiful form, the way we *expect* it to perform . . . administered by people who were conscious of doing something important and who were at their best throughout."

Tom Clark's opinion for a unanimous court in *Seeger* came down on

March 8, 1965, the day the first 3,500 American combat troops landed at Da Nang.

One month later, 20,000 people rallied at the base of the Washington Monument to protest the bombing of North Vietnam. At the demonstration, the president of the militant Students for a Democratic Society called for massive civil disobedience to the draft.

Their protests against the war in Southeast Asia were futile. By the end of 1965, Lyndon Johnson had ordered 184,000 American ground troops to fight in South Vietnam.

Like the majority of Americans, Earl Warren supported the United States presence in South Vietnam. This was a war against communist aggression, and Lyndon Johnson—like Harry Truman, Dwight Eisenhower, and John F. Kennedy before him—was pledged to defend that embattled state.

"Papa Warren," who would later discuss the war with an inquisitive grandson Jeff Warren, "was a complete patriot. He believed in America and he believed in the cause, and he believed that right-thinking people did right things.

"He believed that if we went into war in Vietnam it was for a necessary reason and that nobody in the White House would do it for any other reason but the national interest."

Warren's trust in Johnson remained undiminished, he told columnist Drew Pearson while vacationing in Barbados early in 1966. "He's working hard on Vietnam. . . . He will find some way out."

When Pearson's wife Luvie raked presidential policy as no more than waging war in South Vietnam "till the last American is dead," Warren defended Johnson. The United States, he claimed, "could not pull out of Vietnam without national loss of face."

By the fall of 1966, Warren had become concerned about the escalating conflict, he conceded to Pearson. "The chief danger of Vietnam is that it could be engendering hate for the United States.

"I'm always worried about race war, all the colored races against us, India, Pakistan, the Arabs, Japanese. Three- to four-fifths of the world population is yellow, brown or black."

About the same time, again on a not-for-publication basis, he told magazine writer and later biographer John Weaver, "We are losing a lot of friends over the world because of the fact that we are in that war. It is very difficult for a lot of people to understand why we are there."

Still the conflict grew. As the president increased the number of American troops in Vietnam to 385,000 by the end of the year, Warren continued to defend Johnson's policies.

"I've been for the president. I feel it is my duty to support him." Furthermore, "Johnson had inherited this war."

Sometime after the beginning of 1967, Warren's certainty about presidential policy in Vietnam flagged. He conveyed a sense of doubt about the course of the war, one clerk during the 1966–1967 term observed. "It was more a sadness than a critique," Ken Ziffren added.

The Chief's support of presidential policy dimmed progressively as the war ground on and domestic opposition rose. By the spring of 1967 as many as 350,000 had gathered in New York to hear the Reverend Martin Luther King, Jr., link the escalation of the war to cutbacks in Johnson's Great Society Program. A similar number rallied in Washington to protest the war. On June 23, as many as 1,300 helmeted Los Angeles police with batons flailing scattered 15,000 peaceful demonstrators gathered in front of a hotel where Lyndon Johnson was speaking.

The president was losing control. In August, 1967, Warren declined a personal request from Johnson to visit Vietnam on a fact-finding mission. The judiciary should not become entangled in what was essentially a political issue, he told the president. Regardless of his own feelings, "the brethren would feel involved," Warren explained.

Meanwhile, cases inspired by the war or decided against the backdrop of the conflict in Vietnam continued to come to the Court.

Julian Bond, a leader among the youthful activists who had brought the civil rights movement to the South, won a seat in the Georgia House of Representatives in November, 1964. In response, seventy-five members of that body filed petitions challenging Bond's right to be seated.

Bond had two strikes against him. He was black, one of a scant handful to win elective office in the South. In addition, he had endorsed a statement by the militant Student Non-violent Coordinating Committee proclaiming "sympathy with, and support [of] the men in this country who are unwilling to respond to a military draft."

The House refused to seat him on the ground that his opposition to the war in Vietnam barred him from conscientiously taking the oath to support the state Constitution. Bond sued, claiming his First Amendment rights had been infringed upon.

A three-judge panel upheld Bond's exclusion on the ground that the state constitution left solely to the discretion of each legislative chamber the qualifications of its members. Bond filed for certiorari in the United States Supreme Court; seven of the justices—Clark and Stewart were not recorded —voted to take the case.

Once again, the chief justice led the brethren in a precedent-setting decision. When Georgia's attorney general, Arthur K. Bolton, confidently declared during the November 10, 1966, argument, "The House is the sole judge of qualifications" of its members, Warren asked if that included an unconstitutional qualification.

"Of course that's not good," Bolton conceded. With that, his case collapsed.

Warren bored in. "Would that give us jurisdiction to determine the propriety of the rejection?"

"Yes."

"Where is the dividing line?"

"Whether constitutional rights were violated."

It made no matter if the Georgia House was discriminating against Bond merely because he was black—which Warren seemingly believed—or if it was censuring him for speech that would be constitutionally protected if uttered by a non-officeholder.

When the case came up for discussion in conference the following day, Warren emphatically argued they reverse the lower court and order Bond be seated. Again the brethren were unanimous.

Warren took the opinion. They were for the first time addressing the constitutional issue of the legislature's right to determine the qualifications of its members. Best the Court speak through the chief justice.

His ten-page memorandum to law clerk Benno Schmidt, who would write the opinion, was unusually detailed. Three weeks later, the eight associate justices signed the draft.

Legislator Bond was entitled to the same protection of the First Amendment as Citizen Bond, Warren's opinion of December 5, 1966, held. "The manifest function of the First Amendment in a representative government requires that legislators be given the widest latitude to express their views on issues of policy. . . .

"Just as erroneous statements must be protected to give freedom of expression the breathing space it needs to survive, so statements criticizing public policy and the implementation of it must be similarly protected."

Having done no more than criticize public policy, Bond could not be denied his fairly won seat in the Georgia House of Representatives.*

Bond was among the first to protest the war, but as the American troop commitment in Vietnam grew, so did public opposition at home. And the number of court cases springing from demonstrations.

On the blustery morning of March 31, 1966, David Paul O'Brien and three other young men stood on the steps of the South Boston courthouse and publicly set fire to their draft registration cards.

Indicted by a federal grand jury, O'Brien was convicted of violating a section of the Selective Service Act that made it a crime to mutilate or destroy a draft card. Representing himself, O'Brien told the jury he had

---

* *Bond v. Floyd* effectively overturned a 1919 decision of the Supreme Court sustaining the conviction of Socialist Party chairman and presidential candidate Eugene Debs for attempting to disrupt enlistments during World War I. Debs's sole offense was to give a public speech in which he thundered, "The master class has always declared the war and the subject class has always fought the battles . . ." *Debs,* handed down four months after the armistice, is proof that opinions of even great jurists are shaped by their times. Oliver Wendell Holmes, himself a Civil War hero, delivered the unanimous two-page decision which brushed aside Debs's First Amendment defense. The opinion was signed by Holmes's equally illustrious colleague Louis D. Brandeis.

burned the card "so that other people would reevaluate their positions with Selective Service, with the armed forces, and reevaluate their place in the culture of today, to hopefully consider my [antiwar] position."

The federal court of appeals managed a Solomon-like decision when O'Brien appealed. It ruled as overbroad and therefore unconstitutional the section of the law prohibiting destruction of the card as a symbolic protest. At the same time, it upheld O'Brien's conviction for violating another section of the act that required registrants to carry their draft card at all times.

Both O'Brien and the government filed certiorari petitions in the Supreme Court. Led by Warren, seven justices voted to take up the cases.

At the January 24, 1968, oral arguments, O'Brien's ACLU attorney, Marvin Karpatkin, immediately claimed that burning the draft card was an act of symbolic speech. Thus it was protected by the First Amendment.

Former U.S. Army captain Earl Warren interrupted. Where was the line to be drawn if they accepted destruction of a draft card as symbolic speech? "What if a soldier in Vietnam, in a crowd, broke his weapon? Would it be 'symbolic speech'?"

Like Hugo Black in the sit-in cases before him, the chief justice had reached his limits. At the weekly conference two days later, Warren abruptly abandoned his steadfast defense of First Amendment rights to oppose O'Brien's "symbolic speech" defense.

Warren did not explain his changed position. "This was early in the Vietnam protest era," Larry Simon, a clerk that term, suggested. "He, like a lot of people at the time, thought folks in O'Brien's shoes had plenty of [other] ways they could protest under American law.

"He wants to be cautious with the military. He doesn't want to buck Congress on an issue that is very hot when there certainly is no overwhelming protest movement."

When the brethren agreed unanimously with him, the Chief took the opinion for himself.

Warren instructed Simon, who would draft the opinion, "We don't balance First Amendment rights. When you write this opinion, don't balance." The burning of a draft card was not "speech," Warren stressed.

In fact, that was precisely what they would do—balance David O'Brien's First Amendment rights.

Simon was troubled. "If you have any concept of symbolic speech at all, it is impossible to write an opinion which with intellectual integrity says that the act of burning the draft card is not 'speech.' "

For the court to define "speech" as only verbal would leave paintings and photographs, parades, a school band playing "Dixie" or "The Battle Hymn of the Republic," even the flying of the flag without First Amendment protection.

A week after the oral argument in *O'Brien,* North Vietnamese regulars and Vietcong guerrillas mounted a massive offensive during the New Year celebration. Every provincial capital in the country came under attack dur-

SIMPLE VIRTUES | **487**

ing Tet, an onslaught capped when a suicide squad of nineteen Vietcong broke into the United States Embassy grounds in downtown Saigon.

Tet handed the North Vietnamese a momentary triumph and a crucial political coup. Despite escalating casualties and repeated predictions of victory from both Saigon and Washington, the United States was no closer to an end to the fighting. A month later the American commander in Vietnam, General William Westmoreland, claimed yet another battlefield victory—and asked for 200,000 more troops. Public opinion started a glacial shift in opposition to the war.

All the while, Simon labored on the opinion, even as marines systematically leveled the Vietnamese city of Hue to clear it of attackers. He would not complete his draft until March 4.

Circulated to the brethren, the draft opinion drew only Black's signature. For weeks there was silence. Eventually, the Chief asked Simon, "Is there anything we can do to get this joined, to make it more popular?"

"Yes. We can reject it [draft card burning] on the ground that even though it is speech, it is not protected speech on some rationale."

"How long will that take?"

"I can do that in about twenty minutes."

Warren suggested they adopt a Brennan recommendation that only a compelling state interest would justify infringing on speech. Simon's revision borrowed that formula:

"We cannot accept the view that an apparently limitless variety of conduct can be labeled 'speech' whenever the person engaging in the conduct intends thereby to express an idea." Speech could be curtailed if the government regulation was unrelated to the content and "furthers an important or substantial governmental interest."

The power of Congress to raise an army was sweeping. If Congress required citizens to carry a draft card, that was well within its authority. In effect, those who burned their draft cards were destroying government property used to an overarching end.

The ruling was narrowly drawn. "The basic ability to protest the war was not affected by this decision," Simon maintained. Only Bill Douglas would dissent—and then on the novel contention that a peacetime draft was unconstitutional.

Despite his opinion in the draft card case, Warren had surprising empathy for the antiwar demonstrators, law clerk Paul Meyer recalled a quarter-century later. "He seemed to understand the protest movement. For a man of his age, my expectation would have been that Warren would be more narrow-minded than he was, more fixed in a lot of positions than he was."

When reporters asked the Chief about the wave of student demonstrations, Warren reminded them, "This is a country that was born in protest." He would not deplore the student protest "as long as it isn't violent. It's a way people have of bringing about progress." If nothing else, "it may prove effective in shaking the Establishment out of complacency and smugness."

Warren's affinity to youth, his optimistic estimate of their worth, was reflected in his continuing relationship to his clerks, past and present. The Chief remained a genial father figure; he thought of them as his boys still.

They gathered annually at the National Lawyers Club for a black-tie stag dinner on a Saturday night. After dinner, Warren answered questions frankly, and in confidence, about the Court and its work that year.

The following morning, the Warrens hosted a brunch for the clerks and their families at the Congressional Country Club. It was a reunion the former clerks rarely missed, a treasured moment when they reaffirmed enduring bonds.

Warren continued to take a paternal interest in his current clerks, and their families. To those who sought it, he offered career advice. If they were married, he asked to meet their wives and children. If not, he invariably asked after their parents.

Tyrone Brown's mother, a nurse's aide, had admired the chief justice since 1954 and *Brown v. Board of Education*. "I remember my mother saying for years before that, 'You're going to be my doctor.' After that decision, it was, 'You're going to be my lawyer.' "

The first in his family to graduate high school, young Brown eventually attended Cornell Law School and fulfilled his mother's expectation. When Warren selected him as one of his law clerks in 1967, Brown became just the second black to ever hold that position.*

In awe of Warren, Brown shyly told the Chief his mother wanted to meet him. At that, "Earl Warren was just wonderful." Mrs. Brown rode the train from New Jersey to Washington and a meeting with the chief justice of the United States.

The three gathered in the Chief's office, Warren chatting casually. After a short discussion, the Chief pointedly excused his clerk; he would call Brown when he and his mother were done visiting. A father of six and a mother of five always had much to discuss.

In contrast, the father of Scott Bice, a clerk during the following term, was "a conservative Orange County Republican" who deemed Earl Warren "way out there." He too met the Chief on a visit to Washington.

"It was the one time in my life I have seen my dad sort of sit in awe of somebody. Warren was this *huge* guy who seemed much larger than he was. He had enormous warmth and personality, and exuded a kind of magnetism."

Warren welcomed these visits. They provided a needed voice of reality, a reminder of the concerns of ordinary citizens.

When Warren learned he shared the same birthday, March 19, with clerk

---

* The first was William Coleman, Jr., a magna cum laude Harvard Law graduate who clerked for Felix Frankfurter in the 1949 term. Coleman was later to help write the NAACP briefs in *Brown v. Board of Education,* and eventually to serve in the cabinet of President Gerald Ford.

Markham Ball's firstborn son, the Chief proposed, "When he's old enough to appreciate it, I'll ask him in, and we'll have a birthday lunch together."

Ball took a job in Washington, and forgot about the invitation; the Chief didn't. Seven years later, Mrs. McHugh telephoned to say, "The Chief thinks it's time they had the birthday lunch with Larry Ball."

The Balls, with a scrubbed son in the backseat of their Volkswagen, set off for the Supreme Court. "Driving in, I had a sinking feeling," Mark Ball acknowledged. "What the heck are Larry Ball and the chief justice of the United States going to say to each other? This is going to be a social disaster."

The lunch went off splendidly, Ball said. The birthday boys, one seventy-six, the other nine, chattered on and on about baseball. "Larry distinguished himself by pointing out when the Chief got Nellie Fox and Jimmy Foxx confused. They had a delightful time."

The Chief's genuine respect for young people and their concerns, led him inevitably to reach for two cases that would extend the Bill of Rights to even the youngest Americans.

The first involved fifteen-year-old Gerald Gault, a troubled kid already on juvenile probation when a neighbor complained that young Gault and a friend had placed obscene telephone calls to her. Police picked up the two youths, without telling Gault's parents, and delivered them to the Children's Detention Home.

Probation officers at the facility interrogated young Gault, held him for a period of days without explanation, then finally filed a petition asking that a juvenile court judge declare him a delinquent. The petition stated no reasons.

At Gault's hearing, the judge "didn't feel it was necessary" for the complaining witness to appear. Gault had no attorney who might have defended him against the vague delinquency charge.

Gault was found culpable—apparently on the basis of his own statements. The judge asserted that Gault had admitted making lewd remarks; his parents and a probation officer denied he had. A transcript of the hearing would have settled the issue, but no transcript was made.

The juvenile court judge sentenced Gault to the Arizona State Industrial School "for the period of his minority," a total of six years. (Had Gerald Gault been an adult, he could have received a maximum of a $50 fine and a two-month jail term.)

Finally represented by counsel, an ACLU attorney, Gault appealed to the United States Supreme Court. The State of Arizona argued that juvenile proceedings were not criminal in nature but remedial; thus the state was not obligated to adhere to constitutional requirements as it would in an adult's criminal case.

Six justices led by Warren voted to hear young Gault's appeal. Argued on December 6, 1966, the case came up in conference three days later.

Warren was decisive. Even if a juvenile proceeding was deemed noncriminal, "the same due process must be provided." Gault was entitled to an attorney, to be informed of the charges, to confront witnesses, and to have a transcript.

Black would go further. "Whether or not he's a juvenile, he's being restrained of his liberty. Thus, he's entitled to *all* the guarantees," including the privilege against self-incrimination, a public trial, and a jury.

Abe Fortas was particularly concerned about the "never-never land" of juvenile justice, "the most appalling and dangerous part of the bankrupt estate of our national services." In anticipation of oral arguments in *Gault,* he had devoted a good part of the previous summer researching the problem.

Only Harlan and Stewart had doubts about so radically, so abruptly overhauling a system that had been in place since the Progressive era.

Aware of Fortas's keen interest in the issue, Warren assigned the Gault case to him. Fortas was to deliver on May 15, 1967, an impassioned advocate's decision announcing "under our Constitution, the condition of being a boy does not justify a kangaroo court."

Fortas followed the Chief's lead, adding only that juveniles were to be accorded the privilege against self-incrimination under *Miranda.* Warren was the first to join what he termed "your magnificent opinion," adding enthusiastically, "It will be known as the Magna Carta for juveniles."

Douglas, Clark, and Brennan subsequently joined them; Black and White concurred. Harlan and Stewart would dissent.

Once again the Warren Court had boldly extended the Constitution to the unprotected.

Less than two years later, the justices would return to the question of the rights of juveniles, this time expressly to bring them under the First Amendment.

Unlike Gerald Gault, the Tinker kids and their friend Chris Eckhardt had never been in trouble. They were, in fact, model children, serious students, and unlikely discipline problems.

Mary Beth Tinker was thirteen, an eighth grader at Warren Harding Junior High in Des Moines, Iowa. Her brother John, fifteen, was in the eleventh grade. Christopher Eckhardt was sixteen, and in the tenth grade at Roosevelt High School.

With two others, they were expelled from school on December 16 and 17, 1965, for wearing black armbands to protest the escalation of the war in Vietnam. The suspensions were to remain in effect as long as they insisted on wearing the armbands.

When their parents sought an injunction to prevent school authorities from suspending the children, a federal judge ruled against them. He held the expulsion a reasonable action to prevent a disturbance on campus.

The Tinkers and Eckhardt appealed to the Supreme Court, their attorney arguing his young clients had not been disruptive, had declaimed no speeches, had staged no demonstration. The vote to grant certiorari was a narrow 5–4.

Warren began the conference on November 15, 1968, urging that they reverse the expulsion—a moral victory, no more—on the narrow ground of equal protection. School officials had permitted students to wear other political symbols, campaign buttons, even a Nazi Iron Cross, he pointed out.

With the exception of Black and John Harlan, the brethren agreed with Warren's reasoning. Then Byron White suggested a broader ruling.

"If the authorities are empowered to maintain order, they must be able to classify what disrupts communication among students." The school district had made no such effort.

White's strategy appealed to the Chief. "I could go with Byron."

Warren once more turned to Fortas to write the 7–2 majority opinion. On February 24, 1969, with Mary Beth now a senior in high school, Fortas sternly cautioned that students did not "shed their constitutional rights to freedom of speech or expression at the schoolhouse gate."

Students were "persons" under the Constitution, "possessed of fundamental rights which the State must respect. . . . In the absence of a specific showing of constitutionally valid reasons to regulate their speech, students are entitled to freedom of expression of their views."

For all the ease of *Tinker,* symbolic speech cases continued to trouble Warren when the symbol held up to contempt was one he held dear. Two months after *Tinker,* Warren reversed himself in the last of the symbolic speech cases of the 1968–69 term.

The appeal came from Sidney Street, a New York City resident who had burned an American flag when he learned that James Meredith, the first black to enroll at the University of Mississippi, had been shot from ambush on June 5, 1966.

The first wire service stories reported that Meredith had been killed, prompting Street to set fire to one of his American flags on the sidewalk in front of his home. As a small crowd gathered around the burning flag, a policeman heard Street yell, "If they did that to Meredith, we don't need an American flag!"

The policeman arrested Street for violating a state law that made it a misdemeanor to "mutilate, deface, defile, defy, trample upon, or cast contempt upon an American flag" either by word or deed.

Street was convicted, and given a suspended sentence. His appeals to state courts on First Amendment grounds to no avail, he turned to the United States Supreme Court.

Argued on October 21, 1968, *Street* came up in conference four days later. Warren opened the discussion with an effort to strip constitutional protection from flag-burning.

"The only question is whether New York can punish public burning of the flag. I think the state can do so to prevent riots and the like. It's conduct and not speech or symbolic speech."

Warren was in the minority. The vote was 6–3, with Warren, Black, and Byron White dissenting.

At lunch with his clerks the following day, one of them asked, "What's the theory of your dissent?"

There was a long pause before Warren replied. "Boys, it's the American flag. I'm just not going to vote in favor of burning the American flag."

Paul Meyer sat at the table thinking of his drive from his home in Chicago to Washington a few months earlier. As he drove through the Virginia countryside, he saw the faded billboards urging, "Impeach Earl Warren, the Communist."

He could only shake his head in wonderment. "Here is a man who is viewed as not only a liberal, but somebody who has sold out to the evil forces within the country. And yet, when his fundamental sense of patriotism was impacted . . . his commitment to flag and country rose above everything."

Warren had no legal theory to sustain his opinion; that he would leave to the clerks. He was voting instinctively, not intellectually.

Shortly after the April, 1969, opinions were announced, former law clerk Markham Ball spoke with the Chief about the case. Ball argued that flag-burning was symbolic speech, merely a form of expression, and well within the protection of the First Amendment.

"And the Chief's view on that was that was simply a wrong thing to do. Some things you just don't do. Burning the flag was one of them. Actually, saying certain words in the presence of women was another thing you just didn't do.

"Those are virtues," Ball continued, "values from the heart, from the core of the man."

Earl Warren had begun his Supreme Court career sixteen years before trusting common sense and personal values to find his way to justice. Sixteen years later, he was ending it in the same way.

CHAPTER 39

NEMESIS

THIS WOULD BE THE YEAR OF THE PLAGUE—"A CONTINUOUS nightmare" for Lyndon Johnson, for the Democratic Party, and, eventually, for Earl Warren, chief justice of the United States. The Tet offensive at the end of January, 1968, resulted in a battlefield defeat for communist North Vietnam, but generated a propaganda coup tantamount to political triumph in the United States.

A restive American public, seeing promised victory no closer, began to question the course of the war. The president's popularity ratings tumbled in this election year until hardly one in four favorably viewed his handling of the war.

Opponents of the conflict, particularly the young, rallied to the "Children's Crusade" of Minnesota senator Eugene McCarthy. They buoyed that avowed antiwar candidate to near victory over the president in the New Hampshire primary. Then, when President Johnson refused to reconsider his Vietnam policy, charismatic New York senator Robert F. Kennedy announced he too would run for the Democratic nomination.

Beleaguered Lyndon Johnson, facing further embarrassment in upcoming primaries, abruptly withdrew as a candidate for renomination. With that, the president of the United States became a lame duck, politically helpless before his enemies.

The *annus horribilis* ground on. On April 4, an assassin's rifle brought down the one nationally recognized black leader, Martin Luther King, Jr. In a volatile mixture of sorrow and rage, America's black ghettos exploded;

rioters in the next week torched more than 100 neighborhoods across the nation.

The mutual trust and political alliance achieved in the years since *Brown v. Board of Education* went up in the flames of a hundred ghettos. White, middle-class America lashed out from a frustration as great as black America harbored. Despite civil rights advances, and all the efforts to bring economic prosperity to blacks, it appeared they were tearing down everything that had been built.

The nation seemed wracked by civil insurrections. Authorities in the long, hot summer suppressed racially fueled riots in black communities across the country. Students, homosexuals, environmental activists, and war protesters spilled into the streets.

The sense of lawlessness was overpowering as the presidential primaries accelerated in 1968. Despite a setback in Oregon, late starter Robert Kennedy took a great step toward his party's presidential nomination by capturing California's winner-take-all Democratic primary on June 4.

And then Kennedy was dead. Moments after claiming his victory, the forty-three-year-old Kennedy lay fatally wounded on the floor of the kitchen of Los Angeles's Ambassador Hotel.

The deaths of Martin Luther King, Jr., and Robert Kennedy hit Warren hard, the Chief's law clerk Tyrone Brown recalled. Warren was depressed, "really shaken, I thought, really disturbed."

At lunch with the clerks four days after Kennedy's assassination, "he kept speaking of Bobby as this young, magnetic, vibrant man whose life had been taken away from him at such an early age."

Kennedy's death left Democrats without a unifying candidate, against a resurrected Richard Nixon. The chief justice gloomily predicted Nixon would be elected president in November, a prediction that lent new urgency to Warren's own plans.

For the past months, the chief justice had weighed retirement. He was seventy-eight, well past the undefined but mandatory retirement age he had once suggested for government officials.

He certainly did not need to work. His $40,000 salary as chief justice would continue as retirement income; he would also draw his California pension. In the event of his death, Nina would be comfortable, particularly with the small real estate investments that Ben Swig was guiding. Sister Ethel's death of cancer in June, 1966, relieved him of the $500-per-month he had contributed to supplement her social security check.

His health was as good as a man of his years could expect, he told friends. He wanted to enjoy himself more, to work on behalf of the new World Peace Through Law organization, and to travel with Nina.

His friends were of an age. Almost weekly, it seemed he wrote a letter of condolence to the family of a political ally, a pal of old, or a classmate. John Mullins—"one of the loyal ones," as Helen MacGregor wrote—and

Warren's first vote as district attorney these forty years before, had passed on. Frank Shay, the man Warren had beaten for that post, was seriously ill.

Warren Olney had submitted his resignation as director of the Federal Judicial Center, and had returned to California. Walter Gordon was soon to retire as governor of the Virgin Islands; Warren had made certain that the president would extend Gordon's term an additional year so he could qualify for a federal pension.

Just sixty-seven, Tom Clark had resigned from the Court at the end of the 1966–1967 term. He was making way for his son Ramsey to become attorney general, his resignation eliminating any possible "conflict of interest if his son were the attorney general, appearing before the Supreme Court."

Clark's sacrifice was bittersweet for the chief justice. Longtime acquaintance had grown to warm friendship. At the same time, Clark's resignation opened the door for his son, a liberal with an expansive view of the law; and permitted the president to tap Solicitor General Thurgood Marshall to replace Clark on the Supreme Court.

Lyndon Johnson's selection of Marshall delighted Warren. The newest justice and the Chief were much alike, in background and legal philosophy, said Frank Beytagh, a former law clerk who had later served as an assistant solicitor general under Marshall.

"Neither one of them ever forgot where he came from, nor that the people appearing before them in the Court were real live human beings. The Court might be making law for the whole country, but at the same time they were deciding an individual case that was going to have an effect, positive or negative, on particular people."

There was an additional bond, Beytagh noted. Marshall had argued *Brown* in the high court, and Warren had molded the unanimous decision. They were "forever tied together in history."

While he would enjoy working with Marshall, he feared staying too long as chief justice. Pride dictated resolve. "I'm not going out of here like some of these fellows," Warren promised the visiting Laughlin Waters, elevated to the federal bench in Los Angeles. "I'm going out while I know what I'm doing."

Above all, he did not want to cling to his seat, like Hugo Black or Bill Douglas, past their prime. Both had stayed too long in office, and it saddened Warren.

Black at eighty-two seemed to have lost his bearings; his opinions in recent years were erratic, certainly inconsistent with his earlier sense of jurisprudence. Douglas at seventy, the most brilliant of them all, had grown slovenly in the last few years. As Bill Brennan put it, "He seemed to have lost the interest that was so paramount in everything he did when he started on the Court."

It seemed too that an era was drawing to a close, *his* era of Progressive-inspired reforms, of governmental activism, of a liberal spirit. He had been in public service half a century, since Charles Kasch arranged his first clerkship with the state Assembly in 1919.

It was a good run, but he was politician enough to sense the ebbing tide. In California, Ronald Reagan had defeated Pat Brown for governor in 1966, and almost immediately dismissed Clark Kerr, the president of the University of California, for condoning "the spirit of permissiveness" at Berkeley.

Clark's firing had angered Warren. Despite FBI warnings that the John Birch Society might attack him, the chief justice was one of three invited guests at a faculty protest meeting a month after Kerr's dismissal.

Warren came anyway, in what "was obviously a statement against what Reagan had done." (The apprehensive FBI arranged for the dean of the School of Business Administration, who resembled Warren in bulk and silver hair, to change places with Warren. Ewald T. Grether sat unconcerned and unmolested through the program.)

Warren sensed that Reagan's election in California signaled a tidal shift in public opinion. In June, 1968, the Warren Era in California drew to a close with the primary defeat of Tom Kuchel by an archconservative. Max Rafferty's three-percentage-point margin came from "Impeach Earl Warren" country in the southern portion of the state. The last of California's Progressives was gone.*

Furthermore, his work was done. In the past fifteen years, as son Earl explained, the Court had laid down the legal guidelines in "all major areas of social concern. I think not only is this a factor in his retirement, but also in his contentment."

On June 11, 1968, a week after the fateful California primary, Earl Warren asked Abe Fortas to arrange a visit with the president.

On Thursday morning, June 13, 1968, Earl Warren and Lyndon Baines Johnson spent thirty-eight minutes together in the Oval Office. Warren carried with him a one-sentence letter:

"Pursuant to the provisions of 28 USC, section 371 (b), I hereby advise you of my intention to retire as Chief Justice of the United States effective at your pleasure."

Warren's explanation of his decision was equally brief, according to a White House memorandum for the record. "He came down to say that because of age, he felt he should retire from the Court and he said he wanted President Johnson to appoint his successor, someone who felt as Justice Warren did."

---

* Warren took comfort in the November defeat of Rafferty by Democrat Alan Cranston. "That was a blessing for all Californians because he would have been shoddy representation for our State," Warren wrote Ben Swig on November 6, 1968. The letter is in Box 119, EWP/LC.

In a separate letter of explanation that day, Warren wrote he must eventually bow to his age. "I have been continuously in the public service for more than fifty years. When I entered the public service, 150 million of our 200 million people were not yet born. I, therefore, conceive it to be my duty to give way to someone who will have more years ahead of him to cope with the problems which will come to the Court."

The president asked this "kindest as well as the wisest man" he had ever known, if Warren had a successor in mind. "No, Mr. President, that's your problem," Warren said.*

Johnson pondered for a moment. "What do you think about Abe Fortas?" he asked.

"I think Abe would be a good chief justice," Warren answered.

Warren returned to the court to tell his law clerks of his resignation. They were not greatly surprised, said one of the trio, Larry Simon. "One thing I knew was that Warren had a much better feel for American politics than I did. And it was at that point that I became pretty sure Nixon was going to be the next president of the United States."

Warren would deny strenuously—and with something less than candor —that the timing of his retirement was not politically motivated.

Though not yet nominated, Richard Nixon was already running for the presidency—and using the code words of "law and order" as a campaign theme. Warren Court decisions, he wrote in an article in the November, 1967, *Reader's Digest,* "weakened law and encouraged criminals."

Asserting the Supreme Court should not "become a political issue," Richard Nixon promptly made it one. Given a vacancy on the court, he pledged, "First, since I believe in a strict interpretation of the Supreme Court's role, I would appoint a man of similar philosophical persuasion.

"Second, recent Court decisions have tended to weaken the peace forces —as against the criminal forces—in this country. I would therefore want to select a man who was thoroughly experienced and versed in the criminal law and its problems."

Richard Nixon wanted on the Court only "strict constructionists who saw their duty as interpreting law and not making law. They would see themselves as caretakers of the Constitution, not super-legislators with a free hand to impose their social and political viewpoints upon the American people."

The implicit condemnation of the Warren Court was inescapable. To southerners still smarting from *Brown,* to whites in northern cities worried

---

* According to Richard Mosk, a Warren family friend who served on the staff of the assassination commission, Warren did suggest three people to fill the vacancy: Mosk's father, California Supreme Court Justice Stanley Mosk; Arthur Goldberg, hapless and frustrated as ambassador to the United Nations; and Ramsey Clark, newly named attorney general of the United States. Warren's son-in-law Stuart Brien confirmed this. It may be that Warren made the recommendations only after the defeat of Abe Fortas.

about rising crime rates, to country folk who had lost their veto power in state legislatures, Nixon delivered the siren call.*

The day after Warren's White House visit, at the end of the last conference of the term, the Chief told the brethren of his decision.

The partings were hard. John Harlan had just come by, Warren told the visiting John Weaver. "You know how often John and I disagreed, and vehemently at times, but, we have a feeling for each other."

Two years earlier, Warren had rearranged the Court budget to provide a third law clerk for Harlan, whose eyes were failing; easing the burden would help John stay on, the Chief explained.

"And you know, when John came in to say goodbye, there were tears in his eyes," Warren added, his own eyes moist.

Whispers of the chief justice's retirement raised hackles in the Senate, which would have to vote on Warren's replacement. On June 21, Senators Robert P. Griffin of Michigan and John Tower of Texas stated they would oppose any effort by "lame duck" Lyndon Johnson to name a new chief justice.

The appointment became a political issue. California governor Ronald Reagan claimed Warren had no "right to choose which president he thinks should dominate for the next twenty years the Supreme Court."

Even before Johnson formally nominated a successor, half of the Republicans in the Senate had signed a petition opposing any effort to replace Warren before the November elections with a midnight appointment.

History and law alike were on Johnson's side. John Marshall, generally counted the greatest of the men to sit as chief justice, was confirmed just weeks before President John Adams stepped down.

Five Supreme Court justices in the past half-century had been appointed in the last year of a president's term of office; they included Louis D. Brandeis and Benjamin Cardozo, both of whom would leave a deep imprint on the law. Even this Senate had approved eleven jurists to sit on lower courts in the ten weeks since the president announced that he would not run for reelection.

Senate critics turned on Warren for retiring "at the pleasure of the president." The resignation, Senator Griffin charged, "was not a resignation at all. In so doing, he created the impression of participating with the

---

* The effect of Nixon's politicizing of the Supreme Court can be plotted in public opinion polls. In July, 1967, 45 percent of the public deemed the Supreme Court's performance "excellent" or "good." Two years and a presidential campaign later, just 33 percent judged the Court's record "excellent" or "good." According to the Gallup Poll, "An important factor behind the court's decline in public favor, as judged by the views expressed in surveys, is the growing feeling that the Court is 'too soft' on criminals. Others complain that the rights of the individual are being protected at the expense of society as a whole. Another fairly large group argues that the Court's role should be one of 'interpreting' rather than 'making' laws." The poll is reported in the *Los Angeles Times,* June 15, 1969.

President in a political manipulation to force confirmation of a particular successor."

Whatever the appearance, Warren also had history and law on his side. It was common for federal judges to step down upon confirmation of their successor.

Under the terms Warren laid out, Johnson might have simply accepted the chief justice's resignation. But they had discussed the need for continuity, Warren explained later, "because you don't know from day to day what kind of an issue is going to come before the Court."

Two weeks after the chief justice delivered his letter of resignation, Lyndon Johnson announced he was submitting the name of Abe Fortas to be the new CJ. To fill the vacant seat, he selected former Texas congressman Homer Thornberry, now a judge on the Fifth Circuit Court of Appeals.

Though he counted as many as seventy-four aye votes, Johnson had miscalculated. Fortas plus Thornberry was one Johnson crony too many. Had the president chosen a nonpolitical lawyer or a recognized scholar rather than his old Texas colleague, the outcry might have been muted.

Fortas, long the presidential adviser, had continued in that role after going to the Supreme Court. He had a direct telephone line to the Oval Office on his desk; clerks were warned not to enter if Fortas was talking with the red light on.*

Despite strenuous efforts, Griffin was unable to demonstrate that either Johnson or Fortas had compromised the Court. But the appearance of cronyism rather than merit stained the nomination.

Warren sought to dampen the protest. When reporters in California asked the visiting chief justice about the Fortas nomination, he termed it "a splendid appointment." Fortas, he added, "is a great justice, a great lawyer. I have no doubt he will be a great chief justice."

Six days later, the Chief summoned a rare press conference in the Court's ornate East Conference Room. Standing before the portrait of a stern Chief Justice John Marshall, Warren told newsmen, "As long as a man is President, he has a right to perform the duties of his office."

Warren rejected any argument that a lame duck should not make appointments. Because the Constitution limited a president to two terms, he pointed out, any president in his second term was technically a lame duck.

He declined to answer on political grounds only when he was asked if the timing of his announcement was conditioned on the expectation that

---

* Fortas had talked with Johnson more than 200 times about various governmental matters since going onto the Court. Fortas, of course, was not the first or the last Supreme Court justice to advise the White House. From the first chief justice, John Jay, who doubled as presidential adviser and minister to Great Britain, to Felix Frankfurter, justices had been involved in affairs of state. On the Warren Court, not only Frankfurter and Fortas but William O. Douglas and Arthur Goldberg also had frequent White House contacts. Warren's successor, Warren E. Burger, would talk often with the man who appointed him, Richard Nixon.

Richard Nixon would be elected. "I put all that behind me fifteen years ago."

Similarly denying any political motive, Fortas's opponents attempted to turn his nomination into a referendum on the Warren Court. The common element among Nixon Republicans and southern Democrats who opposed him, Fortas wrote the Chief, "is bitter, corrosive opposition to all that has been happening in the Court and the country: the racial progress, and the insistence upon increased regard for human rights and dignity in the field of criminal law."

Confident just short of disdain, Fortas was to make a grave mistake. He agreed to appear before the Senate Judiciary Committee to offer testimony about his fitness for the post. He thus became the first sitting member of the Supreme Court to submit to questioning by a committee of Congress.

Members of the committee, particularly southern Democrats, homed in on Fortas.

"Mallory," South Carolina's Strom Thurmond raged. "I want that word to ring in your ears—Mallory! A man who raped a woman, admitted his guilt, and the Supreme Court turned him loose on a technicality. And who, I was told later, went to Philadelphia and committed another crime, and somewhere else another crime, because the Court turned him loose on technicalities." *

Fortas was badly shaken. Not only did he not intend to discuss court rulings, but *Mallory* had come down eight years before Fortas took his seat as associate justice. Was he expected to defend the entire record of the Warren Court?

Apparently so. By the fifth day of hearings, a spokesman for the anti-pornography group Citizens for Decent Literature was thundering against the 1957 *Roth* decision and its progeny.

The United States Supreme Court, CDL spokesmen charged, "is directly responsible for the proliferation of obscenity in this country." Any man who would vote for such smut was not fit to sit on the Supreme Court.

Fortas was the scapegoat. "Justice Abe Fortas is not only a friend of President Johnson, he is also a protégé of Earl Warren," Thurmond fumed on the floor of the Senate. "In the 1966–67 term, Justice Fortas agreed with Warren on 97 out of a possible 112 decisions, a record of accord with Warren exceeded only by Justice Brennan.

"If the Senate confirms this appointment, we will be confirming an extraconstitutional arrangement by which the Supreme Court justices can so arrange their resignations as to perpetuate their influence and their ideology on the Supreme Court."

Fortas's critics left no doubt about their true target. As Virginia's Harry

---

* In fact, Mallory was arrested for a rape a second time and acquitted. He was finally convicted of committing a string of burglaries and sentenced to prison in Pennsylvania, according to the *Detroit Free Press,* July 3, 1966.

Byrd put it, "Today's Court badly needs to be brought into balance. Under Mr. Warren, it has become an extremist Court. A majority, which generally includes Mr. Fortas, has taken the Court to the far left."

As the Senate debate ground on, Warren grew more dubious of the outcome. "I'm very much afraid I'm going to have to open up that Court in October," he told a group of college students in Helena, Montana.

Eventually, the Senate would approve Fortas, he predicted. "Between accepting Fortas and keeping me, they are going to take Abe Fortas."

Warren was wrong.

On September 13, 1968, the dean of American University School of Law testified before the Senate Judiciary Committee that Fortas had been paid $15,000 for a series of nine seminars dealing with social aspects of the law after the Court's term ended. The fee had come from a special fund raised from five wealthy businessmen by Fortas's former law partner, Paul Porter.

"The five donors of the fund were not ordinary businessmen," Tennessee Republican Senator Howard Baker asserted. "They were all individuals with extensive business interests in numerous corporations that could at some time become involved in litigation before the Supreme Court of the United States."

Though Fortas had heard no case involving former clients or his law firm, Baker charged the justice had breached the legal canon requiring that judges "should be free from impropriety and the appearance of impropriety." Republicans redoubled their efforts to paint Fortas as an influence dealer with a moral blind spot.

Warren stood steadfast. To those who asked, Margaret McHugh on instructions replied that while the chief justice himself did not accept such fees, "he does not feel that there is anything wrong in accepting honorariums. It is just his way of life not to do so. He has the greatest admiration and respect for Justice Fortas and the other members of the Court."

With Lyndon Johnson twisting arms, the Judiciary Committee eventually voted 11–6 to recommend Fortas. By the third week of September, the Senate was snarled in a filibuster.

While an Associated Press survey suggested Fortas had sufficient votes to win confirmation, the Senate would not get to vote on the nomination. Senate rules permitted unlimited debate until closed by a two-thirds vote of those present and voting. Though a minority could block all business with a filibuster, senators remained reluctant to invoke cloture.

On the afternoon of Tuesday, October 1, the Senate declined to close debate on the Fortas nomination. Needing fifty-nine votes, Fortas's allies mustered just forty-five. Thirty-five Democrats and ten Republicans voted to end the six-day filibuster; twenty-four Republicans and nineteen Democrats voted nay.

Fortas asked the president to withdraw his nomination the following day. He retained his seat on the Court, and his withdrawal halted further attacks on the Warren legacy.

With no replacement in the offing, Warren was caught between upper and nether millstones.

"I couldn't withdraw the letter. That would look terrible," a later Warren law clerk recalled of the Chief's explanation. It would certainly leave the impression he had elected to retire because he feared Richard Nixon would appoint his successor.

As clerk John Keker understood it, "The public appearance, the appearance of propriety, the appearance of things was terribly important to him."

For Warren to withdraw the letter now "would be in his mind a crass admission that he *was* resigning for political reasons." It would tarnish his reputation for rectitude, for personal morality in an immoral world, Keker argued.

That stance "gave moral authority to positions he'd taken, and moral authority is what they needed if they were to survive," Keker said. Warren had no choice.

On Monday, October 7, Earl Warren led the brethren through the scarlet drapes behind the bench to begin his sixteenth term as chief justice of the United States. Two days later, Lyndon Johnson announced that Warren had agreed to stay on, "until emotionalism subsides, reason and fairness prevail."

The term was to be a comparatively quiet one, marked by a handful of important cases among the 3,117 filed. Two were reminders of Warren's early years.

Clarence Brandenburg had invited a television reporter and cameraman to attend the Ku Klux Klan rally on a farm outside of Cincinnati. The resulting story, with its burning cross and muttered curses cast at "niggers" and "Jews," aired both locally and nationally.

It also showed a man in a red, hooded robe, identified as Brandenburg, vaguely threaten, "We're not a revengent [sic] organization, but if our President, our Congress, our Supreme Court, continues to suppress the white, Caucasian race, it's possible that there might have to be some revengeance taken."

An embarrassed Hamilton County prosecutor charged Brandenburg under a state criminal syndicalism law dating from 1919 and the post–world war Red Scare. Twenty-two states, including California, had similar laws that prohibited advocating violence to accomplish political reform.

Four decades earlier, in one of his first cases as a deputy district attorney, Warren had "carried the briefcases" in the prosecution of Alameda County Wobblies. The newly minted deputy was uncomfortable with the charge, but held his tongue.

The United States Supreme Court in 1927 upheld that California statute in the case of clubwoman turned radical social worker Anita Whitney. The state law eventually fell into disuse, supplanted by a more sweeping statute.

Forty-two years later, the issue was back before the high court, brought by a man whose politics stood diametrically to the right of communist

Anita Whitney. The court on June 9, 1969, delivered a unanimous opinion overruling *Whitney* and striking down the law.

Criminal syndicalism laws punished advocacy alone, the unsigned opinion for the Court held. Furthermore, they made it a crime merely to gather to hear someone advocate violence to bring about political change. Because such actions raised no imminent danger to the state, the brethren ruled, the law violated the First Amendment.

In joining the majority, Earl Warren had settled some old business. His vote made belated amends for the Wobbly prosecutions four decades earlier.

The most publicized of the cases in the otherwise quiet 1968–69 term came with a challenge by Harlem congressman Adam Clayton Powell to the House of Representatives itself.

The flamboyant pastor of Harlem's Abyssinian Baptist Church, Powell was denied his seat by a vote of the House on grounds he had misappropriated some $40,000 in office funds to cavort with various women at expensive Caribbean resorts.

While Powell virtually flaunted his affairs—"humility does not appear to be one of his virtues," complained one critic—the odor of racism hung over the March 1, 1967, debate on the floor. As a minister, as a newspaper publisher, as chairman of the House Education and Labor Committee, Powell was a nationally recognized, outspoken black leader. To many in the nation's ghettos, he was a genuine hero persecuted for his "uppity" airs.

A week after the House of Representatives voted 307–116 not to seat Powell, the unhorsed congressman filed suit. He met Article I, Section 2's three constitutional requirements of age, citizenship, and residency. All else was irrelevant, his suit claimed.

For eighteen months, Powell's attorneys pressed his case through the courts, while their client traveled the country defiantly speaking out against the war in Vietnam and against white racism. On November 18, 1968, two weeks after Powell was reelected to a twelfth term by 80 percent of those voting, the Supreme Court granted certiorari.

A Court unafraid of separation-of-powers arguments when reproving the Georgia House of Representatives in the case of Julian Bond would not shrink from a similar rebuff to the Congress of the United States. Only Potter Stewart dissented, on the grounds that the appeal was mooted by Powell's subsequent reelection.

Assuming it was his duty to speak for the Court in a dispute with a co-equal branch of government, the chief justice wrote the decision. Adam Clayton Powell had been unconstitutionally excluded from the Congress, the court held in June, 1969.

Powell was a last statement of the Warren Court's independence, its freedom from political dogma. Events had overtaken the brethren.

Richard Nixon had run a mean-spirited presidential campaign, playing upon fear. He repeatedly assailed Supreme Court decisions that "free the

obviously guilty" and promised to fire Attorney General Ramsey Clark—
as if he were responsible for crime in local communities.

No matter how irrational the attacks, the Republican nominee had found
an issue that resonated with voters, particularly voters fearful of interracial
crime. "It was merely an exercise in the rhetoric of accusation and recrimination which just increased divisiveness throughout the nation," Warren
told writer Jack Pollack later.

Criticism of Court decisions, however baseless, the chief justice could
accept as political invective. But Nixon's unfounded attacks on Clark angered Warren.

In a departure from precedent, Warren publicly praised Clark just four
days before the election. Dedicating the new quarters of the Federal Judicial
Center in Washington, the chief justice pointedly singled out Clark as "a
great attorney general [who] has tried to promote everything that is in the
best interests of this country."

Warren's implicit rebuke of Richard Nixon was not enough. On November 5, 1968, the Republican nominee scored a narrow 500,000-vote victory
over fast-closing Democrat Hubert Humphrey.

The chief justice saw his worst fear realized: Richard Nixon was president-elect, and the question of Earl Warren's retirement "at the pleasure of
the president" remained.

President Johnson, now truly a lame duck, briefly considered a last-
moment appointment of Arthur Goldberg to fill Warren's seat. He dropped
the idea. A man of great pride, Johnson did not wish to risk another rebuff
in the Senate.

If Nixon accepted the pending resignation on his first day in office,
January 20, 1969, the Court would continue to function with eight justices
under Hugo Black's temporary leadership.

But even if Nixon immediately nominated a new chief justice, Warren's
successor could not be confirmed and sworn in until early February. By
then, the justices might have heard arguments in half the cases on the
docket, without the new chief justice.

That strategy risked 4–4 decisions and rearguments, or, equally undesir-
able, a fragmented court issuing plurality opinions that decided individual
cases without settling points of law.

To avert turmoil, Warren took discreet initiative. He asked his son-in-law,
John Daly, a vice president of ABC News, to extend a feeler to the president-elect.

Daly served as messenger. Between tee shots at the Congressional Country Club, he passed on to William Rogers, Nixon's unannounced choice as
secretary of state, the chief justice's concerns for the work of the Court.
Daly suggested his father-in-law would be willing to serve out the judicial
term, and thereby allow a graceful changeover.

Warren would not ask this himself; his resignation was on the table. To
withdraw it would be to risk the charge he was politically motivated—a

point Daly would not have to make but Rogers would understand. However, the president-elect might request the chief justice stay until the end of the term in June.

Rogers conveyed the message, adding his own arguments. The president-elect gained time by leaving Warren in harness. Busy filling Cabinet and sub-Cabinet positions, determined to "clean house" of Democratic loyalists, Nixon would not have to rush the choice of a new chief justice.

On December 4, 1968, President-elect Nixon telephoned the chief justice. According to a carefully worded statement approved by Warren before its release, the two men "had a very pleasant talk."

Virtually a joint communiqué between hostile states, the statement cast Nixon as a gracious winner. "The President-elect said that he thought it most important, in order to avoid serious disruption of the work of the Court, that the effective date should not be until the end of the Term of the Court in June."

Observing the polite rituals of official Washington with what journalist Jack Pollack termed "decorous insincerity," Nixon also asked Warren to swear him in. "The Chief Justice said he was happy to do so and looked forward to the occasion with great pleasure."

On a cold, cold January 20, 1969, the chief justice of the United States, Earl Warren, administered the oath of office to Richard Milhous Nixon, thirty-seventh president of the United States. In measured phrases, Warren read the oath, as Nixon swore to "faithfully execute the office of President of the United States."

Throughout the ceremony, Warren later told a friend, he could not help but think, "But for Nixon, that might have been me taking the oath in 1953. I might have won."

The following day, Warren in his judicial robes went to the East Room of the White House, there to swear in eighty-one members of Nixon's staff. They too pledged to "preserve, protect and defend the Constitution of the United States." *

Warren was to be reminded less than two months later—if reminder were needed—that a Nixon administration would reflect the president's duplicitous nature.

On March 10, 1969, the Court handed down decisions in three cases that raised a single issue: was the government compelled by the Fourth Amendment's prohibition against illegal searches and seizures to turn over to criminal defendants copies of all conversations secretly recorded by its agents?

The solicitor general had argued that nothing in the recorded conversations dealt with the criminal cases. Thus the government should not be compelled to surrender them.

---

* Seven of the men who took the oath that day in the East Room were among those who would serve prison sentences for Watergate-related and campaign finance offenses.

The Supreme Court disagreed, and returned the cases to the trial court. There the judge was to rule whether the wiretaps were illegal, and, if so, whether the recorded conversations had helped the prosecution.

Trailing the three cases were no less than twenty appeals from other defendants, two of them celebrated and their cases closely watched: former heavyweight boxing champion Muhammad Ali, convicted of refusing to be inducted in the draft; and Teamsters' Union president James R. Hoffa, serving an eight-year term for jury tampering.

Two days after this so-called *Alderman* ruling, Bill Brennan received a telephone call from Jack C. Landau, the newly named director of public information for the Department of Justice. Landau explained he had a "very important" matter he wished to discuss with the justice.

Brennan, who knew Landau as a reporter and had recommended him for a Neiman Fellowship at Harvard, agreed to see him. Fifteen minutes later, a nervous Landau was in Brennan's chambers. He was there, he said, "on a mission regarded by the attorney general to be urgent and most important."

Attorney General John Mitchell, Landau stated, had interpreted the wiretap opinions of March 10 "as meaning that the transcript of any conversation, whatever its content, which had been obtained by illegal electronic surveillance would have to be turned over to the defense."

This reading had alarmed the Central Intelligence Agency, the Federal Bureau of Investigation, and the Department of State. Those agencies demanded the government drop any prosecution that might result in turning over transcripts of electronic surveillance on foreign embassies in Washington.

"On the one hand," Landau explained later, "Mitchell wanted to obey the opinion. On the other hand, they wanted to keep the taps on. They couldn't figure a way out."

Every embassy in the capital was under electronic surveillance, Landau told Brennan. (He would later amend that by stating federal agents had forty-six under continuous surveillance and the others surveilled on an intermittent basis.)*

Landau explained that the Department of Justice had assumed that at least three of the brethren had "some official familiarity with the practice" before going on the Court: Byron White as deputy attorney general; Abe Fortas because of his close relationship with Lyndon Johnson; and Thurgood Marshall, from his service as solicitor general.

Landau did acknowledge the Department of Justice was at fault for not formally notifying the Court that foreign embassies were secretly moni-

---

* In a later interview, Landau said he had no quarrel with Brennan's contemporaneous notes of the interview. Landau did say that he carried with him a handwritten list of taps copied from "The Black Book" of the "more than 100 national security wiretaps then under active surveillance." He read "maybe a dozen locations" to Brennan.

tored. To have revealed it though "would be most embarrassing to our foreign relations."

Landau, who had covered the court for the Newhouse Newspapers chain, was elected messenger; the attorney general and the solicitor general, Erwin Griswold, each found protocol or a legal excuse. Furthermore, "they didn't think that submitting something in writing to the Court was wise," Landau said.

What did the attorney general want of the Court? Brennan asked.

According to Brennan's account—Landau claimed to have no memory of it—the emissary replied with what the justices took to be a clumsy threat since there were no bills pending to limit the court's jurisdiction.

As Brennan recorded the interview, Landau "said that the Attorney General had asked him to emphasize that he believed the Department was at fault in the situation and was willing to do anything at all that would help the Court avoid a congressional reaction which might lead either to a constitutional amendment or some legislation to curtail the Court's jurisdiction."

With that, Brennan insisted they meet with the chief justice. "I was scared," Landau the reluctant messenger acknowledged.

Warren was livid. Even years later, as he set down his memoirs, the anger still festered. Warren judged Landau's visit no more or less than an "outrageous attempt" to influence the Court's decision in the twenty trailing cases.

Those cases, including the Ali and Hoffa appeals, "having an identical issue, would normally be accorded the same treatment as in the *Alderman* case. Undoubtedly consternation over a result that would be adverse to wiretapping was the reason for the unusual approach to the Court by Mr. Landau for the Department of Justice."

Warren summoned the brethren to conference on March 17 where Brennan once more recounted Landau's visit. William O. Douglas's reaction paralleled Warren's.

"This was the first instance in the memory of anyone connected with the Court in which the executive branch had made actual threats to the Court," he snapped.

Warren elected to say nothing publicly. There was nothing to be gained by challenging the new administration, "particularly one that had campaigned against the Court on the charge that it was soft on crime."

Warren blamed the blundering approach on the blunt-spoken attorney general. "Mitchell," Landau agreed with Warren, "was not very sophisticated in terms of constitutional law."

On March 24, 1969, the brethren by an 8–1 vote disposed of the trailing cases by relying on the earlier decision. Significantly for Earl Warren, labor thug James R. Hoffa was among the defendants who might benefit.

Warren considered Hoffa "no good," as he privately told columnist Drew

Pearson. "But that doesn't mean we can approve Gestapo tactics in America," he added.

Fifteen years before the chief justice had refused to grant certiorari to Roger "The Terrible" Touhy simply because Touhy was a noted gangster. Since then, Warren had so broadened his vision that he could question the conviction of the nation's most notorious labor racketeer because of governmental tactics.

Within two months, John Mitchell himself would be back in the Marble Palace to visit privately with the chief justice. This time he came intent on dismantling the Warren Court.

His opportunity came with the publication of the May 5, 1969, issue of *Life* magazine containing an article entitled "Fortas of the Supreme Court: A Question of Ethics." *Life*'s William Lambert wrote that Fortas in January, 1966, had accepted a $20,000 check from a charitable foundation headed by financier Louis Wolfson. In return for the sum, the associate justice agreed to advise the Wolfson Family Foundation for a year.

An ethical question arose—at least in the article—because Wolfson and a cohort were then confronting a federal indictment for securities fraud. With no evidence of actual misdeed, Lambert could only ask what other advice or services Fortas might have performed for Wolfson.

Fortas had returned the $20,000—after Wolfson was indicted. Because he had repaid the money before the end of the year, he was not obligated to, nor did he, report it on his income tax return.

During and after his trial, with his conviction on appeal, Wolfson continued to assure friends that the matter would be worked out, sometimes pointedly dropping Fortas's name. But when the Wolfson appeal came before the Supreme Court, Fortas wrote Warren, "Please note that I am disqualified in the above case." He took no part in the case, the court denied certiorari, and Wolfson went to prison.

There was no wrongdoing. At issue, as *The Wall Street Journal* put it, was the fact that "many Washington scandals result from the appearance of wrongdoings, without the allegations ever being proved." *

Rumors quickly made the rounds that the White House and the attorney general had helped Lambert's research. While the reporter denied it—"If anything, I leaked it to the Nixon Administration," he claimed—the White House had eagerly awaited the story.

Two weeks before the article appeared, J. Edgar Hoover and President

* There was nothing to bar judges from serving on outside boards. Warren, like the chief justices before him, was an ex officio officer of the Smithsonian Institution. He also served on the board of the *National Geographic,* and for a five-year period beginning in 1966 was on the advisory committee to review transfers of ownership in the Graham Family trust which owned *The Washington Post.* There is no indication in Warren's Supreme Court records that he was paid for whatever time he might have spent with his fellow *Post* trustees, former Secretary of Defense Robert McNamara, and former Harvard University president James B. Conant. However, trustees are customarily accorded fees.

Nixon agreed there might be as many as four Supreme Court vacancies during Nixon's term: the Warren seat; Harlan, who had grave eye problems; Black, past eighty; and Douglas, "crazy and not in too good health."

Nixon then confided that there might be a fifth vacancy. *Life* magazine was preparing "an exposé" of Fortas, he advised, one powerful enough to force the justice from the bench.*

With publication of the Lambert article, Fortas was wounded, not by evidence of wrongdoing, but by the embarrassing reappearance of the crony or "fixer" image. The administration turned up the heat.

In a carefully calculated campaign, Attorney General Mitchell promised more revelations, then leaked word that the Department of Justice was investigating not only Fortas, but his wife, a former law partner, and his former law firm.

According to Mitchell's plan, Earl Warren would play the decisive role.

Slipping secretly into the Supreme Court through the garage entrance, Mitchell met privately with the chief justice shortly before noon on May 7. In a half-hour meeting, the attorney general turned over to Warren a sealed envelope containing six documents subpoenaed from the Wolfson Family Foundation.

Five of the six only confirmed details of the *Life* story. The sixth, the original contract between the foundation and Fortas, revealed that the consulting arrangement had not been for one year only. Wolfson had agreed to pay Fortas $20,000 a year for as long as he lived, and to continue those payments to his widow after his death.

In effect, Fortas had been on a lifetime retainer of a man later convicted of securities fraud.

The conversation was brief. "I did most of the talking," Mitchell said later.

According to Mitchell, the chief justice was "appreciative" but made no comment. Warren simply said "he would take the matter under advisement."

Mitchell was not surprised. "I wouldn't believe that Earl Warren at this stage of life would be shocked about anything."

In fact, Warren was shaken. The reputation of the Court, *his* Court, was at risk.

Mitchell's revelation stunned Warren. "It was incomprehensible to him," said law clerk Paul Meyer. "It made no sense. To him it was so clearly inappropriate, so clearly wrong. He just couldn't understand how Fortas or anybody on the Court could put himself in that position."

He made no effort to hide his distress, said Margaret McHugh, who saw more of the Chief than anyone else in the Supreme Court building.

---

* Lambert was considered a "special favorite" of White House counsel Charles Colson, according to Mankiewicz, p. 96. Nixon's "dirty tricks" team "rewarded" Lambert by planting a forged cable that purported to link then-President John F. Kennedy with the overthrow and murder of South Vietnamese President Ngo Dinh Diem. Lambert after some months decided the cable was a forgery, and did not go with the story.

"Why would Fortas accept $20,000 a year? It doesn't make any sense." Warren finally confided to Margaret McHugh, "He has to go."

With word that Mitchell had secretly visited the chief justice common currency in Washington, and with reporters closing in on the story, Mitchell turned the screws tighter. The May 12 issue of *Newsweek* quoted the attorney general asserting he had "far more serious evidence."

(Mitchell was not to disclose what, if anything he had. His public relations man, Jack Landau, said he suspected the Department of Justice had turned up suggestions of tax fraud.)

As pressure mounted, Warren summoned a conference of the brethren on Tuesday, May 13. The chief justice quietly laid before them the documents that Mitchell had earlier given to him. In addition, Warren had a statement from Wolfson taken by FBI agents in which the financier flatly stated that Fortas "had made no offer of assistance nor did he indicate he would do anything one way or the other in connection with this matter."

Abe Fortas, dragooned by Lyndon Johnson to sit on the Supreme Court, Abe Fortas, who doubted whether he could step back from the arena at all, threw up his hands. "I have had it. To hell with it."

As onetime Fortas law partner Paul Porter noted, John Mitchell's "political lynching-bee" had worn down the justice. "I think Abe wanted to get off. He was looking for an excuse. He talked about it many times."

On May 14, 1969, Fortas resigned from the Court with the express hope his move would "enable the Court to proceed with its vital work free from extraneous stress." He preceded the man he called "Chief" by a month.

The era of the Warren Court had ended in a whimper.

CHAPTER 40

THE MAN OF GRAVITAS

Shortly before 10:00 a.m. on Monday, June 23, 1969, the eight men gathered in subdued ritual for the last time. They shook hands, then slipped on the black gowns of medieval scholars that marked them as justices of the Supreme Court of the United States.

The crier's announcement sounded in the courtroom: "The Honorable, the Chief Justice and the Associate Justices of the Supreme Court of the United States" and the scarlet curtains parted. For the last time, Earl Warren's Court was sitting in solemn majesty, before a hushed courtroom including the president of the United States, Richard Nixon.

They had drawn near to give attention, as the crier's summons warned, when the president appeared before the Court for the first time in history, to present formally his choice of Earl Warren's replacement.

Warren was determined to step down. His work was done, he repeatedly told friends; the opinions of the Warren Court would live on, modified perhaps, but enduring. The two desegregation rulings, the redistricting cases he thought the most important of his tenure, and the revolution in criminal law wrought by *Mapp, Gideon,* and *Miranda* were irreversible restatements of the American ideal.

A month earlier, Jeffrey Warren, James and Margaret's second son, wrote an impassioned letter to his grandfather, urging him to delay retirement. Jeff feared a Court led by a Nixon appointee, feared too how it would alter the judicial climate in the nation. In his anxiety for the future, Jeff decided this was a terrible world to bring up children.

Grandfather Warren replied on June 15 with what his wife described as the longest handwritten letter she had ever seen him write. The world was an imperfect place, Warren conceded, the future clouded with

> *the Vietnam war, the draft, the arms race, the exhaustion of our resources on military expenditures to the starvation of our domestic problems of poverty, slums, education, environmental pollution, etc.*

Some problems had been met, some were intractable.

> *At the present time we are belatedly paying the price of slavery which we institutionalized for a period of 250 years. Although it was abolished a hundred years ago, the badge of it is still on millions of our citizens, and they, poor souls, are still suffering from the poverty and degradation of it.*

If little had been done to alleviate these conditions until after the Second World War, they had made strides since. Given human nature, progress was not always uniform.

> *Under a democratic form of government, people can vote for poor government as well as good, and, when they do, it often takes time and a lot of effort to undo the bad results.*

When bad government prevailed, the answer was not to tear down. That would leave "the vacuum of *anarchy*" to be filled by repressive autocracies, Warren cautioned.

> *I really believe, Jeff, that what our country needs now is the youth of America—not to destroy what is, but to build—to insist on righting the wrongs of society and during its years of stewardship implement the ideals of Lincoln for "a government of the people, by the people and for the people" so that it will not "perish from this earth."*

To Jeff's urging he not retire, Warren replied,

> *In August it will be fifty-two years since I have had a day out of the public service. Two-thirds of the people of the United States were not born fifty-two years ago. I believe it is time for me to retire. My age (78), my health while not bad is not what it was years ago, and my desire to do some other things, all tell me that this is the time.*

A week after mailing his letter, Earl Warren sat in the center chair behind the long mahogany bench, presiding over his Court for the last time.

He turned first to Justice Thurgood Marshall who read an opinion that concluded the great work of the Warren years. Reversing a 1937 Supreme Court ruling, the Court held 7–1 that under the Due Process Clause the prohibition against double jeopardy applied to the states.

Justice Potter Stewart followed with two decisions of no great moment.

For seventeen minutes, the president of the United States sat quietly waiting. Implicit in the ceremony was an unspoken reminder that here all men were equal, president and layman alike; that the law governed all men.

Warren turned then to Richard Nixon, who advanced to the lectern. "May it please the Court," the president began, with the traditional invocation.

Nixon graciously acknowledged the chief justice's years of public service and Warren's dedication to "his personal family, to the great American family, to the family of man."

During the past sixteen years there had been disagreements over Court decisions, Nixon acknowledged. "But standing above those debates has been the symbol of the Court as represented by the Chief Justice of the United States: fairness, integrity, dignity. These great and simple attributes are, without question, more important than all of the controversy . . ."

The chief justice in turn offered a grave lecture about the role of the Court in the life of the nation. Speaking directly to the president, "because you might not have looked into the matter," Warren noted that the Court so many times spoke "the last word in great governmental affairs. . . ."

> It is a responsibility that is made more difficult in this Court because we have no constituency. We serve no majority. We serve no minority. We serve only the public interest as we see it, guided only by the Constitution and our own consciences. And conscience sometimes is a very severe taskmaster. . . .
>
> It is not likely ever, with human nature as it is, for nine men to agree always on the most important and controversial things of life. If it ever comes to such a pass, I would say that the Court will have lost its strength and will no longer be a real force in the affairs of our country. But so long as it is manned by men like those who have preceded us and by others like those who sit today, I have no fear of that ever happening.

Warren closed with an acknowledgment of his friendship with the men who had sat with him over the past sixteen years—"in spite of the fact that we have disagreed on many occasions." Those disagreements were "not of great importance. The important thing is that every man will have given his best thought and consideration to the great problems that have confronted us."

With that there remained only the last ritual. The outgoing chief justice swore in his successor.

Warren had taken no part in the selection of his replacement, Warren E. Burger, though Warren had predicted Burger's choice in a conversation with Tom Clark. Burger had solid Republican credentials; as chairman of the Minnesota delegation at the fateful 1952 Republican National Convention, Burger had cast the votes that put Dwight Eisenhower over the top.

Burger had court experience; as a judge on the liberal First Circuit Court of Appeals, Burger had gained a reputation for his conservative criticism of his colleagues.

Warren E. Burger took the oath of office, swearing "to do equal right to the poor and to the rich" and "to bear true faith and allegiance to the Constitution."

With that, the outgoing chief justice turned to the crowded courtroom and announced: "I present the new Chief Justice of the United States."

With a single blow of his gavel, Marshal T. Perry Lippitt closed the years of the Warren Court.

While he would maintain an office in the Supreme Court building, Warren took graceful leave of his colleagues. He was of them, but no longer one of them.

For their part, the brethren signed a letter of farewell drafted in Hugo Black's chambers—though not before the senior justice had made a significant editorial change. The draft, probably by a law clerk, stated, "For us it is a source of pride that we have had the opportunity to be members of the Warren Court."

Black, who thought himself the intellectual leader of the court, changed the letter to read: "For us it is a source of pride that we have had the opportunity to be members of the Court over which you have presided during one of the most important and eventful eras of our Nation."

(When Black told reporters a year later that he doubted history would record a "Warren Era," the Chief merely shrugged. "I didn't expect to gain immortality on this job, just a reputation for honesty.")

As going-away presents, the brethren joined by Tom Clark and Albert Goldberg gave Warren the traditional gift of his chair from the courtroom; and a $1,200, custom-made Winchester shotgun. For Nina, there was a bracelet from which hung a single charm, engraved with a replica of the front of the court, and inscribed, "To Nina Warren, First Lady of the Judiciary 1953–1969." *

On Sunday evening, June 29, Warren attended an unpublicized "national tribute" in his honor held on the steps of the Lincoln Memorial. Nearly a thousand people, many of them tourists enjoying a warm summer's night, gathered in front of the steps facing the reflecting pool to listen to the U.S. Army Chorus and speeches honoring the retired chief justice.

Arthur Goldberg praised Warren for enduring "unparalleled abuse" yet remaining "content to rest on the verdict of history for the proper appraisal of his life and works." Warren, still Goldberg's "Chief," "will be remembered not primarily for any particular decision but for his steadfast view that

---

* The gifts were presented on the evening of June 6, aboard the presidential yacht *Sequoia*. Nina Warren wrote a note of remembrance to the missing Abe Fortas, who replied, "Our hearts joined in the tributes that were paid to both of you!" That the exchange is in the Fortas file (Box 353, EWP/LC) suggests, at the least, that Nina wrote with her husband's consent.

. . . the modern world demands that judges, like men in all walks of public and private life, avoid escapism and frankly confront even the most controversial and troublesome justiciable problems."

CBS news commentator Eric Sevareid followed. A frequent visitor to the Warren apartment, Sevareid praised Warren for possessing "that certain quality that helps to hold a diverse people together and move a nation on."

That characteristic was not necessarily eloquence or intellectual attainment, Sevareid continued, but what the Romans called "gravitas"—"patience, stability, weight of judgment, breadth of shoulders. It means that strength of the few that makes life possible for many. It means manhood."

While Warren was leaving the Court, he was hardly retiring. Five years before, he had told his biographer John Weaver that he had no intention of writing his memoirs. "It's all in there," he said, his hand sweeping toward the fifty bound volumes of *United States Reports* recording the Warren years.

Besieged, however, by offers that reached $75,000, Warren signed a contract to write the book he had said he would not write. To former clerk Payson Wolff, Warren explained he was doing it to assure Nina of a secure old age.

He would change his mind too about returning to California. Though that state remained "home, the place I love," Warren elected to stay in Washington because "the things I'm most interested in are rooted there."

According to daughter Virginia, "It just made absolutely no sense to go back to California and start up housekeeping." Her father was seventy-eight, her mother seventy-six. "Their lives were settled. They had no home in California, no furniture. They would have to set up a home if they moved."

But where? "The children were scattered."

Meanwhile, she added, "Father had an office at the court," and a law clerk to assist him with his memoirs and speeches.

There would be many. Speaking engagements would send the Warrens racketing about the world in the next years. The biennial Conferences on World Peace Through Law called them to Bangkok in 1969, Belgrade in 1971, and Abidjan in the Ivory Coast two years later.

At the 1971 conference he was honored "for his landmark decisions upholding human rights which have justly earned him worldwide esteem as a champion of the liberty of man."

Two years later, that organization bestowed its first Human Rights Award on him: "When history reviews the record of our day in terms of man, leadership and their accomplishment in advancing human rights, no name will loom larger than that of Earl Warren."

Travel became their great pleasure. The Chief was quick to accept invitations to give speeches in return for fares and accommodations. The Warrens bracketed the Belgrade conference between stays in Copenhagen, Vienna, Rome—where they were presented to Pope Paul VI—and a Mediterranean cruise with the Swig family. Warren traveled to Tokyo, and returned again to the Philippines on the way to Bangkok.

With Nina he spent two weeks in Geneva in March, 1972, while he attended a conference of the International Labor Organization. They returned to the United States in time to wing off to California, where Warren held seminars with Boalt Hall law students.

The speeches, two of his post-retirement clerks noted, gave him an excuse not to work on his memoirs. "I didn't sense much desire to write a real autobiography, which means coming to grips with your feelings and doing something besides writing the official record," said John Keker.

His public speeches also allowed him to remain involved in the life of the nation. Gradually more outspoken, retired Chief Justice Warren became active Citizen Warren.

Welfare, he argued in an op-ed piece in *The New York Times*, was "not an evil word" when millions of Americans went to bed hungry each night. It was all a matter of who the recipients were, he pointed out.

"When hundreds of millions of dollars are given to bankrupt railroads, failing defense manufacturers, shipping interests and the like, the words 'welfare' or 'relief' are not used. Instead such things are done to 'strengthen the economy.' "

Ending the war in Vietnam, the elimination of poverty, and rooting out religious and racial discrimination became recurring themes of his speeches.

On May 8, 1970, Warren attended the New York Avenue Presbyterian Church services in memory of the four students at Kent State College slain by Ohio National Guard troops five days before. The Chief stood with the congregation at the end of the service, his hand held high in the V-symbol of the antiwar movement.

In a brace of thinly veiled speeches, he scored President Nixon and Vice President Spiro Agnew for exploiting the issue of law and order for political gain. They had raised the issue "in strident terms, but with no discussion of the causes or proposed cures for criminal conduct."

This was raw demagoguery. "The entire campaign was one of harsh rhetoric and a search for scapegoats responsible for the situation," he told an overflow audience of 1,400 at a Johns Hopkins University forum in November, 1970.

Three weeks later, he was the featured speaker at a dinner commemorating the fiftieth anniversary of the American Civil Liberties Union. Once more he condemned the 1968 presidential campaign as "merely an exercise in the rhetoric of accusation and recrimination throughout the nation." *

Nothing in these years provoked him more than what he saw as another

---

* At odds with the ACLU as a district attorney and attorney general, Warren in retirement praised the organization for defending the constitutional rights "of people of all persuasions, no matter how unpopular or even despised by the majority they were at the time." (*The New York Times*, December 9, 1970.) In 1971, he agreed to permit the ACLU of Northern California to use his name on an annual award to be given to prominent civil libertarians. The first recipient was Daniel Koshland, retired president of Levi Strauss and Co. and years before a major financial contributor to Warren's election campaigns.

attack on the Supreme Court by legal conservatives promoting a new National Court of Appeals. Worse still, the "mini-court," as it was quickly dubbed, came tainted by what Warren deemed a personal betrayal.

The mini-court idea sprang from Chief Justice Warren Burger's concern about the Supreme Court's ever-increasing caseload. Burger appointed a seven-member Study Group on the Caseload of the Supreme Court to make recommendations to alleviate the burden.

While the panel included a former Warren law clerk, Peter Ehrenhaft, then practicing law in Washington, Warren was immediately wary. The chairman of the group, Harvard Law professor Paul Freund, had privately disparaged the Warren Court's activism. Two other members were law professors who had written critical articles about the Warren Court's direction. Another was a former president of the American Bar Association, an organization with which the retired chief justice had publicly feuded.

Finally, they had been handpicked by the new chief justice, a conservative chosen for his fidelity to judicial precedent and a constricted view of the Bill of Rights.

As Warren had feared, the Study Group on the Caseload of the Supreme Court concluded, "The Court is now at the saturation point, if not actually overwhelmed." *

To lessen the load, the study group proposed the creation of a National Court of Appeals. That court, composed of seven federal circuit court judges serving three-year staggered terms, would screen all petitions for review now filed in the Supreme Court.

The study group recognized that of all appeals "the great majority, it is to be expected, would be finally denied" by the new National Court of Appeals. "Something of the order of 400 cases a year" would be certified annually to the Supreme Court "for further screening and choice of cases to be heard and adjudicated there."

The report, written by Freund, went on implicitly to criticize the intellectual quality of Supreme Court decisions in recent years. Law clerks spent much of their efforts reading petitions for certiorari, Freund wrote, "but at the cost of sacrificing the time of law clerks that might more fruitfully be applied to research, the critique of drafts of opinions, and service in general as intellectual foils for judges who are inevitably limited in their access to other minds."

Warren had no doubt about where a National Court of Appeals would cut first. Relatively conservative, conditioned to follow precedent, circuit court judges held little sympathy for untutored prisoners raising constitutional challenges on their own behalf.

---

* In Warren's first term, 1953–54, the Court had docketed 1,453 cases. In his last, the 1969–70 term, the Court had 4,172 cases on the docket, a growth of 187 percent. In the two years since, it had swollen even more. The largest part of this increase came in the pauper's petitions for certiorari, particularly from prisoners. They had jumped from 632 to 2,228—252 percent; the *in forma pauperis* cases outnumbered the "paid" cases in Warren's last term, 1,942 to 1,463.

Adoption of a National Court of Appeals, Warren was convinced, "threatened to shut the door of the Supreme Court to the poor, the friendless, the little man." Each one denied the right to appeal to the Supreme Court opened the way for the tidy, lawyerly, paid cases that tended to deal not with constitutional issues but with property rights.

There would be no opportunity for the Supreme Court to reach out and do justice to individuals, Warren told law clerk G. Edward White. To Peter Ehrenhaft, his former law clerk who had served on the study group, Warren wrote a coldly angry note on November 8: "To put it mildly, I was shocked to read in the Sunday *Star* that you and the committee of which you are a member are expected to advance a scuttling of the Supreme Court. I can think of few things which could throttle the Court to a greater extent in its avowed purpose of establishing 'Equal Justice under Law.' "

His sense of betrayal was palpable, and typical of Warren, White said. Throughout his career, the Chief had "demanded absolute loyalty . . ." Once Warren had made up his mind about an issue, "as a former law clerk, you simply did not have any leave to dissent," White added.

On the day he wrote Ehrenhaft, Warren began setting a backfire. In a memorandum to his former law clerks, many risen to prominent positions in the bar and in universities, he wrote:

"I consider this to be of tremendous importance—as a matter of fact, as important as the 50-member Court of the Union which was proposed as a constitutional amendment some years ago but aborted because of its absurdity. In my opinion, this is the same thing in a different disguise."

He was defending the Supreme Court, *his* Supreme Court, and his sense of active jurisprudence, against the academics who sneered at his alleged inattention to legal niceties; against the conservatives whom he had battled since he came to Washington; and, now, against the privileged who saw questions of civil rights crowding property rights from the court's docket.

Warren would speak out against the proposal at every opportunity for the next year. "There are so many special interests which could join together in the secret promotion of it through the Congress that I feel the attack on the proposal should continue," he wrote a friend.

Warren's counterattack on the National Court of Appeals was successful. The proposal faded from sight, particularly as the Court under Burger grew more conservative.

Despite their differing philosophies, chief justice past and chief justice present maintained cordial relations. Burger asked Warren for a signed photograph for Burger's office. The Burgers invited the Warrens to dinner at the Supreme Court, Nina befriending Elvera Burger as Nina had befriended the wives of all the justices.

As time went on, the friendship apparently cooled. According to John Keker, who clerked for Warren during the second year of his retirement, Burger was wary "because Warren had such a powerful reputation. Burger worried about Warren stealing Burger's thunder."

Burger "completely shut Warren out," Keker continued. Warren said "he would have been interested in doing work with the administrative office of the courts, but Burger didn't want him messing around in that area." This was Burger's area of expertise. To ask Warren to head a panel or study group in that area risked sharing credit or even ceding leadership to Warren.

Burger lacked both the stature and the skills to lead a collegial group like the Court. Where Warren had been personally unassuming—even rejecting a $2,000 increase of the salary differential between himself and the brethren—Burger grew increasingly self-important and pompous.

For sixteen years Warren had used the chief justice's traditional small office suite; Burger took over the adjacent conference room and turned it into his personal office. On the collegial Supreme Court, where the chief justice was no more than one among equals, such a move was bound to irritate.

Potter Stewart, probably as even-tempered a justice as sat in these years, scorned Burger as the "show captain." Among themselves, the brethren took to calling Earl Warren "the *real* Chief."

Aware of the friction—Bill Brennan was a frequent visitor in Warren's new office facing the Capitol—Warren spoke carefully in public when asked about the current Supreme Court. Was he concerned that the work of the "Warren Court" might be imperiled? John P. MacKenzie of *The Washington Post* asked Warren on the eve of his eightieth birthday.

"Not in the long run," Warren responded confidently. The school decision, for example, "had wide implications in all areas of life and will continue."

Privately, however, Warren was less certain. The Chief, law clerk G. Edward White said, "was absolutely convinced that Burger and the justices who were now on the Court were going to roll back all the Warren Court's important precedents. They were going to overrule *Miranda*. They were going to overrule *Mapp v. Ohio*. He was just absolutely convinced that was going to happen."

Some of that concern leaked out. When Burger in 1971 wrote a 5–4 majority opinion holding that an illegally obtained confession might be used to challenge the credibility of a defendant, the minority asserted any use of the confession was barred by the *Miranda* decision. Warren fretted but told reporters only mildly, "The new decision is not a repudiation of *Miranda*, but it is not strictly in accord with it."

The Court that Warren knew was changing. Burger was far more conservative than Warren, and Fortas's resignation had opened a seat eventually filled by another conservative Minnesotan, Harry A. Blackmun.

The liberals managed to hold their ground, partly through Bill Brennan's uncanny ability to mold decisions that preserved the core of Warren Court rulings, partly because Warren Burger simply lacked the ability to lead the rethren.

But the years of liberal activism ended.

After thirty-four years on the court, Hugo Black retired on September 17, 1971; medication and illness had impaired his vision, the Alabaman complained. In his seat was Lewis F. Powell, of Richmond, Virginia, a moderate on school integration, and a pillar of the establishment American Bar Association.

Six days after Black stepped down, John Harlan also resigned for reasons of health. He was replaced by William R. Rehnquist, once a law clerk for Robert Jackson, more latterly a lawyer and Republican Party functionary in conservative Arizona.

Both Black and Harlan would be dead before the end of the year. There were so many friends now gone, including George Feldman and Oliver Hamlin, those two uninvited wedding guests from long-ago Oakland.

Warren was eighty years old on March 19, 1971, feted at a formal birthday party that celebrated career and friendships alike. He was a man at peace with his public record and private life. Only one issue seemed to dog his conscience, despite his assertion that he had no "outstanding" regrets: the Japanese evacuation of 1942.

Confidentially he told former clerk and now dean of Boalt Hall Mike Heyman that he regretted his actions. It was an unusual admission.

"He felt bad about what happened," clerk Scott Bice agreed. "In retrospect, given what he had learned over the years, given his heightened sensitivity to racial discrimination and so forth, he recognized that as a very sad day in American history."

Still the stiff-necked Warren resisted any public acknowledgment of responsibility. "That would be showing too much vulnerability," former clerk John Keker theorized. For Warren it was important to maintain the mask of the "public man."

Only through the badgering of his son Earl did Warren relent—in part. The father broke a commitment not to become involved in executive or legislative affairs when he endorsed repeal of the McCarran Act's provision for internment camps for suspected "subversives" in time of war.

"It took a lot of persuading on my part," Earl Junior said. "Others had infuriated him with demands for abject apologies. That's what I had to break down. I was as hard-headed as he was. I argued he should make peace and square away a little history." *

Throughout his career, Warren had drawn a line between his public and private lives, between the personal and the official. Veneer or shell, mask or front, few penetrated it.

What lay behind the screen was "not much different than the average

---

* The Japanese American Citizens League was more forgiving. A JACL statement noted, "Recently there have been published reports that Warren confided in a private conversation that this action was one of his greatest regrets, thus erasing the only flaw in his outstanding record." See *The Oakland Tribune,* July 10, 1974.

American of his time," Keker decided. "He loved his wife, his kids, and wanted success in a pretty conventional way. He believed in conventions."

There were for Earl Warren simple truths, though dismissed as old-fashioned in a more cynical time: a man's character was determined by his willingness not to lie; every man was worthy until he proved himself otherwise; schoolyard rules of fair play were enduring; loyalty to country was true patriotism and loyalty to people true friendship; a man had a responsibility to support his family, to provide for their future; you worked hard and you gave fair value.

These beliefs he had held throughout his life. These were bedrock, the values a man taught his children and sought to live by himself.

The values remained. Their implementation might change.

Over the years, with each new job, Warren conceded, he had learned to see issues differently. But how could a man serve on the Supreme Court for sixteen years and not change—if he was to do his duty?

He had been a district attorney, then attorney general and governor. "Now that he was chief justice of the United States, he had a different job, and he had to think a different way," he told John Keker.

Warren learned from experience. He was older. That he had taken positions as chief justice contrary to earlier arguments did not trouble him.

Because Warren cherished these values, he was first angered, then saddened by Richard Nixon as the convoluted story known as Watergate unfolded.

The investigation of the break-in at the national offices of the Democratic Party—initially dismissed by presidential spokesman Ron Ziegler as a "third-rate burglary attempt"—quickly led to the Committee to Re-elect the President. From there, the stain spread to the former attorney general of the United States, John Mitchell, then on to the White House itself.

Presidential aides managed to keep the lid on the story until after the November, 1972, election, when Richard Nixon buried feckless George McGovern. But despite Nixon's denial that his administration was involved in the burglary, the cover-up came unglued.

One by one, district, federal, and congressional investigators implicated members of the White House staff and others at the heart of the reelection campaign. Campaign functionaries had pulled off what they termed "dirty tricks," the deliberate sabotage of Democratic candidacies. Others had raised huge sums of unreported, illegal cash contributions.

The men closest to the president had known of the planned Watergate burglary, underlings revealed. They had also participated in the subsequent bribery and perjury that amounted to obstruction of justice.

From afar, retired Earl Warren followed the Watergate story. Even vacationing with Ben Swig at the opulent Mauna Kea resort in Hawaii, he daily watched the televised hearings of the Senate Watergate Committee, the volume turned up to accommodate two aging men with diminished hearing and keen interest.

All the while Nixon lie heaped upon Nixon lie, provoking Warren to "a most unjudicial choler," *New York Times* obituary writer Alden Whitman later noted.

"Tricky is perhaps the most despicable President this country has ever had," Whitman quoted Warren from an interview about this time. "He was a cheat, a liar and a crook, and he brought my country, which I love, into disrepute. Even worse than abusing his office, he abused the American people."

By October, 1973, the Nixon presidency was a shambles. Vice President Agnew, who had campaigned across the land demanding law and order, resigned on the tenth. Implicated in a series of petty grafts continuing since his days as a county executive in Maryland, Agnew pleaded no contest to income tax evasion and resigned.

Two days later, the Circuit Court of Appeals for the District of Columbia rejected Nixon's claim that secret tape recordings made in his offices were protected by executive privilege. The court by a 5–2 vote ordered the recordings turned over to District Court Judge John Sirica. The tapes now became the great prize of Watergate.

Though Nixon tried to evade the court order, his control of the presidency slipped away. He made a last effort to block release of the damning tapes with an appeal to the Supreme Court, a court headed by his hand-picked choice, Warren Burger, a court with no less than four of his appointees now sitting.

The embattled president hunkered down as the House of Representatives voted to instruct the chairman of its Judiciary Committee to investigate possible impeachment charges. (Chairman Peter Rodino sought Warren's advice on the selection of a special counsel for the committee's probe; just what Warren told him was not recorded in Warren's files.)

Warren took no pleasure in the fall of Richard Nixon, former law clerk Scott Bice learned during a two-hour visit in May, 1973, with the Chief. "We talked a lot about Watergate, about Nixon, and about how this showed a character that he always thought was there, and the flaws that were in it."

Bice finally asked, "You think impeachment?"

"No," Warren replied. "The American people will not impeach a president."

"He was very sad about how the office, the institution had been sullied. Public office was a way of doing good, of setting a moral tone, of providing moral leadership."

Watergate appalled Warren—yet at the same time it reaffirmed his faith in the American democracy.

In a speech before the National Press Club on December 13, Warren described the unfolding scandal as "conduct debasing our institutions" and a "debacle, the great tragedy of our time . . . cancerous to the body politic."

For attorneys, Watergate was worse still, Warren reminded law school audiences. "[T]he reputation of our profession has recently suffered greatly because a score of lawyers have been convicted or indicted for felonious conduct in the performance of their official duties in the highest reaches of our national government." Among the twenty-one people in and around the White House who had been indicted, sixteen were lawyers. And a seventeenth, the president himself, was in jeopardy.

If there was any bright spot at all amid the "myriad of crimes" known as Watergate, Warren sometimes added, it lay in the fact that ordinary Americans had brought the scandal to light. A security guard faithful to his responsibilities had discovered the burglars. And the federal grand jury bringing the indictments was a goodly sampling of the citizens of Washington, black, white, employed, unemployed, retired, professional and blue-collar men and women.

There was satisfaction in the knowledge that the righteous would prevail, somehow. Earl Warren could not be the stalwart guardian he had once been.

Now in his eighties, he was slower physically—though nothing impeded his attendance at Washington Redskins football games. But the once rosy cheeks were drawn, the skin like old leather, creased in deepening wrinkles. And then there was his heart problem.

In the spring of 1972, Warren went to a doctor, complaining of chest pains. He came away from a battery of tests with a prescription for nitroglycerin capsules.

In the face of the diagnosis Warren was ever stoic. While walking on a brilliant day in the park atop San Francisco's Nob Hill with his son Earl, he announced cryptically, punching his chest with a fist, "You know, I have a little angina."

It was enough for these undemonstrative men who found it so difficult even to express their love. The younger man understood this was more than "a little angina." His father was saying, "I'm not going to be around too long."

The former chief justice still accepted speaking engagements—though doctors, he grumbled, periodically "grounded" him. At the end of January, 1974, in the middle of a four-speech tour of California, he complained he "wasn't feeling well."

Son-in-law Stuart Brien, a pediatrician, arranged for him to be hospitalized in Daniel Freeman Hospital in Inglewood. Tests for "coronary disease" showed he had suffered no heart attack; he needed only rest. After eight days in the hospital, he was released. He was rested, "as well as ever, and I am back in the office on a regular schedule," he assured friends.

He resumed his travels, fulfilling commitments made as long as a year earlier. On Saturday, April 20, 1974, he attended the black-tie dinner his former clerks held for him annually at the National Lawyers Club. The next morning, as was their custom, Nina and Earl Warren hosted the clerks and their wives at a brunch at the Congressional Country Club.

At the end of the week he was in New Orleans to speak at the dedication of a new law building at Loyola University. Two weeks later he was in

California, delivering the commencement address at the University of Santa Clara.

On Tuesday, May 21, 1974, he traveled to Atlanta, Georgia, to receive an honorary doctorate from Morehouse College. In his speech at this small, all-black school, he again warned the National Court of Appeals loomed as a threat to the Supreme Court, "the last forum to which all Americans have free access . . ."

He appealed to the graduates to remember that "everyone, no matter how humble, can have some influence on American life, and one never knows when his acts as an individual might have profound effects."

He was optimistic still. "There are a myriad of instances where one individual has profoundly changed the course of history, and under our system it will always be possible."

There was work yet to be done, work for them, he reminded the black families seated before him. "We are only partway up the mountain we have assayed to climb. We must not falter in the face of recalcitrance born of race prejudice."

It was to be his last public address.

He returned to Washington to confer on Wednesday, May 22, with law clerk Jim Graham regarding research for his memoirs. During their two-hour conversation, Warren recalled an earlier appearance in Georgia during his 1948 whistle-stop tour as the Republican vice presidential nominee.

Because he had stated he would not address a segregated audience, a few blacks had been seated on the speakers' platform. But the rest of the house was segregated, black people in the balcony, whites on the main floor.

"I can see the searching look in their eyes to this day as I told them there should be one law for all men," he told Graham. As he spoke, Warren's face hardened with the conviction that law and social custom had conspired to commit a wrong upon humanity.

In the conversation with Graham he repeated a statement made to the Morehouse graduates the day before. There was "an invidious view which is now held by many: You can't wipe out racial discrimination by law, only through changing the hearts and minds of men."

Warren disdained that as "false credo. True, prejudice cannot be wiped out, but infliction of it upon others can."

This was to be the Chief's last working session at the Court. Two days later, complaining once more of chest pains, he entered Georgetown University Hospital at the insistence of his doctor, Oscar Mann. Water was building up in his chest, so much so that the pain made it difficult for him to sleep.*

---

* According to Arthur Goldberg, Warren said he wanted to enter Bethesda Naval Hospital but needed President Nixon's approval. Nixon reportedly refused, then changed his mind. When Dr. William Lukash, the White House physician, offered to arrange Warren's transfer, Warren in injured pride refused. The anecdote is retold in Pollack, p. 321.

He remained hospitalized until June 2, then stayed confined to the apartment at the Sheraton-Park.

His recuperation went slowly. Margaret McHugh telephoned the apartment for news, then passed on what she had learned to Graham.

June 6: Chief won't be in this week. He's canceled dinner engagements to June 20.

June 19: Warren had a very bad night. Maybe he would be in the following day. Graham's research for the memoirs was piling up, waiting the Chief's return.

June 26: Warren has been away from the Court for five weeks. Nothing Mrs. McHugh has sent to the apartment has been returned, even simple memos requiring only a yes or no answer. Warren's chauffeur commented that the Chief was not doing well.

Edgar and Marjorie Patterson arrived from California. A cranky Earl Warren was waiting for them, perturbed their plane had been late. "I've been waiting for you for hours," he complained.

Three decades before, Governor Warren had encouraged young Capitol policeman Pat Patterson to get an education. Patterson had followed the advice, and eventually was to teach police and community relations at Sacramento State College.

Through the years the Pattersons had telephoned as often as once a month, visiting on occasion. Now Pat Patterson, who had once instructed Governor Warren about growing up black in America, was assuring his friend, "You and I have got a lot of places to go."

Patterson bravely proposed they tour the predominantly black colleges of the South, without fanfare, speaking to the students, just seeing for themselves how integration was working in the South.

"Well," Warren agreed tentatively, "let's set that up when I'm well."

The Pattersons stayed for two hours or more, Marge and Nina doing most of the talking as they sat beside Warren's bed. They talked about the Warren children, now grown, with families of their own; about football games and horse jumping; about those long-ago days in the mansion, the happiest of Nina's life.

Then it was time to go, Nina firmly announcing to the men, "You guys can settle those problems later."

They said good-bye, the governor and his former chauffeur, the two men in tears, the four of them hugging one another.

Warren was having difficulty breathing. The oxygen was not helping.

On July 2, Jim Graham noted in his diary: "No news today. He is now too tired, too weak to shave. He's not reading. This leaves everything uncertain."

That day, having resisted Dr. Mann's orders that he reenter the hospital, Warren finally relented. The diagnosis was congestive heart failure coupled with a coronary insufficiency.

On Wednesday night, July 3, oldest son James flew in from California, while James's son Jeffrey arrived from New York City. The next day, grand-father, son, and grandson gathered in Room 6103 of the Georgetown Hospital.

"He wasn't looking too well," Jeff Warren recalled. To Jeff's frustration, a watchful nurse sat in a corner, refusing to leave.

Papa Warren had lost weight, leaving him just "skin and bones," lying listlessly in the hospital bed. They chatted for a while, then grandfather, father, and son, each in his own time a member of the same select and secret society at Berkeley, convened an informal meeting on this, the traditional meeting night.

As was the custom of their society, each read a favorite poem, first James, then Jeff. When it was his turn, the frail man thumbed through the book until he came to Rudyard Kipling's "The Explorer."

Summoning a strong voice, he read:

"Something hidden. Go and find it. Go and look behind the Ranges—
Something lost behind the ranges. Lost and waiting for you. Go!" . . .

God took care to hide that country till He judged His people ready,
Then He chose me for His whisper, and I've found it, and it's yours!

Yes, your "Never-never country"—yes, your "edge of cultivation,"
And "no sense in going further"—till I crossed the range to see.

God forgive me! No, I didn't. It's God's present to our nation.
Anybody might have found it, but—His whisper came to me.

When Warren finished reading, he threw his arms up over his head, pleased with himself. "Okay, fellas!" he announced.

Son and grandson kissed the old man and left.

They returned the next day, to talk about the law, about recent decisions of the Supreme Court, and about sports. When they finally said good-bye on Friday, Warren had regained his spirits. As son and grandson rose to leave, Warren clapped his hands and promised, "Well, fellas, see you the next time you're back here."

On Monday, July 8, Arthur Goldberg visited. The two former justices discussed the Watergate tapes case, argued that day in the Supreme Court. Warren was adamant in his conviction that the Court not allow the presi-dent to avoid a subpoena by invoking executive privilege.

"No man, not even a king, can put himself above the law," Warren insisted. "I am confident the Court will do its duty, and so will the nation."

The following day, Bill Brennan and Bill Douglas visited at 4:30 P.M., bringing secret word of that day's conference vote. The justices had voted unanimously, 8–0, to compel immediate obedience to the subpoena. The ninth justice, William Rehnquist, had recused himself on the grounds he had worked in the Nixon Department of Justice.

Warren was content. "If Nixon is not forced to turn over tapes of his conversations with the ring of men who were conversing on their violations of the law, then liberty will soon be dead in this nation," he whispered to the two sitting justices.

"If Nixon gets away with that," he continued, "then Nixon makes the law as he goes along—not the Congress nor the Courts."

The Court's decision, which Warren Burger would write, left no chance of that. Richard Nixon's presidency was hung by tape recordings he himself made.

Warren also asked Brennan about the National Court of Appeals proposal. It was failing for lack of support, Brennan replied. Earl Warren seemed to have won his last battle.

When the two visitors rose to say good-bye at 5:30, Warren urged them to stay longer. Mindful of his wasting energy, they excused themselves. Bill Douglas walked from the room in the knowledge he would not see Warren again.

The Chief rested easily in the early evening of July 9, 1974, after the two justices had left. The news from the Court had visibly cheered him. Virginia, there every day, went home to her family; Nina and Honey Bear, summoned from Los Angeles, decided to stay on for a while. Then they too would leave.

Warren lay quietly resting. Suddenly, at 8:10 P.M., his back arched in spasm. The once great chest heaved, and he uttered a single strangled cry.

Earl Warren, fourteenth chief justice of the United States, sank lifeless upon the bed.

AFTERWORD

ARL WARREN WAS BURIED AMONG HEROES AT ARLINGTON NATIONAL Cemetery on the afternoon of Friday, July 12, 1974.

For a day and a half, nine thousand people had filed past his flag-draped coffin in the solemn quiet of the Great Hall of the Supreme Court, plain folks come to pay their last respects.

Another thousand, mostly dignitaries, attended the funeral service at Washington's National Cathedral, including the embattled president of the United States, Richard Nixon. Nearby, the sitting justices of the Supreme Court of the United States filled a pew, men who earlier that week had settled the president's political fate.

Three clerics—an Episcopalian bishop, a Catholic archbishop, and a rabbi —gave benedictions that afternoon for a man unchurched yet deeply moral. Four retired justices who had served with Warren—eighty-nine-year-old Stanley Reed, Tom Clark, Arthur Goldberg, and Abe Fortas, men of such widely differing philosophies—also came to honor the man they all called "Chief."

Twelve days after the body of Earl Warren was laid to rest, his successor, Warren Burger, delivered the unanimous opinion of the Supreme Court: Richard Nixon, no less than any other citizen of the Republic, was obligated to comply with a court order and deliver sixty-four tape recordings of White House conversations to the Watergate special prosecutor.

Nixon had been right to be worried about "the Supreme Court thing." Transcripts of the tapes provided "the smoking gun," proof that the president had violated his oath of office, and had attempted to block investigations of the Watergate burglary.

Facing impeachment in the House of Representatives, and certain conviction in the Senate for high crimes and misdemeanors, Richard Milhous Nixon announced his resignation on August 8, 1974.

Meanwhile, the legacy of Earl Warren loomed larger.

Those who opposed Warren and the "liberal" decisions of his Court expected its successor to rescind or reverse the legal revolution Warren had led. But neither the Burger Court nor *its* successor, the Court over which the conservative William Rehnquist presided, have rescinded the minimal standards established during the years of Earl Warren.

The Burger Court, in large part because its true intellectual leader was William Brennan, remained surprisingly liberal in its decisions. The abortion decision of *Roe v. Wade,* easily the most controversial opinion since *Brown,* flowed directly from the right of privacy rulings of the Warren Court.

The Rehnquist Court has proved more hostile to the poor, the prisoners, and the luckless petitioners once welcome in the Warren Court.

William Rehnquist is not Earl Warren, neither in spirit nor in experience. Over the years, Warren changed his opinions, grew to meet the demands of each new job.

In contrast, Rehnquist's views appeared to be "flash frozen" as a young man, unthawed and unchanged since. He himself told an interviewer in 1985, his opinions had not changed over the years. "I can remember arguments we would get into as law clerks in the early fifties. And I don't know that my views had changed much from that time."

The justices under the intellectually rigid Rehnquist have restricted some rights, particularly the right of appeal in federal courts. In doing so, they overturned a 1963 decision which held that any state prisoner who could demonstrate his or her constitutional rights had been violated was entitled to seek a writ of habeas corpus in federal court.

The Rehnquist Court has tended to be far more solicitous of police and prosecutors' arguments than its predecessors. The justices have permitted warrantless searches of bags and luggage found in automobiles. They have allowed police to search, with permission, the suitcases of bus passengers— invariably members of minorities suspected of smuggling narcotics.

They have reversed a Warren Court decision holding that coerced or involuntary confessions could never be considered "harmless error" in a criminal trial. Chief Justice Rehnquist's 5–4 opinion held that such a confession would not invalidate a conviction if other evidence, independently obtained, supported the guilty verdict.

Furthermore, they have held that prosecutors might use otherwise inadmissible confessions to impeach a defendant's testimony in court.

Still, Court observers agree, while the Rehnquist Court has not expanded civil liberties and civil rights, the conservative judicial revolution has fallen short of expectations.

The major decisions of the Warren years stand, particularly those that fixed the federal Bill of Rights upon the fifty states through "incorporation."

In 1925, the Supreme Court took the first step toward incorporation of the Bill of Rights within the Fourteenth Amendment's guarantee of due process. Freedom of speech and the press, secured from federal intrusion by the First Amendment, were "protected by the due process clause of the Fourteenth Amendment from impairment by the States."

Within fifteen years, the Court had brought the balance of the First Amendment—rights of assembly, of petitioning for a redress of grievances, and of conscience—under the Fourteenth Amendment's umbrella.

Then the Court halted.

Instigated by Hugo Black, in the 1960s, the Warren Court resumed piecemeal incorporation of the Bill of Rights within the Fourteenth Amendment. The right to counsel, to be free from unreasonable searches and seizures, to be protected against self-incrimination and double jeopardy, to confront witnesses in a trial, all these the Court laid upon the states.

By the time Warren stepped down, all the rights embodied in the First, Fourth, Fifth, Sixth, and Eighth Amendments—but for the prohibition against excessive bail—had been applied to the states.

As one civil rights attorney explained, "The big deal about the Warren Court is that it made states toe the mark on constitutional rights."

Meanwhile, a generation later, *Brown* —Warren's great moral teaching— remains the ideal; the United States shall not be two societies, separate and unequal.

The political revolution wrought by the redistricting cases of *Baker v. Carr* and *Reynolds v. Sims* continues. The concept of one-man-one-vote is so simply understood, so fundamental to fairness that it cannot be reversed, even if legislatures were so minded.

The minimal standards the Warren Court created in the field of criminal law with *Miranda, Gideon,* and *Mapp* hold. Police still advise suspects of their rights. Courts still throw out evidence as inadmissible because of police errors. Poor defendants in criminal cases are provided competent lawyers, and free transcripts on appeal.

Curiously, for all the controversy the Warren Court stirred, a surprising number of its decisions that fundamentally changed the law have been accepted without question. The pivotal *Times v. Sullivan* opinion has defined the law of libel since it was handed down in 1963. *Roth v. United States* opened the way for a more mature view of sex and sexual matters in the eyes of the law. The decision in *Sheppard v. Maxwell* still mediates the boundaries between a free and vigorous press and a defendant's right to a fair trial.

As former Warren law clerk and now University of Virginia professor of law G. Edward White noted, the decisions of 1953–1969 seem to have defied the norm of thirty-year cycles of generational change. "Certainly the kind of radical revision of Warren Court decisions that Warren feared and many commentators anticipated have not come to pass. Quite the contrary."

Only in one area, perhaps, does the Warren Court precedent seem tenuous. Conservatives political and religious would like to reverse the School Prayer decision, *Engel v. Vitale,* prohibiting even the most innocuous prayer in public schools. Yet here too the Court, three decades later, has respected precedent.

Any estimate of Warren's career will mark him as one of the seminal figures not only of his own time, but of the years that followed his death. As governor of California, he had the vision to shape the state that would teach America to cope with social and political change in the last half of the century.

As chief justice, Warren ranks among the smallest handful of men to have served on the Supreme Court, "second in greatness only to John Marshall himself in the eyes of most impartial students of the Court as well as the Court's critics."

His achievements are all the more remarkable. Earl Warren was neither a student of government nor a judicial craftsman. Neither was he a legal scholar. He lacked an articulated judicial philosophy beyond the penetrating and constant query, "Is it fair?"

He had only an abiding sense of the public good—that, and a respect for personal values considered old-fashioned or even irrelevant to the business of governing.

Those two qualities, coupled with his own sense of purpose, made him a great leader.

They left the nation, in the words of the Torah passage proclaimed at his funeral, "the memory of the great and the righteous which shall live as an everlasting blessing."

ACKNOWLEDGMENTS

A book like this, seven years in gestation, has many midwives. Some materially assisted, some coached, some coaxed. All helped.

These friends and, in some cases, co-workers, included:

Sam Adams, who read the manuscript;

Herbert Brownell, former attorney general of the United States, who read chapters 20 and 21;

Gene Marine, who read the chapters on Warren's California years, scolding the author for lapses in grammar and fact; and

Fred Okrand, counsel emeritus of the American Civil Liberties Union of Southern California, who lived much of the story here, and read the manuscript for legal errors.

A number of friends provided hospitality to an itinerant writer: Marty and Dennis Renault in Sacramento, too many times to recall without embarrassment; Richard D'Acetis, Elliott Negin, and Marc Okrand in Washington; and in Austin, Texas, Robert and Dagmar Hamilton, Sanford and Cynthia Levinson, and Zipporah Wiseman.

There was hospitality of a different kind offered by the many people I interviewed for this book, including members of the Warren family. They patiently sat for repeated interviews, sometimes reliving painful moments, yet asked nothing of the author. A journalist, a biographer could have asked for nothing more.

In addition, forty-five former law clerks of the Chief, and seven members of the staff of the Kennedy Assassination Commission gave me extended interviews. Bound by pledges of silence, many were speaking of their experience for the first time to an outsider. Their sense of history placed them under obligation to future generations and I regret that some did not live long enough to see the publication of this book.

All of their taped reminiscences, along with six file drawers of research material, have been deposited at UCLA's Department of Special Collections for use by future historians and biographers.

Others too made substantial contributions:

Betty Foot Henderson, whose Sacramento garage yielded reminiscences of the governor's office and mansion during the Warren years, and Wilma Wagner, who also remembered those years fondly;

John Weaver, who opened his own Warren files and heart to this book;

Hugo Black, Jr., for permission to use his father's papers in the Library of Congress;

Lee Coe, for two scarce pamphlets dealing with the Ship Murder Case;

John Ahouse, for his run of *Epic News;*

Scott Powe, who guided me through the Supreme Court's rulings prior to *Plessy;*

the late Leonard Leader, Greg Mitchell, Lisa Rubens, Thor Severson, and Thomas Waltz, all of whom shared their own unpublished research material.

Then there were the librarians and archivists:

the staff at UCLA's Department of Special Collections;

William Roberts, university archivist, Bancroft Library, University of California, Berkeley;

Teddi Akers and Fred Myers of the California State Archives;

Patti Graziano, head librarian at the *Cleveland Plain Dealer;*

Janice Davis and Dennis Bilger of the Harry S Truman Library, Independence, Missouri;

David Wigdor, Frederick W. Bauman, Jr., Mike Klein, and intern Scott Wirz at the Library of Congress Manuscript Division;

Craig St. Clair of the sadly disbanded *Los Angeles Times* History Center;

Claudia Anderson and Ted Gottinger at the Lyndon Baines Johnson Library;

Doug Smith of the Oakland History Collection, Oakland Public Library;

Shinomiya Yae, librarian at *The Oakland Tribune;*

George Schlukbier, chief librarian, *The Sacramento Bee;*

John Gonzales, Sacramento State Library;

Judy Canter, head librarian, and Mike Tuller, *San Francisco Examiner;*

Sharon Hurling, UCLA Microfilm Library;

Karl Kabelac, Department of Rare Books and Special Collections, University of Rochester,

Julia Johnson, head of the Government Publications Library at the University of Southern California;

Mary A. Hollerich, head of the USC Interlibrary Loan Department, and Kathleen Smalldon of her staff; and

Dace Taub, of USC's Regional History Collection.

Three others should be mentioned: David W. McGhee, who worked through the Warren material in the Eisenhower Library; and Michele Trebino and Holly Ziemer, who transcribed some of the taped interviews.

I received timely assistance from West Publishing Corporation, through its Westlaw on-line service; and from Dorothy Molstad, Roxanne Schenzel, and Tim Robinson of that company.

I would also like to acknowledge a grant from the Lyndon Baines Johnson Presidential Library which made possible a productive week in Austin.

My thanks also to friends who lent aid and encouragement: Vince Cosgrove, Robert Dallek, Jack Langguth, Bryce Nelson, Nancy Scott, Paul Wilner, and William Woestendiek;

And to Diane, for ample reason.

Ed Cray
Los Angeles
1988–96

NOTES

In the interest of brevity, the following abbreviations are used in the notes:

CR: *Congressional Record*
DPP: Drew Pearson Papers, Lyndon Baines Johnson Library
EWP/LC: Earl Warren Papers, Library of Congress
EWP/S: Earl Warren Papers, California State Archives, Sacramento. The number following is the file number.
Int.: Interview
JWP: John Weaver Papers, Department of Special Collections, University Research Library, UCLA
LAT: *Los Angeles Times*
NYT: *The New York Times*
OH: Oral History
Sac Bee: *The Sacramento Bee*
SF Chron: *San Francisco Chronicle*
SF Ex: *San Francisco Examiner*

Unattributed interviews are by the author. Copies of these interviews are deposited in the Department of Special Collections, University Research Library, UCLA.

INTRODUCTION

9   Only Abe: Miriam Dinkins Johnson int., January 22, 1991.
10   There was no sudden: Kenny, "California Attorney General," OH, 1979. Pearson's comment is in his undated notes for a biography on Warren in the Lyndon Baines Johnson Library.
10   Warren is: McIntyre Faries OH, p. 93.
10   never set the world: Gunther, p. 18.
10   biggest damn fool: Warren, *Memoirs*, p. 5.
11   will be remembered: Martin Agronsky, quoted in Merrell Small's memoir, "The Country Editor and the Governor," Bancroft Library 77/142, interleaved page after page 512.
11   he will rank: Douglas's appreciation is in *California Law Review*, 58:1, p. 4. He continued, "That rating goes to men who, seeing or sensing the strong tides of events, strive to keep the Constitution modern by making it responsive to current needs."
11   surprised: See "Butterfield to Ehrlichman, October 11, 1971," in *From the President*, p. 327, reporting

a *Life* magazine poll. *Life's* sister publication, *Time,* on January 31, 1944, had decided Warren's record "fails to reveal much promise that he is a potential giant in U.S. history."

11 History is: Earl Warren, Jr., int., July 29, 1991.

CHAPTER 1

16 Son, never let yourself: Weaver, *Warren,* p. 26.

16 He never spent: Warren, *Memoirs,* p. 22.

16 My father: *The Oakland Tribune,* May 17, 1926.

17 I am going: Anna Warren to EW, July 9, 1948, courtesy of Jeffrey Warren.

17 Having lost: Warren, *Memoirs,* p. 14.

17 My boy: Warren, *Memoirs,* p. 15.

18 the ragged edge: Brecher, p. 85.

18 large numbers: *LAT,* June 30, 1894, p. 2.

18 a large group: Warren, *Memoirs,* pp. 12–13. In a conversation with the author on February 19, 1993, Warren biographer John Weaver said, "When he told of the hanging in effigy, all those years later, he gripped the arms of his chair so hard his knuckles were white."

19 were very well mannered: Ruth Smith Henley OH, p. iii.

20 a major crime: Ethel Plank in *The Bakersfield Californian,* June 22, 1966, in JWP, Box 170, File 49.

20 He always liked: Ethel Plank to John Weaver, November 6, 1965, in JWP, Box 170, Folder 49.

20 Earl was an average student: Weaver, *Warren,* p. 22.

20 there was no special promise: Pollack, p. 22. Governor Warren was later to appoint Pauly to the Kern County Board of Supervisors.

21 Father thought: Ethel Plank to John Weaver, November 6, 1965, in JWP, Box 170, Folder 49.

21 shortchanged: Warren, *Memoirs,* p. 27.

21 had quite an analytic mind: Weaver, *Warren,* p. 27.

22 It wasn't that my playing: Pollack, p. 24.

22 get an eyeful: Cavins OH, p. 28.

22 I was dealing: Warren, *Memoirs,* p. 30.

23 I, Earl Warren: Weaver, *Warren,* p. 19.

23 Warren's New Hair Dope: JWP, Box 173, File 72.

CHAPTER 2

24 Well, my boy: Warren, *Memoirs,* p. 32.

24 for a doctor: Pollack, p. 23.

25 As I stood: Warren, *Memoirs,* p. 34.

26 cat and mouse: Warren, *Memoirs,* p. 35.

26 No book: Stone, p. 19.

26 The Freshman: Stone, p. 19.

27 Come on, Pinky: Stone, p. 20.

27 a love between men: Author's not-for-attribution int.

27 the only thing that matters: Jeffrey Warren int., March 3, 1994.

28 pour out his heart: *CR,* June 23, 1955, p. 9062.

28 The supreme issue: Katcher, p. 336.

28 He was called: *CR,* June 23, 1955, p. 9062.

29 The law school: Stone, p. 21.

29 You will never: Weaver, *Warren,* p. 32.

30 I guess I must: Stone, p. 24.

30 The atmosphere: Warren, *Memoirs,* p. 45.

31 to kick the Southern Pacific: Bean, p. 324.

31 Onward, Christian capitalists: Olin, p. 55.

31 Mr. Warren: Warren, *Memoirs,* p. 45.

33 almost in squalor: Warren, *Memoirs,* p. 47.

33 a big man mentally: Pollack, p. 34.

CHAPTER 3

35 a state of flux: Warren, *Memoirs,* p. 52.

36 inspirational: Warren, *Memoirs,* p. 56.

36 womanless, voteless: Lewis S. Gannett, "The I.W.W.," *The Nation,* October 20, 1920, pp. 448–49.

36 The I.W.W. are worse: *SF Chron,* February 16, 1918.

37 Huns of industry: Weintraub, p. 163.
37 I don't think: Whitten, p. 25.
38 I was then so tense: Pollack, p. 47.
38 I had a sense of liberation: Warren, *Memoirs,* p. 61.
39 happy days: EW to Jack D. Maltester, June 28, 1963, in the file "General, 1963," Box 361, EWP/LC.
39 Everything went in Emeryville: Katcher, p. 45.
39 I would frequently: Stone, p. 39.
39 some repulsive informers: Warren, *Memoirs,* p. 62.
40 We were so poor: Nina Warren is quoted in an int. with grandson Jeffrey Warren, March 10, 1994.
41 I spotted him: Stone, p. 46.
41 Actually, he took: Pollack, p. 38.
41 was in no position: Nina Warren int. in Irving Stone Papers, UCLA.
42 had a lot of friends: Katcher, pp. 42–43.

CHAPTER 4

44 unless you were: Jahnsen OH, p. 32.
44 In every county: Walsh int., January 6, 1994.
45 looked like they'd come: Katcher, p. 39.
45 Kid, you're the next: Mullins OH, p. 2.
45 those weren't: Katcher, p. 44.
45 My only objection: Stone, p. 52.
46 because he was ambitious: Shaw OH, p. 10.
46 I knew: Pollack, p. 43.
46 Your program: Mullins OH, p. 6.
47 I believe the quality: *SF Ex,* January 13, 1925.
47 about the worldly ways: Jahnsen OH, p. 6.
48 altogether too demanding: Olney OH, p. 99.
48 It's a great feeling: EW to Drew Pearson, February 7, 1966, in DPP, EW #2 folder.
48 took pride: Olney OH, pp. 105–6.
48 Boy Scouts: Warren, *Memoirs,* p. 103.
48 honorably prosecute: Warren, *Memoirs,* p. 72.
48 he would toy: John D. Weaver, "The Honorable Earl Warren," Part II, *Holiday,* May, 1966, p. 77.
49 Meyers was promptly: Warren, *Memoirs,* p. 78.
49 the most efficient: Pollack, p. 41.
50 an abdominal operation: Warren, *Memoirs,* p. 65.
50 engraved invitations: Warren, *Memoirs,* p. 65.
50 started housekeeping: Nina Palmquist Warren OH.
50 James never wanted: Margaret Warren int., October 1, 1992.
50 marvel how: Nina Warren, "Notes," p. 3, appended to her OH.
51 had to work up: Jahnsen OH, p. 169.
51 his comrades: *SF Ex,* January 20, 1925.
51 When a victim: Coakley, *For the People,* p. 23.
51 a man with: *SF Ex,* February 6, 1925.
51 It has come: *SF Ex,* February 1, 1925.
51 pretty strenuous: Coakley OH, p. 30.
51 Bessie, you leave: Warren, *Memoirs,* p. 83.
52 with the full knowledge: *SF Ex,* July 9, 1926.
52 for the avowed purpose: Open letter from Earl Warren, August 26, 1926, in EWP/S 1.
52 It was more important: Katcher, p. 52.
53 the federal plan: Bean, pp. 365–66; Spence OH.
53 We have a strict rule: Pollack, p. 45.
53 I managed to win: Stone, p. 56.

CHAPTER 5

54 You take care: Warren, *Memoirs,* p. 86.
55 boys and girls: *SF Ex,* November 28, 1927.
55 rum orgies: *SF Ex,* July 30, 1929.
55 Reputations were ruined: Sherry OH, pp. 46–47.
56 I would not recommend: Warren, *Memoirs,* p. 90.

56 Earl Warren would: Cerwin, p. 39.
56 The prosecution: Hichborn, p. 437.
56 If I quit: Coakley OH, p. 37.
57 I can't see how: Warren, Berkeley OH, p. 56.
57 Well, go ahead: Warren, Berkeley OH, p. 56.
57 spectacular only: Warren, *Memoirs,* p. 100.
57 the most sweeping: *SF Ex,* June 18, 1930.
57 became my preoccupation: Weaver, *Warren,* p. 39.
57 How are ya?: Pollack, p. 4.
57 a hell of a politician: Jester OH, pp. 14, 21.
57 You do your job: Jahnsen OH, p. 172.
58 the attitude of fathers: *The Oakland Tribune,* March 13, 1926.
58 I hope: *SF Ex,* September 4, 1931.
58 systematic graft: *The Oakland Tribune,* October 22, 1931.
58 but when you went: Severin OH, p. 13.
59 We shared friendship: Stone, p. 65.
59 representing interests: Warren campaign letter, August 26, 1926, in EWP/S 1.
59 so they couldn't say: Severin OH, p. 13.
59 With Warren: Balaban OH, p. 8.
59 Tell your father: Earl Warren, Jr., int., February 21, 1991.
60 Thank you: Huston, *Pathway,* p. 45.
60 He ran: Coakley OH, p. 57.
60 Let's not fool: Jahnsen OH, p. 148.
60 If you have a man: *Inter-City Express,* December 22, 1965, tipped into the Shea OH.
60 a very tough DA: Resner OH, p. 9.
60 the most intelligent: *The Oakland Tribune,* September 30, 1931; *NYT,* September 30, 1931. Moley later determined he had proclaimed Warren "the best District Attorney in the United States." See his *27 Masters of Politics,* p. 63.
61 plenty of places: Robert Warren OH, p. 4.
62 we got to know: Drew Pearson, "Washington Merry-Go-Round," syndicated column, June 25, 1968.
62 if one believes: Nina Warren Brien OH, p. 22.
62 felt that everybody's: Earl Warren, Jr., int., March 21, 1991.
63 Home is for living: Pollack, p. 52.
63 I feel: EW to J. Frederick Ching, May 6, 1935, in EWP/S 17942.
63 Inevitably we'd get: James Warren OH, p. 11.
63 Unless you had thought: Earl Warren, Jr., int., February 21, 1991.
63 I didn't dare quit: James Warren OH, p. 12.
63 I remember "slacker": James Warren OH, p. 20.
63 one scared kid: James Warren OH, p. 15.
63 In fact: James Warren OH, p. 15.
64 He used to talk: James Warren OH, p. 20.

CHAPTER 6

65 the least susceptible: Bagwell, p. 203.
66 Our government: Bagwell, p. 220.
66 protecting life: Form letter dated August 21, 1934 in EWP/S 57.
66 We made it: EW, "Conversations," p. 78.
66 This is no way: Sherry OH, p. 2.
67 The workers: EW to Robert Wohlforth, November 17, 1938, in *Violations of Free Speech and Rights of Labor,* Part 70, pp. 25717–18.
67 No one ever: Stone, p. 88.
67 You don't break: Arthur Sherry in Pollack, p. 48.
67 I would have burned: *SF Ex,* September 11, 1932. But see the Jester OH, pp. 29–30.
68 the best: Moley is quoted in Warren, *Memoirs,* p. 118. In the *NYT,* September 29, 1931, Moley described Warren as "the most intelligent and politically independent District Attorney in the United States."
68 a run-down-at-the-heel: Powers OH, p. 3.
68 cultivating them: Powers OH, p. 9.
68 the biggest lobbyist: Warren, "Conversations," p. 13.
68 but it wasn't slowing: Jester OH, p. 60.

69   increasing discussion: *The Oakland Tribune,* March 13, 1934.

69   was a Republican: Warren, *Memoirs,* p. 122.

69   Earl represents: Mitchell, p. 238, citing a letter of September 24, 1934.

69   Warren Declares: *The Oakland Tribune,* October 18, 1935.

70   while we stood: James Warren OH, p. 27.

70   Hoover was a beaten man: EW is quoted in Drew Pearson's unpublished proposal for a biography of EW, in DPP, LBJ Library.

70   the first major effort: Schwartz and Lesher, p. 9.

70   Extreme radicalism: Schwartz and Lesher, p. 10. The balance of the quote is from an interview of Deputy District Attorney James H. Oakley by John Weaver in JWP, Box 171, File 60. Warren warmed to FDR, Earl Junior said. "There was more than public courtesy in my father's respect for Roosevelt." Earl Warren, Jr., int., February 21, 1991.

71   I knew I was spoiled: Stone, p. 84.

71   But if you should: Warren, *Memoirs,* p. 110.

72   I did aspire: Warren, *Memoirs,* p. 109.

72   revolutionary at the time: White, *Earl Warren,* p. 34.

72   curb crime: Richard H. Chamberlain OH, p. 4; and Kenny, "My First Forty Years," p. 101.

73   an affable: Burke, p. 23. Merriam's Klan membership was reported in *Epic News,* November 5, 1934.

73   drinking himself: Sinclair, p. 4.

74   he could provide: *Los Angeles Herald,* September 29, 1934, courtesy of Greg Mitchell.

75   the issues confronting: Press release dated October 22, 1934, in EWP/S 49.

75   election would mean: Hill, pp. 81-82.

75   a crusade: Press release dated October 15, 1934, in EWP/S 49.

75   Take California out: EW to "Dear Comrade," undated letter in EWP/S 57.

75   The battle: Radio address, October 22, 1934, in EWP/S 49.

75   Half the unemployed: *Epic News,* October 1, 1934, in EWP/S 49.

75   Heavy Rush of Idle: Sinclair, p. 126.

75   If I am elected: Sinclair, p. 127.

75   for the billboards: Ward Moore in *Frontier,* October, 1953, p. 20.

75   would Russianize: Sinclair, p. 146.

75   to protect us: Press release dated October 30, 1934, in EWP/S 49.

76   The people of California: EW statement, November 6, 1934, in EWP/S 49. Despite his defeat, Sinclair later maintained, "Only we did win. We gave California and all the other states an exciting awareness of what Democracy really is. Franklin Roosevelt was listening to us. And a young district attorney in Alameda County was listening. A fellow by the name of Earl Warren." See *Sac Bee,* September 19, 1958. About the same time, Sinclair also asserted, "Many of the things I was for in 1934 are the law of the land now." From an interview with Ewing Hass, January 11, 1992.

CHAPTER 7

77   the deuces-wild game: Gladwin Hill int., July 10, 1991.

78   it behooves: EW to C. E. Ware, March 17, 1936, EWP/S 212.

78   an outstanding candidate: EW to Ware, EWP/S 212.

78   on other than: EW to Herbert Hoover, June 18, 1935, in EWP/S 157.

79   A united front: Press release dated February 15, [1936,] in EWP/S 68. The committee's history is in H. L. Carnahan to Chester Rowell, January 25, 1936, in the Dickson Papers, UCLA, Collection 662, Box 8, Folder 14.

80   for the sole purpose: Undated statement in EWP/S 157.

80   unpopularity contest: *Newsweek,* May 16, 1936, p. 13.

80   mysterious: *SF Ex,* April 17, 1936. The cartoons ran in the *Examiner* on May 4 and May 5, 1936.

80   Hearst is running: H. L. Carnahan to EW, March 31, 1936, in EWP/S 212.

80   What do you think: Warren, *Memoirs,* p. 112.

80   Well, Mr. President: Warren, Berkeley OH, p. 72.

80   I have never: EW quoted in Drew Pearson Diary, February 6, 1966, in DPP, EW No. 2 file, LBJ Library.

80   the affrontery: H. L. Carnahan to EW, March 25, 1936, in EWP/S 212.

80   One morning: Warren, *Memoirs,* p. 112.

81   He had never been: Warren, *Memoirs,* p. 113.

81   Not the usual thing: In "Earl Warren's Campaigns," p. 48. Warren, Berkeley OH, p. 73, states Hearst himself "said it was a pretty damned good speech."

81   Spending orgy: *SF Chron,* September 18, 1936.

81   first major effort: *The Oakland Tribune,* May 28, 1936. An internal critique scored such rhetoric for damning the New Deal. "Few believed it. Perhaps that was because it was obviously untrue." See Robert Littler to Edward Shattuck, December 7, 1936, in Robert Fenton Craig Papers, UCLA, Collection No. 1177, Box 2, Folder 2.

82 Our defeat: EW to John D. M. Hamilton, December 12, 1936, in EWP/S 193.

82 I believe: "Questionnaire" in EWP/S 201.

82 ships made money: Feingold, p. 79.

82 Alberts had been: Weaver, *Warren,* p. 85. In his Berkeley OH, "Conversations," p. 78, Warren evasively claimed, "I don't know that we ever had any undercover men *in* any union" [emphasis added]. Feingold, p. 68, states that a husband and wife team worked undercover, befriending maritime union men in San Francisco, but never themselves joined a union.

84 the second most important: Lee Coe int., January 22, 1991.

84 Alberts was: Feingold, p. 221.

84 It was a paid: *SF Chron,* September 1, 1936.

84 S.F. Union: Feingold, p. 223.

85 I would never: Feingold, p. 250.

85 I certainly was: EW to Drew Pearson in DDP, proposed book file, ca. August, 1967, LBJ Library.

85 burning desire: Warren, *Memoirs,* p. 118.

85 never heard: Warren, *Memoirs,* p. 119.

85 Well, I guess: Arthur Sherry OH, p. 79.

86 Old Cop-a-Plea: Feingold, p. 330.

86 There is no one: White, *Earl Warren,* p. 39.

CHAPTER 8

88 somewhat of an orator: White, *Earl Warren,* p. 39.

88 I know: Aubrey Grossman OH, p. 4.

88 I don't think: Myron Harris OH.

88 It was one: Lee Coe int., January 22, 1991.

88 the arch-enemy: Miriam Dinkins Johnson int., January 22, 1991.

88 a reactionary: Huberman, p. 22.

88 just another cog: Paul Heide OH, p. 17. Party leader McIntyre Faries in an interview on August 12, 1991, said, "J.R. pretty much made Earl Warren. That didn't necessarily mean they agreed on everything."

88 was hated: Coe int.

88 dragged in the red herrings: *SF Ex,* January 5, 1937.

89 a law-abiding American: Feingold, p. 487.

89 All I want: Feingold, p. 488.

89 ace in the hole: Huberman, p. 13.

89 bluntly stated: Coe, p. 20.

89 is to my mind: Feingold, pp. 489–90.

90 there was a lot: Earl Warren, Jr., int., February 21, 1991.

90 prominently mentioned: Henderson, p. 48, quoting the *SF Chron* of January 28, 1938.

90 I am convinced: *The Oakland Tribune,* February 18, 1938.

90 As you know: EW to John Hamilton, February 11, 1938, in EWP/S 193.

91 They'd bleed: Feigenbaum OH, p. 39.

91 a terrible candidate: Faries OH, p. 65.

91 I didn't think: Asa Call interview with Amelia Fry, February 19, 1975, p. 1, in Bancroft Library 79/102C.

92 Whenever you saw him: Balaban OH, p. 9.

92 is too big: "To the Nisei Voters of California," EWP/S 269. The Japanese Association of America also telegraphed congratulations to Warren upon his victory. See EWP/S 223.

92 outstanding qualifications: *SF Ex,* undated clip, post July 1, 1938.

93 logical choice: *SF Ex,* August 29, 1938.

93 is anxious: Cooper to EW, June 9, 1938, in EWP/S 167.

93 that would make: Kenny, "My First Forty Years," p. 113.

93 I believe: EWP/S 286. Warren's draft on hotel stationery is in this file. The letter is in Stevenson, *Undiminished Man,* pp. 166-67. Cooper suggested Warren follow a similar statement by nationally known Republican Grenville Clark which appeared in *NYT* of April 28, 1938; portions of it obviously inspired Warren.

94 Civil rights: Katcher, p. 109.

94 hollow climax: Warren, *Memoirs,* p. 126.

95 Since he was seven: *SF Ex,* May 17, 1938.

95   Casual, simple: Warren, *Memoirs,* p. 125.
95   I don't believe: Powers OH, pp. 19–20.
96   It was the first: Powers OH, p. 20. The suspect, paroled in 1940, dropped from sight.
96   That's why: Balaban OH, p. 4.
96   quarrelsome: Feingold, p. 725 fn. See also the Jahnsen OH, pp. 138–39; and the Grossman OH, pp. 23–26.

<h2 style="text-align:center">CHAPTER 9</h2>

98   decided to behave: Severn OH, p. 71.
98   to use the State: N. J. L. Pieper to Director, December 20, 1938, FBI 94-1-5619-59.
99   unverified: N. J. L. Pieper to Director, September 12, 1939, FBI 62-21610-5-30.
99   Here are two: Warren, *Memoirs,* p. 128.
99   You will find: *SF Ex,* January 31, 1939.
99   the most corruptive: EW to Sam M. Haskins, December 27, 1938, in EWP/S 327.
99   chief law officer: Section 21, Article V, California Constitution.
100 ingrained bias: Warren, *Memoirs,* p. 142.
100 Do you intend: Warren, *Memoirs,* p. 131.
100 any slot-machine: EW letter dated July 6, 1939, in EWP/S 327.
100 the biggest nuisance: *Los Angeles Examiner,* July 27, 1939.
101 With things like this: Olney OH, p. 173.
101 All the thrills: Henstell, p. 67.
101 Play on the S.S. *Rex:* Olney OH, p. 173.
101 because of political: N. J. L. Pieper to Director, September 8, 1939, FBI document 65-4975-[illegible], courtesy of Ernest Marquez, who is writing a book about Cornero.
102 to spend upon wagers: *Los Angeles Examiner,* July 29, 1939.
102 Three of the four: Cray, "High Rollers on the High Seas," *California Lawyer,* December, 1982, p. 51.
102 The anchored ship: Warren, *Memoirs,* p. 133. The case is reported as *People v. Stralla* (1939), 14 C2d 617.
103 As the chances: Warren, *Memoirs,* p. 130.
103 He doesn't want: MacGregor OH, p. 60.
103 I think they: MacGregor OH, p. 83.
104 looked like everybody's idea: Earl Warren, Jr., int., June 18, 1991.
104 the consummate gentleman: James Walsh int., January 6, 1994.
104 It is a great: EW quoted in notes for EW biography, DPP, LBJ Library.
104 rather intimidating: Walsh int., January 6, 1994.
105 we got to be: Edgar Patterson int., November 20, 1992.
106 an influx of paupers: *NYT,* May 6, 1941. *Edwards v. California* is reported as 314 U.S. 160. The background and impact of the case is in *National Defense Migration,* Part 26, pp. 9969ff.
106 came here to seek: *NYT,* November 25, 1941.
106 Only Earl Warren: *Newsweek,* July 17, 1939, p. 48.
106 type cast: McWilliams OH, p. 36.
107 on perjured testimony: Burke, p. 55.
107 convinced that any lessening: Feingold, p. 670. See *In Re Wallace,* 24 C2d 933, denying Vickerson's claim that the Wehr estate owed her $15,000.
108 a very slim thread: Feingold, p. 676.
108 shocking: *SF Ex,* October 17, 1940.
108 The murderers: Feingold, p. 679.
109 left of center: *Fortnight,* January 27, 1947. On the Communist charges, see *SF Ex,* February 27, 28, and 29, 1936.
109 our old friend: EW to Louis R. Deadrich, April 29, 1935, in EWP/S 17942.
109 slated to be: Hichborn, "California Politics," p. 2803. Radin had dedicated his 1938 book, *The Law and Mr. Smith,* "to my friend Felix Frankfurter."
109 extreme leftist: *The Oakland Tribune,* June 16, 1940.
109 atheistic: *SF Ex,* July 6, 1939. The group faulted anthropologist A. L. Kroeber on the same grounds.
109 couldn't go along: James H. Oakley int., in JWP, Box 171, File 60.
110 speak a word: *The Oakland Tribune,* June 13, 1940.
110 tend to corroborate: *Los Angeles Examiner,* June 14, 1940.
110 soften the blow: *The Oakland Tribune,* June 13, 1940.
110 a compound: White, *Earl Warren,* p. 65.
110 launched forth: From a memorandum dated December 31, 1940, in the "Special Problems" file under "Max Radin," President's Files, University of California Archives, Robert Gordon Sproul

Papers, Bancroft Library, Berkeley, courtesy of Vince Cosgrove. When Radin later sought a federal judgeship, a February 28, 1945, memorandum from the director of the FBI's Domestic Intelligence Division, D. M. Ladd, to the Director, noted, "Warren . . . stated he believed [Radin] was too radical to render unbiased decisions as a judge."

111 black mark: Kenny, "My First Forty Years," p. 140. Later Warren twice appointed Radin to a state commission on uniform codes, a hint that the two men had achieved a rapprochement. David M. Margolick has most thoroughly researched the Radin affair; see his article in *National Law Journal*, September 17, 1979, p. 15.

CHAPTER 10

112 We must realize: A copy of the December 2, 1940, speech is in EWP/S 297.

113 While the most: The "Statement Concerning Civil Rights," October 31, 1940, is in EWP/S 380.

113 he was under: Graves OH, p. 69.

113 that the Attorney General's: Stone, p. 110.

113 Warren didn't think: Adrian Kragen OH, p. 17.

114 Any effort: Stone, p. 114.

114 an active: Graves OH, p. 72.

114 War broke out: Warren's appointment book is in the Bancroft Library, University of California.

114 death and destruction: Goralski, p. 189.

114 Enemy forces: Olson, *State Papers and Public Addresses,* pp. 329-33.

115 We don't have anything: Jahnsen OH, p. 122.

115 all people: *WRA: A Story,* p. 9.

115 the "Yellow Peril": Jester OH, p. 46. Bean, p. 340, asserts Warren shared Webb's view that "persons of Japanese origin had inherent racial traits that rendered them unassimilable and untrustworthy as Americans." See also Schwartz and Lesher, pp. 8 and 11.

115 It should be remembered: A text of the speech is in EWP/S 297.

116 it would be better: Henderson, p. 92

116 point with loving: *LAT,* August 5, 1937. The First Amendment protects both aliens as well as citizens.

116 the most effective: *WRA: A Story,* p. 10.

116 We were told: Kragen int., October 19, 1992.

117 doubt the continued: *SF Ex,* January 4, 1942.

117 all Japanese: Irons, *Justice at War,* p. 38.

117 impossible to distinguish: McKee, p. 107.

117 you have racial: C. B. Horrall to EW, February 19, 1942, in "National Defense Migration," p. 10989.

117 much easier: Olson, *State Papers,* p. 345.

117 persons having: Irons, *Justice at War,* p. 40.

117 There's a tremendous volume: Conn, p. 133.

118 must realize: *The Oakland Tribune,* February 2, 1942.

118 a repetition: Henderson, p. 73.

118 immediate removal: *SF Ex,* January 29, 1942.

118 it was a studied: Grodzins, p. 94.

118 Every alien: *The Oakland Tribune,* February 2, 1942.

118 what we call: Henderson, p. 79.

118 that from Point Reyes: Olney OH, p. 229. The conclusion was faulty, Grodzins points out (pp. 156–157), for the definition of strategic installation covered virtually everything from highways to irrigation ditches, and the maps ignored the fact that the Japanese often bought the land before the strategic installation was built. McWilliams in his OH, p. 29, adds that Japanese truck farmers bought land no one else had wanted.

119 any or all: "Minutes of the California Joint Immigration Committee," February 7, 1942, p. 35, in EWP/S.

119 discriminates against naturalized: Grodzins, p. 93.

119 We'd be in: *NYT,* February 8, 1942, p. 41.

119 an imminent danger: *The Oakland Tribune,* February 12, 1942.

120 the Japanese in California: *Los Angeles Examiner,* February 16, 1942.

120 all Japanese be put: Bird, p. 160.

120 citizens of Japanese extraction: *United States News,* March 6, 1942, p. 28.

120 sensitive areas: Conn, p. 145, fn 58.

120 any and all: Irons, *Justice at War,* p. 63.

120 I have no doubt: Cited in Grodzins, pp. 99–100.

120 For some time: "National Defense Migration," p. 11010.

121 Congressman, there is: "National Defense Migration," p. 11015.

121 we are not straining: See EW to Hoover, 62-57708-5, in EW/FBI, "Cross References," Part II.

121 Many, many Japanese: "National Defense Migration," p. 11015.

121 on the road: "National Defense Migration," p. 11020.

122 These maps show: "National Defense Migration," p. 11017.

122 there was fear: Verne Scoggins int., October 7, 1991.

122 in the interest: *WRA: A Story,* p. 13.

123 Nobody seemed: Richard Bergholz int., January 8, 1992.

CHAPTER 11

125 I thought: Weaver, p. 99.

125 You played: Richard Jennings int., JWP, Box 171, Folder 60.

125 Nobody thought: McIntyre Faries unpublished autobiography, p. 130.

125 What do you want: Margaret Warren int., October 8, 1992.

125 Should Attorney General: Hill, p. 96.

125 A large number: Knowland to EW, October 17, 1941, EWP/S 17837.

126 What have you got: William J. Mailliard OH, p. 6.

126 Why, I couldn't afford: Warren, "Conversations," p. 198.

126 I'm going after them: Stone, p. 116; see also Katcher, p. 158. The correct poll figures are in EWP/S 541.

126 All right: M. F. Small in *Sac Bee,* March 17, 1974.

126 It relieved me: Warren, *Memoirs,* p. 157.

127 Do you think: Adrian Kragen int., October 16, 1992.

127 Warren came: Katcher, pp. 160–61. Warren was extremely sensitive about fund-raising, even denying he did it. "EW simply wants it to be clearly understood that he never, never, never went out chasing campaign dollars." M. F. Small to Warren biographer John Weaver, March 21, 1974, in JWP, Box 175, File 120.

127 I believe: Katcher, p. 159.

127 I can and will: October 15, 1942, campaign speech in JWP, Box 173, File 68.

127 was a run-of-the-mill: Robert and Florence Clifton int.

127 Warren had: Lee Coe int.

127 Anyone who: Burke, p. 252.

128 A Machine's: The quote is on pages 5–6 of the speaker's manual in EWP/S 526.

128 a man might be: Richard Graves is quoted in Katcher, p. 161.

128 We are not: Katcher, p. 161.

128 we are fighting: A text of the June 18, 1942, speech is in EWP/S 541.

128 Warren was his own: Verne Scoggins OH, p. 52.

129 he always seemed: Small, "The Country Editor," p. 381.

129 His father: Robert Fenton Craig Papers, UCLA Department of Special Collections, Collection 1177, Box 1.

129 It was all: Small, "The Country Editor," p. 382.

130 [T]he vast majority: *Sac Bee,* July 16, 1942, cited by Waltz, p. 8.

130 communist radicals: Feingold, p. 711.

130 [I]f elected: Warren's August 8, 1942, speech, quoted in the Stanley Barnes OH, p. 33.

130 I would rather: "Radio Address," August 24, 1942, in EWP/S 541.

130 A system: *Frontier,* March, 1952, p. 5.

131 the moneybags: Warren, *Memoirs,* p. 160.

131 make the attack: Ford Chatters to Whitaker and Baxter, September 2, 1942, in EWP/S 552.

131 predatory interests: *Los Angeles Herald and Express,* October 12, 1942.

131 bitterness, prejudices: *Sac Bee,* October 12, 1942, cited by Waltz, p. 19.

131 so that we may give: Katcher, p. 164.

131 Fellow Americans: Undated "Address by Earl Warren" in EWP/S 537A.

131 I want you to help: Edgar Patterson int., November 20, 1992.

132 Just as I want: *LAT,* November 3, 1942.

132 I told him: Warren, *Memoirs,* p. 162. See also EW to Merrell F. Small, December 10, 1970, in EWP/LC, Box 115.

132 a Joe Kennedy: Fleeson is quoted in Katcher, p. 167.

133 Mother was just broken hearted: Nina "Honey Bear" Brien int., December 4, 1992.

133 a-get-things-done man: Virginia Daly int., July 20, 1992.

133 Warren told me: Hill, p. 99.

133 They're going: Margaret Warren int., October 1, 1992.

133   blue-eyed: Jack Smith in the *LAT,* September 20, 1978, in JWP, Box 171, File 81.
134   From behind Warren: Florence Clifton int., March 3, 1992. See also the Jahnsen OH, p. 204.

CHAPTER 12

137   I want to assure: *Sac Bee,* July 17, 1973.
137   not to talk: Betty Henderson to Cray, August 9, 1992, quoting Edgar Patterson.
138   There is no place: The memorandum of August 15, 1942, is in Sweigert OH, pp. 182ff.
138   I'll bet: Small, "The Country Editor," p. 417.
138   like a civics: Morrie Landsberg int.
138   We got straight: Small, "The Country Editor," p. 111.
139   Verne went: Wilma Wagner int.
139   tremendously good judgment: Chatters OH, p. 81.
139   Some pretty good: Verne Scoggins int.
139   He was never: Earl Warren, Jr., int., February 21, 1991.
139   There will be: Albert C. Wollenberg in *California Law Review,* Vol. 58, No. 3 (1970), p. 7.
139   I had to get: Meyer, pp. 134–35.
139   Governor, you've asked: Merrell F. Small twice tells this story, in the Foreword to the finding list for "Earl Warren Papers, 1924–53, California State Archives, 1976," and in his unpublished "The Country Editor," p. 411.
140   J.R. gave: Scoggins int., October 7, 1991.
140   How are your boys: William S. Mailliard int. in JWP, Box 171, Folder 60.
140   one of the highest-minded: Watkins, p. 579.
140   passing judgment: Richard Graves OH, p. 132. Black journalist J. A. Daly stated in his OH, p. 37, that Warren, asked to appoint Gordon as a deputy district attorney, had declined on the grounds "the time wasn't right for that."
141   He would have danced: Small in the *Sac Bee,* February 27, 1971.
141   the most unscrupulous: EW to Drew Pearson, in undated EW file, DPP, LBJ Library.
141   no ready way: FBI document No. 62-93875-2190, March 31, 1954, in EW "Cross References File," Part II. Apparently hundreds were screened. In just the first ten months of 1953, Warren sought clearance on 142 individuals, according to Document 62-93875-2174.
141   Mr. Warren always: FBI document No. 62-93875-2265, May 7, 1954, in EW "Cross References File," Part II. Charns, p. 48, asserts EW also vetted political opponents, though there is no evidence of this in the documents released.
141   Hello, judge: Betty Henderson to Cray, November 13, 1991.
141   He made the appointment: Chatters OH, p. 160.
141   If you have: Small, "The Country Editor," p. 388.
142   a requirement: A copy of the code, in the California State Library, was forwarded by Wilma M. Wagner.
142   to pick up: Bell int., February 7, 1992.
142   no matter how thin: JWP, Box 171, Box 60.
142   get the facts: Bell int., February 7, 1992.
142   I'm a slow walker: *CR,* March 1, 1954, p. 2380.
142   I've never heard: *Life,* May 22, 1964.
142   he can pronounce: Salinger is quoted in *Newsweek,* May 11, 1964.
142   as if he's running: *Life,* May 22, 1964.
142   a happy gang: Verne Scoggins int., January 5, 1993.
142   impatient with what: White, *Earl Warren,* p. 92.
142   Sure I'm a tough boss: Merrell Small int. in JWP, Box 171, Folder 60.
142   He has no right: Betty Henderson int.
143   There was never: EW to John Weaver, JWP, Box 171, File 60.
143   We did not: Ellen Younglove Fields int.
143   We'd all look: James J. Brown, "Looking Around," *Sac Bee,* April 14, 1967.
143   He was terribly: Mailliard OH, p. 14.
144   Your job: Betty Henderson int.; confirmed by Arlene Tomlinson Hawkins int.
144   We all had: Betty Henderson int.
144   sorry state: A. Alan Post int.
144   We must take: Stone, p. 129.
144   growing at the rate: EW to Drew Pearson, in unpublished proposal for a Warren biography, in Pearson Papers, LBJ Library.
145   like country clubs: W. T. Sweigert int., JWP, Box 171, File 59.
145   Caging men: *The Oakland Tribune,* September 20, 1931.

145   Arrest them: EW to Drew Pearson, Drew Pearson Diary, February 8, 1966, in LBJ Library.

145   Hire them: EW to Drew Pearson, Drew Pearson Diary, February 8, 1966, in LBJ Library.

145   the requirement: Inaugural address, January 4, 1943.

146   This has got: McWilliams's Berkeley OH, p. 50; see also his biography, pp. 112–14.

146   Good men: Sweigert to John Weaver, October 28, 1965, in JWP, Box 171, File 59.

146   He listens: Mailliard OH, p. 11.

147   Warren's timing: Ralph Hoyt quoted in Harvey dissertation, p. 77.

147   maintained personal contact: Scoggins to Cray, October 30, 1991.

147   It's just not right: Helen MacGregor int. in JWP, Box 169, File 52.

147   a serious-minded: Frank J. Taylor, "Man with a New Broom," *Saturday Evening Post,* August 7, 1943, p. 23.

147   completely the creature: "Warren of California," *The New Republic,* October 18, 1943, p. 514.

CHAPTER 13

148   the sports pages: Quoted in "In Memoriam Honorable Earl Warren, Proceedings of the Bar and Officers of the Supreme Court of the United States, Washington, D.C., May 27, 1975," p. 25.

148   If the governor: Mailliard int. with John Weaver, in JWP, Box 171, File 60.

149   as a sounding board: Thor Severson int.

149   I wanted to know: Edmund G. "Pat" Brown int., December 7, 1990.

149   That social ease: Mailliard int. in JWP, Box 171, File 60.

149   All I've ever: Small, "The Country Editor," p. 532.

150   the most ideal: Nina "Honey Bear" Brien int.

150   She made: James Warren OH, p. 3.

150   everything a woman: Brien int.

150   They adored: Virginia Daly int.

150   the best thing: Betty Henderson to Cray, June 18, 1992.

150   Dad wanted: Earl Warren, Jr., OH, p. 12.

151   we just wanted: Daly int.

151   For the others: Brien int.

151   Halt! Who goes there: Earl Warren, Jr., int., June 18, 1991.

151   Somehow we knew: Daly int.

151   He'd talk: Ethel Plank to John Weaver, November 6, 1965, in JWP, Box 170, File 49.

151   The girls could always: Patricia Warren int.

151   Earl was taking: Robert Warren int., June 18, 1991.

151   It was a great time: Robert Warren int., June 18, 1991.

152   She could not bear: Brien int.

152   everything was kind: Robert Warren int., June 18, 1991.

152   because that's what: Robert Warren int., July 9, 1991.

152   I was a shadow: Robert Warren int., June 18, 1991.

152   I became very close: Earl Warren, Jr., int., February 21, 1991.

152   The reason our family: Robert Warren int., June 18, 1991.

152   If you didn't: James Warren, Jr., int.

152   You don't say: Robert Warren int., June 18, 1991. Warren explained that he eventually came to terms with his feelings. "If you can have a relationship with a deceased father, I would say I probably have a better relationship with him now than I ever did."

153   I love you: Earl Warren, Jr., int., November 21, 1992.

153   I always kissed him: Margaret Warren int., October 1, 1992.

153   Very seldom: Robert Warren int., June 18, 1991.

153   He was almost: James Warren, Jr., int.

154   We can produce: *Vital Speeches of the Day,* May 1, 1944, pp. 432–34.

154   with a unity: *SF Ex,* January 8, 1944.

154   black reaction: John Weaver int. of Oliver Carter, May 25, 1966, in JWP, Box 171, Folder 60.

155   record in public: *Time,* January 31, 1944, p. 20.

155   maintained only mild interest: Warren, *Memoirs,* p. 172.

155   the program: Verne Scoggins to Enoch G. Fletcher, January 8, 1944, in Thomas E. Dewey Papers, University of Rochester Library, Series 10, Box 46, File 5.

155   We have fifty: *Time,* January 31, 1944, p. 22.

155   I am not: *SF Ex,* June 18, 1944.

156   To get our boys: Warren's address is reprinted in full in *Vital Speeches of the Day,* July 15, 1944, pp. 538–42.

157 I couldn't honorably: Warren OH, Truman Library, p. 9.

157 Mine was a very happy: Warren OH, Truman Library, pp. 10–11.

157 Warren thought: Scoggins OH, p. 23.

157 the year they tried: Warren OH, Truman Library, p. 9.

157 some agility: Scoggins OH, p. 23.

157 would be laying: *SF Ex,* July 2, 1943.

158 take a long view: Alfred J. Lundberg to EW, July 13, 1943, in EWP/S 3661.

158 [W]ho, I ask you: EW to Lundberg, July 16, 1943, in EWP/S 3661.

159 not in keeping: Warren, *Memoirs,* p. 149. The Supreme Court decision was *Ex Parte Endo,* 323 U.S. 283 (1944).

CHAPTER 14

160 much improved: *SF Ex,* October 21, 1944.

160 a white man had: Margaret Warren int., October 1, 1992. Of the book she could say only it was small and contained statistics on world population.

161 You know: Sweigert OH, p. 67. See also Shea OH, p. 27, and *California Historical Society Quarterly,* 46 (1967), p. 40.

161 If that's the way: Sweigert OH, p. 76. See also Katcher, p. 187.

162 a lot of people: *SF Ex,* December 30, 1944.

162 The Governor's program: *SF Chron,* January 8, 1945.

162 There sure is: M. F. Small in *Sac Bee,* December 21, 1969.

162 trying to: Harvey dissertation, p. 389.

163 My God: *Fortnight,* June 6, 1947.

163 a vote against: Scoggins OH, p. 75.

163 They said: Russel VanArsdale Lee, M.D., OH, p. 36.

163 doctors for all: *Sac Bee,* February 19, 1945.

163 I do not believe: Scoggins OH, p. 20.

163 all suggestions: EWP/S, "Governor's Speech File, 1945."

164 It was not: Faries unpublished autobiography, p. 627.

164 I'm not going: Graves OH, p. 121.

164 What is your degree: M. F. Small in *Sac Bee,* December 21, 1969. A somewhat different account is in Small's unpublished manuscript, "The Country Editor and Earl Warren," p. 128.

164 the power: *Sac Bee,* April 11, 1945.

165 A subterfuge: *Sac Bee,* May 28, 1945.

165 The governor has: *Sacramento Union,* June 5, 1945.

165 In view: Lee OH, p. viii.

165 Let's restore: Henderson, p. 241.

165 It will come: EW to Thomas E. Dewey, Dewey Papers, University of Rochester Library, 4:194:22.

166 I remember a lot: Richard Rodda int., March 23, 1991. Rodda's boss, Herbert Phillips, on the other hand, argued that Warren was a lifelong Progressive. See Phillips, p. 81.

166 Most men: Katcher, p. 189.

166 the Governor's: *The Nation,* February 10, 1945, p. 152.

166 generally, all Republicans: Augustus Hawkins int.

166 that you can't legislate: Earl Warren OH, Truman Library, p. 59.

167 He had a businesslike: Augustus Hawkins int.

167 But there was nothing: Rodda OH, p. 12.

167 Of course it was: Small, "The Country Editor," p. 441.

168 Oh, Jesus: Storke int. with John Weaver, January 27, 1970, JWP, Box 169, File 55.

168 I arrived: Nance Markson int.

169 Just where do you think: Faries manuscript, pp. 630–31.

169 was one of the ones: Richard Carpenter int., October 16, 1992.

169 They're more interested: Katcher, p. 195.

170 [I]t took everything: Graves OH, p. 64.

170 I owe: Graves OH, p. 84. See also Katcher, p. 195.

CHAPTER 15

171 Will you be: *SF Ex,* February 7, 1945. Weaver, p. 142, notes Thomas Jefferson actually said, "If a due participation of office is a matter of right, how are vacancies to be obtained? Those by death are few; by resignation, none."

171 a man: Kenny, "My First Forty Years," p. 83.

172 a fool: *Sac Bee,* September 6, 1945.

172 a definite program: Quoted in *Sac Bee,* September 27, 1974.

172 What was it: Dick Pearce in *SF Ex,* June 6, 1946.

173 You can beat: AP advance obituary, October 22, 1944.

173 It was a wonderful: Virginia Daly int.

173 the best legislation: Small manuscript, p. 2, in EWP/LC, Box 115.

173 a phony: Herbert L. Phillips int., no date, in JWP, Box 171, Folder 60.

173 fake liberal: George Creel, "California's Elephant Boy," *Colliers,* June 8, 1946, p. 77.

173 conducted a very restrained: Stevenson, p. 59.

173 Every four years: Scoggins int., October 7, 1991.

173 to run: Small to John Weaver, June 2, 1967, in JWP. The election over, Warren would telephone again to thank the local contact and ask him to issue a public statement announcing that the committee had been disbanded.

174 A man of his stamp: Harvey dissertation, p. 316.

174 an era of crackpot: *SF Ex,* May 24, 1946.

174 would get so damned: Robert Gros int., May 12, 1995.

174 What burning: Attributed to Eby Ore Jacobs, in JWP, Box 93, File 174.

174 Well, you know: Margaret Warren int., October 8, 1992.

175 We'll take: Small manuscript, p. 16, in EWP/LC, Box 115, "Chief Justice Personal—S."

175 Isn't this a helluva big: Small manuscript in Bancroft Library, 77/142, p. 279.

175 made politicians: *Time,* June 17, 1946, p. 22.

175 unquestionably made him: *The Nation,* June 15, 1946, p. 707.

175 higher ups: Behrens OH, Columbia University, p. 15. Incumbent Frederick F. Houser had opted to run for a Superior Court vacancy in Los Angeles.

175 who had defended: Katcher, p. 205.

175 carpetbaggers: Katcher, p. 204.

176 clearly beyond: Anderson, *Meet the Governor of California,* p. 63.

177 But I take: Harvey dissertation, p. 239, quoting *Sac Bee,* January 6, 1947.

177 This program: EWP/S, Drawer 2852.

177 to quibble: *Sac Bee,* January 21, 1947.

177 trying to frighten: *SF Ex,* February 15, 1947.

177 has done something: *Journal of the American Medical Association,* March 1, 1947, p. 628.

178 then tend: Leary int., October 8, 1992.

178 almost laughingly: Phillips OH, p. 72.

178 This is a plain: *LAT,* March 20, 1947.

178 invisible government: Harvey dissertation, p. 180, quoting a broadcast of June 2, 1947.

179 It's the only time: M. F. Small in *Sac Bee,* August 18, 1973.

179 social consciousness: *Fortnight,* June 16, 1947.

179 California Roosevelt: *Orange County Register,* January 22, 1945.

180 Essentially, he is: *The Nation,* November 29, 1947, p. 583.

180 moderate conservative: Interview with Mary Ellen Leary, October 1, 1992.

180 Breach of the public: Katcher, p. 244. FBI document 45-4031-60, a copy of which was furnished by Ernest Marquez, reports the bribe.

181 It was common: H. Alan Post int.

181 How can it be: Post int.

181 had almost: Warren Olney IV int.

181 He was absolutely: Earl Warren, Jr., int., August 20, 1992.

181 Earl Warren has tried: *LAT,* March 9, 1949.

181 unworthy of his office: Katcher, p. 245.

181 he thinks: *LAT,* March 9, 1949.

182 What drove Olney: Leary int., January 6, 1993.

182 the limitations of all: *Inside USA,* p. 18.

CHAPTER 16

183 What about: Warren int., Truman Library, p. 3.

183 Your governor: *NYT,* June 13, 1948. Truman jocularly wrote Warren on the twelfth, "As you may know, I inducted you into the Democratic Party when I was in Sacramento."

183 I am sure: *Fortnight,* July 2, 1948, p. 10.

183 He couldn't have: Earl Warren int., Truman Library, p. 3.

184 not necessarily: Transcript of a press conference (at the National Press Club?), in "Presidential Campaign Files, Issues, 1948," EWP/S 637.

184 when to be: Leary is quoted in Henderson, p. 404.

184 I am making: *LAT,* October 9, 1946.

184 fully aware: Small, "The Country Editor," p. 324.

184 talking things: *LAT,* June 8, 1947.

184 rising political figure: *LAT,* June 5, 1947.

185 Warren thought: Jones OH, p. 21.

185 at the solicitation: Warren, *Memoirs,* p. 240.

185 Sure, I'd like: *Fortnight,* February 27, 1948, p. 5.

185 no interest: *LAT,* January 10, 1948.

185 It was a real: Mailliard OH, p. 13.

185 get an FEPC: The *Sun* quote is from the April 13, 1948, issue; the *Press* quote from the March 22 number; and the *Afro-American* extract from the April 3 paper. All are cited in an undated, but circa April 16, "Governor's Office Inter-Office Memorandum, Sacramento," filed in EWP/S 1925. The fact that Verne Scoggins was tracking the national press suggests how serious was Warren's bid for the nomination.

186 I am sure: "Address by Governor Earl Warren," NBC, May 16, 1948, in EWP/S 621.

186 My wife has asked: Murrow int., June 2, 1948, in EWP/S 637.

186 The plan: Helen MacGregor to "My Dear," June 17–22, 1948, in JWP, Box 174, File 95.

187 It was thoroughly: MacGregor to "My Dear."

187 the only man: Smith, *Thomas E. Dewey,* p. 18.

187 but in the process: Small, "The Country Editor," p. 339.

188 You could never: Drew Pearson Diary, October 26, 1966, in DPP, LBJ Library.

188 I sure don't want: Earl Warren, Jr., int., February 21, 1991.

188 he felt: Wilkins int., June 18, 1991.

188 He demanded: Wilkins int., June 18, 1991.

188 A lot of us: Katcher, p. 226.

189 What made: JWP, Box 169, File 37.

189 Pop, I had: Small, "The Country Editor," p. 350.

189 For the first time: Jack Smith in the *LAT,* March 13, 1991. One reporter joked that the streetcar was named Desire, a mock reference to the Tennessee Williams play.

189 We have: Smith, *Thomas E. Dewey,* p. 501.

189 only a miracle: *Newsweek's* Ernest K. Lindley is quoted in Smith, *Thomas E. Dewey,* p. 502.

189 One day: Sweigert manuscript, JWP, Box 171, File 59.

189 Well, Bob: *Whistle Stop: Harry S. Truman Library Institute Newsletter,* Summer 1973, p. 2.

189 They struck fire: Kyle Palmer OH, *LAT,* p. 78.

189 I don't believe: Earl Warren OH, Truman Library, pp. 22–23.

190 But Tom: Small, "The Country Editor," p. 356.

190 There would be: Earl Warren, Jr., int., February 21, 1991.

190 we are very: *Off the Record,* p. 149.

190 gluttons of: Smith, *Thomas E. Dewey,* pp. 32, 518.

191 And I know: Gallagher OH, p. 18.

191 well-intentioned: *SF Ex,* September 21, 1948, and October 1, 1948. For his part, Truman said, "Governor Warren is a good man and an excellent public servant. I cannot, and will not, hurt him to gain the Presidency." See *California Law Review,* 58 (1970), p. 3.

191 a fine American: *Kansas City Times,* September 23, 1948.

191 What is your: "Press Conference with Governor Earl Warren," September 24, 1948, in EWP/S 6457.

191 if any: *SF Ex,* September 25, 1948.

191 If Dewey: Samuel Brightman OH, Truman Library, p. 55.

191 I'm so low: Walter Jones OH, p. 21. Apparently Warren griped, off the record, to other correspondents as well. See the Samuel Brightman OH, Truman Library, p. 12.

192 The Democrats aren't making: Earl Warren int. in Truman Library, pp. 15–16. See also *NYT,* October 27, 1948.

192 They just thought: Earl Warren int. in Truman Library, p. 17.

192 Do you think: *Whistle Stop: Harry S. Truman Library Institute Newsletter,* Summer 1973, p. 3.

192 I think you're: Graves OH, p. 85.

192 He has reached: Small, "The Country Editor," p. 358.

192 a mere tail: *NYT,* October 30, 1948.

193 Don't you know: *SF Ex,* November 3, 1948. Art Shay, *Life's* bureau chief, provided details in a letter.

193 He didn't seem: Margaret Warren int., October 8, 1992.

193 What do you know: Andy Logan, "Around City Hall," *The New Yorker,* October 5, 1992, pp. 80–81.

193   Thank God: *Sac Bee,* July 20, 1969.
193   Yes, I have: *SF Ex* and *NYT,* November 4, 1948.
194   It looks great: *Fortnight,* November 19, 1948, p. 11.
194   monstrous patchwork: *Sac Bee,* November 18, 1948.
194   There is no: Edwin F. Self, "Man Without a Party," *Frontier,* March 1952, p. 5.

CHAPTER 17

195   He'd taken lessons: Katcher, p. 241.
195   not let one drop: Mary Ellen Leary int., October 6, 1992.
196   It's quite: *Sac Bee,* May 14, 1949.
196   an entering wedge: Warren radio broadcast of June 7, 1949, in Warren speeches file, EWP/S.
196   all that power: *LAT,* May 21, 1975.
196   a nucleus: Velie, "The Secret Boss of California," *Colliers,* August 13, 1949, p. 12.
197   There isn't a short cut: Velie, "The Secret Boss of California," *Collier's,* August 20, 1949, p. 60.
197   a decent sort: Samish and Thomas, *The Secret Boss,* p. 113. Samish does not seem to have contributed openly to Warren's campaigns.
197   I'm the governor: A typescript of Samish's address of August 25, 1939, is in the John Randolph Haynes Papers, UCLA, Collection 1241, Box 74, Franklin Hichborn file.
197   The game was: H. Alan Post int., December 1, 1992.
197   Samish was a kind: Gladwin Hill int., July 10, 1991.
197   on matters: Velie, "Secret Boss," August 13, 1949, p. 13.
197   They didn't want: Small, "The Country Editor," p. 113.
198   tried to keep: Richard Rodda int.
198   That's the way: *Collier's,* August 13, 1949, p. 71.
198   the few who flout: Phillips, *Big Wayward,* p. 125.
199   The only amount: *SF Chron,* March 9, 1949.
199   Graft Here: *LAT,* March 12, 1949.
199   first mistake: Samish and Thomas, *The Secret Boss,* p. 14.
199   could be very rough: John Moss int.
200   It'll be easier: Clark Kerr OH, p. 5.
202   apparently in order: Stewart, p. 109.
202   Warren then came: Kerr OH, p. 3.
202   what the Quakers: Clark Kerr int.
202   He didn't use: Katcher, p. 253.
202   We must not permit: "Address by Governor Earl Warren," NBC Broadcast, May 16, 1948, in EWP/S 621.
202   The Legislature has: Governor's Press Conference, March 26, 1948, in EWP/S 1925.
203   If necessary: *SF Ex,* May 16, 1945.
203   small, willful: Henderson, "Earl Warren and California Politics," p. 333.
203   without any thought: The minutes of the regents' meeting are quoted in White, *Earl Warren,* p. 119.
203   campus politicians: Katcher, p. 253.
204   I don't believe: White, *Earl Warren,* p. 119.
204   sadistic attacks: Warren, *Memoirs,* p. 218.
204   blanket accusations: *NYT,* June 19, 1950, p. 1, and *SF Ex,* June 19, 1950. For a different interpretation of Warren's anticommunism, see Edward R. Long, "Earl Warren and the Politics of Anti-Communism," *Pacific Historical Review* 51 (1982), pp. 51–70.
205   I am of: California *Senate Journal,* September 20, 1950, p. 13.
205   loyalty comes: *The Oakland Tribune,* October 4, 1950. Warren makes no mention in his *Memoirs* of the Levering oath or two later oaths required of local government and public school employees. Two years later, the state Supreme Court unanimously held the university oath unconstitutional on the ground that the legislature had preempted the field, and the regents could not usurp the legislature's prerogative. With that, Warren claimed validation for his stand against the regents' oath. At the same time, the Court upheld the legislature's Levering oath. See *Tolman v. Underhill,* 39 Cal. 2d 708, and *Pockman v. Leonard,* 30 Cal. 2d 676.

CHAPTER 18

206   had been running: Warren, *Memoirs,* p. 201.
206   the political grind: Pearson, *Diaries,* p. 69. However, Warren confidant Merrell Small said later, "All along thoughts of the Presidency were in Warren's mind, and the realization that he needed to

continue as Governor in order to have a political base." See Long, "Earl Warren and the Politics of Anti-Communism," *Pacific Historical Review* 51 (1982), p. 59, fn. 37.

207   gigantic proportions: *Fortnight,* September 30, 1949, p. 10.

207   What I'm going to do: Sam Yorty int.

207   The Republicans: *Sac Bee,* September 11, 1949.

208   standing out: Chaudet OH, p. 33.

208   not because: Kyle Palmer int., *LAT* Historical Archives, p. 17.

208   for the good: *LAT,* January 11, 1950.

208   after his father: Gladwin Hill int.

208   We're endorsing: EW to Drew Pearson in DPP, Proposed Book "The Chief" file, LBJ Library.

208   The Republican machine: James Roosevelt in *Frontier,* November, 1950, p. 7.

209   beholden to no one: Warren speech file in EWP/S, February 3, 1950.

209   I am going: Warren speech file in EWP/S, February 3, 1950.

209   No one: Scoggins OH, p. 11.

209   But Sir: A copy of the note was forwarded by Smith's mother, Bernice Smith, at the request of Betty Henderson.

209   I feel: Small, "The Country Editor," p. 436.

210   a two-fisted: Retired Arizona Senator Barry Goldwater is quoted in Halberstam, *The Fifties,* p. 313.

210   the opening round: Morris, p. 323.

210   shrewd, pudgy: Morris, p. 588.

210   I say to you: Mankiewicz, p. 36.

211   was not a gentle: Hale Champion int.

211   No, we're not: Earl Warren, Jr., int., February 21, 1991. Nixon biographer Roger Morris places this meeting sometime in January, 1950.

211   I have: Warren speech file, May 6, 1950, in EWP/S.

211   as is the California custom: *NYT,* June 19, 1950.

211   None of the Republican: *NYT,* June 19, 1950.

212   is being deliberately: Morris, p. 542.

212   a notorious: Morris, p. 580.

212   exactly opposite: Ambrose, *Nixon: Education of a Politician,* p. 217.

212   pink right down: Morris, p. 598.

212   Tricky Dick: Ambrose, *Nixon: The Education of a Politician,* p. 216.

212   that it is neither good: Warren address to the Board of Directors, Truman Library, April 28, 1973. Warren's opinion of Chotiner is in Richard Rodda, "Earl Warren: 'One of the Giants,' " *Sac Bee,* February 27, 1977.

213   I'm just interested: *Sac Bee,* October 29, 1950.

213   a fellow: Palmer int., p. 27. Chotiner claimed a share of the credit for the strategy. See Katcher, p. 257. Holt would later serve in Congress.

213   I hope and pray: Katcher, p. 261.

213   The newspaper report: *Sac Bee,* November 5, 1950; Morris, p. 609; and Katcher, p. 261, all slightly different.

213   Every voter: Mazo and Hess, p. 75.

213   Did you know: Morris, p. 610.

214   Both he and I: *LAT,* November 4, 1950.

214   Oh, Daddy: Nina "Honey Bear" Brien int.

215   Mother, take: *Saturday Evening Post,* February 3, 1951.

215   Betty, what: Letters from Betty Foot Henderson, February 25, 1992, and August 14, 1994, provided both description and conversation.

215   benevolent: Warren, *Memoirs,* p. 199. Afterward Mrs. Shattuck bitterly referred to the governor as "SOB Warren." See EW to Drew Pearson in DPP, Proposed Book "The Chief" file, LBJ Library.

215   very satisfactory: *SF Ex,* November 10, 1952.

216   It was just like: Earl Warren, Jr., int., June 18, 1991.

216   She never left: Brien int.

217   almost miraculous: EW to Richard Falk, December 20, 1950, in Bancroft Library 72/39 C.

217   What would the average: Mary Ellen Leary int., October 1, 1992. The medical bills were smaller than they might have been. At least one specialist, Herzl Friedlander, M.D., never submitted a bill. Sacramento's doctors traditionally treated elected officials and their families free of charge, Junius Harris had advised Friedlander. Harris seemingly also saw to it that the hospital, of which he was one of the founders, rendered only a token bill. Friedlander int., July 8, 1991.

CHAPTER 19

218 Warren dominated: Mildred Younger int.
218 People say: Robert Warren int.
219 California: Nixon to Palmer, February 17, 1951. Palmer forwarded the letter to EW. It is now in EWP/S 17790.
220 American Gibraltar: Ambrose, *Eisenhower,* p. 498, supplementing Herbert Brownell int., February 14, 1992.
220 Pretty much: Jones OH, pp. 6, 23.
220 It's a politician's problem: Herzl Friedlander, M.D., int.
220 I think: Robert Warren int., July 9, 1991.
220 remarkable progress: EW to Hoover, April 17, 1951, in FBI document 94-1-5619-96; and Friedlander int.
221 Without any: Special Agent in Charge, Los Angeles to Hoover, June 30, 1951, FBI document 94-1-5619-98.
221 strenuous and callous: Quoted in Harvey, p. 275.
222 the communists: Morris, p. 630.
222 It is a sad: *LAT,* April 12, 1951.
222 leading Eisenhower backer: The story ran October 15, 1951. The unnamed backer was probably Pennsylvania senator James Duff, a Warren friend.
223 until the snow: As writer Gene Marine quoted Senator Clair Engle.
223 an opportune diagnosis: Friedlander int.
223 Harris supervised: Verne Scoggins int., September 10, 1991. *Bee* editor Walter Jones was one of the few told the truth.
223 The presidency: *SF Ex,* November 15, 1951.
224 be done first: *Sac Bee,* November 15, 1951.
224 The only time: Small, "The Country Editor," p. 560.
224 try to go back: *LAT,* November 17, 1951.
224 We cannot afford: Warren, *A Republic,* p. 43. See, too, the long interview of Warren in *U.S. News & World Report,* May 2, 1952, pp. 38ff.
225 intra-abdominal: *SF Ex,* November 22, 1951.
225 Is it true: M. F. Small in the *Sac Bee,* March 15, 1970.
225 They opened: Warren, *Memoirs,* p. 253.
225 You know, you and I: Edgar Patterson int., September 13, 1991; November 20, 1992; January 4, 1993.
226 enlightened Republican: Smith, p. 590.
226 The General: Memorandum, Governor's Press Conference, January 7, 1952, in EWP/S 1929.
226 My father: Earl Warren, Jr., int., July 29, 1991.
226 the candidacy: Werdel quoted in McCormac OH, p. 94.
227 The voters: *LAT,* January 15, 1952.
227 abandoned Republicanism: J.A. Smith to EW, March 4, 1952, in Truman Library, Official File, California—Y. See also the *Los Angeles Examiner,* March 5, 1952.
227 venomous: *LAT,* June 3, 1952.
228 disappointed office seekers: *SF Ex,* May 22, 1952.

CHAPTER 20

229 a reasonable chance: "Notes on Governor's Statements in Telephone Call to Mary Ellen Leary," June 9, 1952, in EWP/S.
230 He had: Earl Warren, Jr., int., September 19, 1993.
230 an almost total: Morris, p. 651.
230 Now, what: Faries OH, p. 2.
230 A lot of these people: Faries OH, pp. 2–3.
231 This was a sign: Katcher, p. 283.
231 We permitted: Warren, *Memoirs,* p. 251. The seven included Ray Arbuthnot, Patrick Hillings, Jack Drown, Warren Brock, John Krehbiel, and Frank Jorgensen, an alternate. Harrison Call was a last-minute substitute for a delegate unable to go. Arbuthnot int., August 5, 1991.
231 The names: Laughlin Waters int., September 3, 1991.
231 would be free: Henderson, p. 385.
231 well before: Smith, *Lucius D. Clay,* pp. 601–2. See also Morris, p. 686.
231 We had some: Smith, *Lucius D. Clay,* p. 602.
232 in a position: *LAT,* June 1, 1952.

232 the strongest candidate: A copy of the "Dear Friend" letter is the Pre-Presidential Papers of Richard Nixon, "Earl Warren, Jr." [sic] file, Box 799, National Archives, Pacific Southwest Region.

232 If you're going: Mellon OH, p. 7.

232 I told Palmer: Warren, *Memoirs,* p. 251.

233 Dick, what do: Patrick Hillings int.

233 He didn't get: Hillings int.

233 In the event: *LAT,* July 6, 1952.

233 gave his own: Mazo, p. 92.

233 either that: Dinkelspiel OH, p. 3.

233 the only realistic: Dinkelspiel OH, p. 5.

234 who was most: Hillings int.

234 Had he done enough: Finch int.

234 it was going: Hillings int.

234 I think he: Mellon OH, p. 10.

234 to try and get: Hillings int.

234 As expected: Mazo, p. 92.

234 The chemistry: Richard Bergholz int.

234 there were kind: Waters int.

234 Dick would never: Margaret Warren int., October 8, 1992.

234 seemed gripped: *LAT,* May 13, 1962. In his *Memoirs* (p. 251), Warren disclaimed any knowledge of Nixon personally urging they bolt.

235 Warren was convinced: *Sac Bee,* July 15, 1973; Small was not on the train.

235 It became apparent: Jorgensen OH, p. 68.

235 A delegate cannot: Phillips is quoted in JWP.

235 simmering with: *SF Ex,* July 5, 1952.

236 You trust me: *LAT,* July 6, 1952.

236 the balance of power: *NYT,* July 3, 1952.

236 moral issue: Katcher, p. 292.

237 Well, of course: Mellon OH, pp. 9, 27.

237 must have known: Hillings Int.

237 But I just couldn't: Small, "The Country Editor," p. 504.

238 Imagine my surprise: Warren, *Memoirs,* p. 252.

238 There is no: Quoted in Morris, p. 662.

238 I know enough: *NYT,* July 8, 1952.

238 Neither Warren nor I: Ambrose, *Education,* p. 558.

239 sensitivity to human: Warren, *Memoirs,* p. 253.

239 on a collision: Halberstam, p. 208.

239 Taft begged me: Drew Pearson Diary, February 5, 1966, in Warren, Earl, #2 file, DPP, LBJ Library.

240 Twenty: McIntyre Faries int., August 12, 1991.

240 I didn't feel: Knowland, Columbia OH, p. 28; corroborated by Faries OH, p. 12. A year and one-half later, Warren noted, Taft was dead, and Bill Knowland would have been president of the United States. "Bill Knowland always seemed frustrated and bitter after that convention," Warren told Drew Pearson.

240 I think: Knowland OH, Eisenhower Library, p. 18.

240 If anyone: Hill, *Dancing Bear,* p. 105, which gives no source for the quote. Herbert Brownell, in a letter to the author on December 16, 1993, asserted the statement "seems inconsistent with everything I know about the matter. I certainly never heard Eisenhower claim that Earl Warren cinched the nomination for him, and I do not believe he felt that way."

CHAPTER 21

241 He was bitter: Maryalice Lemmon int.

241 I never felt: "Conversation with Chief Justice Earl Warren," reprinted in *CR,* October 1, 1969, p. 28054.

241 We have a traitor: Davis is quoted in Morris, p. 719.

242 All we wanted: Smith, *Lucius D. Clay,* p. 598.

242 The delegation: *SF Ex,* July 9, 1952. Delegate Grant C. Ehrlich concurred with the estimate in an interview on October 21, 1993.

242 he wants Knowland: Faries int., August 12, 1991.

242 an administration: *SF Ex,* July 11, 1952.

243 I can't get: Faries OH, p. 22. Apparently they had forgotten Warren awaited their call at the Blackstone Hotel.

243 The Eisenhower and Taft: Knowland OH, Eisenhower Library, p. 19.

244 I'm authorized: Faries int., August 12, 1991. Faries OH, p. 23. Herbert Brownell, in a letter of December 16, 1993, maintained that Eisenhower asked him that evening to seek opinions of the leaders of Eisenhower delegations about possible vice presidential nominees. Thus Lodge would not have been authorized to make the offer at that moment.

244 a great ticket: SF Chron, July 13, 1952.

244 a great honor: SF Ex, July 12, 1952.

244 He never forgets: William Mailliard int., JWP, Box 171, Folder 60.

244 The California delegation: Nixon, My Six Crises, p. 300.

244 There was always: Hillings int.

245 was particularly: H. H. Clegg to Mr. Tolson, September 22, 1952, FBI 94-1-5619-146.

245 The whole idea: New Republic, September 29, 1952, p. 3.

245 respectable Republican: Morris, p. 832.

245 He was asked: Katcher, p. 296.

245 I don't know: SF Ex, September 11, 1952. According to Earl Warren, Jr., his father thought Stevenson "would have made a very fine president." Int., February 21, 1991.

246 Well, Mr. President: Warren OH, Truman Library, p. 42.

246 At the Republican: SF Ex, October 5, 1952.

246 the only commitment: Ewald, p. 78. Elbert Tuttle in his Columbia OH, pp. 71–72, states that Warren Burger of Minnesota carried the request from Brownell to Warren. According to Tuttle, Burger told Warren that "he could have the first appointment that he wanted under the new administration" if he held on to his delegates. Brownell denies it in his autobiography, p. 118.

247 in line for: Katcher, p. 297.

247 I want you to know: Schwartz and Lesher, p. 16. Brownell, p. 165, and in an interview on September 6, 1991, placed the telephone call in December, "just before Eisenhower left for Korea." In fact, the president-elect secretly left New York on November 29.

247 A silly time: Phillips, p. 161.

248 I had been: JWP, Box 169, File 52. Warren proposed his Capitol Police driver, Edgar Patterson, also take a seat on the CYA. Just beginning his studies in criminology at Sacramento State College, Patterson declined.

248 A party wheelhorse: SF Ex, April 26, 1953.

248 I've been thinking: Brownell, p. 165. Brownell was uncertain of the date. On June 16, 1953, the White House asked the FBI to run a name check on Warren. Such checks were perfunctory exercises prior to federal appointment. The FBI responded merely by copying Warren's biographical entry in Who's Who. See FBI File 162-69527-34958.

249 THANKS FOR MESSAGE: Brownell, p. 165.

249 Herb Brownell tells me: Mailliard OH, pp. 42–44.

250 My firm and long-standing: "Statement by Governor Earl Warren, Thursday, September 3, 1953," in EWP/LC Box 15.

250 wearing a path: McIntyre Faries int., August 12, 1991.

250 [N]either he nor I: Eisenhower, Mandate, p. 228.

251 not to make: Eisenhower, Mandate, p. 227.

251 You are needed: Scoggins OH, p. 84.

251 Yes, the agreement: Earl Warren, Jr., int., February 21, 1991.

251 to gain a more: Eisenhower, Mandate, p. 228.

251 my relationship: "Memorandum," in Brownell Berkeley OH, p. 25.

252 The main reason: Brownell int., November 30, 1993.

252 I think he would: Brownell int., November 30, 1993.

252 low-key: Brownell, Advising Ike, p. 167.

252 two old friends: Brownell, Berkeley OH, p. 65.

252 he had been: "Memorandum," in Brownell OH, Berkeley, p. 25.

252 did not feel: "Memorandum," in Brownell OH, Berkeley, p. 8.

252 He was very firm: Brownell int., November 30, 1993. Ewald, p. 80, quotes Brownell describing Warren as "cocky." Brownell reconsidered: "Perhaps I spoke too strongly. In retrospect, I don't think that was the proper word."

252 Are you generally: Brownell int., February 14, 1992.

253 I can guarantee: Life, May 22, 1964, p. 117.

253 The White House: Maryalice Lemmon int.

253 the smartest politician: Palmer int., LAT archive, p. 82.

253 Warren would: Raymond Moley, "Knight of Nonpartisanship: Earl Warren," in Farrelly and Hinderaker, p. 227.
254 most tax-ridden: *SF Ex,* January 25, 1953.
254 to take California: Harvey, p. 212.
254 government was not: Katcher, p. 308.
254 If Hiram Johnson: Katcher, p. 309.
255 My mind: *SF Ex,* October 2, 1953.
255 I will not: Earl Warren, Jr., int., August 20, 1992.
255 I want you: Herzl Friedlander int.
255 Without your loyalty: Clint Mosher in the *SF Ex,* October 3, 1953.
255 let his hair down: Joe Lipper int.
255 Here I was born: "Farewell Message to the People of California," October 2, 1953, courtesy of Verne Scoggins.

CHAPTER 22

259 I, Earl Warren: Copies of the oaths, and the commission are in EWP/LC, Box 360, General 1953–1956 file. Details of the ceremony are taken from Merrell F. "Pop" Small to "Dear Maury," October 6, 1953, courtesy of Morris Landsberg; and the *SF Ex,* October 6, 1953.
260 this capable and loyal: Black's eulogy is in 346 U.S. VII.
262 I believe: DDE to "Dear Milton," October 9, 1953, in DDE Diary Series, Box 3, Eisenhower Library.
263 vehemence: Simon, *The Antagonists,* p. 159.
263 is a very attractive: Simon, *The Antagonists,* p. 222.
264 Warren thought: Philip Wilkins interview.
266 I shall consider: Burton to Eisenhower, October 1, 1953, in DDE (Ann Whitman) Administration File, Box 36, Eisenhower Library.
268 ceremonial rosettes: "Felix Frankfurter to Brethren," May 18, 1953, in EWP/LC, Frankfurter correspondence file.
268 A Chief must: Frank, *Marble Palace,* p. 78.
268 I've always thought: Transcript of a PBS interview by Abram Sacher, February, 1972, in EWP/LC, Box 846.
269 available for many services: Warren, *Memoirs,* p. 261.
270 perfectly miserable: Warren, *Memoirs,* p. 272.
270 It's a job: JWP, Box 169, File 41.
270 She could have: Patricia Warren int., August 22, 1991.
271 the Japanese situation: Margaret Olney int., October 19 and 22, 1992. See also the Hansen OH, p. 55, and the Sherry OH, p. 87, where EW seemed less willing to defend the decision of 1942.

CHAPTER 23

272 He brings: Schwartz, *Super Chief,* pp. 147–48.
273 an air of amity: Flynn int.
273 no notoriety: Warren, *Memoirs,* p. 280. The case is *Voris v. Eikel,* 346 U.S. 328 (1953).
273 I ran: Mrs. Robert McHugh int.
273 I just thought: Margaret Bryan int., August 20, 1992.
274 Act to promote: Quoted by Kluger, p. 72.
274 the exact rights: *Plessy v. Ferguson,* 163 U.S. 537 (1896).
275 Our Constitution: 163 U.S. 537, 559.
276 impair and inhibit: *McLaurin v. Oklahoma State Regents,* 339 U.S. 637 (1950).
277 would have been: Frankfurter to Stanley Reed, May 20, 1954, quoted in Schwartz, *History,* p. 286.
278 This is the first: Schwartz, *History,* p. 286.
278 Indian children: California School Code, Division 3, Part 1, Chapter 1, Article 1, Sections 3.3 and 3.4, adopted in 1929. The "Indian" label served to exclude children of Mexican descent.
278 Most Negroes: Pearson's notes of August 21, 1967, for a biography of EW are in the LBJ Library.
278 I can see: Memorandum from Jim Graham, January 21, 1994.
279 I insist: Quoted in Kluger, p. 665.
279 *Plessy* was a disastrous: Jim Graham, "Memorandum to File" regarding "Conversation with E.W. on May 22, 1974," courtesy of Jim Graham.

279 could not use: Transcription of a Warren speech dated December 11, 1972, in CBS Interview collection, Box 3, LBJ Library.

279 You know: Earl Warren, Jr., to John Weaver, in JWP, Box 169, File 38.

280 Sometime to every: Alexander M. Bickel, "Is the Warren Court Too 'Political'?" *New York Times Magazine,* September 25, 1966, reprinted in Levy, p. 217.

280 the baddest nigger: Kluger, p. 172.

280 He handled it: Earl Pollock int.

280 in Virginia: Kluger, p. 674.

281 The Court has finally: Schwartz, *Super Chief,* p. 86.

281 it seemed: Kluger, p. 678.

281 Only the *fact:* Kluger, p. 678.

281 It would be unfortunate: Schwartz, *Super Chief,* p. 86.

282 Of course, there was no: Schwartz, *Super Chief,* p. 87.

282 However passionately: Kluger, p. 684.

282 new law: Kluger, p. 681.

282 to talk it over: Kluger, p. 683.

283 Each justice would: Earl Warren's Brandeis int. broadcast on PBS, in Box 846, EWP/LC.

283 I think it was: EW's Brandeis int., in Box 846, EWP/LC.

283 Let's have: Frankfurter's notes on the conference are quoted in Schwartz, *History,* p. 297.

283 He followed: Flynn int.

284 Stan, you're all by yourself: Kluger, p. 698.

284 The Chief Justice: Kluger, p. 698.

284 He didn't want: Pollock int.

285 to say that: Schwartz, *History,* p. 302.

285 It wasn't anything: Flynn int.

285 were prepared: EW "To the Members of the Court," May 7, 1954, in "Segregation State Cases" file, Box 571, EWP/LC.

286 a beautiful job: Douglas to Warren, May 11, 1954, in "Segregation State Cases" file, Box 571, EWP/LC.

286 magnificent job: Burton Diary entry for May 8, 1954, Library of Congress Shelf No. 17858, Reel 4.

286 in order to demonstrate: Warren, *Memoirs,* p. 286.

286 I am authorized: Warren's reading copy is in "Segregation State Cases" file, Box 571, EWP/LC.

287 We come then: *Brown v. Board of Education,* 347 U.S. 483.

287 a wave of emotion: Warren, *Memoirs,* p. 3.

CHAPTER 24

288 Today I believe: Burton to "Dear Chief," May 17, 1954, in Box 571, "State Segregation Cases" file, EWP/LC.

288 *This* is a day: Frankfurter to "Dear Chief," May 17, 1954, in Box 571, "State Segregation Cases" file, EWP/LC.

288 could not possibly: Frankfurter to Learned Hand, quoted in Steamer, *Chief Justice,* p. 66.

288 What a pleasure: Schwartz, *Super Chief,* p. 148.

289 under the domination: *NYT,* February 20, 1954. The same charges are slightly amplified in L. B. Nichols to Clyde Tolson, February 20, 1954, FBI document 77–61323–62.

289 one of the finest: *LAT,* February 21, 1954.

289 the biggest lot: *NYT,* February 20, 1954.

290 No greater honor: EW to "Dear Mr. President," March 19, 1954, in Presidential Correspondence, October 5, 1953–1963 file, Box 105, EWP/LC.

290 a social upheaval: Robert L. Carter, "The Warren Court and Desegregation," in Saylor, ed., *The Warren Court,* p. 55. Carter provides a convenient list of later Warren Court decisions striking down segregation in public facilities.

290 The decision won't: *U.S. News & World Report,* May 28, 1954, p. 22.

290 We are going: *NYT,* May 18, 1954, p. 20.

290 I will maintain: *NYT,* May 18, 1954, p. 20.

290 South Carolina will not: *Newsweek,* May 24, 1954, p. 25.

290 flagrant abuse: *NYT,* May 18, 1954, p. 20.

290 was pretty bad: Clark OH for the LBJ Library, p. 20.

290 after *Brown:* Margaret Bryan int., February 15, 1994.

291 I think Justice Black: Warren int. by Abram Sacher, for PBS, February, 1972, in Box 846, EWP/LC.

291 It doesn't matter: Gunther int., March 25, 1993.

291 sound judicial: *NYT,* May 18, 1954, p. 20.
291 If today's judges: Bozell, pp. 53–54. For other scholarly criticisms of the decision, see Herbert Wechsler, "Toward Neutral Principles of Constitutional Law," *Harvard Law Review,* 73 (1959), pp. 1ff.; and Louis Pollak, "Racial Discrimination and Judicial Integrity," *University of Pennsylvania Law Review,* 108 (1959), pp. 1ff.
291 had abandoned: AP dispatch to *Sac Bee,* May 18, 1954.
291 The Court took: Lytle, p. 159.
292 During the dinner: Warren, *Memoirs,* p. 291.
292 These are not: Warren used the term "Negroes" in his *Memoirs.* Schwartz, *Super Chief,* p. 121, gives the pejorative word, probably relying on an uncredited interview with a clerk. Ewald, p. 83, an Eisenhower apologist, acknowledges that a decade later he personally heard the retired president use the identical expression.
292 It isn't what: This not-for-attribution quote is from an author's interview. The informant added, "I do believe it because I got it from as direct a source as you can get—and it's not Eisenhower."
292 and with it: Warren, *Memoirs,* p. 291.
292 Dwight Eisenhower: Margaret McHugh int.
292 To the vast: *SF Chron,* May 18, 1954.
293 When you travel: Rankin is quoted in Warren's *Memoirs,* p. 374.
293 the argument: Gunther int., March 25, 1993.
293 whatever it may: *The Oral Argument Before the Supreme Court in Brown v. Board of Education of Topeka, 1952–1955,* pp. 413-15.
294 be rather cruel: Schwartz, *Super Chief,* p. 117, relying on Black and Frankfurter notes of the conferences.
294 deliberate effort: Warren's notes of the conference are in "Segregation Cases, 1955," Box 574, Nos. 1–5, EWP/LC.
295 racial discrimination: *Brown v. Board of Education,* 349 U.S. 294 (1955).
295 Felix's favorite: Gerald Gunther int., March 25, 1993.
295 at the beginning: Frankfurter to EW, May 27, 1955, in Box 574, Nos. 1–5, "Segregation Cases, 1955," in EWP/LC. The all-deliberate-speed standard would remain in effect until *Griffin v. Prince Edward County Board of Education,* 377 U.S. 216 (1964).
295 the harvest: Frankfurter to EW, May 31, 1955, in Box 574, Nos. 1–5, "Segregation Cases, 1955," in EWP/LC.
296 "Good faith": EW to Honorable Walter A. Huxman, November 14, 1955, in Box 574, Nos. 1–5, "Segregation Cases, 1955," in EWP/LC.
296 Eisenhower was annoyed: Herbert Brownell int., September 17, 1992.
296 there can be no: Eisenhower, *Mandate,* p. 230. He would note at a September 3, 1957, press conference, "You cannot change people's hearts merely by laws." (Eisenhower, *Public Papers* [1957], p. 640.) Six days later he signed the first civil rights bill since the Civil War.
296 to eliminate: Anthony Lewis, "A Talk with Warren," p. 129.
296 almost a traumatic: Lewis, "A Talk with Warren," p. 129.
297 Daddy wasn't sure: John Weaver undated interview of William S. Mailliard, in JWP, Box 171, Folder 60.
297 because he had: Virginia Daly int.
298 Argue, argue: McDermott in the *Sac Bee,* July 14, 1974.
298 This has been: Gunther int., April 1, 1993.
298 his answer: Kragen in *California Law Review,* 58, No. 3 (1970), p. 32.
298 sometimes Warren would say: Adrian Kragen int.
299 The best years: *Sac Bee,* October 30, 1977.
299 I've found: *SF Chron,* July 11, 1954.
299 The work here: EW to Earle C. Anthony, June 25, 1954, in "Personal Correspondence A," Box 1, EWP/LC.
300 has certain qualities: *NYT,* March 5, 1954.

CHAPTER 25

301 I don't believe: Margaret Bryan int., August 22, 1992.
301 it took: Richard Flynn int.
301 he had considered: Clayton, p. 232.
301 a fight: Earl Pollock int.
301 was a very decent guy: Gerald Gunther int., March 25, 1993.
302 Frankfurter spent: Oliver OH, p. 6.
302 He wanted: Wolff int.

302 I think he could: Flynn int.

302 did not have: Stern int.

303 I am willing: Gunther int.

303 I was shocked: Anthony Lewis, "A Talk with Warren," p. 128. Bernard Schwartz maintained that Warren told attorney and friend Edward Bennett Williams this was the one decision he would have changed. See *Super Chief,* p. 134. *Irvine* is reported at 347 U.S. 128.

304 And I being: Lewis, "A Talk," p. 128.

304 trying not: Wolff int.

304 Well, he was going: Gunther int.

306 the Senator: "Supreme Court Notes from Other Justices, 1954," in Box 336, Harold Burton Papers, LC.

306 was in constant: Newman, p. 195.

306 The Supreme Court: Clayton, p. 124.

307 may have been: Anthony Lewis int.

307 and things: Moody int., February 8, 1994.

307 I don't think: Wolff int.

307 I often thought: Stewart is quoted in Schwartz, *Super Chief,* p. 134.

307 a Court for the correction: Schwartz and Lesher, p. 132.

307 the jobs used: Schwartz and Lesher, p. 133.

308 to members: *Evelyn Rice v. Sioux City Memorial Park Cemetery,* 348 U.S. 880 (1954) and 349 U.S. 70 (1955).

308 a next step: Wolff int.

308 This woman: Schwartz, *Super Chief,* p. 156, apparently relying on Hugo Black's notes of the conference.

309 It's moot: Wolff int.

309 improvidently granted: *Rice v. Sioux City Memorial Park,* 349 U.S. 70.

309 the biggest flop: Wolff int.

309 The Chief was on: Gunther int.

309 This was the justice's: Gunther int. Warren seems to have destroyed most of his conference notes, and with them his formal records of the votes to grant certiorari.

310 That's what you get: Samuel Stern ints., September 11, 18, 1994.

310 turned the Chief: Gunther int.

310 I think he learned: Gunther int.

310 Sometimes he would ask: Wolff int.

310 but he was strongly: Moody int., February 8, 1994.

311 Help yourselves: Wolff int.

311 He disliked heartily: Wolff int.

311 He simply said: Flynn int.

312 the Court system generally: James Browning int.

312 to live and die: Unpublished article by Martin Agronsky in Box 6, EWP/LC. There was no explanation why Agronsky, a well-regarded journalist, did not publish his article, but obviously he felt confident enough of its accuracy to send a draft to Warren.

313 There is small: *Sac Bee,* May 18, 1954.

313 Do people have so low: Unpublished article by Martin Agronsky in Box 6, EWP/LC.

313 This has been: "Personal Presidential Ambitions Disavowed File," Box 104, EWP/LC, no date. The statement was released to the press late Friday afternoon, April 15, 1955.

313 You not only: "Harold Burton 1953–1957" file, in Box 349, EWP/LC.

313 typical of the straightforwardness: *NYT,* April 16, 1955.

314 I know the Chief Justice: Hagerty, *The Diary of James C. Hagerty,* p. 245.

314 I will run: Pollack, *Earl Warren,* p. 9.

314 that the Supreme Court: Eisenhower Diary, January 30, 1956, in Ann Whitman Diary Series, Eisenhower Library.

314 it would be: Eisenhower Diary, January 30, 1956, in Ann Whitman Diary Series, Eisenhower Library.

315 Opposed: Quoted in Ambrose, *Eisenhower: The President,* pp. 293–94.

315 Why on earth: Pollack, p. 7. Stevenson said he wished Warren would run. "Whoever won, at least the Republic would be secure."

CHAPTER 26

316 He had one: Curtis Reitz int.

316 Tall, broad-shouldered: Miriam Troop to Cray, October 5, 1992. Ms. Troop's original drawing is now in the National Gallery of Art.

316 He had a compass: Arthur Rosett int.

317 My own belief: Newman, p. 471.

317 evaluated in terms: Warren address at the University of Chicago School of Law, May 28, 1958, courtesy of Dallin H. Oaks.

317 He wasn't tied: Reitz int.

317 Yes, but is it fair: A number of Warren's former clerks and newsmen mentioned the question, but none could recall a specific oral argument in which he asked it.

317 is simply a mature: Quoted in *Life,* May 22, 1964, p. 118.

318 not in high regard: Schwartz, *Super Chief,* p. 180.

318 Courts-martial were: Schwartz, *Super Chief,* p. 181.

318 The simple question: Schwartz, *Super Chief,* p. 243.

319 I do not conceive: Simon, *The Antagonists,* p. 237, fn.

319 they were bound: Graham Moody int., February 8, 1994.

319 Such clashes: Frankfurter to EW, undated letter in Box 353, EWP/LC.

319 The Chief talked: Harold Ward, quoted in Newman, p. 471.

319 If anyone complained: Newman, p. 471.

319 He would very strongly: Stern int., September 11, 1994.

319 Whether one saw: William Allen int.

319 learning from actual: Warren int. by Abram Sacher, Brandeis University, February, 1972, in Box 846, EWP/LC.

319 really a shock: Warren int. by Abram Sacher.

320 with no legal basis: "Declaration of Constitutional Principles," *CR,* March 12, 1956, pp. 4460, 4515.

320 The Supreme Court: "The Supreme Court Must Be Curbed," *U.S. News & World Report,* May 18, 1956, p. 50.

321 no loss to the U.S.: Schwartz, *Super Chief,* p. 183.

321 My general: Stern int., September 11, 1994.

321 Sedition against: *Pennsylvania v. Nelson,* 350 U.S. 497, at 505.

321 Something has got: Murphy, *Congress and the Court,* p. 87.

321 politicians instead: Schwartz, *Super Chief,* p. 183.

321 We made a mistake: Murphy, *Congress and the Court,* p. 88.

322 You have heard: Unpublished "Hearings on S. 4050, S. 4051, and S. 4047," Senate Judiciary Committee, Internal Security Subcommittee, June 26, 1956. The criticism stung Warren. See his *Memoirs,* p. 325.

322 Members of the Court: EW to L. Harold Anderson, May 28, 1956, in "Personal Correspondence —A," EWP/LC.

322 querulous: Kenneth Ziffren int., September 3, 1992.

324 We were glad: Rice, p. 121. Information on the Brennan appointment was drawn from Brownell's *Advising Ike,* p. 180, and Sherman Adams's OH for the Eisenhower Library, p. 242.

324 I don't expect: Nat Hentoff, "Profiles: The Constitutionalist," *The New Yorker,* March 12, 1990, p. 54.

324 I was introduced: Hentoff, p. 54, quoting a 1987 National Public Radio interview.

324 a couple: Larry Temple int., April 5, 1994.

324 I always encourage: Schwartz and Lesher, p. 270.

324 the Jesus Quartet: Herbert Mitgang, reviewing Bernard Schwartz, *Main Currents in American Legal Thought,* in *NYT,* July 7, 1993.

324 The more I get: White, *Earl Warren,* p. 180.

324 hard-core liberal: White, *Earl Warren,* p. 181, quoting Frankfurter to Hand, June 30, 1957.

325 The dignity: *Mesarosh v. United States,* 352 U.S. 9.

326 a veritable Pandora's box: 353 U.S. 680. Caute, *The Great Fear,* pp. 135–38, provided details of Matusow's career.

326 Warren was: de Grazia, p. 275.

326 If anyone: de Grazia, p. 274, quoting *Newsweek,* May 11, 1964.

327 a withering function: White, *Earl Warren,* p. 252.

327 an abuse of freedom: EW's handwritten draft of his unissued opinion is in the *Roth v. United States* file, Box 579, EWP/LC.

327 whether to the average: 354 U.S. 489.

328   without unnecessary: Cray, *The Enemy in the Streets,* p. 129.
328   And that's all: I. Michael Heyman int.

CHAPTER 27

329   was anything but: Warren int. by Abram Sacher, Brandeis University, February, 1972, in Box 846, EWP/LC.
330   Boys, I have never felt: Curtis Reitz int.
330   The Whittaker vote: Jon Newman int.
330   At our trial: Ben Dobbs int., May 1, 1990.
331   I've just received: Dobbs int. The actual letter has not surfaced.
331   calmer times: 341 U.S. 494, at 581.
331   advocate the overthrow: "Statement of Attorney General Earl Warren Concerning Civil Liberties," October 31, 1940, in EWP/California, F3640:380.
331   We must test: Address at Centennial Celebration for Robert M. LaFollette, Sr., reprinted in *CR* (1955), p. 9063.
331   garden variety: Warren, *Memoirs,* p. 5; *Sac Bee,* May 5, 1948.
332   Who is getting picked on: John Ely int.
332   have proved: Schwartz, *Super Chief,* p. 232, quoting the Burton and Frankfurter conference notes.
332   clear and present: *Schenck v. United States,* 249 U.S. 47.
332   dumb: Yarbrough, p. 190.
332   once a preeminent: Yarbrough, p. 191.
332   concrete action: 354 U.S. 298, at 319–20.
333   starts with preconceived: EW speech to law enforcement officers, ca. 1939, in EWP/S F3640: 331. Warren also scored a Senate subcommittee led by Robert LaFollette, Jr., which revealed that Warren as district attorney had purchased tear gas for use in controlling pro-labor demonstrations.
333   irresponsible: EW to Hiram W. Johnson, January 25, 1940, in EWP/S, F3640: 17961.
333   any question: Quoted by Anthony Lewis in Sayler, et al., *The Warren Court,* p. 15.
334   removed themselves: *Watkins v. U.S.,* 354 U.S. 178.
334   unthinkable: EW to "Dear Felix," June 5, 1957, in EWP/LC, Box 580, "Watkins No. 1" file.
334   personal vendetta: *Ibid.*
335   Our form: 354 U.S. 234, at 250.
335   only be called: Lewis in Sayler et al., *The Warren Court,* p. 17.
335   in sharp contrast: Walker, p. 243.
335   Warren read: *Time,* July 1, 1957, p. 13.
336   reasserting its ancient: *NYT,* June 18, 1957.
336   There is implicit: *Christian Science Monitor,* June 19, 1957.
336   arrogant incompetence: The newspaper editorials are quoted in Lytle, pp. 130 ff.
336   selected from a cult: "Twenty Years of Court Packing," *U.S. News & World Report,* December 12, 1958, p. 116.
336   extreme solicitude: *U.S. News & World Report,* December 13, 1957, p. 75.
336   a partisan agent: Quoted in Lytle, p. 145.
336   he had been: Warren, *Memoirs,* p. 5.
337   clear lack: Benno Schmidt int.
337   If I were president: Graham Moody int.
337   was the biggest: EW int., LBJ Library, p. 7; later in Warren, *Memoirs,* p. 5. Ambrose, *Eisenhower,* vol. II, p. 190, and Ewald, p. 85, quote the president in similar comments at other times.
337   I wish I could: Rusher, p. 63, without citing a source.
337   I'm satisfied: Adams OH, p. 121.
337   Yes, two: Nat Hentoff, "The Constitutionalist," *The New Yorker,* March 12, 1990, p. 45.
338   he felt: Michael Smith int.
338   How much more: Jeffrey Warren int., March 10, 1994.
338   the modern Thaddeus: *CR* (1957), p. 10672.
338   judicial limitation: *CR* (1957), p. 10471. The CJ's *Mallory* file (EWP/LC Box 436, No. 521) is very thin. This suggests the justices thought it a straightforward, noncontroversial case. Frankfurter wrote one draft and made only slight revisions.
338   rummaging: 353 U.S. at 682.
338   out of business: *CR* (1957), p. 10741.
339   A victory greater: Quoted in Murphy, *Congress and the Court,* p. 130.
339   Horace, you never: Albright int., JWP, Box 173, File 73.
339   There should be: JWP, File 60.

339 Democracy has: EW speech of November 12, 1956, reprinted in Warren, *Public Papers,* pp. 98–99.

339 tireless, fearless: "Address by the Honorable Earl Warren, July 6, 1957," in Box 89, Folder 1, Post-Presidential File, Harry S. Truman Library.

340 I had understood: Page 2 of Pearson's handwritten notes in the file "Proposed Book, The Chief," in DPP, LBJ Library.

340 They're always worried: Drew Pearson Diary, February 6, 1966, DPP, LBJ Library.

340 If the courts lean: AP dispatch to the *Sac Bee,* July 25, 1957.

340 The report was: AP dispatch to the *Sac Bee,* July 25, 1957.

341 snide: Warren, *Memoirs,* p. 323.

341 a disservice: Warren, *Memoirs,* p. 324.

341 girlish giggles: As described by Nina Warren in a note to Betty Henderson.

CHAPTER 28

342 prayerfully: *Arkansas Gazette,* September 3, 1957, courtesy of Keri McKenzie Kemble. The paper's editor, Harry Ashmore, had privately praised the Court's handling of the integration cases. See Ashmore to EW, May 31, 1955, in *Brown* file, EWP/LC.

342 If any racial: *Arkansas Gazette,* September 5, 1957.

343 Go back: Halberstam, *The Fifties,* p. 674.

343 with every means: *NYT,* September 6, 1957.

344 Two, four: Chafe, p. 158.

344 abhorred the idea: Brownell int., September 17, 1992.

344 *not* to enforce: Ambrose, *Eisenhower,* vol. II, p. 420.

344 to get as little: *Newsweek,* October 7, 1957.

345 The time has not: Eisler, p. 151.

345 there was a sense: I. Michael Heyman int.

346 some bad law: Butler OH, pp. 39, 43.

346 May it please the Court: Heyman int.

346 recognized that time: Transcript of hearing, *Cooper v. Aaron,* August Special Term, 1958, pp. 49–50, in Box 584, EWP/LC.

346 It gave me: Warren, *Memoirs,* p. 13.

346 Mr. Butler: Transcript, pp. 89 ff.

347 We knew: Simon, *The Antagonists,* p. 230.

347 notoriety given: Warren, *Memoirs,* p. 298.

347 his attitude: Eisler, p. 152.

348 The constitutional rights: *Cooper v. Aaron,* 358 U.S. 13.

348 caused quite a sensation: Warren, *Memoirs,* p. 298.

348 the lawyers of the South: Frankfurter to C. C. Burlingame, November 12, 1958, quoted in Dunne, p. 350.

348 Felix was: Simon, *The Antagonists,* p. 232.

348 There was havoc: Newman, p. 475.

348 I think that: Butler OH, p. 31.

348 When the institutional integrity: Franklin int.

349 more than $1,000: *New York Journal-American,* September 29, 1958. The president of the United States was similarly "double-dipping," drawing both a military pension and his $100,000 annual salary.

349 It is crystal clear: The Reverend George W. Cheek, Sr., D.D., "The Pending Tragedy in the South," n.p., n.d. Cheek is identified as former minister of the Alabama Avenue Presbyterian Church, Selma, Alabama. The pamphlet is in the Black Papers, Library of Congress, Box 335, "Post September, 1958" file.

349 treason's biggest victory: Murphy, *Congress,* p. 127.

349 front man: Cray, *General of the Army,* p. 686.

349 By a process: *CR,* July 26, 1957, p. 12806, and reprinted in *Limitation of Appellate Jurisdiction of the United States Supreme Court,* Part I, pp. 2ff.

350 have brought glee: *Limitation,* II, p. 195.

350 I have seen: *Limitation,* II, p. 97.

350 The choice: *Limitation,* II, p. 209.

350 Therefore, the Court: *Limitation,* II, p. 637.

351 They fail: *Limitation,* II, p. 589.

351 *Salus populi: Limitation,* II, p. 587.

351 the most revered: Gunther, p. 653, *NYT.*

351 contrary to the maintenance: *Limitation,* II, p. 200.

351 unwise: Murphy, *Congress,* p. 161.

351 such a statute: Gunther, p. 661.

352 reverse the Court: *CR,* August 20, 1958, p. 17313.

352 cause us grave: "Report of the Conference of State Chief Justices, 1958," p. 36.

CHAPTER 29

354 absolutely fascinating: I. Michael Heyman int.

354 would precipitate: Jon Newman int.

355 The Chief: Dallin Oaks int., February 25, 1994.

355 Don't worry: Oaks int., February 25, 1994.

355 Chicago was: Oaks read from his November 6, 1957, journal entry in an int. on February 25, 1994.

355 put the screws: Heyman int. As an academic, Heyman would eventually become dean of the law school and chancellor at Berkeley.

355 he would talk: Scott Bice int., January 19, 1994.

356 He went for: Oaks int., February 25, 1994.

356 What he cared about: Larry Simon int.

356 Most of these: Jesse Choper int.

356 He seizes on facts: Oaks int., February 25, 1994.

356 God damn it: From an interview with a source close to the chief justice.

356 where personal rights: Int. with a Warren clerk on a not-for-attribution basis.

356 There were some: Heyman int.

357 I'm just troubled: Choper int. The case is *Torcaso v. Watkins,* 358 U.S. 450.

357 The fact that: Schwartz, *Super Chief,* pp. 382–83, probably quoting Tom Clark's conference notes.

357 a lot of influence: Choper int.

357 This is the result: Henry Steinman int.

357 the received law: Heyman int.

358 And when he wrote: Newman int.

358 There is no: Warren's draft in "Nos. 572, 415, 710" is in EWP/LC, Box 579, *Perez v. Brownell* file.

358 It makes no difference: Schwartz, *Super Chief,* p. 316, quoting Black's conference notes.

358 the power to denationalize: *Perez v. Brownell,* cited in Schwartz, *Super Chief,* p. 317.

358 If the priceless: Schwartz, *Super Chief,* p. 317.

359 The basic concept: *Trop v. Dulles,* 356 U.S. 100–101.

359 The Court must not: Oaks int., February 25, 1994.

360 the dungaree Navy: Frank, *The Warren Court,* p. 135.

360 interested in people: Simon int.

360 turn out to be: Frankfurter to Hand, October 29, 1958, on Part III, Reel 27, Frankfurter Papers, Harvard Law School.

360 I am a lawyer: Clayton, p. 217.

360 at the crack of dawn: Harriet Potter to EW, October 21, 1958, in EWP/LC, Box 358, "Potter Stewart."

360 in dissent frequently: Marc Franklin int.

361 without the state: Schwartz, *Super Chief,* p. 324, quoting Tom Clark's conference notes.

361 there isn't a man: Frankfurter to Brennan, January 7, 1959, quoted in Schwartz, *Super Chief,* p. 325.

361 dazzling high-wire: Caute, *The Great Fear,* p. 149.

362 ultimate value: 360 U.S. 126.

362 I think he saw: John Weaver int. with I. Michael Heyman, in Folder 59, Box 171, JWP.

362 that the country was: Franklin int.

362 A five-year: Quoted in Murphy, *Congress and the Court,* p. 238.

362 A very spotty year: Franklin int.

362 He was an instinctive: Schwartz and Lesher, p. 67.

362 He had an incredible: Peter Taft int., March 10, 1992. Taft was a nephew of Warren's old political rival Robert Taft.

362 At the same time: Unpublished Martin Agronsky article in Box 6, EWP/LC.

363 I hope you agree: EW to Hugo Black, February 27, 1958, in "Earl Warren File," Box 62, Hugo Black Papers, LC.

363 Court gossip: Oaks int., February 25, 1994.

363 a little private: Oaks int., February 25, 1994.

363 quite a few: Mrs. Tom C. (Mary) Clark int.

363 Here the Chief: Oaks int., February 25, 1994.

363 wondrously like: Schwartz, *Super Chief,* p. 311.

363 went on at great: Anthony Lewis int., April 8, 1994. The case was *Caritativo v. California,* 357 U.S. 549.

364 You are a damned liar: *Los Angeles Examiner,* July 1, 1959.

364 You people: Schwartz and Lesher, p. 154.

364 I was taught: Warren, *Memoirs,* p. 344.

364 I don't know: EW to "Dear Shay," August 3, 1959, in "Sherman Minton" file, Box 357, EWP/LC.

364 heartsick about: Naomi Nover to "Dear Mr. Chief Justice," June 30, 1959, in Box 91, EWP/LC.

364 son of a bitch: Laughlin Waters int.

364 To say something: Oaks int., February 25, 1994.

CHAPTER 30

366 Word went out: Henry J. Steinman, Jr., int. in Folder 60, Box 171, JWP.

367 stretching exercises: Miriam Ottenberg in *The Washington Star,* March 19, 1961, and Anthony Lewis in *NYT,* March 19, 1961, provided details of Warren's daily routine.

367 who has been concerned: Anthony Lewis in *NYT,* March 19, 1961.

368 I just can't: James E. Clayton in *The Washington Post,* March 19, 1961.

368 prisoner of the cozy: William O. Douglas to "Dear Chief," July 14, 1960, in Box 351, EWP/LC; and the Edmund G. Brown OH.

368 too young: EW int. with John Weaver, File 37, Box 169, JWP.

368 No American: Undated draft of letter to "Dear Mrs. Kennedy," in "President Correspondence, 10/5/53–1963," Box 105, EWP/LC.

368 I remember him: Jacqueline Kennedy to EW, December 20, 1963, in "President Correspondence, 10/5/53–1963," Box 105, EWP/LC.

369 Warren was always: Fred Dutton int.

369 They both had: Robert Warren int., July 9, 1991.

370 brought into the fold: Arthur Rosett int.

370 He had a fantastic: Murray Bring int.

370 The right thing: Murray Bring int.

370 an indefensible: *NYT,* April 25, 1961.

371 Chief Justice: *Time,* May 5, 1961, p. 17.

371 degraded the Court: Quoted in Urofsky, p. 124.

371 in his personal: Quoted in Urofsky, p. 125.

371 A lot of the old: Rosett int.

371 the criminal: *People v. Defore,* 242 N.Y. 13. The exclusionary rule was earlier pronounced in *Weeks v. United States,* 232 U.S. 383.

372 the security of one's privacy: *Wolf v. Colorado,* 338 U.S. 27.

373 a confidential: Douglas concurring in *Mapp v. Ohio,* 367 U.S. 643.

374 I care deeply: Frankfurter to "Dear Brethren," January 30, 1962, in William O. Douglas, 1961–63, Box 351, EWP/LC.

374 shocks the conscience: *Rochin v. California,* 342 U.S. 165, in which a doctor pumped the stomach of an arrestee for two pills hastily swallowed as Los Angeles sheriff's deputies swarmed into his home.

374 I never thought: Jahnsen to Weaver in JWP, Box 171, Folder 60. The California Supreme Court in 1922 had ruled that "when competent evidence is produced in a trial, the courts will not stop to inquire or investigate the source from which it comes." See *People v. Mayen,* 188 Cal. 237.

374 he thought the: Earl Warren, Jr., int., March 21, 1991.

374 Wouldn't this be: Schwartz, *Super Chief,* p. 393.

375 Well, we're just: Jesse Choper int.

375 Frankfurter was livid: Choper int.

375 You've had that dissent: Choper int.

375 There is no war: *Mapp v. Ohio,* 367 U.S. 643.

375 So terribly important: Earl Warren, Jr., int., March 21, 1991.

376 Pepsi-Cola: R. Markham Ball int.

376 one of the worst: Notes for Biography dated August 14 [1968] in DPP, EW file.

377 If he has: Dempsey to John Weaver, April 20, 1965, in File 60, Box 171, JWP.

377 The moral principle: *U.S. v. Mississippi Valley Co.,* 364 U.S. 548–49.

377 crude, heavy-handed: Frankfurter to Harlan, n.d., quoted in Yarborough, p. 130.

377 decision did not: Warren, *Memoirs,* p. 315.

378 He hated obscenity: Choper int.

378 indeed astonishing: *Times Film Corp. v. Chicago,* 365 U.S. 69.

378 It is axiomatic: *Times Film Corp. v. Chicago,* 365 U.S. 75.

378 I really hate: Choper int.

CHAPTER 31

379 by the hog lot: Irons and Guitton, *May It Please the Court,* p. 8. Other information was drawn from Schwartz and Lesher, *Inside the Warren Court,* pp. 184–87.

379 the most important: Warren, *Memoirs,* p. 306.

380 the petitioners ask: *Colegrove v. Green,* 328 U.S. 549.

380 big city: Press release from Information Service, University of Virginia, October 8, 1961, in the Brennan Library of Congress papers, Box 69, Folder 2.

380 So it really: James Adler int.

380 politically expedient: Warren, *Memoirs,* p. 310.

380 a sorry day: Speech of Attorney General Earl Warren to the Associated Farmers, December 2, 1940, in EWP/S F3640:297.

381 Frankfurter unleashed: Schwartz, *Super Chief,* p. 412. Schwartz identified Brennan as his source in an int. on March 17, 1994.

381 I'll be the sixth: Newman, p. 517.

381 Mr. Wilson: Irons and Guitton, p. 14.

382 I don't think: Schwartz, *Super Chief,* p. 416.

382 he was most troubled: Henry Steinman int., quoting Roland Homet, Jr.

382 had the utmost: William Dempsey int.

382 The Court's authority: 369 U.S. 267.

383 And Frankfurter: Murray Bring int.

383 Whittaker sort: Adler int.

383 You know, I don't: Quoted in Bring int.

383 advise me: Statement dated March 16, 1962, in Box 358, EWP/LC.

383 was a great force: Edwin O. Guthman int.

383 I thought: Guthman and Shulman, p. 116.

384 Bill, it is: EW to "Bill" undated but probably March 26, 1962, in Folder 2, Box 70, Brennan papers, LC.

384 inevitable: Anthony Lewis, "Historic Change in the Supreme Court," *NYT Magazine,* June 17, 1962.

385 There was dismay: Roland Homet int.

385 a second seizure: EW to the brethren, April 25, 1962, in Box 354, EWP/LC.

385 To retain my seat: Frankfurter to "My Dear Mr. President," August 28, 1962, in Box 354, EWP/LC.

386 save Goldberg: Theodore C. Sorenson, "Memorandum for the President," March 29, 1962, in President's Office Files 88A, JFK Memorial Library.

386 There is nobody: Schwartz and Lesher, p. 207.

386 Almighty God: Quoted in the script for *CBS Reports'* "Storm Over the Supreme Court," Part II, broadcast March 13, 1963, p. 1.

387 A person: *Sac Bee,* July 27, 1974.

387 God save: Schwartz, *Super Chief,* pp. 440–41.

387 I wonder: Choper int.

387 They put: Clayton, p. 17.

387 I know of nothing: *CR,* June 28, 1962, pp. 10840–41.

387 This is not: *CBS Reports'* "Storm Over the Supreme Court," Part II, broadcast March 13, 1963, p. 20.

387 shocked and frightened: Clayton, p. 18.

388 shocking and scandalizing: *LAT,* June 26, 1962.

388 deconsecrated: *CBS Reports'* "Storm Over the Supreme Court," Part II, broadcast March 13, 1963, p. 21.

388 another step: *NYT,* June 26, 1962.

388 disintegration: Clayton, p. 18.

388 I vividly: Warren, *Memoirs,* pp. 315–16.

388 the hysteria: EW to Thomas J. Cunningham, October 15, 1962, in "Court Correspondence on Cases" file, Box 365, EWP/LC.

388 a very easy: *NYT,* June 28, 1962.

388 It might be: James Corman to John Weaver, March 29, 1965, in JWP.

389 WANTED FOR IMPEACHMENT: A copy of the brochure is attached to FBI document 62-87267-150, dated September 4, 1961, in Warren's FBI file. The Los Angeles office of the FBI said the Cinema Organization Guild was "known to the bureau as an 'anti-organization,' especially known for its anti-Semitic literature."

389 limited government: AP dispatch to *Sac Bee,* September 16, 1957.

389 knowingly accepting: *CR,* April 12, 1961, p. 5612.

390 actually Dwight Eisenhower's: Alan F. Westin, "The John Birch Society: Fundamentalism on the Right," *Commentary,* August, 1961, p. 96.

390 Communist influences: Westin, "The John Birch Society," p. 95.

390 is now so strongly: Welch's *The Politician* is quoted in *CR,* April 12, 1961, p. 5667.

390 Why Chief Justice Warren: AP dispatch to *SF Ex,* August 5, 1961.

390 They talk: Warren, *Memoirs,* p. 314. The sarcastic tone may be that of Luther Nichols, the Doubleday editor who finished the book after Warren's death in 1974.

391 Those things: *NYT Magazine,* October 19, 1969, p. 133.

391 I wouldn't impeach: *The Boston Globe,* November 13, 1961.

391 All he wants: *Newsweek,* December 4, 1961, p. 18.

391 not the proper: *SF Ex,* December 14, 1961.

392 that they had reason: Drew Pearson Diary, December 2, 1966, in DPP.

392 I'll have to get: Drew Pearson column in *The Washington Post,* August 30, 1961.

392 Signboards such as this: EW to Robert B. McConnell, June 16, 1965, in "General 1965" file, Box 362, EWP/LC.

392 the theory: EW to Brown, March 26, 1963, in "General 1963" file, Box 361, EWP/LC.

392 I can understand: Earl Warren's OH for the LBJ Library, p. 5.

392 extremism in the defense: *NYT,* January 6, 1985.

392 only seasoned men: Schwartz and Lesher, p. 227.

CHAPTER 32

395 He felt: Gordon Gooch int.

396 Warren had: Conversation with Agnes Williams, April 11, 1994.

396 When we got: Gooch int.

397 He was always: James Corman int.

397 Well, Harry: Corman int.

397 Republicans soured: Augustus Hawkins int.

397 I instinctively: Edmund G. Brown int., December 7, 1990.

397 more forthcoming: Fred Dutton int.

398 It was a very: Hale Champion int.

398 for one reason only: Untitled press release dated July 26, 1962, in National Archives Pacific Southwest Region, Pre-Presidential Papers of Richard Nixon, Box 799, Earl Warren, Jr., file.

398 It would have been: McGrory OH, JFK Library.

398 a bad man: M. F. Small to John Weaver, January 6, 1973, in Box 169, JWP.

399 Uncle Chiefy: Caroline Zecca int., with details provided by her father, Richard Dinner, January 20, 1994.

399 the best thing: As inscribed in the dedication to EW's posthumous *Memoirs.*

399 story of human: "Topics of the Times," *NYT,* November 1, 1992. See also Warren's *Memoirs,* pp. 230–31.

400 You know, Jim: Margaret Warren int.

400 Just think: James Warren, Jr., int.

401 It was quite: Jeffrey Warren int.

401 No, no: Murray Bring int.

401 He knew how important: Robert Gros int. Law clerk William Dempsey made the same observation in an interview on March 24, 1994.

401 It took forever: Roland Homet, Jr., int.

401 wonderment as to: EW to Brennan, October 5, 1959, in "Brennan '56–'59" file, Box 348, EWP/LC.

402 He'd be walking: Gooch interview.

403 The question: Lewis, *Gideon's Trumpet,* p. 79, which provided many of the details in this section.

404 a denial: *Betts v. Brady,* 316 U.S. 455, at 462.

404 It was obvious: Henry Steinman int. Steinman specifically denied the assertion in Schwartz, *Super Chief,* p. 408, that Warren issued instructions to his clerks to be on the alert for such a case.

404 Right to counsel case: Steinman int.

405 There is nowhere: Steinman int.

406 black Monday: Clayton, p. 233.

406 once a geographical: *Gray v. Sanders,* 372 U.S. 368.

406 I agree: *Gray v. Sanders* file, Box 604, EWP/LC.

407 will be a little: McIntyre Faries int., July 25, 1991.

408 a legal Gordian Knot: Schwartz, *Super Chief,* p. 479.

408 They sell us: *Charlotte Observer,* February 3, 1960.

409 believes a store owner: EW's undated notes in "Sit-In Cases" file, Box 604, EWP/LC.

409 we will have: Schwartz, *Super Chief,* p. 481, without citing the source.

409 as nearly a unanimous: EW to "Dear Bill" Douglas, May 18, 1963, in "Sit-In Cases" file, Box 604, EWP/LC.

409 When a state: *Peterson v. City of Greenville,* 373 U.S. 244.

410 the trend: *U.S. News & World Report,* July 1, 1963, p. 72.

410 Court historians: *Milwaukee Journal,* September 29, 1963, quoted in *CR,* September 30, 1963, p. 18318.

411 But really: Quoted in *CR,* October 21, 1963, p. 19849.

411 tragically late: *The Washington Post,* October 5, 1963.

CHAPTER 33

412 a terrible: Margaret Bryan int.

412 It was reported: EW to Jim Bishop, May 8, 1973, in "Kennedy Assassination Committee, General Correspondence, 1969–1974," Box 758, EWP/LC.

412 It was a bizarre: Frank Beytagh int.

413 We were joshing: EW to Jim Bishop, May 8, 1973.

413 It was like: EW interview with John Weaver, January 1, 1966, in File 60, Box 171, JWP. A number of people commented on Warren's affection for the Kennedys, including son Robert, grandson Jeffrey, secretary Margaret McHugh, and law clerks Frank Beytagh and Ken Ziffren.

413 He was very: Margaret McHugh int.

413 a great and good: The eulogies are reprinted in *CR,* November 25, 1963, p. 22695.

414 He told me: Earl Warren, Jr., int., June 18, 1991.

414 He just wasn't: McHugh interview.

414 They told me: EW int. by the historian of the Warren Commission, Alfred Goldberg, a copy of which is in the "Warren Commission General Correspondence File," Box 758, EWP/LC. Warren substantially told the same story to Abraham Sacher of Brandeis University, a copy of which is in Box 846, EWP/LC; and in his LBJ Library OH.

415 making a determined: USIA memo, November 25, 1963, by Donald L. Wilson, acting director, to Bill Moyers, in File 1359, Box 55, Office Files of Bill Moyers, LBJ Library.

415 far more incredible: Richard H. Nelson OH, LBJ Library, p. 44.

415 And I thought: Goldberg int. of EW for the commission.

415 I told him: Drew Pearson, "The Chief Justice," unpublished manuscript in Box 6, EWP/LC.

416 The President told me: Goldberg int. of EW for the commission.

416 We don't know: Sacher int. of Warren, p. 17.

416 Well, Mr. President: Sacher int. of Warren, p. 18. See also the transcript of LBJ's telephone call to Senator Kuchel, November 29, 1963, at 8:25 P.M., LBJ Library.

416 It took a lot: Beytagh int.

417 I don't have much: "Telephone Conversation between the President and Senator Russell," November 29, 1963, 8:55 P.M. (The transcript differs slightly from the actual recording.)

418 the only guy: Warren Olney IV int., August 26, 1992, quoting FBI agents.

418 attempting to establish: Memorandum from Cartha DeLoach to "Mr. Mohr," December 12, 1963, FBI file number 62-109090-36. Hoover denied responsibility for the attack on Olney in a memorandum for Mr. Tolson, et al., dated June 22, 1964, in 62-109090-176.

419 He *was* my father's: Earl Warren, Jr., int., September 19, 1993.

419 Truth is: David Belin speech, National Press Club, March 26, 1992.

419 What do you think: Joseph Ball int.

419 Then we will: Drew Pearson Diary, October 26, 1966, in "Earl Warren No. 2" file, DPP.

420 a major strain: Sam Stern int.

420 in more or less: *NYT,* December 17, 1963.

420 We checked: W. David Slawson int.

420 because the agents didn't: Slawson int.

420 a lot of inaccuracies: David Belin int.

420 FBI reports: Ball int. "No one tried to touch or guide us," Warren told the commission's historian. "The White House never gave us an instruction, *never, never* even looked at our work until I took it up to the President." See the Goldberg int. of EW, p. 2.

421 was a real breach: Slawson int. For Hoover's actions, see FBI document 94-1-5619, dated December 17, 1963, and filed in 62-109090-37; Hoover to Tolson, et al., dated February 5, 1964, in 100-106670-297; and *NYT,* November 29, 1985.

422 a surface case: Goldberg int. of EW, p. 3.

422   The facts: Warren, *Memoirs,* p. 362.
422   If I were still: *NYT,* November 22, 1966. Eight years later, he reiterated this. See the Goldberg int., p. 9.
422   One person: David Belin speech, National Press Club, March 26, 1992, courtesy of David Belin.
422   No one could: Goldberg int. of EW, p. 5.
422   in a conspiracy: Goldberg int. of EW, p. 3.
422   I don't doubt: Undated notes in DPP, in file "Warren, CJ, Earl #1," in LBJ Library.
423   I am quite: Undated notes in "Warren, CJ, Earl #1," DPP.
424   Big brother: *U.S. News & World Report,* August 17, 1992, p. 36.
424   felt that he: Earl Warren, Jr., int., July 7, 1991.
424   But the fellow: EW int., LBJ Library, p. 22. A local official who heard the Ruby interview secretly gave a lengthy report of it to the FBI. That informant "feels Ruby has definitely deteriorated mentally to a considerable degree." See FBI document 44-24016-1638, in File 62-109090.
424   little Mrs. Kennedy: Drew Pearson Diary, Wednesday, October 26, 1966, in DPP.
425   so horrible: Warren, *Memoirs,* p. 371. Warren also recommended that the government use the power of eminent domain to acquire and preserve "all the artifacts of the assassination" taken up by investigators.
425   The public was: Goldberg int. of EW, p.4.
425   So Marina Oswald: Belin, *Final Disclosure,* p. 47.
425   a little spitfire: August 21 [1967] notes in "Proposed Book 'The Chief' " file, DPP.
426   might not be published: Drew Pearson, "The Chief Justice," unpublished manuscript in Box 6, EWP/LC.
426   I have never cussed: Pearson manuscript in Box 6, EWP/LC.
426   any additional: *The Nation,* November 29, 1993, p. 653.
427   no suggestions: Quoted in *The Nation,* November 29, 1993, p. 653. In July, 1966, Kennedy told Richard Goodwin, "I never thought it was the Cubans. If anyone was involved it was organized crime. But there's nothing I can do about it. Not now." See Goodwin, *Remembering America,* p. 465. On "The J.F.K. Cover-Up," generally, see *Newsweek,* November 22, 1993, pp. 58ff.
427   relentless as a: Howard P. Willens int., April 9, 1965, in Folder 60, Fox 171, JWP.
427   It was taking: Earl Warren, Jr., int., September 19, 1993.
427   It would have been: August 21 [1967] notes in "Proposed Book 'The Chief' " file, DPP.
427   Ford wanted: August 21 [1967] notes in "Proposed Book 'The Chief' " file, DPP.
427   furious about it: Goldberg int. of EW, p. 7.
427   far too many: William H. Jordan, Jr., OH, LBJ Library, p. 14. Jordan was Russell's executive secretary. Russell had trouble accepting Specter's single-bullet theory.
427   The Commission has: *Report of the Warren Commission, NYT* edition, p. 41.
428   It was remarkable: Goldberg int. of EW, p. 7.
428   considerable information: *Report of the Warren Commission,* p. 44.
428   they had done: Frank Beytagh int.
429   was probably done: Fred Warner Neal int., and Neal to author, March 23, 1993. A professor at Claremont Graduate School, Neal had known Warren for a decade.
429   One can't say: Howard P. Willens int., April 9, 1965, in Folder 60, Fox 171, JWP.
429   That commission: Robert Warren OH, p. 38.
429   This has been: *Sac Bee,* ca. October 1, 1964, in Weaver files.
429   Nothing: Notes for EW biography in EW file, DPP.
429   The report is: Drew Pearson Diary, October 26, 1966, DPP.
429   Warren's position: Belin interview, June 11, 1992.
429   I don't think: Goldberg int. of EW, p. 10.
430   the problem of trying: *CR,* August 30, 1967, p. 24496, quoting an int. of Epstein on CBS.
430   gadfly: Posner, p. 412, quoting then–CBS Television reporter Dan Rather. Governor Connally termed Lane a scavenger. Joe Ball said of Lane, "He has all the glib approach of a circus barker and just about as much behind his argument." See transcript of Associated Press Managing Editors panel, November 17, 1966, in File 145, Box 178, JWP.
430   underhandedness: Kenneth Ziffren int., September 9, 1992.
430   These were: Epstein, *Inquest,* p. xviii.
430   the ultimate act: Ziffren int., September 9, 1992.
430   fast and loose: EW to Dr. John K. Lattimer, February 3, 1972, in Kennedy Assassination Commission, General Correspondence 1969–74 file, Box 758, EWP/LC.
430   to do something: George Reedy int., April 15, 1994.
431   What possible: File 37, Box 169, JWP.
431   I took him: Belin int. Ball, Slawson, and Specter expressed similar sentiments in interviews with the author.

431 I have read: Sacher interview of EW, p. 19.
431 There were no: Goldberg interview of EW, p. 4.

CHAPTER 34

433 a lengthy memorandum: Frank Beytagh int., June 27, 1994.
433 the desire: Kenneth Ziffren int., September 3, 1992.
434 He took all: Beytagh int., June 27, 1994.
434 Legislators represent: *Reynolds v. Sims,* 377 U.S. 533.
434 My congratulations: Goldberg to "Dear Chief," March 13, 1964, in Reapportionment Cases File, Box 503, EWP/LC.
434 your very fine: Both Black's and Douglas's notes are in Reapportionment Cases File, Box 503, EWP/LC.
435 that these adventures: Yarbrough, p. 151.
435 Possessed of an equal: Brennan is quoted in *NYT,* April 13, 1989, p. A18.
435 finished its work: *CR,* March 1, 1965, p. 3873–74.
435 I would be very: *LAT,* September 17, 1964.
435 redress constitutional: *NYT,* September 16, 1964.
435 There is nothing: Max Freedman in the *LAT,* September 17, 1964.
435 All who are devoted: *LAT,* October 12, 1964.
435 Nina and I: EW to Storke, October 31, 1964, in "Chief Justice Personal—S," Box 115, EWP/LC.
436 too doctrinaire: *Newsweek,* May 11, 1964, p. 11.
436 All in all: Ernest Havemann, "Storm Center of Justice," *Life,* May 22, 1964, p. 122.
436 The Supreme Court: *Life,* May 22, 1964, p. 122, three weeks before *Reynolds* came down.
436 I was just wrong: Schwartz, *Super Chief,* p. 504.
436 After a while: Jesse Choper int.
437 You don't give: Jeffrey Warren int., March 3, 1994.
437 Why in the hell: Storke to John Weaver, January 31, 1966, in File 55, Box 169, JWP.
437 merely the application: Anthony Lewis, "A Talk with Warren on Crime, the Court, the Country," *NYT Magazine,* October 19, 1969, p. 130.
437 most of those problems: EW interview with Abraham Sacher, Box 846, EWP/LC.
437 ultimately had: Theodore Boehm int.
437 one of extraordinary: *NYT,* June 20, 1964.
438 We took them out: Jahnsen OH, p. 171.
438 In Montgomery: The ad is reprinted as a frontispiece in Lewis, *Make No Law.*
438 this monstrous: Lewis, *Make No Law,* p. 121.
438 support to an inference: 376 U.S. 254, 294.
439 at least in the area: Schwartz, *Super Chief,* p. 532, apparently relying on Tom Clark's papers.
440 Otherwise, we will: The undated note is in Warren's file on the case, EWP/LC.
440 one of the enduring: Newman, p. 533.
440 a profound: *Times v. Sullivan,* 376 U.S. 254, 270.
440 We get two: McIntyre Faries int., July 25, 1991.
440 My name is: Warren, *Memoirs,* p. 295.
441 shoved his stack: Califano, p. 54.
441 I'm not sure: James Corman int.
442 The fundamental question: Irons and Guitton, *May It Please the Court,* p. 268.
442 How far do you drive: Irons and Guitton, p. 268.
442 [T]he Act: *Heart of Atlanta v. United States,* 379 U.S. 241.
442 I agree: In "Heart of Atlanta" file, 1964 Term, EWP/LC.

CHAPTER 35

443 He loved you: Gertrude Minton to EW, in Box 356, EWP/LC.
443 a great man: Press Release in Frankfurter Correspondence File, Box 353, EWP/LC.
444 there was talk: EW int., LBJ Library, p. 29.
444 the most compelling: Goldberg to "My Dear Brethren," July 26, 1965, in Box 355, EWP/LC.
444 wrong war: Arthur J. Goldberg int. No. 1, LBJ Library, p. 3.
444 poor Arthur: Scott Bice int.
444 would play: Goldberg int., LBJ Library.
444 camouflage with which: Kalman, p. 16.
445 sacrosanct: Kalman, p. 193.

445 God almighty: Murphy, *Fortas,* p. 171.
445 Immediately after: Black to EW, in "Black Correspondence 1963–1968" file, Box 347, EWP/LC.
445 To the best: Fortas OH, LBJ Library.
445 He's a good man: James Warren OH.
445 a great and powerful: *Yale Law Journal,* 84 (January, 1975), p. 407.
446 We'd sit down: Douglas Kranwinkle int.
446 God damn it: Scott Bice int.
446 The Chief was livid: Tyrone Brown int.
446 For two weeks: *Brooks v. Florida,* 389 U.S. 413, at 414.
447 We'll put that: Brown int.
447 It got rid: Jesse Choper int.
447 for an abstract: Schwartz, *Super Chief,* p. 379.
447 a most fundamental: *Poe v. Ullman,* 367 U.S. 497, at 547–48.
448 was outraged: Yarbrough, *John Marshall Harlan,* pp. 312–13.
448 This is the most: Schwartz, *Super Chief,* p. 577.
448 The right of a husband: Schwartz and Lesher, *Inside,* p. 230.
448 Penumbras, formed: *Griswold v. Connecticut,* 381 U.S. 479.
449 just viciously evil: Newman, p. 557.
450 are slavery laws: Irons and Guitton, p. 280, which also provided some of the history of the case detailed here.
450 The denial of cert: Gerald Gunther int., March 25, 1993.
450 How do we know: Wilma Dykeman and James Stokely, "Inquiry into the Southern Tensions," *NYT Magazine,* October 13, 1957, p. 20.
451 very seriously embarrass: Schwartz, *Super Chief,* p. 159.
451 was furious: Schwartz, *Super Chief,* p. 161.
451 leaves the case: *Naim v. Naim,* 350 U.S. 985.
451 We twice: Gunther, *Learned Hand,* p. 667, fn.
451 total bullshit: Gunther int., March 25, 1993.
452 I think it is: *McLaughlin v. Florida,* 379 U.S. 184 at 198.
452 Almighty God: 388 U.S. 1, at 3.
452 like a red flag: Benno Schmidt int.
452 a kind of roving: Schmidt int.
453 Warren was quite: Schmidt int.
453 If Black: Schmidt int.
453 The freedom to marry: *Loving v. Virginia,* 388 U.S. 1, at 11.
453 I can't see: Schwartz, *Super Chief,* p. 715.
453 Why should: *Levy v. Louisiana Charity Hospital, New Orleans,* 391 U.S. 68, at 70.
454 These decisions: *Levy v. Louisiana* and *Glona v. American Guarantee Co.,* 391 U.S. 68, at 76.

CHAPTER 36

455 I think we are: Kenneth Ziffren int., September 3, 1992.
455 help him: *Leyra v. Denno,* 347 U.S. 556.
456 The abhorrence: *Spano v. New York,* 360 U.S. 315, at 320.
457 It will do nothing: Cray, *Enemy in the Streets,* p. 143.
457 They realized: Michael Smith int.
457 the good ones: Ziffren int.
458 bizarre: *Miranda v. Arizona,* 384 U.S. 436.
458 was called upon: Irons and Guitton, p. 217.
458 I believe: Schwartz, *Super Chief,* p. 589.
459 I feel guilty: Brennan to "Dear Chief," May 11, 1966, in File 2 of 4, Box 45, Brennan Papers, LC.
459 Negro defendants: Box 617, EWP/LC.
459 It's a disease: Drew Pearson Diary, February 4, 1966, in DPP.
459 Was entirely: Fortas is quoted in Schwartz, *Super Chief,* p. 589.
459 [T]he prosecution: *Miranda v. Arizona,* 384 U.S. 436, at 444.
460 One. We do not: EW's reading copy of the opinion is in Folder No. 3, Box 617, EWP/LC.
460 Gideon: Graham, *The Self-Inflicted Wound,* p. 158.
460 We might as well: Cray, *Enemy in the Streets,* p. 152.
460 so detached: Cray, *Enemy in the Streets,* p. 152.
460 the judicial rules: Quoted in *CR,* August 22, 1966, p. 20128.
460 another set: *LAT,* June 15, 1966.

461 decisions which hamper: Cray, *Enemy in the Streets,* p. 152. For Hoover's responsibility, see Louis Nichols Official and Confidential File, Reel 1, and Charns, p. 162, n. 100.

461 excessive: Cray, *Enemy in the Streets,* p. 152.

461 Bronx Man: Graham, *The Self-Inflicted Wound,* p. 185.

461 now making: John Weaver undated int. of Oscar Jahnsen, ca. 1965, in Folder 60, Box 171, JWP.

462 Deliver me: Jester OH, p. 66.

462 we were really: I. Michael Heyman int.

462 This opinion: Goldberg to EW, June 14, 1966, in "Goldberg, 1964–1969" file, Box 354, EWP/LC.

462 throwing society: EW speech at Bohemian Grove, July 30, 1965, in Box 818, EWP/LC.

462 Thinking persons: *NYT,* September 12, 1965.

463 [N]one of us: EW to Edward P. Morgan, June 25, 1966, in Miranda No. 4 file, Box 617, EWP/LC.

463 It is always: Anthony Lewis, "A Talk with Warren on Crime, the Court, the Country," *NYT Magazine,* October 19, 1969, p. 35.

463 is just so much: Morrie Landsberg, "A Conversation with Chief Justice Earl Warren," June 24, 1969.

463 he spent: James Gaither int.

464 more correspondents: "Report of Special Committee on Publicity in Criminal Trials to the Section of Criminal Law of the American Bar Association," n.d., but ca. 1935–1936, p. 7, in F3640:17603, EWP/S.

464 I think this violates: Schwartz, *Super Chief,* p. 544.

464 over and over: Gaither int.

465 the commercial objectives: *Estes v. Texas,* 381 U.S. 532, at 571.

465 Quit Stalling: *The Cleveland Press,* July 30, 1954.

465 the biggest: *Time,* November 22, 1954.

466 increasingly prevalent: *Sheppard v. Maxwell,* 384 U.S. 333. Three decades later, Sheppard's son claimed to have found DNA evidence that would exonerate his dead father.

466 They didn't: Details of the case are in Irons and Guitton, p. 200, and *Terry v. Ohio,* 392 U.S. 1.

467 Police officers: Irons and Guitton, p. 203.

467 In view: *Terry v. Ohio,* 392 U.S. 1, at 24.

CHAPTER 37

469 to banish: *South Carolina v. Katzenbach,* 383 U.S. 301, at 308.

469 What happened: Kearns, p. 229.

470 nearly a century: *South Carolina v. Katzenbach,* 383 U.S. 301, at 337.

470 This is a tax: Newman, p. 568.

471 a blank check: Newman, p. 569.

471 mistreated: Newman, p. 548.

471 does not represent: Newman, p. 549.

471 all seem to want: Black and Black, *Mr. Justice and Mrs. Black,* p. 112.

472 The State: *Adderley v. Florida,* 385 U.S. 39, at 47.

472 In the history: "Justice Black at 75: Still the Dissenter," *NYT Magazine,* February 26, 1961.

472 Hugo changed: Newman, p. 570.

472 is not allowed: *NYT,* December 14, 1966.

472 He's going to stay: Anthony Lewis int.

473 is based: Black, *A Constitutional Faith,* pp. 10–11.

473 Judges may also: Black, p. 14.

473 Look, Hugo: Schwartz, *Super Chief,* p. 629.

473 Nothing is more: *U.S. v. Brown,* 381 U.S. 437, at 444. Archie Brown, a resident of Oakland and a critic of Warren since the Shipboard Murder Case, was also one of the defendants in *U.S. v. Yates,* handed down on Red Monday, 1957.

474 successors: Chapter 108, Laws of the State of Arizona, Twenty-fifth Legislature, Section 38-231.

474 The law said: Barbara Elfbrandt int.

475 They can't limit: Schwartz, *Super Chief,* p. 624.

475 This Court: Black dissenting in *Kingsley International Pictures v. Regents,* 360 U.S. 684 at 690.

475 uncanny ability: de Garzia, p. 505.

475 the sex: de Grazia, p. 501.

476 book burning: Schwartz, *Super Chief,* p. 619.

476 not the quality: *Kingsley Books, Inc. v. Brown,* 354 U.S. 436, cited by White, *Earl Warren,* p. 255.

477 three elements: *A Book Named "John Cleland's Memoirs of a Woman of Pleasure" v. Massachusetts,* 383 U.S. 413 at 418.

477 leer of the sensualist: *Ginzburg v. United States,* 383 U.S. at 468.

477 Ginzburg stood: Schwartz and Lesher, *Inside the Warren Court,* p. 245.

477 is now finally: Quoted in de Grazia, p. 511.

478 To Be Hung: Retold by Elizabeth Black, in *Mr. Justice and Mrs. Black,* p. 140.

478 the greatest: "It Is the Earl Warren Court," *NYT Magazine,* March 13, 1966, p. 30.

478 not since: Reprinted in *CR,* March 29, 1966, p. 7199. The *Post-Dispatch, Bee,* and *Chronicle* articles are also reprinted here.

479 The president: Undated int. with James Warren, in Folder 60, Box 171, JWP.

479 He has emerged: *Washington Post,* March 21, 1966.

480 Whatever doubts: Goldberg to EW, October 11, 1965, in Box 354, EWP/LC.

480 We must offer: EW to Weaver in File 39, Box 169, JWP.

CHAPTER 38

481 a purely ethical: Irons, *The Courage of Their Convictions,* p. 156.

481 belief in: Irons, *Courage,* p. 158.

482 very pleased: Irons, *Courage,* p. 174.

482 I don't know: Schwartz, *Super Chief,* p. 570.

482 People ought: Earl Warren, Jr., int., March 21, 1991.

482 is whether a given: *Seeger v. U.S.,* 380 U.S. 163, at 166.

482 the beneficiary: Irons, *Courage,* p. 175.

483 Papa Warren: Jeff Warren int., March 3, 1994.

483 He's working hard: Pearson diary entry for February 7, 1966, in EW No. 2 file, DPP.

483 till the last: Pearson Diary, February 9, 1966, in EW No. 2 file, DPP.

483 The chief danger: Pearson notes for proposed book "The Chief," dated August 21 [1966], in DPP.

483 We are losing: File 39, Box 169, JWP.

483 I've been for: Undated entry, ca. early 1967, in Pearson notes, DPP.

484 It was more: Ken Ziffren int., September 9, 1992.

484 the brethren would: Pearson notes for proposed book "The Chief," dated August 21, [1966], in DPP.

484 sympathy with: Lewis, *Make No Law,* p. 235.

484 The House is the sole: Schwartz, *Super Chief,* p. 667, citing a *U.S. Law Week* report.

485 The manifest: *Bond v. Floyd,* 385 U.S. 116, at 135.

486 so that other: *U.S. v. O'Brien,* 391 U.S. 367, at 370.

486 What if: Schwartz, *Super Chief,* p. 683.

486 This was early: Larry Simon int.

486 We don't balance: Simon int.

487 Is there anything: Simon int.

487 We cannot accept: *U.S. v. O'Brien,* 391 U.S. 367, at 376.

487 The basic ability: Simon int.

487 He seemed: Paul Meyer int.

487 This is a country: *SF Chron,* June 16, 1967.

487 it may prove: *SF Ex,* November 17, 1968.

488 I remember my mother: Tyrone Brown int.

488 a conservative: Scott Bice int.

489 When he's old enough: R. Markham Ball int.

489 didn't feel: Walker, *In Defense of American Liberties,* p. 254. Other details are from Kalman, p. 252.

490 the same due process: Schwartz, *Super Chief,* p. 673.

490 never-never: Kalman, p. 250.

490 under our Constitution: 387 U.S. 1, at 28.

490 your magnificent: EW to Fortas, March 17, 1967, in *Gault* case file, EWP/LC.

491 If the authorities: Schwartz, *Super Chief,* p. 736.

491 shed their constitutional: *Tinker v. Des Moines Independent Community School District,* 393 U.S. 503.

491 If they did: *Street v. New York,* 394 U.S. 76.

492 The only question: Schwartz, *Super Chief,* p. 733.

492 What's the theory: Meyer int.

492 Impeach Earl Warren: Meyer int.

492 And the Chief's: R. Markham Ball int.

CHAPTER 39

493   a continuous: Johnson, *The Vantage Point,* p. 532.
494   really shaken: Tyrone Brown int.
494   one of the loyal: MacGregor to John Weaver, File 52, Box 169, JWP.
495   conflict of interest: Mrs. Tom C. (Mary) Clark int.
495   Neither one: Frank Beytagh int., June 29, 1994.
495   I'm not going: Laughlin Waters int.
495   He seemed: Nat Hentoff, "The Justice Breaks His Silence," *Playboy,* July, 1991, p. 122.
496   the spirit: Cannon, *Ronnie and Jesse,* p. 232.
496   was obviously: Clark Kerr int.
496   all major areas: *Sac Bee,* June 15, 1969.
496   Pursuant to the: EW to "My dear Mr. President," June 13, 1968, in Box 360, EWP/LC.
496   He came down: The June 13, 1968, memorandum by James R. Jones is in Box 350, Collection FG 535/A, LBJ Library.
497   I have been: EW to LBJ, June 13, 1968, in Box 667, Retirement Folder, EWP/LC.
497   kindest as well: Johnson to EW, April 30, 1968, in Presidential Correspondence File, Box 105, EWP/LC.
497   No, Mr. President: Earl Warren OH for the LBJ Library, p. 31.
497   One thing: Larry Simon int.
497   weakened law: Dunne, p. 409.
497   become a political: *NYT,* August 9, 1968; Kohlmeier, p. 91.
497   First, since I: File 146, Box 180, JWP.
497   strict constructionists: *NYT,* November 3, 1968.
498 · You know: John Weaver int.
498   right to choose: *NYT,* June 24, 1968.
498   was not a resignation: *CR,* October 1, 1968, p. S11684.
499   because you don't: Earl Warren int., LBJ Library, p. 30.
499   a splendid: *LAT,* June 30, 1968.
499   As long: *NYT,* July 6, 1968.
500   is bitter: Fortas to "Dear Chief," July 25, 1968, in Fortas Correspondence, Box 352, EWP/LC.
500   Mallory: *Nominations of Abe Fortas and Homer Thornberry,* p. 191.
500   is directly: de Grazia, p. 538.
500   Justice Abe Fortas: *CR,* July 8, 1968, p. 20154.
501   Today's Court: *CR,* September 9, 1968, p. 26144.
501   I'm very much: *CR,* September 27, 1968, p. 28592, reprinting an article in the *Charlotte Observer* of August 25.
501   The five donors: *CR,* September 26, 1968, p. 28263.
501   he does not feel: McHugh to John Blankley, October 4, 1968, in General Correspondence File, 1968, Box 363, EWP/LC.
502   I couldn't withdraw: John Keker int.
502   until emotionalism: UPI dispatch, October 10, 1968.
502   We're not a revengent: 395 U.S. 444, at 446.
503   humility: Hamilton, p. 462, quoting Ohio Republican Congressman Samuel L. Devine.
504   It was merely: Pollack, pp. 283–84.
504   a great attorney general: AP dispatch, November 1, 1968.
505   had a very pleasant: "Proposed Statement for the Press by President-elect Nixon," in EWP/LC.
505   decorous: Pollack, p. 286.
505   But for Nixon: Herb Klein int.
506   very important: Untitled Brennan "recollection" dated March 18, 1969, in Brennan Correspondence, 1967–1974, Box 348, EWP/LC.
506   On the one hand: Jack Landau int., September 7, 1995.
506   some official: Brennan "recollection."
507   they didn't think: Landau int.
507   said that the Attorney General: "Brennan recollection."
507   I was scared: Landau int.
507   outrageous attempt: Warren, *Memoirs,* p. 340.
507   having an identical: Warren, *Memoirs,* p. 341.
507   This was the first: Douglas, *The Court Years,* p. 259.
507   particularly one: Warren, *Memoirs,* p. 341.
507   Mitchell was not: Landau int.
507   no good: Warren is quoted in Pearson's proposal for a Warren biography, DPP.

508 Please note: Fortas to Warren, March 26, 1969, in EWP/LC.

508 many Washington: *CR,* May 5, 1969, p. 11263.

508 If anything: Charns, p. 101.

509 crazy and not: J. Edgar Hoover to Clyde Tolson, April 23, 1969, in *Louis Nichols Official and Confidential File, Reel 1.*

509 I did most: Shogan, p. 248.

509 It was incomprehensible: Paul Meyer int.

510 Why would Fortas: Margaret McHugh int.

510 had made no: Murphy, *Fortas,* p. 568.

510 I have had it: Paul Porter OH, LBJ Library, p. 37.

510 enable the Court: Abe Fortas to EW, May 14, 1969, in "Abe Fortas 1969–1974" file, Box 353, EWP/LC.

CHAPTER 40

512 the Vietnam war: EW to "Dear Jeff," June 15, 1969, courtesy of Jeffrey Warren.

513 his personal family: 395 U.S. VII.

513 because you might: 395 U.S. VII. Warren's sure-handed draft of the statement is in Warren Burger Correspondence File, Box 347, EWP/LC.

514 to do equal: A copy of the oath is in the Burger correspondence file, Box 347, EWP/LC.

514 For us it is: Schwartz, *Super Chief,* p. 630, citing the Black Papers at LC. The Marshall papers, Box 49, contain the edited version.

514 I didn't expect: *The Washington Post,* March 15, 1971.

514 unparalleled abuse: *CR,* July 1, 1969, p. S7390.

515 It's all in there: File 38, Box 169, JWP.

515 home, the place: File 39, Box 169, JWP.

515 It just made: Virginia Daly int.

515 for his landmark: William S. Thompson in *American Bar Association Journal,* October, 1974, p. 1236.

516 I didn't sense: John Keker int.

516 not an evil: *NYT,* May 13, 1972.

516 in strident terms: *SF Ex,* November 15, 1970.

516 merely an exercise: *NYT,* December 9, 1970.

517 The Court is now: "Report of the Study Group on the Caseload of the Supreme Court," (Washington, D.C.: Federal Judicial Center, n.d. [1972]), p. 9.

517 the great majority: "Report of the Study Group," p. 18.

517 Something of the order: "Report of the Study Group," p. 21.

517 but at the cost: "Report of the Study Group," p. 7.

518 threatened to shut: Associate Justice William Brennan in *Harvard Law Review,* Vol. 88 (1974), p. 4.

518 To put it mildly: EW to Ehrenhaft, November 8, 1972, in "National Court of Appeals No. 1" file, Box 773, EWP/LC.

518 demanded absolute: G. Edward White int.

518 I consider this: "Memorandum to My Law Clerks," in "National Court of Appeals No. 1" file, Box 773, EWP/LC.

518 There are so many: EW to Jefferson B. Fordham, September 3, 1973, in "National Court of Appeals No. 1" file, Box 773, EWP/LC.

518 because Warren had: John Keker int.

519 show captain: *LAT,* June 26, 1995.

519 the *real* Chief: Int. with a former Supreme Court law clerk who asked for anonymity.

519 Not in the long run: *The Washington Post,* March 15, 1971.

519 was absolutely: White int.

519 The new decision: AP dispatch to *NYT,* March 19, 1971.

520 outstanding: Quoted by Trude B. Feldman in the *Miami Herald,* reprinted in *CR,* July 29, 1974, p. 25422.

520 He felt bad: Scott Bice int.

520 That would be showing: Keker int.

520 It took a lot: Earl Warren, Jr., int., August 20, 1992.

520 not much different: Keker int.

521 Now that he: Keker int., paraphrasing EW.

521 third-rate burglary: Kutler, p. 189.

522 a most unjudicial: Alden Whitman, "Alden Whitman's Golden Oldies," *Esquire,* April, 1975, p. 83.

522 We talked a lot: Bice int.

522 conduct debasing: AP's standing obituary, April, 1974.

522 The reputation: Address at Loyola University, New Orleans, April 27, 1974, in Box 837, EWP/LC.

523 myriad of crimes: EW to Eugene V. Rostow, March 5, 1974, in "Court General 1974" file, Box 365, EWP/LC.

523 You know: Earl Warren, Jr., int., February 21, 1991.

523 as well as ever: EW to John Weaver, March 25, 1974, in File 40, Box 169, JWP.

524 the last forum: "Address delivered by Honorable Earl Warren," May 21, 1974, in Box 837, EWP/LC.

524 I can see: Jim Graham int.

524 an invidious view: Memorandum of "Conversation with E.W. on May 22, 1974," dated July 15, 1974, courtesy of Jim Graham.

525 I've been waiting: This meeting was reconstructed from interviews with Patterson on September 13, 1991, and November 20, 1992.

525 No news: Graham int.

526 He wasn't looking: Jeff Warren int., March 3, 1994.

526 skin and bones: James Warren OH, p. 49.

526 Something hidden: The full text is in *Rudyard Kipling's Verse: Definitive Edition* (New York: Doubleday, 1940).

526 Okay, fellas: James Warren OH, p. 49.

526 No man: Pollack, p. 326.

527 If Nixon: Douglas, *The Court Years,* p. 238.

AFTERWORD

529 the Supreme Court: Kutler, p. 513.

530 flash frozen: Savage, p. 38.

531 protected by the: *Gitlow v. New York,* 268 U.S. 652.

531 The big deal: Alexander Cockburn quoting Morton Stavis, president of the Center for Constitutional Rights, in *LAT,* June 27, 1991.

532 Certainly the kind: G. Edward White int., June 29, 1994.

532 second in greatness: Abraham, pp. 239–40.

SELECTED BIBLIOGRAPHY

Abraham, Henry J., *Justices and Presidents,* 1st and 3rd eds. (New York: Oxford University Press, 1974, 1992).

"Acts of Executive Clemency of California" (Sacramento: California State Printing Office, 1943–1954).

Agnew, Spiro, *Go Quietly—or Else* (New York: William Morrow, 1980).

Ambrose, Stephen E., *Eisenhower: Soldier, General of the Army, President-Elect* (New York: Simon and Schuster, 1983).

———, *Eisenhower: The President* (New York: Simon and Schuster, 1984).

———, *Nixon: The Education of a Politician, 1913–1962* (New York: Simon and Schuster, 1987).

[Anderson, A. J.], *Meet the Governor of California* (Pasadena, Calif.: Login Printing Co., [1948]).

Bagnell, Beth, *Oakland: The Story of a City* (Novato, Calif.: Presidio Press, 1982).

Baker, Leonard, *Brandeis and Frankfurter* (New York: Harper & Row, 1984).

Barger, Bob, "Raymond L. Haight and the Commonwealth Progressive Campaign of 1934," *California Historical Quarterly,* XLIII (1964), pp. 219–30.

Bass, Jack, *Unlikely Heroes* (New York: Simon and Schuster, 1981).

Bean, Walton, and James J. Rawls, *California: An Interpretive History* (New York: McGraw-Hill, 1988).

Belin, David W., *Final Disclosure* (New York: Charles Scribner's Sons, 1988).

Beytagh, Francis X., Jr., "On Earl Warren's Retirement: A Reply to Professor Kurland," *Michigan Law Review,* 67 (1968–1969), pp. 1477–92.

Bickel, Alexander M., *Politics and the Warren Court* (New York: Harper & Row, 1966).

Bird, Kai, *The Chairman* (New York: Simon and Schuster, 1992).

Black, Hugo L., *A Constitutional Faith* (New York: Alfred A. Knopf, 1968).

Black, Hugo L., and Elizabeth Black, *Mr. Justice and Mrs. Black* (New York: Random House, 1986).

Blue and Gold, The, Published by the Junior Class (Berkeley: 1908–1915).

Bonelli, William G., [and Leo Katcher], *Billion Dollar Blackjack* (Beverly Hills: Civic Research Press, 1954).

Bozell, L. Brent, *The Warren Revolution* (New Rochelle, N.Y.: Arlington House, 1966).

Branch, Taylor, *Parting the Waters* (New York: Simon and Schuster, 1988).

Brecher, Jeremy, *Strike!* (San Francisco: Straight Arrow Books, 1972).

Brennan, William J., "Chief Justice Warren," *Harvard Law Review,* 88 (1974), pp. 1–5.

Brodie, Fawn M., *Richard Nixon: The Shaping of His Character* (New York: W. W. Norton, 1981).

Brownell, Herbert, with John P. Burke, *Advising Ike* (Lawrence, Kans.: University Press of Kansas, 1993).

Burke, Robert E., *Olson's New Deal for California* (Berkeley and Los Angeles: University of California Press, 1953).

Burton, Harold H., "Diary," Library of Congress Microfilm No. 17858, Reels 4 and 5.

Califano, Joseph A., Jr., *The Triumph and Tragedy of Lyndon Johnson* (New York: Simon and Schuster, 1991).
Cannon, Lou, *President Reagan: The Role of a Lifetime* (New York: Simon and Schuster, 1991).
————, *Ronnie and Jesse: A Political Odyssey* (Garden City, N.Y.: Doubleday and Co., 1969).
Cashman, Sean Dennis, *America in the Age of the Titans* (New York: New York University Press, 1988).
Caughey, John Walton, *California* (New York: Prentice-Hall, 1940).
————, *California: A Remarkable State's Life History,* 4th ed. (Englewood Cliffs, N.J.: Prentice-Hall, 1970).
Caute, David, *The Great Fear* (New York: Simon and Schuster, 1978).
Cerwin, Herbert, *In Search of Something* (Los Angeles: Sherbourne Press, 1966).
Chafe, William H., *The Unfinished Journey* (New York: Oxford, 1986).
Charns, Alexander, *Cloak and Gavel* (Urbana: University of Illinois Press, 1992).
Chiasson, Lloyd, "The Japanese-American Encampment," *Newspaper Research Journal* (Spring, 1991), pp. 92–107.
Clayton, James, *The Making of Justice* (New York: E. P. Dutton, 1964).
Coakley, J. Frank, *For the People* (Orinda, Calif.: Western Star Press, 1992).
Coe, Lee, "The Ship Murder: The Story of a Frameup" (San Francisco: King-Ramsay-Conner Defense Committee, n.d. [ca. 1937]).
Conn, Stetson, "The Decision to Evacuate the Japanese from the Pacific Coast," in Kent Roberts Greenfield, *Command Decisions* (Washington, D.C.: Office of the Chief of Military History, Department of the Army, 1960). pp. 125–50.
Conrat, Maisie and Richard, *Executive Order 9066* (San Francisco: California Historical Society, 1972).
"Conversation with Chief Justice Earl Warren, A" (Sacramento: McClatchy Broadcasting, 1969).
Cook, Blanche Wiesen, *The Declassified Eisenhower* (Garden City, N.Y.: Doubleday & Company, 1981).
Cox, Archibald, *The Court and the Constitution* (Boston: Houghton Mifflin Co., 1987).
————, *The Warren Court* (Cambridge, Mass.: Harvard University Press, 1968).
Cray, Ed, *The Big Blue Line* (New York: Coward McCann, 1967).
————, "California, Here I Come," *California Lawyer,* December 1986.
————, *The Enemy in the Streets* (New York: Anchor Books, 1972).
————, "High Rollers on the High Seas," *California Lawyer,* December, 1982, pp. 49–51.
————, "It Was Lies, All Lies!" *California Lawyer,* September, 1983, pp. 42ff.
————, "The Longshoreman and the Law," *California Lawyer,* October, 1985, pp. 48–51.
Creel, George, "California's Elephant Boy," *Collier's,* June 8, 1946, pp. 20ff.
Crouch, Winston W., and Dean E. McHenry, *California Government,* rev. ed. (Berkeley and Los Angeles: University of California Press, 1949).
Dallek, Robert, *Franklin D. Roosevelt and American Foreign Policy* (New York: Oxford University Press, 1979).
Daniels, Roger, *The Politics of Prejudice* (Berkeley: University of California Press, 1977).
Dawley, Alan, *Struggles for Justice* (Cambridge, Mass.: The Belknap Press, 1991).
Dean, George, "Warren of California," *The Commonweal,* October 3, 1947, pp. 592ff.
Dilliard, Irving, ed., *One Man's Stand for Freedom* (New York: Alfred A. Knopf, 1963).
Donovan, Robert J., *Eisenhower: The Inside Story* (New York: Harper and Brothers, 1956).
Dorsen, Norman, ed., *The Evolving Constitution* (Middletown, Conn.: Wesleyan University Press, 1987).
Douglas, William O., *The Court Years, 1939–1975* (New York: Random House, 1980).
Downey, Sheridan, *They Would Rule the Valley* (San Francisco: n.p., 1947).
Dunne, Gerald T., *Hugo Black and the Judicial Revolution* (New York: Simon and Schuster, 1977).
"Earl Warren—a Tribute," in *California Law Review,* Vol. 58, No. 1 (1970), pp. 1ff.
Eisenhower, Dwight D., *Mandate for Change, 1953–1956* (Garden City, N.Y.: Doubleday and Company, 1963).
Eisler, Kim Isaac, *A Justice for All* (New York: Simon and Schuster, 1993).
Epstein, Edward Jay, *Inquest* (New York: Viking Press, 1966).
————, "Shots in the Dark," *The New Yorker,* November 30, 1992, pp. 47ff.
Ernst, Morris L., *The Great Reversals* (New York: Weybright and Talley, 1973).
Ewald, William Bragg, Jr., *Eisenhower the President* (Englewood Cliffs, N.J.: Prentice-Hall, 1981).
"Executions in California, 1943 Through 1963," California Department of Corrections, Research Division (Sacramento, Calif.: March 31, 1965).
Farrelly, David, and Ivan Hinderaker, *The Politics of California* (New York: The Ronald Press, 1951).
Feingold, Miriam, "The King-Ramsay-Conner Case: Labor, Radicalism and the Law in California, 1936–1941," unpublished Ph.D. dissertation (Madison: University of Wisconsin, 1976).
Ferrell, Robert H., ed., *The Diary of James C. Hagerty* (Bloomington, Ind.: Indiana University Press, 1983).
Fleischer, Lawrence, "Thomas E. Dewey and Earl Warren: The Rise of the Twentieth-Century Urban Prosecutor," in *California Western Law Review,* 28 (1991–92), pp. 1–50.
Foote, Robert Ordway, "The Radical vs. Conservative Issue in California," *The Literary Digest,* September 8, 1934, pp. 7–8.

Ford, Robert S., *Red Trains in the East Bay* (Glendale, Calif.: Interurbans Publications, 1977).

Frank, John P., *Marble Palace* (New York: Alfred A. Knopf, 1958).

———, *The Warren Court* (New York: Macmillan, 1964).

Frankfurter, Felix, "Chief Justices I Have Known," *Virginia Law Review,* 39 (1953), pp. 883ff.

From the President: Richard Nixon's Secret Files (New York: Perennial Library, 1989).

Frost, Richard H., *The Mooney Case* (Stanford, Calif.: Stanford University Press, 1968).

Gentry, Curt, *Frame-up: The Incredible Case of Tom Mooney and Warren Billings* (New York: W. W. Norton, 1967).

———, *J. Edgar Hoover: The Man and the Secrets* (New York: W. W. Norton, 1992).

Girdner, Audrie, and Anne Loftis, *The Great Betrayal* (New York: Macmillan, 1969).

Gitlin, Todd, *The Sixties,* rep. ed. (New York: Bantam, 1989).

Goldman, Roger, and David Gallen, *Thurgood Marshall: Justice for All* (New York: Carroll & Graf, 1992).

Goodman, Richard N., *Remembering America* (Boston: Little, Brown and Co., 1988).

Goralski, Robert, *World War II Almanac, 1931–1945* (New York; G. P. Putnam's Sons, 1981).

Gordon, Rosalie, *Nine Men Against America* (New York: Devin-Adair Company, 1961).

Graham, Fred P., *The Self-Inflicted Wound* (New York: Macmillan, 1970).

Graham, Susan K., "A Study of the Effects of Racism on Media Coverage," unpublished paper prepared for Journalism 505, University of Southern California, December 11, 1991.

Grant, H. Roger, ed., *Brownie the Boomer* (DeKalb, Ill.: Northern Illinois University Press, 1992).

Gressman, Eugene, William O. Douglas, and Williams S. Thompson, "The World of Earl Warren," *American Bar Association Journal,* October, 1974, pp. 1228ff.

Grodzins, Morton, *Americans Betrayed* (Chicago: University of Chicago Press, 1949).

Gunther, Gerald, *Learned Hand* (New York: Alfred A. Knopf, 1994).

Gunther, John, *Inside USA* (New York: Harper, 1947).

Guthman, Edwin O., and Jeffrey Shulman, *Robert Kennedy: In His Own Words* (New York: Bantam Press, 1988).

Haldeman, H. R., *The Haldeman Diaries* (New York: Putnam, 1994).

Hamilton, Charles V., *Adam Clayton Powell, Jr.* (New York: Atheneum, 1991).

Hampton, Henry, and Steve Fayer, *Voices of Freedom* (New York: Bantam Books, 1990).

Harris, Richard, *Justice* (New York: E. P. Dutton, 1969).

Harrison, Gordon, "Warren of California," *Harper's Magazine,* June, 1952, pp. 27ff.

Harvey, Richard Blake, "The Political Approach of Earl Warren, Governor of California," unpublished Ph.D. dissertation (University of California, Los Angeles, 1959).

Haveman, Ernest, "Storm Center of Justice," *Life,* May 22, 1964, pp. 108ff.

Healey, Dorothy, and Maurice Isserman, *Dorothy Healey Remembers* (New York: Oxford University Press, 1990).

Henderson, Lloyd Ray, "Earl Warren and California Politics," Ph.D. dissertation, University of California, Berkeley, 1966 (Ann Arbor, Mich.: University Microfilms, 1982).

Henstell, Bruce, *Sunshine and Wealth: Los Angeles in the Twenties and Thirties* (San Francisco: Chronicle Books, n.d.).

Hill, Gladwin, *Dancing Bear* (Cleveland: World Publishing, 1968).

Hichborn, Franklin, "California Politics—1891–1939" (Unpublished manuscript in UCLA Department of Special Collections, Collection 1242, Boxes 180–182).

———, *The System as Uncovered by the San Francisco Graft Prosecution* (San Francisco: The James H. Barry Company, 1915).

[Huberman, Leo, attrib.] "Punishment Without Crime" (San Francisco: King-Ramsay-Conner Defense Committee, n.d. [1940]).

Huston, Luther A., *Pathway to Judgment* (Philadelphia: Chilton Books, 1966).

Investigation of Organized Crime in Interstate Commerce, Hearings before the Special Committee to Investigate Organized Crime in Interstate Commerce, United States Senate, 81st Congress, 2nd Session, Parts II, X (Washington, D.C.: Government Printing Office, 1950).

Investigation of the Assassination of President John F. Kennedy, Hearings Before the Select Committee on Assassinations of the U.S. House of Representatives, 95th Congress, 2nd Session, September 18–21, 1978. (Washington, D.C.: Government Printing Office, 1978).

Irons, Peter, *The Courage of Their Convictions* (New York: The Free Press, 1988).

———, *Justice at War* (New York: Oxford University Press, 1983).

Irons, Peter, and Stephanie Guitton, *May It Please the Court* (New York: The New Press, 1993).

Jaffe, Julian F., *Crusade Against Radicalism: New York During the Red Scare, 1914–1924* (Port Washington, N.Y.: Kennikat Press, 1972.

JFK: The Book of the Film (New York: Applause Books, 1992).

Johnson, Haynes, *Sleepwalking Through History* (New York: W. W. Norton, 1991).

Johnson, Lyndon Baines, *The Vantage Point* (New York: Holt, Rinehart and Winston, 1971).

Kalman, Laura, *Abe Fortas* (New Haven, Conn.: Yale University Press, 1990).

Katcher, Leo, *Earl Warren: A Political Biography* (New York: McGraw-Hill Book Company, 1967).

Kearns, Doris, *Lyndon Johnson and the American Dream* (New York: Harper & Row, 1976).

Kelley, Stanley, Jr., *Professional Public Relations and Political Power* (Baltimore, Md.: Johns Hopkins Press, 1956).

Kenny, Robert W., "My First Forty Years in California Politics," (Unpublished manuscript in Special Collections, UCLA Library).

Kluger, Richard, *Simple Justice* (New York: Alfred A. Knopf, 1976).

Kohlmeier, Louis M., Jr., *"God Save This Honorable Court!"* (New York: Charles Scribner's Sons, 1961).

Kurland, Philip B., "The Supreme Court and Its Judicial Critics," *Utah Law Review,* 6 (1959), pp. 457–66.

Kutler, Stanley I., *The American Inquisition* (New York: Hill & Wang, 1982).

Leader, Leonard, *Los Angeles and the Great Depression* (New York: Garland Publishing, Inc., 1991).

"Legal and Constitutional Phases of the WRA Program," United States Department of the Interior, War Relocation Authority (Washington, D.C.: U.S. Government Printing Office, n.d. [post-1944]).

"Legislative Investigative Report, Submitted by H. R. Philbrick, December 28, 1938," unpublished, in UCLA Special Collections as JK 8745 A86L.

Levy, Leonard W., *The Supreme Court Under Earl Warren* (New York: Quadrangle Books, 1972).

Lewis, Anthony, "Earl Warren," in Leon Friedman and Fred L. Israel, eds., *The Justices of the United States Supreme Court, 1789–1978,* Vol. 4 (New York: Chelsea House, 1980).

———, *Gideon's Trumpet* (New York: Random House, 1964).

———, *Make No Law* (New York: Random House, 1991).

———, "The Supreme Court and Its Critics, *Minnesota Law Review,* 45 (1961), pp. 305–32.

———, "A Talk with Warren on Crime, the Court, the Country," *New York Times Magazine,* October 19, 1969, pp. 34ff.

Lichtenstein, Nelson, ed., *Political Profiles: The Johnson Years* (New York: Facts on File, 1976).

Limitation of Appellate Jurisdiction of the United States Supreme Court, Hearings before the Subcommittee to Investigate the Administration of the Internal Security Act and other Internal Security Laws of the Committee on the Judiciary, United States Senate, 85th Congress, 1st Session, on S. 2646, Part 1, 1957; 2nd Session, Part 2, 1958 (Washington, D.C.: U.S. Government Printing Office, 1957, 1958).

Loewy, Arnold H., "The Warren Court as Defender of State and Federal Criminal Laws," *The George Washington Law Review,* 37 (1969), pp. 1218ff.

Lytle, Clifford M., *The Warren Court and Its Critics* (Tucson: The University of Arizona Press, 1968).

Lytle, Clifford M., Jr., *The Warren Court and Its Political Critics,* Ph.D. dissertation, University of Pittsburgh, 1963 (Ann Arbor, Mich.: University Microfilms, 1964).

McCloskey, Robert G., *The Modern Supreme Court* (Cambridge, Mass.: Harvard University Press, 1972).

[McKee, Ruth E.,] *Wartime Exile: The Exclusion of the Japanese Americans from the West Coast,* United States Department of the Interior, War Relocation Authority (Washington, D.C.: Government Printing Office, n.d.).

McWilliams, Carey, *California: The Great Exception* (New York: Current Books, 1949).

———, "Earl Warren—a Likely Dark Horse," *The Nation,* November 29, 1947, pp. 581ff.

———, *The Education of Carey McWilliams* (New York: Simon and Schuster, 1979).

———, "Government by Whitaker and Baxter," *The Nation,* April 14, 1951, pp. 346ff.; April 21, 1951, pp. 366ff.; May 5, 1951, pp. 418ff.

———, *Prejudice* (Boston: Little, Brown and Co., 1949).

———, *Southern California: An Island on the Land,* 2nd ed. (Santa Barbara and Salt Lake City: Peregrine Smith, Inc., 1973).

———, "Warren of California," *New Republic,* October 18, 1943, pp. 514ff.

Mankiewicz, Frank, *Perfectly Clear* (New York: Quadrangle, 1973).

Margolick, David M., "Earl Warren's Past: The Forgotten Blemish," *National Law Journal,* September 17, 1979, p. 15.

Mazo, Earl, *Richard Nixon: A Political and Personal Portrait* (New York: Harper and Brothers, 1959).

Mazo, Earl, and Stephen Hess, *Nixon: A Political Portrait* (New York: Harper & Row, 1968).

Medalie, Richard J., *From Escobedo to Miranda* (Washington, D.C.: Lerner Law Book Co., 1966).

Meyer, Agnes E., *Journey Through Chaos* (New York: Harcourt, Brace and Company, 1944).

Miller, Loren, *The Petitioners* (Cleveland, Ohio: Meridian Books, 1966).

Mitchell, Greg, *The Campaign of the Century* (New York: Random House, 1992).

Moley, Raymond, *Politics and Criminal Prosecution* (New York: Minton, Balch and Company, 1929).

Morris, Roger, *Richard Milhous Nixon: The Rise of an American Politician* (New York: Henry Holt, 1990).

Mowry, George E., *The California Progressives,* rep. ed. (Chicago: Quadrangle, 1963).

Muir, Florabel, *Headline Happy* (New York: Henry Holt, 1950).

Murdock, Steve, "The Man Behind the Warren Mask" (San Francisco: The Daily People's World, n.d. [1948]).

Murphy, Bruce Allen, *The Brandeis-Frankfurter Connection,* rep. ed. (Garden City, N.Y.: Anchor Press, 1983).

———, *Fortas* (New York: William Morrow, 1988).

Murphy, Walter F., *Congress and the Court* (Chicago: University of Chicago Press, 1962).

Murray, Robert K., *Red Scare: A Study in National Hysteria* (Minneapolis: University of Minnesota Press, 1955).

Nagel, Robert F., "How the Right Learned to Love Earl Warren," *California Monthly,* October, 1982, pp. 50ff.

National Defense Migration, Hearings before the Select Committee Investigating National Defense Migration, House of Representatives, 77th Congress, Parts 26, 29 (Washington, D.C.: Government Printing Office, 1942).

Nelson, Steve, James R. Barrett, and Rob Ruck, *Steve Nelson: American Radical* (Pittsburgh, Penn.: University of Pittsburgh Press, 1981).

Newman, Roger K., *Hugo Black: A Biography* (New York: Pantheon, 1994).

North, Mark, *Act of Treason* (New York: Carroll & Graf, 1991).

Oglesby, Carl, *Who Killed JFK?* (Berkeley, Calif.: Odonian Press, 1992).

Olin, Spencer C., Jr., *California's Prodigal Sons* (Berkeley and Los Angeles: University of California Press, 1968).

Olson, Culbert L., *State Papers and Public Addresses,* selected by Stanley Mosk (Sacramento: California State Printing Office, 1942).

O'Reilly, Kenneth, *Racial Matters* (New York: The Free Press, 1989).

Parmet, Herbert, *Eisenhower and the American Crusades* (New York: Macmillan, 1972).

———, *Richard Nixon and His America* (Boston: Little, Brown, 1990).

Pearson, Drew, *Diaries, 1949–1959,* edited by Tyler Abell (New York: Holt, Rinehart and Winston, 1974).

Phillips, Herbert L., *Big Wayward Girl* (Garden City, N.Y.: Doubleday & Co., 1968).

———, "Warren of California," *The Nation,* May 24, 1952. pp. 495ff.

Pollack, Jack Harrison, *Earl Warren: The Judge Who Changed America* (Englewood Cliffs, N.J.: Prentice-Hall, 1979).

Prange, Gordon W., Donald M. Goldstein, and Katherine V. Dillon, *At Dawn We Slept* (New York: McGraw-Hill Book Company, 1981).

Proceedings of the Attorney General's Conference on Crime Held December 10–13, 1934 (Washington, D.C.: Government Printing Office, 1934).

Proceedings of the First National Parole Conference (n.p., n.d. [U.S. Government Printing Office, 1939]).

Rappleye, Charles, and Ed Becker, *All-American Mafioso; The Johnny Rosselli Story* (New York: Doubleday, 1991).

Rehnquist, William H., *The Supreme Court: How It Was, How It Is* (New York: William Morrow, 1987).

Report of the Joint Fact-Finding Committee on Un-American Activities in California, Senate, California Legislature, 55th Session (Sacramento, 1943).

Report of the Study Group on the Caseload of the Supreme Court, Federal Judicial Center (Washington, D.C., 1972).

Report of the Warren Commission on the Assassination of President Kennedy, New York Times ed. (New York: Bantam Books, 1964).

Rice, Arnold S., *The Warren Court: 1953–1969* (Millwood, N.Y.: Associated Faculty Press, Inc., c. 1987).

Richard Nixon's Secret Files, ed. by Bruce Oudes (New York: Harper & Row, 1989).

Richardson, James, *For the Life of Me* (New York: G. P. Putnam's Sons, 1954).

Richmond, Al, *A Long View from the Left: Memoirs of an American Revolutionary* (Boston: Houghton Mifflin Co., 1973).

Rusco, Elmer Ritter, "Machine Politics, California Model: Arthur H. Samish and the Alcoholic Beverage Industry," unpublished Ph.D. dissertation (University of California, Berkeley, 1960).

Rusher, William A., *The Rise of the Right* (New York: William Morrow, 1984).

Ryckman, Charles S., "Warren of California," *Cosmopolitan,* April, 1944, pp. 42ff.

Salvatore, Nick, *Eugene V. Debs: Citizen and Socialist* (Urbana: University of Illinois Press, 1982).

Samish, Arthur H., and Bob Thomas, *The Secret Boss of California* (New York: Crown Publishers, 1971).

Savage, David, *Turning Right: The Making of the Rehnquist Supreme Court* (New York: John Wiley & Sons, 1992).

Sayler, Richard H., Barry B. Boyer, and Robert E. Gooding, Jr., eds., *The Warren Court: A Critical Analysis* (New York: Chelsea House, 1969).

Schneiderman, William, *Dissent on Trial: The Story of a Political Life* (Minneapolis, Minn.: MEP Publications, 1983).

Schoenebaum, Eleanora W., *Political Profiles: The Eisenhower Years* (New York: Facts on File, 1977).

Schultz, Bud, and Ruth Schultz, *It Did Happen Here* (Berkeley and Los Angeles: University of California Press, 1989).

Schwartz, Bernard, *A History of the Supreme Court* (New York: Oxford University Press, 1993).

———, *The New Right and the Constitution* (Boston: Northeastern University Press, 1990).

———, *Super Chief: Earl Warren and His Supreme Court* (New York: New York University Press, 1983).

———, *The Unpublished Opinions of the Warren Court* (New York: Oxford University Press, 1985).

Schwartz, Bernard, with Stephen Lesher, *Inside the Warren Court* (Garden City, N.Y.: Doubleday & Co., 1983).

Scobie, Ingrid Winther, *Center Stage: Helen Gahagan Douglas: A Life* (New York: Oxford University Press, 1992).

Selvin, David F., *Sky Full of Storm* (Berkeley: University of California Institute of Industrial Relations, 1966).

Severn, Bill, *Mr. Chief Justice: Earl Warren* (New York: McKay, 1968).

Shogan, Robert, *A Question of Judgment* (Indianapolis, Ind.: The Bobbs-Merrill Co., 1972).

Simon, James F., *The Antagonists* (New York: Simon and Schuster, 1989).

———, *Independent Journey: The Life of William O. Douglas,* rep. ed. (New York: Penguin, 1981).

———, *In His Own Image* (New York: David McKay Company, 1973).

Sinclair, Upton, *I, Candidate for Governor and How I Got Licked* (Los Angeles: End Poverty League, Inc., 1935).

Singer, Donald Lee, "Upton Sinclair and the California Gubernatorial Campaign of 1934," unpublished Master of Arts thesis (University of Southern California, Los Angeles, 1966).

Slackman, Michael, "The Orange Race: George S. Patton, Jr.'s Japanese-American Hostage Plan," *Biography,* 7 (1984), pp. 1ff.

Small, Merrell F., "The Country Editor and Earl Warren," unpublished manuscript in the Bancroft Library, University of California, Berkeley.

Smith, Beverly, "Earl Warren's Greatest Moment," *Saturday Evening Post,* July 24, 1954, pp. 17ff.

Smith, Jean Edward, *Lucius D. Clay: An American Life* (New York: Henry Holt, 1990).

Smith, Richard H., "Towns Along Tracks," unpublished Ph.D. dissertation (University of California at Los Angeles, 1976).

Smith, Richard Norton, *Thomas E. Dewey and His Times* (New York: Simon and Schuster, 1982).

———, *An Uncommon Man* (New York: Simon and Schuster, 1984).

Steamer, Robert J., *Chief Justice: Leadership and the Supreme Court* (Columbia: University of South Carolina Press, 1986).

Stevenson, Janet, *The Undiminished Man* (Novato, Calif.: Chandler and Sharp, 1980).

Stewart, George R., *The Year of the Oath* (Garden City, N.Y.: Doubleday & Co., 1950).

Stone, Irving, *Earl Warren* (New York: Prentice-Hall, 1948).

Storke, Thomas M., *California Editor* (Los Angeles: Westernlore Press, 1958).

"Supplement to the *Kern Standard,* Reports of the Grand Jury" (Bakersfield, Calif.: A. C. Maude Pub., 1895).

Swisher, Carl Brent, *Historic Decisions of the Supreme Court,* 2nd ed. (New York: D. Van Nostrand Company, 1969).

Theoharis, Athan, *From the Secret Files of J. Edgar Hoover* (Chicago: Ivan R. Dee, 1991).

Theoharis, Athan, and John Stuart Cox, *The Boss: J. Edgar Hoover and the Great American Inquisition* (Philadelphia: Temple University Press, 1988).

Thomas, Evan, *The Man to See* (New York: Simon and Schuster, 1991).

Thompson, Fred, *The I.W.W.: Its First Fifty Years* (Chicago: Industrial Workers of the World, 1955).

Truman, Harry S., *Memoirs,* rep. ed. (New York: New American Library, 1955).

Tushnet, Mark, ed., *The Warren Court in Historical and Political Perspective* (Charlottesville: University Press of Virginia, 1973).

Urofsky, Melvin I., ed., *The Douglas Letters* (Bethesda, Md.: Adler & Adler, 1987).

Velie, Lester, "The Secret Boss of California," *Collier's,* August 13, 1949, pp. 11ff.; August 20, 1949, pp. 12ff.

Vestal, Theodore Merrill, "The Warren Court and Civil Liberties," doctoral dissertation, Stanford University, 1962 (Ann Arbor, Mich.: University Microfilms, n.d.).

Violations of Free Speech and Rights of Labor, Report of the Committee on Education and Labor, 77th Congress, 2nd Session, Senate Report No. 1150, Parts I–IV (Washington, D.C.: Government Printing Office, 1942); 78th Congress, 1st Session, Senate Report No. 398, Part V (Washington, D.C.: Government Printing Office, 1943).

Walker, Samuel, *In Defense of American Liberties* (New York: Oxford University Press, 1990).

Waltz, Thomas, "A Narrative History of the 1942 California Gubernatorial Campaign Through the Sacramento Bee," unpublished paper prepared for History 191B, California State University, Spring, 1989.

Ward, Estolv Ethan, *The Gentle Dynamiter* (Palo Alto, Calif.: Ramparts Press, 1983).

Warren, Earl, *Memoirs* (New York: Doubleday, 1977).

————, *The Public Papers of Chief Justice Earl Warren* (New York: Simon and Schuster, 1959; rep. Westport, Conn.: Greenwood Press, 1974).

————, *A Republic, if You Can Keep It* (New York: Quadrangle Books, 1972).

Wasby, Stephen L., ed. *"He Shall Not Pass This Way Again"* (Pittsburgh, Penn.: University of Pittsburgh Press, 1990).

————, *The Impact of the United States Supreme Court* (Homewood, Ill.: The Dorsey Press, 1970).

Watkins, T. H., *Righteous Pilgrim* (New York: Henry Holt, 1990).

Weaver, John D., "Happy Birthday, Earl Warren; What Say You to Those Who Come Next?" *West, Los Angeles Times,* March 8, 1970, pp. 9ff.

————, *Warren: The Man, the Court, the Era* (Boston: Little, Brown, 1967).

Weinstein, James, *The Decline of Socialism in American, 1912–1925* (New Brunswick, N.J.: Rutgers University Press, 1984).

Weintraub, Hyman, "The I.W.W. in California, 1905–1931," Master of Arts thesis, University of California, Los Angeles, 1947.

Wells, A. J., *The San Joaquin Valley of California* (San Francisco: Passenger Department, Southern Pacific Company, 1908).

Wells, Tom, *The War Within* (Berkeley: University of California Press, 1994).

Werstein, Irving, *Pie in the Sky* (New York: Delacorte, 1969).

Westin, Alan F., "The John Birch Society: Fundamentalism on the Right," *Commentary,* August, 1961, pp. 93–104.

White, G. Edward, *The American Judicial Tradition* (New York: Oxford University Press, 1976).

————, *Earl Warren: A Public Life* (New York: Oxford University Press, 1982, 1987).

————, "Earl Warren as Jurist," *Virginia Law Review,* 67 (1981), pp. 461–551.

White, J. Patrick, "The Warren Court Under Attack: The Role of the Judiciary in a Democratic Society," *Maryland Law Review,* 19 (1959), pp. 181ff.

White, William Allen, *Autobiography* (New York: The Macmillan Company, 1946).

Whitten, Woodrow C., "Criminal Syndicalism and the Law in California: 1919–1927," Transactions of the American Philosophical Society, New Series, vol. 59, Part 2, 1969.

Whitman, Alden, "Alden Whitman's Golden Oldies," *Esquire,* April 1, 1975, pp. 82ff.

Woodward, Bob, and Scott Armstrong, *The Brethern,* rep. ed. (New York: Avon, 1981).

WRA: A Story of Human Conservation, United States Department of the Interior, War Relocation Authority (Washington, D.C.: Government Printing Office, n.d.).

Yarborough, Tinsley E., *John Marshall Harlan: Great Dissenter of the Warren Court* (New York: Oxford University Press, 1992).

ORAL HISTORIES

•

Dwight D. Eisenhower Library
Abilene, Kansas

Sherman Adams
Herbert Brownell, 1967–68; 1977
Clarence Manion

•

Lyndon Baines Johnson Library
University of Texas
Austin

Hale Boggs	James C. Hagerty	John J. McCloy
Ramsey Clark	D.B. Hardeman	Richard H. Nelson
Tom Clark	Leon Jaworski	Paul Porter
Clark M. Clifford	William H. Jordan, Jr.	Larry Temple
John Sherman Cooper	Nicholas Katzenbach	Homer Thornberry
Abe Fortas	Thurgood Marshall	Robert E. Waldron
Arthur J. Goldberg		

•

John Fitzgerald Kennedy Library
Columbia Point
Boston

William O. Douglas
Felix Frankfurter
Mary McGrory, Peter Lisagor, and George Herman
Leander Perez, Jr.

•

Robert F. Kennedy Oral History Program
John Fitzgerald Kennedy Library
Columbia Point
Boston

William O. Douglas

•

Los Angeles Times History Center

Kyle Palmer

•

Oral History Program
UCLA
Los Angeles

Robert W. Kenny
Carey McWilliams
Ellis E. Patterson

•

Oral History Research Office
Columbia University
New York

Earl C. Behrens
Richard C. Butler
William Fife Knowland
Edward P. Morgan
Chalmers Roberts
Robert C. Storey
Elbert Tuttle

•

Regional Oral History Office
Bancroft Library, University of California
Berkeley

Horace Albright
Robert S. Ash
Maryann Ashe
Edith Balaban
Stanley Barnes
Nina Warren Brien
Germain Bulcke
Omar Cavins
Richard H. Chamberlain
Ford Chatters
Joseph W. Chaudet
Gordon Claycombe
Florence McChesney Clifton
Robert Clifton
John W. Cline, M.D.
J. Frank Coakley
John C. Cuneo

Thomas Cunningham
E. A. Daly
McIntyre Faries
E. J. Feigenbaum
Marguerite Gallagher
Mary Gallagher
Aubrey Grossman
Cornelius Haggerty
Oliver D. Hamlin
Victor Hansen
Myron Harris
Albert E. Hederman, Jr.
Paul Heide
Beverly Heinrichs
Ruth Smith Henley
Oscar J. Jahnsen
Lowell Jensen

Lloyd Jester
Miriam Johnson
Robert W. Kenny
Clark Kerr
William F. Knowland
Adrian Kragen
Ralph Kreiser
Thomas H. Kuchel
Russel VanArsdale Lee
William Mailliard
Manford Martin
Ernest McMillan
Rollin McNitt
Carey McWilliams
Thomas J. Mellon
John Mullins
John Francis Neylan

Warren Olney III
Robert B. Powers
Herbert Resner
Bryl Salsman
Vern Scoggins
Clarence Severin
Mary Shaw

Willard W. Shea
Arthur H. Sherry
U. S. Simonds
Homer R. Spence
W. T. Sweigert
Beach Vasey
Francis E. Vaughan

Ernest H. Vernon
Earl Warren
Earl Warren, Jr.
James Warren
Nina Palmquist Warren
Robert Warren
Albert C. Wollenberg, Sr.

•

Harry S. Truman Library
Independence, Missouri

William L. Batt
Samuel C. Brightman
Oliver J. Carter
Clark M. Clifford
Harold I. McGrath
Walter Trohan
Earl Warren

•

Author's Interviews

James Adler, January 18, 1994
William Allen, February 8, 1994
Robert L. Anderson, October 14, 1992
Ray Arbuthnot, August 5, 1991
Joseph Ball, October 16, 1990
R. Markham Ball, February 14, 1994
David Belin, June 12, 1992
James R. Bell, February 7 and 13, 1992
Richard Bergholz, January 9, 1992
Francis Beytagh, June 27 and 29, 1994
Scott Bice, January 19, 1994
Theodore Boehm, February 4, 1994
Nina "Honey Bear" Brien, December 4, 1992
Murray Bring, February 15, 1994
Edmund G. "Pat" Brown, December 7 and 14, 1990
Tyrone Brown, March 3, 1994
Herbert Brownell, September 6, 1991; February 14, 1992; August 19, 1992; November 30, 1993
James Browning, February 22, 1994
Margaret A. Bryan, August 20, 22, and 23, 1992; September 1, 1992; February 15, 1994
Lillian Carlson, October 25, 1990
Richard "Bud" Carpenter, October 16 and 20, 1992
Hale Champion, February 10, 1994
Theodora Hymes Chioino, August 5, 1993
Jesse Choper, January 14, 1994
Kenneth Chotiner and Florence Chotiner, August 24, 1991
Mrs. Tom Clark, April 5, 1994
Florence "Susie" Clifton and Robert Clifton, March 3, 1992
George R. Cochrane, February 25, 1994
Lee Coe, January 22, 1991
James Corman, March 5, 1993
Elva Crispin, September 6, 1991
Phyllis DeCroix, September 6, 1991
William Dempsey, March 14, 1994
Richard Dinner, January 20, 1994
Ben Dobbs, May 1, 8, and 14, 1990
Fred Dutton, February 17, 1994
Grant C. Ehrlich, October 21, 1993
Barbara Elfbrandt, May 16, 1991
John Ely, February 12, 1994
Bill Fairbank, September 12, 1991
McIntyre Faries, August 9 and 12, 1991

Ellen Younglove Fields, August 5, 1992
Robert Finch, July 24, 1991
Dennis Flannery, March 17, 1994
Richard Flynn, February 8, 1994
Marc Franklin, February 10, 1994
Herzl Friedlander, M.D., July 8, 1991
Leonard Friedman, December 1, 1992
James Gaither, April 5, 1994
Gordon Gooch, February 17, 1994
James Graham, January 6, 1994
Mary Elizabeth Graham, July 31, 1991
Ewald Grether, August 29, 1993
Robert R. Gros, April 18, May 12, 1995
Jackie H. Grunwald, August 19, 1991
Gerald Gunther, March 25 and April 1, 1993
Edwin O. Guthman, April 20, 1992
Ewing Hass, January 11, 13, and 16, 1992
Arlene Tomlinson Hawkins, February 16, 1993
Augustus Hawkins, March 12, 1992
Dorothy Healey, October 25, 1990
Betty Foot Henderson, August 28, 1991
Ira Michael Heyman, February 17, 1994
Gladwin Hill, July 10, 1991
Patrick Hillings, July 26, 1991
Roland Homet, March 4 and 8, 1994
Miriam Dinkins Johnson, January 22, 1991
Alice Jones, September 6, 1991
John Keker, February 22, 1994
Clark Kerr, August 25, 1993
Phyllis Chotiner Kogen, September 7, 1991
Adrian Kragen, October 16 and 19, 1992
C. Douglas Kranwinkle, January 27, 1994
Jack Landau, September 7 and 14, 1995
Morris Landsberg, March 21, 1991
Mary Ellen Leary, October 1, 6, and 15, 1992; January 5 and 6, 1993
Maryalice Lemmon, September 3, 1993
Helen Lima, November 11, 1990
Joe Lipper, February 10, 1994
Marguerite Magee, September 9, 1991
Frank Mankiewicz, July 20, 1992
Ben Margolis, October 4, 1990
Nance Markson, February 19, 1993
Margaret (Mrs. Robert) McHugh, February 3, 1994
Paul Meyer, March 1, 1994
Ross Miller, October 23, 1992
Graham Moody, February 8 and April 19, 1994
Richard Mosk, August 17, 1992
Stanley Mosk, August 13, 1992
John Moss, June 17, 1991
Jon O. Newman, January 25, 1994
Dallin Oaks, February 25 and March 4, 1994
Warren Olney IV, August 26, 1992
Mrs. Warren Olney III, October 19 and 22, 1992
Jerry Pacht, March 23, 1992
Edgar "Pat" Patterson, September 13 and 21, 1991; November 20, 1992
Stella Pauw, September 10, 1991
Earl Pollock, March 3, 1994
H. Alan Post, December 1, 1992
Harry Pregerson, March 25, 1993
Margaret Price, September 10, 1991
George E. Reedy, April 15, 1994
Curtis Reitz, June 28, 1994

Charles Rhyne, August 5, 1992
Richard Rodda, March 23 and July 16, 1991
Arthur Rosett, February 17, 1994
Benno Schmidt, February 25, 1994
Leah Schneiderman, October 20 and November 16, 1990
Bernard Schwartz, March 17, 1994
Verne Scoggins, October 7, 1991; January 5, 1993
Thor Severson, July 16, 1991
Phyllis Shafter, September 10, 1991
Samuel Slaff, August 15, 1986
W. David Slawson, April 9, 1992
Michael Smith, June 27, 1994
Elizabeth Snider, February 15, 1992
Arlen Specter, August 4, 1994
Elizabeth Spector, September 20, 1990
Loretta Stack, November 13, 1990
Bea Steinberg, September 23, 1990
Henry Steinman, February 24, 1994
Samuel Stern, September 11 and 18, 1994
Peter Taft, March 10, 1992
Larry Temple, April 5, 1994
Wilma Wagner, September 6, 1991
James Walsh, January 6 and 13, 1994
Earl Warren, Jr., February 22, March 21, June 18 and July 29, 1991; August 20, 1992; September 19, 1993;
    July 8, 1995
James Warren, Jr., March 15, 1994
Jeffrey Warren, March 3, 10, and 11, 1994
Margaret Warren, October 1 and 8, 1992
Patricia Warren, August 20 and 22, 1991
Robert Warren, June 18 and July 9, 1991
Laughlin E. Waters, September 3, 1991
John Weaver, December 22, 1993
Caspar Weinberger, February 17, 1994
T. Edward White, June 29, 1994
Philip Wilkins, June 18, 1991
Payson Wolff and Helen Wolff, September 21, 1992
Samuel W. Yorty, January 9, 1992
Mildred Younger, September 7 and 12, 1991
Caroline Zecca, September 17, 1993
Elizabeth Ziegler, February 13, 1992
Kenneth Ziffren, August 26 and September 3, 1992

INDEX

police practices
  jurisdiction over, 303–4
  see also criminal procedure
poll taxes, 470–71
Pollack, Jack Harrison, 252*n,* 504, 505
Pollock, Earl, 280, 284–85, 291
Polsdorfer, Agnes, 59
Poor Laws, English, 106
pornography, *see* obscenity
Porter, Paul, 445, 501, 510
Post, H. Alan, 197
Powell, Adam Clayton, 503
Powell, Lewis F., 520
Powers, Robert, 68, 95–96
powers, separation of, 435
prayer, school, 386–89, 407–8, 435, 436, 480,
  532
Pregerson, Harry, 397
Preparedness Day bombings, 36, 106
press, freedom of, 437–40, 531
  trial coverage and, 463–66
prison reform, 68
prisoners' rights, 446–47
privacy, right to, 447–54, 530
probable cause, 467
Progressivism, 27–28, 90, 154, 156, 184, 201,
  221, 224, 410, 495–96
  in California politics, 31, 36, 42, 44–45, 56,
  69, 73, 74, 76–78, 91, 93, 106, 127, 128,
  138
  and citizens' advisory groups, 145
  Frankfurter and, 302
  health care and, 161, 162, 165
  juvenile justice system and, 490
  legal aid and, 67
Prohibition, 48, 55, 60, 70, 78, 176, 197, 372
Project Alert, 391
public accommodations, desegregation of, 408–
  410, 441–42
Public Health Service, U.S., 170
public transportation, integration of, 320, 383
Pullman Palace Car Company, 18
Purcell, Charles H., 140

Quinn, John, 27

racial discrimination, 160–61, 225–26, 524
  in criminal cases, 440–41
  miscegenation laws and, 309–10, 449–43
  in public accommodations, 408–10, 441–42
  redress of, *see specific decisions*
  in voting, 381, 437, 469
  see also segregation
Radin, Max, 108–11, 445
Rafferty, Max, 496
Railroad Men's Non-Partisan League, 129
Ramsay, Ernest G., 83–86, 88, 89, 93, 96, 107–
  109, 130, 254
Rankin, J. Lee, 293, 325, 345, 376–77, 418–20,
  423–27
Ransdell, William C., 460
Rayburn, Sam, 267, 367

Reader's Digest, 497
Reagan, Ronald, 282*n,* 496, 498
Reconstruction, 274, 344, 437
Reconstruction Finance Corporation, 267
Red Monday, 332–38, 340, 349, 350, 448*n*
Redding Chamber of Commerce, 128
Redicher, Lorraine, 48
redistricting, *see* apportionment
Redlich, Norman, 419
Redrup v. New York (1967), 477*n*
redress of grievances, petitioning for, 531
Reed, Stanley, 259, 260, 267, 268, 308, 451
  and anticommunism, 332
  calls for impeachment of, 338*n*
  at EW's funeral, 529
  retirement of, 330, 369
  and school desegregation, 277, 281–84, 291,
  295
  and tainted evidence, 304
Reed, Thomas Harrison, 27–28
Reedy, George, 430
Rehnquist, William H., 336, 520, 526, 530–31
Reichel, William V., 155, 156
Reitz, Curtis, 316, 317, 333*n*
Republican Party, 10, 42, 66*n,* 105, 147, 254,
  263, 289, 397
  in Alameda County, 42–46, 53, 69, 71
  anticommunism in, 202–5, 338
  apportionment ruling opposed by, 480
  Burger and, 513
  in California state politics, 72–82, 90–94, 99,
  107–10, 113, 114, 125–32, 139, 146, 162,
  164–66, 172–77, 180–81, 194, 196, 198,
  201–2, 207–11, 248, 397–98
  and Fortas's appointment as Chief Justice, 500,
  501
  and Jenner bill, 352
  and John Birch Society, 392
  in 1932 election, 70
  in 1940 election, 106
  in 1944 election, 153–56
  in 1948 election, 183–94, 368, 524
  in 1952 election, 219–24, 226–46, 513
  in 1956 election, 296*n,* 313–14
  in 1960 election, 368
  in 1964 election, 435
  in 1968 election, 504
  Progressives in, 28, 31, 44–45
  Rehnquist and, 520
  in South, 437
  and Supreme Court appointments, 247, 250,
  251, 265
  during World War II, 117
restaurants, segregation in, 408–10
Reston, James "Scotty," 300, 336
restrictive covenants case, 167, 276
Retail Credit Association, 289*n*
Reynolds, D. M., 110*n*
Reynolds v. Sims (1964) 433–37, 439–40, 480,
  531
Rhetoric (Aristotle), 273
Rhyne, Charles, 293, 341*n,* 345, 351